Writer's Northwest Handbook

3rd Edition

Writer's Northwest Handbook
3rd Edition

Published by
MediaWeavers
Rt 3 Box 376
Hillsboro, OR 97124

Publishers & Editors
Dennis Stovall, Linny Stovall

Editorial Assistants
Judy Binder
Penny Olien
William Woodall

Advertising Sales
Darlene Fesler

Art
Geoff Sauncy

ISBN 0-936085-07-X
ISSN 0896-7946

Table of Contents

Table of Contents

Introduction to the 3rd Edition

This book is a synthesis of what's going on in NW writing and publishing — a reflection of an incredibly dynamic scene. Drama. Tension. Suspense. They're all here. With the personalities to match. There is also a burgeoning sense of community that encircles us. We don't take it for rude regionalism, but the sense that place is important to understanding and feeling is strong among us. It is offered here in a way which we hope highlights its reality and provides proof of its potential in the broader context.

The Northwest enjoys some of the finest writers working today — in all genres. To list names would only be an invitation to accidentally omit someone, so we'll skip it. But that fact of numbers and quality, which definitely abets the creative growth of new writers, is part of the place. The more of us working and in contact, the more we write and the better we write. Which is in keeping with the recent attention to literacy in our society, and with the renewed stress on writing in our schools.

The regional upsurge in small press publishing, which is cataloged in this book, is part of a larger phenomenon. Independent publishing is booming, with several exciting regional centers appearing.

Writer's Northwest Handbook has evolved in the midst of this dynamic. We believe that the material included represents the incredible variety and vitality present in our continental corner — without losing sight of its relationship to the whole. In doing this new edition, we tried to incorporate your suggestions for improvements and new features. Let us know how we've done.

The articles, essays, and interviews are all new. And for that we thank all the writers whose excellent efforts appear here. Their bylines and credits are worth a second look. They have willingly given their time and talent to help other writers.

Media Weavers is an imprint of Blue Heron Publishing, Inc. We are the same folks, but Blue Heron also publishes the Walt Morey Adventure Library and plans other imprints. Media Weavers publications serve the community of the written and printed word: writers, publishers, teachers, librarians, editors, illustrators, printers, agents, and interested bystanders. Because *Writer's Northwest Handbook* promotes the role and recognition of books, it is an official resource of the Oregon Center for the Book in the Oregon State Library.

Thanks for buying this edition. May it be a useful tool for you. And may your most creative period be before you.

— DS & LS

Acknowledgements

Compiling and editing this book was an immense task. On the editorial and production side, we want to thank three people who were critical to its production: Judy Binder, who provided organizational skills and quality editing of every type of copy we threw her way; William Woodall (WW after articles), who quite simply wrote and edited his way through a stack of work faster than a speeding bullet; and Penny Olien, who was a stalwart in the trenches during the entire battle to revise the listings and edit copy.

Darlene Fesler took on the task of selling advertising for the section in the back that helps support this project. And boy did she help. The price would be a buck or two higher without her efforts.

Geoff Sauncy has given us his art again. This time his medium was electronic. His software graphics tool was FullPaint for the Apple Macintosh. The cover illustration was then touched up with Adobe Illustrator88. Geoff's Blue Heron is the logo of Blue Heron Publishing, Inc.

Thanks are due the Washington State Arts Commission for a grant that paid some Washington writers, the Oregon Arts Commission for a grant to incorporate its *Oregon Literary Directory* in the *Handbook*, and the Oregon Center for the Book for a production grant.

For those with an interest in technique, we used the following tools, type and facilities: Three Apple Macintosh computers networked with MacServe, a 40 meg LaCie hard disk, a 50 meg Jasmine hard disk, an E-Machines' Big Picture large screen monitor, PageMaker3 from Aldus, FileMaker4 from Claris, Illustrator88 from Adobe, Microsoft Word, and an Apple LaserWriter II NT (for proofs). The typefaces are Times, Helvetica, and Optima from Adobe. Page images were set to film or paper at Portland Advertising Typography by Kevin McDonald on a Linotronic 300. Printing and binding were done by WCP of Tualatin, Oregon.

We would like to dedicate this book to our parents. They lent encouragement when it was most needed, appreciating the value of *Writer's Northwest Handbook* and the front-loaded effort required to publish it. By seniority then: Harold, Pete, Ruth, and Red (who died June 16, 1988).

—DS & LS

Western Voices

I See by My Outfit
by Robert Sheckley

I see by my outfit that I am a writer. I am wearing my Banana Republic photojournalist's vest with the pockets so numerous that you need a crib sheet to locate them all. I am wearing my Nike Air Shoes. I must be an Oregon writer. I also have on my plaid backwoods style workshirt bought in Bloomingdale's in New York. Clipped to the upper pocket is my peerless Mont Blanc fountain pen. If any proof were needed that I am a writer, that would surely do it. You don't carry around a 250-dollar fountain pen (which I bought in Spain for 60 dollars) just to write a shopping list.

I have other writerly marks. Come into my home and look at my Macintosh. Observe the books on the shelves in my bedroom. I wrote all of them. So I'm a writer, right?

Then why is it that I never seem to know how to write? It's obvious I know how to write. Check out them books there. I wrote them all. Who says I don't know how to write?

But I don't. The fact is, I write, but I don't know how. Since I am an intellectual, I find this state of affairs deplorable. Sometimes I think I'd rather know how to write than to actually do it. Sometimes I think there must be a better way. Sometimes I look at the project in hand and a cloud of despair settles over my head leaving me in a double fog, the one regional, the other personal. Sometimes I think that, even though I don't know how to write, I'll bet I could write a pretty good book on how to write.

I take myself out to the bookstores and look at books on how to write. Every once in a while I buy a new book on how to write. I always think, this is it at last! I'm going to say a word here about books on how to write.

As much as anything else, a book on how to write was instrumental in starting me writing. I am referring to *Writing and Selling* by Jack Woodford. It's dated now, and much of its advice is worthless. What in hell is a syndicate story, anyhow? The market must have collapsed before the Second World War. But what Woodford gives is good attitude. It was encouraging to me, dreamy, literary, show-off kid that I was, to read Woodford's growl about getting it down on paper and never mind the theories. Woodford was so tough-minded! How was I to know he was confined to an institution when he wrote the book, or slightly later, perhaps? And what difference would it have made? Crazy Woodford preaching tough-mindedness. He gave me the fantasy of being a tough-minded pulp writer who sat in front of the typewriter with a felt hat perched on the back of his head, cigarette glowing in the ashtray, inevitable cup of coffee beside him. I loved it. That was my idea of heroism.

Next came Polti, with his *Thirty-Six Dramatic Situations*. On the cover it says it is used by thousands of successful authors. No doubt also by thousands of unsuccessful ones. I never got anything out of it except a sense of delight at Polti's bold categorization of all dramatic situations, whether correct or not.

In recent years I have gotten a lot out of Peter Elbow's *Writing with Power*. Where do they get these titles? Elbow is talking about free-form writing, just set your clock for five or ten minutes and let 'er rip. I was doing this long before I ever read Elbow, but his saying it made it legitimate for me.

Some other books on writing I've enjoyed hanging out with, but am too lazy to precis for you: — *A Writer's Time*; *Comedy Writing Secrets*; *The Essence of Fiction*; *Techniques of the Selling Writer*; etc.

You can get something out of almost any book on how to write. But it might be good to forget the how-to aspect. Either you're the sort who can do exercises from a book or you're not. I'm not. What I get out of these books is a nice long chat with a professional. Or at least a fellow traveler.

None of these books seem applicable to science fiction. I glance at and then put aside the books on writing science fiction by my fellow professionals. They seem to be filled with good advice, but none of it seems to pertain to me. I couldn't write

---

> *"Amazing what rotten, light-minded and unworkable characters come to you when you're sitting down in a state of High Seriousness determined to Perpetrate Fiction."*

---

science fiction their way. I learned to write science-fiction by trying to write something *like* science fiction, figuring I'd get to the real thing later, when I knew more about it. I didn't know then that the longer you live the less you know, and the less capacity you have to *do* anything about your ignorance even if you *could* learn something. I hope I'm not losing you? thank you, it was good for me, too. What was I saying? Oh, yes, the way to write, for example, is not to do what I just did, interject (or even introject) yourself into the matter, gratuitously. Fiction is a controlled dream, we learn from John Gardner, in *On Writing Moral Fiction*, *On Becoming a Novelist*, etc. Gardner, speaking for the traditional novel, the well-beloved realism, says, in effect, "Author, keep your nose out of the story. Don't mar the reader's pleasure by bringing up matters extraneous." Right, I say. But I prefer to read Italo Calvino. His *If on a Winter's Night a Traveller* is a classic not only in the art of fiction, and also in the subtler art of Pleasing Yourself During the Writing of Your Novel — a topic not touched by other pundits.

Someone should write a book, not on how to write, but on how to manage the deeper problem, how to balance the needs of self-expression with the requirements of form. Or, to phrase it a little differently, How to Enjoy Yourself While Fictionalizing Assiduously. Just take a look at writers. You'll soon see that most of them don't have any fun, certainly not when they're writing, probably not much any other time, either. They can't afford to have fun writing because everyone knows that fiction is a deadly serious business, a practice beloved of mankind and illuminating in the highest degree, profound even when humorous, filled with symbols, double-entendres, compassion, hard-edged action, and many other good things. Fiction, we learn, is one of the highest forms of artistic endeavor, and one must go about it seriously, even if one is writing humor.

Armed with this attitude, and in a fatal state of High Seriousness, the writer starts his novel with a character whose character must be expressed in dossier. This is dull and unpleasant work. The writer must actually interview the character as if he were applying for a job. As he is, of course: he is applying to be the hero of your story. But does he have the necessary qualifications? Most do not. Amazing what rotten, light-minded and unworkable characters come to you when you're sitting down in a state of High Seriousness determined to Perpetrate Fiction. Sorry, sir, you won't do, your problems are too diffuse, what we wanted was someone with a rather more pointed problem, not this vague *angst* you suffer from. Heartbreaking, but you have to say it. What a pity most of the characters who walk across the *tabula rasa* of your mind aren't interested in your literary criteria. Your imagination knows, even if you don't, that the play-pleasure principle is not to be reduced to something as vulgar as

finding an appropriate character to fit your novel.

Novel-writing is unfair to authors. Characters you can have fun with fit nowhere. Plots that you enjoy have no logic.

No simple answer. Nor can you solve it by going to the opposite extreme. It will never do to become Mr. Natural, say to hell with all that formal stuff, I write as I please. What you please to write usually doesn't read well. It isn't interesting! If you are writing a story for an audience, you must, you simply must, play the fiction game. Write for your readers, by all means. But not too hard. Amuse yourself. But not too much. Always change your mind. Don't sweat it. Forget everything, including these words, and write your tale. Then read it over quickly. If it doesn't sicken you too much, ship it out to somebody who might buy it.

That's what it comes down to for me. On the other hand, maybe there's a better answer in a book somewhere. ❖

Robert Sheckley is a well-known freelance science fiction writer, now moving into mysteries. He has written about 40 books, 10 are short story collections, the rest are novels — widely translated, some with heavy gutturals. Sheckley lives in Portland.

Ursula K. Le Guin Interview
by Jane Elder Wulff

Getting the word out.

That's what writers have to do at some point, somehow, if their lives are not to be wasted in the great abundance of nature's excess, along with apple blossoms, tadpoles, and all the other detritus of infinite possibility.

Getting the word out. Emily Dickinson did it by stuffing scraps of envelopes in the backs of drawers: that's one way. Media Weavers and Writer's Northwest Handbook exist to help writers find more reliable ways.

Toward that end, we talked with a Northwest writer who has been eminently successful in transmitting her message to the world. Ursula K. Le Guin is an immensely prolific writer whose work first appeared in the '60s as science fiction, has transcended all genres to become one of the most respected Americans writing today.

WNH: How did you get started?

Le Guin: By sending out manuscripts endlessly, short story and fiction and novel, and for ten years, getting them back. By sending out poetry manuscripts, which I did begin to publish here and there in my 20s. And then finally, breaking through, first into one of the little scholarly quarterlies with a short story, and then very soon after that into a commercial market, one of the science fiction magazines, also with a short story. So I began absolutely the way most writers do, by just sending stuff.

WNH: After the breakthrough, how did things develop?

Le Guin: I was very lucky in getting into science fiction. I thought, okay, this is a name they're willing to stick on what I

write — fantasy, science fiction, it's fine with me, I didn't care what they called it.

WNH: You weren't worried about getting categorized?

Le Guin: No! I wanted to get published! I had been sending stuff out for ten years and getting rejection slips. As a writer, how could I take myself seriously if I'd kept sending it out and nothing had gotten published except some little poems?

WNH: I understand your first four novels were brought out by Ace Books.

Le Guin: Ace was the major science fiction publisher at the time, a paperback rip-off market if there ever was one, with a very clever editor, Don Wollheim, who now is DAW Books. Don was never afraid to take on a new author or a slightly different, experimental book. In fact, he was less conservative then than he is now. It's interesting how these things change.

Meanwhile I managed to get some non-genre short stories published here and there. I got myself an agent, a lovely agent (Virginia Kidd) who's always been ready to take whatever I send her. Okay, from then on it's simply a matter of getting a little more name. By then I'm an established science fiction writer winning prizes and stuff. I begin to get a little clout, I begin to be able to write less what editors and publishers think they want and more what I want. The freedom of success.

WNH: Noel Young's Capra Press of Santa Barbara joined your long list of publishers in the '70s, first with poetry, then with fiction. What prompted your decision to work with a small Western publisher?

Le Guin: When I can, I will go to a Western publisher,

because I'm a Westerner (a Portland resident, born in Berkeley) and I don't want everything to be in the East. I don't want to feed the illusion New York has that it's the center of this country. It's anything but — and particularly now.

There used to be a real network of publishers, editors, and writers that centered in New York, a genuine support network. It was very professional. It was useful to the art of writing. These days, I think that network's broken down. The publishers have all bought each other out and then sold out to corporations which know nothing about publishing or books and are looking only for commercial quick profit. The whole publishing scene is in a mess, a real breakdown condition — which is another good reason for going to a small regional publisher. You're strengthening the big network instead of the little, local, Eastern cartel of 'big-name' publishers.

WNH: What of the genuine support network that many people see developing regionally, in the Northwest and elsewhere?

Le Guin: I hope it'll develop nationally. I was more willing 20 years ago to accept this kind of control coming from New York, because there was some justification. They *were* good at what they did. And they did distribute the books marvelously. You could write in the West, get published in New York and be distributed all over the country. *Distribution* — that's what we want, as authors.

I don't think the New York system is working so well anymore. The big distribution, the big bucks are all for books which aren't even really books, they're products, ground out by the baloney factories and the best seller mills. And that's not the kind of thing I'm interested in reading or doing.

I'm talking about serious writing here; I'm talking about fiction; and I don't pretend to any knowledge of anything else. But my point is exactly that every time a good book can get itself published by a non-New York publisher and get some real distribution, maybe win an award or something, we do strengthen the larger network. We also strengthen the West Coast network, which I'm particularly interested in, because I live here. It gives me real pleasure to deal with my own kind of people.

WNH: For an untried author with a fiction book manuscript, what are the alternatives?

Le Guin: It depends so much on your book. If it's a book which you seriously believe has commercial potential, then your immediate advantage in going to the big New York publisher is money up front, good royalties, and excellent distribution. That book will get into all the bookstores.

If you're dealing with a small publisher, they don't have the instant money to give you, though their royalties may be excellent. Their distribution can be good, or it can be very local indeed. I would say when you're dealing with a small publisher, find out how they distribute, where they distribute. Because it's heartbreaking to get a book published, perhaps a beautifully printed job, and then realize they don't know how to sell it.

WNH: Why bother to go to a small publisher at all?

Le Guin: First, because the big publishers probably will not take your book if it is in any way innovative, or genre-busting, or hard to classify. Most of them want a predictable, safe, imitative product — especially from an unknown writer, whose 'name' won't 'sell.' Not all of them; not always; but these days it seems that risk-taking is increasingly left to the smaller publishers.

And then, there is the pleasure of dealing on a small scale with real people, instead of with faceless entities in New York. That's a solid, valid reason. It's a kind of moral reason, really. It's doing business on a scale that is human instead of totally commodified.

WNH: Human values have shaped your associations with other writers as well as with publishers. You belong to the Authors League and the Writers Guild, and you're a founding member of Science Fiction Writers of America and, more recently, Northwest Writers Inc.

Le Guin: But I think the other bonding force, really the one I've been most active in, is teaching. Workshops. I love writing workshops. It's selfish. I get so much from the young writers. I get so much. The interplay is so exciting to me.

There's also the kind of thing which is really a spin-off from workshops — small groups of writers, unpublished or just beginning to get published, who get together and criticize their work, workshop style. I might have got myself to join one of those groups if there had been any, but there weren't, you see, when I was coming up. That's a phenomenon of the last 15 or 20 years, and one I encourage. Because a workshop lasts a week or two, and you go back home alone with your manuscript...we do need some mutual support. I just didn't know how to find it when I was young.

It can go too far. I would also put in a word of warning. Little groups can become little cliques that read each other's manuscripts and admire them. But a writer of determination and talent is going to break out of that little circle eventually. It won't be big enough.

WNH: You have taught science fiction writing at Clarion in Seattle and with Tony Wolk at Portland State University, but your workshops have been harder to put a name to.

Le Guin: The one at Haystack in 1987, I wanted to call 'Subversive Writing.' The director wisely said, 'I don't know...' We called it 'Innovative Writing' which was just loose enough. We wanted people who were writing outside the genres, interested in women's writing, oral work, stuff like that. We tried to get people who were working on the fringes and the margins — and by golly, we got some, too. It was a wonderful workshop. Really interesting people. I like to keep pushing.

WNH: Writers work alone. They're such solitary folks. And they tend to be isolationists. And yet — you have to get your work out.

Le Guin: They tend to be introverted people, which is disapproved of by our society. All of a sudden, you have to become an extravert, and a salesman, all the rest of it. That's the key point. I think the hardest point for a writer who hasn't published yet is that changeover from the private artist working alone to this public individual offering something to a totally uncaring commercial market. That is exactly the point at which support from other writers who have been through it or are going through it is wonderful. I didn't have it. I just struggled on. A lot of people never get that support. You can do without it. But you have to be kind of bullheaded. Determined. ❖

Jane Elder Wulff, a freelance writer, has received an Artist Trust Project Grant to support work on her current novel. "I'm exactly at the point to which Ursula refers, the 'key point' of going public. A nice time to be meeting her!"

Interview with Colleen McElroy
by Carol Orlock

Colleen McElroy has published seven collections of poetry, including Bone Flames *and* Queen of the Ebony Isles, *and recently published her first collection of short stories,* Jesus and Fat Tuesday. *Her play about Harriet Tubman,* Follow the Drinking Gourd, *was produced by the Seattle Children's Theatre, and she has also written screenplays. She is Professor of English at the University of Washington.*

WNH: You began writing in your mid-thirties, but were you studying and learning about writing before that?

McElroy: While I was growing up I spent so much time listening to language. At home, I was a listener, but I always carried tales right out the door with me. I'd listen to how it was told and then tell it my own way. I guess I was training myself to be a writer.

WNH: Were there writers you admired while you were in school?

McElroy: We knew about Langston Hughes and Phyllis Wheatley. They were available because I had two aunts who were school teachers, and they knew what to buy. But we're still talking about a school system where, at that time, they had Negro History *Day*. In those days, the school system tried to teach me that all writers were white, male and dead. I came of age in the '50s and I was not reflected on *Father Knows Best*. If you saw a Black face on programs like that, which was very rare, it was either the good Samaritan scene or the delivery — the maid or the service person.

WNH: So you crossed cultural barriers to take yourself seriously as a writer, and you continue crossing barriers, working in poetry, fiction and playwriting. Do you need to pause between them?

McElroy: There are connections. Once I became more involved with character in fiction, I developed ways of using those details in poems. Now the poem's characters are not just there, they're moving as well. In fiction I think I'm making my eye work first, and then the ear comes much later. With poetry it's the ear that's working first, and then the eye catches up with it.

"In those days, the school system tried to teach me that all writers were white, male and dead."

WNH: What do you find most central in the three genres?

McElroy: I love language. I love the way it sounds. I love exploring what's been left out in a conversation. I think a good fiction writer learns to put in only what's said so that you can understand what's been left out. I like hearing the bits of dialogue, which is why playwriting intrigues me. Though what I hear in my head is not always what the actor's going to do with it later.

WNH: You've worked with theatre groups and you've also published with both commercial and university presses. Can you compare these experiences?

McElroy: My experiences with presses have been relatively good. I can't classify one as better than the other. I look for a press that's going to distribute, is able to fight the tide of the quick sale. Poetry doesn't move like that. It's not the big press versus the small press but one just involves more people. And so the politics will be very different.

WNH: Speaking of politics, there's a lot of talk these days about a women's aesthetic, or a Black aesthetic, academic perspective — how do you see that? Do you feel any pressure to fit into those categories?

McElroy: Oh God, yes. Most of the time, though, the pressure comes as afterthought, as part of a review of my work. I don't think you can separate the racism and sexism out in publishing. It's sometimes unspoken, but it's there. I tend to take a dim view of reviewers who can only compare me to other Black women. I've seen them groping to stretch me to fit Gwendolyn Brooks, Alice Walker, Toni Morrison. Spare me! And knowing, of course I don't write like they do, I have to write from the perspective I have. That kind of classification allows people to be selective, and so, perhaps a lot of women don't get published because they don't fit someone's definition of the Black female aesthetic academician.

"Most of the geography of creativity is populated by self doubt."

WNH: Do you find differences in this between the commercial, academic or literary presses?

McElroy: Commercial presses and book sellers tend to go with the trends and will say, "That doesn't sell. That's out." What do you mean, it's out? What do you mean it's out to speak about issues that are pertinent, relevant? They're really saying they think of the American public as being fickle, some mindless, spineless glob out there that can be changed from one kind of thing to another overnight. I always tell my students if you don't want just the quickie autobiography of the latest rock star, then you've got to frequent small book stores. You've got to support independent presses.

WNH: If you were starting out now as a writer, is there other good advice you would give yourself?

McElroy: I would hope I wouldn't have to know as much about writing and publishing as I do now. It was very fortunate that I started with the blind faith of my own talent. I didn't have a notion of comparing myself to other people, and because of that I had to do a lot of things on my own, and those were good. I just went along paying attention to what I was doing. It gave me a sense of wonder, the right to experiment without having censorship. A writer lives in a land of self doubt. Most of the geography of creativity is populated by self doubt. All of those little obstacles spring up in the middle of the road as you're walking toward this story or that poem.

WNH: So knowing too much about publishing could keep one from writing?

McElroy: Knowing all that only creates more of the same kind of self-doubt that we all have to deal with anyway. And sometimes if you're very young, you don't know how to fend it off. I write because I love language, and I want to communicate with language, I want to use it as a tool. To me, language is the dancer's body and the sculptor's clay, you want to make it do something that it wouldn't do under other circumstances. And getting published tells me one-half of what I need to know when I try the next bit of language. Too often we teach young writers that when you are published you can rid yourself of the responsibility of change. And you can't do that. Go ahead and seek publication but understand that there's a responsibility that comes with it.

WNH: To continue developing as a writer?

McElroy: Right. ❖

Carol Orlock's novel *The Goddess Letters* was published in 1987, and her work has also appeared in *Calyx, Clinton Street Quarterly,* and *Ms. Magazine.*

Joyce Thompson: A Woman of Obsessions
by Sherry Alexander

Novelists and parents are obsessed, according to Joyce Thompson.

"Writing fiction requires an intense investment of one's self — an obsession, really, to face ideals in one's own life. It is the same with parenting," she says.

Thompson speaks from experience. Her own passion for fiction in its purest form drove her from a profitable career as a "pen for hire" to that of a successful novelist with eight books to her credit.

"I don't think of myself as successful on a day-to-day basis. Success is fleeting. It's important for me to be a full-time professional and a full-time mom, so I am. It's that simple."

Despite the fact that she tends to make her commitment to dual careers sound easy, Joyce readily admits that the twelve month combination of mom/writer requires sacrifices.

Her writing schedule, for instance, must be matched to school and day care center hours so as to be available for Alexandra, age nine, and Ian, age four, when they return home. And, occasionally, deadlines looming on the horizon necessitates pumping herself up with caffeine in order to meet them. However, Thompson feels the rewards far outweigh the sacrifices.

"I believe in my work, and I believe in my motherhood. Since the alternatives are not acceptable to me, I have to keep things balanced. To do this, I have learned to take one day at a time. Problems are dealt with as they arise, and I don't go looking for them either. Balancing my careers means I let the easy be easy so that I have enough energy to handle the hard stuff when it comes. And believe me, it comes. Every novelist will agree with that. There are no guarantees in fiction. Only possibilities."

Joyce's teaching of other writers centers on these possibilities. She feels fiction is most valid for people who want to tell a story that can touch another human being. She cautions writers to learn to honor and trust their intuition, to discipline their muse, to be patient with their work, and to be careful consumers.

"There are so many classes, seminars, conferences, and teachers out there that we must all be very careful of what we take into our souls. Writing, whether it is non-fiction or fiction, requires integrity. We should be willing to determine our needs for additional instruction, and then investigate which instructor will help us meet our goals. Probably the best advice I can give to someone with a burning desire to write a novel is to read, read, read, so as to get a sense of the possibility."

Joyce Thompson really cares about writers. Since 1980, she has taught the finer points of her craft to hundreds of students. "There are skills that are basic to all types of writing, and I readily pass these on to individuals who take my class. But I want them to have more. I don't take, nor do I seek, criticism very well. Yet, I've found I relish it when it comes from a colleague I respect. Through the years, my goal has been to see each group of people develop continuing relationships as colleagues ... to learn to trust their instincts ... to be highly critical and extremely nurturing of each other's work. And, I must admit, it is an enviable situation. I've witnessed astonishing breakthroughs."

"...my work must hold the promise that I will come out somewhere I've never been before. It's the same with parenthood."

Breakthroughs are not foreign to Joyce Thompson either. Five years ago, she was one of the hottest new women writers in the United States. A contract for her fourth novel, *Conscience Place,* had just been signed, and Hollywood moguls were vying for the movie rights. She had become the darling of fiction, and it scared her to death.

"Something in me knew I wasn't ready for success, so I backed off." Thompson's retreat was an act of self-preservation. She was pregnant with her second child and was locked into marriage that produced an unstable environment. "I've spent the last five years making my life stable," she says. "Now I feel I can commit myself to my career." And, commit she has!

Joyce supports herself and her children with the income she generates from her work. "Sometimes, things are a little leaner than I like, but I have no complaints. In fact, my children have actually been able to go to places like Disneyland. Of course,

Continued

that's because someone else paid our way so I could work on a novelization. But the kids didn't care who was paying. They just had fun.

"This business can be stressful on a family if you let it be. I choose not to let it. My work is part of my own survival, and taking time out for human events is very important to me. This may sound a little corny, but I pray. I feel it is necessary for me to tap into something that is bigger than me on a daily basis. My father passed away a few months ago. I decided that I wanted to be part of his passing, so I put my novel on hold and spent his last remaining months with him and my mother. It felt good to be there. By the end of July, I found I had taken care of all the little details associated with death. For the first time in my career, I felt successful, yet I had absolutely nothing left to give.

"As women, we are trained to give. However, we fail to realize that there won't be anything left to give if we don't take care of ourselves. After my father's death, I checked into a hotel and slept. I needed to be quiet—to take care of myself. Then I was ready to face the obsessions of life."

Joyce offers a final word of advice to would-be novelists: "Don't forsake the integrity of your work. Maintain it. If you are willing to put your integrity at stake, your work will always be successful to you. Writing needs passion, but it also needs honesty. I have found my work must hold the promise that I will come out somewhere I've never been before. It's the same with parenthood."

According to Joyce Thompson, novelists and parents are obsessed. "I can't think of a better passion," she laughs. "Can you?" ❖

Sherry Alexander writes a parenting column for *Food Day*, a supplement of the *Oregonian* in Portland, has written four books on parenting topics, and is working on her first novel.

Northwest Asian-American Literature
by Lawson Fusao Inada

It's my privilege to be asked to do a piece on Northwest Asian-American literature for this publication, and since it is a *handbook* I want to offer something handy — a list of sources sort of like a, say, menu of specials. Which I hope you're already familiar with. So why not start off with a little story.

This happened a couple of summers ago right here in Ashland, Oregon. Just an hour or so in one evening; just a conversation, actually — but since I was part of it, let's assume that it has relevance to the subject at hand. And just for the fun of it, perhaps you can pretend to be the other man.

Anyway, I got a phone call, see, and this guy said he was in town and wanted to interview me. Was from Tokyo, had landed in Seattle and met some folks who said, "Well, if you're interested in Asian-American literature, you might as well stop by and see Lawson on your way to L.A." Okay, why not. No problem.

It turned out we were about the same age, both English profs even, so communication promised to be easy; however, he immediately announced that he was at the "number one" university, was writing up a piece for a "leading" journal, and had recently published a study of Australian literature with a "top-ranked" company.

So there we were in my outback study. I was giving it my best shot, trying to be a worthy subject — put on some Coltrane to smooth us through my duller moments as I showed him some of the work I was doing: a review of Native American poet Wendy Rose's new book; some prose-in-progress for Chicano poet Gary Soto's hometown Fresno collection; the new poem I would read at the Puyallup Fairgrounds, upon the unveiling of George Tsutakawa's sculpture commemorating the site of Camp Harmony, one of our "assembly centers" during World War II...

That sort of thing. The stuff I do. The man took some notes, certainly, but I could tell from what he didn't say, from how things just stopped, dropped, without benefit of follow-through, that communication wasn't really happening. Words were heard, all right, but meaning wasn't meeting eye to eye.

(Look at it this way: I am, after all, the descendant of peasants; Inada, after all, does mean "ricefield"; and not only am I not a "real" Japanese, here I am carrying on in this cultural upstart of a country, stuck way the heck out here in Boondock Prefecture and relegated to teaching at some kind of Southern Ainu State College. You get the picture: say, an audition for a Bartles & Jaymes commercial...)

"They...picked up on the lingo, the opportunities, and whatever else the land had to offer — racism, legislation, the camps..."

So let's talk Tinsel Town. That ought to be meaningful, real, fun. Be sure to check in with the East West Players, our oldest and most prominent theater company. Why, just last summer, I had a blast working with their troupe, taking our creativity to disadvantaged regions of the city and... "I can't understand why none of you has achieved the stature and status of Sessue Hayakawa."

I had to laugh, for suddenly I had a vision of my grandfathers in their youth — Mitsumi Inada and Busuke Saito, Sessue's contemporaries — a couple of lean, muscular, intense, good-looking dudes, "Oriental sex symbols" for real; these were men with the vision, guts, smarts, and gumption to strike out for parts unknown and make a go of it; they play the role of slaves on Hawaii plantations before making it to the Northwest and working their way to California. Now here comes this professor fella in a rental car retracing their tracks, setting out to discover America; they found it, made it, on their knees, feet, backs, and, oh no, didn't fade away with the advent of the talkies; yes, indeed — picked up on the lingo, the opportunities, and whatever else the land had to offer — racism, legislation, the camps…

So as their grandson, I said what they would have said: "Welcome to America." He was a nice enough guy. I trust the feeling was mutual. Perhaps we'll work together in the future. There's much to be learned among us.

Now we're "live" — a bright blue morning full of fall. I've got three books on my desk to share, each of the tradition, which continues to continue. It *is*; we *are*: Welcome to the territory.

1. *No-No Boy*, John Okada. This is his first and only novel; it was published by Tuttle in 1957, didn't sell, and went quickly out of print; some of us (Jeff Chan, Frank Chin, Shawn Wong, myself — Asian-American writers, the editors of *Aiiieeeee!*, Howard University Press) found it, knew immediately what we had (greatness speaks for itself; recognizing No-No Boy as a classic was a snap), and reprinted it with our own money in 1976; John died at 47 in 1971, and we never had a chance to meet him.

John is a contemporary of, say, Baldwin and Mailer; he was raised in the International District, Asian-American Seattle; his father was a pioneering railroad man; John's younger brother is *the* Frank Okada, the painter of international fame and art professor at the University of Oregon; John went through journalism school at the University of Washington and Columbia.

No-No Boy takes place in post-war Seattle and Portland; it's about, well, love, family, strength, integrity, existence, the aftermath of the still-unfolding camp experience, including the resistance. It's about an individual, a people, a country, the human condition. John, I mean to tell you — this book keeps getting better and better and bigger and bigger. For those who haven't read it — you're in for an experience.

No-No Boy is now available from the leading publisher of Asian–American literature. For a free brochure of the entire line, write: University of Washington Press, PO Box 50096, Seattle, WA 98145.

2. *Turning Shadows into Light*, edited by Mayumi Tsutakawa and Alan Chong Lau. Subtitled "Art and Culture of the Northwest's Early Asian/Pacific Community," this book was published in 1982 as "a new collection of essays, photographs, artwork and literature which delves into the cultural life of Northwest Asian-Americans from the turn of the century to the beginning of the Second World War." From way back, in our vital communities, we had our newspapers, theaters, culture, creativity…

This is a very lovely production — an invaluable historical document and a showcase of established artists, past and present. It's available from our Northwest Asian-American newspaper: *International Examiner*, 318 Sixth Avenue South, Seattle, WA 98104.

3. *The Seattle Review* (Padelford Hall GN-30, University of Washington, Seattle, WA 98195) Volume XI, Number 1, Spring/ Summer 1988. A special Asian-American issue, edited by

---

"From way back, in our vital communities, we had our newspapers, theaters, culture, creativity…"

Shawn Wong. By now, you're getting the correct impression that Seattle is the hub of our territory; it just goes to show what some well-earned, well-deserved access can do, for the benefit of everyone. The University of Washington, with its press, this review, and a bonafide Asian-American Studies program, is a key player; moreover, many of our writers have come through its creative writing courses. Then, too, we've got representation in the various community arts agencies, political venues…

(What about Portland? Good question. Well, it certainly didn't help matters when the Japanese-American community was removed during the War; sure, quite a few families returned to the city, scattered here and there, but that solid, central, substantial core community is gone forever. But I can envision it as such a happening place — from up by Powell's Books to down by the river, with 14 hotels, a multitude of stores, restaurants, churches, organization, the whole bit, with commerce coming in from miles around… Ah, Shi-ta Machi — "down town" - now you're gone…)

This star-studded collection — essays, drama, poetry, fiction — can hold its own, page for page, with anything else produced in America. Besides Northwesterners, there are established writers from throughout the nation (including a startling contingent from Hawaii) and Canada, with hints of the future from relative newcomers to the continent. The authors are too numerous to mention; you'll see. ❖

Lawson Fusao Inada is the author of *Before the War*, the first volume of poetry by an Asian-American published by a major firm; also an editor of two major Asian-American anthologies: *Aiiieeeee!*, Doubleday, 1976, and *The Big Aiiieeeee!*, Howard University Press, forthcoming.

"Most of the geography of creativity is populated by self-doubt." —Colleen McElroy

Wally McRae, Rancher Poet
by Jeri D. Walton

"The writing of poetry is preceded by the appreciation and recitation of poetry," says Wally McRae, third generation rancher on Rosebud Creek in Montana. "I started reciting poetry and stories to my parents, my aunt and uncle, and my parent's friends before I could read. One year, after a Christmas program in my sister's one-room country school, the teacher asked if there were any contributions from the community. My parents poked me in the back and I went up on stage and delivered a Christmas piece. I was four or five at the time."

Wally began writing poetry and limericks for his high school newspaper *The Shoveler*, but writing in quantity was an outgrowth of public speaking engagements and being the master of ceremonies at art events. By the early 1970s publications were printing his work and he was performing his own poems at events such as rodeos, art auctions, and the Montana Governor's Award for the Arts banquet.

Although his poem "Reincarnation" has entered the cowboy poetry traditions as a recitation, and he is kept busy traveling throughout the West as a guest lecturer, speaker, and entertainer, McRae considers himself first and foremost a rancher. "If you are going to write occupational poetry, first you have to be something. Ranchers are very past and future oriented. That is one of the keys to why I write poetry. My poetry is a way to express those feelings and frustrations.

"I don't really believe I fit the category of cowboy poet, a lot of what I write is not cowboy, but rancher. So I guess rancher poet would be more accurate. My poetry is a little broader and not restricted to just cowboy. That gives me more freedom and is liberating because so much cowboy poetry is being written to-

---

"If you are going to write occupational poetry, first you have to be something."

---

day. The main reason I started writing poetry was that I had reservations about coal-oriented industrialization. I felt that some of the cultural values, traditions and beliefs of the agricultural and livestock ranching community should be expressed so that people could understand us. There were some historical and oral traditions that would be better remembered if recorded in a rhymed and metered form."

When McRae is not working on his ranch or writing poetry, he is kept busy by his community involvement. He is chairman of the board of a local bank, serves on the First Interstate Holding board headquartered in Billings, and is part of the Rosebud Protective Association, an affiliate of Northern Plains Resource Council. He is also a member of the Coal and Cattle Company Theater. He has been involved in about twenty of their performances over the years as actor and director. In 1986 he wrote and directed one of the melodramas that they performed.

When asked about performing on stage he replied, "The first time I recited one of my own poems on stage was as a part of a speech. I was surprised at the effectiveness of poetry in getting an idea or message across to a group of people. I have found that sometimes your best poems do not perform well, and sometimes an easily performed poem does not do well on paper. One of my favorite poems, 'Grass-Fat Steers,' does not do well on stage. I tend to shy away from 'Reincarnation' because it is done so much. 'Put That Back...Hoedown' is one of those poems that is so much better performed than written down because of the intricacies of the beat. I am one of a very few that does not actually perform on stage: I recite my poems. Sometimes I move around and act but I usually tend to stick to the podium and recite."

Many cowboy poets place a strong emphasis on becoming financially successful with their work. McRae, however, does not. Ranching is his livelihood, and the crafting of his poems is as much a challenge to him as it is an expression. He does not simply write a poem, but rather in the crafting of verse experiments with meters within the body of a poem so that the mechanics are as much a statement of originality as the rhyming structures or the content.

He especially appreciates friends and fellow poets like Mike Korn, Mike Logan, Baxter Black and others for their constructive criticisms. After he finishes a new poem he likes to call these friends and get their ideas and opinions. He reads the work of others, McRae says, not only to understand the tradition and styling but because "As I pay more attention to other's poetry, I can see my own poetry improve."

In closing, McRae said, "I see a disturbing trend of audiences tending to influence the types of poems that we do on stage. More and more I see that in order to be successful a lot of us poets are tending to select humorous poetry because we get more bang for the buck, a more prolonged response out of the audience, which I feel is unfortunate. If I do more than one poem, I go against the grain and do include some serious poems, because I feel that they are just as important even though the response is not as large and as audible. I think Baxter Black's 'Buckskin Mare' is the best poem ever written and it is especially significant that it is not a funny poem. It is a very serious poem and has gone much beyond a lot of the more shallow poetry that is being written today. We need to resist the tendency for humor and not abandon the more serious things." ❖

McRae is the author of two published books and his third is to be released in the winter of 1989, entitled *Things of Intrinsic Worth*. His poetry reflects the life he leads and the day-to-day trials, tribulations, tragedy and humor of ranching in the 1980s.

Jeri D. Walton is publisher/editor of Outlaw Books Publishing Company located in Bozeman, Montana. She is also the author of the quarterly *Outlaw Newsletter* that helps poets and authors keep track of Western events, other authors, new books and poetry gatherings. For more information, write to Outlaw Books, Box 4466, Bozeman, MT 59772 or call (406) 586-7248.

How Poetry Lives in the West: Interview with Robert Wrigley

While it may seem like a long journey from East St. Louis to Lewiston, Idaho, Robert Wrigley has made the trip successfully and even managed to maintain his sense of humor. He's been the recipient of nearly a dozen awards and fellowships. His poems have appeared in numerous magazines and anthologies across the U.S., and he's published two books, *The Sinking of Clay City* (Copper Canyon Press, 1979) and *Moon in a Mason Jar* (University of Illinois Press, 1986).

Wrigley is currently an Associate Professor of English at Lewis Clark State College. He continues to write and publish poems, and spends many days on the road each year giving readings around the country. He gave *Writer's Northwest Handbook* some forthright observations on small presses and the state of the poetic arts in this country.

WNH: How did you end up in the West? What did you find here that made you settle? Or where did you find it?

RW: In Montana. Montana's where I got absolutely hooked on living in the West. I went to Southern Illinois University for my B.A., and then went to Montana for my MFA.

WNH: Was that because Richard Hugo was there?

RW: No, I applied to four MFA programs, Columbia, Iowa, Montana and Oregon. Oregon and Columbia turned me down. Then I looked at the map and said, this one here, this looks much more interesting. That was a fortuitous decision. I'm much happier here than I might have been elsewhere.

WNH: Where Hugo lives larger than life still?

RW: Oh, he does. He really was a great teacher and one of the best people I've ever known. Once he met you, he always remembered you. It was a great part of his personality.

WNH: How did your experience with him make you work differently as a poet, or does it?

RW: I guess I got this philosophy from Hugo, one which takes the pressure off in some ways. Being a poet in this country means that you're going to be a failure no matter how successful you are, so therefore, failure ought not to be at all surprising. It's not, and if you're willing to fail, said Hugo, chances are you will succeed more often. Anytime you approach the paper needing to write something, you have to be willing to fail; otherwise, you're not taking any gambles.

WNH: Has it made a difference being in the West, somewhat isolated from the so-called cultural centers of the country?

RW: I think there is a tendency for editors anywhere else to see Idaho as a return address and do a double take. Idaho? You know, it's their problem. You look at Oregon, you see writers who live there and Washington, writers who live there, and even Montana, writers who live there. And then there's Idaho, which is sort of a vacuum. A lot of that has to do with the culture of the state; it may have a lot to do with the education, the way education is funded and approached in this state. We don't have many writing programs in this state. We have a writer's program now at Lewis Clark State, an undergraduate writing program, but right now Idaho may be one of the few states in the Union that doesn't have an MFA program.

WNH: So there's no center like Missoula.

RW: No, and that is one serious lack that Idaho has. On the other hand, all four of the college towns have vital reading series. We had a great reading series this year.

WNH: This vacuum means that there won't be a feeling of community among the writers.

RW: Yeah. One thing I noticed in my travels in the East, though, is that I don't think there are communities of writers in the East any more than there are communities of writers in the West. There are just more writers. There are cliques, there are coteries, there are little groups, little Mafias in a way, here and there throughout the East, and a writer in the East probably knows 200 other writers within a hundred miles of where he's at, but I don't think that gives them any sense of community necessarily.

> *"…I don't see any built-in blessings or built-in virtues in a small press, but the good small presses are heroic. I mean, they're making a contribution to American letters that so far exceeds what most commercial publishers are doing that it's just not even funny."*

WNH: Do you find it hard to market your poems, to send them out into the world?

RW: You have to have a real belly for rejection, to be able to accommodate a whole lot of rejection. I understand Truman Capote never got a rejection slip. First of all, I find that difficult to believe. Second of all, I wish I'd known that. I was doing some editing and I'd have solicited some of his and rejected it, just so he would have had the experience. [laughter] Send this back and we'll take it the second time.

WNH: Keeping your books in print is always a problem. The way the industry is changing, do you see that getting better or worse?

RW: No one really knows what's gonna happen now. That's one of the reasons I like university presses, they're good about that. You don't see university press books of poetry remaindered. You never find one in a "deadlist" catalog. I get a lot of $2.98 hardcover poetry books in deadlists that have been remaindered by Viking or Random House.

That's another catastrophic thing that happened recently. Publishing is Rupert Murdock. Rupert Murdock soaked up Harper & Row and the first thing he did was disconnect Harper & Row from its distribution. Harper & Row distributed Illinois, the University of Illinois books, and Pittsburgh Press books and other university press books and that didn't look so hot on the ledger, so that was gone. Now, Illinois is with CUP Services out of, I think, New York, which is Cornell University Press. I don't know, we'll see. I don't know if the distribution is going to be as good or not.

WNH: Does that make you think more about the small presses?

RW: Oh absolutely. But I think small presses need to work

Continued

very, very hard at distribution. And any publisher ought to publish a book that looks good, that's handsome. In fact, I think books ought to be handsome and I think books ought not to be full of typos and blunders. That's inexcusable. You take a look at the best small presses, Copper Canyon and Gray Wolf and North Point and Confluence and you'll find boo-boos every now and then, but certainly no more than you'll find in the trade publishers' books.

I think there are a lot of people who start small presses not because they love literature so much, but they see it as a way to make a name for themselves. There are a lot of venal people in small presses just as there are venal people in large presses, so I don't see any built-in blessings or built-in virtues in a small press, but the good small presses are heroic. I mean, they're making a contribution to American letters that so far exceeds what most commercial publishers are doing that it's just not even funny. ❖   —WW/WNH

Working in the West, for the West
An Interview with William Kittredge

William Kittredge was raised in eastern Oregon and left the family farm in his mid-thirties. Throughout his writing career he's been concerned with the land, however, with the ways humans use it and abuse it, with the ways we perceive it and receive life from it. Kittredge's work includes We are Not in This Together (Graywolf Press, 1984) and Owning It All (Graywolf Press, 1987), and he contributed to the making of the film, Heartland. His strong commitment to the region and its artists shines through in the following interview, in which he speaks at length about two of his current involvements, the Hellgate Writer's organization and an upcoming anthology of Montana writing which will be published in November, 1988.

Writer's Northwest Handbook: What was the initial reason for beginning Hellgate Writers?

William Kittredge: We started this Hellgate Writers thing, frankly, to raise money. The University couldn't do the things they used to do.

WNH: With all the visible literary activity around here, didn't the University consider it that important?

WK: Not enough. Also, I think they relied on the fact that we'd go out and figure out another answer.

WNH: Has your fund raising been successful?

WK: We've raised $15,000 or $20,000 in grants. We've had great luck and great local support. Everybody liked the programs. Normally, when you get somebody fairly well known on the campus, you get a campus audience. But, for instance, with this last "poetry for people" thing, getting it almost completely off campus — in the Congregational Church and places like that — suddenly we got a whole different audience. A big audience of townspeople. An audience we really want to connect with.

One of the things about Hellgate Writers is that it tries to impress upon people that these types of communities like Missoula — an old logging camp connected to a university — are really going to have to change. Agriculture, mining, and logging are not going to bail the economy out any more. They're going to have to get recreation and other kinds of industries. They'll come if the right cultural things are here. And it's advertised.

WNH: How do you see this developing in literary terms?

WK: As a regional center. It's something that many people,

myself included, have very consciously made our concern.

WNH: We've seen an amazing number of little groups as we've toured the state. Do you have some plan in mind to include the disparate groups?

WK: Yes, to the degree they'd like to participate. Once we get going and get outside of Missoula, we'd love to do things all over the place. For instance, next year we're planning a conference in Helena with Arnie Melina of Second Story Cinema. We want to do things with Yellowstone [Arts Center]. Groups like this.

WNH: With your "poetry for people" series you weren't just off campus, you went into the schools, the prison, and the library.

WK: That's right. We want to do more of that. All we can do. Of course, that makes funding easier too. A lot of people don't give a damn if we have another reading in Missoula or not. But if you get them out into the world — participating in the world in some way — that makes a big difference.

WNH: Tell us about your anthology project.

WK: We're doing a big anthology of Montana writing to be out the first of November, 1988. Annick Smith and I are the

---

"Most tribes and reservations are understandably not interested in celebrating the centennial of Montana."

---

editors. Jim Welch, Bill Bevis at the University, and Rich Roeder who works in the Governor's office, and Mary Blew, from Lewiston, are on the editorial board. We spent a couple of years, got a lot of grants, including one for $25,000 just to publish it. The Historical Society will publish it and the University of Washington Press will distribute it. It's 800 pages. Some books aren't as long as the table of contents. It ranges from the oral traditions to tales from the present.

We begin with a whole thing by Native American writers, with an introduction by James Welch. Writers include D'Arcy McNickle, Gray Stone Coates, Maclean, Welch, McGuane, and Crumley — and there's Wayne Ude, Mike Moon,

Spike VanCleve, Richard Brautigan, David Quamman, David Long, Mary Blew.

WNH: Will this work further develop people's feelings for the region?

WK: Yes. Regional cultures are so easy to understand. They're specific. And they're humanly understandable in terms of scale, in terms of size. The Northwest is a place. It's a culture. My God, it's as big as France. And it's as clearly identifiable as France.

But in doing this anthology we found something interesting. In spite of the incredible role that Butte played in the state's history and the conflicts from the beginning between the mine owners and miners, which made this state more liberal than either Idaho or Wyoming, and helped to create an environment for good written material — in spite of that, we couldn't find one good piece on underground mining in Butte.

We are finding some powerful examples of writing by the Native Americans, however. We realized almost at once that we had a real political problem. Most tribes and reservations are understandably not interested in celebrating the centennial of Montana. So another researcher went out to gather their stories.

And that's a whole field that is enormously rich, and which no one has touched.

What's happening is that at the moment there's a huge movement of interest in Native American writing. We get a few Native Americans at the University. There are a few in the anthology. The last one in the book is Deborah Earling, who's probably about twenty-five. She's from a little reservation town near here and is studying for her MFA at Cornell right now. Curt Dueker is another one, a guy who was an undergraduate here, went to Columbia, and is now down in Berkeley. Roberta Hill Whiteman is another wonderful poet. But there aren't as many as you'd hope.

Most of the transcriptions of the old stories are boring anthropological stuff, but the exceptions show what wonderful stories are out there. Powerful. Elegant. There's great native storytelling all over the place out there. And the young Native American writers, for the most part, are not conversant with it.

WNH: Are these writers being published anywhere else, in magazines or journals?

WK: No. I think this anthology will be an absolute revelation to this state. It's all good stuff. ❖ —WW/WNH

Say It with Cash
by Peter Sears

How many foundations west of the Mississippi River devote their funding to contemporary writing and publishing? You can count them on one hand. How many regional workshops for marketing assistance to small press publishers have been held in the 1980s anywhere in the country? You can count them on one hand. How many state arts agencies west of the Mississippi River employ a full-time literary coordinator? You can count them on one hand. Nationally, only 4% of public arts agency money goes to the written arts, and from foundations only 1% (*Foundation News*, Spring 1986).

For all the hue and cry about literacy, for all the sincere well wishing of in-state and regional writers, for all the palaver about the gap in publishing serious literature as a result of the major commercial houses publishing less and less serious literature, for all the changes in tax laws that have crippled writers, for all the listing of the literary arts as a primary arts discipline by the NEA and state arts agencies, for all this and a lot more, the support is simply not there. Support of dollars and services for contemporary writing and publishing is so negligible that the value of competing for it is questionable.

Here is the informed passion of Terry Melton, Director, Western States Arts Federation (WESTAF), from a 1987 public hearing in Portland: "Go to any state arts agency, go to the NEA itself, and you will see: literature is not getting a square shake…. Think of all the emphasis on literacy, and deservedly so, but not just literacy, but the substance of it, serious literature!"

WESTAF became so concerned about the sorry state of support for the written arts that it commissioned David Fraher to do a comprehensive survey of the western states arts agencies in

1981. Mr. Fraher found that not only was support for the written arts (called "literature" or the "literary arts" in arts administrative terminology) no higher than the national norm, but the percentage of funding within various categories was lopsidedly out of whack with the interests of those allegedly being served, writers and publishers.

His findings: at the very bottom was small presses, receiving only 2% of all funding to the written arts (1981 WESTAF report, page 42). Next up was fellowships to writers, at 3% — and next, literary magazines at 5%. Where does the funding go? Next up was a miscellany of "others" at 6% and, then, still heading up, readings at 13%. These five categories accounted for only 29% of the total funding to the written arts.

The remaining 71%? Consumed by one category: payment to writers participating in AIE (Arts in Education), an artist residency program, called in Washington State, AIR, Artists in Resi-

---

"…visual arts and the literary arts frequently indulge in the upstartish practice of presenting new art."

---

dence. A wonderful program for the enrichment it provides schools and community programs. But not a program that should account for almost three quarters of the monies going to the written arts. Not by any criterion. The 71% to AIE writers does reveal, though, how little funding goes to what writers and pub-

Continued

lishers value — 71% is ten times more than the combined 7% going to small presses and literary magazines. No wonder WESTAF acted on the report by launching the WESTAF Annual Book Awards!

How did Oregon and Washington fare in David Fraher's WESTAF report? They ranked first and second respectively in funding to the written arts (page 42). This isn't surprising. Oregon and Washington lead the west, for example, in the number of small presses and literary magazines. Furthermore, they are the first to initiate an interstate literary program (1988).

So let's look at "literature" funding in a western state where the statistics are comparatively favorable to the written arts. Here is Oregon 1986-1989. The following include only project grants. That means grants to organizations. Neither fellowships nor AIE are included.

Literature Funding, Oregon Arts Commission (OAC) 1986-1989:

Year	Requests	Grants	Requested	Awarded	%Total
1986	19	13	$42,900	$12,573	1.5
1987	19	12	$45,797	$13,925	1.8
1988	20	9	$54,185	$15,780	1.1
1989	14	11	$44,555	$14,905	2.7

The percentage of total grant funding awarded to literature in 1988 is lower than it would have been had OAC not received a major increase in its budget from the state legislature earmarked specifically for "Oregon Arts Challenge," a program of grants to nine organizations with budgets of over $400,000. This accounts for $711,484 of the grants awarded, or about half.

Given the particularity of 1988 funding, literature's percentage of the total funding has slightly increased. Yet, how much does this advance mean when set against comparable statistics of the other arts disciplines? The visual arts have led the way all four years with an average 12.4% of the total funding. Here is a listing by discipline and percentage of the total grant funding.

Discipline	Average % of Total Grant Funding 86-89
Visual Arts	12.4
Music	11.1
Theatre	10.6
Media Arts	4.0
Opera	2.8
Dance	2.7
Crafts	2.0
Literature	1.8
Folk Arts	1.1
Design	.4
Photography	.2
Interdisciplinary	.2

These percentages can be doubled, basically, if one is comparing funding by discipline, because 50.5% of the total grant funding over the four years has gone to community arts organizations and AIE. Their grants are not broken down by discipline.

Literature still holds eighth place with a measly 3.6%. That is dead last among the supposed four major disciplines: visual arts, performing arts, media arts, and literary arts. Even media arts is well ahead of literature at 8%. In fact, each of the performing arts — music, theatre, dance, and opera — is well ahead of literature. As to the performing arts in general, their combined total percentage of 55.4% is not only more than twice the visual arts per se, but is still more than the visual arts, crafts, design, photography, and folk arts put together!

In short, literature and the media arts together account for about a tenth, the visual arts about a third, and the performing arts about a half. The funding statistics say there are only two primary arts disciplines, performing and visual.

Given these statistics, to speak of the literary arts as one of four major arts disciplines is a misnomer. And this, if anything, seems to be the trend in public arts agency funding. Why? More aggressive efforts to seek funding? More and better grant applications? Perhaps.

More likely, it is because there are more performing arts organizations; project grants are awarded to organizations. Perhaps it's because the performing arts offer events for which people can dress up and see something that is familiar to them, whereas the visual arts and the literary arts frequently indulge in the upstartish practice of presenting new art.

Yet, when it comes right down to it, what art form can challenge the written word for delivering its evocative, memorable power in such a condensed space and to so many people, so quickly, and for so little money? ❖

Peter Sears comes from a background in education and writing prior to working at the Oregon Arts Commission as Community Services Coordinator. Since there is no literature coordinator, the few staff-assigned projects in literature go to him.

Two private sources of substantial support for the literary arts follow — while the Oregon Institute of Literary Arts is devoted solely to literature in Oregon, Artist Trust services are only for Washington artists and cover all medias.

Artist Trust, 517 Jones Building, 1331 3rd Ave., Seattle, WA 98101. Phone: (206) 467–8734. Services include: Quarterly journal, mailing list of Washington artists in all disciplines, information clearinghouse, information on health care providers, public art education and advocacy, annual awards of twenty or more fellowships of $5,000 to artists for creative time, project grants up to $750 in support of new work.

Oregon Institute of Literary Arts, PO Box 10608, Portland, OR 97210. Phone: (503) 223–3604. Services include: Oregon Book Awards of $1,000 are given for outstanding works in the categories of fiction, creative nonfiction, poetry, drama, and special awards for contributions to Oregon literature; also, in 1988 six writing grants ranging from $1,350 to $1,750 were awarded as well as five publishing grants of $1,000 each.

Small Press Publishing: The Vital Signs

Those of us who write feel it in our guts. New York draws us. The measure of American publishing success is there, among the towers of babble, on the umpteenth floor of a building that's just like the one next to it — and the next. But we know the Grail is there. Somewhere. We pursue.

Yet the giants of publishing, like an old forest, were once the small guys who sank their roots in this nation's cultural Mecca, who grew tall on the fertile words of those they published. Too tall, some would say, for those at the top have lost sight of the ground. The real lifeblood of writing and publishing is always where its existence is most fragile — at the edges of the field, in the small clearings that admit light to the forest floor.

Small presses are where the new, the experimental, the totally whacked out, the uneconomical, the borderline, the raw,

---

"Where a dense thicket of important and healthy publishers once stood, there are only a few, though the multitude of names often persist as imprints of the new communications conglomerates."

---

and the untested are found. But that's only half the story, because small presses are also solid, conservative, profitable, enduring, boring, and basic to the continued development of American culture. Enigmatic, to say the least.

The heroic historical center is less central all the time. Small press publishing, like writing, requires at base a pencil, paper, postage, and maybe a phone — plus the time (money) and inclination to live constantly at risk. Clearly there are lots who fit the description. And their levels of sophistication range from the base described to the latest high tech publishing computers.

While the measure of success for most writers remains purchase by a major trade house, that's probably not where they were first published. And if the trend continues, it's not where they will wind up. There are forces at work in the forest.

Greed motivates much of this motion. Corporate giants have cut the ranks of the major houses through successive buyouts, mergers, and other mega-bucks deals. Where a dense thicket of important and healthy publishers once stood, there are only a few, though the multitude of names often persist as imprints of the new communications conglomerates. The results are disturbing.

More books are published by these few than ever before by the many, but that's tough to attribute to the winnowing of the ranks. On the contrary, the consolidation toward virtual monopoly in the mass communications biz has been because we are reading more than ever and the industry has gotten rather appealing as an investment. Not to mention the clearly understood matter of power that control of media represents.

There may be more new books published, but since when is "more" the criteria for better? The types of books published represent a narrower set of interests. The titles are necessarily less representative of the breadth of available literary work. And the essential corporate decision-making process is being steadily removed from the hands, hearts, and minds of bookpeople and

placed under the jurisdictions of accountants. MBAs as the arbiters of contemporary culture.

It's one of the reasons that the shelf life of a new title is frequently so short that the author's celebration is interrupted by the news that the book is out of print. In the crass world of big time commercial publishing, the break even point for a book is significantly higher than it would be for a small press. And with so many titles offered in each season's new list, no one can afford to devote attention to marketing books with marginal sales. Cultural responsibility is sacrificed in such an environment.

Books and publishers must make money, or they simply won't survive. But a big publisher can abandon and destroy large numbers of books simply because they are not generating a high enough profit. Not that they weren't selling, mind you. On the other hand, the investment of time, cash, and emotion required of a small press for each title puts an entirely different cast on the question of taking any book that sells steadily out of print.

As a result, a growing number of writers are looking to small presses for relationships in which the cash nexus is not the only motivation. Some are returning to small presses after succeeding on the system's terms. For others it is a matter of wanting to be a real part of one's own publication.

According to John Baker, editor of *Publishers Weekly*, there are over 16,500 viable small press publishers in the country today. That semi-official count is corroborated by others in the industry. But the unofficial feeling is that there are closer to 100,000 in the subterranean world of independent publishing. It's almost like a national sideline, this writing and publishing thing. Yet the majority of publishers are not visible because they directly serve highly defined markets; their books seldom appear on the shelves of bookstores or libraries.

"Small Press" has generally referred to the literary and fine letterpress publishers who continue to extend the arts and crafts. They are now the smallest segment of the small presses, outpaced by the growing ranks of small commercial trade publishers who compete with the major publishers in one or a few markets, and by the publishers who are the sole servers of narrow niches. Together, these segments of the industry, including many authors/publishers, constitute the future of American publishing. They are not the swept aside leavings of the major markets, but the sources of innovation and intellectual vigor. The torch-

---

"According to John Baker, editor of **Publishers Weekly,** *there are over 16,500 viable small press publishers in the country today."*

---

bearers of literacy and liberty.

The incredible number of independent, small publishers is partly a response to the dynamics of the whole industry. The shrinking of the ranks of major houses left generous space for small presses to flourish. Titles which might once have had a chance with a big press, despite expectations of low initial sales, are now available to the small presses. Books with small mar-

Continued

kets, or regional markets. Experimental books. Poetry. And reprints of solid out-of-print titles. All these are likely candidates for small press publication.

Clearly there are important choices for authors who want their work to survive, who believe that the real test is the satisfaction of readers — not only accountants.

There are certainly writers who will publish with a small house at first, figuring that such a step brings them closer to real success, i.e., New York. Others, who are less dazzled by the glitz of the big time, understand that a small press may well guarantee them tangible, durable success — perhaps a more modest success, and perhaps a smaller advance, but better royalties and a higher likelihood of staying in print, which means better income for longer and increased chances of subsequent publication.

The big publishers were once all small. Because they had to fight for their spaces, aggressively define their goals, and solve problems with imagination instead of money, they gave as good as they got. American literature is better off for that. Now they have matured. Even become overripe. And a new crop of origi-

> *"They [small presses] are not the swept aside leavings of the major markets, but the sources of innovation and intellectual vigor. The torchbearers of literacy and liberty."*

nal, imaginative, and aggressive small publishers is breathing life into the world of the written and printed word — offering real hope for the future. ❖ —DS

Writing without Bias
Suggested Book List from the Seattle Public Library

Associated Press Stylebook and Libel Manual
This style manual gives preferred terminology for referring to racial origin or handicaps.

Avoiding Handicapped Stereotypes: Guidelines for Writers, Editors and Book Reviewers
FROM: Interracial Books for Children Bulletin, Vol. 8, No. 6 and 7, 1977.

Disabled - Yes; Handicapped - No: The Language of Disability

Dumond, Val
"SHEIT": A No-Nonsense Guidebook to Writing and Using Nonsexist Language. c1984

Guidelines for Non-Sexist Language in APA Journals. American Psychologist 32 (June 1977) p. 486-94.

Guidelines for Reporting and Writing About People With Disabilities. 2nd edition.

Images of Disability in Media

Language Barrier. c1981. Discussions of terms used to refer to people with disabilities.

Macmillan Publishing Company. Committee for Creating Positive Sexual and Racial Images in Educational Materials.
Guidelines for Creating Positive Sexual and Racial Images in Educational Materials. c1975.

McGraw-Hill Book Company
Guidelines for Bias-Free Publishing
Contains guidelines for equal treatment and fair representation of the sexes, minority groups and disabled people.

McGraw-Hill Book Company
McGraw-Hill Style Manual: Concise Guide for Writers and Editors. c1983. Sec. 12-6: Bias-Free publishing.

Media Need Guidelines for Reporting on Blindness and Low Vision. c1985.

Miller, Casey & Kate Swift
Handbook of Non-Sexist Writing. c1980
Gives suggestions for writers who are "committed to equality as well as clarity in style."

Sexist Language: A Modern Philosophical Analysis
ed. by Mary Vetterling-Braggin. c1981. A study of the implications of sexist language as well as a comparison of sexist and racist language.

United Cerebral Palsy Association
Watch Your Language!: No No's for the Media Regarding the Disabled

Without Bias: A Guidebook for Nondiscriminatory Communication. c1982.
How to avoid using discriminatory language when talking about people's age, sex, disabilities and race.

How-to

Writing for an Audience of One
by Ursula Hegi

At a recent writers' workshop, one of my students brought up a question that I'm asked many times: "How soon do you think of your audience when you write fiction?"

When I begin a short story, I write for an audience of one — myself. It's too soon to think of a market, a certain editor. If I started a manuscript for a specific magazine, I believe it would fail. It wouldn't be mine any longer.

To preserve the integrity of my work, I need to write the first few drafts for myself, discovering what I mean, discovering what the story is about.

Gradually, as the content of the story emerges for me in subsequent drafts, I begin to think of my readers. Is the story as clear to them as it is to me? Do I need to bring out the connections more? Is the point of view appropriate to the story? The voice? Does the plot emerge from the characters? Can my readers see my characters the way I see them? As writers, we are aware that our readers only see what's on the page — not in our minds. Though a manuscript may make sense to us because of what we know about the characters beyond the realm of the story, our readers only see what's on the page.

For me, revision is easier than a first draft. In a first draft I have to face a blank page or the blank screen of my computer, drawing whatever will appear from deep inside me. Writing a first draft can fill me with incredible despair. Or joy. But after I finish a first draft, I have something to work with, something I can touch and hold like a lump of clay that contains the shape I envisioned; it is up to me to free that shape from the surrounding mass of material I can't use, to scrape away anything superfluous, to add whatever the work needs.

And so I revise, ten or twenty or fifty times, as long as it takes for the fiction to become clearer, to reveal its meaning to me and — eventually — to my readers. Yet, their interpretation does not have to be the same as mine.

After I complete several drafts, I often bounce the story off two or three trusted writer friends, people I've stayed in contact with since graduate school. They send the manuscript back to me with their notes and questions. We do this for each other.

A few weeks ago I read that Toni Morrison (*Beloved, The Bluest Eye, Song of Solomon*) said in an interview that her characters are her audience; she writes for them. I'm intrigued by that approach, intrigued enough to want to try it. It keeps the audience where it belongs in early drafts of fiction — within the writer, within the writer's imagination.

After I have completed a manuscript, I think about the best possible market. Do I want to send this story to the Atlantic Monthly? To Prairie Schooner? To the North American Review? It's essential for writers to know what magazines publish — not to write for them, but to send them appropriate submissions. Over the years I have talked with many editors who complain that most of the unsolicited manuscripts they receive are totally inappropriate for their magazines. "Please, no more crash stories," warns an editor of an in-flight publication for passengers.

My students ask me: How do you know when a manuscript is finished? How do you make sure you don't hold on too long? Aside from the obvious considerations about craft, it often comes down to a gut feeling, a sense of having completed the story, of having taken it as far as I can. Some writers say a story is never finished — it's abandoned. I've heard painters say the same thing about their work.

But until I reach that place where I feel my story is completed and ready to be abandoned to my readers, I write for an audience of one — myself — breathing the manuscript until it has revealed its meaning to me. ❖

Ursula Hegi is the author of *Intrusions* and *Unearned Pleasures and Other Stories*. She directs the M.F.A. program in creative writing at Eastern Washington University. This article is made possible in part by a grant from the Washington State Arts Commission.

Overflow and Reflection: Writing and Rewriting
by William Woodall

"Poetry is the spontaneous overflow of powerful feelings...recollected in tranquility."
— William Wordsworth, from the Preface to the second edition of *Lyrical Ballads*.

The great Romantic poet urged writers to take time for emotional reflection during the creative process. We might say that writing *is* rewriting. When we approach our work, whether it be verse or prose, fiction or non-fiction, with this fact in mind, the creation of a first draft goes more smoothly. As we proceed to rewrite in an analytically creative way and begin to see that rewriting is not an amorphous task, we can do that part of the work more efficiently and end up with a better poem, article or story.

Let's look at the "overflow" first, to see what this attitude brings us in the way of specific techniques. The underlying idea is that the first draft is always just that. Since we know it's not

Continued

the finished product, our aim is to get it written as quickly as possible. What can we do to help accomplish this?

Although we disliked doing it in high school, making an outline remains one of the biggest aids to getting the first draft written. Knowing where we're going makes the opening easier to write. There's no need to spend time and energy polishing the first sentence or the first paragraph now. We'll write it as it comes and get on with the rest of the piece.

Now that we've started, let's do some things that help keep the words flowing. During the rewriting we will take time to find just the right verb or the perfect adjective. If the first word that comes to mind now isn't the right one, circle it, or put parentheses around it, and go on. When the phrase or clause feels wrong, insert a question mark and keep writing. If a passage really needs to be reworked, but it just won't come, put a big RW!! in the text. This approach gives us fewer excuses to stop writing, and the markers will draw our attention to places which need work. Remember, this version won't leave the house.

Now that it's on paper, or in the machine, what about the "reflection?" Let it sit for a day or two, or at least an hour, even if the editor is banging on the door. Then proceed to rewrite with this fact in mind: it's impossible to make all the necessary corrections in one more reading. Since we'll be going through our story, essay or poem more than once anyway, let's focus on one particular problem at a time. On the first trip back through the "cold" first draft, check the overall organization and the transitions between the paragraphs or stanzas. Even if the piece is experimental fiction, the reader must be able to follow it. Begin polishing the opening and looking critically at the words.

Next, go through and look at every verb. Try to replace linking verbs — am, is, are, was, etc. — with action verbs wherever that's possible. Choose verbs and constructions that shorten sentences or create movement while they contribute to the over-all tone or direction of the piece. Eliminate the passive voice, unless it's specifically called for, and don't forget to use the thesaurus.

The third time through look at grammar and punctuation. If something doesn't look right, read it aloud. Ears may be more accurate than eyes, especially late at night when the piece has to go out the next morning. This practice always helps in sorting out the trouble spots, and it also provides some critical distance needed for evaluation.

One reading should be focused exclusively on spelling. Start from the back and read the entire piece forward a word at a time. This exercise will be difficult to do at first, but misspellings really show up.

Now ask the question, "When I read this work, do I get from it what I want my readers to get?" It's useful to recall the main idea or the reason for writing the piece. Every word, sentence and paragraph should move the reader toward the conclusion.

Looks like it's ready to go now, but let it rest again, then look at it as if it's just come back in the SASE. Pretend to be the editor. Ferret out the weaknesses and run through the rewriting process again.

Seems like a lot of work? It is, but it's time that most writers will take anyway. If we do it in an organized, analytical fashion, that time will be more productive and the quality of the work which goes out will be better. The percentage of sales to submissions will improve, too, and that's what we're all after.

William Woodall is a writer, carpenter & musician who lives in the mountains of southwestern Idaho. He edited the award-winning literary magazine, *cold drill*, in 1974.

A Month in the Life
by Lewis Green

Adventure. Romance. Travel. And 10 months of every 12 attached by fingers to a word processor; by ear to a telephone; by eyes to stacks of notes, press releases, maps and books; and by heart to a vocation.

Travel writing, like any job, is more work than fantasy. It, too, is often a struggle.

Life's tussle begins early, usually about 7 a.m. Eyes barely slits, feet numb to the cold, the cat and I dance our way to the kitchen. She becomes one with her Science Diet, I with my thoughts. Hunched over the last of the corn flakes, yesterday's words are rewritten while today's take shape. An hour later, the battle between work and play ensues. There seems always a reason to avoid writing, always an excuse to be lazy, and no one but me to say how the day is to be spent.

The sun shines, William Kennedy's newest novel sits half-read, and Volunteer Park awaits fresh and green. The conflict rages — fun or food, sun or shelter, for those are the choices. To not work is to not eat. Today, I eat — writing wins out over sloth.

The word processor whines to life. On command, it reveals a page conceived from a seed planted several months ago at *Northwest,* the Oregonian's Sunday magazine. It was still winter, then. Thinking of warmer days, I wrote a two-page query suggesting an adventure, a week-long white-water trip down the Snake River. Like all good stories, this one needed a fresh angle. And to fulfill the promise of the best kind of travel writing, I followed in the footsteps of William Least Heat Moon, who paved *Blue Highways* with an aphorism: "A true journey, no matter how long the travel takes, has no end."

I knew from research, letters to departments of tourism and telephone calls to outfitters, that dozens of guides pack travelers into Hells Canyon, but only one braves those waters in dories — seventeen-foot-long, seven-foot-wide wooden boats. No rubber rafts, no jet boats, just rigid crafts unbending to the river's power. The dories added a touch of the unusual, increased the element of danger and delivered this proposal from the depths of the ordinary to the heights of an event. The editor agreed.

Our working relationship went back two years, so she knew I would deliver. It wasn't always that way. In the beginning, an assignment required more than a good idea and a well-written proposal. She needed evidence of my skills; I needed to justify my existence as a travel writer. So with that first query went three of my best tear sheets and a resumé detailing my writing background.

For me, the procedure is similar with every new editor. Not so for all writers: some may choose the personal approach, the face-to-face meeting; others might work speculatively (unpub-

---

"…I faced Hells Canyon again, this time more frightened by my own words than I ever could be by a dory coming within inches of a rocky death."

---

lished writers have no other choice). In most instances, publications dictate the method: For example, a few magazines, and nearly all newspapers, prefer finished manuscripts over queries. Mostly, I shy away from taking such risks. It makes more sense to spend a week creating a proposal, than a month producing an unassigned manuscript. The reasons are obvious. If the editor isn't interested in the idea or finds your style inappropriate or finds the article unworthy of print, time, money and ego suffer the greatest indignity fostered on writers — rejection. (Heavy editing of a purchased article claims a close second.) I take my rejection in small doses, swallowing it in the form of proposals turned down rather than manuscripts returned.

As for the Hells Canyon article, there was no need to deal with hurt feelings. Assignment in hand, I anticipated the trip. This time, costs would be minimal. The outfitter had invited me as his guest. Although I am loathe to ask for a "freebie," the reality of economics demands acceptance of such graciousness when it is offered. While some magazines pick up expenses, most expect the writer to do whatever is necessary to finance the trip (a very few refuse to accept a story created out of complimentary experiences).

Before leaving for Lewiston, Idaho, to meet the outfitter, I gathered information on Hells Canyon, the Snake River and the outfitters who operate on it. When it came time to write the story, my notes would be useful in filling out the article.

Then, the day arrived, the adventure began. With notebooks, pens and micro cassette recorder packed safely away, I crawled into a dory armed with knowledge of the trip and my outfitter, prepared to waste little time asking questions already answered elsewhere and eager to discover the elusive Hells Canyon. I spent the next week participating, watching, listening and interviewing, all the while taking careful notes. Adventure ended and back in Seattle wearing the pink skin of overexposure, I answered the bell. Wordzilla, the beast of writerdom, and I squared off in the ring.

I mulled the story over, tested unwritten leads, devised outlines. Meanwhile, I worked on other proposals and wrote an article on country inns for a national magazine. The *Northwest* piece would earn me $250. It would be economic suicide to spend too much time courting it. Other work had to be accomplished. But, as always, when the pieces of the story began coming together, I set other work aside to concentrate on telling the Snake River story.

Monday arrived. Cat fed, stomachs soothed, excuses laid aside, I cleared my desk of unfinished business, reread my notes and created mental pictures of the trip. On Tuesday, I gave life to the computer and stared fruitlessly at its blank face. All that preparation, all that forethought, melted like the snows of July on Mt. Hood. Words never come easy to me.

An hour passed, two, lunch arrived, and but one paragraph, some 100 words, hung limply from the screen. By late afternoon, however, the experience found translation in words, phrases, sentences and paragraphs. And by Thursday, my first efforts, some five rewritings, were put to bed. I needed time to relax, time to forget this story.

The following Monday, I faced Hells Canyon again, this time more frightened by my own words than I ever could be by a dory coming within inches of a rocky death. As best I could, never feeling completely confident in my abilities, I cleaned the piece up. Tuesday morning, I mailed it. To the post office, I presented several weeks of research, a week of thought, a week of writing. Return mail delivered a contract, then a paycheck and, finally, a published piece with little to no editing. My rewards.

With every success comes the question: What made this story work, what made the article worthy of print? It wasn't inverted pyramids, the who, what, when, where, why and how

---

"Travel writing is feature writing. It employs the best techniques of fiction. A good story fulfills a dream."

---

of newspaper stuff.

Travel writing is feature writing. It employs the best techniques of fiction. A good story fulfills a dream. Most readers will never experience the trip, whether it's as exciting as racing down the Snake River or as ordinary as a weekend at a bed and breakfast. Therefore, the story must be brought to life, otherwise why would it be read? Words must convey smells and sounds, sights and sensations. Descriptive nouns and active verbs must be employed to create a story of vivid detail. Transport the reader's mind. The beast grows weak against an onslaught of good writing.

It is a struggle but a necessary one. Editors are not easily fooled by drivel, neither are good travel writers. Knowing that and wanting to avoid real work, Samantha (my hungry companion) and I continue our morning treks into the kitchen, she being led by her stomach, I by my heart. ❖

Lewis Green is a Seattle-based travel writer whose most recent book is *The Bed and Breakfast Traveler* from Globe Pequot Press.

Updating the Contemporary Romance
by Margaret Chittenden

There have been changes in the romantic novel in recent years. If you are aware of them, you'll have a better chance of selling your submission. Of course, nothing takes the place of studying recent novels from cover to cover, but here are a few areas to consider.

People: Years ago the heroine was always a virgin. In many romance lines, this is no longer necessary. She can be 'experienced,' though she should still not be promiscuous. She is stronger, more independent than she used to be. She usually has an interesting career. She may be ready for a permanent relationship, but she isn't sitting around waiting for Prince Charming to drive up in his Cadillac and give meaning to her life. Beware of making her militantly feminist though, don't have her snarling at the hero if he opens a door for her — it's necessary for her to *like* men, or at least this particular man.

It's okay for the heroine to have some flaws. She should be attractive, but she doesn't have to be perfect. She doesn't have to ski like an expert *and* play the piano by ear *and* sing as well as Barbra Streisand *and* know everything there is to know about the inner workings of her car, while at the same time whipping up little gourmet dinners and looking ravishingly lovely. She can worry about her weight. She can use makeup to improve her looks. Create an independent, competent, intelligent heroine by all means. Wonderwoman no.

Our hero is also changing. He used to be tall, dark, and brooding, extremely wealthy and much older than the heroine. He was often domineering if not brutal. He might grab the heroine's wrists or ankles and pin her to the bed or floor. Today's heroine would karate chop him if he tried something like that. He is now more often sensitive, tender, gentle, sympathetic. He

---

"The main thing to remember about hero and heroine is that they should be real live three-dimensional interesting *people."*

---

can even have a sense of humor. However, don't take the hero directly from macho to wimp. Nobody wants a hero who is maudlin or namby-pamby. He should still be a reasonably strong man, an admirable man, a successful and sexy man.

The main thing to remember about hero and heroine is that they should be real live three-dimensional *interesting* people.

It's also necessary to use contemporary dialogue and references. I can usually gauge the age of a writer by the references she uses. Recently, I read a manuscript in which the twenty-five-year-old heroine listened to Stardust on the radio, used Chanel No. 5, and waltzed. When you are writing contemporary romance, your novel should reflect contemporary life.

Place: American settings have come into their own, whether rural or big-city. Small Town U.S.A. can be romantic. However, there's still room for exotic foreign settings, though the heroine should be American. Whatever setting you use, try to avoid any resemblance to a travel guide. Descriptions of place should be brief and vivid, preferably given as part of the action.

If you do use an overseas setting, keep it in a contemporary framework. If you set your novel in England, for example, don't set it in a castle or a mansion, don't make your hero an Earl or a Lord — they're all impoverished anyway. London is a lively trend-setting city with lively trend-setting people. Write about *them*.

Plot: Forget formula. Plots are no longer strictly linear and simplistic. "Boy meets girl, boy loses girl, boy marries girl", is not acceptable without some interesting twists and turns. Most romance publishers do put out guidelines, but while these are helpful, it is best to use them only as a framework for a story that is original and interesting and imaginative.

Situations should be contemporary. Arranged marriages or marriages of convenience are out. The other woman as a major plot device is out. (Especially if she's the hard-faced mean bitch of tradition.) Heroines who loll in bubble baths while musing on the hero are out. She's more likely to take a shower — with the hero. Believability is in. Realism is in. Current issues are in, especially in romance lines where subplots are encouraged. It pays to remember you are writing romance, however. You can use situations that are contemporary and realistic without getting into too many negative aspects. You do require conflict though, *believable* conflict, not tame misunderstandings that could be cleared up if the hero and heroine just once sat down and talked.

Love scenes: You've probably noticed that contemporary romance has been getting spicier. However, love should still be the main ingredient in a love scene. Violence and rape do not belong in the romantic bedroom. Love scenes should be an integral part of the growing relationship between hero and heroine, not something that's thrown in for titillation. Read guidelines to discover how various editors feel about love scenes.

Because of our changing times, there's been some discussion among writers and editors about the use of contraception in romance novels. So far, there is a wide difference of opinion. Some editors and writers feel the element of fantasy would be destroyed. Others feel a responsibility to young readers. The jury is still out. If contraception is used, it should certainly be done in a discreet manner.

Viewpoint: Many editors are now asking for part of the book to be in the hero's viewpoint. This offers a considerable challenge, but adds immeasurably to the interest of the novel. Beware of making your hero react in the same way as your heroine, however. Men and women are not the same.

To conclude: Quality is important. The romance novel *can* be an art form. There is certainly no reason why a romance novel cannot be a good book. Take time to rewrite. (I take eight to twelve months for every book I write.) Make your novel the best it can possibly be before sending it out. Check all facts for accuracy. Editors and readers are sophisticated people, they *know* when you haven't researched thoroughly. Cut out the extra adjectives and adverbs. Use *he said* or *she said*, rather than obscure substitutes. Write simply and clearly.

One thing hasn't changed: If you have writing talent and are willing to work hard and accurately, if you have enough imagination to be original and are sufficiently young at heart to write of contemporary situations in a contemporary style, if you believe in love, if you believe that writing about love can be just as worthwhile as writing about death and destruction, and that your book is worth all the talent and skill and care that you can bring to it, then you'll find an editor and a reader waiting for you with open arms. ❖

Margaret Chittenden (aka Rosalind Carson) has published three children's books, four romantic suspense novels, one occult horror novel, and two mainstream books, the most recent, *Forever Love*, is a murder mystery with a background of reincarnation.

Copyright © 1988 Margaret Chittenden

How to Write Ads
by Larry Leonard

A* ad in the ad biz could take any number of forms. It might be a newspaper ad, a magazine ad, a radio spot, a TV spot, the instructions on a tea bag, the copy on a button, the text of a brochure or annual report, a page of technical explanation for some arcane gizmo, a funny cartoon strip…. God knows what it might be.

The principle for all is the same. Your job is to sell something.

My method of copywriting is cowardly. As I have never felt I had any talent at all, I try to find out why somebody would *want* to buy the thing. I do this by asking the clients why they think somebody would want to buy it. Then I wake up the agency account executive and ask him why anybody would want to buy it. Then, I ask the competition why they think it's a piece of crap.

This is mostly done by telephone.

When I know how everybody feels, I have a quick grounding that usually leads me in one way or another. THIS GIZMO IS THE ONLY BLUE ONE ON THE MARKET!

That is my "unique selling proposition."

From that, I develop my "concept."

A "concept" is a premise. A theme, if you will. Sometimes it cannot even be expressed in words. That was the case with the Alaska Airlines Eskimo.

Advertising people are terribly insecure, so, no doubt, if you run in and say, "Eureka! I've got it! We don't have to say a word! We just put a blue Eskimo on the tail!", someone somewhere will attach the line: "Nobody knows Alaska like Alaska knows Alaska!", which means absolutely nothing.

But, they've covered all the bases, and will feel better.

Sometimes, words are truly perfect, as was the case with my mortuary campaign for the Little Chapels Of The Chimes.

"Face it, prepare for it, then forget about it. And, enjoy life."

Once you have your concept, the battle is almost over. Write a headline that will, WITHOUT ANY GODDAMN PUNS, catch the potential customer's attention and pose an implied or direct question that *drags* him into the text.

In the text, begin by enlarging on the headline, then offer the solution to the problems/opportunities just expanded, then ask for the order.

One ad or a campaign, it's the same. In the campaign, you just find other ways of saying the same thing over and over again.

SOME GENERAL TIPS

Every cute headline that could be written already has been.

When asked to produce something by an agency, just call the technicians who do it commercially and communicate panic. The TV stations, radio stations, commercial recording studios, magazines, newspapers and printers out there are *interested* in helping you do your job.

> *"The most elegant concepts I've ever been credited with I stole."*

Print copy is meant to be read. TV and radio are "heard". A thirty-second TV spot should time out to 27" (seconds).

Listen to people when you're doing your research. The most elegant concepts I've ever been credited with I stole. (Never from other ad people. Always from those so-called "non-creative" types who make, use, sell, or buy the product or service in question.)

Write at least a dozen creative concept lines. Then, trust your feelings. When the right one pops up, it'll give you a thrill.

Remember that advertising is a business, *not* an art form.

Advertising is team work. Express your beliefs, but bear in mind that an eighty-word headline may be difficult for the artist to get on a one column by three-inch newspaper ad.

When possible, find out *where* the ad will appear. An ad for cigarette rolling papers in *Rolling Stone* might need a slightly different treatment when it runs in *Reader's Digest*.

Remember there are two reasons why people spend money. Because they want something, and because you have supplied rational reasons why they need it. If you can subtly imply the first and directly support the second, their minds and hearts will follow. ❖

* The editors argued with the author and lost.

Larry Leonard of Dairy Creek, Oregon has been a copywriter and creative director for ad agencies; he is also a freelance writer, and Breitenbush recently published his novel, *Far Walker*.

Copyright © 1988 Larry Leonard

Surviving as a Playwright in the Pacific Northwest
by Charles Deemer

When I tell people that I am a playwright who lives in Portland, Oregon, they smile at me as if I were a hobbyist; when I tell them I don't have a nine-to-five job, they regard me with disbelief. Playwrights belong in New York or Los Angeles. How on earth can a playwright survive in the Pacific Northwest?

With great difficulty. Yet there appear to be great numbers of us attempting to do just this. The Northwest Playwrights' Guild, headquartered in Seattle with an active chapter in Oregon, has a healthy membership. How many of these members do not have to support their scriptwriting work with steadier, if more mundane, incomes is difficult to say.

What advice, then, do I have for Northwest playwrights seeking markets for their work? First and foremost, establish your credibility. For the past three years, every play I have written has been commissioned. My plays have been premiering in Oregon, primarily in Portland, for a decade now, including specialized plays, such as Oregon historical drama. In fact, when people look for someone to write a play with an Oregon historical theme, they likely come to me or to Eugene's Dorothy Velasco, since we have established track records in the genre.

How does one get a track record? By having plays produced. How does one get plays produced? By finding a director interested in your work. This, in my view, is the first and most

> **"...Circulate your work everywhere in the regional market until you find a director who responds with enthusiasm."**

important step for a playwright to take: circulate your work everywhere in the regional market until you find a director who responds with enthusiasm. In my own case, I found two directors/producers in Portland, Steve Smith and Gary O'Brien, each an artistic director at a theater company, and I can realistically say that without their support I very well may have remained unproduced in the Northwest (for which reason I would no longer be living here).

Get produced, gain credibility, and many projects will come to you. Likely not enough to make a living, however, and so the playwright must find other ways to market his or her skills. Film and television projects come readily to mind, but I have little expertise in marketing in these areas. I've worked in both genres but again the projects came to me as commissions, from Oregon Public Broadcasting or independent producers, because of my high visibility as a playwright in the Oregon marketplace. And such visibility and success feed on themselves: the wider one is known, the more work one gets, the still wider one is known.

Teaching is another way a playwright can market craft. I do workshops and am active in the Portland Artists-in-the-Schools program but I try to limit this kind of activity because I never get my own work done when I'm teaching. My own work has first priority. Thus, not only teaching, but commissions themselves can be frustrating because generally one has less artistic freedom when someone else is buying the product ahead of time.

Commissions are welcome, to be sure, and pay better than royalties; but, in my case, three years of writing commissioned plays exclusively has led me to change my situation.

I recently founded my own theater company, called Counterpoint, and am attempting to create my own marketplace, specializing in simultaneous-action drama, a new theatrical form in which, without exactly trying, I've become something of a pioneer. My first play in this form was commissioned and produced by Steve Smith, who also commissioned a sequel, and both projects were highly successful in Portland. I used these opportunities to learn about this exciting new genre, an environmental drama that has scenes occurring simultaneously throughout the space at hand (in my case, a mansion and a riverboat). But since commissions in the form were coming more slowly than my sense of the growing marketplace for this kind of drama, for the first time in three years I decided to write something without a guaranteed paycheck.

In other words, when the marketplace didn't come to me, I decided to go to the marketplace. I may succeed or I may fail but at least I am not sitting around waiting for something to happen. Which suggests another kind of advice: keep your eyes and ears open, be familiar with the marketplace for theater and related opportunities, and respond accordingly. Surely there are many more qualified playwrights living in the Northwest than concrete opportunities for their work to be produced. This makes for a "survival of the fittest" kind of environment, and those playwrights are going to succeed who have something to say, the craft with which to say it, producer/director collaborators who like what they say, marketing imagination and, perhaps most importantly, endurance.

It took me two years of hustling before anyone in Portland would do a play of mine, even though I moved to town with good credentials, an M.F.A. and East Coast productions. I stayed around and hustled because I wanted to live where I do. I could make more money in a larger marketplace but I've never regretted my decision. I also never forget that playwriting is, at root, a collaborative art, and I often thank my good fortune in finding the likes of Steve Smith and Gary O'Brien, my frequent producers and directors.

For one seeking to establish a playwriting career in the Pacific Northwest, the beginning is to find your Smith, your O'Brien. And the more one writes, of course, the more scripts one will have to circulate among potential collaborators. Playwriting, in the final analysis, is first and foremost writing, albeit a highly specialized kind of writing. The first obligation of a writer is to write.

And that's worth repeating: the first obligation of a writer is to write. ❖

Charles Deemer writes for stage, screen, television and print media. He is Artistic Director of Counterpoint: A Simultaneous-Action Theater Company and Editor of *Sweet Reason: A Journal of Ideas, History and Culture.*

A Dialogue for Self-Publishers
by Mark Jaroslaw

Deborah: They sent my manuscript back again. One more time, and I'm calling the *Guiness Book of World Records*.

Mark: You sound cynical.

Deborah: Me? Cynical? I like being treated like a leper by every publisher in New York.

It sometimes begins with cynicism, or even the demands of a runaway ego.

But more often, self-publishing is motivated by a savvy intuition of what the reading public might enjoy, and how you — the writer — can meet that need. Nowadays, thousands of self-published titles (typically nonfiction) are showing up every year, proving that more writers than ever are deciding to take control of their works.

Should you self-publish? Well, consider this:

As both writer and publisher, you're your own boss, have absolute editorial control, enjoy all the profits, and the new tax advantages are terrific. What does all this independence cost? Plenty. Self-publishing is no small-ticket item, and dollars and cents are just one measure. You also have to figure how much time, energy, diligence and commitment you're willing to invest.

Whether or not to self-publish is a big decision. But if you do take the plunge, I wish you luck and stamina. In the meantime, you're invited to eavesdrop on the the following dialogue:

D: I've read a few articles about self-publishing. But I'm still not clear what it is.

M: It's the power we have as writers to see our work become books without many of the usual middlemen.

D: That's what confuses me. I'm a writer, not an expert on marketing, production or promotion. Does that mean I can't self-publish?

M: Absolutely not. Self-publishing is the art of collaborating. It's having a vision for your book, and letting qualified artists, and other pros, help you achieve that vision. As publisher, you don't have to wear ALL the hats. Just know how and where to find the people who wear them best. Now, tell me about your book.

D: It's about food and American history. The two things I love most. I'm calling it, "The Pioneer Bread Book: A Toast to the Old Northwest." It's got some great oral histories, and a hundred or so terrific recipes. It's Julia Childs in a covered wagon.

M: Interesting concept, and it has several strengths. First, it's nonfiction. Bookstores and book distributors love good, well-researched nonfiction. Second, your approach to the subject sounds unique, which means little or no competition. Third, your title should appeal easily to identifiable groups.

D: Does it bother you that it's too regional?

M: Not a bit. It makes it easier reaching your audience. That's one of the nice things about self-publishing. You can establish a track record in your own back yard before deciding whether it's worth going national.

D: So, what's the first step?

M: A formal marketing plan. Identify the special-interest groups you think will have an interest in your book. In your case, I'd start with historical societies. Gift and gourmet shops. Cooking groups. Maybe museums, too. Decide how you want to let them know about your book, and what message will reach them best.

D: You said self-publishing was a matter of collaborating. Sounds like it could get expensive.

M: There's no getting around it. Self-publishing *can* put a strain on your budget. But if it's money well spent, it can only improve your book's chance of success. For example:

Books meant for the commercial market need to be designed. And, unless you're skilled in that area, you'll need a graphic artist to prepare your cover and lay out the interior pages. The bill could be $500 or more.

"You're looking at an investment of between $5,000 and $7,000 to launch a 250-page paperback, with, say, 3,000 copies."

A professional typesetter will be needed to convert your manuscript or computer disc into photo-ready copy for the printer. Typesetters charge several dollars per finished page.

Then, there's the printer. To get the best price, you'll need one that specializes in quantities typical of a self-publisher (usually 1,500 to 3,500 copies). To give you an idea, I printed 3,300 copies of a 256-page paperback. The bill was $4,000.

Then there's promotion. The tab depends on how much geography you want to cover, how much you want to spend on promotional materials, whether you want to invest in ads, and whether you need the assistance of a public relations freelancer. Promotion can run a few hundred or a few thousand dollars.

D: You're talking real money here. I could probably buy a new car for what it would cost to publish my book.

M: Pretty close. You're looking at an investment of between $5,000 and $7,000 to launch a 250-page paperback, with, say, 3,000 copies.

D: But from what I've read, I can design the book myself, and draw up the pages on my computer printer.

M: That's true. Self-publishing is as collaborative as you want it to be. But book distributors and bookstores are getting more selective all the time. And if a book has a homemade quality, they may decline to carry it. If that happens, you could end up with a bedroomful of unsold books.

D: OK. Now, what about pricing? I don't want to underprice my book, but I don't want to scare people away either.

M: You can't go wrong by pricing your book within a dollar or two of your competition. But if you want a helpful formula, try what I call the Rule of Eight.

Simply divide the number of books you're printing into the cost of the printing itself. That gives you a "unit cost." Once you have that, multiply it by eight for an approximate retail price. That should cover expenses, and offer a fair return on your in-

Continued

vestment. If your price seems too low, raise your price to market level; if it's too high, cut expenses.

D: Someone told me that all self-published books need an identifying number of some sort. How do I get one?

M: Years ago, the book industry developed a numerical code to help bookstores, schools, and libraries distinguish one book from another for ordering purposes. Now, every book that's published is entitled to an International Standard Book Number (ISBN). It's a 10-digit number, and acts like the book's "fingerprint."

You can get the numbers at no cost. Just call a New York publishing outfit called R.R. Bowker (area code 212); they'll send you an ISBN information kit.

D: None of the self-publishing articles I've read have much meat in them. Can you recommend any books on the subject?

M: Yes. Two of the most practical are Tom and Marilyn Ross's *Complete Guide to Self-Publishing* (Writer's Digest Books), and Dan Poynter's *The Self-Publishing Manual* (Para Publishing). You can order them through a college bookstore if they're not available locally.

D: OK. So, let's say I decide to self-publish. Give me the hard, cold realities. Slowly.

M: All right. We'll pretend your book was professionally designed and typeset, and the cover price is $12.95. You print 3,000 copies, and the price for everything comes to $6,000.

You approach a distributor — like Seattle's big regional distributor, Pacific Pipeline. They place your book all over the Northwest, and charge you 15% of the book's cover price. Of course, the stores have to make a profit. So Pipeline gives them the usual 40% from the cover price.

When the dust settles, your $12.95 has been reduced by 55%. Your share is $5.83.

D: Sounds like the distributors and bookstores are playing hardball. Is that $5.83 my net profit?

M: No, your gross profit. Remember, you still have to pay off a $6,000 investment.

But, you would be into profit in no time. Somewhere after 1,100 copies. And if you sold your book by mail — and earned the full $12.95 — you'd be into profit after about 500 copies. So, you can see why it pays to take your marketing plan seriously. Those special-interest groups could translate into mail-order sales.

D: Okay, okay, I'm convinced. But now I've got a million questions. Can I get bank financing for my book? How many copies should I print? Where can I find someone to design my book? How can I get on the Donahue show?

M: One step at a time. First, analyze your budget. Next, read a book on self-publishing. Then, test your idea on some of the special-interest groups in your marketing plan. When you're ready, move. And one more thing: To help bring your book closer to reality, do something toward it — no matter how insignificant — every day. ❖

Seattle resident Mark Jaroslaw conducts publishing workshops. He is a former Los Angeles journalist whose latest title is, *The Book in You: A Resource Guide for Northwest Self-Publishers.*

Literary Agents
by Dan Levant and Elizabeth Wales

While working in the sales department of a large New York publishing house I met an author who appeared instinctively to know more about publishing than my company did. And we were publishing his book. He breezed in and out of the company's Madison Avenue offices, confident and purposeful, always with pertinent questions, helpful information and exciting new promotion plans. If he had an agent, I never saw him or her.

Many authors simply do not need the services of an agent because they have a knack for the business of publishing. Or, sometimes an author meets a supportive and responsive editor in the right house early on in his career. However, most writers — and it is estimated close to 75% of all writers — eventually work with literary agents.

Exactly what does agent representation mean and exactly what do agents do? Agents serve writers, representing writers' work to the national book publishing industry. Secondarily, agents sell all rights retained by the author to interested and appropriate markets.

While in practice literary agents' services vary remarkably, there are some basic services that all writers should expect from agents and there are policies that are widely shared within the literary agency business:

• Agents should know where to sell marketable work, which rights to market, and where those markets might be.

• Generally, though there are always exceptions, on behalf of the author the agent offers domestic (U.S.) trade hardcover rights to appropriate publishers. The book publisher, who signs a contract for trade hardcover rights, normally holds second serial rights, trade paperback rights, mass-market paperback rights, book club rights, and sequel or next-book options. The sale of these rights is the publisher's responsibility, although an agent may play an active role, particularly with a well-known author.

• The agent usually retains, on behalf of the author, first serial rights, translation rights, character rights, T.V.-film-dramatic presentation rights, and foreign rights. The sale of these rights is the agent's responsibility.

In order to successfully sell a work and obtain maximum returns from the sale of rights, the agent must be in regular contact with publishing editors, subsidiary rights buyers, and foreign rights and film representatives.

• Negotiating a contract with a publisher is the critical juncture for both the agent and the author. A thorough understanding of publisher contracts and close attention to key contract items that will affect the author's income are all special responsibilities, and presumably skills, of the agent.

• Most literary agencies that serve the book publishing industry encourage new writers and, therefore, accept unsolicited queries. However, unsolicited manuscripts are less commonly reviewed by agencies.

• Any material that arrives at an agency without a SASE (stamped self-addressed envelope) is at risk of not being reviewed and is at risk of not being returned. Use SASE.

• Some agencies provide editorial services, ghostwriters,

> *"Decisions within publishing firms about what to publish are often very arbitrary, swayed by publishing trends, market demand, executive dictates, and the habits and tastes of the editors, sales, and marketing decision makers."*

---

collaborators, and translators. Check an agency's services if you require this type of support.

• Generally, an agent will review a writer's query and then ask, or not ask, to see the book proposal or manuscript.

An agent will do a better job selling a book and all its associated rights if he or she is enthusiastic about the book. Sometimes an agent's reaction to a work does tell the writer something about the writing or the market for the title, but just as often the agent's response to a work is his or her own and simply reflects personal opinions and tastes. If the first agent is not interested in your work, try another agent. If the first agent is interested, be sure the agent is committed to your work and that his or her policies and services fit your expectations and needs.

• Some agencies charge a reading/evaluation fee. Be very careful that you know what services you require and how much they will cost before you engage in "for fee" services. An evaluation may give you feedback or some editorial and marketing advice, but usually carries no assurances for possible publication.

• Literary agents earn commissions on all the work they sell. For years an agent earned 10% of the writer's domestic (U.S.) earnings. Recently, dozens of agencies have increased the commission to 15%, which often decreases in steps to 10% if the book's earnings break through specified ceilings.

• An author's advance, royalties, and rights earnings are usually paid to the agency account. The agency then deducts their commission and pays the author. Consequently, the author should trust the agent absolutely. The burden of responsibility lies with the agent to monitor royalty and other earnings to see that they are accurate and issued in a timely manner.

• Most agencies depend solely on commissions for their income. Many agencies will bill an author, or deduct from the author's earnings, photocopy costs, foreign postage costs, and messenger service costs; that is normally all an author should expect in terms of expenses that are passed on from the agency.

Know in advance what an agency's charges are for expenses accrued while representing your work: make certain they are reasonable and nominal.

If you decide to look for representation, you should spend some time carefully choosing an agent. Shop around. Check the listings in *Literary Agents of North America* or the *Literary Market Place*. Ask friends who are writers if they know of any agents they can recommend. Do not swoon into the arms of the first agent who shows an interest in your work. Talk to prospective agents. Know their track records. Go over the services and policies of each agency. Make sure you feel comfortable with the agent and trust him or her absolutely. If the agent does not use a written agreement — which is generally a good idea — review with the agent the terms of your relationship and the terms of representation.

A good agent can be enormously helpful to the career of a writer. He or she can organize a writer's writing business and bolster the writer's earnings. But, an agent cannot change the market. The market is difficult and quirky. Decisions within publishing firms about what to publish are often very arbitrary, swayed by publishing trends, market demand, executive dictates, and the habits and tastes of the editors, sales, and marketing decision makers.

In the commercial business of publishing, someone must have the confidence that there is a market for your book. It can even be a small market, preferably well-defined, but the confidence in that market is critical.

The challenge for an agent who believes in your manuscript or proposal is to find a publishing champion for your work. An agent wants to see that your book is published — and published right. And that you get paid for your efforts. ❖

Dan Levant and Elizabeth Wales have recently established a Seattle-based literary agency with the primary objectives of representing Pacific Northwest authors to the national book publishing industry. Dan Levant worked as an agent in New York City (principal at Madrona Publishers). Elizabeth Wales was associated with Oxford University Press, the Strand Bookstore, and Viking Penguin.

Literary Agents, Debby Mayer. New York: Poets and Writers, 1983. Describes what agents do, how much they charge, and how to find an agent. Concise and helpful with interesting anecdotes about author-agent experiences.

Literary Agents of North America, 3rd Edition. New York: Author Aid/Research Associates International, 1988. A listing of about 500 U.S. and Canadian literary agencies with a brief description of their services and policies.

How to be Your Own Literary Agent, Richard Curtis. Boston: Houghton Mifflin, 1983. A top agent, Curtis reveals the ins and outs of his trade and his own techniques for dealing with publishers, negotiating contracts and handling financial matters.

The Writer's Survival Manual: The Complete Guide to Getting Your Book Published Right, Carol Meyer. New York: 1984. Well-organized and readable summary description of the book publishing industry — all with the writer's objective of getting published right as the focus of concern.

Book Design, an Invisible Art

by Susan Applegate

We all know what a manuscript looks like, and we all know what a book looks like, but how does the one get turned into the other? They are very different. A manuscript is usually typewritten and double spaced on 8 1/2" x 11" paper. The sheets are separate and their number is usually large enough to make them hard to control, and reassemble, when dropped. A book is smaller and always easier to handle and read: it's typeset and bound along one edge.

We are so used to books that we don't think about how their familiar shape came to be. Often when I tell someone I'm a book designer, the response is a blank look followed by: "Oh, you mean you design covers." Well, the cover needs to be designed, but so does what goes between the covers.

Technical Background Is Necessary

Deciding how a manuscript can best be presented in book form involves quite a bit of technical knowledge. The art of it comes with an understanding of standard formats and how to use them or change them to achieve a certain look. Knowing the history of books and typesetting is invaluable, because history has established conventions that we take for granted, but miss when they're not followed.

The choice of typeface alone can greatly influence the tone of a book. Careful design can ease the production process. For example, a manuscript that is marked carefully and clearly with typesetting instructions will be typeset smoothly and quickly, saving time and money while producing a better product.

Knowledge of the book-manufacturing process is essential to book design. Book printers work with certain set multiples of pages, and designing a book to fit within these multiples is most efficient. The number of book pages the manuscript will make is flexible, and depends upon the size of the type, the space between the lines of type, the width of the margins, etc. By varying these elements the length of the book can be manipulated.

The example is from a cookbook I designed. As you can see, the finished page doesn't look like the manuscript. The changes from manuscript-page layout to book-page layout required many clear and conscious decisions, plus carefully written instructions for the typesetter, who also had a sketch to help her visualize the final product. The end result was a cookbook that is easy to read from a greater-than-normal distance and pleasing to the eye.

I didn't expect cooks using the book to consciously think: "My, this book is nicely designed." Good book design is something that should not be noticed. It's there to enhance and harmonize with the text, to make the information as accessible as possible and not to interfere in any way with the reading.

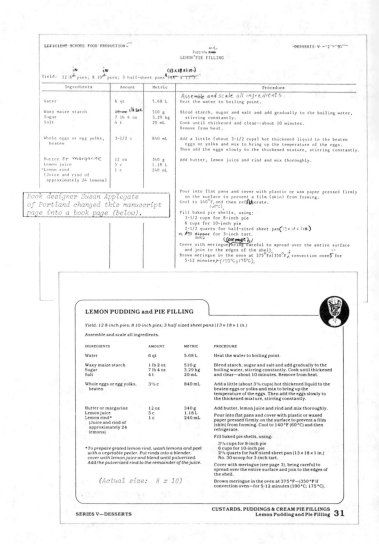

Book designer Susan Applegate of Portland changed this manuscript page into a book page (below).

Cover Design

The cover of a book is very important. It must reflect the content, and explain what the book is about, verbally and visually. People really do judge books by their covers. The cover must be so attractive that it makes even the casual browser pick up the book.

Successful covers don't just appear spontaneously from the imagination of the designer. They are carefully planned with much sketching and rearrangement of elements. The time, money, and energy invested in cover design is well spent because the cover is the most important marketing tool of the book.

A starting point in cover design is an ordering of elements. What is most important? (It may not be the title.) What comes next? What is tertiary? More that three levels of emphasis probably won't work — too busy. Continuing to analyze in one-two-three order while sketching and rearranging eliminates unacceptable layouts.

In *Back Talk*'s cover the most important element, to my eye, is the title within the dark rectangle. The rectangle, with the type

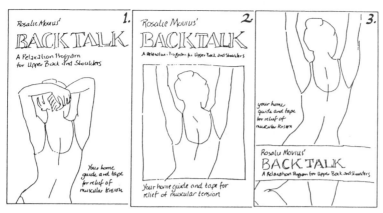

DESIGNER'S NOTES

1-2 Rejected rough sketches.

3   I realized I was getting close to a workable design when I did this.

4   I varied the elements, especially the figure.

5   Here the final layout was carefully worked out and I hand drew the letters to look like display typesetting.

reversed (white on dark), ties the title, author's name, and subtitle together as the number-one element. Second in importance is the illustration, which is a picture of what the booklet is about. Third, and much less important, is the sentence to the left, which gives more information about *Back Talk*. If your eye sees the illustration as most important, that is okay because the layout, as your eye moves down the illustration, leads you to the title.

By comparing the finished cover with the sketches you can see how the cover of *Back Talk* evolved.

For More Information

The Design of Books, by Adrian Wilson, is an excellent, easy-to-read book about this invisible craft. *Editing by Design*, by Jan White, does not deal directly with books, but does explain the design process clearly, and makes interesting reading. As the title suggests, Mr. White discusses the relationship between words and design. ❖

Susan Applegate is a graphic artist, book designer, and owner of Publishers Book Works in Portland. She likes talking to people, invites queries, and has information available about her services. This information first appeared, in slightly different form, in *Publishing Northwest* (a quarterly publishing-industry newsletter from Te-Cum-Tom Enterprises in Coos Bay, Oregon).

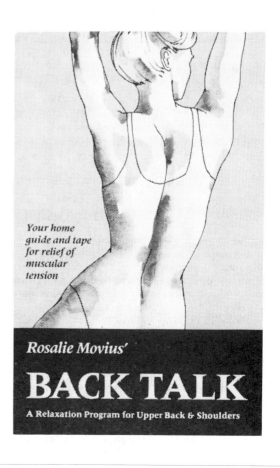

Book Publicists
by Anne Damron

A book publicist is a trained professional who can get the most media coverage for a book — regardless of the subject. Authors working with an established publishing house are assigned a publicist (mid-sized houses usually have only one) with whom they will work on promotion from the day the contract is signed. Small publishers may hire a freelance or consulting publicist, or assign someone from their staff. A good publicist will gauge the publicity opportunities for the book based, in part, on the author's willingness to promote.

Most publicists send their authors a detailed questionnaire at the time of contract signing. Common questions highlight the author's previous television and radio experience (if the author has none, the publicist may hire a trainer), journals and magazines that might do a book review, important questions that the book answers, etc. This information helps the publicist create a plan which will best utilize the author's experience and skills.

"The average publicity life for a book is three to six months."

Planning allows the publicist to ensure, for example, that travel editors discover a book *before* the peak travel season ends, that bookstores have advance planning for promotions, and that excerpts can be placed in appropriate magazines. Publicity tours — especially multi-city tours — are usually scheduled four to six months in advance. Most magazines also require that much lead time for book reviews. *Publishers Weekly* and *Library Journal* need 15 or more weeks.

Publicists keep abreast of the author's schedule changes (heaven forbid that "The Today Show" call and the publicist be unable to find the author because he or she is cruising to Alaska!). Skilled publicists won't promise an appearance on "Oprah" or "Donahue," and will do their best to help the author understand the odds of such an appearance or a review in the *New York Times Book Review.*

Savvy authors ask their publicists what the plans are for the five main areas of publicity opportunities. *Customers* (the readers) will see reviews, mentions of the book in news releases picked up by the media, and via direct mail. *Bookstores* aid the publicity effort by running advertisements in their newsletters, sponsoring a reading or a booksigning, or having autographed copies on hand. *Library* sales benefit from promotion, since most librarians buy books after seeing reviews or receiving a direct mail flyer. Authors should ask about *subsidiary rights* at the time of contract signing. Book club sales can be a tremendous publicity boost. A good publicist won't overlook promotion to the profitable *non-traditional markets*: the military, premium sales, specialty shops, export, catalogs.

Good publicists give their authors lists of what they will and won't (or can't afford to) do to promote a book, so the author won't have to ask. The marketing and advertising departments can do the same. Publicists should provide ample supplies of catalogs and other promotional materials to the author, as authors are usually the best advertisements for their books. Regular communication with the author is essential so that both parties know who is doing what, where and when.

The average publicity life for a book is three to six months. Most publicists will continue to promote a book as part of their line, as a tie-in with newly released books, or as it fits into current events. Publicists who handle more than one book, often up to 40 per year, have to move on to other projects.

Many authors become their own publicists, especially as the book gets older. Others move on to other writing projects leaving the book to sell itself. However, an active author can greatly prolong the life of a book. ❖

Anne Damron is the 1988 President of Book Publicists Northwest and the Publicity and Promotions Manager at The Mountaineers Books.

Basic Definitions of the Publishing Industry

A *publisher* contracts with writers for manuscripts, makes all the decisions determining how the book looks, assumes all financial responsibility for the book manufacturing, handles and assumes responsibility for marketing the books to the public, and pays the writer a royalty. Money is made from book sales. Publishing is often confused with printing — they are not interchangeable.

Printers put ink on paper. Someone else makes the decision about where the ink goes. Publishers pay printers.

Graphic artists and *book designers* are hired by publishers to help decide what a book will look like.

A *typesetter* converts the words of a manuscript into the proportional letters called typesetting. Like the printer, the typesetter follows the directions of someone else.

A *self-publisher* is a person in the business of publishing who also is the author of the book being published.

A writer with a manuscript will always find a *vanity press* interested in his or her manuscript. The vanity press is a type of so-called publisher that makes money from authors rather than from selling books to the public. Vanity presses are to be avoided. It is cheaper to self-publish.

The distinction between publishing and printing did not exist in Ben Franklin's time. He was, by these definitions, a self-publisher who also did his own design, typesetting, and printing. The technology of all these fields has grown very complex since then, more than any one person can master successfully.

Publishing is a very risky business and there are many more hopeful writers with manuscripts than publishers. Thus competition is stiff for the major publishers, most of whom are based in New York, and many writers in the Northwest consider self-publishing. In fact, our local culture would be *much less* rich without our local publishing industry.

—Susan Applegate

Marketing the Book Package
An Interview with Solstice Press

Patricia Hart and Ivar Nelson, owners of Solstice Press, have been publishing words in a variety of shapes and styles for over ten years. Their publications company in Moscow, Idaho, The North Country Book Express, publishes magazines — notably the six-year-old Palouse Journal — *and catalogs. Solstice Press is a non-fiction, trade book publisher which not only produces books directly but also creates "packages" with larger publishing houses. Their first book on cross country ski trails was published in 1978; they now publish four or five books a year and have a 20-book backlist.*

Writer's Northwest Handbook: How did you two start working together?

Ivar Nelson: When Pat and I met, she was working on a publication at the library, and I had Book People (a book store in Moscow), so already we were in the printed word business. Our concept at that time was to sell other people's books as a wholesaler. That would create the marketing pipeline into which we would then put our own books.

WNH: So each of you was thinking independently of publishing when you got together?

IN: Yes, the goal was to become a book publisher. So the next thing we did was production work for other people. And both wholesaling and production work were valuable, because we learned by doing.

WNH: Like all small presses you must have some trouble with cash flow. What do you do when times are tight?

Patricia Hart: What evens out cash flow during those times are package books. That's a sure thing. You're actually being paid for everything. We still do some catalog work for clients, too, as well as university contracts and things for the local historical society.

IN: Packaging has its problems, though. We sold a package to Dial, then Doubleday bought them, and they couldn't have cared less. You've got a classical case that authors run into, too, which is that you have something going with a publisher and your editor leaves. And when that happens, you might as well just forget it because it's so personal with those people in New York, with the big publishers. You've sold your book to one editor, and that editor is your advocate in-house. When that editor is gone, you don't have an advocate. They'll go ahead and do the book, but it'll be rather limp. That's what happened to our camping books.

WNH: How do you make these packaging arrangements?

PH: When I talk to an editor about packaging a book, we agree on press run, the price of the book, the size of the book. This is based on a proposal. What they want is a description, the market, something about the author, and less than a chapter, because a chapter really stresses them out.

I'm selling to the editor, so the editor and I work until we get something that will fly. One of the reasons we are successful is that we have no grand illusions about press runs. And the number people in New York are running is very small. They're running 5,000 at a time.

We arrange to have a certain amount of money for the mechanical end — that is, all of your editorial talent up to the mechanical stage, and they give a hunk of money for that.

IN: They are much more willing to give bigger advances than they are royalties. They have a real problem with the percentages on royalties. They have offered 8% on wholesale.

PH: At this point, you're selling tacos — I mean one penny — it's practically nothing.

IN: But they're quite willing to give enormous advances.

"We figure we have about 15 seconds when we first show the idea to a New York editor."

As a small press, we want to give big healthy royalties because everybody takes the risks together, but we don't want to give the money up front. So it's very much the opposite of that.

PH: Then they may pay a third, a third, and a third, usually while we're producing it. We figure out what we could make in royalties on the first press run, and they're happy to give it. But it's up front — no risk to the author or to us.

IN: That's on contract usually. It may be an advance with half on contract, half on the galleys.

WNH: And then you split that advance with the author?

IN: We take an agent's cut and pass on the rest to the author. That's the traditional way they work. They're used to giving advances. It doesn't bother them at all.

It's very funny selling to them. It's just like we teach in class: a magazine has seven seconds when somebody's looking at it on the magazine rack. We figure we have about 15 seconds when we first show the idea to a New York editor.

WNH: Is this a written proposal?

PH: This is you: "Hello — what do you think?"

WNH: How does this packaging help the author?

PH: What you do when you're packaging is that you can get distribution for your authors you'd never be able to afford yourself.

WNH: Have you tried selling the book yourself for awhile and then selling it to New York?

PH: We've never had any luck with that. One of the reasons is that when we were selling it ourselves, we were selling it to the trade. But I think if you did it without doing the trade, if you sold 30,000 copies, then New York might pick it up. Thirty thousand seems to be the magic number. And they'll really go with it.

IN: When our *North American Wild Game Cookbook* went into three printings, we thought that was the chance. So we ran all around New York and they wouldn't go for it. They couldn't understand somebody shooting a deer. That was too much for them.

WNH: How about the mix of your books?

PH: Probably 90% of our book ideas are generated by Ivar or me, and then we go out and look for an author. Because of that, when you see a certain set of interests, it reflects what we thought were good book ideas. That's very eclectic. There's just no overlap. If I had it to do over again, I'd do a number of books on one particular and narrow subject. ❖   —WW/WNH

The Fine Art of Getting Published
by Knute Berger

Current estimates place the number of magazines published worldwide at between 60,000 and 100,000. In the U.S. alone, there are some 16,000 different magazines, forming a nearly $16 billion industry, according to the Magazine Publishers Association. If each of those U.S. magazines published an average of a dozen articles a month (a conservative figure), that would translate into more than 2,300,000 articles — 70% to 90% of which are freelance written.

So, with all this mass of verbiage, is there class? Does this vast quantity of published words mean that we are saying what we are saying better than ever before — so much better that we're cranking it out and lapping it up in record proportions?

Of course not. And it is the troubling contradiction between quality, quantity and public taste that baffles many writers — especially those waiting for their first taste of printers ink. Many writers complain loudly and justly about not being able to get their own good work accepted by publishers when literally dozens of inferior writers are collecting accolades, guest spots on Donahue and — worst of all — checks at the postbox.

The complaints are justified, but publishing is not based upon justice. The system of decision making stems from the fact that it is a business, first and foremost. Decisions, by and large, are made for bottom line reasons: Will it sell? Is there a market? Can the Japanese printers do it for less? How quickly can a completed manuscript be in my hands? Is someone else making money selling stuff just like it?

If you recognize from the beginning that there's little fairness in the system, you will save yourself a lot of frustration. But knowing there is a system — with general rules and considerations — ought to be some consolation.

"Publishing is a bit like the fashion industry: it works with long lead times."

At *Washington* magazine, and at every other magazine I have worked at, we are deluged with ideas. If anything exceeds the output of our publishing industry by 25 million times, it is the output of ideas. On my desk this morning, I have story proposals relating to the sea urchin gonad industry, quilting, Fort Nisqually, local aerobatic performers, Washington's best liars, a museum devoted to coin minting errors, the story behind a family's success making pasta, Puget Power's 100th anniversary, a father-son basketball coaching dynasty and a woman who cares for abandoned minority children. And that's just a sampling.

Each week, we receive perhaps fifty query letters or manuscripts, plus half a dozen book proposals (and to date we've only published one book.) We may also get another twenty or thirty phone calls from writers pitching ideas over the phone. Unless it's my mother, they are invariably told to put it down on paper and send it in so it can make the rounds among the three editors on our staff who review all ideas that come our way.

The most successful commercial writers, whether they are magazine freelancers or authors of books, are people with ideas, and if there is any secret to The Fine Art of Getting Published, it is the strength of ideas themselves. Publishers feed on them. I don't know where *Washington* magazine would be if they didn't flow in from our readers, our contributors and our staff. We may never do a major feature on sea urchin gonads, but I will defend to the death someone's right to send me that idea.

The longer I am in this business, the more I am impressed with the power of good ideas. They usually are self-evident and require very little discussion among editors who know what they are doing.

The next question is: what constitutes a good idea? Well, good ideas have several common characteristics. First, a good idea is one that fulfills a genuine need — preferably a growing need. It may be a need for entertainment, a need for information, a societal need for greater awareness — whatever. If an idea is needed — if its time has come — it will eventually be given the life it deserves. Eventually.

Another characteristic of a good idea is that it gets better as time goes by. Ideas grow and change — let the ones to which you commit yourself improve with time. If your idea is good now, but will get better in a year or two, you've just bought yourself the time to sell it. Stay away from trends. Publishing is a bit like the fashion industry: it works with long lead times. The clothes you see in *Vogue* are already old news to the designers planning next year's line. So too with publishers.

In publishing, good ideas are defined in another way. A good idea is one matched to the needs and character of the publishing company considering it. That's why 10 or 100 different companies may consider the same idea and only one will accept — the idea must fit in with the goals and aspirations of the editors and, through them, the company they work for. You have no control over those goals and aspirations — you can't convince them to rethink their philosophies or standards. You must stick by your idea and find the right partner for it. Some ideas have many potential partners — usually the kinds of ideas that show up on the bestseller lists and in mass circulation magazines. Often, however, good ideas have only a couple of potential mates, and your job is to find them.

This is the part that most writers find painful — finding their publishing mates. There is no equivalent of a singles bar to hang out in and find one. Some have ideas that are best handled by a dating service — literary agents — but first, they have to get the agent, a process many find as painful and as difficult as finding a publisher. There is no easy answer to this problem. The simple fact is, if you have an idea and want to sell it, you also have the responsibility of doing your homework: looking at publishers' catalogs to see what types of books they are publishing, reading trade publications and magazines to see what their editors are choosing.

It is amazing to me how few writers do this. At *Washington*, we get article submissions from all over the country. Nothing wrong with that, but why people would propose articles to us about things in Iowa or Florida is beyond me. But they do. There is no quicker way to alienate an editor than to insult him or her with an idea that is so inappropriate as to prove that you have not read his or her publication. You've just confirmed the editor's worst fears that grip him on the way home at night after a brutal day at the office: no one appreciates what I do.

The process of researching and learning the publishing business, if you are going to be part of it as a freelance writer, is essential and, quite frankly, if it is too distracting or painful for you, you are better off doing something else. The minute you ask for money for your work, you are entering into an arena where the rules are made by people other than yourself — and they will expect you to play by those rules. This is true whether you receive an advance from a publisher, a grant from an arts organization or an assignment from your local magazine.

The flipside is the service that is performed, and the pleas-ure there is in seeing a good idea come to life and reach its audience, which is, after all, what publishing is all about: delivering the audience. To fill a true need, to supply information that has a positive impact on our lives — to teach, to enlighten, to enrich — all these are the fulfilling aspects of this line of work. It completes the creative process we are all partners in. ❖

Knute Berger, Executive Editor, *Washington* magazine. Edited by John Willson from a speech delivered on Governor's Writers Day, 1987, at Washington State Library, Olympia.

The Ethics of Simultaneous Submissions
by John Willson

Technology and a burgeoning literary magazine market fuel a growing practice

"Is it OK to send my work to more than one magazine at the same time?"

Writers just beginning to send out their poems and stories frequently ask me that question, and I've always answered with an emphatic "no," explaining that in sending your work to a magazine, you're entering a time-honored trust between writer and editor that the work isn't being sent elsewhere.

However, in recent years I've noticed the phrase "simultaneous submissions OK" in directories and newsletters that list literary markets, and I'm beginning to find writers who simultaneously submit their work as a matter of course.

Joseph Bruchac points to a number of factors in attitude shifts toward simultaneous submissions in an article in the *Greenfield Review Literary Center Newsletter* (1/87)*. These include the rapidly growing market of literary magazines, and computer/word processing technology which enables a writer to easily produce multiple "originals" of a given poem or story.

Feeling the very foundation of submissions ethics trembling beneath me, I wrote a simultaneous submissions survey and sent it to the editors of 65 literary magazines and presses in the Northwest. It consisted of two yes-or-no questions: 1) Do you as editor of your magazine/press consider simultaneous submissions? 2) Has your policy toward simultaneous submissions changed in recent years?

> *"We like to be told that it is a simultaneous submission in the cover letter."*
> *—Bronwyn Pughe,* **Cutbank**

The total response — 57% of the surveys I sent out — was immediate, and the numbers surprised me. Over half the magazines, including some well-established ones, *do* consider simultaneous submissions. The wide range of policies, reflected in editors' written replies, revealed even more; very few surveys came back without additional comments. Several editors at-tached two-page, single-spaced letters. It was clearly a topic about which most editors felt strongly.

Responses from editors who *do* consider simultaneous submissions reflect a variety of views, but a few generalizations can be drawn regarding their policies. First, a large portion of magazines consider simultaneous submissions out of sympathy for the writer. They cite long reporting times — the time it takes for editors to accept or turn down a writer's work — as the reason for allowing a writer to send his or her work elsewhere at the same time. A comment by David Memmott, *Ice River* editor, is typical: "Most small mags/presses have voluntary editors and little or no staff, and consequently take longer to respond to submissions. Writers in our time face a publish-or-perish milieu which forces them to get more work into print before they publish books."

The second common motive behind considering the policy is simply hunger for material; in the midst of an expanding literary magazine market, some editors see themselves in competition for a finite quantity of good poems and stories. John Gogol of *Mr. Cogito* puts it succinctly: "We want good poems — don't care *how* they come!"

There is an ironic flipside to the reasoning that considering simultaneous submissions helps writers because most magazines have long reporting times: by encouraging writers to submit to more than one place at a time, the policy increases the bulk of manuscripts going out to magazines, flooding editors' desks and therefore actually extending reporting times.

Further, it's clear that many writers are sending out their work simultaneously regardless of the policies of the magazines they send to. Such indiscriminate submissions have many editors irate, including Scott Preston of Wind Vein Press — which does accept simultaneous submissions: "... the problem of rote submission, by people who have never read my mags, bothers me a great deal...I sometimes think that the number of writers' guides, publications, indexes and assorted trivia damage the small press world as much as they assist it."

Continued

The most extreme abuse of simultaneous submissions happens when writers both submit to and publish a given work in more than one place, leading to the key ethical — and sometimes legal — issue raised by editors who do not consider simultaneous submissions. A case in point comes from Linda Clifton, whose *Crab Creek Review* recently switched to a "no" policy: "Several authors have not only simultaneously submitted, but, without telling us, simultaneously accepted, placing our copyright in jeopardy."

Describing a typical scenario, Editor Larry Dennis addresses a hypothetical writer who has submitted a story to *Eotu* and had it accepted. Having paid the writer for First North American Serial Rights — the right to be the first North American publication to publish a piece of writing — Dennis sends the

---

"…it's a waste of our bloody time to accept something only to find out it has been accepted by someone else. We don't want to duke it out with other magazines."
— The Editors, Fine Madness

---

story down the long line toward production, which includes typesetting, layout, advertising placement, artwork, and printing.

Dennis goes on to describe the turn of events: "So now I get a letter from you (the writer) saying, 'You know that 6,000 word story I sent you? Well, *Jawhammer Annual* just sent me $1,000 for it so you'll have to pull it.'"

"My response is immediate. 'Yeah? Right? Get real. Your story, the one I sent you $5 for, is going to print, so you'll have to send that $1,000 check back.'"

"That's the simultaneous submission in action. And it happens *every time*, just like that. For the writer it's a gamble. You send out the story to eighteen magazines, odds are it will be bought. If it isn't you lose postage.

"Sometimes I take the gamble. If it's a really good story, worth a lot to me because my readers will enjoy it, I figure I can win. I buy the story from you cheap, then, what! it's in print and that guy with the $1,000 check, well, gee, I guess he loses. And so do you."

Beyond the ethical and legal considerations, editors who do *not* consider simultaneous submissions emphasize time and the work involved in reviewing submissions. John Witte, *Northwest Review* editor, explains: "Our staff of expert editors donate their time without pay, and devote many hours considering a work for publication. If, after a poem or story has been accepted, we learn that it has been taken elsewhere, we have wasted considerable effort lavished on it, leaving in our editorial craw a sharp, stuck object."

The issue finally comes down to honor and responsibility.The policy of accepting simultaneous submissions mainly benefits the writer — it doesn't save editors any time or effort — so the very least a writer can do is assume responsibility for his or her submissions. In turn, editors should make their policies clear wherever possible.

I therefore make the following suggestions, borrowed from Joseph Bruchac with a few of my own added:

1) Writers should learn the submissions guidelines of any publication they send to. These can be found in the magazines themselves and often in listings of literary markets. If the magazine states that it *does not* consider simultaneous submissions, then it's unethical for you to send that magazine a piece you are submitting elsewhere.

2) When simultaneously submitting your work to magazines which *do* consider simultaneous submissions, state in your cover letter that you are doing so. Otherwise, the editor must assume that he or she has exclusive consideration of your work.

3) Needless to say then, if one magazine accepts your work, you should notify the other magazines of this immediately.

4) Given the increased practice of simultaneous submissions, it would be a further act of good faith for a writer *not* simultaneously submitting to indicate this.

5) Editors should clearly state their policies in their guidelines.

6) Writers should keep careful records of where and when work is sent, who it is sent to and what the reply is.

7) If a magazine has neither accepted nor turned down your work within a reasonable amount of time — Bruchac suggests three months — send a short query letter with SASE regarding its decision. ❖

*"The Ethics of Multiple Submissions" by Joseph Bruchac. *Greenfield Review Literary Center Newsletter*, 2 Middle Grove Rd., Greenfield Center, NY 12833.

John Willson co-edits *Exhibition*, the art and literary magazine of the Bainbridge Island Arts Council. He is a recipient of Academy of American Poets and Pacific Northwest Writers Conference Awards.

Magazines/Presses which **do** consider simultaneous submissions:	Magazines/Presses which **do not** consider simultaneous submissions:
Bellingham Review/Signpost Press	*Backbone*
Calyx	Bellowing Ark Press
Capilano Review	*Calapooya Collage*
Catalyst	*Crab Creek Review*
cold-drill/Ahsahta Press	*Dog River Review*
Cutbank	*Event*
Ellensburg Anthology	*Fine Madness*
Eotu	*Northwest Review*
Ergo!	*Oregon East Magazine*
From the Woodpile	*Poetry Northwest*
Ice River	*Poetry Today*
Jeopardy	*Poets. Painters. Composers.*
Malahat Review	*Room of One's Own*
Mississippi Mud	*Silverfish Review*
Mr. Cogito	*The Village Idiot*/Mother of Ashes Press
NRG/Skydog	*West Coast Review*
Portland Review	
Prism International	
Rhyme Time/Hutton Publications	
Wind Vein Press	
The Written Arts	

Writing & Editing: Strange & Necessary Bedfellows
by Gillian Conoley

I think the act of writing is a truly mysterious process, unique to each individual writer. I don't believe in the hocus-pocus stereotype of the artist as someone who goes around in a trance all the time, who suffers and despairs until the next burst of inspiration, but I do think that each writer, each good writer, must find his or her own way out of the mire in a highly individual fashion, and must be steadfast enough in the task to accept awkwardness as a kind of grace.

As for myself, I find it necessary to shut out everything, all noisy fragments of twentieth century existence, every jingoism of the mass media that invades the house in the form of hyped junk mail, free detergent samples, pre-recorded phone solicitations. I shut the door of my study and imagine the hectic, empty messages of our post-Laconian age dissolving. For me, writing is like finding an oasis where I can see again, and rename everything, where language can be rescued, where words can return to their original, exotic states.

Curiously, it was through editing that I learned this most helpful tool of ignoring the other world so I could create my own. One of my first post-college jobs was as a Dallas newspaper reporter and editor in the mid-70s, just before the brooding silence and muffled beeps of the computer filled America's newsrooms, forever turning them into places of hushed, anxiety-filled quiet. The room I walked into for my first "real" job was filled with the glorious din and ra-ta-ta-tat of typewriters. The men did not wear fedoras, nor the women sharp shoulderpads à la Barbara Stanwyck, but the newsroom was full of tough talk, exasperated editors, cigarette smoke because no one had yet learned to say no. Most especially between the hunger-filled hours of 11 a.m. to the approaching 2:30 deadline, there was a steady stream of unrelenting noise. It was wonderful.

Still, once I had gathered enough material from the outside to compose a story, I couldn't think in all the noise. Think or die,

> *"At* **Willow Springs,** *we look for work that uses fresh language fully engaged in the power of telling, work that exhibits an imagination that is not afraid to test its boundaries."*

get paid or don't, my colleagues said. I wiped the green from behind my ears, and soon I wasn't hearing anything but my own thoughts. Four years later I gave up newspaper writing and editing altogether and wrote what I had been hiding away at home — poetry. Now, two collections of poetry later, I find myself again in the role of an editor, this time as a literary magazine editor, and I am most grateful for the lesson in necessary noise reduction, as it is a movable skill, whether I am in the silence of my own study, shutting out the nagging, doubting voices of my subconcious, or in the *Willow Springs* (a magazine published at Eastern Washington University) office, trying to make a deadline to our typesetter while staff members are sorting through our burgeoning stacks of manuscripts.

In my experience there are other ways in which writing and editing crosspollinate, ways far more mysterious or perhaps more utilitarian than this. For example, I think a good literary magazine, one that is responsible to the literary climate of its time, must have a clearly defined and recognizable editorial vision, just as a writer must, over the years, develop a way of seeing, a way of perceiving the world that is particular and individual. This is no easy task, and calls for diligence on the part of the editor and the writer.

Both as editor and writer I am interested in new possibilities for language, in drawing it into riskier associations than those we find in "plain style" mimetic prose or poetry. In our post-structural, post-nuclear, post-industrial time, it's no secret that the word is endangered, that meaning is floating somewhere outside of our tired, inky signifiers. I'm most interested in work that admits this problem, and yet forges ahead, renewing that language at every turn rather than despairing of its shopworn qualities, or worse, actually engaging in them. I think some of my interest in language results directly from those years working with newspapers, where all the richness of life and event is encapsulated in a vocabulary calibrated to an eighth-grade intelligence and comprehension, in a language dulled, deadened, made palatable for "easy readability."

At *Willow Springs*, we look for work that uses fresh language fully engaged in the power of telling, work that exhibits an imagination that is not afraid to test its boundaries. Everyone on the staff is also a writer, so we try to get the work read, back, or accepted as soon as possible, and we try to live up to our high standards, perhaps the most difficult task of editing.

When each issue arrives, there is great celebration, and an unexpected joy fills the office. Each staff member (and most especially our managing editor) works late stuffing padded envelopes out to subscribers and contributors, to libraries and bookstores. Perhaps more at this time than any other, I see editing as a collective, creative act, a process that involves not only the writers presented, but most especially in our case, a motley and enthusiastic crew of editors who are also writers, who love literature and its future, language and the imagination, enough to make sure we send necessary messages to one another before returning to the solitude of writing, to the lone workhorses of our desks, richer for the contact.

Gillian Conoley's poetry collections include *Some Gangster Pain* (Carnegie-Mellon University Press) and *Woman Speaking Inside Film Noir,* (Lynx House Press). She teaches at Eastern Washington University's MFA Program, and is the editor of *Willow Springs*. This article is made possible in part through a grant from the Washington State Arts Commission.

Copyright Law — Friend or Foe?
by Sally E. Stuart

Ten years ago a copyright law went into effect that protects writers and gives them clout in their dealings with editors. When writers understand their rights and wisely use the power granted them, they will find this law a boon to the profession.

However, as with any law, the clear-cut lines of right and wrong can lose their focus when publishers or writers do not understand the law, or try to alter its function to suit their own particular needs. The professional writer must not only learn all he can about the rights granted him under Public Law 94-553, but be prepared to stand up for those rights against all comers.

The first thing to understand is that everything you write is copyrighted from the moment it reaches a tangible form, such as a final draft. This protection is automatic and should not be confused with registering a copyright, which requires a form and a fee. That copyright protection lasts for your lifetime, plus 50 years, and you control how and when your writings may be used.

It is not necessary to register your copyright unless you fear infringement. In general, that means when you have created something highly original, done a great deal of research, or have compiled original statistics. The registration fee for individual works is $10, and must be accompanied by Form TX (for all types of published/unpublished nondramatic literary works). Forms are available through the Copyright Office, Publications Section LM-455, Library of Congress, Washington, DC 20559, (202) 287-8700.

You may register groups of material under one $10 fee. For example, you may copyright all your unpublished works for the year by putting them in a binder under a title such as, "The Unpublished Works of John Doe — 1989." All your published works can be combined in the same way only if each individual piece carried its own copyright notice when published. You will have to ask publishers to include that notice for you. The binder of material, plus the $10 fee must be accompanied by Form TX and Form GR/CP.

Writers are responsible for including their copyright notice on a manuscript when it is submitted for publication. The notice must include the word or symbol for copyright (C with a circle around it), the date, and author's name: Copyright 1989 Jane Doe. This notice should appear at the top of the first page of each manuscript. Such inclusion will give you automatic copyright protection, and indicate to the editor that you wish to retain control of the copyright. Since all editors do not understand this, it is best to also mention what rights you are offering, such as "First Rights Offered."

To sell all rights means that you lost control of the copyright, and the right to resell or reprint the work in the future. It is an outright sale, like selling a car. The publisher may reprint it or sell reprint rights to other publishers without further payment to you.

You can no longer sell all rights without realizing it. Such a transfer of rights must now be in writing. A publisher's intention to purchase all rights will usually be mentioned in a letter of acceptance. If you offer first rights, and the publisher has not made known his intention to buy all rights, he has, in fact, not bought all rights (no matter what he says later). If you do sell all

rights, those rights may be reclaimed after 35 years — if you ask for them.

If no mention of rights is made by either you or the publisher at the time of sale, you have sold non-exclusive rights. He then has the right to print your piece, and to reprint it as often as he likes in any succeeding issues of that particular periodical, without paying you additional reprint fees.

If you are selling to a non-copyrighted publication, be sure to ask that your piece be printed with your copyright notice. That way, your piece will be protected even though the periodical as a whole is not. If they should fail to carry your copyright notice, the law does provide a way to correct such an error. Send to the copyright office for information on how to make that correction. Likewise, innocent infringers, misled by the omission or error in the copyright notice, are shielded from liability.

When you sell a book, all rights are negotiated in the contract and then the publisher will copyright the book in the name of the publisher or the name of the author. The author should ask that the copyright be registered in his name. If it is registered in the publisher's name, when the book goes out of print, the publisher could refuse to return the rights to the author for 35 years after publication or 40 years after the grant of copyright, whichever comes first.

One of the biggest attempts to divert the original intent of the law is by publishers who send contracts that state the piece you want to sell is "work for hire." Technically, work for hire is work another party commissions you to do, such as work done as a regular employee of a company or as a specific assignment. It was not intended for use by an editor to buy all rights in his regular dealings with freelancers, even on assigned articles. Such a contract makes it impossible to reclaim the rights, even after 35 years. Freelancers are advised to protect themselves and other writers by refusing to sign such contracts, except under their legitimate use.

There are some things that cannot be copyrighted, such as titles, ideas, plans, methods, systems, concepts, plain facts, and statistics. So, if you publish an article on how to make margarine-tub birdhouses, your copyright will prevent others from copying your presentation of that idea, but they are free to write another article on the same topic as long as they word it differently. The idea for a margarine-tub birdhouse can be used by anyone.

If you understand the copyright law and take advantage of the protection it offers, it will become a trusted ally. But, if you let yourself be trapped into selling all rights to publications not paying enough to warrant it or signing work-for-hire contracts, that same friend will turn on you and become a formidable enemy, eating away at your rights as an author. ❖

Sally E. Stuart is a full-time, freelance writer, and the author of a dozen books including the *Inspirational Writers Market Guide* (to be published by Writer's Digest in 1989), and *Copyright Not Copycat: A Writers Guide to Copyright.*

Tips on Magazine Distribution from Small Changes
by Sheri Basom & David Spiekerman

The market for magazines in the Pacific Northwest is diverse, sophisticated, and growing. Readers here like unusual specialty magazines as well as the mainstream kind. Our retail outlets are big and small, including newsstands, bookstores, grocery stores, and specialty stores. Though the retailer makes only 25% on the sale of a magazine compared to the 40% made on the sale of a book, magazines are periodicals and sell quickly once on the shelf.

The Northwest was a magazine backwater as recently as 10 years ago. One magazine wholesaler typically served each of the

> *"The social ferment of the '60s and '70s and the advent of the computer have generated the creation of hundreds of new specialty magazines in the last ten years."*

magazine outlets exclusively. And magazine selection was limited to mainstream titles chosen for their profitability, not their content. Today, half a dozen specialty magazine distributors serve the Northwest. The social ferment of the '60s and '70s and the advent of the computer have generated the creation of hundreds of new specialty magazines in the last ten years. Small, alternative distributors have taken root and blossomed in the Northwest to sell these new titles.

Magazine distribution is unique in that unsold issues can be returned to the wholesaler for credit. As a "guaranteed sale," magazines are a good risk, especially for specialty stores which retail a product line that can be enhanced by a display of informative, germane periodicals. For example, a store which sells massage paraphernalia and supplies does well with a magazine rack of health and New Age titles.

A prospective magazine publisher looking for distribution for his/her product in the Northwest needs to consider several variables. First, what is the territory served by the distributor? Our company, for example, distributes to customers in Alaska, British Columbia, Alberta, Montana, Idaho, Washington, Oregon, California, and Nevada. Most other magazine distributors in the Northwest distribute their products to single metropolitan areas only.

Second, in what kind of retail outlets do you want your magazines? Some stores and chains restrict their wholesale purchases to a select few. For reasons of efficiency, exclusive retail outlets have decided to buy from a limited number of vendors. So ask your potential distributors where they can and cannot sell.

Third, what is the purpose of the distributor and how does that affect their choice of new titles? Some distributors put profit first, second, and last and will pick up any kind of title if it generates money. Pornography distributors are a gross example of this kind. Other distributors exclude titles that run against their philosophical, ethical, and political grain, their world outlook. Seeing the distributors' lists of publications also will indicate to you whether or not the area on which your magazine focuses is represented and to what degree.

Fourth, how good a selling job does the distributor perform? Are their sales increasing year to year? How many retail accounts do they have? How long have they been in business? What is their reputation with other publishers and with their retail outlets?

Fifth, how punctual is the distributor in paying the bills? Ask other publishers. There are some distributors who will be slow payers. You need the money for your next issue, and they may have your money parked elsewhere.

If you cannot hand over the distribution with full faith, then you need to make another choice. In this business, good magazines die because of poor distribution, and bad magazines thrive because of great distribution. Do your homework. ❖

David Spiekerman has worked for four years distributing magazines in the Pacific NW. He has been published in national magazines such as *East West* and *Organic Gardening*, and keeps abreast of the ever-changing magazine scene.

Check List

1. SUBJECT: Are you regional or small? Does your product have a broader focus? Will you want national exposure? What category do you fit in? (Examples: general, Northwest, art, literature, health, women, New Age, politics, etc.)

2. LAYOUT: For magazines: Name of magazine and packaging need to be on the top third of the cover so it will show on the newsstand. Standard size is 8 1/2 x 11. Larger sizes are very difficult to display, smaller ones get lost. An exception is small journals which may be grouped together. For calendars: Once again, large oversize are difficult to display and impossible to ship. Cardboard inserts and shrink wrapping keep the product stiff and new.

3. SUPPORT: You can advertise the product by providing some flyers for promotion. You may want to provide your own displays or racks.

4. TIMING: Magazines: Be current with dates! Or use volume numbers. A May issue in July doesn't work. Calendars: The following year's calendars are sold from January through March. Example: 1988-89 calendars are shown in January. Distributors put together their catalogs June-August.

5. DISTRIBUTION: Distributors know where to place your product. We watch sales and restock when the store runs low or out of stock. For the store, we provide service by bringing the stock, watching the sales, and providing more product. We can also let the retailer know how well something is selling.

Continued

6. TERMS: Discounts range from 50-60% to the distributor. Books and calendars are 40% off retail to the stores. Magazines are 25% off retail. The store can return magazines and calendars which don't sell for wholesale credit.

Returns policy: When do you need the returns from the distributor? In what form? Whole copies, mastheads or covers, or affadavits (statement of return)? Affadavits are simplest for us. Many of our customers requiring whole copy returns pay for shipping.

How to ship: UPS is common and most reliable. They can always trace lost items and will pay for anything insured. USPS and common carrier (truck) are fine for large shipments.

Payment terms: Be clear about when you want payment. For magazines, it is common not to pay for an issue for 30 days after the next one is received. If you publish quarterly or less frequently, you may want to make other arrangements.

7. FOLLOW-UP: Call the distributor and send sample copies. If you do market research, please let us know which stores are already interested. ❖

Eleven years ago Shari Basom started Small Changes, a wholesale distributor of magazines and calendars throughout the Northwest.

The Basics of Libel
by Douglas A. Edmunds

Our courts have stated that good reputation is probably the dearest possession that a man has, and once lost is almost impossible to regain. Shakespeare put it this way:

Good name in man and woman, dear my lord,
Is the immediate jewel of their souls:
Who steals my purse steals trash; 'tis something, nothing;
'Twas mine, 'tis his, and has been slave to thousands;
But he that filches from me my good name
Robs me of that which not enriches him
And makes me poor indeed.

— *Othello*, Act 3, Scene 3

The pieces of the libel puzzle:

Most attempts to completely define libel either understate or overstate its scope; with that disclaimer in mind, I'll define a libel action as proof of at least four necessary elements:

1. The defendant (or someone he is closely associated with) communicated (orally or in writing) to a third person. That communication could be a book, magazine, newsletter, or a broadcast, speech, etc. Of course, you can write whatever you want without liability provided you keep it to yourself, but there is not much profit in it. The tough cases involve internal memoranda, drafts, etc., that are read by third persons, but only within the publisher's organization.

2. In that communication somewhere is a purportedly factual statement which could reasonably be understood to be about the plaintiff. A lot of cases have focused on mistaken identity; the test is not whether you intended to say it about this particular person, but rather, that that's the message that was conveyed. And it isn't necessary that you have identified the person by name; "the mayor of the largest city in Oregon" will do. Fiction writers take note: check out those names of people you place in distant cities; you are not immune from libel.

It has to be a statement of fact, not expression of opinion. But couching a statement in opinion-type language ("as I see it,

Jones is a thief") may not be enough to redeem you, especially if the statement isn't the kind of thing that is usually a matter of opinion. Likewise, quoting someone else as saying the defamatory statement ("Jones said that Smith is a thief") attaches his libelous statement to you.

3. The statement is defamatory. The statement will usually be considered defamatory if it has a tendency to harm the reputation of the plaintiff, so as to lower him in the estimation of the community or to deter third persons from associating or dealing with him. But actual loss of reputation is not essential, though it may be a factor in the severity of the damages awarded.

The new piece of the puzzle:

Until recently, the law of defamation was a matter of state law. Each state had its own working definition of the elements of the basic case and of the defenses. But starting with a U.S. Supreme Court decision in 1964 called *New York Times vs. Sullivan*, we have entered an era in which First Amendment rights of free speech and expression have been applied to defamation actions. This brings us to the newest element of the case:

4. If the plaintiff is a public official or someone who has voluntarily injected himself into a public controversy, then the plaintiff will have to show that the defendant acted with "actual malice." This is a catch phrase for showing that the defendant either *knew* the communication was false or that it was made with *reckless disregard* to whether it was false or not.

As a result of the U.S. Supreme Court decisions, there are several new factors, not yet fully clarified, that apply to libel law:

1. The judge has to determine the status of plaintiff as a public figure, private figure, or somewhere in between, in order to decide what elements apply.

2. The plaintiff has to be able to prove "actual malice" if he is categorized as a public figure.

3. All other plaintiffs have to make some showing of fault on the part of the defendant. The Supreme Court has left it up to each individual state to decide what degree of fault will be re-

quired, and there is no uniformity.

4. An award of punitive damages, in most cases, now requires proof of "actual malice."

Defenses: Truth is a defense; so is consent; some persons have such a high degree of privilege that it is called an "absolute" privilege to say what they want (usually limited to judges in the courtroom and politicians on the debating floor); others have what are called "qualified" privileges (which means privileged, so long as a specific interest worth protecting is at risk). Most of these are matters of state law, and subject to a lot of variation of interpretation.

Assuming that the plaintiff establishes his case, the damages that may be awarded to him are compensation for injury to reputation and feelings. If he can also show actual malice, he may be able to recover "punitive" damages, the damages that add a lot of zeros to the bottom line.

Guidelines to follow:

Here are a few pointers on libel to consider as you pursue your writing career.

1. *Libel is an unavoidable risk of writing*. As a writer, your ethics should be paramount. You can't write your best if you fear being sued.

2. *Read your contract to see what it says about the costs of defending libel actions*. Even if you win, a libel suit will cost plenty to defend. Most likely your publisher will also be a named defendant. How much of the cost of defense is he going to bear? Does he claim authority to settle, and charge it back to you?

3. *Don't rely on this article or any book for the answers to real life problems*. Libel law is changing. Even with the U.S. Supreme Court setting certain standards, it is still predominantly a matter of state law; those subtle nuances which can mean the difference between a sizeable judgement or verdict for the defense. Check the publication dates of the books you read on libel.

4. *If you are desktop publishing, you must know what risks you face and how to reduce them*. Editorial comment, photographs, cartoons, and paid advertisements are all potential areas for libel actions. You need to be aware of how defamation is defined in your state. You need to know the requirements and benefits of the retraction laws. You should consider insurance coverage that will at least pay your costs of defense if available at a reasonable price. You should also know something about the closely related legal action of invasion of privacy.

Author's Disclaimer: New cases are being decided almost daily that re-interpret the law. It is hazardous to guess what directions the law will take in the future. This article is not a substitute for legal counsel, which you should seek in the appropriate circumstances. ❖

Douglas A. Edmunds is an attorney licensed in Oregon and Washington, and welcomes you to sign up for his free quarterly newsletter on Author Law.

Tools of the Trade: Computers
by Steve Johnson

Introduction

"When Hemingway starts on a project he always begins with a pencil, using a reading board to write on onionskin typewriter paper. He keeps a sheaf of the blank paper on a clipboard to the left of the typewriter, extracting the paper a sheet at a time from under a metal clip which reads 'These Must be Paid.' He places the paper slantwise on the reading board, leans against the board with his left arm, steadying the paper with his hand , and fills the paper with handwriting which through the years has become larger, more boyish, with a paucity of punctuation, very few capitals, and often the period marked with an x. The page completed, he clips it face-down on another clipboard which he places off to the right of the typewriter. Hemingway shifts to the typewriter, lifting off the reading board, only when the writing is going fast and well, or when the writing is, for him at least, simple: dialogue, for instance." (From Writers at Work, Paris Review)

"If I had to give up writing on my computer, I would feel I had returned to scraping letters in cuneiform on clay tablets.... The writing itself is far more serious than on the typewriter. There is no punishment for revising and revising again.... Writing on the screen has a fluidity that makes compromise with what you envision silly." (Marge Piercy, Whole Earth Software Review)

I remember the moment when the first book I produced myself came rolling off a giant web press. Hardly the historic moment of the first Bloomsbury book, to me it was an important milestone. With the book at home, where nothing could keep my ego in check, I would set it on the table and sneak up on it from various angles. I didn't want to look too closely, knowing I would find typos or crooked headlines (rub-on letters). We bound the book with a rented industrial stapler. The cover, one of the best parts of the book thanks to John Larson (Press 22), sat there beaming back at me. The insides were "typeset" using the state of the art electronic typewriter of its time (1972), the IBM Executive.

When I look at that book now it seems like the first draw-

Continued

ings done by one's child in kindergarten. And, reflecting on those self-publishing days, makes the state of the art of writing and publishing with computers in this desktop publishing era all the more poignant.

The first computer I wrote with was made by Vector Graphics, Inc., one of dozens of companies that tried to gain a part of the small computer market before Big Blue (IBM) entered the picture in 1981. By today's standards, the computer was about as modern as a 1950s television set. It was, to me, all very mysterious. As with a 1950s television set you either learned how to fix the thing, or saw the repairman often. Most likely both. It was like listening to Pachelbel on an eight-transistor radio.

I never really expected to become a computer "technotwit," and even though today many of my colleagues associate me with computers, I still only think of computers as a means to an end. My first use of a computer, even before I had my own, was to communicate with the rest of the world by participating in an early online communication system, and by logging on to database systems like DIALOG. Even though I talked and read about the wonders of computers as organizers of information that might reveal patterns we couldn't see with the naked mind, I continued to do my own creative thinking and writing with paper and pens.

It wasn't until 1984 that I met the machine of my dreams. Like all manifestations of my dreams, she wasn't exactly what I expected. In fact, the first time I saw her at an exhibition in Denver, it struck me as a rather homely, ineffectual thing. It was the first Macintosh, the Mac 128. In 1983 I met Mark Vermillion who was getting Apple's Community Affairs Program off the ground, a wonderful scheme to seed computers in nonprofit organizations around the country so they could create social change networks by using the computers as communicating workstations. When Mark and I struck an agreement about seeding several computers in Portland for a community computer center, I took several Apple IIEs and Macintoshes — little realizing how much this funny Macintosh computer was going to change my life.

Over the years I've had to deal with many forms of prejudice against computers. In 1976 I was almost tarred and feathered at a neighborhood meeting for suggesting the use of a computer to create a skill bank of a neighborhood's resources; at other times I have had to listen to writers pooh-pooh computers as just another consumer fad. I listen to such arguments with a grain of salt. It's fine, I think, to say that most of the great writers have had nothing but ink and paper; but it's an insult to the many talented people involved in publishing — the typesetters, graphic designers, illustrators, binders, printers, and even the nameless people who make the pens and paper — to think that writing is a lonely art performed on a desert island. And, along the way, technology is used to create the final product from good pens to typesetting equipment and printing presses. Computers are a part of the technology of writing and publishing.

In the first years I used a computer for some part of my writing, but I seldom used it for first drafts. Sitting in front of a screen was more intimidating than sitting in front of a whirring IBM Executive typewriter. Only a pen and paper are polite enough to be still while your mind struggles for the right word, or wanders through free associations looking for meanings.

While I am daily in awe of how a computer has enhanced my own writing, I will also freely admit the computer has brought us such deadly blessings as five-pound novels where cutting and pasting giant chunks of text from one place to another, with subtle transitions lost in the shuffle, passes for the art of editing.

Hardware

While I describe software available for both Macintosh and IBM-compatible hardware, it is clear to me, and many others, that the Macintosh is setting the standard as the writer's best toolchest. Well respected publishing analyst, Johnathan Seybold says, the Macintosh is:

"At the forefront of most of the exciting things that are happening in publishing. It is the personal computer that was designed for publishing applications. It has set the standard for user personal computer graphics and user interface. It is attracting much of the best new software for monochrome and color graphics design, page composition, presentations, and HyperText, as well as for integration of the written word, graphics, and sound."

The Four Basic Writer Software Programs

There are four types of software that I recommend for the writer:

- Idea outliners
- Word processors
- Spelling checkers and word finders
- Page layout programs

1. Idea Outliners

Outliners allow you to put your thoughts into an outline form and arrange and rearrange them any way you like. Outlines are hierarchical lists: lists with levels. Given that some ideas are more important than others, elements of most outlines are at different levels. Each single line of text, or headline, represents a level of thought. A headline can have subheadlines under it, and in turn, each of the subheadlines can have subheadlines, and so on.

Since high school I've disliked outlines, which I've regarded on a par with diagraming sentences. But the outliner I use on my Macintosh (More) has become an important tool for my writing. One of my worst habits as a writer has been to fill my brain with the whole shebang until it weighs me down like the bladder of a tavern on a Friday night. Then, by the time I sit down to write, the screen (or paper) stares back at me, and I realize like a tourist in Kansas that every direction seems about the same. Where to begin? With an idea outliner I let the ideas flow out in any crazy pattern that comes to mind, then slowly rearrange them. The process works better, I think, for technical writing than for creative writing, but it helps for both.

Some features of outlining software:

Expanding and collapsing: Expanding a headline will reveal all subordinate levels. Collapsing allows you to hide from view any headlines or windows subordinate to the headline you select. A wonderful way to metaphorically clean up your mind.

Importing and exporting: It is important that you can move information back and forth from an outliner to your word processing program.

Text window option: Some outliners allow you to attach more extensive text related to any outline item. The text is hidden unless specifically called for, and thus the outline can remain simple and clean.

Sorting options: With sorting you can sort in descending or ascending order any of the headlines at any one level. Great for alphabetizing lists.

Typestyles: Some outliners may only allow you to use one typestyle per file. This may not be important if you only use the outliner for rough drafts, but critical if you want to use the outline as a finished product.

Presentation features: Some outliners allow you to highlight headlines with bullets, and incorporate graphics, borders and rules, and make tree charts. All useful features if you want to turn your outline into transparencies or slides for presentations.

2. Word Processing Programs

The word processing software market is a well established market. Unless you buy your software from a street vendor selling hot watches too, you will probably get most of the standard features associated with word processing, i.e. ability to format type (at least underlining, boldface, italic), cut and paste sections of copy, search for and replace words, and basic document formatting features (line spacing, margins, headers, footers).

But, word processing has come a long way, and new programs are emerging with features that create mush out of that neat category created by the computer industry, desktop publishing (see more on that later). The following are some things to keep in mind when buying word processing software, and a summary of some of the latest and bravest features of word processors that might be handy for writers.

What you see is what you get (WYSIWYG). With today's programs you can format text on the screen that closely resembles the final product. With some of the most advanced software packages, (sometimes referred to as page layout programs or document processing software) you can see it exactly as it will appear, including the typestyle, graphics, and rules and borders, all laid out in multi-column format. Some programs have a "page preview" display which will show you in miniature what a page, and sometimes even facing pages, will look like when printed.

Clutter on the desktop. Sometimes the manufacturers go a little haywire, and, as with car dashboards, the clutter on a screen can distract from the primary task at hand. Likewise, too little information can be equally frustrating. But there are enough options to make most anyone happy and productive.

Importing and exporting text. The program you choose should have the ability to read files written in other word processing programs. Minimally, programs will have the ability to read and produce files in text-only, (sometimes referred to as ASCII) format. Many programs have specific translators for different programs. This can be especially helpful if you do collaborative projects or send writing to publishers on disks. You should be forewarned that this importing and exporting business is still rough.

Tabs. A Nobel prize awaits someone who makes an easy to use and reliable tabbing feature for word processing programs. I've yet to find a program that doesn't have some glitches. Human error is part of the problem. We are creatures of habit, used to the tab reality of typewriters. With the proportionally spaced lettering that desktop computers use, tabs are a delicate, cantankerous process. There are no perfect solutions except to try the tabbing features before purchasing.

Cleaning up mistakes. Make sure the program has ways to recover from mistakes. The program should have an "undo" function, allowing you to change your mind after you have cut a large chunk of text or done other actions. And if you are not sure you will remember to use the save command (saving what you have written from temporary memory to permanent disk memory), then buy a program that saves automatically, or better yet allows you to toggle between automatic and forced saving.

Ease of accessing often-repeated functions. Depending on the type of writing you do, there are features you will use more frequently. For example, if the program allows you to change typestyle and size, then the feature should be something that only takes a nanosecond to change. You'd be surprised how irritating a delay in accessing a feature is when you have the creative juices flowing.

For the perpetual Ph.D. candidate. If you are doing technical writing, report writing, or still finishing a dissertation, you should investigate the programs with advanced features. Most programs will allow you to place headers and footnotes. But some provide elegant tools for multiple footnotes, and others, such as the current Cadillac of word processors for the Macintosh, Fullwrite Professional, create an automatic table of contents, index and bibliography.

Brainstorming and writing. Some word processing programs have built-in outliners, allowing you to shift back and forth between an outline of your work and the full text. Although the outlining features within word processors are improving, the one I've used most often, Microsoft's Word, is still cumbersome and I end up doing brainstorming in a dedicated idea outliner like More.

Precision control of spacing. Thanks to the desktop publishing rage, word processing programs are increasingly including more precise ability to control letter and line spacing. In most page layout programs and in some word processing programs you can control the spacing (called tracking) between letters, between certain awkward letter pairs (called kerning), between words, and move words or letters above or below the base line of a sentence. A good word processing program will also allow you to have fine control over line spacing (leading). These features, along with automatic hyphenation programs are what can make your final product resemble true typesetting.

Spelling checkers and word finders. Some of the newer, monstrous, word processing programs even have built in spelling dictionaries and word finders or thesauruses. Having these features as part of your word processor is a real plus — you don't have to load up another program to check for correct spelling.

Integrating graphics into your writing. Again, a feature that caught on through desktop publishing, now some word processors allow you to integrate graphics in your writing. The simplest kind of program allows for placement of a graphic, but you will not be able to have text on the same line. Also, most programs allow for placement of the graphic only; once in place

Continued

it cannot be manipulated. More advanced programs will allow you to place text and graphics in a variety of formats, and even include drawing tools to manipulate the graphics (at least simple boxes and rules) or draw them right in place.

The kitchen sink too. Beyond all these features there are still more. A posted note feature allows you to post an electronic equivalent of a sticky note on a document. It is there as an editorial comment and won't be printed. Glossaries allow you to create a list of words or phrases that will be automatically typed in when you type in an abbreviation representing the longer word or phrase. A calculation function will allow you to add (but usually only add) a row of numbers. Although if you are interested in this kind of feature you might want to get an integrated program like Microsoft Works that includes word processing along with database management, spreadsheet, and telecommunications.

3. Spell Checkers and Word Finders (Thesauruses)

Since I was in the wrong line when they handed out synapses for spelling, I've eagerly waited for automatic spelling checkers. Spell checking programs are not perfect yet, but are worth their price. With 70,000 to 100,000+ dictionaries, today's programs can help you find some of the most embarrassing typos and spelling errors; however, they will not find all your mistakes. For example, a spelling program will miss words that actually spell another word you didn't intend to use, e.g. *then* rather than *than*. Also, a program may find a misspelled word but it may not know how to offer the correctly spelled word unless you are at least in the ballpark.

Word finders or thesaurus programs are the next best writer's tools; while not things you would want to depend on to replace the eternal muse, the programs can still help you past some writer's blocks.

At the fringe of these programs are those variously called grammar or style checkers. And that's where I draw the line between usefulness and fluff. The programs are accessed similarly to spell checkers and word finders, most often as separate programs, occasionally as part of a word processing program. You run your piece of writing through the program and back come comments about your writing style. One program even provides a reading level and interest level analysis of your program — about as appropriate as having a high school freshman grade a William Burroughs novel. Another program will tell you if you have used any sexist and prejudicial jargon, a barely useful, at most comical, way of looking at your writing. The best feature of these programs, something available in spell checkers anyway, is a writing analysis that includes a word count broken down by number of nouns, adjectives, etc.

Since a spell checker is your most likely word processing add-on, let's look at some of the features you should consider.

Accessible in what manner. Is it a program that has to be loaded separately, or is it a part of a specific word processing program, or accessible for any word processing program, e.g., as a desk accessory on the Macintosh. If it is a stand-alone program then what word processing programs will it work with? Some spell checkers will require that the document be put in text-only (ASCII) format. This means you may have to reformat it after corrections are made. **Double words.** Will it check for double words, e.g. *the the*, *and and*, etc. Some programs will additionally check for inappropriate double spaces.

Additional dictionaries. Does it allow you to add words to the dictionary, or use supplemental dictionaries (medical, legal, scientific dictionaries, etc.)? **Interactive program vs. batch programs.** An interactive program allows you to check spelling as you write. Make sure it has a way to turn this feature off and on easily or you may never get any writing done. **Homonym checking.** Will it allow you to turn on and off a feature that will provide you with homonyms, e.g. *tacks* and *tax*, etc.? **Skipping words.** The ability to force the program to skip over certain words in a document. For example, the first time it finds a unique word (not in its dictionary) you should be able to add it to the dictionary so it won't pause each time. Also, a good feature is the ability to skip a word just in the current document without adding it to the dictionary (when you are using a word in a unique way).

4. Page Layout Programs

Page layout programs, sometimes referred to as page composition programs, allow you to compose pages as you might in the past only have done with manual cut and paste and a light table. The current generation of page layout programs have several handy features not yet available with most word processing programs.

Some important features in page layout programs to keep in mind include the following.

Importing and exporting text. The ability to import both graphics and text from a wide variety of sources is important for page layout. Most page layout programs are not sophisticated word processors, so it is important to be able to do writing and editing in word processing programs and then import the text into the page composition program.

Importing graphic images. Computer graphics generation is the most rapidly expanding area of computing today. Pictures, in the form of digital clip art (drawn with drawing programs) or scanned (using digital scanners) can be imported for use in documents. But there are several standards used for imported pictures. The page layout program you choose should be able to use several types of image formats including: TIFF format (used by scanners); EPS (encapsulated PostScript, used by programs like Adobe Illustrator), PICT (used by object-oriented drawing programs), and MacPaint or bit-mapped images.

Letter, word, and spacing controls. In a good layout program you should be able to control spacing in several ways. First off, you should be able to control the kerning and tracking — adjusting the spacing between letters and words to improve their readability. While kerning adjusts the amount of space between certain awkward letters, leading adjusts the amount of space between lines, and tracking controls over-all letter and word spacing. You should be able to control the spacing between lines as well as make adjustments for individual words (or lines) by moving the characters up or down from the baseline (the normal horizontal placement of characters) in small increments.

Hyphenation is an important feature of layout programs because it allows you to fit more text on a given line by splitting a word into two or more parts. It is an especially important feature when using small column widths with fully-justified type.

Graphic tools. There are a wide variety of graphics tools available in many page layout programs. Some programs allow for cropping and scaling of images; as well as producing shades of gray, fill patterns, rules and borders (with different weights or sizes of lines), as well as circles, ovals, boxes, and pen patterns.

Special features. There are still other useful features to consider, including text flow around graphics, spelling dictionaries, glossaries, style sheets, master pages (allowing for batch production of pages with uniform features), crop marks, color separations, and thumbnail page previews.

The Future of Writing: Some Predictions

Within a couple of years laser printers will be standard and anything less than the quality we associate with that will seem farcical. Laser printers will drop in price to be competitive with yesterday's daisywheel printers.

Graphics, including scanned images and halftone photographs, will be the fastest growing and most intriguing part of the computer market. Scanners and telefax machines (in Japan they are already more popular than desktop computers) will be sold in great numbers and will drop dramatically in price.

Hypertext programs like HyperCard are not a fad. Advances in these programs will usher in new ways of communicating that we can only imagine now. New forms of electronic writing that will include photographs, animation, and sounds will bring forth a new kind of artist.

Within a couple of years there will be multi-purpose graphic design centers everywhere that will make the single-purpose printer, typesetter or layout shop obsolete. At these centers, such as the Krishna Copy Center in Berkeley, you will be able to access elegant technology to help you publish anything under the sun.

Page layout programs may disappear as a separate market; replaced by intelligent word processing programs that do the same thing, and other programs that will incorporate many of the features of page composition programs.

As more professional typesetters and graphic designers begin to use computers for their work, a market will evolve for sophisticated page composition programs and graphics programs. These programs will not be as easy to use, but will have many sophisticated features such as photographic touch-up, and wonderful features for manipulating text, and creating new typestyles on the spot.

Mass storage devices such as CD ROM and optical disks will change the computer industry. It will be routine for small computers to come equipped with large storehouses of knowledge.

Database manager software, traditionally thought of as an earnest tool for data crunchers and mass mailers, will become a tool for artists. Imagine what Nabokov could have done with his crazy card-index system (used to record images and coincidences) with a good database management system. Over the years, who knows what patterns he might have seen using a database system. Really intelligent database systems that will be something like HyperCard on the Macintosh, and polished versions of expert system software (software that attempts to duplicate an individual's expertise) will open up a new world for writers and creative thinkers, allowing them to communicate their obscure psychological findings with the scientists of the world. ❖

Steve Johnson has self-published over a dozen books, and has been editor or publisher of magazines and newspapers, including *RAIN* magazine, an international technology assessment journal. He is chairperson of a national consortium of nonprofit computer resource centers. Names of hardware and software mentioned in this article are the trademarked property of their manufacturers, and are so identified here in order to keep the symbol ™ from disrupting the text.

"For me, writing is like finding an oasis where I can see again, and rename everything, where language can be rescued, where words can return to their original, exotic states."
— Gillian Conoley

Tips

SELF-PUBLISHING CHECKLIST

The following is a list of many important tasks for self-publishers. This is by no means comprehensive and should be supplemented by research into book publishing practices. Adequate preparation and thoughtful business judgement will save you time, energy, and money.

Book Concept
- The author has the ability to complete this project
- Potential market has been checked
- Niche is identifiable among competing titles
- Read and learn about self-publishing and book promotion
- Determine if sufficient funds are available to produce and promote your book, based on projected costs. If subsidy publishers are being considered, investigate them thoroughly before investing

Writing Process
- Writing schedule has been developed
- Preliminary subject research
- Detailed research and interviews
- Book outline and chapter development
- First draft of manuscript
- Draft evaluation and fact check
- Revisions (as many as necessary to produce final draft)
- Production of art work

Preliminary Details
- Establish your publishing company
- Register for International Standard Book Number, Cataloging in Publication data, and Advance Book Information.
- Get at least four typesetting bids (also photo screens and PMTs)
- Get at least six printing bids (ink, paper, cover, and binding)
- Mail manuscripts to any key contacts (for cover reviews)
- Consult with editor, graphic artist, book designer
- Establish price of book (review all costs, necessary profit margin, and what the market can bear)
- Find distributor(s) and plan all sales methods to be used

While Book is Typeset and Printed (or sooner)
- Design pre-publishing or first sales brochure
- Obtain list of target book reviewers (send galleys if possible)
- Obtain endorsements, if appropriate
- Set up accounting system and business materials
- Determine advertising mediums and budget
- Obtain mailing lists for direct promotion (check into joint mailings with publishers of compatible books)
- Design media kits

When Books are Ready to Sell
- Register for copyright
- Mail review and promotional copies (also media kits)
- Begin all test advertising, mailings, and direct promotions
- Plan participation in book fairs and target events
- Supply distributors and sales outlets

Additional tips
- Check into local writers' and publishers' organizations
- Attend regional retail book shows
- Consult other self-publishers and experts for advice (at all stages)
- Consider speaking engagements, seminars, and publicity tours

Young Writers & Writers for the Young

Writing for Children
by Nita Slater

If you had no idea what the weather was like outside, how would you dress? In the same way, it is important that we are aware of the market and its trends in order to know what will sell. There is freedom of expression in today's children's books. Sales are on the rise in all categories. Books line the bookstore shelves in brighter colors, more-glorious-than-ever illustrations, and livelier animation.

Parents remember books they loved as children. They encourage their children to read the classics which are back in grand style and selling well — *The Three Musketeers*, *Jane Eyre*, *Aesop's Fables*, *Tom Sawyer* and *The Little Engine That Could* (retold by Watty Piper), just to name a few.

There is an increasing number of "Activity Books" for toddlers and pre-school age children. They have pop-up characters and stories told on cassettes. Many of these are non-fiction — *Dinosaurs*, *Early Humans* (*The Prehistoric World*), *Why Are We Getting A Divorce?*, *Why Was I Adopted?* For the very young, *Word Books For Baby*, *Shapes*, *Chippy Goes to The Dentist*, and many more. Walt Disney is still a safe haven in fiction and fantasy for the lighter side of children's storytelling. For beginning readers, the Serendipity Books engage in fiction/fantasy stories with a light moral lesson included.

Teen romances are one of the hottest selling, fastest growing markets. Serial books for age twelve and up deal with young romance, careers, and travel. If you're writing for money and not love, this arena is probably for you. But don't stop here. The categories go on into science fiction, fantasy, nature, mystery and mysticism.

There is still a clear need for more nonfiction books for children aged four through twelve years. Writers need to address subjects that are difficult for adults as well as children to handle — death, divorce, physically and mentally handicapped children, braces, doctors and dentists.

We have obviously become more aware and more sensitive to the needs created by today's changing society and their affect on our children. Much like adults, children want to sort out their own needs and feelings. Books give them the ability to do this on a personal level, no matter what the age. Children are as individual as adults, and, like adults, are searching for the true self. Only they are just beginning the search. What kind of books would appeal to you on such a quest? Many publishers are reevaluating and expanding their lists to meet the growing audience of young readers. There may be many books on similar subjects, but a fresh viewpoint might mean there is room for your book too.

Write to please yourself. As a child, what emotional needs did you have? What were your fantasies? Where did your dreams take you? Events may change but basic needs don't. We still long for the same things — love, security, safety and happiness. Stories need an "inner truth." Without it there isn't much of a story. G.K. Chesterton wrote: "Children know themselves innocent and demand justice. We fear ourselves guilty and ask for mercy."

If there is truly magic in our lives, I believe it resides in the hearts and minds of our children. They experience life with a keen sense that remains untouched by the socially accepted buffers built into an adult world. Perhaps those of us who write, and who wish to write children's books, are trying to extend and encourage these refreshing feelings of existence. ❖

Nita Slater is the co-author of a children's book, and has written a book of poems.

Society of Children's Book Writers

If you are not sure where to place your literary pen, you might want to check out The Society of Children's Book Writers (SCBW). This organization was formed in Los Angeles around 1970 by a group of freelance writers. It acts as a network for the exchange of knowledge among children's writers, editors, publishers, illustrators and agents. We in the Northwest are fortunate to have a local chapter.

The SCBW-NW was formed to meet the concerns of those writers and illustrators who are writing for children, or want to, in Oregon, Washington and Idaho. To serve this end, it has developed local workshops dealing with such topics as: Basics for Beginning Writers, Why Do You Want to Write for Children?, and Picture Books in Particular. The topics and guest speakers offer variety, interest and challenge to the writer/illustrator. There are panel discussions, open critiques, workshop groups with publishers, authors, agents, editors, and professional illustrators. Group critiquing is available on a regular basis. Board meetings are quarterly and the group publishes a quarterly report containing upcoming events and special articles.

For Oregon, you may contact SCBW-NW through Margaret Bechard, Regional Advisor, 12180 S.W. Ann Place, Tigard, OR 97223. Phone: (503) 639-5754.

The Seattle group meets the first Wednesday of the month at 7:30 at Seattle Pacific University. For information, contact Linda Wagner, The Society of Children's Book Writers — Washington, 186320 NE 202nd St., Woodinville, WA 98072. Phone: (206) 481-4091.

Regional Literature & Juvenile Readers
by Mac Swan

Mrs. Higham marched back and forth in front of the shined blackboards on the first day of Freshman English, a three-page dittoed handout (on 14-, not 11-inch paper) held in focus at arm's length. From this "recreational reading list" each of us would, she commanded with firmly set jaw and hawklike eyes, choose a minimum of two books each semester. We were to read them completely, thoroughly, and to report upon them for the benefit of the rest of the class.

In the ensuing 40 or so minutes, Mrs. Higham, the flying ends of her gray hair sharp in the light against the blackness of the chalkboards, introduced the books: "You all have friends." She searched the faces for one of us who might not. "Does friendship have any limits? What would you do if your friend

---

"From this 'recreational reading list' each of us would, she commanded with firmly set jaw and hawklike eyes, choose a minimum of two books each semester."

---

accidently killed someone? How would this change your friendship?" Immediately in front of me, (seated in accord with the alphabet), Martha Susan circled *Of Mice and Men*. "What would you do if you were kidnapped and taken aboard a sailing ship? You might like Stevenson's adventure story, " Mrs. Higham continued.

Hers was a virtuoso teaching performance. She walked up and down the aisles, talking sometimes from the back of the room, and when she came to A.B. Guthrie's book, *The Big Sky,* she cast the hook which caught me: If we wanted to read this book, we should ask our parents first, she told us. "Some parts," she said with eyes wide over her spectacles, "require a 'mature' reader." That night, hidden beneath the covers in my basement room, flashlight in hand, I entered the world of Boone Caudill, Jim Deakins, Dick Summers and Teal Eye.

What I had expected in my libidinous imaginings while listening to Mrs. Higham was not what I found. Guthrie's expert storytelling transported me to the early 1800s, to the fur trading days on the Missouri and Teton rivers. When the characters fought their way over Marias Pass in the bitterness of winter, my knowledge of that region was tied to theirs; their geography and mine were the same, and that kinship evaporated the mists of time between their experience and my own.

Works grounded firmly in one's own geographic region hold special fascination for readers of all ages, but more especially for young readers struggling to define themselves and their relationship to the larger world. Students in my Montana Literature class take great delight in reading stories about places they know. The setting of Richard Hugo's and James Welch's poems about "The Only Bar in Dixon," the Salish-Kootenai reservation and the Mission Church of D'Arcy McNickle's *The Surrounded*, and the Big Blackfoot River of Norman Maclean's *A River Runs Through It* form immediate bonds between reader and literature. For the students, regional familiarity eases the establishment of kinship with the work's characters and events.

As they make use of stories to mirror and define their own experiences, readers seek out books which speak directly to them about both the uniqueness and the commonality of their place. Unfortunately for the juvenile reader seeking contemporary fiction, the selection is limited. Excellent works exist reflecting the West of years ago — Doig's *This House of Sky,* Huey Call's *Winter Wheat* for example — but for the most part, the juvenile's experience in the contemporary West is being overlooked. The social stability of the past, even here, is crumbling. Montana's young adults often must choose between getting a job or keeping the closeness of their family, friends and community. It is this West which needs exposure in juvenile literature, a West where bad guys no longer wear black hats, where independence and all its concomitant side-effects bend necessarily toward interdependence, where horse sense needs to outpace the horse.

William Kittredge has said that all good literature is regional. I agree. And while geographical setting does not determine literary quality, quality regional literature holds particular fascination for young readers. Geographical and cultural familiarity can provide that important first step into the literary world of wider experience for the young reader. Places overlooked in their closeness emerge new, redefined, reborn through the stories which grow from them. ❖

Mac Swan, a derelict from the radical '60s, currently poses as a teacher and writer in the quiet town of Polson, Montana. He is writing a teacher's source book on Montana writers.

"Writing a first draft can fill me with incredible despair. Or joy."
—Ursula Hegi

Fight Censorship: Students Must Practice Real Life Thinking
by Reva Luvaas

Why have a high school newspaper explore socially significant issues? Why not stick to "safe" topics like club news, sports, senior spotlights and district announcements? Why teach students responsible journalism, accurate, well-researched facts, objective reporting and effective quotes? Why not avoid a professionally trained teacher's guidance and sense of responsibility and give school officials the power to censor, not only school newspapers, but plays and other "school-sponsored expressive activities?"

These questions are part of the debate centered around a recent Supreme Court decision in the Hazelwood School District v. Kuhlmier case. According to Idaho's *Lewiston Tribune*, January 14, 1988, "The court held that in activities that are 'part of the school curriculum' and might seem to carry its imprimatur, officials may bar dissemination of student statements about drugs, sexual activity, pregnancy, birth control, connected political issues and other matters when doing so would serve 'any valid educational purpose.'"

The reality of this censorship doesn't hit home until it involves you. As a high school journalism teacher, I found that out. My censorship accident occurred when my Lapwai High School student reporter wrote "Take Control; Birth Control." On May 15, 1987, a research article on planned parenthood and the high teen pregnancy rate in the United States accompanied "Baby Boom: Fad or Responsibility," a feature on the school's Teen Parenting class. Neither work seemed obscene, libelous or disruptive to the educational process, the limits placed on reporters in the precedent-setting 1969 Tinker case.

The research for "Take Control," found in the Lapwai High and Nez Perce County libraries, was listed as a bibliography. Also included were results of a confidential Lapwai student survey, grades eight through twelve, indicating that out of the 126 students surveyed, "52% have had sex, but only 63% of those who have had sex use birth control. Of those who do use birth control, 53% do not use it every time they have sex." The student reporter compares this with teenagers throughout the country, to point out the risk of sexual activity and to briefly outline birth control practices. As Tribune reporter Jim Fisher asserted in his January 17, 1988 editorial, the student writing was "clinical, not sophomoric." The article ends:

"Of course, there is another method that is a sure way to not get pregnant — abstinence. Abstinence is choosing NOT to have sex. Intercourse is just one of the many ways you can express loving feelings for someone."

The result of "Take Control" was not a letter to the editor, but journalism guidelines approved by the school board, insisting that the principal review all future articles when proposed, and again, the same articles when ready to print. The principal had power to censor any that would offend or infringe upon the religious or moral standards of the readers. The Hazelwood decision basically upheld those guidelines eight months later.

At the time the guidelines were imposed, I wrote a letter of protest to the principal saying that I would prefer not to teach journalism under these conditions. Another teacher, asked to advise journalism while I was on a previously arranged year's leave of absence, declined and also wrote a letter to the principal. Two attempts by the students to produce a school paper were made this last school year on their own time. Currently, there is no school paper at Lapwai.

My stand on the Lapwai guidelines puts me on the side of the dissenting Supreme Court Justices, Brennan, Marshall and Blackman in the Hazelwood case. They state that:

"The court deviates from precedent in approving brutal censorship and thought control in the high school. This decision violates the First Amendment's prohibitions against censorship of any student expression that neither disrupts classwork nor invades the rights of others. It denudes students of much of the First Amendment protection that Tinker itself prescribed. The obscure triangle of rationales given by the majority does not withstand analysis and teaches students they needn't respect the diversity of ideas that is fundamental to the American system...The court teaches youth to discount important principles of our government as mere platitudes. The young men and women at Hazelwood expected a civics lesson, but not the one the court teaches them today."

According to Mike Simpson, NEA Office of General Counsel, "advisors who fail to wield a heavy blue pencil may find their jobs at risk because the principal objects to what their students write." He adds, "the legal reasoning used in Hazelwood could be applied to severely limit the right of teachers to speak freely in the classroom or to assign outside readings."

From my censorship "accident," I know well of what he speaks. Lapwai Superintendent, Robert Sobotta, raised a valid point in the *Lewiston Tribune*, January 14, 1988, when he reacted to my preference not to return to the advisor's position if the guidelines remained in force, by saying, "we can't force her

> *"The court deviates from precedent in approving brutal censorship and thought control in the high school."*

into it..., but then if it were in the job description it would present another dilemma."

A spinoff censorship occurred when the Lapwai High teachers were asked not to talk to reporters about the controversy over the school newspaper guidelines during the school day. Mr. Sobotta was appointed by the school board as spokesman in the matter. In the Lewiston High School's *The Bengal's Purr*, November 6, 1987, he said, "too many people were calling the teachers during the school time and it just gave them an out so that they didn't have to be bothered. We're satisfied in our own community with what's going on. We just want it over."

But censorship is not over. Reading lists and library books, as well as speech, drama and journalism classes are under constant scrutiny. One thing is sure, this school district is not the only one experiencing a shift of gears. Censorship flourishes nationwide. Educators, writers and librarians, all of us involved with any form of language use, must face directly the responsi-

Continued

bility we have in formulating the law of the land, the guidelines of a school district and the atmosphere of a classroom.

Happily, there are steps that can be taken to handle censorship when it occurs and steps to take to avoid its occurrence in the first place. There are many support groups available for teachers and school districts which want to work together for the students' benefit. (See side bar.) We can start at home by evaluating the processes we have set up for reviewing materials and for handling complaints. We can elect to say something or remain silent. We can join professional organizations that support freedom of thought. We can work to avoid censorship "accidents" without sacrificing the freedom to think, to learn and to speak. ❖

Reva Luvaas is president of the Inland Council of Teachers of English, serves on SLATE (the political arm of the National Council of Teachers of English), and is the coordinator for the Bitterroot Teachers Network which deals with a Foxfire approach to teaching.

For More Information on Censorship:

The Journalism Education Association, PO Box 99, Blue Springs, MO 64015 offers the services of The Student Press Law Center, also a brochure, *First & Foremost*, on policy development since the Hazelwood case.

National Coalition Against Censorship, 135 W. 43rd St., New York, N.Y. 10036, 212-944-9899, offers information, guidelines, books, surveys.

Washington Coalition Against Censorship, 5503 17th Ave. NW, #604, Seattle, WA 98107, 206-547-1910.

Books published by the National Council of Teachers of English which are not on censorship itself, but are relevant to this issue: *How Writing Shapes Thinking* by Judith A. Langer & Arthur N. Applebee; *Talking Into Writing* by Donald L. Rubin & William M. Dodd; *Response to Student Writing* by Sarah Warshauer Freedman.

Starfire: How to Fire up Student Writers
by Chris Weber

"Lively music flowed from Grandpa's harmonica. I stood in the entryway near the living room listening, and thinking how much his life was like his music. The high notes were for his travel around the world. The low notes were for his work on the farm. There were many low notes and many tasks for him to complete. He always blew into each hole exactly the right way, and the perfect tune floated from the small instrument. Likewise was his performance on Hillcrest Acres, the farm. Grandpa was the harmonica, his life was the song."
—Sarah Creedon, 12, Lake Oswego

The above is an excerpt from *Treasures 2: Stories & Art by Students in Oregon*. It is the second in a series of student publications by the Oregon Students Writing & Art Foundation, a non-profit organization, and a division of The Oregon Reading Association. The Foundation was created four years ago to fill a need of teachers and students.

In 1984 some of my students wanted to create their own contest for other students. Along with designing the first contest poster, they helped me develop some of the guidelines and rules, as well as select the name for the contest — Starfire. To my students, Starfire meant that special time and place when words fly on the page and the student writer is in a private world filled with fiery energy. The students and I ran the first Starfire Writing & Art Contest just for the Portland area. Four months later the winners were published in *Brother Holocaust & Other Stories*.

In 1985 the Foundation developed and sponsored the second Starfire Writing & Art Contest, which was the first opportunity statewide for Oregon students to publish. Approximately nine hundred students participated in that contest. Writing and artwork from ninety-one authors and sixty artists were chosen to

be published in *Treasures: Stories & Art by Students in Oregon*, which took a year and ten thousand dollars to produce. We had two thousand copies printed, and seventeen hundred have sold.

In the year following the release of *Treasures*, through grants and successful book sales from over twenty states, we began building up the funds necessary to start on our next publication project — *Treasures 2*.

The first step was another Starfire contest. This time more than two thousand students from over 56 towns and cities throughout Oregon (grades 1-12) submitted their stories, and seven hundred students sent in their art. In deciding the winners, teachers and student editors of the Foundation's staff read the entries judging them for voice, the power of the words, and honesty, the extent to which the student authors invested themselves in their writing. Art teachers and student artists of the Foundation's staff looked at expression, detail, and composition in evaluating the art.

Once the winners were selected, work began on *Treasures 2*. Teachers, professionals, and students helped with mass mailings, editing, and graphic design. On a day-to-day basis, I had the good fortune to work with Anh Hua and Yen Nguyen, two excellent high school students and fine young people. They were involved in all operations of the Foundation: planning, inputting, editing, sales, accounting, public relations, clerical work, training of other student editors, and graphic design. We were all a hard-working family building a beautiful book and long-lasting friendships.

Treasures 2 was published after two years. The biggest problem, of course, was the cost, which ran over twenty-one thousand dollars. The Collins Foundation helped with a contribution of $10,000.

The projected budget for *Treasures 3: Stories & Art by Stu-*

dents in Japan and Oregon is over sixty-thousand dollars during a three-year period. The first step in raising money is to sell out the first run of *Treasures 2*, so we've begun working on a promotional package about the Foundation and *Treasures 2* to reach teachers in Oregon, Japan, and other interested geographic areas. At the rate it's selling, the first run of two thousand copies should be sold out within the next seven months. Then we plan on doing a second printing.

The response to *Treasures 2* has been fantastic. The student authors and artists of *Treasures* and *Treasures 2* have been singled out for special recognition by their school districts. Some have been promoted to advanced writing classes. In Beaverton, Oregon, all of the student contributors went before the school board to receive certificates from the Superintendent. A student in Washington County was invited to speak to another school about the writing process, and other students have been interviewed by the media. Many shared their experiences with teachers at teachers' conferences, and others participated in public readings. Recognition of the students' achievements and praise for their accomplishments continues to grow.

You may order *Treasures* and *Treasures 2* through Media Weavers. If you would like more information about the Oregon Students Writing & Art Foundation and its next project — *Treasures 3: Stories & Art by Students in Japan and Oregon*, write:

Chris Weber, Director
The Oregon Students Writing & Art Foundation
P.O. Box 2100
Portland, Oregon 97208-2100
(503-232-7737)

Chris Weber is founder and director of the Oregon Students Writing & Art Foundation. He is also a full time ESL teacher for the Portland Public Schools.

"This winter, we received our copy of *Treasures*. The students read it constantly and recommend favorite stories to each other. They use *Treasures* to get ideas for topics and styles of writing. It definitely motivates them to write. A frequent comment is, 'A kid wrote this story. I can write, too!' Our three winners are respected by their classmates. This year, every pupil in my class wants to enter their story in the contest."
—Adele Cerny, Teacher, John Day

"It's great (being published) because I get to see something I've worked on enjoyed by other people."
—Morgan Long, Student Author, Portland

"Sometimes I wonder if from these experiences I can help somebody else. I hope so...perhaps a small somebody like me."
—Heather Rivers, Student Writer, Mollala

"*Treasures* and *Treasures 2* have shown my students that they CAN communicate to people they have never even met through writing. These books have given them a sense of pride and a feeling that through writing they have authority in our world. To see my students pass around the books, poring over every story and illustration, is to look at the faces of pride."
—Sue Morgan, Teacher, Grants Pass

Report from a Young Publisher
by Annie Workman

I started writing when I was about three years old when I wrote a story about Bert and Ernie as cavemen. I kept writing, and entered a story of mine in a Young Authors Convention.

When my brother got a job shoveling snow, I wanted to earn money, too. I created a magazine about my parents called *Computer Life* and sold it to them. They suggested that I do more, so I started my own magazine. It went from *Vista Cruiser U.S.A.* to *Muddy Pickup U.S.A.* to *Slug Bug U.S.A.* Now it's called *Rainbow Magazine*, and is produced in a newsletter format. I charge $.50 per issue, and I send it out to relatives and friends, and anyone else who subscribes once a month. My sixth grade teacher, Mr. Rickert, along with my parents, encouraged me a lot. My grandpa also encourages me by sending me mystery stories that he writes. Those are fun to read.

My magazine is usually about four to six pages long. I started out doing them all by hand. My parents decided to help me out, so they gave me an old typewriter. Nowadays I do my magazine on computer (an Amiga using Pagesetter). Right now I only have about twelve subscribers. The subscription ends this August, and I might take a break for awhile. When I start writing again, I want to make it bigger and better in order to get more subscribers.

Earlier this summer I went to the Clayton Institute for the Arts in Denver, Colorado. They have Creative Writing, Music Composition, Dance, Visual Arts, and Theatre. The Creative Writing classes are very good, and if you have finished sixth through eighth grade and are interested in learning a lot about writing, I strongly suggest going there.

I will keep writing for as long as I can. I have written an article for *The Market Guide for Young Writers*, too.

I write a lot of different types of articles in my magazine. Every month I have an advertising column that sells things like potholders. I also write a story about the funny things my best friend Jana Jaraczeski and I do together. I call it "Ann & Jan." I also put a "Recipe of the Month" in each month, which I get out of my mom's foreign foods cookbook. I usually put a poem or two in, and sometimes I put an article in about facts that I learned in school on a certain subject. ❖

Annie Workman, from Great Falls, Montana, is 12 years old. She won honorable mention for her entry in *Cricket Magazine* Contest, and wrote an article for the *Market Guide for Young Writers*.

Resources for Young Writers

What follows is a sampling of resources for students who want to stretch beyond the borders of their classroom writing projects. These are only some of the many contests, writing programs, and publications that may entice a young writer. The publishers of this book would like to hear from you — students, parents, teachers, and publishers — if you care to add to this list. Any updates will be listed in the quarterly newspaper, *Writer's NW*, which serves as a supplement to *Writer's Northwest Handbook*.

Alaska

Writings from Alaska Schools is an annual publication from the Alaska Council of Teachers of English, PO Box 3184, Kodiak, AK 99615. Contact: David Jaynes. All Alaskan students are invited to submit samples, which are then judged and edited by ACTE. The 1987 anthology contained work from 80 schools representing many different grade levels and types of writing.

The Alaska State Writing Consortium Newsletter, Department of Education, PO Box F, Juneau, AK 99811. Contact: Annie Calkins at 907-465-2841. The Consortium is the Alaskan version of the Writing Project (a writing program for teachers which exists in most states); the newsletter announces contests for young writers and lists student newsletters and magazines.

Pencils of the Stars, considered the oldest continually published poetry journal in Alaska for young writers, publishes work from elementary children of the Anchorage School District. The Mielke family provides ten yearly awards in honor of Margaret Mielke, Alaska's first poet laureate.

Idaho

Northwest Inland Writing Project Newsletter, Elinor Michel, College of Education, University of Idaho, Moscow, ID 83843. Phone: 208-885-6586. Quarterly newsletter focuses on classroom approach to writing. Student work produced in writing workshops is accepted in limited amounts.

Contact Lynn Meeks, Language Arts Consultant at the State Department of Education, Len B. Jordan Office Building, 650 W. State, Boise, ID 83720 for information on writing programs.

Montana

The Montana Division of the American Association of University Women sponsors an annual essay contest with prizes, open to all Montana students, grades 10–12. For information and guidelines contact: Julianne Perrault, 20200 W. Dickerson #58, Bozeman, MT 59715.

Contact Edward Eschler, English & Social Studies Specialist, Office of Public Instruction, Helena, MT 59620 for information on writing programs.

Often the Teachers of English organization in each state will sponsor writing contests. Check out the Montana Association of Teachers of English & Language Arts, c/o Rebecca Stiff, President, Helena High School, Helena, MT 59601.

The Montana Writing Project may also have contacts for young writers. Contact: Dr. Beverly Ann Chin, Director, Montana Writing Project, Department of English, University of Montana, Missoula, MT 59812.

The Missoula Reading Council sponsors a statewide young authors conference for elementary through eighth grade. The conference includes workshops, speakers, and a display of books students have made. There are no qualifications or fees for the display, except that the student submit through a teacher.

Ghost Town Quarterly has a section reserved for student material called Students' Corner. Any student from kindergarten through 12th grade may submit material. Send for guidelines with a self-addressed, stamped envelope (SASE) to: *Ghost Town Quarterly*, PO Box 1163, Anaconda, MT 59711.

Oregon

Oregon Student Magazine Contest is sponsored by the Oregon Council of Teachers of English and Eastern Oregon State College. The contest is open to students and teachers publishing student writing in a magazine format where all aspects of the project are worked on by students and teachers. Awards six prizes of $100 each. Contact: George Venn, English Department, Eastern Oregon State College, La Grande, OR 97850.

High School Journalism Contest sponsored by Oregon Press Women. Categories for features, photography, news, editorial. Contest is judged by professional journalists. First place winners are entered in the National Federation of Press Women Contest. Guidelines are sent to Oregon high schools. Contact: Glennis McNeal, PO Box 25354, Portland, OR 97225.

Oregon Writing Festival is an annual event co-sponsored by the Oregon Council of Teachers of English and the Oregon Department of Education, hosted by the University of Oregon. Includes workshops, speakers, and sharing groups where students read their writings.

Young Writers Fiction Contest is sponsored by *Northwest Magazine, The Oregonian*, 1320 SW Broadway, Portland, OR 97201. It is for residents of Oregon age 30 or under; one short story per entry.

The Oregon Students Writing & Art Foundation has published two anthologies of student writing (and is working on a third). Students take part in all aspects of this project. Contact the Foundation c/o Chris Weber, PO Box 2100, Portland, OR 97208-2100.

Physicians for Social Responsibility Writing Contest is open to Oregon students grades 7-12. The subject is "I Can, We Can Overcome War." Prizes. For guidelines, write PSR at 921 SW Morrison, Suite 500, Portland, OR 97205.

The Asterisk, Oregon Press Women, Inc., PO Box 25354, Portland, OR 97225-0354. The newspaper for prize-winning high school journalists.

Skipping Stones, c/o Aprovecho, 80574 Hazelton Rd., Cottage Grove, OR 97424. Phone: 503-942-9434. New quarterly seeks writing in every language, artwork, and photography from and for children.

Young American, America's Newsmagazine for Kids, PO Box 12409, Portland, OR 97212. Accepts work from young writers.

Washington

Washington State has over 20 young authors'/writers' conferences. They offer a variety of workshops, nationally known children's authors, speakers, manuscript sharing, prizes, critiques, T-shirts and souvenirs. Dates, sites and speakers change each year. Most are held in the winter and spring. For information contact: Fred Bannister, Supervisor, Reading/Language Arts, IPS Division, Old Capitol Bldg. FG-11, Olympia, WA 98504.

Young Voices, a Thurston County magazine of children's writing, is interested in stories, articles and poems from elementary or middle school writers. Contact the magazine at PO Box 2321, Olympia, WA 98507; phone: (206) 357-4683. —LS

Regional Presses and Publications

Some offer markets for young writers, others specialize in topics for parents, teachers, and/or youth. Check them out in the market listings section for more information.

Adopted Child
Alaska Council of Teachers of English
The Asterisk
Blue Heron Press
The Book Shop/*Children's Newsletter*
Bright Ring Publishing
Centerplace Publishing Company
Childbirth Education Association
Coalition For Child Advocacy
Council for Indian Education
Creative Children
Enfantaisie
First Alternative Thymes
Flashes
The Charles Franklin Press
Ghost Town Quarterly
Havin' Fun, Inc.
Heron Books, Inc.
Home Education Magazine
Home Education Press
Images
Kid Care Magazine
Kids Lib: Oness Press
Legacy House, Inc.
LUNO: Learning Unlimited Network of Oregon
Markins Enterprises
Monte Publishing Company
Nerve Press
Northwest Inland Writing Project Newsletter

Our Little Friend
P.R.O. Newsletter of Oregon
Parenting Press, Inc.
Pathways
Paws IV Publishing Co.
The Pedersens
Peel Productions
Portland Family Calendar
Press Porcepic Ltd.
Primary Treasure
Saturday's Child
Seattle's Child/Eastside Project
Seattle's Child Publishing
Skipping Stones
Teaching Home
Teaching Research Infant and Child Center News
TGNW Press
Titania Publications
Totline
West Coast Baby Magazine
Wheel Press
Young American, America's Newspaper for Kids
Young Voices

Not regional, but unique, is the *Market Guide for Young Writers* by Kathy Henderson, Shoe Tree Press, PO Box 356, Belvidere, NJ 07823, $12.95 paperback.

Tips

WRITER'S DAILY JOURNAL

- Date

- Work performed (project or client):

- Phone calls (number, purpose, and results):

- Appointments (time, location, and purpose):

- Expenses:

- Income (source, project, invoice number):

- Correspondence:

- Notes:

QUERY & MANUSCRIPT LOG

Subject or title:

Date completed/mailed:

Query/manuscript:

Publication:

Editor's name:

Photos or artwork included:

On-spec/assignment:

Pays on publication/acceptance:

Date returned or accepted:

Date published:

Payment:

Profiles:
Magazines, Presses, Groups

Mississippi Mud: It's Not What You'd Call an Office Job But It's Kept Me Off the Streets
by Joel Weinstein

When I look back over the fifteen years I've put into my magazine, *Mississippi Mud*, I feel something like the ringmaster of a traveling sideshow. It's been a small and ragtag operation for all of its life. The writers and artists I've published have all had their different acts, a few of which, it's seemed to me, could have gone well with a fly-by-night carnival. By putting the magazine on newsstands around Portland — and, increasingly, in all parts of the country — I've tried to offer to anyone who would shell out a few pennies a bit of a ride through America's literary funhouse.

Fifteen years. I've always looked on dedication in others with a mixture of admiration and condescension, at bottom glad that I'm not stuck in the rut of an office job or the care and feeding of a number of other souls. But then fifteen years in the literary magazine business is astonishing longevity, and I have to marvel that it's me that's been doing it. When I pose the question to myself, I get the same smartass answer I give to those who ask me why I do it at all: the magazine has a life of its own.

For several years the process of embellishing the presentation of my first love, writing, kept me absorbed in the magazine. I looked at turn-of-the-century popular magazines and advertising of all kinds. Since I liked to locate *Mississippi Mud* near the edge of high culture — although on the bleacher-seat side — I sought writing that had both the narrative soundness of those early popular magazines and the undercurrents and the innovations of style that best captured the darkness of life in America at the end of the twentieth century. By using fine papers and discrete touches of color and creating layouts that emphasized elegance of typography and classical page borders, I could hark back to the glory days of magazine publishing. Yet the magazine has a distinctly modern cast because of the often harrowing, urban-centered writing and the eerily visionary artwork that accompanies it.

But it was the occasional dramatic sidetrack that really got me excited about publishing *Mississippi Mud*. At about the ten-year mark, I was despairing to a friend, as I often did, that the magazine was a pathetic thing financially. She suggested that I put out a *Mississippi Mud* calendar. Now this seemed to me like a preposterously conventional thing to do, but when I mentioned this to an astute European artist, he said, "Oh, you mean like the medieval books of hours." All of a sudden this was a stupendous idea: a tenth anniversary issue that was a desk calendar, both a savage parody of and a tribute to a religious book that was among the most beautiful manuscripts ever printed.

The *Mississippi Mud* Book of Days became the most complicated project I'd ever undertaken, but the result was hugely satisfying. It was gorgeous. It had six colors of ink — one for each season, plus two for additional sections — and each month was illustrated by a different artist. There were religious holidays that I made up: Beaster and the Pantylost and the Utterance of the Seven Illegible Oaths. There were the anniversaries of notable literary events like the day A.A. Milne was eaten by a bear. Amidst all of this folderol was fiction and poetry by the cream of Northwest writers. To celebrate its publication I had a party: a show of the original art, a reading by the writers, a band that rocked into the night and 65 pounds of barbecued chicken.

The Book of Days did not make me rich as I'd wildly hoped. This outburst was followed by several years of more or less routine publishing. About a year and a half ago, a friend who directs Portland's highly successful artist-run gallery, Blackfish,

---

> *"I've tried to offer to anyone who would shell out a few pennies a bit of a ride through America's literary funhouse."*

---

suggested I think about having a show there. I'd long been intrigued by how I might incorporate sculpture into the magazine, and I realized that a gallery show might be the means to do that. Rummaging through some manuscripts, I discovered, in much the way I'd previously come up with themes for the magazine, that many of them dealt with family life.

I made poster-sized broadsides of the written works and gave each one to an artist who created or lent a painting, drawing, print, photograph or sculpture to the show. I then conceived of a way for visitors to walk through the gallery as a reader might thumb through the magazine, trying to create a certain progression of mood and color and thought that conveyed, as a whole, the sweet poignance, the maddening irony and the ineffable but deeply familiar mystery of family life in America in our time. I also had the writers record their poems and stories on cassettes which, with musical interludes composed and performed especially for the show, were made into a tape that played endlessly during the show.

There were 34 writers, artists and musicians in "Family Life." Frequently the sense of collaboration was profound. I gave a sculptor a story that was densely worded, syntactically weird and riddled with displacements of voice and time. Underneath its convolutions was a story of powerful, deeply-felt emotion. The sculptor told me at first that she hated the piece, but

Continued

after some prodding from me she persisted, and, to my delight, she created a sculpture that embodied what I regarded as the story's best features.

It has been difficult to know how to follow "Family Life." *Mississippi Mud* will continue to hit the newsstands. Although I'm notoriously slow at turning manuscripts around, I continue to derive great pleasure from reading what comes to me in the mail, marveling at the variety, oddness and vitality with which people try to be writers, and I continue to feel a strong connection with these people.

I do think that literary magazines offer otherwise unpublished writers these small consolations: in the hope of getting published at all, writers begin to impose a discipline on themselves that, hopefully, will lift their work out of the personal, solitary realm of the journal and the diary; if they do catch some editor's attention — and, miraculously, their words find their way into print — these will be read by an audience that is somewhat larger than the one comprised of wives and boyfriends, mothers, aunts and co-workers; and finally, this is one of the few opportunities that writers have to experiment, play, lash out, fool around, and, by their very outrageousness, find a receptive ear for their work.

Beyond the magazine, some new form awaits *Mississippi Mud*. I haven't the foggiest idea what that might be, but I'm not worried. A painter friend and I have been talking about producing a puppet show. What could be more fitting for a traveling sideshow like *Mississippi Mud*? ❖

Joel Weinstein, a writer and graphic designer, has published *Mississippi Mud* for 15 years.

Northern Lights Magazine, Interview with Don Snow

Writer's Northwest Handbook: The masthead in your magazine opens with this statement:

Northern Lights is a bimonthly publication of the Northern Lights Research and Education Institute, a nonprofit, tax-exempt education foundation. Northern Lights Institute analyzes issues concerning the future of the Northern Rockies — Idaho, Montana and Wyoming — for the benefit of citizens who want to develop and implement responsible public policies.

WNH: How would you describe the Institute?

Don Snow: If Northern Lights were in Washington DC, it would be called a think tank. But we haven't acted like a conventional think tank. We don't publish dreary, numbers-bound, grey reports that keep us respectable from an academic vantage point, or any vantage point…. We have really tried to keep a human face in everything. The magazine has fit fairly well with that motivation. It has been the most human-spirited thing in the organization; it has been the organization's soul.

WNH: What's been the response to the magazine?

DS: It's a critical success and a market failure.

WNH: What went wrong in the market?

DS: We never achieved a level of self-sufficiency to the extent that subscriber income supported the operating costs of the publication. As long as the Institute was able to subsidize the cost of certain issues through related grants, we were fine. If we had a grant to do something on the Missouri River, you're going to hear about that in the magazine.

We didn't want it to operate on any subsidy, though. We never wanted the magazine to be a newsletter. We wanted the magazine to be feistier, more independent than that, intellectually. We wanted it to build a very vigorous constituency both for itself and for the organization, and we needed to achieve a level of self-sufficiency to do that. We didn't pay people great wages, but we didn't exploit the beejeesus out of them either.

WNH: What about advertising?

DS: That became a rock in a hard place. A regional publication, limited market. Where is Northern Lights? Would a Missoula biz want to advertise in it? We only have a few hundred Missoula subscribers.

Over a period of time we were confident, however, based on the rates of return we were getting on very small direct mail hits, 2,500 to 5,000. We were getting 4% returns. Religiously. Sometimes 7%. Paid subscribers.

So we said, we've done this for two years. How much money would it take for us to do a huge campaign — which in the real publishing world is a tiny campaign — to get ourselves up to sufficiency? We determined it would cost somewhere between 40,000 and 50,000 bucks. So I wrote a proposal and went out and raised the money from private philanthropy, grants, and

---

"It's a critical success and a market failure."

---

in one case, a small loan. Spent 40,000 of the 50,000. Did almost 100,000 pieces of mail. Deluxe mail. We got a rate of return that was a tiny fraction of 1%. We don't know exactly what happened.

Right smack in the middle of the campaign, the stock market crashed. We don't know to what extent that had a dampening influence. People started to get real worried about disposable income. It wasn't an expensive publication, but in this region 16 bucks is 16 bucks.

WNH: These weren't just regional lists?

DS: Hell, all over the place. In some instances, national. *The Utne Reader* list is national. We used *Mother Jones* in about a seven-state area. We used *Harpers* in a six-state area. We're a long way from being professionals, obviously. But it was a fairly crafty strategy.

So we got this dismal return, and we regrouped to begin asking the hard questions. Are we going to spend the last

$10,000? Why would we do that? What are we going to do now? The answer is that we're going to radically cut the costs of the publication. Number One. Number Two, we don't want to feel like Sisyphus — we're going to assume that this publication has a limited market. That's going to be our assumption. Our policy now is anybody who ever subscribed to *NL* magazine, whether they let their subscription lapse, or they gave us hundreds of dollars because they loved it so much, gets it from now on. It's like public radio. You don't have to do anything to get it. But the understanding is that if you don't give something back to it, there's not going to be public radio anymore.

WNH: What is the readership?

DS: The total list is pushing 6,000. Which is respectable, but we never had a current, paid subscriber list that topped — I think, our highest point was 3,100.

WNH: How will this new policy affect your ads?

DS: What can we tell an advertiser? Are our readers real likely candidates for using mail order? Should we get Banana Republic to advertise? We really can't honestly answer that. We did a reader profile. We found out demographics, average income. It's an impressive readership. It's highly educated, very much like the *Altantic, Harpers, New Yorker*. They make good incomes. They are united in a love they have of this region, no matter where they live. But beyond that, it's a fairly ill-defined bunch.

We're appealing to a different kind of character than the usual public interest member. There're a lot of people who have sort of odd or maverick political persuasions. We've disgusted a lot of liberals. We've menaced conservatives. We haven't told anybody exactly what they want to hear, so that it validates their pictures of the universe. It turns out that *NL* is a different kind of character. It's clearly a liberal leaning kind of thing, yet the last edition pisses all over the liberal community.

WNH: What's the continuing relationship to the Institute if you want the paper to be feisty and independent?

DS: It's feisty within limits. So if we're getting into water issues, we want to talk about water issues in a very lively and engaging way, a much more journalistic way, rather than mere analysis.

We want that to continue, but we want to upgrade the sophistication and the respectability — the credentials of the magazine — a little bit. In other words, we want it to be somewhat less prepared by freelancers who have otherwise no relationship to the Institute. ❖   — WW/WNH

Genesis of a Press: Honeybrook
by Donnell Hunter

After two weeks tutelage under Tree Swenson of Copper Canyon Press (as part of the 1981 Port Townsend Writers conference where we printed broadsides of our own poems and those of the visiting poets), I had so much fun I wanted to find a letterpress of my own. In June, 1983 one became available when the *Rigby Star* changed ownership in my home town. So, with the help of my son and his pickup and the rental of a forklift from the lumberyard, I loaded up the 1899 version of a 12 x 8 Chandler and Price letterpress, and headed for Rexburg, Idaho. My dream was about to come true.

For a moment it looked like it was going to evaporate when the press toppled off the second forklift I rented and smashed onto the concrete driveway of my home. But after twenty dollars' worth of welding and some patience rewinding a smashed spring — learned Chandler and Price were no longer in business so I couldn't buy parts — I was in business. I borrowed some type cases from the Ricks College Library and ordered some Centaur type from McKenzie-Harris Type Foundry in San Francisco. By the next April I had my first chapbook of poetry, *The Frog in Our Basement,* under the Honeybrook Press imprint. The name came from a farm my great-grandfather owned in Pennsylvania in the late 1700s.

When William Stafford visited our Ricks College Campus for a poetry reading, I showed him my press in my garage and gave him a copy of my book. He asked if I had any other projects in mind. I said I had one in mind I hoped to arrange that week. I took a deep breath. "I'd like to do a chapbook of your poems." He said, "Well, I'm not sure I've got anything suitable at the present." I thought it was a polite "not interested." Next morning after he had read the poems in my book and made a couple of comments about them, I said I was serious about wanting to print a chapbook for him, but if I was too presumptuous, just tell me so. He said it wasn't that, and he would see if there might be something he could find.

Four days later the manuscript for *Stories and Storms and Strangers* arrived in the mail. A friend did a line drawing for the cover, and I printed an edition of 400 copies before it got too cold in my garage to keep working.

In 1985 I got a request from a friend to do a chapbook of her haiku. That led to another request from a poet in Virginia, as well as one from one of Stafford's friends in Washington, and before I knew it I had six books in print, including two of my own and a second Stafford chapbook, *Brother Wind.* With my earnings I bought two more type faces, Italian Old Style and Deepdene. And I had enough projects each summer to keep busy until school started. This included three chapbooks printed for Confluence Press.

I have learned to make my own linoleum blocks and line drawings for photoengravings for illustrations. I still consider my printing mostly a hobby, but it's been a hobby that has paid its own way. One bookseller in California has collected every title I've done, as have the libraries of the University of Washington and the University of Oregon. This month I received a similar order from Boise State University Library and am shipping two copies of all thirteen titles I have printed in today's mail.

Continued

This afternoon — after finishing writing this article — I hope to make three print runs on paper I dampened last night for my own (fifth) chapbook, *Songs of the River*, so I can keep on schedule with my original goal to print a chapbook of my own poems each year. While a letter press is slow and handsetting type can be tedious, there is nothing like its clarity and texture. Not to mention the fun of doing your own work with your own hands in an old-fashioned way. ❖

Donnell Hunter is proprietor and sole laborer at Honeybrook Press, and teaches at Rexburg College, Rexburg, Idaho.

Oregon State University Press
by Jo Alexander

There are about 85 university presses in the U.S., ranging in size and output from the well-known giants like California, Yale, and Chicago, through the smaller but well-established presses like Nebraska and Kansas, to the tiny — like the Oregon State University Press. OSU Press is the only university press in the state, and one of only a handful in the Pacific Northwest; by anyone's standards it is very small, publishing only half a dozen books a year. But all university presses, from the largest to the smallest, have certain things in common.

We are all committed to publishing high quality scholarly books. We are all connected in one way or another to an institution of higher education; most university presses depend on their host institution for the financial support that makes possible the publication of important books that rarely sell very many copies. We all rely heavily on faculty members at our own and other universities to help us make judgments on the merits of manuscripts we are considering for publication; while a commercial publisher might sign a contract with an author on the basis of a hunch, we put each manuscript through a rigorous review process before making a publication decision. Few of us, however,

---

"The more esoteric the subject matter, the easier it is to target the audience…"

---

publish only strictly scholarly books; most of us are attempting to pay for the publication of those scholarly books by publishing some more popular titles, often on regional topics.

OSU publishes scholarly books in a limited range of disciplines and books of particular interest to the Pacific Northwest region. We are often asked whether authors must be OSU faculty; the answer is no — we will publish books by anyone, if the subject matter is appropriate and the manuscript is thoroughly researched and clearly written. All manuscripts must be approved by the Press's staff, peer reviewed by one or more outside readers, and then discussed and recommended for publication by the Editorial Board, so the decision-making process is quite lengthy. If you have a book-length manuscript that you would like us to consider, please send a query letter first. Our print run is usually in the range of 1,000 to 2,000 copies, most of which are sold to academics and libraries.

We promote our books primarily through direct mail. The more esoteric the subject matter, the easier it is to target the audience, buy a mailing list, and mail fliers. We also rely heavily on getting reviews in the scholarly journals; while it often takes a couple of years for a review to be published, a good review in a reputable journal is worth waiting for. We rarely if ever buy space advertising; the cost is prohibitively expensive and, contrary to authors' beliefs, it does not sell many books. Even the larger presses, which do advertise, do so as a means of making a statement about their interest in a particular scholarly field, rather than to sell a specific title.

Like most university presses, we also publish regional titles of interest to a broader audience. In 1987, for example, we published *Marking the Magic Circle*, a collection of poetry, essays, and fiction by Eastern Oregon author George Venn, and *William L. Finley: Pioneer Wildlife Photographer*, a book of fascinating historical photographs from the region. We would like to do more of this kind of publishing in the future.

One kind of publishing we rarely undertake is poetry. Occasionally, the Press has, for one reason or another, taken a volume of poetry, with mixed results. One surprise winner was *Westerns* by Richard Dankleff, published in 1984, which received an enthusiastic review in *Publishers Weekly* and went into a second printing within six months. But that doesn't happen often! The Press's policy on poetry is not to encourage submissions; if something slips through onto my desk and is truly extraordinary, we might consider it. I apologize to all the poets out there with no publishing outlets. I know it's really hard to get published. But it's also difficult for a publisher to promote and market poetry, and we don't think we are well equipped to do a good job.

We would be glad to send a catalog to anyone who would like to know more about Oregon's only university press. Write: OSU Press, Waldo Hall 101, Corvallis, OR 97331-6407. ❖

Jo Alexander has been Managing Editor of the OSU Press since 1984. A native of England, she worked for the University of London Press for 13 years before coming to the U.S. in 1974 (just in time to watch Nixon's resignation speech on the TV in a hot basement apartment on New York's lower East Side).

Small Press, Small College: A Positive Confluence

When it comes to making things run at Confluence Press, Jim Hepworth does it all. Yet, he'll be the first to admit that without a great deal of help from many sources, he would be unable to carry on the work of this active press. Not only does Confluence publish five books per year, the press has an active workshop and intern program as well. In order to clearly see the press, we need to look at the many roles Jim fills, including publisher, marketing expert, teacher, and editor.

For twelve years Confluence has published poetry, fiction and non-fiction from the friendly confines of Lewis Clark State College in Lewiston, Idaho. As the publisher, Jim must balance two sets of problems. When *Writer's Northwest Handbook* (WNH) talked with him in June of 1988, he spoke about the first of these conflicts, the demands of the marketplace versus the desire to publish what he likes.

"I don't really know a good small publisher who doesn't aspire to sell books," he observed. Yet he went on to tell us about a book of haiku which Confluence had just published which was "a complete flop financially. I like being able to say, okay, I'm not doing this because we've got a market, but this is a good story…That's fun."

Another conflict arises because of his affiliation with the college, which creates a certain pressure to publish subsidized books or literary journals not of his choosing. When *The Slackwater Review,* a campus magazine, had dwindled to a circulation of two hundred, Jim chose to put his energies into projects he felt were more productive.

Managing the business side of publishing takes an enormous amount of Jim's time, just as it does in all small press operations. He has to find the money to support the work, then try to sell the books once they've been published. WNH asked him to explain these two aspects of his work.

"The school puts up about 13% of our overall budget," he said. "Then we get another maybe 13% from the ICA [Idaho Commission on the Arts]." He raises scholarship money, gives lectures, and is "Mr. Promotion and Publicity for the literature and languages division [of the college]." The press also receives grant support from the National Endowment for the Arts, and additional money comes in from book sales.

Marketing help comes from a variety of sources as well. Kampman & Company distributes Confluence Press books — along with over 70 other small presses — with a focus on the eastern half of the country. Jim doesn't have the animosity towards New York that some small publishers exhibit. He sees the need to reach this market, to sell books wherever books are purchased.

In the western part of the country word of mouth still sells. Jim also uses direct mail and relies heavily on the author's promotion of his or her own work. All this work takes time and energy, since little money is available to throw at the problems. "The trouble is," he concluded, "that every book is a new product. That's the thing I hate about publishing…if you just have Crest toothpaste to market all your life, you can get real good at it…."

Jim does have some student help to deal with the myriad tasks of the office and the business. Besides teaching his two classes, he trains interns and then quickly loses them. "You just train your help," he observed, "and then you get somebody good and that person leaves…. I would like to see what would happen if I could just have one person who carried over from year to year, semester to semester…."

This work is invaluable for the students, however. Every student who's gone through the program is either in graduate school or is working. "And that's something," Jim concluded.

In and around all this other work, Jim does what all small press people love the most: he deals with the literature. He seeks new writers and good books. For this work the press has received numerous awards, including Western States Book Awards in poetry, fiction, and non-fiction, the Pacific Northwest Booksellers award, and special exhibiting privileges at the World Book Fair.

Jim takes part of the credit for this success, but he's also generous with his thanks. "We're a literary publisher," he says. "We exist primarily because of the generosity of the public…. The fact that a little college is willing to spread out its own little wing and be protective: it's almost an anomaly."

Like publishers everywhere, Jim Hepworth is always looking for the next good book. He sums it up this way:

"I don't care what subject it is, there's no subject too small for a good book and there's no subject too big for a good book…. Once you have that good book, there's plenty of room out there. It's getting the good book that's the problem, and that book creates its own audience." ❖ —WW/WNH

Publishing Success in Montana — American Geographic

Writer's Northwest Handbook interviewed Mark Thompson, Publications Director of American Geographic, to find out how a small publishing company became large enough to work a deal with Random House.

Writer's Northwest Handbook: Would you tell us a little about the history of your press?

Mark Thompson: The magazine [*Montana Magazine*] was begun in spring, 1970, as a quarterly, then went to bimonthly in '78. We started books in 1980 with the first of our color books — *Montana Mountain Ranges*. We've done 15 books in the Montana series, and we're now out in seven other states, including Oregon, Wyoming, Vermont and Minnesota. We just sent off a book on New Hampshire. So we've evolved slowly into our

Continued

current form, American Geographic Publishing.

WNH: Your books aren't exactly like other photographic books. Are they a natural outgrowth of your magazine work?

MT: Our books are different. These aren't literary books. They're stories of the land and the people, and how they interact. They're photo books with a little more text. We hit a unique scene, between the coffee table books and the travel guide books. We have more photos than most of the guide books, more text than most of the coffee table books.

In any event, our background is color and the magazine. People associate *Montana Magazine* with that center section of color photography. As a result of the magazine, we had a tremendous stock of photography.

WNH: So these books mostly grew out of your photography stock?

MT: Yes, but that's beginning to change too. It wasn't long after our books started coming out before there was the California Geographic Series, and the Utah Geographic Series, and they weren't ours. We needed to get busy in a hurry, and get out where we wanted to be. So there was a tremendous run of titles for us in 1987. As a result of that, we weren't working out as far in advance as we wanted so we were using all this stock photography. But as we get out in '89 and '90, we will be assigning photography and the books will be even better than they are now.

"These aren't literary books. They're stories of the land and the people, and how they interact."

We're getting subject areas that are narrow enough that we really have to assign photographers. We just can't get stock of some things that we want to do. And if it's really contemporary and fresh, we really have to have contemporary and fresh photographers.

WNH: When you go into other states are you using people there or sending people in?

MT: A little of both. We worked with a writer who had been married to a woman from Vermont, and that writer had done two books for us already. As one of those gypsy photographer types, he can go anywhere, and if he can survive and take photos, he'll do it. In that case, we sent out our own guy. We try to find local sources if we can, though. In New York we're using a fellow from Boston, a wonderful, wonderful writer — the best. So it's nice when we stumble on them and can afford them.

WNH: Does it matter if you use regional writers and photographers?

MT: It really doesn't matter, but it can cut the lead time. It's pretty frightening to sit in Helena and have spent a week on the phone talking with writers in Vermont, and say, yeah OK, this one's it. And not have met any of them. This is the first year I've had to sign contracts with authors that I haven't met. And I don't want to do it anymore.

WNH: What about distribution?

MT: Distribution is all Random House, except the Montana books.

WNH: Are you packaging them for Random House?

MT: No, we're the publisher. This is our first full year with them. They're teaching us a lot about the trade because we're not national book publishers yet. I hope they're benefiting from it as well.

WNH: Are you making more money?

MT: It's hard to tell. It's already bad enough in this business: the money comes so late after you've spent it, but it's compounded by dealing with a large distributor, because they're behind another phase of it. So we really honestly don't know yet.

WNH: Is the budget shared for the marketing?

MT: Yes, that is shared. They have notions about marketing books that are based on dealing with James Michener and folks like that. They call us up and want to know what our hotel budget's going to be for the author tour, and we say, what author tour? TV? What are you talking about?

WNH: When did you start with Random House?

MT: The first books they handled from us were our fall books in '87. We wanted to get into other states. It seemed the most logical way to have a national distribution. It's not everyone who has the brass to walk up to the door of Random House, and say, you guys really need us, but our publisher does have that kind of brass. And it worked.

I think it was a coincidence, and that Random House was looking to acquire some smaller publishers, not acquire financially, but to have some other small publishers from diverse backgrounds in their stable, so to speak. They have some funny little titles, and I guess we're one of their funny little titles.

WNH: I understand that you have your printing done in Hong Kong. How has that affected your work?

MT: As a result of our printing in the Orient, we stumbled into some things. Our publisher is primarily an adventurer, that's what he does best. And he had a chance to venture to Vietnam, and concluded to do a book on Vietnam.

WNH: Will this open up the Pacific Rim idea for you?

MT: We really need to look at other markets, so we're just beginning to think and talk about it. We're finding out how much it costs to have a book translated and trying to make some contacts in consulates and foreign trade associations. Meanwhile, we'll keep doing what we're doing now. ❖ —WW/WNH

"…if there is any secret to The Fine Art of Getting Published, it is the strength of ideas themselves. Publishers feed on them."
—Knute Berger

Northwest Native American Writers' Association

This group started in July, 1987 in order to promote the visibility of Native American writers, as well as oral and written literature. It is a non-profit organization whose primary objective is the publication of the *Northwest Native American Writer's Literary Resources*. The publication will list Native American writers, poets and storytellers from the Pacific Northwest, including writers from other nations who reside in and have invested tenure in the NW. Other Native American authors, who by native language groups which cross state boundaries are a part of the NW area, will be included in the publication.

Membership is open to NW Native American writers, storytellers and poets. Inclusion in the *Literacy Resources* is limited to published, accredited, or in some way, professional writers. The intent is not to be exclusive, but to introduce legitimate Native American writers to other writers, educators, editors, publishers and the public. Membership is participatory.

NWNAW members are available for readings, classroom discussions and consultation on Native American literature curriculum. The group has held readings at Portland State University for Native American Awareness Week, and at the Interstate Firehouse Cultural Center in Portland. It provides extensive listings of works by Native American authors and has published a 19-page folio of broadsides which sells for $10.

Contact: Northwest Native American Writers Association (NWNAW), PO Box 6403, Portland, Oregon 97228, or phone Elizabeth Woody (503) 232-3513. ❖

The Federation of British Columbia Writers

The largest writers' organization in BC, the Federation of British Columbia Writers is a non-profit group of professional and aspiring writers in all genres. It is an activist group, serving as a liaison between writers and the government, lobbying for increased pay, promoting Federation members' books, and striving for greater visibility for writers.

The following is excerpted from literature put out by the Federation.

We are members of the B.C. Book Promotion Council, First Night, the Ad Hoc Coalition for B.C. Artists, the Burnaby and Vancouver Community Arts Councils. We are awaiting word on our membership in the Cultural Alliance, the Public Lending Rights Commission and the Canadian Repography Collective.

We meet regularly with representatives from the Canadian Society of Children's Authors, Illustrators and Performers; the Writers' Union; Kootenay School of Writing; the Periodical Writers of Canada; the Playwrights Union; Women and Words; the League of Poets; and the Freelance Editors Association of Canada (FEAC).

These activities have permitted more effective promotion of our programs throughout the province and increased cooperative efforts. These efforts include: FEAC's telephone and answering machine are located in our Vancouver office; we are negotiating with OWL for shared space in Penticton; the Writers' Union has provided research material used by our Federation; our Naramata Conference saw Colin Browne of Kootenay School and Leona Gom of Women and Words doing "Blue Pencil Cafes;" and, we are becoming an effective referral service for people seeking writers and writers seeking assistance.

We have grown from 200 members to over 600 in less than a year, thanks to a well planned and executed membership drive. Colin Browne, W.P. Kinsella, Jane Rule, Barry Broadfoot, Spider Robinson, Robert Bringhurst, George Payerle, Jurgen Hesse, Christie Harris, Peter C. Newman, Bill Bisset, David Watmough, George Woodcock, Sandy Duncan, Alan Twigg and Susan Musgrave are some of our members.

We have successfully completed our JobTrac project, "Literary rites: a competition," which attracted over 700 entries, and production of the *Literary Arts Directory*, copies of which are included with the grant application.

We have begun a reading series, Writers Bridging Cultures, to spur interest in writers of minority cultures in Canada. This project is receiving support from the Secretary of State, Multiculturalism.

Our first province-wide conference held in Naramata, "Balancing the Books," allowed our members to meet and talk about the business of writing. The evaluation forms indicate the need for an annual conference for our members and other interested writers.

The *Writers in the Classroom Directory* should be completed by the end of June for use in B.C.'s schools this fall.

This year we hope to repeat the competition; update our members' directory; increase regional participation; co-sponsor workshops, like "Literary Groceries" with Kootenay School; further expand the membership drive; continue to organize readings; and act as a referral service. ❖

Multicultural Playwrights' Festival
by Nikki Louis

In keeping with its longstanding commitment to ethnic artists, The Group Theatre company produced its first annual American Minority Playwrights' Festival in 1985. Designed to present the work of Black, Native American, Chicano/Hispanic, and Asian-American playwrights, the Festival sought scripts from ethnic writers from all over the country. A panel of theater professionals selected "finalists," who received workshop productions, and "semi-finalists," who were represented by a one-time rehearsed reading.

Playwrights from the first three festivals have gone on to productions at various theaters around the country. Kermit Frazier, last year's finalist and a semi-finalist two previous years, recently won a $10,000 McKnight Fellowship from the Minneapolis Playwright's Center. The 1986 winning play, *Tea*, by Valina Hasu Houston, received productions in New York and San Diego. Bill Yellow Robe from Montana recently won a Jerome Fellowship of $5,000 and a one-year residency at the Minneapolis Playwright's Center.

Last year, the Northwest Playwrights Guild joined The Group in co-sponsoring a Forum to inaugurate the third annual festival. Maria Irene Fornes, whom the Guild brought to Seattle

---

"Approximately 90% of the plays produced by American regional theaters in the last three years had all-white casts."

---

to conduct a two-week playwriting workshop, was guest speaker and discussed the working relationship between playwright and director.

This year's event, now renamed the MultiCultural Playwrights' Festival, was held July 3, 1988 at the University of Washington's Ethnic Theater. An initial selection process narrowed the nearly 200 submissions under consideration to 70. The jury further narrowed the list to 25, then subsequently selected two scripts for full workshop productions and six for rehearsed readings.

"To my knowledge, this is the only professional festival of its kind in the country," states Festival Director Tim Bond, referring to its multicultural focus. This year, the number of winning playwrights attending the Festival has more than doubled (he expects seven of the eight playwrights to come to Seattle). "Furthermore, the number auditioning for parts in the festival has significantly increased."

"It is important to support the writers," states Jacqueline Moscou, King County Arts Commissioner, "whose vision comes from their culture." "And it's important to let the people in those cultures know that there is a voice out there representing them," adds Laura Esparaza, Assistant to the Festival Director.

That is not to say there is nothing of interest for the playgoer or the playwright who is not a member of the cultural groups represented in the Festival. "Preserving the origins from which

our writers speak while sparking the recognition of universal themes is what the Festival is all about," says Bond. "The Festival began out of The Group Theatre's need to give greater representation to some of the non-white cultural groups in our society. Approximately 90% of the plays produced by American regional theaters in the last three years had all-white casts," he says. "The audiences are mainly middle and upper-class whites. There is a fear on the part of artistic directors and producers that these audiences will not respond to material that is too far outside the realm of their daily lives."

"But I believe that's a fallacy," Bond states. "These audiences are interested in seeing plays about societies other than their own. This is clearly evidenced in the recent successes of such plays as *Fences* by August Wilson, *Roosters* by Bill Sachez-Scott, *The Colored Museum* by George Wolfe, *The Kiss of the Spider Woman* by Manuel Puig. All of these plays have received popular acclaim and are being produced across the country with regularity. American regional theatre is 25 years old, and the audiences are ready to see multi-ethnic casts and plays about minorities."

Bond also emphasizes that the intent of theFestival is to promote the playwright, not the play. And in this regard, the focus of the festival is not ethnocentric — there is no restriction of or requirement for the subject matter of the plays, simply that writers be people of color. Many ethnic playwrights explore themes other than those of their own ethnic culture, knowing that they are also part of an American culture.

The Group Theatre has evolved in the last decade from a small band of ethnic actors to one of the state's finest professional theater companies. It has produced over 75 plays, 3 playwrights festivals, workshop programs and touring project, and in 1986 became the only theater company in Washington State to receive the Governor's Arts Award for artistic excellence and outstanding contribution to the community. ❖

Nikki Louis, a second generation Japanese-American who spent her early years interned in an Idaho relocation camp, is a writer/performer. She is a member of the Steering Committee of the NW Playwrights Guild, and a founder of Playwrights-In-Progress. This piece is adapted from an article in the June, 1988 issue of *The Arts*, King County Arts Commission newsletter.

Northwest Association of Book Publishers
by Joe Stein

Seven years ago five women began meeting regularly in one another's homes to commiserate on the scary business of publishing. Rank amateurs printing books! But they found support, and the energy and zeal to succeed.

Thanks to these small beginnings, today there is the Northwest Association of Book Publishers (NWABP) with more than 150 members who have produced over 700 titles. As it grew, NWABP's care, planning and effort have widened toward the goal of professional publishing. A significant number of people who dropped out were "vanity" authors, but vanity is out of place with the high standards of this group. On special occasions NWABP exhibits the scores of book titles of its members. At every meeting, members unveil at least one new title. In this atmosphere, small wonder that many ears went up when Michael Powell, of Powell's Books, was heard to say, "We indulge hobbyists, we do business with professionals."

In the past few years the association has sought to define and refine its identity as a service — for, by, and of its members. One committee promotes exhibits across the continent, another works constantly on organization, and the board of directors seeks always to upgrade standards. Before each monthly meeting, a one-hour seminar for new members explores the arcane rudiments of publishing.

The inexperienced are apt to race ahead, unaware that writing the book is only the first step, easy compared to the problems of distribution. NWABP fosters a careful plan of production, promotion and distribution before taking the big plunge. When mistakes get made anyway, the experienced hands are there with counsel.

Paulette Jarvey's company, Hot Off the Press, Canby, (five employees) accounts for 60 how-to craft titles. That is in press runs of 10,000 books each, altogether 1.5 million books marketed in the U.S., Canada and Australia.

Another of the founders, Judy Majors, Apple Press, Milwaukie, has topped 500,000 books so far. She has eight sugar-free cookbook titles, and sold two more to Random House.

Among the early joiners, Kiki Caniff began with a book she wrote about Sauvie Island. The publisher flubbed it, so she formed her own KI-2 Enterprises, Portland, and made an immediate success with *Oregon Free*. It is now in its third edition. Last year her latest, *The Northwest Golfer,* sold 5,000 copies within three months of publication.

We find no NWABP publisher who started with big money. Susan Joyce and Doug DuBosque (Peel Productions) got started by taking over the marketing of their full-color children's book *Peel, the Extraordinary Elephant*. School visits as well as newspaper, radio and TV coverage helped create a demand for a reprint for *Peel* as well as new titles, including *How do you draw dinosaurs?* and a cassette version of *Peel*.

Another success, Barbara Harris, Portland, has a single title, *Microwave Cooking*. Created for kitchen use, it was an overnight hit at publication in 1974. That was before NWABP, but Harris still likes the support of the group. She's made 28 printings, a total of 750,000 copies.

Of a more literary line in public and current affairs are the titles of Circa Press, Lake Oswego. Owner Bob Brooks wrote the first three, but has two more in the works by outside authors. His first book (science fiction) *The Brain People and the New Humans* was followed by *Free Will — An Ultimate Illusion,* and *The Human Position*.

Interport USA, Portland, the gardening enterprise of George G. Van Patten, has made two solid hits, the first, *Growing Marijuana Indoors*. He began with little more than loose change, did his own typesetting, layout and pasteup, and printed on Multilith. He says this proved the book would sell, "and it started my cash flow."

To beat the controversy about his first volume, Van Patten scrubbed (on a word processor) every reference to marijuana from the text, and published the second. *Gardening Indoors Illustrated* is widely accepted in the garden community. Interport USA distributes through wholesalers and stores over the nation, but two-thirds of his sales come by mail. It has marketed 80,000 books in five years.

Richard L. Lutz, 1988 president of the group, sold 12,000 sets of a cassette tape series before he published the book, *Feel Better! Live Longer! Relax*. The former head of the Oregon State Hospital, Richard and his wife, Mary, own Dimi Press, Salem.

Donna Matrazzo, Communicom, Portland, in 1980 struck out on her own after a bad publishing experience; she took over *The Corporate Script Writing Book*. This year she did her seventh printing, reaching 15,000 copies so far. Donna relies heavily on mail order distribution.

Experience in real estate sales led Heather Kibbey of Panoply Press to write and publish *How to Finance a Home in Oregon*, which answers common questions in that field. With two co-authors, Panoply Press has since done a second book and four audio tapes. Total output has hit 15,000 books and 6,000 cassettes.

At the same time, Kibbey works in partnership with Cheryl Long, Culinary Arts, Lake Oswego. The firm now has five books in print, two by outside authors, and has marketed 20,000 books to date.

There are many others, but this brief account samples the range of books under the NWABP aegis. Broadly non-fiction, juvenile, and how-to, NWABP also represents some fiction, religion, art, and poetry. And by the rules, members must write and publish at least one book. On the roster are a number of services, viz., layout, editing, design, typesetting, printing, graphics, artwork, promotion and distribution, among its non-voting members.

It's clear each publisher is unique — sure, each book is unique — but NWABP members have common characteristics. They work in earnest, tirelessly, at the ever-exciting challenge of bringing books to market. The seven years past promise a bright future for professional publishers. None dare call them small. ❖

Joe Stein, 1987 vice-president of NWABP, has written on science, aeronautics, space and public affairs in the freelance market. In 1985, he published his book, *Lift*, "what helicopter people do for people," which went to a second printing.

Idaho Commission on the Arts Programs for Writers

• Yearly literature fellowships

• Apprenticeships in areas such as creative writing, playwriting, and the book arts

• AIE residencies

• Project grants to presses and organizations presenting community readings and workshops for writers

• Sudden Opportunity Program which provides up to $600 for an Idaho artist to take advantage of an immediate artistic opportunity

• The Idaho Writer-In-Residence Award — An Idaho writer tours twenty communities in two years and receives a $10,000 stipend. Selection for the the 1990-91 Writer-In-Residence will be made in the fall of 1989.

• Touring — Applications will be taken in the summer of 1988 for Western writers wishing to tour in Idaho. Accepted authors will be placed on the Idaho Commission on the Arts 1989-90 Touring Roster of booking by presenting organizations.

• Governor's Arts Award — Writers and patrons of literature are eligible for special biennial awards for both excellence and support of the arts. The next awards will be given during the Centennial Year 1990.

Contact:
Idaho Commission on the Arts
304 W. State
Boise, Idaho 83720
208-334-2119 ❖

Montana Arts Council Programs

The Montana Arts Council (contact Julie Cook, Director of Artists Services), New York Block, 48 North Last Chance Gulch, Helena, MT 59620, (406) 443-4338, offers the following programs that involve creative writers:

Artists in Schools/Communities program — places writers in school and community residencies for one week to one month. Applications reviewed by advisory committee of writers and teachers. Accepts applications from throughout the U.S. Application deadline, approximately March 1 of each year. Write for information in late December.

Individual Artist Fellowship program — awards $2,000 to Montana writer based on excellence of work. Applications reviewed by panel of writers. Applicants must be Montana residents. Application deadline, approximately May 1 of alternating years (1989, 1991). Write for information in February.

First Book Award program — provides publication of a writer's first book. Manuscripts reviewed by two selected jurors. Applicants must be Montana residents. Application deadline, approximately May 1 of alternating years (1990, 1992). Write for information in February.

ArtistSearch — monthly newsletter-like publication provides information about workshops, competitions, awards, and other opportunities for writers. Open to both in-state and out-of-state artists. No deadline. Write for registration form.

In addition to these programs, writers may be interested in contacting the following three Montana organizations about their regular literary programming:

Hellgate Writers, 143 South 5th East, Missoula, MT 59801

Regional Writers Project, Yellowstone Art Center, 401 North 27th St., Billings, MT 59101

Second Story Cinema/Helena Film Society, 9 Placer St., Helena, MT 59601. ❖

Oregon Arts Commission Literary Opportunities

In addition to opportunities available in all the arts — individual fellowships, Artists In Education, and project grants:

Across the River is the Washington/Oregon reading exchange, a program that combines a Washington writer and an Oregon writer reading together in three rural sites in each state. Six writers from Oregon and six from Washington participated in the pilot program in 1988.

Literary Mailings are periodic mailings of professional interest to the field.

Assistance to the Editors of OCLAM is support of the editors of Oregon College Literary/Arts Magazines (OCLAM) for their biennial meetings, sponsored by Oregon regional arts councils.

Pacific Northwest Literary Calendar is a computerized literary events calendar accessible by a personal computer with telecommunications capability and available, therefore, to most of the over 200 public libraries in the state, most Oregon regional arts councils, and some writing organizations and writers. A monthly printed calendar is posted in many bookstores, universities, colleges, coffeehouses, and community centers around the state. It is the first joint project of the Oregon State Library and the Oregon Arts Commission.

OPAC Writing Compendium is a computerized trust of resource information stored under the **NEWS** file on the Oregon Public Access Catalog (OPAC) based at the Oregon State Library. **FUND** is a listing of sources of fellowships and grants for writers and writing organizations; **CON** lists literary contests of poetry, short fiction, novellas and novels, and nonfiction; **SERV** displays books and resource materials for both the professional writer and the neophyte; and **NL** is the newsletters of Pacific Northwest writing organizations.

Oregon Small Presses and Literary Magazines will be a comprehensive listing of all publications of Oregon small presses, nonprofit and commercial, and comparable data of the literary magazines. The directory is a joint project of the Oregon State Library and the Oregon Arts Commission, and will list the public libraries of Oregon, and the bookstores of Oregon, Washington, Idaho, Montana, and Alaska that are members of the Northwest Book Sellers Association.

Young Writers, an annual statewide writing contest for high school students, has not been assigned program funding, so its fate is unknown at this time. ❖

Literary Arts and the Washington State Arts Commission

The Washington State Arts Commission (WSAC) has a number of ways to serve the literary arts in the State of Washington. Opportunities exist for writers and publishers of poetry, prose and literary criticism, and sponsors of literary arts activities.

Writers and poets can conduct residencies in educational institutions through the **Artist-in-Residence Program.** The agency is beginning to explore the concept of literary and two-dimensional or three-dimensional artists collaborating on **Art in Public Places** projects. And through its membership in the Western States Arts Foundation, the Commission participates in the **Western States Book Awards**, presented to outstanding authors and publishers of fiction, creative non-fiction and poetry.

The Commission's competitive grant program, the **Partnership Program**, provides funds for artistic projects to non-profit arts organizations, including non-profit presses. Other presses and publications that cannot obtain that IRS designation may apply under an "umbrella agency" such as a library, arts council or arts commission. The Partnership Program offers funding for information/resource sharing, literary arts publications, magazines, anthologies, and various marketing and pro-

motional activities. The program also assists with literary projects in educational institutions when the project is not a normal school function and serves the general public.

The Commission provides direct support to individual artists through the **Artist Fellowship Program**. Unrestricted awards of $5,000 apiece are made in even-numbered years to practicing professionals in the literary arts. Applicants must have at least five years of professional artistic achievement, currently reside in Washington state, and not be enrolled in an educational degree program in the field in which they are applying.

Across the River is the Washington/Oregon Writers' Exchange, a program that combines a Washington writer and an Oregon writer reading together in rural sites in both states. Six writers from Washington and six from Oregon have participated in this pilot program.

Write to the Washington State Arts Commission, 110-9th & Columbia Building, Mail Stop GH-11, Olympia, WA 98504-4111, or call (206) 753-3860, for more information about any of the Commission's programs. Ask to receive our bi-monthly newsletter, *Washington Arts*, to keep abreast of deadlines and new opportunities. ❖

Tips

FREELANCE RATE CHART

The following rates are based on information obtained from freelancers and communications consulting firms located in the Northwest. These fees should only be used as guides for setting your own rates, based on your experience and location.

Advertising copywriting	$15-50/hour
Annual reports	$20-45/hour
Articles (ghosted)	$10-35/hour
Articles (with writer's byline)	$10-25/hour or % of fee paid
Book (ghosted)	$15-35/hour or flat fee
Book (with credit)	$10-30/hour or % royalty
Brochures	$15-45/hour or flat fee
Business letters	$15-35/hour
Company newsletters	$30-100/page or $15-30/hour
Corporate history	$500 & up flat fee or contract wage
Editing	$12-20/hour
Family history	$12/hour & up
News releases	$20-40/page
Promotional or public relations	$15/hour & up (expenses extra)
Readings of poetry or nonfiction	$20/hour & up
Research for writing projects	$10/hour & up
Resume writing	$30/each and up
Scriptwriting	$15/hour & up or by negotiated rate
Speeches	$20-80/hour
Technical writing	$15-60/hour
Typing (nontechnical)	$0.75-1.75/page
Typing (technical by transcription)	$1-4/page
Writing/publishing consulting	$20-60/hour

Tips, Tables, & Forms

Sample News Release

Your Letterhead

News Release
Date

For Immediate Release
Contact: Your name
        Your phone number(s)

Strong lead sentences make news releases more effective. Let the first sentence position your book as a solution to a problem or as an answer to a need. The first paragraph should mention the name of your book, as well as your name.

A news release should answer the who, what, where, when, and why news questions. Who will be interested in this book and why? What is the book about? When was the book published? Why was this book written and published? The information must "sell" the editor on the importance and timeliness of your book. Your credentials, as the author, will also help to gain credibility and human interest.

Ideally, this release should only require one page. It should be typed, double spaced, and on your company letterhead. If practical, it may be personalized to the editor.

The final information should contain the price and availablility details. Be sure to include your company address, as well.

The book's title
Author's name
Size, cover style, and binding
ISBN number and Library of Congress Card Catalogue number
Publication date
Price

#
(signifies the end)

Effective Book Proposals

Book proposals are the sales tools of writers. Yours must be outstanding if it is to gain an editor's attention and effectively "sell" the concept of your book.

For a proposed work of fiction, this presentation must give the editor information about you and your story. Proposals for novels are completely dependent on sample chapters and a synopsis — and, unless you are a published author, the complete manuscript must be available (when requested). A nonfiction book must be proposed in a similar manner, except that the manuscript does not always have to be completed in advance of a "go-ahead" from the editor. Frequently, nonfiction works will be purchased — or earn some level of commitment — solely on the basis of the proposal.

The following tips focus on proposals for nonfiction works:

• Present your concept in the first few pages.

State the case for publishing your manuscript. A good place to begin is with the reason you wrote (or will write) this book. Describe the situation that points to the need for it. Next, summarize how your book will satisfy this need. Explain why your book will be different from others that are already on the market. Offer some evidence of who will read it and why.

It is also valuable to synopsize your book in this introductory section. This will be proof that your work accomplishes what you said it would in the opening presentation. An effective way to follow the synopsis is with a review of your qualifications. This may include professional credentials, experience, or educational background. The closing statement should summarize the major "selling" points you are trying to get across to the editor.

• The big "sell" should follow your introduction.

Since the editor is now familiar with your basic concept, it is time to get down to the business aspects of such a publishing project. In detail, describe the audience, the marketability (why people will buy the book), the competition (and why your book is better or different), and any other sales information you've compiled. The more specific you can be, the better. After all, your publisher must make a business decision — will this book be a profitable investment.

• The outline must be detailed and give the editor a complete "feel" for the book's contents.

Each chapter title should be followed by a couple of paragraphs that review what is to be covered and the approach to the material. Important information should be highlighted. Write this in a style that reflects how you will write the manuscript. Also, it is a good idea to include a couple of representative chapters. This will allow the editor to become more familiar with your style.

• Describe the publishing details to the editor.

What is the length of your book — in words or manuscript pages? Will photos or art be used? Is there a particular book design that you believe is best suited? How long after the contract is signed will the manuscript be completed?

• Include a current résumé and biography.

Convince the editor that you are the best person to write this book. If you have significant writing experience, it will help to sell the project. You may wish to enclose clips of your published work or reviews of other books that you have written. Basically, the key is to emphasize your strengths and qualifications.

"Some writers say a story is never finished — it's abandoned."
—Ursula Hegi

Sample Manuscript Format

```
Your name                          Publication name
Your address                       Copyright data
Your phone number                  Rights being sold
                                   Word count




                        TITLE OF ARTICLE
                         Your byline



     Your title and byline should begin halfway down the page.
The manuscript should be typed, double spaced on clean bond
paper. Each page, after the first, should have a heading with
part or all of the title, your last name, and the page
number. Do not staple your pages together.


     You should avoid using correction fluid, cross-outs, and
written-in corrections — editors appreciate "perfect"
submissions because they are easier to read and edit. Some
editors do not accept dot matrix printed submissions, so
check their requirements before sending your manuscripts. Be
sure to use the correct postage on submission packages. "On
speculation" submissions should include an envelope with
return postage, if you wish it returned.


     A cover letter should always be included with your
manuscript. This will remind the editor of your query and
introduce your manuscript.
```

Irresistible Queries

A query letter is a sales pitch to a busy editor. It must accomplish its purpose in seconds if the offering is to have a chance of publication. Which means that this first impression must be better than 90% of its competitors, or rejection is likely. The article or book idea is on the line.

Put yourself in the editor's place. How would you decide which ideas to accept?

Approximately 40% of the queries you receive miss the mark. They propose subjects inappropriate for your publication, suggest topics recently used, or offer ideas unacceptable in content or appearance.

After rejecting these, you quickly separate those submitted by writers you know and trust. The rest are judged by factors such as approach, style, topic, author's credentials, proposed length, availability of art work or photos, and various subjective criteria — like how you feel after a nasty drive to the office.

As you skim each query, you read the opening paragraph, looking for a lead sentence that grabs your attention. This sentence should draw you in by making you curious about the article's topic. Sometimes a reference to a statistic or a little-known fact provides the "hook." The effectiveness of a query's lead should represent the effectiveness of the article's lead.

As many as half of the queries on your desk may contain promising leads. Now, you look for second (and possibly third) paragraphs that give you larger doses of the writer's style. They should also give you a deeper understanding what will be covered in the proposed article.

At this point, some of the queries really excite you. But a few remind you of recent articles in competing publications. And some do not fit with coming themes. Your final "cut" is made after rereading the paragraphs describing the articles and authors. In these sections, you look for appropriate article lengths, completion dates, and other details that match your publication's needs. You feel more comfortable with an author who has written for your publication or similar ones. A couple of article clips on similar subjects are welcome enclosures. Also, you give extra consideration to authors who are in especially good "positions" to do the work — due to their contacts, expertise, educational background, or professional qualifications.

The winners are the survivors of this process. These few freelancers receive "go-aheads" — on speculation or on assignment.

The following tips have been solicited from Northwest-based periodical and book publishers, as well as from freelancers' experiences:

- Article queries should be limited to one page in length. They should be typed, single spaced, and use a business letter format.
- The author's credentials should never be exaggerated, but his or her strengths must always be emphasized.
- Look for creative approaches (slants) in presenting common subjects.
- Provide hooks to which the editor (and readers) may directly relate.
- Show a sincere interest in your subject.
- Be sure that your query and article writing style matches that of the publication.
- Always read several back issues of the target publication so that you are familiar with its format and style, and so you are aware of recently covered topics.
- Carefully follow instructions in the publication's writer's guidelines.
- Always include a self-addressed stamped envelope (SASE) with queries.
- Direct your queries to the specific editor for your type of submission.
- Don't be afraid to adjust the format of your query to effectively present your idea. In some cases, the use of long quotes or "bullet" highlighted statements may be the best way to hook the editor.
- Suggest a title for your article, if you have an especially good idea.
- Stay away from gimmicks in your queries. Don't use brightly colored paper or inappropriate enclosures to get the editor's attention.
- Keep your queries neat, clean, and free of typos. ❖

Always include a self-addressed, stamped envelope with your query or manuscript submission.

Sample Query Letter

Date

Editor's name
Editor's address

Dear (editor's name):

The lead of your query may be the actual lead that you
will use in your article. It must attract the editor's
attention and draw interest to your topic and approach.
Write the query just as you would write a letter to a
friend.

The second paragraph should contain some details about
your subject and the point of the article being
proposed. Your writing style should continue to be as
it would in the article. Statistics, quotes, or
important facts should be mentioned to reflect your
preliminary research. Without giving away the entire
story, you must write enough here to entice the reader
-- an editor -- into wanting to know more. If you have
done your job properly, the editor will ask you to send
the complete manuscript.

You should include a paragraph discussing how you will
present the story, naming individuals to be interviewed
or resources to be used. Explain why this article will
interest the publication's readers. Tell the editor
how long the article will be and whether photos or art
work would be available. Also, say when the piece
could be completed.

Finally, state your qualifications for writing this
article. Mention your recent publishing credits or, if
none exist, why you are in the best position to write
this article. Include clips of articles similar to
that which is being proposed in this query. Follow the
instructions in the publication's writer's guidelines
and those listed in *Writer's Northwest Handbook*.

Sample Photo Release

```
┌─────────────────────────────────────────────────────────────┐
│                        PHOTO RELEASE                          │
│                                                               │
│  For value received I grant permission to ..................., │
│  its successors, licensees and assigns, to publish and copyright for all purposes, │
│  my name, pictures, and information concerning myself and my property photographed at │
│  ............................................................... │
│  on the ...................day(s) of ......................... 19............ . │
│                                                               │
│                                                               │
│  Signature (or name if subject is a minor)..................... │
│  Parent (if subject is a minor)................................ │
│  Date ................................. Editor/Dept. ........... │
│  Photographer                                                 │
│  ............................................................. │
└─────────────────────────────────────────────────────────────┘
```

Feel Free to Copy and Use.

Sample Expense Report

```
┌─────────────────────────────────────────────────────────────┐
│                       EXPENSE REPORT                          │
│                                                               │
│                                                               │
│  Name............................................................ │
│  Address......................................................... │
│  City/State/Zip.................................................. │
│  Phone........................................................... │
│                                                               │
│  Project......................................................... │
│  Date assigned/approved............................. By......... │
│  Expenses incurred                                            │
│                                                               │
│                                                               │
│  Receipts [  ] enclosed    [  ] available upon request        │
│                                                               │
│  Make check payable to........................................ │
└─────────────────────────────────────────────────────────────┘
```

Look beyond the newsstands and bookstore shelves to find markets for your writing

Try the following:

- **Business libraries**
- **Government agencies**
- **Industry & professional associations**
- **University departments**
- **Federal depository libraries**
- **State libraries**

What to submit

Article queries:
- A catchy lead
- A sense of the depth & breadth of your article
- Details on slant & presentation
- A brief biographical paragraph

Nonfiction manuscripts:
- Cover letter
- Outline or synopsis
- Sample chapters or the ms
- Biographical sketch or résumé

Fiction manuscripts:
- Cover letter
- Synopsis or outline
- Sample chapters or the ms

Notes

Introduction to the Market Listings

HOW TO USE THIS SECTION

The listings follow the index section. All entries are alphabetical (see the conventions note below), and there is a separate entry for each publishing operation or imprint (even when several reside at the same address). However, a single listing may appear in more than one of the indexes, if it publishes a range of subjects.

There are three major indexes: book publishers, periodical publishers, and newspapers. Each of these indicates state of residence and up to three subject areas. The tabular format allows one to scan quickly for those titles which match specific criteria, i.e., periodicals in Montana that publish poetry. The subject matter published by each is indicated by numbers, which are identified in the accompanying key. There are also several subject indexes for areas most requested by readers.

If you cannot find entries for a subject, don't give up. Some of those surveyed indicated no indexing information or too much. In either case we've tried to assign the appropriate codes. Often the names of publishers or publications suggest the subject matter. In other cases, names of presses may be totally misleading. To ensure greater success, scan for similar subjects; then read the listings for detail. The indexing subjects are necessarily general. Many publications and publishers are interested in a broader range of topics than included in the index. If you cannot discern subject areas or interest in submissions from a listing, you may want to query the publisher for complete information. When doing so, always include a self-addressed, stamped envelope, and do not submit material without first getting an OK from the publisher.

INDEXING & LISTING CONVENTIONS

We have adhered to certain rules in alphabetizing. When cardinal numbers (1000, etc.) appear at the beginning of titles they are indexed before letters; you will find them at the beginning of the list and indexes, before the "A"s. Titles beginning with "The" are indexed by the second word (except for The Dalles). Listings with the same name are indexed alphabetically by name+state. Titles such as "Mary Smith Publishing" should be indexed in "Smith," but check "Mary," too. Where abbreviations or acronyms are used at the beginnings of titles we have tried to expand them so that they are indexed on the full name, i.e., "B.C." or "BC" are alphabetized as "British Columbia." It was not always possible to do this, so please check all possibilities before giving up.

ABBREVIATIONS AND TERMS

We have used a number of standard abbreviations in the listings. These include: *SASE* (self-addressed stamped envelope), *ASAP* (as soon as possible), *ds* (double spaced), and *ms & mss* (manuscript(s)). *Sub* may mean either subscription or submission, and should be clear from the context. *Circ* means circulation, and *w/* means with. If you are sending a query or submission from one country to another you must include return postage in the form of an *IRC* (International Reply Coupon) available from your post office. The terms *biannual* and *biennial* are confusing, since the former means either twice a year (semi-annual) or every two years (biennial). Oh, the joys of English.

INCLUSIONS, EXCLUSIONS, & ACCURACY

We have attempted to cull those which do not belong here. Surveys were mailed (using a "clean" list) to all known publications and appropriate organizations. (To those who responded, we extend our appreciation.) When surveys were not returned, we had to assume that there were no changes to these listings.

We have expended thousands of hours in careful research, entry, editing, proofreading and proofreading and proofreading. Take the possibility of changes since publication into consideration when you query or submit. Phone calls, letters, or current editions of publications, or catalogs of publishers, will keep you from wasting your time — or the time of the wrong editors.

Every effort has been made to show the breadth of writing and publishing in the NW. Listings which are not writers' markets are nevertheless research and reading resources. Together they are tools for access to information, ideas, and art — and they are vehicles for delivery of those things to others.

FREE UPDATES

Writer's NW is a quarterly tabloid devoted to the same themes and audiences as this book. Each issue includes updates to these listings, along with articles, reviews, and a calendar of NW writing-related events. As you use *WNH*, please pass along corrections, changes, new listings, dead listings, entries which don't belong, and your suggestions for making *WNH* more useful. *Writer's NW* is free — well, almost — to *Handbook* readers. To receive yours, send your name and address to Media Weavers, Route 3 Box 376, Hillsboro, OR 97124. Because the newspaper project is so costly, we request contributions, though they are not required. Thanks in advance for your help in keeping the *WNW* and *WNH* alive.

Market Subject Key

001	Abstracts/Indices	044	English	087	Native American
002	Adventure	045	Entertainment	088	Natural History
003	Agriculture/Farming	046	Environment/Resources	089	Northwest
004	Alaska	047	Family	090	Old West
005	Americana	048	Fantasy/Sci Fi	091	Oregon
006	Animals	049	Fashion	092	Outdoor
007	Anthropology/Archaeology	050	Feminism	093	Peace
008	Antiques	051	Fiction	094	Philosophy
009	Architecture	052	Film/Video	095	Photography
010	Arts	053	Fishing	096	Picture
011	Asia	054	Food/Cooking	097	Poetry
012	Asian American	055	Forestry	098	Politics
013	Astrology/Spiritual	056	Gardening	099	Prison
014	Avant-Garde/Experimental	057	Gay/Lesbian	100	Psychology
015	Aviation	058	Genealogy	101	Public Affairs
016	Bicycling	059	Geology/Geography	102	Publishing/Printing
017	Bilingual	060	Government	103	Recreation
018	Biography	061	Health	104	Reference/Library
019	Biology	062	History, American	105	Religion
020	Black	063	History, Canadian	106	Rural
021	Boating	064	History, General	107	Satire
022	Book Arts/Books	065	History, NW/Regional	108	Scholarly/Academic
023	British Columbia	066	Home	109	Science
024	Business	067	How-to	110	Senior Citizens
025	Calendar/Events	068	Humor	111	Sex
026	Canada	069	Idaho	112	Socialist/Radical
027	Chicano/Chicana	070	Industry	113	Society
028	Children (By/About)	071	Labor/Work	114	Sociology
029	Children/Teen	072	Land Use/Planning	115	Sports
030	Collecting	073	Language (s)	116	Student
031	College/University	074	Law	117	Technical
032	Commerce	075	Liberal Arts	118	Textbooks
033	Community	076	Literary Crit/Reviews	119	Trade/Associations
034	Computers	077	Literature	120	Travel
035	Conservation	078	Lumber	121	Urban
036	Consumer	079	Maritime	122	Visual Arts
037	Counter Culture	080	Media/Communications	123	Washington
038	Crafts/Hobbies	081	Medical	124	Women
039	Culture	082	Men	125	Writing
040	Dance	083	Military/Vets	126	Handicapped
041	Drama	084	Minorities/Ethnic	130	Other/Unspecified
042	Economics	085	Montana		
043	Education	086	Music		

This key provides access to cross-indexing and allows speedy location of listings based on rather specific criteria. There are two general ways to make use of it: either before or after locating listings.

Before looking through either the indexes or the listings, study the key above and select the subject numbers of interest to you. Then turn to the major indexes on the following pages and scan the key numbers column for your selections.

Or, while browsing through either the major indexes or the listings, you may refer to this table when the text is insufficient.

Book Publishers

Periodical Publishers

Newspapers

Script Publishers & Others

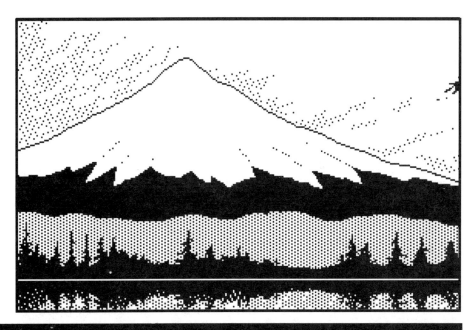

Selected Special Category Indexes: States

Alaska Publishing

Abbott Loop Christian Center
Adventures
AK Sea Grant
Aladin Printing
Alaska Angler Publications
Alaska Business Monthly
Alaska Council of Teachers of English
Alaska Dept of Labor, Research & Analysis
Alaska Dept. of Fish & Game
Alaska Flying Magazine
Alaska Geographic
Alaska Heritage Enterprises
Alaska Historical Commission
Alaska History
Alaska Illustrated
Alaska Journal
Alaska Jrl of Cmmrce
Alaska Magazine
Alaska Medicine
Alaska Native Language Center
Alaska Native Magazine
Alaska Natural History Association
Alaska Nurse
Alaska Outdoors
Alaska Pacific University Press
Alaska Quarterly Review
Alaska Review of Soc & Econ Conditions
Alaska State Writing Consortium
Alaska State Writing Consortium Newsletter
Alaska the Mag of Life on the Last Frontier
Alaska Today
Alaska Trails
Alaskan Bowhunter
Alaskan Byways
The Alaskan Viewpoint
Aleutian Eagle
ANC News

Anchorage Daily News
Anchorage Times
Arctic Environmental Info & Data Center
Ascii
Balcom Books
Black Current Press
Bulletin
Camp Denali Publishing
Capital City Weekly
The Denali Press
Epicenter Press, Inc.
Fairbanks News-Miner
Fathom Publishing Company
Firsthand Press
From The Woodpile
The Frontiersman
O.W. Frost Publisher
Geophysical Institute
Great Northwest Pub. & Dist. Company
Heartland Magazine
Homer News
Horizons Alaska Magazine
Howell Publishing Company, Inc.
In Common
Institute of Social & Economic Research
Intertext
Henry John & Company
Ketchikan News
Kodiak Mirror
The Milepost
Mooncircles
New River Times
The Newspoke
The Next War
Northwest Arctic NUNA Nugget
Old Harbor Press
Out North Arts & Humanities, Inc.
Outpost
The Ovulation Method Newsletter
Paws IV Publishing Co.
The Pedersens
Pelican Publications
Permafrost
Perseverance Theatre
Pressing America
Rainforest Publishing

Ramalo Publications
Review of Social & Economic Conditions
Sea Grant Program
The Senior Voice
Sentinel
Solstice Press
The Sourdough
Southeastern Log
Spirit Mountain Press
That New Publishing Company
This is Alaska
Tundra Drums
Tundra Times
Institute of Marine Science Elmer E. Rasmuson Library
University of Alaska Museum
University of Alaska Press
User-Friendly Press
Vanessapress
We Alaskans
White Mammoth
Windham Bay Press

British Columbia Publishing

A.R.C. Publications
Aardvark Enterprises
The Advocate
Aerie Publishing
Agent West Weekly
AKHT Publishing
Alberni District Historical Society
Alive Books
Amphora
Anian Press
Antiques & Collectibles
Antonson Publishing Ltd.
Arbutus Publications, Ltd.
Arsenal Pulp Press Book Publishers, Ltd.
Art Gallery of Greater Victoria
Arts B.C.
Arts & Crafts News
Automotive Retailer
Azure Press

Barbarian Press
Beautiful British Columbia
Ben-Simon Publications
Blackfish Books
The Boag Foundation Ltd.
Boating News
Bold Brass Studios & Publications
Bowen Island Historians
B. C. BookWorld
B.C. Business Magazine
B.C. Farmways
British Columbia Genealogical Society
B.C. Historical News
B.C. Hotelman
BCIT Link
British Columbia Library Association Newsletter
B.C. Lumberman Magazine
British Columbia Medical Journal
British Columbia Monthly
B.C. Naturalist
B.C. Orchardist
B.C. Outdoors
B.C. Professional Engineer
British Columbia Railway Historical Assn
B.C. Studies
B.C. Teacher
Burnaby Historical Society
Butter-fat Magazine
Callboard
Campbell's Publishing Ltd.
Canada Poultryman
Canadian Aquaculture Magazine
The Canadian Biker
Canadian Literature
The Canadian Press
Canadian Truckers
Canadian West Magazine
Canho Enterprises
Capilano Courier
The Capilano Review
Cappis Press
Centre Publications
CGA Magazine
Chanticleer
Cloudburst Press
Common Ground
communiCAtion

Community Digest Magazine
Construction Sightlines
Cove Press
Crook Publishing
Democrat
Discovery Press
Diver (Vancouver, BC)
Douglas & McIntyre Publishers
Ekstasis Editions
The Elder Statesman
Empress Publications
Enterprise
Equinews
Esquimalt Lookout
Estrada Publications and Photography
Event
Event
Fine Art & Auction Review
Flight Press
Footprint Publishing Company
Fountain Books
The Fraser Institute
Fur Bearers
Georgia Straight
The Globe & Mail
Good Medicine Books
Granny Soot Publications
Gray's Publishing, Ltd.
Haralson Enterprises
Harbour Publishing
Harbour & Shipping
Heartwood
Hi Baller Forest Magazine
Horizons SF
Horsdal & Schubart Publishers, Ltd.
Housewares Canada
Il Centro, Newletter of Italian Canadian Community
Integrity Publications
Interior Voice
International Prospector & Developer
Island Books
Joint Development Trading Company Ltd.
Journal of B.C. English Teachers' Association
Kabalarian Philosophy
Kamloops Museum &

Archives
Key to Victoria
Kinesis
Klassen & Foster Publications
Lambrecht Publications
Light-House Publications
Lightship Press Ltd.
Line
Log House Publishing Company Ltd.
Logging & Sawmilling Journal
Logistics & Transportation Review
Lumby Historians
The Malahat Review
The Martlet
Milestone Publications
Mining Review
MIR Publication Society
Monday Magazine
Mosaic Enterprises, Ltd.
Mountain News
Musings
Nanaimo Historical Society
NC Publishing
Nechako Valley Historical Society
Nerve Press
New Star Books
News & Views
North Island Gazette Printers&Publishers
Northern Times Press
Nursery Trades BC
Oolichan Books
Open Road Publishers
ORC Enterprises Ltd.
Other Press
Outlook
The Overseas Times
Pacific Affairs
Pacific Educational Press
Pacific Northwest Agencies Inc.
Pacific Yachting
Panda Press Publications
Pandora Publishing Ltd.
Panorama Publication Ltd.
Parallel Publishers Ltd.
The Peak
Pemberton Pioneer Women

Philam Books, Inc.
Photography at Open-Space
Pioneer News
Playboard Magazine
Plus (Vancouver, BC)
Polestar Press
Pope International
  Publications
Poptart
Potboiler Magazine
Press Gang Publishers
Press Porcepic Ltd.
Preston & Betts
PRISM International
The Province
Provincial Archives of
  British Columbia
the raddle moon
Railway Milepost Books
Raincoast Books
Raxas Books
The Reader
Red Cedar Press
Repository Press
Resource Development
Rhino Press
Richmond Review
RNABC News
Room of One's Own
Sandhill Publishing
Sea Kayaker
Select Homes
Shires Books
The Silver Apple Branch
Skookum Publications
Skyword
Slug Press
The Smallholder Publishing
  Collective
The Snow Man Press
Socialist Party of Canada
Solstice Books
Solus Impress
Sono Nis Press
Gordon Soules Books
  Publishers Ltd.
Special Interest Publications
THE SUN - EDITORIAL
Sunfire Publications Ltd.
Swedish Press
Talonbooks
Technocracy Digest
Theytus Books
Trail City Archives
Training Associates Ltd.
Truck Logger
Trucking Canada - Western
  Edition
True North/Down Under
Truth on Fire (Hallelujah)
Truth on Fire (Hallelujah)
TV Week
University of British
  Columbia Press
U of V, English Literature
  Studies Monograph
  Series
U of V, Western
  Geographical Series
Update
Urban Design Centre Society
THE VANCOUVER
  COURIER
Vancouver History
Vancouver Magazine
Vancouver Symphony
VCC
Vitamin Supplement
W.S. Productions
Donald E. Waite
  Photographer & Publisher
  Co.
Wavefront
West Coast Review
Western Fisheries
Western Living
Western Trucking
Westworld Magazine
Whistler Publishing

Whitehouse Publishing
Woman to Woman Magazine
Woman To Woman
  Magazine
Wood Lake Books, Inc.
Word Works
Writing Magazine
Wynkyn Press
xPress
Yellow Hat Press

Idaho
Publishing

AAG-AAG!
Ad Lib
The Adjusting Entry
Adopted Child
The Advocate
AHI Newsletter
Ahsahta Press at Boise State
  University
Aldrich Entomology Club
  Newsletter
American Dry Pea & Lentil
  Assn Bulletin
Appaloosa Journal
Backeddy Books
Blue Scarab Press
Boise Business Today
Boise Cascade Quarterly
Boise Idaho Register
Boise Magazine–Idaho
  Annual Inc.
BSU Focus
Boise State U. Western
  Writers Series
BSU/Search
The Book Shop/Children's
  Newsletter
Bookmark
Cache Valley Newsletter
The Caxton Printers, Ltd.
Central Idaho Magazine
Christian Outlook
Classical Assn of the Pacific
  NW Bulletin
Classics Unlimited, Inc.
Cloudline
Coeur d'Alene Homes
  Messenger
cold-drill Books
cold-drill Magazine
Confluence Press, Inc.
Contempory Issues
  Clearinghouse
Cranial Academy Newsletter
Crusader
Cruzzin Magazines
Current News
Currents
Dairyline
Echo Film Productions
Economic Facts/Idaho
  Agriculture
El Centinela
Em-Kayan
Emerald House
The Emshock Letter
Engineering Geology/Soils
  Eng Symposium
EOTU Magazine
Ex Libris
Farm & Ranch Chronicle
Flashes
The Flyfisher
Flyfishing News, Views &
  Reviews
Fox Reading Research
  Company
Frontier Publications
Gem Paperbacks
Gem State Geological
  Review
Golden Eagle
Great Blue Graphics
Heated Closet

Hemingway Western Studies
  Series
Highway Information
Opal Laurel Holmes
  Publisher
Honeybrook Press
Horse Times
Hyde Park Press
Idaho
The Idaho
Idaho Archaeologist
The Idaho Argonaut
Idaho Arts Journal
Idaho Business Review
Idaho Cities
Idaho Citizen
Idaho Clean Water
Idaho Conservation League
  Newsletter
Idaho Council on Economic
  Ed. Newsletter
Idaho County Free Press
Idaho English Journal
Idaho Farm Bureau News
Idaho Fish & Game News
Idaho Forester
Idaho Foxfire Network
Idaho Genealogical Society
  Quarterly
Idaho Grange News
Idaho Humanities Council
  Newsletter
Idaho Law Review
Idaho Librarian
Idaho Motorist
Idaho Museum of Natural
  History
Idaho Pharmacist
Idaho Potato Commission
  Report
Idaho Power Bulletin
Idaho Press-Tribune
Idaho Register
Idaho Senior Citizen News
Idaho State Historical
  Society
Idaho State Journal
Idaho State University Press
The Idaho Statesman
Idaho, The University
Idaho Thoroughbred
  Quarterly
Idaho Voice
Idaho Voter
Idaho Wheat
Idaho Wildlife
Idaho Wool Growers
  Bulletin
Idaho Yesterdays
Idahoan
Idahobeef
Idahonian/Palouse Empire
  News
Idaho's Economy
IEA Reporter
IHSA News
Impressions Publishing
  Company
In-sights
Incredible Idaho
INCTE Newsletter
Info
Inky Trails Publications
IPEA News
IWUA Alert
Journal of Health, Physical
  Education,
Journal of the Idaho
  Academy of Science
Journal of the Nez Perce Co.
  Hist. Soc.
Junction City News
KID Broadcasting
  Corporation
Lacon Publishers
Lacoz Chicana
Latah Co. Genealogical Soc.
  Newsletter
Latah County Historical

Society
Latah Legacy
Legacy House, Inc.
Lewiston Morning Tribune
The Light Spectrum
Limberlost Press
Line Rider
Listen: Journal of Better
  Living
Little Red Hen, Inc.
Marketing Reports & Trade
  Leads
Mineral Land Publications
Modern & Contemp. Poetry
  of the West
Mole Publishing Company
Mother of Ashes
Mountain Light
Mountain Meadow Press
Mushroom, the Journal
Mystery Time
New Breed News
The News Examiner
News & Reports
Northwest Anthropological
  Research Notes
Northwest Inland Writing
  Project Newsletter
Nutrition Notebook
Open Path Publishing
The Optimist
Our Little Friend
Owyhee Historical Society
  Bulletin
Owyhee Outpost
Pacific Press Publishing
  Association
Packrat Press Books
Painted Smiles Inc.
Palouse Journal
Pandora's Treasures
Paradise Creek Journal
Pathways
Pea & Lentil News
Peak Media
Planned Parenthood
  Association of Idaho
Points & Picas Magazine
Portfolio
Post Register
Potato Grower of Idaho
Potlatch Times
Primary Treasure
The Printer's Devil
Property Tax Charges
Quest for Excellence
R.N. Idaho
Randy Stapilus Ridenbaugh
  Press
The Redneck Review of
  Literature
Rendezvous
The Retort
Rhyme Time Poetry
  Newsletter
Rolling Drum Press
Rural Property Bulletin
St. Alphonsus Today
Satellite Dealer Magazine
Satellite Guide
Satellite World
Shoban News
Signs of the Times
Smoke Signals
Smurfs in Hell
Snake River Alliance
  Newsletter
Snake River Echoes
Snowmobile West
Solstice Press
Solus Impress
Speaking of Taxes
Spice West Publishing
  Company
Steppingstone Press
Stonehouse Publications
Sugar Producer
Sun Valley Books
Sun Valley Center for Arts

and Humanities
Sun Valley Magazine
Sunrise Tortoise Books
Syringa Publishing
Thorn Creek Press
Time to Pause
Timeless Books
The Times News
Treasure Valley Good News
Treasure Valley This Week
Trestle Creek Review
Tri County Special Services
Two Magpie Press
Center for Business
  Development & Research
The University News
University of Idaho Press
Upper Snake River Valley
  Historical Society
Videosat News
The Village Idiot
The Voice
Mark West Publishers
Western Banker Magazine
Western Newsletter
Westwind Publishing
Whitman-Latah Republic
Wind Vein Press/White
  Clouds Revue
Writer's Chapbook
Writer's Info
Writing Pursuits
Yellow Jacket Press

Montana
Publishing

Aero Sun-Times
Agri-News
Alternative Energy
  Resources Org.
American Geographic
  Publishing
Anaconda Leader
Art West Magazine
Artist Search/Montana Arts
  Council
J. Arvidson Press
Barlow Press
Beartooth Networks, Inc.
Big Sky Business Journal
The Big Timber Pioneer
Bigfork Eagle
BikeReport
Billings City Reader
The Billings Gazette
The Billings Times
Birkworks Publishing
Bitter Root Valley Hist.
  Newsletter
Bozeman Chronicle
The Bread and Butter
  Chronicles
Buckskin Press, Inc.
Bugle
Circle
The Coming Revolution
Community Living
  Publications
Computer Innovations Desk
  Top Publish
Council for Indian Education
Courier-Pioneer-Advertiser
Creative Children
CutBank
Dillon Tribune-Examiner
The Direct Express
The Drift Group
EMC Retort
Exponent
Fade in Publications
Falcon Press Publishing Co
Flower of Truth Publishing
The Foundation Afield
Ghost Town Quarterly
Glacier Natural History
  Assn, Inc.

Great Falls Montana
  Catholic Register
Great Falls Tribune
Greycliff Publishing Co.
Griggs Printing & Publishing
Gros Ventre Treaty
  Committee
H.B. Publications
Haker Books
Hard Row to Hoe
Hot Springs Gazette
Hungry Horse News
The Independent Record
Kalispell Inter-Lake
Kalispell News
Kutenai Press
Lang Publications
J. Larsen Publishing
Lewistown News-Argus
Life Scribes
Livingston Enterprise
MAAE Rhythm
Madison County History
  Association
Madisonian
Manx Publishing Co.
Message (Condon, MT)
Miles City Star
Missoulian
Montana Artpaper
Montana Arts Council
Montana Business Quarterly
Montana Crafters Inc.
  Review
Montana Crop & Livestock
  Reporting Serv
Montana Department of
  Labor & Industry
Montana English Journal
Montana Historical Society
  Press
Montana Kaimin
Montana Magazine
Montana Newsletter
The Montana Poet
Montana Sen. Citizen News
Montana Standard
Montana, the Magazine of
  Western History
Mountain Press Publishing
  Company
Mountain View Publishing
  Company
MSU Exponent
Multiples Press
Native American Education
  Newsletter
Northern Lights
Old Farm Kennels
Old Violin-Art Publishing
Outlaw Newsletter
Perceptions
Pictorial Histories
  Publishing Company
Pioneer Publishing Company
Ponderosa Publishers
The Portable Wall/Basement
  Press
Postcard/Paper Club
  Newsletter
Seven Buffaloes Press
SmokeRoot
Societry for Industrial
  Archeology
Stay Away Joe Publishers
Stonechild Press
Stoneydale Press Publishing
  Company
U of M, Publication in
  History
Valley Farms
Western Business
Western Horizons Books
Western Livestock News
Western News
G.M. White
Whitefish Pilot
Whitehall Ledger
Wildlife-Wildlands Institute

Oregon Publishing

1000 Friends of Oregon Newsletter
ACAPella
AcreAGE
The Active Pacifist
Ad-Dee Publishers, Inc.
Adventures In Subversion
Advocate
Aesthetics West
Agadir Press
Agri-Times
Albany Democratic-Herald
Alchemy
Alioth Press
The Alliance
Aloha Breeze
Amadeus Press
Amateur Brewer Information
Frank Amato Publications
American Indian Basketry Magazine
American Institute for Yemeni Studies
American Rhododendron Society Journal
American-Nepal Education Foundation
Americas Focus
Amity Publications
Angst World Library
Animal Aid
Animator
The Antique Doorknob Publishing Company
Aozora Publishing
APA-EROS
Aphra Behn Press
Apostolic Book Publishers
Apple Press
Applegate Computer Enterprises
Arabian Horse Country
The Archer
Architectural Lighting
Areopagitier Press, Inc.
Argus Observer
ARMA Newsletter
Arrowood Books, Inc.
Artist's Notes
Artoonist
The Arts Council of Southern Oregon Newsletter
Arts East/Eastern OR Reg. Arts Council
Asia Cable
AOI News Digest
Associated Press
Associated Publications, Inc.
The Asterisk
Astrology Night
Astrology West Magazine
Athena Press
Ray Atkeson
Auto Trader
Automotive News of the Pacific Northwest
Aviation News
Axis
Baker Democrat-Herald
Bandon Historical Society
Bandon Western World
Barclay Press
Bardavon Books
Barleycorn Books
Barometer
Marlene Y. Bastian
Mary Anne Bauer Productions
Beacon
Beacon
The Bear Facts
The Bear Wallow Publishing Company
Beautiful America Pub Co

Beaver Briefs
Beaver Publications
Beaverton Arts Commission Newsletter
Beaverton Business Advocate
Bedous Press
Beef Industry News
Before the Sun
Benton Bulletin
Berry Fine Publishing Company
Berry Patch Press
Bethel Publications
Beynch Press Publishing Co.
Beyond Words Publishing Inc.
Bible Temple Publications
Bicentennial Era Enterprises
Bigoni Books
Binford & Mort Publishing
Bioenergy Bulletin
Black Sheep Newsletter
Blatant Image: a Magazine of Feminist Photography
Blind John Publications
BLM News, Oregon & Washington
The Bloodletter
Blow
Blue Heron Publishing
Blue Mountain Eagle
Bluespaper
Bob Book Publishers
Bonanza Publishing
Book Production Associates
Bookletter Newsletter
BookNotes: Resources for Small & Self-Pubs
Braemar Books
Breitenbush Publications
Bridge Tender
The Bridge
The Bridge
Broadsheet Publications
The Broadside
Brown Penny Press
Brown's Business Reporter
Buckman Voice
Bulletin
The Bulletin
Burns Times-Herald
The Business Journal
Business Network News
Business News
Byline
Calapooia Publications
Calapooya Collage
Calyx, A Jrl of Art & Lit by Women
Calyx Inc.: Calyx Books
Canby Herald/North Willamette News
Cannon Beach Gazette
Capital Press
Carefree Cooking Company
Carnot Press
Cascade Automotive Resources
Cascade Farm Publishing Company
Cascades East
Castalia Publishing Company
Catchline, Ski Business News
Catholic Sentinel
CBA Bulletin
Cedar Island Press
Center for Urban Education
Centerplace Publishing Company
Central America Update
Central Oregonian
Chain Saw Age
Chin Up Beacon
Chinkapin Press, Inc.
Christian Update
Chronicle

The Chronicle
Circa Press
Circle
Citizen Action
The City Open Press
Clackamas County News
Clatskanie Chief
The Clatsop Common Sense
Claustrophobia: Life-Expansion News
Clear Water Journal
Clients Council News
Clinton St. Quarterly
Coast Tidings
Coast to Coast Books
Coffee Break
Collegian
Colonygram
Columbia Communicator
The Columbia Press
Comic Relief
Commercial Review
COMMUNICOM
Commuter
Comparative Literature
The Compass
The Competitive Advantage
Computer Able News
Computer & Electronics News
The Computing Teacher
Connections
Connections Journal & Resource Directory
Conscious Living Foundation
Construction Data & News
Contacts influential
Continuing Education Publications
Controversy in Review
The Cookbook Factory
Coquille Valley Sentinel
Coriolis Publishing Company
Corvallis Gazette Times
Cottage Grove Sentinel
Council Human Rights/Latin Amer.
Courier 4
The Courier
The Court Scribe
Creative News n' Views
The Crescent
Crook Co. Historical Society Newsletter
Cross Cultural Press
Crow Publications, Inc.
Crowdancing Quarterly
Cryptogram Detective
Culinary Arts Ltd.
Cumtux
The Current
Curry Coastal Pilot
Curry County Echoes
Curry County Reporter
The Cutting Edge
The Daily Astorian
Daily Barometer
Daily Emerald
Daily Shipping News
The Daily Tidings
Dayton Tribune
Dead Mountain Echo
Dee Publishing Company
Denali
Desert Trails
The Digger
Dilithium Press & Portland House
Dimi Press
Dioscoridus Press, Inc.
Discovery
Dog River Review
Dog-Eared Publications
Doll Mall
Doves Publishing Company
The Downtowner
Dragonfly

The Drain Enterprise
Drelwood Publications
Duane Shinn Publications
Eagle Signs
Early Warning
The Earthling
Earthtone
Earthwatch Oregon
East Oregonian
The Eastern Beacon
Eastern School Press
Echo Digest
Educational Digest
The Eighth Mountain Press
Elan Northwest Publishers
Elegance Design Publications
Enchantment Publishing of Oregon
Encore Arts in Performance Magazine
Endeavor
Enfantaisie
Ensemble Publications, Inc.
The Enterprise Courier
Entertainment Publications, Inc.
Environmental Law
ERIC Clearinghouse on Educational Mgmt.
Essence
Eurock
Events Magazine
The Extender
Extension Service Publishers
Eye of the Raven
Fanatic Reader
Farah's, Inc.
Fedora
The Fernglen Press
FINNAM Newsletter
Finnish American Literary Heritage Found
FIR Report
Firehouse Theater
First Alternative Thymes
The Florian Group
Florist & Grower
Flyfishing
The Flying Needle
Flying Pencil Publications
Focus
Forelaws on Board
Forest Industries Telecommunications
Forest Log
Forest Planning
Forest Watch/CHEC
Forest World
Fountain Publications
Fox Publishing Company
The Free Agent
Free-Bass Press
Freighter Travel News
Friendly Press
Front Row
Fryingpan
Future Science Research Publishing Co.
Gable & Gray, The Book Publishers
Gadfly Press
Gahmken Press
Gaining Ground
Galley Proofs
Galloway Publications, Inc.
Garren Publishing
The Gated Wye
Genealogical Forum of Portland Bulletin
Geo-Heat Center Bulletin
Geological News Letter
The Georgian Press Company
Geriatric Press, Inc.
Gilgal Publications
GIS/CAD Mapping Solutions
Glass Studio Magazine

Goal Lines
The Golden Eagle
The Gorge Current
Gospel Tract Distributors
Grants Pass Daily Courier
Grapevine Publications, Inc.
Graphic Arts Center Publishing Company
Gray Power
Grayfellows, Inc.
Greener Pastures Gazette
Greer Gardens
Gresham Outlook
Grey Whale Press
The Griffin Press
Group 1 Journal
HACK'd
Hampshire Pacific Press
Hapi Press
Harvest House Publishers
Harvest Magazine
Havin' Fun, Inc.
Headlight Herald
Health Education League of Portland
Health News and Notes
Healthview
HearSay Press
Helstrom Publications
Heppner Gazette-Times
Herald & News
Herb Market Report
The Hermiston Herald
Heron Books, Inc.
Heron's Quill
High & Leslie Press
Hillsboro Argus
Janice McClure Hindman Books
Historic Preservation League of Oregon Newsletter
Historical Perspectives: Oregon State Archives
The Hollywood Star
Hood River News
Horsemanship
Hot Off The Press
House by the Sea Publishing Company
House of Humor
Howlet Press
Hubbub, A Poetry Magazine
Hulogos'i Cooperative Publishers
Hyperlink
Ice River
Iconoclast
IFCC News
Illinois Valley News
Image Imprints
Image West Press
Images
Impact
In Focus
In Stride Magazine
Incunabula Press
Indian Feather Publishing
Infoletter
Information Center
Information Press
Inner Growth Books
Institute for Quality in Human Life
Inst. for Study of Traditional Amer-Ind Arts
The Insurgent Sociologist
Interact
Interport U.S.A., Inc.
The Interwest Applied Research
InUNISON
Investor's Clinic
ISBS, Inc.
IWA Woodworker
Jackson Creek Press
Jalapeno Press
Janes Publishing
Janus Press
The Jason

JC/DC Cartoons Ink
Jean's Oregon Collections
Jefferson Review
Jewish Review
Jomac Publishing Inc.
Jordan Valley Heritage House
Journal of Personality Assessment
Journal of Pesticide Reform
The Journal of the Oregon Dental Assn
Junior League of Engene Publishers
Juniper Ridge Press
Just Out
Karanda Books
KBOO Program Guide
Keizertimes
Keyboard Workshop
Ki2 Enterprises
Kid Care Magazine
Kids Lib: Oness Press
Kindred Joy Publications
Kiowa Press
Klamath Falls Publishing
Klamath Pioneer Publishing
KMG Publications
Krause House, Inc.
KSOR Guide to the Arts
La Posta: A Journal of American Postal History
Lake County Examiner
Lake Oswego Review
The Lamron
Land
Landmark
Lane County Living
Lane Regional Air Pollution
Larry Langdon Publications
The Lariat
Lavender Network
LC Review
Lebanon Express
Letter to Libraries
LFL Associates
Library & Information Resources for the NW
Life Press
Lifeprints
Lifeworks Letter
Limousin West
Lincoln County Historical Society
The Linews
Listen To Your Beer
Lithiagraph Classifieds
Livestock Express
Llama World
The Log
Lord Byron Stamps
Loud Pedal
Love Line Books
LUNO: Learning Unlimited Network of Oregon
Lynx House Press
The Madras Pioneer
Magpie
Sal Magundi Enterprises
The Mail Tribune
Malheur Enterprise
Management Information Source Inc.
Management/Marketing Associates, Inc.
The Marijuana Report
Marketing Index International Pub
Markins Enterprises
Master Gardener Notes
Master Press
Maverick Publications
Mazama
McKenzie River Reflections
MCS Enterprises
Media Weavers, Inc.
Mediaor Company
Message Post: Portable Dwelling Info-Letter

Valley Herald
Valley Times
Van Dahl Publications
Vanguard
Vanguard
Veda News
Venture Communications
Vernier Software
Vet's Newsletter
The Villager
Vincentury
Virtue
Vision Books
Visions
The Voice
W.H. 1
Walking Bird Publishing
Wallowa County Chieftan
Warner Pacific College Art & Literature Magazine
Warner World
Washington Stylist and Salon
Watermark
We Proceeded On
Weather Workbook Company
Webb Research Group
Welcome to Planet Earth
Wells & West Publishers
West Hills Bulletin, Mt. Tabor Bulletin
West Lane News
West Side
Western Aluminum News
The Western Doll Collector
Western Engines
Western Horizons Press
Western Investor
Western Trailer & Mobile Home News
Western Wood Products Association
Westgate Press
Westridge Press
Westwind Review
What's Happening
Wheaterstone Press
Wheel Press
White Ribbon Review
Wild Oregon
Wilderness House
Wildlife Safari Newsletter
Wildwood Press
Willamette Collegian
The Willamette Jrl of the Liberal Arts
Willamette Kayak & Canoe Club
Willamette Law Review
Willamette Press
Willamette Week
The Willamette Writer
Windsor Publications, Inc.
Windyridge Press
Wistaria Press
Womanshare Books
Womanspirit
The Women's Yellow Pages
Womyn's Press
Woodburn Drag Script
Woodburn Independent
Woodstock Independent News
Tom Worcester
Words & Pictures Unlimited
Words Press
World Peace University
The World
World Wide Publishing Corporation
Writer's NW
Writer's-In-Waiting Newsletter
YIPE
Young American, Amer's Newspaper for Kids
Zap News
The Zig Zag Papers

Washington Publishing

55 And Over
A.R.O. Publishing
Aberdeen Daily World
Abraxas Publishing
Academic Enterprises
ACRL Newsletter
Actinidia Enthusiasts Newsletter
ADCIS News
Adventure Northwest
Advocate
Ag Marketer
Agarikon Press
Age of Achievement
Aglow Magazine
Aglow Publications
Agri Equipment Today
Alaska
Alaska Airlines Magazine
Alaska Construction and Oil
Alaska Fisherman's Journal/Ocean Leader
Alaska Northwest Publishing Company
Alcoholism & Addiction Magazine
Alcoholism/The National Magazine
ALKI: The Washington Library Assn Journal
Allied Arts Newsletter
Allied Arts of Seattle
Altitude Medical Publishing Company
Ampersand Publishing
Anacortes American
Analysis and Outlook
Ananse Press
Ansal Press
Aperature Northwest Inc.
Apropos
Arches
The Archive Press
Argos Guidelines
Argus Magazine
Ariel Publications
Arlington Times
Arnazella's Reading List
Artist Trust
The Arts
ASA Publications
Asian Music Publications
Auto and Flat Glass Journal
Baby
Back Door Travel
Backbone: A Journal of Women's Lit
Backlash
Backwater Press
Bainbridge Review
Ballard News-Tribune
Bassett & Brush
Bay Press
Bay Side Publishing & Printing
Bayless Enterprises Inc.
BCS Educational Aids, Inc.
Beacon Hill News
Beacon Hill Press of Seattle
Bear Creek Publications
Bear Tribe Publishing
Beginning Press
Bellevue Art Museum
Bellevue Journal-American
Bellingham Herald
The Bellingham Review
Bellowing Ark
Bellowing Ark Press
Bench Press
The Bicycle Paper
Bilingual Books, Inc.
Bingo Today
Bippity-Boppity Books
Birds' Meadow Publishing Company, Inc.

Black Heron Press
Black on Black
Black Powder Times
Blue Begonia Press
Blue Heron Press
Blue Raven Publishing
Bluestocking Books
Boredom Magazine
Botany Books
Bottom Line Press
Box Dog Press
Bremerton Sun
Brewster Quad-City Herald
Bricolage
Bright Ring Publishing
Broken Moon Press
Brooding Heron Press
Brussels Sprout
Bulletin of the King Co. Medical Society
Business Magazine
Buttermilk Road Press
Butterworth Legal Publishers
Cain-Lockhart Press
Call - A.P.P.L.E.
Camas-Washougal Post-Record
Campus Magazine
CANOE Magazine
Capitol Hill Times
Caronn's Town & Country w The Crib Sheet
The Cascade Publishing Company
Cashmere Record
Catalyst
Catalytic Publications
CCLAM CHOWDER
CCW Publications
Celestial Gems
Center for East Asian Studies
Center for Pacific Northwest Studies
The Center Press
Central County Press
Central Kitsap Reporter, Bainbridge Island Profiles
Ceramic Scope
CETUS Jrl of Whales/Porpoises & Dolphins
Channel Town Press
Chelan Valley Mirror
Chess International
The Chewalah Independent
Childbirth Education Association
Chinook Observer
The Christ Foundation
Christian Zion Advocate
The Chronicle
Circinatum Press
CIRI-BETH Publishing Company
The City Collegian
Clark Publishing, Inc.
Cleaning Consultant Services, Inc.
Coalition for Child Advocacy
Coastal Press
Collegiate
Columbia Basin Herald
COLUMBIA The Magazine of Northwest History
The Columbian
Columbiana
Communicator
Computer Education News
Computer Learning Systems Inc.
Concerning Poetry
Concrete Herald
Conscience & Military Tax Campaign
Constant Society
Consultant Services

Northwest, Inc.
Consumer Resource N.W.
A Contemporary Theatre
Contractors Weekly
Cooper Point Journal
Copper Canyon Press
Copyhook
Copyright Information Services
Coulee City News-Standard
Courier-Herald
Courier-Times
Cowles Publishing Company
Cowlitz County Advocate
Cowlitz-Wahkiakum Senior News
Crab Creek Review
Crabtree Publishing
Craft Connection
The Craft Network/The Craft Directory
Crafts Report
Crosswind
Crystal Musicworks
Current
Current Concepts-Oral/Maxillofacial Surg
Current Lit Publications, Inc.
CVAS
Cybele Society
Daily Bulletin
The Daily Chronicle
Daily Evergreen
Daily Journal American
The Daily News, Port Angeles
The Daily Olympian
The Daily
Dalmo'ma
Darvill Outdoor Publications
Davenport Times
Dayton Chronicle
Deals & Wheels
The Desktop Publishing Journal
DHA and Associates Publishing Company
Dialogue - Thoughtprints
Dispatch
Dragon Gate, Inc.
Dream Research
The Duckabush Journal
Duckburg Times
Earshot Jazz
Earth View, Inc.
East is East
East Washingtonian
Eastern Washington State Historical Soc
Eastland Press
Eastside a la Carte
Eastside Courier-Review
Eastside Writers Association Newsletter
Echo
Ecotope Group
Edge Art Press
Edmonds Arts Commission Books
The Edmonds View
Edwards Publishing Company
Ruth Edwins-Conley, Publishing
Elder Affairs
Elephant Mountain Arts
Ellensburg Anthology
Ellensburg Daily Record
Elliott Press
Emerald City Comix & Stories
Emergency Librarian
Empire Press
emPo Publications
Empty Bowl Press
The Empty Space
Engineering News-Record
Enterprise
Entreprenurial Workshops

ERGO! Bumbershoot's Literary Magazine
ESQ
Estrela Press
Et Cetera
Europe Through the Back Door Travel Newsletter
The Everett Herald
Evergreen Pacific Publs.
Evergreen Publishing
Exhibition
Facts Newspaper
Fairchild Times
Fairhaven Communications
Family Tree Pony Farm
Fantasy and Terror
Fantasy Football
Fantasy Macabre
Farm Review
Fax Collector's Editions, Inc.
Features Northwest
Federal Way News
Ferndale Record, Inc.
The Fiction Review
N.H. Fieldstone Publishing
Findhorn Publications
Fine Madness
Finnish Connection
Harriet U. Fish
The Fisherman's News
Fishing and Hunting News
Fishing Holes Magazine
Fishing Tackle Trade News
Fjord Press
Focus on Books
Footnotes
Judy Ford & Company
Foreign Artists, Poets & Authors Review
The Foreword
Forks Forum & Penninsula Herald
Fort Lewis Ranger
Four Five One
The Fox Hunt
Franklin County Graphic
The Charles Franklin Press
Fredrickson/Kloepfel Publishing Company
Free Press
Free! Newsletter of Free Materials/Services
Freedom Socialist
The Freighthoppers Manual
Friends of the Trees Yearbook
Friendship Publications, Inc.
Frontier Printing & Publishing
Frostfox Magazine
Function Industries Press
Future in Our Hands
Garnet Publishing
Gasworks Press
Gazette
Gazette-Tribune
Gemaia Press
General Educational Development Inst.
Geologic Publications
Getting Together Publications
Daniel W. Giboney
Globe
Globe Peguot Press - Western Office
Globe Publishing Co.
Glover Publications
Gluten Intolerance Group of NA
Golden Adler Books
Golden Horizons, Inc.
Golden Messenger
Goldermood Rainbow
Golf Sports Publishing
Goliards Press
Gonzaga University Press
The Goodfruit Grower Magazine

Bruce Gould Publications
The Grange News
Grant County Journal
Gray Beard Publishing
Herbi Gray, Handweaver
Grays Harbor County Vidette
Great Expectations
Great Expeditions
Green Bough Press
Greenwood Publications
The Group Theatre Company
Gryphon West Publishers
Guide Magazine
H.T.C. Publishing Co. (Hot Tub Cooks)
Had We But, Inc.
Haiku Zasshi Zo
Hancock House Publishers Ltd.
Hand Voltage Publications
Hands Off
Harbor Features
Harbor Press
Harstine House
Hartley & Marks, Publishers
Heliworld Press
Henry Art Gallery
Herald
Heritage Music Review
Heritage Quest
Heritage Quest Press
Hewitt Research Foundation
Hidden Assets
Shaun Higgins, Publisher
Highline Times & Des Moines News
The Hispanic News
Historical Gazette
Historical Society of Seattle & King Co.
Holden Pacific, Inc.
Holistic Resources
Holtz-Carter Publications
Home Education Magazine
Home Education Press
Homes & Land Magazine
Homestead Book Company
Hook & Needle Times
Hound Dog Press
House of Charles
How To Travel Inexpensively
The Howe Street Press
HTH Publishers
Hundman Publishing
Hunt Magazine
Hydrazine
I Can See Clearly Now
Idaho Farmer-Stockman
Illuminator
Imagesmith
Imaginationary Books
In Context
In. S. Omnia
Independent
Independent
Independent
Info Alternatives
Inland Country
Inland Register
Innkeeping World
Inscriptions
Insight Northwest
Insurance Adjuster
Insurance Week
Interface
Intermountain Logging News
International Communication Center
International Examiner
Intuition Trainings
Island Publishers
Island Spring
Issaquah Press
IYE (in your ear magazine)
Jacada Publishing Company

Totline	Urquhart Associates, Inc.	Wash 'n Press	Washington State Library	West Coast Baby Magazine	Wind Row
Touch the Heart Press	Vagabond Press	The Washington Alumnus	Washington State Migrant Ed News	Western Cascade Tree Fruit Assn Quarterly	Winn Book Publishers
TOWERS Club, USA Newsletter	Valley American	Washington Arts	Washington State University Press	The Western Flyer	The Wire Harp
Toy Investments, Inc.	Valley Herald	Washington Cattleman	Washington Teamster Newspaper	Western Journal of Black Studies	Wise Buys
Trail Breakers	Valley Optimist	Washington Clubwoman	Washington Thoroughbred	Western Publishing	WLA Highlights
Trainsheet	Valley Record & North Bend Record	Washington Cookbook	Washington Trails Assn.	Western Viking	Wood Bone Fire
Traveller's Bed & Breakfast	Valley View Blueberry Press	Washington Crop/Livestock Reporting Service	The Washington Trooper	Westside Record Journal	Woodford Memorial Editions, Inc.
Triad Ensemble	Vancouver Columbian	Washington Farmer Stockman	Washington Water News	Westwind	Word Power, Inc.
Tribune	Vandina Press	Washington Food Dealer Magazine	Washington Wildfire	Wheat Life	Wordware
Truck Art	Vardaman Press	The Washington Grange News	Washington Wildlife	Whidbey News Times & Whidbey Today	Work Abroad Newsletter
Tumwater Action Committee Newsletter	Vashon Point Productions	The Washington Horse	Washington Women	White Salmon Enterprise	Workingman's Press
Turman Publishing Co.	Vashon-Maury Island Beachcomber	Washington Insurance Commissioner	Washington's Land & People	Whitman College Press	World Without War Council
Turock Fitness Publishers	Vector Associates	Washington Library News	WashPIRG Reports	Whole Air	Writers Information Network
Twin Peaks Press	Vector Publishing	Washington Magazine	Waterfront Press Company	Wicazo Sa Review	Writer's Publishing Service Company
Umbrella Books	Velosport Press	Washington Newspaper	Waterlines Magazine	Wiggansnatch	The Written ARTS
Union-Bulletin	Vernon Publications	Washington Professional Publications	Watermark Press	Wilbur Register	WSEO Dispatch
Uniquest Publications	Victory Music Review	Washington Sea Grant Program	Waves	Wildfire	Michael Yaeger
University Herald	The Video Librarian	Washington State Bar Assn.	R.M. Weatherford Press	Wildfire	Yakima Herald-Republic
U of W, Graduate School of Business	Vidiot Enterprises Views	Washington State Historical Soc.	Wednesday Magazine	The Willapa Harbor Herald	Yakima Nation Review
U of W, Ofc of Publications	Vintage Northwest		Weekly	William & Allen	Yakima Valley Genealogical Soc Bulletin
University of Wash. Press	Leo F. Vogel		Welcome Press	Willoughby Wessington Publishing Company	Ye Galleon Press
University Press of the Pacific	Void Press		Wenatchee Daily World	Willow Springs	Young Pine Press
Upword Press	Wahkiakum County Eagle		Wenatchee News Agency Inc.	Wilson Publications	Young Voices
	Warren Publishing House				Your Public Schools

Selected Special Category Indexes: Subject Areas

Ag/Forestry/Gardening

Academic Enterprises
AcreAGE
Actinidia Enthusiasts Newsletter
Aero Sun-Times
Ag Marketer
Agri Equipment Today
Agri-News
Agri-Times
ALKI: The Washington Library Association Journal
American Dry Pea & Lentil Assn Bulletin
American Rhododendron Society Journal
Animal Aid
Appaloosa Journal
Arabian Horse Country
Beef Industry News
Black Sheep Newsletter
BLM News, Oregon & Washington
Botany Books
The Bread and Butter Chronicles
B.C. Farmways
B.C. Orchardist
Butter-fat Magazine
Canada Poultryman
Canadian Aquaculture Magazine
Capital Press
CETUS Jrl of Whales/Porpoises & Dolphins
Coulee City News-Standard
Dairyline
The Digger
Earthtone
Economic Facts/Idaho Agriculture
Equinews
The Extender
Extension Service Publishers
Farm & Ranch Chronicle
Farm Review
Fins and Feathers (Idaho Edition)
Florist & Grower
Forest Industries Telecommunications
Forest Log

Forest Planning
Forest Watch/CHEC
Forest World
The Foundation Afield
Friends of the Trees Yearbook
The Goodfruit Grower Magazine
The Grange News
Green Bough Press
Hartley & Marks, Publishers
Herb Market Report
Horse Times
Horsemanship
Hound Dog Press
Idaho Farm Bureau News
Idaho Farmer-Stockman
Idaho Forester
Idaho Grange News
Idaho Potato Commission Report
Idaho Thoroughbred Quarterly
Idaho Wheat
Idaho Wool Growers Bulletin
Idahobeef
Info
Infoletter
Interport U.S.A., Inc.
IWUA Alert
Journal of Pesticide Reform
Juniper Ridge Press
Ketch Pen
Klamath Falls Publishing
Land
The Lariat
Legacy House, Inc.
Limousin West
Line Rider
Livestock Express
Llama World
Logging & Sawmilling Journal
Marketing Reports & Trade Leads
Master Gardener Notes
Midgard Press
Montana Crop & Livestock Reporting Serv
Montana Farmer-Stockman
Montevista Press
Native Plant Society of Oregon Bulletin
Northwest Edition
Northwest Lookout

Northwest Nurserystock Report
The Northwest Palate
Northwest Roadapple, Nwsppr for Horsemen
Northwest Seasonal Worker
NW Unit Farm Magazines
Northwest Wool Gatherer's Quarterly
Nursery Trades BC
Nutrition Notebook
Offshoot Publications
Old Farm Kennels
OMGA Northwest Newsletter
Onion World
Oregon Association of Nurserymen
Oregon Birds
Oregon Farm Bureau News
Oregon Farmer-Stockman
Oregon Future Farmer
Oregon Grange Bulletin
The Oregon Horse
Oregon Jersey Review
Oregon Wheat
Oregon Wildlife
Oregon's Agricultural Progress
Ornamentals Northwest
Pacific Coast Nurseryman Magazine
PAWS
Pea & Lentil News
Peel Productions
The Permaculture Activist
Permaculture with Native Plants
Pet Gazette
POME News
Potato Country
Potato Grower of Idaho
The Pullman Herald
Radiance Herbs & Massage Newsletter
Seattle Aquarium
Seattle Audobon Society
Seven Buffaloes Press
Silver Bay Herb Farm
Sinsemilla Tips
Small Farmer's Journal
The Smallholder Publishing Collective
SONCAP News
The Sproutletter
Standard-Register

Sugar Producer
The Dalles Weekly Reminder
Timber!
Timber Press, Inc.
Timberbeast
Tomorrow's Forest
Trout
U.S. Department of Ag, Forest Service
U of O, Forest Industries Management Center
Washington Cattleman
Washington Crop/Livestock Reporting Service
Washington Farmer Stockman
The Washington Grange News
The Washington Horse
Washington Thoroughbred
Washington Water News
Washington Wildlife
Washington's Land & People
Western Cascade Tree Fruit Assn Quarterly
Western Livestock News
Wheat Life
Whitehouse Publishing
Wildfire
Wildlife Safari Newsletter
Wildlife-Wildlands Institute
Windsor Publications, Inc.
Ye Galleon Press

Arts: Fine, Allied, & Applied

ACAPella
Aesthetics West
Agri-News
The Alaskan Viewpoint
Allied Arts Newsletter
Allied Arts of Seattle
Amadeus Press
Amateur Brewer Information
American Geographic Publishing
American Indian Basketry Magazine
Animator
Arabian Horse Country
Architectural Lighting

Art Gallery of Greater Victoria
Art West Magazine
Artist Search/Montana Arts Council
Artist Trust
Artist's Notes
Arts B.C.
The Arts Council of Southern Oregon Newsletter
Arts & Crafts News
Arts East/Eastern OR Reg. Arts Council
The Arts
Asian Music Publications
Bay Press
Beaverton Arts Commission Newsletter
Before the Sun
Bellevue Art Museum
The Bellingham Review
Beyond Words Publishing Inc.
Black Powder Times
Black Sheep Newsletter
Blatant Image: a Magazine of Feminist Photography
Bluespaper
Braemar Books
British Columbia Railway Historical Assn
Broadsheet Publications
Brussels Sprout
Bugle
Bulletin
Business Magazine
Calyx, A Jrl of Art & Lit by Women
Canho Enterprises
Carefree Cooking Company
Caronn's Town & Country w The Crib Sheet
Center for Urban Education
Ceramic Scope
The City Open Press
Common Ground
COMMUNICOM
A Contemporary Theatre
The Cookbook Factory
Crab Creek Review
Craft Connection
The Craft Network/The Craft Directory
Crystal Musicworks
Current

The Current
Dog River Review
The Duckabush Journal
Earshot Jazz
Echo Film Productions
Ellensburg Anthology
emPo Publications
The Empty Space
Encore Arts in Performance Magazine
Eurock
Events Magazine
Fanatic Reader
Fine Art & Auction Review
Firehouse Theater
The Flyfisher
Focus
Forest World
The Free Agent
From The Woodpile
Front Row
Function Industries Press
Galley Proofs
Glass Studio Magazine
Globe Peguot Press - Western Office
Herbi Gray, Handweaver
The Group Theatre Company
HearSay Press
Henry Art Gallery
Heritage Music Review
Historic Preservation League of Oregon Newsletter
Holtz-Carter Publications
Homestead Book Company
Hook & Needle Times
Idaho Arts Journal
Idahoan
Images
Inst. for Study of Traditional Amer-Ind Arts
International Communication Center
Jeopardy
Jimmy Come Lately Gazette
Journal of Health, Physical Education,
KBOO Program Guide
Keyboard Workshop
KID Broadcasting Corporation
KSOR Guide to the Arts
La Posta: A Journal of American Postal History
Listen To Your Beer

The Washington Horse
Washington Insurance Commissioner
Washington Professional Publications
Washington Stylist & Salon
Washington Teamster Newspaper
Washington Water News
Washington Women
Washington's Land & People
Western Aluminum News
Western Banker Magazine
Western Business
Western Cascade Tree Fruit Assn Quarterly
Western Fisheries
The Western Flyer
Western Investor
Western Livestock News
Western Trailer & Mobile Home News
Western Trucking
Western Wood Products Assn
Wheat Life
Wildfire
The Willamette Writer
The Women's Yellow Pages
Work Abroad Newsletter
Writer's NW

Children

Adopted Child
Alaska Council of Teachers of English
The Asterisk
Blue Heron Press
Blue Heron Publishing
The Book Shop/Children's Newsletter
Bright Ring Publishing
Centerplace Publishing Company
Childbirth Education Association
Coalition For Child Advocacy
Council for Indian Education
Creative Children
Enfantaisie
Estrada Publications and Photography
First Alternative Thymes
Flashes
Focus on Books
The Charles Franklin Press
Ghost Town Quarterly
Green Bough Press
Havin' Fun, Inc.
Heron Books, Inc.
Home Education Magazine
Home Education Press Images
Kid Care Magazine
Kids Lib: Oness Press
Legacy House, Inc.
Lighthouse Magazine
LUNO: Learning Unlimited Network of Oregon
Markins Enterprises
Monte Publishing Company
Nerve Press
Open Hand Publishing, Inc.
Our Little Friend
P.R.O. Newsletter of Oregon
Parenting Press, Inc.
Pathways
Paws IV Publishing Co.
The Pedersens
Peel Productions
Portland Family Calendar
Press Porcepic Ltd.
Primary Treasure
Rainbow Press
Saturday's Child

Seattle's Child/Eastside Project
Seattle's Child Publishing
Skipping Stones
Street Times
Teaching Home
Teaching Research Infant and Child Center News
TGNW Press
Titania Publications
Totline
West Coast Baby Magazine
Wheel Press
Young American, Amer's Newspaper for Kids
Young Voices

Fiction

Adventures In Subversion
Alchemy
Angst World Library
Aperature Northwest Inc.
Arrowood Books, Inc.
Arsenal Pulp Press Book Publishers, Ltd.
Artoonist
Backbone: A Journal of Women's Lit
Barbarian Press
Barlow Press
Beacon
Before the Sun
The Bellingham Review
Bellowing Ark
Bellowing Ark Press
BikeReport
Black Heron Press
The Bloodletter
Blue Heron Publishing
Boise Magazine–Idaho Annual Inc.
Bookmark
Box Dog Press
Braemar Books
Breitenbush Publications
British Columbia Monthly
Calyx, A Jrl of Art & Lit by Women
Calyx Inc./Calyx Books
The Capilano Review
Cappis Press
Caronn's Town & Country w The Crib Sheet
Catalyst
Center for Urban Education
Chanticleer
Christian Outlook
Clear Water Journal
Clinton St. Quarterly
cold-drill Books
cold-drill Magazine
Comic Relief
Common Ground
Confluence Press, Inc.
Crab Creek Review
Crowdancing Quarterly
Current
Current Lit Publications, Inc.
CutBank
Dalmo'ma
Denali
Dog River Review
The Downtowner
Dragon Gate, Inc.
The Duckabush Journal
Edmonds Arts Commission Books
Ruth Edwins-Conley, Publishing
Ellensburg Anthology
Emerald City Comix & Stories
emPo Publications
Empty Bowl Press
The Emshock Letter
EOTU Magazine

ERGO! Bumbershoot's Literary Magazine
Essence
Event
Exhibition
Fanatic Reader
Fantasy and Terror
Fantasy Macabre
The Fiction Review
Fine Madness
Fjord Press
Four Five One
The Free Agent
From The Woodpile
Globe Publishing Co.
Hapi Press
Heartwood
Heated Closet
Horizons SF
House of Humor
Howlet Press
Hydrazine
Ice River
Inky Trails Publications
Interior Voice
Intertext
IYE (in your ear magazine)
The Jason
JC/DC Cartoons Ink
Jeopardy
Kiowa Press
Kutenai Press
Lighthouse Magazine
Line
Lynx House Press
The Malahat Review
The Marijuana Report
Matrix
Maverick Publications
Midnight Shambler
Mississippi Mud
Montana Arts Council
Montana Review
Mooseyard Press
Mother of Ashes
Ms. Leroy Press
Multnomah Press
Mystery Time
Nerve Press
Senior Writers Network News
New Woman Press
The Next War
Northern Lights
Northwest Magazine
Northwest Passage
Northwest Review
NRG Magazine
Oolichan Books
Oregon Authors
Oregon English
Outlaw Newsletter
Owl Creek Press
The Pacific Review
Panda Press Publications
Paper Radio
Passages Travel Magazine
Pathways
Performance Press
Permafrost
Poe Studies
Poetic Space
Poetry Exchange
Poets. Painters. Composers.
The Pointed Circle
Poptart
The Portable Wall/Basement Press
Portland Magazine
Portland Review
Potboiler Magazine
Press Porcepic Ltd.
Pressing America
PRISM International
Pulphouse
The Quartz Press
Rain
Read Me
The Real Comet Press

The Redneck Review of Literature
Repository Press
Rhapsody!
Rickereall Creek House
The Rose Arts Magazine
Rosewood Press
Runaway Publications
Ruralite
Sandpiper Press
Science Fiction Review
The Seattle Review
Seattle Star
Charles Seluzicki, Fine Press Series
Seven Buffaloes Press
Sign of the Times-a Chronicle of Decadence
The Silver Apple Branch
Silverleaf Press
Skydog Press
Slightly West
Small World Publications
Snohomish Publishing Company
Spindrift
Stories & Letters Digest
Studio 403
Talonbooks
Testmarketed Downpour
TGNW Press
Tidewater
Time to Pause
TIPTOE Literary Service
Trace Editions
Trout Creek Press
TV Week
University of Idaho Press
University of Portland Review
Upword Press
Vagabond Press
Vashon Point Productions
The Village Idiot
Vintage Northwest
Leo F. Vogel
Warner Pacific College Art & Literature Magazine
Wash 'n Press
Wavefront
West Coast Review
Western Newsletter
Westwind
Wheel Press
Willow Springs
Wood Bone Fire
Writer's Publishing Service Company
Writer's-In-Waiting Newsletter
Writing Magazine
Writing Pursuits
The Written ARTS
Michael Yaeger
Young American, Amer's Newspaper for Kids

History/Biography

Alaska Heritage Enterprises
Alaska Historical Commission
Alaska History
Alaska Pacific University Press
Alberni District Historical Society
American Indian Basketry Magazine
Areopagitier Press, Inc.
Art West Magazine
Baker Democrat-Herald
Bandon Historical Society
Bayless Enterprises Inc.
The Bear Wallow Pub. Co.
Beautiful America Publishing Company

Beaver Briefs
Binford & Mort Publishing
Bitter Root Valley Hist. Newsletter
The Boag Foundation Ltd.
Boise State U. Western Writers Series
Bowen Island Historians
The Bridge
British Columbia Genealogical Society
B.C. Historical News
B.C. Outdoors
British Columbia Railway Historical Assn
Burnaby Historical Society
Buttermilk Road Press
Calapooia Publications
Callboard
Canadian West Magazine
Cascades East
The Caxton Printers, Ltd.
COLUMBIA The Magazine of Northwest History
Cowlitz County Advocate
Crook Co. Historical Society Newsletter
Cumtux
Curry County Echoes
Dioscoridus Press, Inc.
Douglas & McIntyre Publishers
Eastern Washington State Historical Soc
Edmonds Arts Commission Books
FINNAM Newsletter
Finnish American Literary Heritage Found
Harriet U. Fish
Fjord Press
Footprint Publishing Company
Frontier Printing & Publishing
The Frontiersman
Genealogical Forum of Portland Bulletin
The Georgian Press Company
Good Medicine Books
Gray's Publishing, Ltd.
Haralson Enterprises
Harvest Magazine
Heritage Quest
Heritage Quest Press
Historic Preservation League of Oregon Newsletter
Historical Gazette
Historical Perspectives: Oregon State Archives
Historical Society of Seattle & King Co.
Horsdal & Schubart Publishers, Ltd.
Idaho Genealogical Society Quarterly
Idaho State Historical Society
Idaho Yesterdays
Idahoan
Journal of Everett & Snohomish Co. Hist.
Journal of the Nez Perce Co. Hist. Soc.
Kamloops Museum & Archives
Kindred Joy Publications
La Posta: A Journal of American Postal History
Landmarks
Latah Co. Genealogical Soc. Newsletter
Latah County Historical Society
Latah Legacy
Legacy House, Inc.
Lincoln County Historical Society

Lumby Historians
Madison County History Association
Melior Publications
The Messenger
Montana Historical Society Press
Montana, the Magazine of Western History
Monte Publishing Company
Montevista Press
Mountain Light
Museum of History & Industry
Musings
Nanaimo Historical Society
Nechako Valley Historical Society
The Next War
Niche Press
Northwest Discovery
Northwest Historical Consultants
Northwest Passages - Hist. Newsletter
Nugget Enterprises
Old Harbor Press
Old News
Old Stuff
Olympic Publishing, Inc.
Oolichan Books
Oregon Committee for the Humanities
Oregon Focus
Oregon Historical Quarterly
Oregon Historical Society News
Oregon Historical Society Press
Oregon State University Press
Owyhee Historical Society Bulletin
Owyhee Outpost
Pacific Northwest Labor History Assn
THE PATRIOT
The Pedersens
Pemberton Pioneer Women
Pictorial Histories Publishing Company
Pika Press
Pioneer Press Books
Pioneer Trails
Printery Farm
Provincial Archives of British Columbia
The Quarterdeck Review
Rainy Day Press
Red Cedar Press
Roseburg Woodsman
Runaway Publications
Sagittarius Press
Sherman County For The Record
Skagit County Historical Society
Skookum Publications
Snake River Echoes
Solstice Press
Sono Nis Press
Sourdough Enterprises
Southern Oregon Historical Society
Spencer Butte Press
Spirit Mountain Press
Springfield Historical Commission
Sunfire Publications Ltd.
Sweet Reason: A Journal of Ideas, Hist/Cult
The Table Rock Sentinel
The Dalles Weekly Reminder
Timberbeast
The Touchstone Press
Trail Breakers
Trail City Archives
The Trainmaster

The Extender
Finnish Connection
Forest Log
Fredrickson/Kloepfel
 Publishing Company
Freedom Socialist
Gahmken Press
The Gated Wye
GIS/CAD Mapping
 Solutions
Guide Magazine
Hartley & Marks, Publishers
HearSay Press
Heartwood
Hemingway Western Studies
 Series
Heron Books, Inc.
Highway Information
Historical Perspectives:
 Oregon State Archives
Hound Dog Press
Idaho Cities
Idaho Citizen
Idaho Council on Economic
 Ed. Newsletter
Idaho Voice
Idaho Voter
Idaho's Economy
Impact
Information Press
Inner Growth Books
Insight Northwest
Institute of Social &
 Economic Research
The Insurgent Sociologist
The Interwest Applied
 Research
Investor's Clinic
Jennifer James, Inc.
Jewish Review
The Journal of Ethnic
 Studies
Journal of Financial &
 Quantitative Analysis
Journal of Personality
 Assessment
KBOO Program Guide
Landmark
Limberlost Press
Listening Post - KUOW FM
The Marijuana Report
Medic Publishing Company
Mercury Services Inc.
Merril Press
Metamorphous Press
Metrocenter YMCA
Monday Magazine
Montana Business Quarterly
Northwest Arts
Northwest Construction
 News
The Northwest
 Environmental Journal
Northwest Ethnic News
Northwest Examiner
Northwest Public Power
 Bulletin
ODOT News
Oregon Arts News
Ore Cncl on Alchlsm &
 Drug Abuse Nwslttr
Oregon Economic
 Development Department
Oregon Humanites
Oregon Libertarian
Oregon Public Employee
Oregon State University
 Press
Oscillator
Pacific
Pacific Affairs
Pacific Banker
Pacific Northwest Executive
Pacific Northwest Magazine
Packrat Press
Pallas Communications
Passage
The Peak
Playful Wisdom Press

Portland Business Today
Pressing America
Princess Publishing
Property Tax Charges
Puget Sound Business
 Journal
The Quartz Press
Rain: Resources for Building
 Community
Rainbow News
The Real Comet Press
Recovery Life
Reflections Directory
Review of Social &
 Economic Conditions
The Rose Arts Magazine
Seattle Art Museum Program
 Guide
Seattle Business Magazine
Seattle Chinese Post
Seattle Monthly
Seattle Weekly
Signal Elm Press
The Silver Apple Branch
Sinsemilla Tips
Siskiyou
Siskiyou Journal
Skipping Stones
The Sneak Preview
Socialist Party of Canada
Southern Willamette
 Alliance
The Southwestern
 Sovereignty, Inc.
Speaking of Taxes
Special Child Publications
Spokane Area Economic
 Devel Council
Sprague Advocate
Sweet Reason: A Journal of
 Ideas, Hist/Cult
The Dalles Weekly
 Reminder
Tumwater Action Committee
 Newsletter
Center for Business
 Development & Research
University of Alaska Press
University of Idaho Press
U of O, Bureau of
 Governmental Research/
 Service
University of Portland
 Review
Urban Design Centre Society
Vancouver Magazine
Vancouver Symphony
Venture Communications
Vernon Publications
The Voice
Washington Arts
The Washington Grange
 News
Washington Magazine
Washington State Bar Assn.
The Washington Trooper
Washington Water News
WashPIRG Reports
Welcome Press
West Hills Bulletin, Mt.
 Tabor Bulletin
Western Journal of Black
 Studies
Westgate Press
White Ribbon Review
The Willamette Jrl of the
 Liberal Arts
Willamette Law Review
Willamette Week
World Without War Council
WSEO Dispatch

Women

Adopted Child
Aglow Magazine
Aglow Publications
The Alliance
Apropos
Backbone: A Journal of
 Women's Literature
Bear Creek Publications
Blatant Image: a Magazine
 of Feminist Photography
Calyx Inc./ Calyx Books
Caronn's Town & Country w
 The Crib Sheet
Castalia Publishing
 Company
Centerplace Publishing Co.
Chanticleer
Childbirth Education
 Association
Coalition For Child
 Advocacy
Coeur d'Alene Homes
 Messenger
Douglas & McIntyre
 Publishers
Edmonds Arts Commission
 Books
The Eighth Mountain Press
The Charles Franklin Press
Freedom Socialist
Galley Proofs
Grey Whale Press
Harvest Magazine
Home Education Magazine
Home Education Press
Hot Springs Gazette
Inland Country
InUNISON
Kinesis
Laughing Dog Press
Lavender Network
Lesbian Contradiction: A
 Jrnl of Irreverent
 Feminism
Lifeline America
Lifeworks Letter
Listen: Journal of Better
 Living
Madrona Publishers, Inc.
Manufactured Homes
 Magazine
Midwifery Today
The Mobile/Manufactured
 Homeowner
Moonstone Press
Mountain Meadow Press
New Star Books
New Woman Press
Northwest Women in
 Business
Oregon Business Women
Ore Cncl on Alchlsm &
 Drug Abuse Nwslttr
The Ovulation Method
 Newsletter
P.R.O. Newsletter of Oregon
Parenting Press, Inc.
Pemberton Pioneer Women
Pennypress, Inc.
Perceptions
Performance Press
Phinney Ridge Review
Planned Parenthood
 Association of Idaho
Playful Wisdom Press
Portland Family Calendar
Press Gang Publishers
Printery Farm
Progressive Woman
Quarterly Review
Room of One's Own
The Rude Girl Press
Ruralite
Saturday's Child
The Seal Press
Seattle's Child/Eastside
 Project

Select Homes
Silverleaf Press
Spiritual Women's Times
Views
Virtue
Washington Women
West Coast Baby Magazine
White Ribbon Review
Wildfire
Woman to Woman Magazine
Womanshare Books
Womanspirit
The Women's Yellow Pages
Womyn's Press
Writer's Info

Writing Publishing Language Library

Aardvark Enterprises
ACRL Newsletter
Aesthetics West
Alaska Native Language
 Center
Alaska Quarterly Review
Alaska State Writing
 Consortium Newsletter
ALKI: The Washington
 Library Assn. Journal
Amphora
Arnazella's Reading List
Barlow Press
Bilingual Books, Inc.
Blue Heron Publishing
Boise State U. Western
 Writers Series
Book Production Associates
The Book Shop/Children's
 Newsletter
Bookletter Newsletter
Bookmark
BookNotes: Resources for
 Small & Self-Pubs
B. C. BookWorld
British Columbia Library
 Association Newsletter
Bulletin
Cain-Lockhart Press
Calapooya Collage
Canadian Literature
CCLAM Chowder
Clear Water Journal
Coast to Coast Books
Colonygram
COLUMBIA The Magazine
 of Northwest History
Comparative Literature
Concerning Poetry
Controversy in Review
Copyright Information
 Services
CutBank
CVAS
The Denali Press
The Desktop Publishing
 Journal
Eastside Writers Association
 Newsletter
Emergency Librarian
Enfantaisie
ERGO! Bumbershoot's
 Literary Magazine
Et Cetera
Event
Fanatic Reader
The Fiction Review
Fine Madness
Finnish American Literary
 Heritage Found
Finnish Connection
Fjord Press
Focus on Books
Footnotes
Foreign Artists, Poets &
 Authors Review

Function Industries Press
Galley Proofs
Green Bough Press
Hard Row to Hoe
HearSay Press
Hot Springs Gazette
Idaho English Journal
Idaho Librarian
Idaho State University Press
In. S. Omnia
Information Press
Inscriptions
Intertext
Journal of B.C. English
 Teachers' Association
Laughing Dog Press
LaVoz Newsmagazine
Letter to Libraries
Lewiston Morning Tribune
Library & Information
 Resources for the
 Northwest
Life Scribes
Limberlost Press
Line
Literary Markets
Media Weavers, Inc.
The Minnesota Review
Modern Language Quarterly
Montana Newsletter
Montana Review
Monthly
Senior Writers Network
 News
Niche Press
North American Post
Northwest Inland Writing
 Project Newsletter
Northwest Notes
Northwest Review
The Northwest Review of
 Books
Old Violin-Art Publishing
Open Hand Publishing, Inc.
Oregon Assn of Christian
 Writers Nwslttr
Oregon Authors
Oregon Committee for the
 Humanities
Oregon Library Foundation
 Newsletter
Oregon Library News
Oregon Publisher
Oregon State Poetry Assn
 Newsletter
Overland West Press
Owl Creek Press
Parlie Publications
PNLA Quarterly
Poe Studies
Poetry Exchange
Poetry Today
Portland Scribe
Powell's Books
Pressing America
Prime Times
The Printer's Devil
The Printer's Northwest
 Trader
Publishing Northwest
 Newsletter
the raddle moon
The Reader
Red Cedar Press
Reference & Research Book
 News
Rendezvous
Repository Press
Rhapsody!
Romar Books
Sakura Press
Satellite Guide
Satellite World
Scitech Book News
Seattle Weekly
Second Language
 Publications
Charles Seluzicki, Fine Press
 Series

Sesame
Shining Knight Press
SmokeRoot
Snohomish Publishing
 Company
The Sourdough
Spotlight
Spotlight Northwest
Sweet Reason: A Journal of
 Ideas, Hist/Cult
Tidewater
TIPTOE Literary Service
TOWERS Club, USA
 Newsletter
Trace Editions
Elmer E. Rasmuson Library
University of British
 Columbia Press
University of Portland
 Writers
U of V, English Literature
 Studies Monograph
 Series
U of W, Office of
 Publications
Washington State Library
Washington Women
Watermark
Western Newsletter
The Willamette Writer
Willow Springs
Wind Vein Press/White
 Clouds Revue
WLA Highlights
Writer's Chapbook
Writer's Info
Writers Information Network
Writer's NW
Writer's-In-Waiting
 Newsletter
Writing Magazine
Writing Pursuits

Notes & Updates

1000 Friends of Oregon Newsletter, 400 Dekum Building, 519 S.W. 3rd, Portland, OR 97204. Monthly. Query w/SASE. Newsletter on issues of Oregon land use, development and environment. Index: 35, 91, 101.

55 And Over, 121 Mercer Street, Seattle, WA 98109. 206–282–3499. Monthly. No submission info. Query w/SASE. Index: 110.

A.R.C. Publications, PO Box 3044, Vancouver, BC V6B 3X5. Publisher. No submission info. Query w/SASE. Index: 130.

A.R.O. Publishing, PO Box 31667, Seattle, WA 98103. Publisher. No submission info. Query w/SASE. Index: 130.

AAG-AAG!, PO Box 6, Kendrick, ID 83537. Editor: Carolyn Gravell. Periodical. Circ. 400. No submission info. Query w/SASE. Index: 97.

Aardvark Enterprises, 192 Balsam Place, Penticton, BC V2A 7V3. 604–492–0272. Contact: J. Alvin Speers. Publisher of 3-4 softcover, subsidy books a yr. Publication for author by arrangement. Guidelines/sample. Index: 67, 102, 104.

Abbott Loop Christian Center, 2626 Abbott Road, Anchorage, AK 99507. Publisher. No submission info. Query w/SASE. Index: 105.

Aberdeen Daily World, 315 South Michigan, PO Box 269, Aberdeen, WA 98520. 206–532–4000. Daily newspaper. No submission info. Query w/SASE. Index: 33.

Abraxas Publishing, 439 Kirkland Way, PO Box 312, Kirkland, WA 98033. Publisher. No submission info. Query w/SASE. Index: 130.

Academic Enterprises, PO Box 666, Pullman, WA 99163-0666. 509–334–4826. Self-publisher of 1 softcover book a yr. Not a freelance market. Index: 3, 19, 118.

ACAPella, PO Box 11, Days Creek, OR 97429. Editor: Eleanor Davis. 503–825–3647. Quarterly. Circ. 300. Sub. $10. "No one receives any remuneration for the publication in *ACAPella* of their original gospel music or poetry." Nonfiction, poetry. "Purpose of our organization is to assist and encourage members in the writing of gospel music and poetry, and provide timely articles about the state of the art." Sample available $1. Index: 86, 97, 105.

AcreAGE, PO Box 130, Ontario, OR 97914. Editor: Marie A. Ruemenapp. 503–889–5387. Monthly tabloid "distributed free to rural residents of Oregon and Idaho and related agri-business firms of the region.... We're interested in anything agriculturally oriented that will help our readers farm or ranch better, or entertain them." Payment: Money on publication. Rights purchased: 1st. Query w/SASE. Phone query OK. Reports in 2 wks. Publishes in 1-2 mos. Nonfiction, photos. Photos: $7.50 for 1st and $5 for others; 35mm B&W with articles; occasionally buys cover photos (color slides). "We encourage you to send us your exposed B&W film, preferably Tri-X and we will develop it here. Negatives will be returned." Tips: "*AcreAGE* is a very localized magazine, and as such, rarely uses material that isn't about farmers and ranchers in eastern Oregon and southern Idaho. Index: 3, 24, 45.

ACRL Newsletter, Washington State University, Owen Science & Engineering Library, Pullman, WA, 99164-3200, Contact: Editor. Periodical. No submission info. Query w/SASE. Index: 104, 108, 109.

Actinidia Enthusiasts Newsletter, 1466 Chelan, WA 98816. Editor: Michael Pilarski. For kiwi enthusiasts. No submission info. Query w/SASE. Index: 3, 19, 56.

The Active Pacifist, 454 Willamette, Eugene, OR, 97402. Editor: Gary Kutcher. Monthly periodical. No submission info. Query w/SASE. Index: 93.

Ad Lib, University of Idaho Law Library, Moscow, ID, 83843. Editor: Trish Cervenka. Irregularly published periodical. No submission info. Query w/SASE. Index: 74.

Ad-Dee Publishers, Inc., 2736 Lincoln Street, Eugene, OR 97405. No submission info. Query w/SASE. Index: 130.

ADCIS News, Miller Hall 409, Western Washington University, Bellingham, WA 98225. Periodical. No sub. info. Query w/SASE. Index: 31.

The Adjusting Entry, PO Box 2896, Boise, ID 83702. Editor: Joyce Kasper. 208–344–6261. Ads: same. Quarterly aimed at CPAs. Circ. 1,500. Sub. membership. No pay. Byline given. Phone query, dot matrix, and photocopies OK. Reports in: varies. Technical information. Index: 24, 42.

Adopted Child, PO Box 9362, Moscow, ID 83843. 208–882–1181. Editor: Lois Melina. Monthly. Sub.$20. Circ. 3,000. Freelance ms accepted. Pays: money, copies on publication. Rights purchased: All. Byline given. Query with clips, ms, SASE. Photocopies, computer disc OK. Accepts: nonfiction. The newsletter uses a journalistic style with the author interviewing appropriate news sources on all types of adoptions. Some topics covered: bonding & attachment, how to talk to children about adoption, parenting, issues faced by the adopted adolescent. Guidelines available; sample/$1.75. Index: 28, 47, 114.

Adventure Northwest, PO Box 1715, Auburn, WA 98071. Editor: Kerry Ordway. 206–863–4373. Monthly on NW travel for "upper middle class" audience about 45 yrs. old. Circ. 75,000. Buys 75 mss/yr. Payment: Money on publication. Byline given. Rights purchased: 1st. Query with mss, SASE. Dot matrix OK. Simultaneous submissions OK to non-competing markets. Publishes submissions in 2-6 mos. Nonfiction: 800-1,000 wds, $25-$100. Guidelines/sample available. Index: 120.

Adventures, Sheldon Jackson College, 801 Lincoln, Sitka, AK, 99835. Contact: Editor. No submission info. Query w/SASE. Index: 31.

Adventures In Subversion, PO Box 11492, Eugene, OR 97440. Contact: John Zerzan, Dan Todd. 503–344–3119/503–345–1147. Self-publisher of occasional flyers and papers which present a "critical contestation of contemporary capitalism and its spurious opposition." Not a freelance market. Index: 71, 107, 112.

Advocate, Mt. Hood Community College, 26000 S.E. Stark, Gresham, OR, 97030. 503–667–7253. Newspaper. No submission info. Query w/SASE. Index: 31.

Advocate, PO Box 327, Sprague, WA 99032. 509–257–2311. Weekly newspaper. No submission info. Query w/SASE. Index: 33.

The Advocate, Vancouver Bar Association, 4765 Pilot House Road, West Vancouver, BC V7W 1J2. Editor: D.P. Roberts, QC. Periodical. No submission info. Query w/SASE. Index: 74, 113.

The Advocate, PO Box 895, Boise, ID 83701. 208–342–8958. Editor/Ads: Linda Watkins-Heywood. Monthly. Sub. $25. Circ. 2,800. Pays copies. Byline given. Submit ms. Dot matrix, photocopies OK. Reports in 6 wks. Nonfiction. "General interest, law-related topics; max. 6 pgs, typed, ds. If want notice of acceptance, please specify." Sample/$2.50. Index: 69, 74.

Aerie Publishing, Deep Bay, Vancouver Island, RR 1, Bower, BC V0R 1G0. Publisher. No submission info. Query w/SASE. Index: 130.

For lists of abbreviations and the key to index numbers, see "How to Use this Section" on page 75.

Writer's Northwest Handbook   99

Aero Sun-Times, 44 N. Last Chance Gulch #9, Helena, MT, 59601. 406–443–7272. Editor: Wilbur Wood. Periodical. Accepts nonfiction, poetry, photos, cartoons, other. Index: 3, 46.

Aesthetics West, PO Box 5149, Eugene, OR 97405. Contact: Robert Travis. 503–343–8278. Pub. of 2 books a yr. Print run: 100-2,500. Rarely accepts freelance material. Softcover, originals, and subsidy books. Query w/SASE. Photocopies & simultaneous submissions OK. Nonfiction, fiction, poetry, photos, plays, cartoons. "Avant garde art and cultural fiction and nonfiction, with original art. Book-length (ca 100 pp) or substantial fraction thereof. Unique perspective absolutely necessary." Index: 22, 122.

Ag Marketer, PO Box 1467, Yakima, WA 98907. 509–248–2452. Monthly. No submission info. Query w/SASE. Index: 3, 24.

Agadir Press, PO Box 2015, Corvallis, OR 97339. Publisher. No submission info. Query w/SASE. Index: 130.

Agarikon Press, PO Box 2233, Olympia, WA 98507. Publisher. No submission info. Query w/SASE. Index: 130.

Age of Achievement, 835 Securities Bldg., Seattle, WA, 98101. Contact: Editor. Quarterly. No submission info. Query w/SASE. Index: 130.

Agent West Weekly, 1425 W. Pender Street, Vancouver, BC V6E 2S3. Editor: Douglas W. Keough. 604–688–0481. No submission info. Query w/SASE. Index: 130.

Aglow Magazine, PO Box I, Lynnwood, WA 98046-1557. Contact: Publications Department. 206–775–7282. Ads: Barbara Joseph. Bimonthly for charismatic Christian women. Circ. 15,000. Sub. $9. Uses 7 mss per issue. Payment: Money on acceptance. Byline given. Rights purchased: 1st. Query w/SASE. Photocopies OK. Reports in 6 wks. Nonfiction, fiction. Look for "Christian solutions to the problems faced by today's women. We pay up to $.10/word depending on amount of editing. 1,500 wds is best length for us." Guidelines/sample available. Index: 105, 124.

Aglow Publications, Box 1, Lynnwood, WA 98046-1557. Contact: Publications Department. 206–775–7282. Publisher of 12 softcover originals a yr. Print run: 10,000. Payment: Royalties. Rights purchased: 1st. Query with sample chapters, SASE. Photocopies OK. Reports in 6 wks. Publishes in 6-12 mos. Nonfiction. Look for "Christian solutions to problems faced by today's women. To 50,000 wds." Guidelines/catalog available. Index: 105, 124.

Agri Equipment Today, PO Box 1467, Yakima, WA 98907. 509–248–2457. Monthly. No sub. info. Query w/SASE. Index: 3, 24.

Agri-News, PO Box 30755, Billings, MT 59107-0755. Editor: Rebecca Tescher. 406–259–4589. Weekly agricultural tabloid interested in "cottage industry." Circ. 18,000. Writers must have expertise in agriculture. Payment: Money. Query w/SASE. Phone query OK. Nonfiction: 750 wds for $20-$35 on Montana & Wyoming ag-related stories/profiles. Fillers: 500-1,000 wds for $15-$25 on "farm taxes, ag-related business, gardening, knitting & crafts." Photos: B&W, good quality, $5, as used. Tips: "Must be useful to Montana & Wyoming agrarians." Guidelines/sample available. Index: 3, 38, 85.

Agri-Times Northwest, Box 189, Pendleton, OR 97801. 503–276–7185. Editor: Virgil Rupp. Weekly newspaper, Eastern WA, OR, ID. No submission info. Query w/SASE. Index: 3.

AHI Newsletter, Len G. Jordan Bldg., Rm. 300, 650 W. State Street, Boise, ID 83720. Editor: Tom Rybus. Published 3 time a yr. Circ. 6,500. No submission info. Query w/SASE. Index: 130.

Ahsahta Press, Dept. of English, Boise State University, 1910 University Drive, Boise, ID 83725. 208–385–1246. Contact: Tom Trusky. Publisher of 3 softcover originals or reprints a yr. Print run: 500. Payment: copies for 1st & 2nd printing; 25% royalties commence with 3rd printing. Rights purchased: 1st. "We read samplers only (15 poems) sent Jan-Mar SASE." Reports in 2 mo. "Poetry of the American West. Spare us conventional verse, clone Stafford/Snyder stuff, Jesus-on-Mt. Ranier, or anything that jingles. We are not interested in photographs of Mt. Ranier (or Hood), or sensitive line drawings/lithos of same. We are interested in your poetry. Guidelines included in catalog. Sample: $6.45 ppd. Index: 89, 97.

AK Sea Grant, 138 Irving #11, Fairbanks, AK, 99775. Contact: Editor, Book publisher. No submission info. Query w/SASE. Index: 4.

AKHT Publishing, 2420 Parkview Drive, Kamloops, BC V2B 7J1. No submission info. Query w/SASE. Index: 130.

Aladin Printing, PO Box 364, Palmer, AK, 99645. Contact: Editor. Book publisher. No submission info. Query w/SASE. No submission info. Query w/SASE. Index: 130.

Alaska, Alaska NW Publishing Company, 130 Second Avenue, Edmonds, WA 98020. 206–774–4111. Monthly. No submission info. Query w/SASE. Index: 4, 45, 103.

Alaska Airlines Magazine, 1932 First Avenue, Suite 503, Seattle, WA 98101. Periodical. No submission info. Query w/SASE. Index: 4, 45, 120.

Alaska Angler Publications, PO Box 8-3550, Fairbanks, AK 99708. Publisher. No submission info. Query/SASE. Index: 4, 53, 103.

Alaska Business Monthly, PO Box 102696, Anchorage, AK, 99510. Editor: Paul Laird. Periodical. No submission info. Query w/SASE. Index: 4, 24.

Alaska Construction and Oil, 109 W. Mercer, Seattle, WA 98119. 206–285–2050. Monthly. No submission info. Query w/SASE. Index: 4, 24.

Alaska Council of Teachers of English, PO Box 3184, Kodiak, AK, 99615. Editor: David Jaynes. Book Publisher. No submission info. Query w/SASE. Index: 28, 43.

Alaska Department of Labor, Research & Analysis, PO Box 1149, Juneau, AK 99802-2000. Publisher. No submission info. Query w/SASE. Index: 4, 42, 71.

Alaska Department of Fish & Game, PO Box 3-2000, Juneau, AK 99802-2000. 907–465–4112. Editor: Sheila Nickerson. Bimonthly magazine. Sub: $9. Circ: 12,000. Occasionally takes freelance material, mostly staff written. Pays: $.07 wd on publication. Rights acquired: 1st. Byline given. Submit ms, SASE. Dot matrix, photocopies, simultaneous submissions OK. Reports in 1 mo. Publishes in 6 mo. Accepts nonfiction on Alaska wildlife resources only. Photos: B&W $10-$25; color $25-$35; cover $100, back $50. Guidelines available. Sample/$2. Index: 4, 53, 92.

Alaska Fisherman's Journal/Ocean Leader, 1115 N.W. 46th Street, Seattle, WA 98107. 206–789–6506. Monthly. No submission info. Query w/SASE. Index: 4, 24, 53.

Alaska Flying Magazine, Pouch 112010, Anchorage, AK 99511. Editor: J.R. Lasley. 907–488–4345. Periodical. No submission info. Query w/SASE. Index: 4, 15, 120.

For lists of abbreviations and the key to index numbers, see "How to Use this Section" on page 77.

Alaska Geographic, Alaska Geographic Society, PO Box 93370, Anchorage, AK 99509. Editor: Penny Rennick. 907–563–1141. Quarterly. Circ. 20,000. Sub. $30 for membership in Alaska Geographic Society. Payment: Money on acceptance. Byline given. Rights purchased: 1st. Query w/SASE. Photocopies and simultaneous submission OK. Reports in 1 month. Nonfiction, photos. "Each issue devoted to specific topic, thus written proposals suggesting a topic are best initial approach. Mss are lengthy with finished issues ranging from 100-300 pages. Geography/natural resources in the broadest sense." Rates approx. $100 printed page. Photos: 35mm color. $100 full pg; $50 half pg; good captions with photos. No guidelines, but will answer letters promptly. Sample available. Index: 4, 88, 120.

Alaska Heritage Enterprises, 945 W. 12th Avenue, Anchorage, AK 99501. Publisher. No submission info. Query w/SASE. Index: 4, 64.

Alaska Historical Commission, Department of Education, 524 W. 4th Avenue, Suite 207, Anchorage, AK 99501. Publisher. No submission info. Query w/SASE. Index: 4, 43, 65.

Alaska History, Alaska Historical Society, PO Box 100299, Anchorage, AK 99510. 907–276–1596. Editor/ads: James H. Ducker. Sub. $5. Circ. 1,000. Publishes 2 softcover journals a yr. Accepts unsolicited/freelance mss Uses 3 per issue. Pay: Copies. Rights purchased: 1st. Byline given. Submit: Ms w/SASE. Dot matrix, photocopy OK. Reports in 2 mos. Publishes in 6 mos. Accepts: Nonfiction. Ed. hint: Photos and maps desired. Sample: $5. Index: 4, 62

Alaska Illustrated, 4341 MacAlister Dr., Anchorage, AK 99515. 970–243–1286. Editor: Kevin Cassity. Self-publishes 1-3 softcover Alaska, travel books a yr. Accepts freelance submissions. Payment terms vary. Submit query w/SASE. Dot matrix, photocopied, simultaneous OK. Reports in 4-6 wks. Publishing time varies. Accepts nonfiction and photos. Index: 4, 120.

Alaska Journal, Box EEE, Anchorage, AK 99509. Editor: Terrence Cole. Periodical. No submission info. Query w/SASE. Index: 4.

Alaska Journal of Commerce, 800 W. Fifth Ave., Ste. 410, Anchorage, AK 99501. 907–272–7500. Editor: S. J. Suddock. Ads: L. Brown. Weekly business newspaper. Sub. $49. Circ. 5,000. Uses 1-3 freelance mss per issue. Payment on publication, rates vary. Acquires 1st rights. Byline given. Submit by assignment only, SASE. Photocopied, computer disk w/hard copy OK. Reports in 2 wks. Publishing time varies. Accepts nonfiction, cartoons. Photos: B&W or color print. "Some travel features." Tips: press releases welcome. Samples available. Index: 4, 24, 42.

Alaska Magazine, Box 4005, Anchorage, AK 99509. Monthly on natural resources and non-urban life in Alaska/Western Canada. Circ. 150,000 to college educated readers, 35 and older. Payment: Money on acceptance. Byline given. Rights purchased: 1st. Submit ms w/SASE. Dot matrix OK. Publishes submissions in 4-12 mos. Non- fiction: 2,000 wds for $50-400. Photos: 35mm color, $25-$200 (cover). Sample $2. Index: 4, 106.

Alaska Medicine, 4107 Laurel Street, Anchorage, AK 99504. Editor: William Bowers, M.D. 907–562–2928. Periodical. No submission info. Query w/SASE. Index: 4, 61, 81.

Alaska Native Language Center, P.O. Box 900111, University of Alaska, Fairbanks, AK 99775-0120. 907–474–7874. Publishes 4-6 softcover orig. books a yr. No unsolicited mss. Circ. 1,000-2,000. "Scholarly publishing in and about Alaska's Native languages. Catalog/sample. Index: 4, 73, 108.

Alaska Native Magazine, PO Box 220230, Anchorage, AK 99522-0230. Not a freelance market. Index: 4, 87.

Alaska Natural History Association, 2525 Gambell, Anchorage, AK 99503. Publisher. No submission info. Query w/SASE. Index: 4, 88.

Alaska Northwest Publishing Company, 130 Second Avenue S., Edmonds, WA 98020. 206–774–4111. Editor: Ethel M Dassow. Circ. 2,000-10,000. Publishes 10-12 hard/soft/orig/reprints a yr. Accepts unsolicited mss. Query with clips/SASE. Accepts: Nonfiction. "From 50,000-100,000 wds informal prose re: history, geography, resources, people of Alaska, Canada, the Pacific Northwest states. Also 1st-person experience narratives, preferably upbeat and outdoor-oriented. Royalty: 10% of gross. *No* juveniles, poetry, fiction, politics, economics. Photos: B/W, color trans., B/W drawings. *No* sex, drugs, vulgarity, racism, psychological studies, explorations of physical or mental illness; no muckraking. Controversial material *must* explore all angles fairly." Guidelines/catalog available. Index: 2, 4, 7.

Alaska Nurse, Alaskan Nurses Association, 237 E. 3rd, Anchorage, AK 99501. Periodical. No submission info. Query w/SASE. Index: 4, 61, 81.

Alaska Outdoors, Box 6324, Anchorage, AK 99502. Editor: Christopher M. Batin. 907–276–2672. Periodical. No submission info. Query w/SASE. Index: 4, 92, 103.

Alaska Pacific University Press, 4101 University Drive, Anchorage, AK 99508. 907–564–8304. EditorAds: Jan Ingram. Publisher of 1-2 hard/soft books a yr. Accepts unsolicited submissions. Pay: royalties on publication. Rights acquired: All. Submit ms, SASE. Dot matrix, photocopies OK. Reports in 3 mo. Publishes in 1 yr. Accepts: nonfiction, fiction, poetry; with Alaskan focus, its people, places, and history. Book length determined by topic and information presented. Index 4, 62, 87.

Alaska Quarterly Review, Department of English, University of Alaska/Anchorage, 3221 Providence Drive, Anchorage, AK 99508. No submission info. Query w/SASE. Index: 31, 44, 76.

Alaska Review of Social & Economic Conditions, University of Alaska, 707 A. Street, Anchorage, AK 99501. Editor: Ronald Crowe. 907–278–4621. Periodical. No submission info. Query w/SASE. Index: 4, 42, 114.

Alaska the Magazine of Life on the Last Frontier, Box 4-EEE, Anchorage, AK 99509. Editor: Tom Gresham. 907–563–5100. No submission info. Query w/SASE. Index: 4.

Alaska State Writing Consortium, c/o Alaska Dept. of Education, PO Box F, Juneau, AK 99811. 907–465–2841. Editor: Annie Calkins. Annual journal. Sub. $5. Circ. 500. Accepts submissions from Alaskan teachers. Guidelines available. Sample $5. Index: 4, 43.

Alaska State Writing Consortium Newsletter, c/o Alaska Dept. of Education, PO Box F, Juneau, AK 99811. 907–564–2841. Editor: Annie Calkins. Bimonthly during August-May. Sub. $51 out of state. Circ. 1,100. Uses freelance material. Pays copies on publication. Byline given. Submit ms. Photocopied OK. Reports in 1-2 wks. Publishes in 1-2 mos. Accepts nonfiction, fiction, poetry, cartoons. Topics: "Writing across the curriculum, writers residencies with children and adolescents, computers and writing, ties between oral language and writing and reading." Index: 43, 125.

Alaska Today, Department of Journalism, University of Alaska/Fairbanks, Fairbanks, AK 99701. Periodical. No submission info. Query w/SASE. Index: 4, 31, 101.

Alaska Trails, 7624 Duben Avenue, Anchorage, AK 99504. Publisher. No submission info. Query w/SASE. Index: 4.

For lists of abbreviations and the key to index numbers, see "How to Use this Section" onpage 75.

Writer's Northwest Handbook   101

Alaskan Bowhunter, PO Box 190629, Anchorage, AK 99519-0629. Contact: Bill Nixom. No submission info. Query w/SASE. Index: 115.

Alaskan Byways, PO Box 211356, Anchorage, AK 99521. Editor: Lisa M. Short. Periodical. No submission info. Query w/SASE. Index: 4, 120.

Alaskan Viewpoint, HCR 64, Box 453, Seward, AK 99664. 907–288–3168. Editor: Lory B. Leary. Publisher of annual arts & crafts "who's who" and temporarily suspended monthly art newspaper, planned to be resumed in 1989. Query w/SASE. Index: 4, 10, 38.

Albany Democratic-Herald, Box 130, Albany, OR 97321. 503–926–2211. Daily newspaper. No submission info. Query w/SASE. Index: 33.

Alberni District Historical Society, PO Box 284, Port Alberni, BC V9Y 7M7. 604–723–3006. Publisher of the "occasional" soft/orig. book. Not a freelance market. Index: 18, 26, 33.

Alchemy, Portland Community College, 12000 S.W. 49th Ave., Portland, OR 97219. College literary magazine. Editor could change yearly. SASE for guidelines. Index: 31, 51, 91.

Alcoholism & Addiction Magazine, PO Box 31329, Seattle, WA 98103. 206–547–2217/800–252–6624. Editor: Neil Scott. Ads: Les Miller 800–342–6237. Bi-monthly magazine. Sub. $24. Circ. 30,000. Uses freelance material. Pays in copies. Acquires 1st rights. Byline given. Submit ms, SASE. Dot matrix, photocopied OK. Accepts nonfiction, fiction, poetry. Topics: addiction recovery–treatment/assistance programs, family dynamics, intervention, research, medical implications, legislation, etc. Tips: 850-2,000 word articles. Guidelines available. Sample $5. Index: 61, 100.

Alcoholism/The National Magazine, PO Box 19519, Seattle, WA 98109. Bimonthly. No submission info. Query w/SASE. Index: 61.

Aldrich Entomology Club Newsletter, University of Idaho, Department of Entomology, Moscow, ID 83843. Irregular periodical devoted to insects. No submission info. Query w/SASE. Index: 19, 31, 109.

Aleutian Eagle, PO Box 406, Dutch Harbor, AK 99692. 907–562–4684. Weekly newspaper. No submission info. Query w/SASE. Index: 33.

Alioth Press, PO Box 1554, Beaverton, OR, 97075. 503–644–0983. Editor: Mark Dominik. Publishes hardcover reprints. Does not accept unsolicited submissions. Index: 130.

Alive Books, 202-8592 Fraser Street, Vancouver, BC V5X 3Y3. Publisher. No submission info. Query w/SASE. Index: 130.

ALKI: The Washington Library Association Journal, The Library MS-84, Eastern Washington University, Cheney, WA 99004. 509–359–7893. Editor: V. Louise Saylor. Quarterly journal. Sub. $14. Circ. 1,200. Uses freelance material. Pays copies on publication. Byline given. Submit query w/clips, ms, phone. Dot matrix, photocopied, simultaneous, electronic/modem OK. Accepts nonfiction, photos, cartoons. Topics: libraries and all related issues for people concerned with libraries. Tips: 1,000-2,500 wds depending on topic. Photos: B&W glossy w/ captions. Guidelines & sample available. Index: 22, 55, 75.

The Alliance, PO Box 14742, Portland, OR 97214. Monthly of the Oregon Coalition of Alternative Human Services. News and views by/for progressive activists: political, environmental, feminist, and labor. No submission info. Query w/SASE. Index: 37, 50, 98.

Allied Arts Newsletter, P.O. Box 2584, Bellingham, WA 98227. 206–676–8548. Editor: Miriam Barnett. Circ. 500+. Sub. $15. Monthly newsletter. Accepts unsolicited/freelance mss No pay. Phone query OK. Photocopy OK. Reports in: 15th of the month. Accepts poetry, photos, cartoons. "Will print anything related to visual, performing, or literary arts." Index: 10, 86, 122.

Allied Arts of Seattle, 107 South Main, Room 201, Seattle, WA 98104. 206–624–0432. Publishes a newsletter 6 times a yr. "We are not publishers but we have published a few titles such as 'Art Deco', 'Impressions of Imagination:Terra Cotta Seattle', and 'Access to the Arts'." Index: 10.

Aloha Breeze, PO Box 588, Hillsboro, OR 97123. Weekly newspaper. No submission info. Query w/SASE. Index: 33.

Alternative Energy Resources Organization, 324 Fuller - C4, Helena, MT 59601. Publisher. No submission info. Query w/SASE. Index: 35.

Altitude Medical Publishing Company, 5624 Admiral Way, Seattle, WA 98116. No submission info. Query /SASE. Index: 61, 81.

Amadeus Press Inc., 9999 SW Wilshire, Portland, OR 97225. 503–292–0961. Editor: Richard Abel. Ads: Michael Fox. Publishes 10 music-related hardcover, originals, reprints per yr. Accepts unsolicited submissions. Acquires all rights. Submit query w/clips. Dot matrix, photocopied OK. Reports in 3-4 wks. Index: 86.

Amateur Brewer Information, PO Box 546, Portland, OR 97207. Publisher. No submission info. Query w/SASE. Index: 38.

Frank Amato Publications, PO Box 02112, Portland, OR 97202. Publishes hard/ softcover originals, reprints; also 2 fishing magazines. Accepts unsolicited submissions. Query w/clips, ms, SASE. "Interested in nonfiction book proposals–most subjects." Catalog available. Index: 53

American Dry Pea & Lentil Association Bulletin, PO Box 8566, Moscow, ID 83843. Editor: Harold Blain. Trade monthly. Circ. 350. No submission info. Query w/SASE. Index: 3, 24.

American Geographic Publishing, PO Box 5630, Helena, MT, 59604. Editor: Mark Thompson. 406–443–2842. Publishes *Montana Magazine*, regional photo books with text (15 in the Montana Series and seven other states). No submission info. Query w/SASE. Index: 59, 92, 95.

American Indian Basketry Magazine, PO Box 66124, Portland, OR 97266. Editor: John M. Gogol. 503–233–8131. Quarterly of photo-essays on Native American basketry and crafts. Interested in history, biography, artistic methods and materials used. Heavily dependent on quality photos. Tips: Thorough understanding of Native American arts and crafts is important. No submission info. Query w/SASE. Index: 38, 64, 87.

American Institute for Yemeni Studies, Portland State University, History Department, PO Box 751, Portland, OR 97207. Publisher. No submission info. Query w/SASE. Index: 31, 84.

American Rhododendron Society Journal, 17701 S.W. West View Rd., Lake Oswego, OR 97034. 503–653–2664. Editor: Adele Jones. Quarterly sent with membership in American Rhododendron Society. Sub. $20 mbr. Circ. 6,000. Uses several freelance mss per issue. No pay. Byline given. Submit ms, SASE. Phone query, dot matrix, photocopies, computer disc OK. Reports in 2-4 wks. Publishes usually within 1 yr. Looking for: rhododendron & azalea theme, all material is related to this interest. Guidelines available. Sample/$3. Index: 56.

American-Nepal Education Foundation, 2790 Cape Meares Loop, Tillamook, OR 97141. Contact: Hugh B. Wood. Publisher. No submission info. Query w/SASE. Index: 43, 84.

Americas Focus, 2000 S.W. 5th Avenue, Portland, OR, 97201. Editor: Donald Bassist. Periodical. No submission info. Query w/SASE. Index: 130.

For lists of abbreviations and the key to index numbers, see "How to Use this Section" on page 77.

102 Market Listings

Amity Publications, 78688 Sears Road, Cottage Grove, OR 97424. No submission info. Query w/SASE. Index: 130.

Ampersand Publishing, PO Box 943, Mukilteo, WA 98275. No submission info. Query w/SASE. Index: 130.

Amphora, The Alcuin Society, PO Box 3216, Vancouver, BC V6B 3X8. 604–688–2341. Quarterly newsletter. Sub. $24/yr. Cdn. Circ. 325. Accepts freelance material. No pay. Acquires 1st rights. Byline given. Submit ms, SASE. Dot matrix, photocopied OK. Publishes 1st issue w/available space. Accepts nonfiction, photos. Topics: book arts, calligraphy, book collecting, book binding, etc. Sample $5 Cdn. Index: 22.

Anaconda Leader, 121 Main Street, Anaconda, MT 59711. 406–563–5283. Biweekly newspaper. No sub. info. Query w/SASE. Index: 33.

Anacortes American, PO Box 39, Anacortes, WA 98221. 206–293–3122. Weekly newspaper. No sub. info. Query w/SASE. Index: 33.

Analysis and Outlook, PO Box 1167, Port Townsend, WA 98368. Editor: R.W. Bradford. Monthly. No submission info. Query w/SASE. Index: 130.

Ananse Press, PO Box 22565, Seattle, WA 98122. Publisher. No submission info. Query w/SASE. Index: 130.

ANC News, Alaska Native Coalition, c/o 310 K St., Suite 708, Anchorage, AK, 99501. Contact: Editor. Periodical. No submission info. Query w/SASE. Index: 130.

Anchorage Daily News, PO Box 149001, Anchorage, AK 99514-9001. 907–786–4200. Daily newspaper. No submission info. Query w/SASE. Index: 33.

Anchorage Times, PO Box 40, Anchorage, AK 99510. 907–263–9000. Daily newspaper. No submission info. Query w/SASE. Index: 33.

Angst World Library, 1160 Forest Creek Road, Selma, OR 97535. Publisher of fiction. No submission info. Query w/SASE. Index: 14, 51.

Anian Press, 1871 E. Pender Street, Vancouver, BC V5L 1W6. Publisher. No submission info. Query w/SASE. Index: 130.

Animal Aid, Animal Aid, Inc., 408 S.W. 2nd, Rm 318, Portland, OR 97204. Periodical. No submission info. Query w/SASE. Index: 6.

Animator, Oregon Art Institute, Northwest Film & Video Center, 1219 S.W. Park Avenue, Portland, OR 97205. Editor/Ads: Kathy Clark. 503–221–1156. Quarterly on film, video, public relations, media. Circ. 2,000. Sub. $6 individual, $10 institution. Payment: Copies on acceptance. Byline given. Submit ms w/SASE. Nonfiction, photos, cartoons. Sample available. Index: 10, 52, 122.

Ansal Press, 8620 Olympic View Drive, Edmonds, WA 98020. Publisher. No submission info. Query w/SASE. Index: 130.

The Antique Doorknob Publishing Company, 3900 Latimer Road N., Tillamook, OR 97141. No sub. info. Query w/SASE. Index: 130.

Antiques & Collectibles, 2776 Bourquin, Sta. 304, Box 8000, Abbotsford, BC V2S 6H1. Editors: Don & Kathy Wright. 604–852–3608. Periodical. No submission info. Query w/SASE. Index: 8, 30.

Antonson Publishing Ltd., 1615 Venable Street, Vancouver, BC V5L 2H1. No submission info. Query w/SASE. Index: 130.

Aozora Publishing, 131 Ash Street, PO Box 95, Myrtle Point, OR 97458. No submission info. Query w/SASE. Index: 130.

APA-EROS, Sylvia, c/o Correspan, PO Box 759, Veneta, OR, 97487. Contact: Editor. Bimonthly periodical. Accepts freelance material. Submit query w/clips, SASE. Accepts nonfiction, fiction, poetry, other. Sample $2. Index: 39, 45, 82.

Aperture Northwest Inc., PO Box 12065, Seattle, WA 98102. Contact: Richard K. Woltjer. Publisher of directories. Not a freelance market. Index: 1, 77.

Aphra Behn Press, 13625 S.W. 23rd, Beaverton, OR 97005. Contact: Suzanne Graham. 503–646–0471. Publisher of 1-2 nonfiction, softcover originals a yr. Press run: 500-5,000. Accepts freelance submissions. Payment: 8-12% royalties, on retail minimum price, with "average advance." Reports in 2 wks. Publishes in less than 1 yr. Query w/SASE. Dot matrix, photocopies and simultaneous submissions OK. Mss from 60,000 to 100,000 wrds on "popular science — technology — prefer medical, biological, engineering, cosmological, philosophical." Tips: "Informative, with self-help orientation, socio-economic commentary or philosophy of science." Index: 61, 81, 109.

Apostolic Book Publishers, 9643 N. Lombard, Portland, OR, 97203. Contact: Editor. Book publisher. No submission info. Query w/SASE. Index: 105.

Appaloosa Journal, Appaloosa Horse Club, Inc., PO Box 8403, Moscow, ID 83843. 208–882–5578. Editor: Betsy Lynch. Ads: Chris Olney. Sub $15. Circ. 15,000. Monthly. Accepts unsolicited mss on spec. Uses 2 freelance mss per issue. Pay: Money, copies on publication. Byline given. Submit query w/ clips & SASE. Dot matrix, photocopies OK. Reports in 6-8 wks. Accepts nonfiction, photos (5x7 or larger B/W glossies/color prints/color transparencies). Pays "$0-$300 depending on length, content, & presentation, illustrations & photos, and whether or not is audience-specific (relating to Appaloosa horses and their owner/trainers). Accepts training, breeding, health and management, human interest and personality profiles as they relate to the Appaloosa breed." Guidelines/sample: $2.50+$1 post. Index: 6, 103.

Apple Press, 5536 S.E. Harlow, Milwaukie, OR 97222. 503–659–2475. Editor: J. Majors. Publishes 8 health and travel related softcover originals per yr. Does not accept unsolicited submissions. Submit query w/SASE. Dot matrix, photocopied, simultaneous, electronic, computer disc OK. Reports in 4 wks. Publishes within 1 yr. Index: 61, 120.

Applegate Computer Enterprises, 470 Slagle Creek Road, Grants Pass, OR 97527. 503–846–6742. Self-publisher of 1 softcover book a yr on personal computers. Print run: 2,000. Not a freelance market. Catalog available. Index: 34.

Apropos Magazine, PO Box 1295, Bellingham, WA 98227. Monthly of health, beauty, fashions for women. Sub. $5/yr. No submission info. Query w/SASE. Index: 36, 49,124.

Arabian Horse Country, 4346 S.E. Division, Portland, OR 97206. Monthly. No submission info. Query w/SASE. Index: 6, 38, 103.

Arbutus Publications, Ltd., PO Box 35070, Sta. E, Vancouver, BC V6M 4G1. No submission info. Query w/SASE. Index: 130.

The Archer, 2285 Rogers Lane NW, Salem, OR 97304. 503–363–0712. Editor: Winifred Layton. Quarterly. Sub. $8. Circ. 200. Uses 45 freelance mss per issue. Pays copies on publication. Byline given. Submit ms, SASE. Reports in 1 month. Publishes in 6-12 mos. Poetry, not over 30 lines. Tips: "Be sure name, address are on each page. Tmany ignore this necessity!" Sample $2. Index: 97.

Arches, Office of Public Relations, University of Puget Sound, Tacoma, WA 98416. Editor: Gregory W. Brewis. Periodical. No submission info. Query w/SASE. 31.

For lists of abbreviations and the key to index numbers, see "How to Use this Section" on page 75.

Architectural Lighting, 859 Willamette St., PO Box 10460, Eugene, OR, 97440. 503–343–1200. Editor: Charles Linn. Ads: Robert Joudanin. Monthly Magazine. Sub. $49. Circ. 50,000. Uses freelance material. Pays copies, other. Acquires 1st rights. Byline given. Submit query w/clips, ms, phone. Dot matrix, electronic subs OK. Reports in 1-3 mos. Accepts nonfiction. Guidelines available. Sample $5. Index: 9.

The Archive Press, 2101 192nd Avenue S.E., Issaquah, WA 98027. Publisher. No submission info. Query w/SASE. Index: 130.

Arctic, Environmental Info & Data Center, University of Alaska, 707 A Street, Anchorage, AK 99501. Publisher. No submission info. Query w/ SASE. Index: 4, 88, 109.

Areopagitier Press, Inc., 9999 S.W. Wilshire, Portland, OR 97225. 503–292–0961. Editor: Richard Abel. Ads: Michael Fox. Publishes 4 hardcover original, reprint books a yr. Accepts unsolicited submissions. Acquires all rights. Submit query w/clips. Dot matrix, photocopied OK. Reports in 3-4 wks. Accepts history-related nonfiction. Index: 62, 64.

ARGOS GUIDELINES, Penrhyn Publishing, PO Box 2109, Renton, WA 98056. Contact: Editor. Periodical. No submission info. Query w/ SASE. Index: 130.

Argus Magazine, 2312 Third Avenue, Seattle, WA 98121. Editor: John S. Murray. 206–682–1212. Periodical. No submission info. Query w/ SASE. Index: 130.

Argus Observer, 1160 S.W. Fourth Street, Box 130, Ontario, OR 97914. 503–889–5387. Daily newspaper. No submission info. Query w/SASE. Index: 33.

Ariel Publications, 14417 S.E. 19th Place, Bellevue, WA 98007. No submission info. Query w/SASE. Index: 130.

Arlington Times, PO Box 67, Arlington, WA 98223. 206–435–5757. Weekly newspaper. No submission info. Query w/SASE. Index: 33.

ARMA Newsletter, 777 Pearl St., Eugene, OR, 97401. 503–687–5047. Editor: Karen Goldman. Irregularly published. No submission info. Query w/SASE. Index: 130.

Armory Publications, PO Box 44372, Tacoma, WA 98444. No submission info. Query w/SASE. Index: 130.

Arnazella's Reading List, Bellevue Community College, Bellevue, WA 98007. Literary magazine. Query w/SASE. Index: 31, 76.

Arrowood Press, Inc., PO Box 2100, Corvallis, OR 97339. 503–753–9539. Editor: Lex Runciman. Publisher of 1-2 hard/softcover books per year of general literary interest. Unspecified payment schedule. Query w/SASE before submitting. Nonfiction, fiction, poetry, plays. Index: 51, 77, 97.

Arsenal, Pulp Press Book Publishers, Ltd., Box 3868 MPO, Vancouver, BC V6B 3Z3. Contact: Tom Osborne. 604–687–4233. Publisher of 5-8 softcover originals per yr. Print run: 500-1,000. Payment: Royalties: 15% of net sales. Query w/SASE (Int'l reply coupon if from USA). Dot matrix, photocopies, simultaneous submissions and electronic OK. Reports in 2-3 mos. Publishes in 1-2 yrs. Non- fiction, fiction, poetry. "We specialize in short runs designed for a small, literary-oriented audience. We are open to most works which fall in the above 3 categories, with the exception of 'mass-market' designed mss." Catalog available w/SASE. Index: 23, 51, 97.

Art Gallery of Greater Victoria, 1040 Moss Street, Victoria, BC V8V 4P1. Publisher. Unspecified payment schedule. Nonfiction. Guidelines available. Index: 10.

Art West Magazine, PO Box 1799, Bozeman, MT 59715. Editor: Helori M. Graff. 406–586–5411. Bimonthly of wildlife and Western & American realism, aimed at collectors. Interested in historical as well as contemporary pieces. Uses photo-essays and profiles of artists, galleries and museums. Query w/SASE. Nonfiction, photos. Guidelines/sample available. Index: 10, 30, 62.

Artist Search, Montana Arts Council, New York Block, 48 N. Last Chance Gulch, Helena, MT 59620. 406–443–4338. Editor: Julie Cook. Monthly arts publication. Circ. 2,000. Accepts unsolicited/freelance mss. "This is a newsletter that includes space for artists to communicate with other artists. Very little poetry, fiction or essay publication." Index: 10, 85.

Artist Trust, 517 Jones Building, 1331 Third Ave., Seattle, WA, 98101. 206–467–8734. Contact: David Mendoza. Not-for-profit foundation, quarterly journal of information by, for, and about individual artists in all medias in Washington State. Index: 10, 39, 122.

Artists Notes, Lane Regional Arts Council, 411 High St., Eugene, OR, 97401. 503–485–2278. Editors: K. Wagner, D. Beauchamp. Monthly periodical. Sub. $20-29. No submission info. Query w/SASE. Index: 10.

Artoonist, 4620 SW Beaverton-Hillsdale Hwy. Ste. B1, Portland, OR 97221. New periodical. Articles, cartoons. No submission info. Query w/ SASE. Index: 68.

Arts B.C., Cultural Services Branch, Parliament Building, Victoria, BC, V8V 1X4. Editor: Dawn Wallace. Quarterly periodical. No submission info. Query w/SASE. Index: 10.

Arts & Crafts News, Burnaby Arts Council, 6450 Gilpin Street, Burnaby, BC V5G 2J3. Editor: Laura Jacobson. Quarterly of news and articles "concerning the arts and craft making and marketing." Circ. 10,000. Byline given. Phone query. Dot matrix, simultaneous submissions OK. Nonfiction. Tips: "We are non-profit. Although we accept articles gladly, we cannot offer payment." Sample available. Index: 10, 23, 38.

The Arts, King County Arts Commission, 828 Alaska Building, Seattle, WA 98104. Editor/Ads: Joan Mann. 206–344–7580. Monthly newsletter of the King County Arts Commission. "We welcome articles, photographs, drawings, but such material must be accompanied by a SASE." Index: 10, 39, 123.

The Arts Council of Southern Oregon Newsletter, 236 E. Main, Ashland, OR, 97520. 503–482–5594. Editor: Gregory N. Leiber. Periodical. Circ. 8,000. No submission info. Query w/SASE. Index: 10, 33.

Arts East, Eastern Oregon Regional Arts Council, RSI House, Eastern Oregon State College, LaGrande, OR 97850. 1–800–452–8639 x1624. Editor: Anne Bell. Accepts unsolicited/freelance mss. No pay. Byline given. Dot matrix, photocopy OK. Accepts nonfiction, poetry, photos, cartoons. "Arts East is a newsletter concerned with art-related events, programs and profiles in Eastern Oregon, SE Washington and West Idaho. There is occasional need for freelance pieces. Sample. Index: 10, 31.

J. Arvidson Press, PO Box 4022, Helena, MT 59601. Publisher. No submission info. Query w/SASE. Index: 130.

ASA Publications, 6001 6th Avenue S., Seattle, WA 98108-3307. No submission info. Query w/SASE. Index: 130.

For lists of abbreviations and the key to index numbers, see "How to Use this Section" on page 77.

104   Market Listings

Ascii, PO Box 222, Eagle River, AK 99577. Publisher. No submission info. Query w/SASE. Index: 130.

Asia Cable, 1248 S.W. Larch, Portland, OR, 97034. Editor: John Vezmar. Periodical. No submission info. Query w/SASE. Index: 130.

Asian Music Publications, School of Music, University of Washington, Seattle, WA 98105. No submission info. Query w/SASE. Index: 11, 31, 86.

AOI News Digest, Associated Oregon Industries, 1149 Court N.E., Salem, OR 97301. Monthly. No submission info. Query w/SASE. Index: 24, 91.

Associated Press, 1320 S.W. Broadway, Portland, OR 97201. 503–228–2169. News bureau. No submission info. Query w/SASE. Index: 130.

Associated Publications, Inc., P.O. Box 13390, Portland, OR 97213. 503–287–6115. Dealer magazine for small engine outdoor power equipment. Editor: Victor Graf. Ads: Donn Lawty. Circ. 22,000. Sub.: $9yr., $15/2 yr. Accepts unsolicited/freelance mss. "No consumer/user-oriented articles please!" Pays money on acceptance, $5/photo, more for specialized, high-quality or color. Byline given. Submit ms w/SASE. Dot matrix, photocopied, simultaneous, computer disk OK. Reports in 1 month. Accepts nonfiction, photos (B/W glossy, 3x5 or larger). Sample: $1+post. Index: 117.

The Asterisk, Oregon Press Women, Inc., PO Box 25354, Portland, OR, 97225-0354. Editor: Jean C. Connolly. Quarterly newspaper for prize-winning high school journalists & photographers.. No submission info. Query w/SASE. Sample $2. Index: 28, 29, 116.

Astrology Night, Oregon Astrological Association, PO Box 6771, Portland, OR 97228. Periodical. No submission info. Query w/SASE. Index: 13, 24.

Astrology West Magazine, 9513 S.W. Barbur Boulevard, #120, Portland, OR, 97219. Editor: Richard Rogers. Periodical. No submission info. Query w/SASE. Index: 13.

Athena Press, 431 E. Main, Box 597, Athena, OR 97813. 503–566–3452. Weekly newspaper. No submission info. Query w/SASE. Index: 33.

Ray Atkeson, 1675 S.W. Westwood Drive, Portland, OR, 97201. Contact: Editor. Publisher. No submission info. Query w/SASE. Index: 130.

Auto and Flat Glass Journal, PO Box 12099, Seattle, WA 98102-0099. 206–223–0861. Trade monthly. No submission info. Query w/SASE. Index: 24.

Auto Trader, PO Box 23369, Tigard, OR, 97223. 503–244–2886. Contact: Editor. Weekly periodical. Does not use freelance material. Index: 36.

Automotive Retailer, 1687 W. Broadway, #302, Vancouver, BC V6J 1X5. Editor: Donald C. Dingwall. 604–731–2108. Trade periodical. No submission info. Query w/SASE. Index: 24.

Automotive News of the Pacific Northwest, 14789 S.E. 82 Dr., Clackamas, OR, 97015-9624. Editor: Bradley A. Boyer. Monthly periodical. No submission info. Query w/SASE. Index: 36.

Aviation News, Oregon Aeronautics Division, 3040 25th Street S.E., Salem, OR, 97310. 503–378–4880. Editor: Ann Snyder. Periodical. No submission info. Query w/SASE. Index: 15.

Axis, Western States Chiropractic College, 2900 N.E. 132nd, Portland, OR 97230. 503–256–3180. Newspaper. No submission info. Query w/SASE. Index: 61, 81.

Azure Press, PO Box 2164, 2417 Beacon Avenue, No. 3, Sidney, BC V8L 3S6. Publisher. No submission info. Query w/SASE. Index: 130.

Baby, Creative Services International, 1920 Broadway, Vancouver, WA 98660. Editor: Mike Weber. 206–696–1150. Periodical. No submission info. Query w/SASE. Index: 130.

Back Door Travel, 120 4th Avenue N., Edmonds, WA 98020. Editor: Mike McGregor. 206–771–8303. Quarterly on budget travel, "helping people to travel as 'temporary locals'... interested in personal accounts about meeting people, traveling on a budget, discovering new places." Circ. 6,000. Sub. free. Uses 2-3 mss per issue. Payment: Copies. Byline given. Rights purchased: 1st, 2nd, 3rd. Query with ms, SASE. Dot matrix, photocopies, simultaneous submissions OK. Nonfiction, poetry, photos, cartoons. "Articles should be practical, how-to, destination-oriented travel pieces...Our readers range from just planning a first trip to just returning from the tenth trip. Information about alternate modes of travel (bicycle, trekking) are welcome." Sample: Free. Index: 120.

Backbone: A Journal of Women's Lit, PO Box 95315, Seattle, WA, 98145. Editor: Lauren Fortune. Periodical. No submission info. Query w/SASE. Index: 77, 124.

Backeddy Books, PO Box 301, Cambridge, ID 83610. Publisher. No submission info. Query w/SASE. Index: 130.

Backlash, 4128 Fremont Ave. N., Seattle, WA, 98103. 206–547–9669. Editor: Dawn Anderson. Bimonthly periodical. No submission info. Query w/SASE. Index: 130.

Backwater Press, 7438 S.E. 40th, Mercer Island, WA 98040. Publisher. No submission info. Query w/SASE. Index: 130.

Bainbridge Review, PO Box 10817, Bainbridge Island, WA 98110. 206–842–6613. Weekly newspaper. No submission info. Query w/SASE. Index: 33.

Baker Democrat-Herald, PO Box 807, Baker, OR 97814. Editor: Gary Middleton. 503–523–3673. Ads: Susan Truscott. Daily newspaper. Circ. 3,500. Sub. $50. 25% of each issue is freelance. Payment: $.50 per col/inch on publication. Byline given. Rights purchased: 1st. Query w/ms, SASE. Photocopies OK. Nonfiction, photos. Sample: Regular rate + postage. Index: 33, 65, 103.

Balcom Books, 320 Bawden Street, No. 401, Ketchikan, AK 99901. Publisher. No submission info. Query w/SASE. Index: 130.

Ballard News-Tribune, 2208 N.W. Market, Seattle, WA 98017. 206–783–1244. Weekly newspaper. No submission info. Query w/SASE. Index: 33.

Bandon Historical Society, PO Box 737, Bandon, OR 97411. Historical publisher on Bandon, Oregon and environs. Index: 65.

Bandon Western World, Box 248, Bandon, OR 97411. 503–347–2423. Weekly newspaper. No submission info. Query w/SASE. Index: 33.

Barbarian Press, 12375 Ainsworth Road, R.R. #5, Mission, BC V2V 5X4. 604–826–8089. Editors: Jan & Crispin Elsted. Publishes 3 hard/

For lists of abbreviations and the key to index numbers, see "How to Use this Section" on page 75.

Writer's Northwest Handbook   105

softcover original, reprint books a yr. Accepts unsolicited submissions. Pay in copies on publication. Submit query w/clips, ms, SASE. Dot matrix, photocopied OK. Reports in 6 wks. Publishing time variable. Accepts nonfiction, poetry, translations. Topics: "Strong interest in block printing, especially wood engraving. We print limited edition books, so do not have wide distribution. Our emphasis is on quality of production & text." Photos–suitable graphic media for letterpress. Index: 77, 97.

Barclay Press, 600 E. 3rd Street, Newberg, OR 97132. Publisher. No submission info. Query w/SASE. Index: 130.

Bardavon Books, PO Box 1378, Ashland, OR, 97520. 503–773–7035. Publisher. No submission info. Query w/SASE. Index: 130.

Barleycorn Books, 290 S.W. Tualatin Loop, West Linn, OR 97068. Publisher. No submission info. Query w/SASE. Index: 130.

Barlow Press, P.O. Box 5403, Helena, MT 59604. 406–449–7310. Editor: Russell B. Hill. Circ. 500-1,000. Publishes 2 soft/orig./reprint books a yr. Accepts unsolicited mss. Pays by arrangement. Submit query w/clips, ms, SASE. Dot matrix, photocopies, simultaneous, computer disk OK. Reports in 2 mo. Publishes by arrangement. Accepts nonfiction, fiction, poetry. "Especially interested in traditional fiction set in the modern or historic Northwest; also interested in nonfiction compilations of letters, diaries, clippings, journals, etc. from the Northwest." Has published both letterpress and offset titles. Guidelines/sample. Index: 22, 51, 85.

Barometer, Western Wood Products Association, 1500 Yeon Bldg., Portland, OR 97204. Weekly which publishes statistical reports. Not a freelance market. Index: 1, 24.

Bassett & Brush, W. 4108 Francis Avenue, Spokane, WA 99205. Publisher. No submission info. Query w/SASE. Index: 130.

Marlene Y. Bastian, 24042 NE Treehill Dr., Troutdale, OR 97060. 503–669–7800. Self-publisher of 1 softcover book. Not a freelance market. Index: 36, 67.

Maryanne Bauer Productions, PO Box 02467, Portland, OR 97202. Publisher. No submission info. Query w/SASE. Index: 103.

Bay Press, 914 Alaskan Way, Seattle, WA 98104. 206–447–1871. Editor: Thatcher Bailey. Publishes 3-6 art and cultural criticism books per yr. Press run 5,000. Pays 5%/cover/advance and payments twice yearly. Reports in 4 wks. Publishes within 1 yr. Submit query, SASE. Dot matrix, photocopied OK. Accepts nonfiction. Topics focus on contemporary arts criticism and conceptual art projects. Catalog available. Index: 10.

Bay Side Publishing & Printing, 9629 Evergreen Way, Everett, WA., 98204. 206–353–7388. Publisher. No submission info. Query w/SASE. Index: 130.

Bayless Enterprises Inc., 427 9th North, Seattle, WA 98109. Contact: George Bayless. 206–622–6395. Self-publisher of two softcover maritime books per yr. Print run: 7,500. Not a freelance market. Index: 65, 79, 103.

BCS Educational Aids, Inc., PO Box 100, Bothell, WA 98206. Publisher. No submission info. Query w/SASE. Index: 43.

Beacon, Southwest Oregon Community College, Coos Bay, OR 97420. 503–888–2525 x304. Editor: John Nolan. College literary magazine. Editor could change yearly. SASE for guidelines. Index: 31, 51, 91.

Beacon, University of Portland, 5000 N. Willamette Blvd., Portland, OR 97203. 503–283–7376. Newspaper. No pay. Byline given. Query w/ SASE. Opinion pieces for editorial page and articles on entertainment in the Portland area considered. Preference given to students and faculty. Query w/SASE. Index: 31, 43, 45.

Beacon Hill News, 2720 S. Hanford Street, Seattle, WA 98144. 206–723–1300. Weekly newspaper. No submission info. Query w/SASE. Index 33.

Beacon Hill Press of Seattle, 1845 41st Avenue E., Seattle, WA 98112. Publisher. No submission info. Query w/SASE. Index: 130.

Bear Creek Publications, 2507 Minor Avenue E., Seattle, WA 98102. Editor: Kathy Shea. Publisher of 1-2 nonfiction, softcover originals per year for parents/expectant parents. Press run: 2,000. Accepts freelance material. Query with outline, sample chapters, SASE. Photocopies, simultaneous sub.s' OK. Reports in 1 month. Publishes in 6 mos. Payment and rights negotiable. Index: 47, 67.

The Bear Facts, The Citizens' Utility Board of Oregon, 2637 S.W. Water, Portland, OR 97201. 503–227–1984. Consumer affairs periodical. No submission info. Query w/SASE. Index: 36, 91.

Bear Tribe Publishing, PO Box 9176, Spokane, WA 99209. 509–326–6561. No submission info. Query w/SASE. Index: 130.

The Bear Wallow Publishing Company, High Valley Foothill Road, Union, OR 97883. 503–562–5687. Editor: Jerry Gildermeister. Publisher of 1 hardcover, nonfiction book a yr. Print run 5,000-10,000. Does not accept unsolicited submissions. Index: 5, 62, 90.

Beartooth Networks, Inc., Box 1742, Billings, MT, 59103. Editor: Lee Lemke. Publisher. No submission info. Query w/SASE. Index: 130.

Beautiful America Publishing Company, P.O. Box 646, Wilsonville, OR 97070. 503–682–0173. Contact: Beverly Paul. Ads: Carla Laurent. Publisher of 12 hard/softcover books per yr. No unsolicited mss. Pay: Copies, royalties, advance on acceptance. Rights purchased: 1st. Byline given. Submit query w/ clips. Accepts nonfiction, poetry, photos (color or B/W). Sample. Index: 62, 87, 120.

Beautiful British Columbia, 929 Ellery Street, Victoria, BC V9A 7B4. Editor: Bryan McGill. 604–384–5456. Periodical. No submission info. Query w/SASE. Index: 23.

Beaver Briefs, Willamette Valley Genealogical Society, PO Box 2083, Salem, OR 97308. Quarterly. No submission info. Query w/SASE. Index: 58, 91.

Beaver Publications, 15605 N.W. Cornell Road, Beaverton, OR 97006. Publisher. No submission info. Query w/SASE. Index: 130.

Beaverton Arts Commission Newsletter, 12500 S.W. Allen Blvd., Beaverton, OR 97005-4727. 503–644–2191. Index: 10.

Beaverton Business Advocate, Beaverton Area Chamber of Commerce, 4800 S.W. Griffith Drive #100, Beaverton, OR 97005. Editor: Jerri Doctor. 503–644–0123. Periodical. No submission info. Query w/SASE. Index: 24.

Bedous Press, PO Box K, Beaverton, OR 97075. Publisher. No submission info. Query w/SASE. Index: 130.

Beef Industry News, Oregon Cattlemens Association, 400 S.W. Broadway, Portland, OR 97205. 503–281–3811. Periodical. No submission info. Query w/SASE. Index: 3, 24, 91.

Before the Sun, PO Box 14007, Salem, OR 97309. 503–399–5184. Periodical. Circ. 400. Sub. $2.95. Byline given. Rights purchased: 1st. Query

For lists of abbreviations and the key to index numbers, see "How to Use this Section" on page 77.

106   Market Listings

w/SASE. Dot matrix, photocopies OK. Nonfiction, fiction, poetry, plays, cartoons, other reproducable artwork. "Topics range anywhere from science fiction to political essays. Our main objective is to provide a variety of mss that could be read by anyone. Length not to exceed 3,000 wds with 1,500 the average." Photos: high contrast B&W. "We'd like to see BTS on a waiting room table. Stories should be short/clean." Sample: $2.95. Index: 41, 51, 97.

Beginning Press, 5418 S. Brandon, Seattle, WA 98118. 206–723–6300. Publishes 3 softcover original books a yr. Press run: avg. 6,000. Does not accept unsolicited submissions. Index: 36, 61, 105.

Bellevue Art Museum, 10310 N.E. 4th Street, Bellevue, WA 98004. Publisher. No submission info. Query w/SASE. Index: 10.

Bellevue Journal-American, 4339 134th Place S.E., Bellevue, WA, 98004. 206–641–4130. Editor: Joanne Kotker. Periodical. No submission info. Query w/SASE. Index: 130.

Bellingham Herald, 1155 North State Street, PO Box 1277, Bellingham, WA 98227. 206–676–2600. Daily newspaper. No submission info. Query w/SASE. Index: 33.

The Bellingham Review, The Signpost Press, PO Box 4065, Bellingham, WA 98227. 206–734–9781. Editor: Shelley Rosen. Semiannual magazine of poetry, drama, art, fiction. Sub $4. Circ. 800. Pay: 1 copy + sub on publication. Byline given. Query, SASE. Photocopy, simultaneous submission OK. Reports in 2 wks -3 mo. Publishes in up to 1 yr. Accepts nonfiction, fiction, poetry, photos, plays, reviews. Sample/$2. Index: 41, 51, 97.

Bellowing Ark, PO Box 45637, Seattle, WA 98145. 206–545–8302. Editor: Robert R. Ward. Bimonthly. Sub. $12. Circ. 1,000. Uses about 30 mss per issue. Pays in copies. Byline given. Submit ms, SASE. Publishes in 2-4 mo. Accepts nonfiction, fiction poetry. Topics: "literary works in the American Romantic tradition, ie., think of Roethke, Whittier, Emerson, Lindsay. Mostly poetry, fiction and serializations...but other forms sometimes used (plays, essays). Some short autobiography used for "Literal Lives" section...we do not hesitate to publish newcomers if the work is right." Sample $2. Index: 51, 97.

Bellowing Ark Press, PO Box 45637, Seattle, WA 98145. 206–545–8302. Editor: Robert R. Ward. Publishes 2-4 softcover original books a yr. Press run usually 1,000. Not accepting unsolicited submissions at present. Pays royalties. Publishes fiction, poetry. Index: 51, 97.

Bench Press, 3100 Evergreen Point Road, Bellevue, WA 98004. Publisher. No submission info. Query w/SASE. Index: 130.

Ben-Simon Publications, PO Box 318, Brentwood Bay, BC, V0S 1A0. Contact: Editor. Publishes 1-2 hard/softcover originals, reprints a yr. Press run: 1,000-3,000. Accepts unsolicited submissions. Submit query, sample chap., SASE. Dot matrix, photocopied OK. Reports ASAP. Accepts nonfiction. Catalog available. Index: 130.

Benton Bulletin, Box 351, Philomath, OR 97370. 503–929–3043. Weekly newspaper. No submission info. Query w/SASE. Index: 33.

Berry Fine Publishing Company, 5963 Walina SE, Salem, OR 97301. Publisher. No submission info. Query w/SASE. Index: 130.

Berry Patch Press, 3350 N.W. Luray Terrace, Portland, OR 97210. Publisher. No submission info. Query w/SASE. Index: 130.

Bethel Publications, Route 1, Box 1, Lyons, OR 97358. Publisher. No submission info. Query w/SASE. Index: 130.

Beynch Press Publishing Co., 1928 S.E. Ladd Ave., Portland, OR 97214. 503–232–0433. Contact: Alyce Cornyn-Selby. Publishes 2 softcover books a yr. on communication. Not a freelance market. Index: 24, 100.

Beyond Words Publishing Inc., Pumpkin Ridge Rd., Rt. 3, Box 492B, Hillsboro, OR 97123. 503–647–0140. Editor: Cynthia Black. Publishes 5-10 hard/softcover books a yr. Accepts unsolicited submissions. Payment negotiated, on publication. Acquires all rights. Submit query w/clips, SASE, phone. Mac computer disk OK. Reports in 3 mos. Publishes in 6 mos. Accepts nonfiction, fiction, photos, children's. Topics: self-help, New Age. Index: 61, 95.

Bible Temple Publications, 7545 N.E. Glisan Street, Portland, OR 97213. Publisher. No submission info. Query w/SASE. Index: 105.

Bicentennial Era Enterprises, PO Box 1148, Scappoose, OR 97056. 503–684–3937. Self-publisher of softcover books. Not a freelance market. Index: 42, 60, 98.

The Bicycle Paper, PO Box 842, Seattle, WA 98111. Editor: Barclay Kruse. 206–329–7894. Ads: Peggy Steward. 206–827–6339. Bimonthly of general interest on bicycling. Circ. 4,000. Sub. $4.50. Unspecified payment schedule. Guidelines/SASE. Index: 16, 115.

Big Sky Business Journal, PO Box 3263, Billings, MT, 59103. Editor: Evelyn Pyburn. Newspaper. No submission info. Query w/SASE. Index: 24.

The Big Timber Pioneer, PO Box 190, Big Timber, MT, 59011. Editor: Becky Oberly. Newspaper. No submission info. Query w/SASE. Index: 130.

Bigfork Eagle, 5299 Montana Hwy 35, Bigfork, MT, 59911. 406–837–5131. Contact: Editor. Newspaper. No submission info. Query w/SASE. Index: 33.

Bigoni Books, 4121 N.E. Highland, Portland, OR 97211. No submission info. Query w/SASE. Index: 130.

BikeReport, PO Box 8308, Missoula, MT 59801. Editor: Daniel D'Ambrosio. 406–721–1776. Published 9 times a year for touring bicyclists. Circ. 18,000. Sub. $22. Uses 9 mss per issue. Payment: Money, copies on publication. Byline given. Rights purchased: 1st. Query with ms, SASE. Dot matrix, photocopies OK. Nonfiction, fiction, cartoons. "We like imaginative pieces that use cycling as a starting point to investigate or reveal other topics." They could include anything relating to tours in the USA, foreign countries, or any essay with cycling as a theme. Guidelines available; sample/$1. Index: 16, 51, 120.

Bilingual Books, Inc., Outdoor Empire Publishing, 511 Eastlake Avenue E., Seattle, WA 98109. No submission info. Query w/SASE. Index: 17, 73.

Billings City Reader, 1348 Main, Suite 104, Billings, MT, 59105. Editor: Cathie Dorweiler. Newspaper. No submission info. Query w/SASE. Index: 33.

The Billings Gazette, PO Box 2507, Billings, MT, 59103. Arts Editor: Christine Meyers. Newspaper. No submission info. Query w/SASE. Index: 33.

For lists of abbreviations and the key to index numbers, see "How to Use this Section" onpage 75.

The Billings Times, 2919 Montana Ave., Billings, MT, 59101. Contact: Editor. Newspaper. No submission info. Query w/SASE. Index: 33.

Binford & Mort Publishing, Box 42368, Portland, OR 97242. Contact: Pauly Gardenier. 503–221–0866. Publisher of 10-12 hard/softcover books and reprints per year on themes of Western Americana, history, biography, travel, recreation and reference. Payment: variable advance to established authors; 10% royalties. Query w/SASE. Dot matrix OK. Reports in 2-4 mos. Publishes in 1 yr. Nonfiction, on above themes, with emphasis on NW/Pacific Coast. Fiction: only if heavily historical. Index: 18, 65, 103.

Bingo Today, Dart Publishing, Inc., 616 - 222nd Place N.E., Redmond, WA 98053. 206–868–2962. Ads: Rim Miksys. Biweekly for bingo players/managers. Circ. 20,000. Not a freelance market. Index: 45, 103.

Bioenergy Bulletin, Bonneville Power Administration, PO Box 3621, Portland, OR, 97208-3621. Editor: Tom White. Bimonthly periodical. No submission info. Query w/SASE. Index: 60.

Bippity-Boppity Books, 915 W. 12th, Spokane, WA, 99204. Book Publisher. No submission info. Query w/SASE. Index: 130.

Birds' Meadow Publishing Company, Inc., 1150 N. Olson Road, Coupeville, WA 98239. No submission info. Query w/SASE. Index: 130.

Birkworks Publishing, PO Box 883, Helena, MT, 59624. Editor: Jeff Birkby. Publisher. No submission info. Query w/SASE. Index: 130.

Bitter Root Valley Historical Newsletter, Bitter Root Valley Historical Society, Hamilton, MT, 59840. Contact: Editor. Quarterly. No submission info. Query w/SASE. Index: 65.

Black Current Press, Gutenberg Dump, PO Box 1149, Haines, AK, 99827. Book Publisher. No submission info. Query w/SASE. Index: 97.

Black Heron Press, PO Box 95676, Seattle, WA 98145. 206–523–2637. Contact: Jerry Gold. Publisher of 2 hard/softcover fiction books per yr. Press run 500-5,000. Accepts unsolicited mss. Pays royalties. Submit ms w/SASE. Dot matrix, photocopies, simultaneous OK. Reports in 2-4 mo. Publishes in 1 yr. Accepts nonfiction, fiction. "Any topic, but must be emotionally moving without being sentimental, or can be intellectually stimulating." Catalog $1.25. Index: 51, 77, 83.

Black on Black, Northcity Press, PO Box 55021, Seattle, WA, 98155. Periodical. No submission info. Query w/SASE. Index: 20.

Black Powder Times, PO Box 842, Mount Vernon, WA 98273. 206–336–2969. For black powder firearms enthusiasts. No submission info. Query w/SASE. Index: 38, 103, 115.

Black Sheep Newsletter, 1690 Butler Creek Rd., Ashland, OR 97520. 503–482–5901. Editor: Kent Erskine. Ads: Dona Zimmerman. Quarterly about animal fiber raising and use of animal fibers. Circ. 2500. Sub. $10/yr. Accepts freelance mss. Pays copies on publication. Rights purchased: 1st. Byline given. Submit ms. Dot matrix, photocopies OK. Accepts nonfiction, photos (B/W & color). Sample $2.50. Index: 6, 38.

Blackfish Books, 1851 Moore Avenue, Burnaby, BC. No submission info. Query w/SASE. Index: 130.

Blatant Image: a Magazine of Feminist Photography, 2000 King Mountain Trail, Sunny Valley, OR, 97497-9799. Irregular periodical. No submission info. Query w/SASE. Index: 50, 95.

Blind John Publications, 2740 Onyx Street, Eugene, OR 97403. No submission info. Query w/SASE. Index: 130.

BLM News, Oregon & Washington, Bureau of Land Management, PO Box 2965, Portland, OR, 97208. 503–231–6275. Editor: Jeanne Glenn. Periodical. No submission info. Query w/SASE. Index: 55, 60, 101.

The Bloodletter, Friends of Mystery, PO Box 8251, Portland, OR 97207. Editor: Debbara Hendrix. Newsletter published 3-5 times a yr. Circ. 500. Accepts unsolicited freelance material. Byline given. Photocopied OK. Accepts nonfiction, cartoons. Topics: "any aspect of mystery." Sample available. Index: 51.

Blow, Grey Whale Productions, 4820 S.E. Boise, Portland, OR, 97206. Editor: Karol Ann Kleinheksel. Periodical. No submission info. Query w/SASE. Index: 130.

Blue Begonia Press, 225 S. 15th Avenue, Yakima, WA 98902. 509–452–9748. Editor: Jim Bodeen. A fine hand letterpress publisher/printer of poetry originals. Press run: 250-300. Accepts poetry for two books per yr. "We don't encourage submissions. There's tmuch to do as it is. We're not interested in adding another book to a poet's resume...A manuscript needs to be important enough for one person working nights to want to do it by hand." Pays in copies on publication. Query w/SASE. Catalog and samples available. Index: 97.

Blue Heron Press (Books), **Microaccess** (Newsletter), PO Box 5182, Bellingham, WA 98227. 206–671–1155. Contact: Mitch Lesoing/Carol Anderson. Publisher of 3 softcover books a yr. No unsolicited mss. Query with clips, SASE. Reports in 6-8 wks. Publishes in 6-12 mos. Accepts nonfiction, fiction, photos. Topics: computer education materials, children's books, outdoor recreation (boating, hiking, fishing). "Stock photos & graphics sometimes purchased at std. rates." Index: 29, 34, 103.

Blue Heron Publishing, Inc., Rt. 3, Box 376, Hillsboro, OR 97124. 503–621–3911. Contact: Dennis Stovall, Linny Stovall. Publishes writing related books under Media Weavers imprint (*Writer's Northwest Handbook* and *Writer's NW*, a quarterly newspaper). Publishes the Walt Morey Adventure Library (reprints from the author of *Gentle Ben*). Interested in doing other reprints of young adult fiction. Query w/SASE. Index: 29, 51, 125.

Blue Mountain Eagle, 741 W. Main Street, Box 69, John Day, OR 97845. 503–575–0710. Weekly newspaper. No submission info. Query w/SASE. Index: 33.

Blue Raven Publishing, PO Box 5641, Bellevue, WA 98006. 206–643–2203. No submission info. Query w/SASE. Index: 130.

Blue Scarab Press, 234 S. 8th St., Pocatello, ID, 83201. Editor: Harald Wyndham. Publisher. No submission info. Query w/SASE. Index: 130.

Bluespaper, 3438 SE Caruthers St., Portland, OR 97214. 503–231–5605. Editor: Mark Goldfarb. Quarterly. Sub. free. Circ. 10,000. No submission info. Query w/SASE. Index: 86, 89.

Bluestocking Books, 1732 32nd Avenue, Seattle, WA 98122. No submission info. Query w/SASE. Index: 130.

The Boag Foundation Ltd., 576 Keith Road, West Vancouver, BC V7T 1L7. Publishes socialist books on social and historical topics. Query w/SASE. Index: 64, 112, 113.

Boating News, 26 Coal Harbour Wharf, 566 Cardero Street, Vancouver, BC V6G 2W6. Periodical. No submission info. Query w/SASE. Index: 21, 92, 103.

For lists of abbreviations and the key to index numbers, see "How to Use this Section" on page 77.

Bob Book Publishers, 22910 Bland Circle, West Linn, OR, 97068. Editor: Bobby Lynn Maslen. Publisher. No submission info. Query w/SASE. Index: 130.

Boise Business Today, Boise Chamber of Commerce, PO Box 2368, Boise, ID 83701. Editor: Lee Campbell. Monthly devoted to issues of interest to the Boise area business community. No submission info. Query w/SASE. Index: 24, 69.

Boise Cascade Quarterly, Boise Cascade Corporation, One Jefferson Square, Boise, ID 83728. Editor: Don Hicks. Corporate quarterly. Circ. 100,000. No submission info. Query w/SASE. Index: 24.

Boise Idaho Register, PO Box 2835, Boise, ID 83701. Newspaper. No submission info. Query w/SASE. Index: 33.

Boise Magazine–Idaho Annual Inc., 211 W. State St., Boise, ID 83702. 208–344–4642. Editor: Alan Minskoff. Ads: Diana Henderson. Bi-monthly. Sub. $12.95. Circ. 5,000. Uses freelance material. Pays money on publication. Acquires 1st rights. Byline given. Query w/clips. Photo-copied, computer disc OK. Reports in 4-6 wks. Publishing time varies. Accepts nonfiction, fiction, poetry, photos, cartoons. Topics: city/regional, not connected with any government. Guidelines available. Sample $2.50. Index: 33, 51, 97.

BSU Focus, Boise State University, 1910 University Drive, Boise, ID 83725. 208–385–1577. Editor: Larry Burke. Quarterly magazine. Circ. 43,000. Accepts unsolicited/freelance mss. Pays money on publication. Rights purchased: 1st. Byline given. Query w/ clips. Dot matrix, photo-copy, simultaneous, etc. OK. Reports in 1 wk. Publishes in 3-4 mos. Accepts nonfiction, many topics. Sample. Index: 31.

BSU/Search, Boise State University, 1910 University Drive, Boise, ID 83725. Editor: Larry Burke. Semiannual. Circ. 1,000. No submission info. Query w/SASE. Index: 31.

Boise State University Western Writers Series, Department of English, Boise State University, 1910 University Drive, Boise, ID 83725. Contact: James H. Maguire. 208–385–1246. Publisher of 5 nonfiction, softcover books per year of "critical introductions to the lives and works of authors who have made a significant contribution to the literature of the American West." Print run: 1,000. "Those who write for us are usually members of the Western Literature Association or read the association's journal, *Western American Literature*." No pay. Rights purchased: All. Query w/SASE. Photocopies OK. Reports in 1 month. Publishes in 5-10 yrs. Guide & catalog available. Index: 18, 31, 76.

Bold Brass Studios & Publications, PO Box 77101, Vancouver, BC V5R 5T4. No submission info. Query w/SASE. Index: 130.

Bonanza Publishing, 62560 Stenkamp Rd., Bend, OR, 97701. Editor: Rick Steber. Book publisher, hard/softcover. Press run: 5,000-10,000. Does not accept unsolicited submissions. Index: 130.

Book Production Associates, Box 3289, Portland, OR 97208. Contact: Beth Howell/Dick Mort. 503–281–4486. Short run self-publisher of softcover books in most categories. No unsolicited mss; query. Dot matrix, photocopies & modem OK. Index: 102.

The Book Shop/Children's Newsletter, The Book Shop, 908 Main Street, Boise, ID 83702. Editor/Ads: Lori Benton. 208–342–2659. Biannual newsletter reviewing new children's titles, mostly read by parents, teachers, and librarians. Circ. 250. Sub. free. Uses 2 mss per issue. Byline given. Query with ms, SASE. Phone queries, photocopies OK. "We are interested in book reviews only. Copy should be limited to seven paragraphs." Guidelines and sample available. Index: 29, 76.

Bookletter Newsletter, Bookloft, 107 E. Main St., Enterprise, OR, 97828. Periodical. No submission info. Query w/SASE. Index: 22.

Bookmark, Library, University of Idaho, Moscow, ID 83843. Editors: Richard Beck & Gail Eckwright. Semiannual periodical. Circ. 1,000. No submission info. Query w/SASE. Index: 22, 76, 77.

BookNotes, PO Box 555, West Linn, OR 97068. 503–233–2637. Editor: Cliff Martin. Quarterly provides marketing help for small publishers, self-publishers. Not a freelance market. Sample $5. Index: 24, 102, 125.

Boredom Magazine, PO Box 85817, Seattle, WA, 98145. Editor: Patrick McCabe. Periodical. No submission info. Query w/SASE. Index: 130.

Botany Books, 1518 Hayward Ave., Bremerton, WA 98310. 206–377–6489. Self-publisher of softcover books. Accepts no mss. Index: 56, 67.

Bottom Line Press, 3247 63rd Avenue S.W., Seattle, WA 98116. No submission info. Query w/SASE. Index. 130.

Bowen Island Historians, R.R. 1, Bowen Island, BC V0N 1G0. Publisher. No submission info. Query w/SASE. Index: 64.

Box Dog Press, PO Box 9609, Seattle, WA, 98121. 206–454–4078. Contact: Editor. Publishes softcover books. Press run: 40-100. Accepts unsolicited submissions. Reports in 4 wks. Accepts fiction, poetry, photos, cartoons. Catalog available. Index: 51, 68, 97.

Bozeman Chronicle, 32 S. Rouse, Bozeman, MT, 59715. 406–587–4491. Editor: Rob Dean. Daily newspaper. No submission info. Query w/ SASE. Index: 33.

Braemar Books, PO Box 25296, Portland, OR 97225. 503–292–4226. Self- publisher of 1 softcover book per year for record collectors, music stores, radio stations. Print run: 500. Not a freelance market. Index: 30, 77, 86.

The Bread and Butter Chronicles, Seven Buffaloes Press, PO Box 249, Big Timber, MT 59011. Editor: Art Cuelho. Semiannual with essays and columns on contemporary American farmers and ranchers. Sub. $2.50. No submission info. Query w/SASE. Sample: $1 SASE. Index: 3, 85, 89.

Breitenbush Publications, PO Box 02137, Portland, OR 97202. Contact: Paul Merchant. 503–230–1900. Publisher of 5–10 hard/softcover originals and reprints per yr. Payment: Royalties. Query with outline, sample chapters, SASE. Photocopies OK. Reports in 3 mos. Publishes in 1-2 yrs. Accepts nonfiction: "Human interest. No travel guides. Nothing over 250 pages." Fiction: "Author must be represented in magazines. 250-300 page limit." Poetry (currently accepting few poetry mss): "Author must have significant exposure in magazines before book publication." Tips: "Breitenbush has a full schedule. Please query first." Catalog available $1. Index: 51, 97.

Bremerton Sun, 545 Fifth Street, PO Box 259, Bremerton, WA 98310. 206–377–3711. Daily newspaper. No submission info. Query w/SASE. Index: 33.

Brewster Quad-City Herald, PO Box 37, Brewster, WA 98812. 509–689–2507. Weekly newspaper. No submission info. Query w/SASE. Index: 33.

Bricolage, c/o Creative Writing Office, Department of English, GN-30, University of Washington, Seattle, WA 98195. Periodical. No submission info. Query w/SASE. Index: 31.

For lists of abbreviations and the key to index numbers, see "How to Use this Section" on page 75.

Writer's Northwest Handbook   109

Bridge Tender, 9070 S.W. Rambler Lane, Portland, OR 97223. Quarterly. No submission info. Query w/SASE. Index: 130.

The Bridge, Danish American Heritage Society, 29672 Dane Lane, Junction City, OR, 97448. Editor: Arnold N. Bodtker. Semiannual periodical. No submission info. Query w/SASE. Index: 65, 84.

The Bridge, Portland Community College, 12000 S.W. 49th, Portland, OR 97219. 504–244–6111. Editor: Po Smith. Ads: Chris Mootham. Newspaper published 32 times a yr. Uses freelance material. Pays $.50/column inch on publication. Acquires 1st rights. Byline given. Query w/clips, SASE. Dot matrix OK. Accepts nonfiction, photos. Topics: consumerism, entertainment, computers. Photos: B&W only, $10 on publication. Sample for postage. Index: 31, 34, 36.

Bright Ring Publishing, PO Box 5768-MW, Bellingham, WA 98227. Contact: Mary Ann F. Kohl. 206–733–0722. Publisher of 1 softcover children's book per yr. Press run: 2,000-5,000. Payment: Royalties. Query with ms, SASE. Dot matrix, photocopies, simultaneous submissions, electronic OK. Reports in 6 wks. Publishes in 1 yr. Nonfiction, fiction, photos, illustrations. "Prefer works that work as children's picture books, teacher's how-to books, or parent/teacher activity books...all respecting the child as a creative, unique individual. Length: 128-160 pages for activity books, multiples of 8 for picture books. Topics: art, drama, music, independent creative activity for kids...Anything that involves copying adult models or following detailed directions would not appeal to our philosophy." No guidelines but personal response guaranteed w/SASE. Index: 29, 43.

B.C. Bookworld, 940 Station St., Vancouver, B.C. V6A 2X4. 604–684–2470. Editor: Alan Twigg. Circ. 40,000. Sub. $2/issue. A tabloid newspaper, "with new stories about books and authors related to B.C." Accepts unsolicited/freelance mss. Pays money on publication. Rights purchased: None. Byline given. Submit: ms w/SASE. Photocopy OK. Accepts nonfiction, photos (photos necessary). Hints: "Keep it educational & brief & true." Index: 22, 23, 125.

B.C. Business Magazine, 550 Burrard Street, Vancouver, BC V6C 2J6. Editor: R.A. Murray. 604–669–1721. No submission info. Query w/SASE. Index: 23, 24.

B.C. Farmways, RR #1, Old Salmon Arm Road, Enderby, BC V0E 1V0. Periodical. No submission info. Query w/SASE. Index: 3, 23.

British Columbia Genealogical Society, PO Box 94371, Richmond, BC V6Y 2A8. Publisher. No submission info. Query w/SASE. Index: 23, 58.

B.C. Historical News, Box 35326, Station E., Vancouver, BC V6M 4G5. Quarterly. No submission info. Query w/SASE. Index: 23, 63, 65.

B.C. Hotelman, 124 W. 8th Street, North Vancouver, BC V7M 3H2. Editor: Vivian Rudd. 604–985–8711. Periodical. No submission info. Query w/SASE. Index: 23, 24.

BCIT Link, B.C. Institute of Technology, 3700 Willingdon Avenue, Burnaby, BC V5G 3H2. 604–434–5734. Periodical. No submission info. Query w/SASE. Index: 31.

British Columbia Library Association Newsletter, 883 W. 8th Ave., Vancouver, BC, V5Z 1E3. Contact: Editor. Periodical. No submission info. Query w/SASE. Index: 104.

B.C. Lumberman Magazine, Box 34080, Station D, Vancouver, BC V6J 4M8. No submission info. Query w/SASE. Index: 23, 24, 78.

The British Columbia Medical Journal, 115-1665 W. Broadway, Vancouver, BC V6J 5A4. 604–736–5551. Editor: W. Alan Dodd, MD. Ads: Doug Davison. Monthly professional journal. Sub $30. Circ 6,600. Freelance ms accepted. No pay. Byline given. Submit ms. Computer disc OK. Accepts medical/medically-related/ scientific articles — 2,500 wds. Photos: 5x7 B&W glossy. Sample/ $4. Index: 81, 119.

British Columbia Monthly, PO Box 4884, Bentall Station, Vancouver, BC V7X 1A8. Monthly literary publication. Index: 14, 51.

B.C. Naturalist, 100-1200 Hornby Street, Vancouver, BC V6Z 2E2. Editor: Dick Stace-Smith. 604–687–3333. Periodical. No submission info. Query w/SASE. Index: 35, 88, 109.

B.C. Orchardist, #3-1115 Gordon, Kelowna, BC V1Y 3E3. Editor: Ron Wade. 604–763–1544. Periodical. No submission info. Query w/SASE. Index: 3, 23, 24.

B.C. Outdoors, 202-1132 Hamilton Street, Vancouver, BC V6B 2S2. Editor: Henry L. Frew. 604–687–1581. Monthly magazine on outdoor subjects: hunting, fishing, conservation and other outdoor recreation in Western Canada. Nonfiction, photos. No submission info. Query w/SASE. Guidelines available. Index: 35, 63, 103.

B.C. Professional Engineer, 2210 W. 12th Avenue, Vancouver, BC V6K 2N6. Editor: Mike Painter. 604–736–9808. Periodical. No submission info. Query w/SASE. Index: 23, 24.

British Columbia Railway Historical Association, PO Box 114, Victoria, BC V8W 2M1. Self-publisher of softcover books on B.C. railway history. Print run: 3,000. Unspecified payment schedule. Rights purchased: All. Query with ms, SASE. Dot matrix, photocopies OK. Nonfiction, photos. Catalog available. Index: 38, 63, 103.

BC Studies, University of British Columbia, 2029 W. Mall, Vancouver, B.C. V6T 1W5. 604–228–3727. Editor: Prof. Allan Smith. Quarterly journal. Sub. $16. Circ. 900. Uses freelance material. No pay. Submit query w/clips. Dot matrix, photocopied OK. Reports in 1-3 mo. Publishes up to 1 yr. Accepts nonfiction: scholarly articles on any aspect of human history in B.C. Catalog, sample available. Index: 23, 108, 114.

B.C. Teacher, 105 2235 Burrard Street, Vancouver, BC V6J 3H9. Editor: Nancy Flodin. 604–731–8121. Periodical. No submission info. Query w/SASE. Index: 23, 43.

Broadsheet Publications, PO Box 616, McMinnville, OR 97128. Contact: Wilma Grand Chalmers. 503–472–5524. Self-publisher of 1 softcover book per year for adult music listeners. Not a freelance market. Index: 45, 86.

The Broadside, Central Oregon Community College, College Way, Bend, OR 97701. 503–382–2743. Newspaper. No submission info. Query w/SASE. Index: 31.

Broken Moon Press, 330 Del Monte Avenue, Tacoma, WA 98466. Publisher. No submission info. Query w/SASE. Index: 130.

Brooding Heron Press, Waldron Island, WA 98297. Publisher. No submission info. Query w/SASE. Index: 130.

Brown Penny Press, 18130 Hwy. 36, Blachly, OR 97412. Publisher. No submission info. Query w/SASE. Index: 130.

For lists of abbreviations and the key to index numbers, see "How to Use this Section" on page 77.

Brown's Business Reporter, PO Box 1376, Eugene, OR 97440. 503–345–8665. Editor: Dennis Hunt. Weekly newsletter. Sub. $45. Circ. 1,300. Uses 0-1 freelance mss per issue. No pay. Byline given. Dot matrix, photocopied, simultaneous, electronic, computer disc OK. Publishes in 2-3 wks. Accepts business "briefs," 150-300 wds. Sample, SASE. Index: 1, 24.

Brussels Sprout, Vandina Press, PO Box 1551, Mercer Island, WA 98040. 206–232–3239. Editor: Francine Porad. Brussels Sprout publishes a poetry journal 3 times/yr. Sub.: $11 U.S., $12 Canada, $15 others. Accepts unsolicited/freelance mss. "We look for haiku that captures the 'haiku moment' in a fresh way. Artwork featured in each issue, using 8-12 pieces from the one artist." No pay. Rights sought: 1st. Byline given. Submit ms w/SASE. Dot matrix, photocopy OK. Reports in 3-5 wks. Publishes in 3-5 mo. Accepts haiku, senryu. Guidelines available. Sample: $4 U.S., $5 Canada, $6 others. Index: 10, 97.

Buckman Voice, Buckman Community Association, 3534 S.E. Main, Portland, OR 97214. Periodical. No submission info. Query w/SASE. Index: 33.

Buckskin Press, Inc., PO Box 789, 220 McLeod Street, Big Timber, MT 59011. Publisher. No submission info. Query w/SASE. Index: 130.

Bugle, Rocky Mountain Elk Foundation, Route 3 Wilderness Plateau, Troy, MT 59935. Editor: Lance Schelvan. 406–295–5424. Ads: Bob Munson. Quarterly on elk conservation, hunting. Circ. 60,000. Sub. $12.50. Uses 4 mss per issue. Pays copies on publication. Byline given. Dot matrix, photocopies, simultaneous submissions OK. Reports in 30 days. Nonfiction, fiction, photos, cartoons. "Anything relating to elk: habitat, management, biology, hunting, art." Tips: "Will accept 'popular' articles of a more technical nature in addition to hunting stories." Photos: prefer 35mm transparencies. Sample $3. Index: 19, 35, 95.

Bulletin, Alaska State Council on the Arts, 619 Warehouse Avenue, Suite 200, Anchorage, AK 99501. Editor: Suzi Jones. 907–279–1558. Alaska arts news. No submission info. Query w/SASE. Index: 4, 10.

Bulletin, Genealogical Forum of Portland, Inc., 1410 S.W. Morrison, Ste. 812, Portland, OR, 97205. 503–227–2398. Editor: Ruth C. Bishop. Ads: Wilfred Burrell. Quarterly periodical. Sub. $15/mbr. Circ. 900. Uses freelance material. Submit ms, SASE. Reports in 8 wks. Accepts nonfiction, poetry, other. Sample $1/SASE. Index: 58.

Bulletin of the King Co. Medical Society, PO Box 10249, Bainbridge Island, WA 98110. 206–682–7813. Professional publication, 11 times per yr. No submission info. Query w/SASE. Index: 24, 61, 81.

The Bulletin, 1526 N.W. Hill Street, Bend, OR 97701. 503–382–1811. Daily newspaper. No submission info. Query w/SASE. Index: 33.

Burnaby Historical Society, 6719 Fulton Avenue, Burnaby, BC V5E 3G9. Contact: Una Carlson. Self-publisher of historical pieces on the Fraser River area. Not a freelance market. Index: 23, 65.

Burnaby Writers' Society Newsletter, 6450 Gilpin St., Burnaby, BC V5G 2J3, Canada. Editor: Eileen Kernaghan. Monthly membership newsletter. Index: 125.

Burns Times-Herald, 355 N. Broadway, Box 473, Burns, OR 97720. 503–573–2022. Weekly newspaper. No submission info. Query w/SASE. Index: 33.

Business Journal, Box 14490, Portland, OR 97214. Editor: Robert Fisher. 503–233–0074. Weekly periodical covering business in the greater Portland area. Circ. 10,500. Freelance market, buys 2-4 mss per issue. Payment: Money on publication. Query w/SASE. Phone query, dot matrix OK. Reports in 1-2 wks. Publishes in 2-6 wks. Nonfiction: 800-1,200 wds at $3 per published column inch on local business. Guidelines available w/SASE; sample: $1. Index: 24.

Business Magazine, 1920 Broadway Street, Vancouver, WA 98663. Editor: Scott Frangos. 206–696–1150. Ads: Francis Fisher. Bimonthly periodical. Circ. 3,500. Freelance market for photos only: need 4-color cover and feature photos. Rates negotiable. Index: 24, 42, 95.

Business Network News, Direct Media, 4755 SW Watson, Beaverton, OR, 97005. 503–295–4657. Contact: Editor. Monthly periodical. No submission info. Query w/SASE. Index: 24.

Business News, 220 Cottage NE, Salem, OR 97301. 503–581–1466. Editor: Jeff Marcoe. Biweekly periodical. Sub. $6. Circ. 1,350. Uses freelance material. Byline given. Submit by phone. Photocopied OK. Accepts nonfiction. Sample available. Index: 24, 42, 101.

Butter-Fat, PO Box 9100, Vancouver, BC V6B 4G4. 604–420–6611. Editor: Grace Hahn. Ads: Carol Paulson. Monthly magazine for dairy industry. Sub. $8/yr. Circ. 4,000. Accepts freelance material by assignment only. Byline given. Index: 3, 24.

Buttermilk Road Press, 5210 Butterworth, Mercer Island, WA 98040. 206–232–1267. Editor: Amos L. Wood. Self-publisher of originals. Index: 65, 89, 103.

Butterworth Legal Publications, 15014 NE 40th St., Ste. 205, Redmond, WA 98052-5325. 206–881–3900. Editor: Ray Krontz. Publishes hard/softcover, looseleaf books. Accepts unsolicited submissions. Nonfiction: books and services for lawyers and others in the legal community, primarily treatises, practice manuals, and rule or statute compilations. Authors are compensated by means of negotiated royalties. Publishes state-specific titles for OR, WA, & AK. Proposals for national titles are passed on to Publishing Director in Massachusetts. Index: 72, 74.

Byline, Rogue Community College, 3345 Redwoods Hwy., Grants Pass, OR 97526. 503–479–5541. Contact: Editor. College newspaper. Index: 31.

Cache Valley Newsletter, Rt. 3 Box 273, Preston, ID 83263. Editor: Newell Hart. Monthly. Circ. 400. No submission info. Query w/SASE. Index: 33.

Cain-Lockhart Press, PO Box 1129, 19510 SE 51st St., Issaquah, WA 98027. 206–392–0508. Self-publisher of two softcover books a year. Not a freelance market. Index: 11, 73, 120.

Calapooia Publications, 27006 Gap Road, Brownsville, OR 97348. Contact: Margaret Carey/Patricia Hainline. 503–466–5208 or 503–369–2439. Publishers of regional histories, not presently accepting mss. Catalog available. Query w/SASE. Index: 65.

Calapooya Collage, Western Oregon State College, Monmouth, OR 97316. 503–838–1220. Editor: Thomas Ferte. Annual literary journal produced and written by the staff and students, but including works and articles by noted professional writers and other non-students. Circulated nationally. Published Aug. 1. Accepts freelance material. Pays in copies. "All submissions must be typed ds, and accompanied by a SASE." Nonfiction, fiction: 1,700 wds. Poetry: any type, length. Sponsor of the annual $700 Carolyn Kizer Poetry Awards. Index: 31, 76, 97.

Call - A.P.P.L.E., 290 S.W. 43rd, Renton, WA 98052. 206–251–5222. Editor: Kathryn Hallgrimson Suther. Ads: Dave Morton. Monthly com-

For lists of abbreviations and the key to index numbers, see "How to Use this Section" on page 75.

Writer's Northwest Handbook   111

puter-related magazine. Sub. $21. Uses freelance material. Pays money on publication. Acquires 1st rights. Byline given. Electronic submissions OK. Accepts nonfiction, fiction, photos. Topics: GS hardware & programming; Apple II programming, tutorial, applications. Guidelines available. Sample $3. Index: 34.

Callboard, Box 114, Victoria, BC V8W 2M1. Annual. Accepts freelance material. Byline given. Rights purchased: All. Submit ms w/SASE. Dot matrix, photocopies OK. Nonfiction, photos w/article. Sample available. Index: 65.

Calyx, A Journal of Art & Literature by Women, PO Box B, Corvallis, OR 97339. 503–753–9384. EditorAds: M. Donnelly. Published 3 times a yr. Sub. $18. Circ: 2,500. Most articles by freelance writers. Pays copies on publication, money when grants allow. Byline given. Submit ms w/ SASE. Dot matrix, photocopies, simultaneous submissions OK. Reports in up to 6 mo. Publishes in 3 mo. Accepts fiction, poetry, photos, art, book reviews, essays, interviews; work by women — fine literature and art. Guidelines available. Sample $6.50 + $1.25 S&H. Index: 10, 51, 77.

Calyx, Inc.: Calyx Books, PO Box B, Corvallis, OR 97339. 503–753–9384 or 503–753–3110. Editor/Ads: Margarita Donnelly. Publisher of 4 hard/softcover original books by women. Print run 1,500-10,000. No unsolicited submissions. Pays royalties. Dot matrix, photocopies, computer disc OK. Reports in 1 yr. Publishes in 1-2 yrs. Accepts fiction, poetry, art. Topics: fine literature & art by women. Catalog available. Index: 51, 77, 124.

Camas-Washougal Post-Record, PO Box 1013, Camas, WA 98607. 206–834–2141. Weekly newspaper. No submission info. Query w/SASE. Index: 33.

Camp Denali Publishing, PO Box 67, McKinley Park, AK 99755. No submission info. Query w/SASE. Index: 130.

Campbell's Publishing Ltd., 1150 Rockland Avenue #210, Victoria, BC V8V 3H7. Contact: Betty Campbell. Publisher of NW travel guides. No submission info. Query w/SASE. Index: 89, 120.

Campus Magazine, W. 827 25th Ave., Spokane, WA, 99203. Contact: Editor. Free periodical. No submission info. Query w/SASE. Index: 31.

Canada Poultryman, 605 Royal Avenue, New Westminster, BC V3M 1J4. Editor: Anthony Greaves. 604–526–8525. Trade periodical. No submission info. Query w/SASE. Index: 3, 6, 24.

Canadian Aquaculture Magazine, 4611 William Head Road, Victoria, BC V8X 3W9. Editor: Peter Chettleburgh. 604–478–9209. Ads: Deirdre E. Probyn. Quarterly. Circ. 1,000. Sub. $14 (Cdn.). Uses 2-3 mss per issue. Payment: $.10 wd on publication. Byline given. Rights purchased: First. Query w/SASE. Phone query, dot matrix, photocopies, electronic OK. Nonfiction, photos, or drawings. Topics: "Readable profiles on fish farmers, processors and research facilities; technical, how-to articles; in-depth analysis of political and resource issues with a bearing on Canadian aquaculture industry." Guidelines available; sample/$3.50. Index: 3, 24, 35.

Canadian Biker Magazine, PO Box 4122, Sta. A, Victoria, BC V8X 3X4. 604–384–0333. Editor/Ads: W. L. Creed. Magazine, 8 issues/yr. Sub. $19.95/12 issues. Circ. 20,000. No submission info. Query w/SASE. Guidelines available. Sample $3.00. Index: 115.

Canadian Literature, Univ. of British Columbia, 2029 W. Mall, Rm. 223, Vancouver, B.C. V6T 1W5. 604–228–2780. Editor: W. H. New. Ads: B. Westbrook. Quarterly journal. Circ. 2,250. Rarely accepts unsolicited submissions. Pays in money, copies on publication. Acquires 1st rights. Query w/clips, SASE. Reports in 1 wk. Publishes in up to 2 yrs. Accepts poetry, criticism. For Canadian writers and writing; average 10 printed pages. $5 per printed page, $5 poems. Sample cost varies. Index: 31, 76, 97.

Canadian Press, 1445 W. 43rd Ave., Vancouver, BC, V6H 1C2. Contact: Editor. No submission info. Query w/SASE. Index: 130.

Canadian Truckers, 4250 Dawson Street, Burnaby, BC V5C 4B1. Trade periodical. No sub. info. Query w/SASE. Index: 24, 71.

Canadian West, PO Box 3399, Langley, BC V3A 4R7. 604–576–6561. Editor: Garnet Basque. Quarterly tabloid on pioneer history of B.C., Alberta and the Yukon. Sub. $12/yr. Circ. 8,000. Uses 4-5 freelance mss per issue. Pays 3-5 cents/word on publication. Acquires 1st rights. Byline given. Submit ms, SASE. Dot matrix, photocopied OK. Reports in 6-8 wks. Publishes as space available. Accepts nonfiction. Topics: historical–ghost towns, mining, lost treasure, Indians, shipwrecks, rocks, gems & bottles, robberies, battles, etc. "All articles should be accompanied by suitable artwork/photos. Factual accuracy is required". Guidelines available. Sample $4. Index: 23, 63, 90.

Canby Herald/North Willamette News, 241 N. Grant Street, Box 250, Canby, OR 97013. 503–266–6831. Weekly newspaper. No submission info. Query w/SASE. Index: 33.

Canho Enterprises, Box 937, Kelowna, BC V1Y 7P7. Contact: A. Davison. Publishes 2 softcover, original, educational, historical dramas annually. Print run: 5,000. Accepts freelance material. Payment: Money, 25 copies. Rights purchased: All. Query w/outline, SASE. "Must be easy, clear reading, researched and proofread. Do not send if going out to others." Reports in 1-2 mos. Publishes in 1-2 yrs. Nonfiction, plays. "Our book dramatizations are based on true life, are informative, and illustrated; are important on all school library shelves, some college level, but easy reading; are 'general interest' and Library of Congress card numbers; historically valuable in USA for all ages with new revelations." Catalog available. Index: 41, 43, 89.

Cannon Beach Gazette, 132 W. Second, Box 888, Cannon Beach, OR 97110. 503–436–2812. Biweekly newspaper. No submission info. Query w/SASE. Index: 33.

CANOE Magazine, PO Box 3146, Kirkland, WA, 98083. 206–827–6363. Editor: Dave Harrison. Ads: Glen Bernard. Bimonthly. Sub. $11.97. Circ. 55,000. Uses 15 freelance mss per issue. Pays money on publication. Acquires 1st, other rights. Byline given. Submit query w/clips, ms. Reports in 1 mo. Accepts nonfiction, photos. Guidelines available. Sample $3. Index: 92, 103.

Capilano Courier, Capilano College, 2055 Purcell Way, North Vancouver, BC V7H 3H5. Contact: News Coordinator. 604–986–1911. Ads: Imtiaz Popat. 604–980–7367. Biweekly. Circ. 2,000. Accepts freelance material. Byline given. No pay. Query w/SASE. Photocopies OK. Nonfiction, fiction, poetry, photos, cartoons. Topics: Education, student related issues. Guidelines/sample available. Index: 31, 43, 97.

The Capilano Review, 2055 Purcell Way, North Vancouver, BC V7J 3H5. Editor: Dorothy Jantzen. 604–986–1911. Quarterly literary and visual arts magazine, "publishing only what its editors consider to be the very best work being produced." Circ. 1,000. Sub. $12. Accepts freelance material. Payment: $40 maximum/$10 minimum and copies on publication. Byline given. Submit ms w/SASE. Photocopies, electronic OK. Reports in 6 mos. Fiction, poetry, photos, plays. "We are most interested in publishing artists whose work has not yet received the attention it deserves. We are not interested in imitative, derivative, or unfinished work. We have no format exclusions." Guidelines available; sample/$3. Index: 14, 31, 51.

Capital City Weekly, PO Box 2010, Juneau, AK 99803. 907–789–4144. Weekly newspaper. No sub. info. Query w/SASE. Index: 33.

For lists of abbreviations and the key to index numbers, see "How to Use this Section" on page 77.

112 Market Listings

Capital Press, Box 2048, Salem, OR 97308. Editors: K. Palke, C. Homan. 503–364–4431. Weekly newspaper of agriculture and forestry for "farmers, ranchers, small acreage producers and small woodlands owners." Circ. 30,000. Payment: Money on publication. Byline given. Rights purchased: First. Query w/SASE. Phone query, dot matrix OK. Reports in 1-2 wks. Publishes in 1-2 mos. Nonfiction: 10-20 column inches for 90 cents/inch, on ag, livestock and small woodlands. Photos: B&W glossies ($10) or color slides ($15). Index: 3, 55.

Capitol Hill Times, 2720 S. Hanford, Seattle, WA 98144-6599. 206–323–5777. Weekly newspaper. No submission info. Query w/SASE. Index: 33.

Cappis Press, Publishers, 1119 Oscar St., Victoria, BC V8V 2X3. 604–420–2580. Editor: Mary Hoel. Publishes 3 hard/softcover originals, subsidy books a yr. Press run: 5,000-10,000. Accepts some unsolicited submissions. Pays royalties on publication. Acquires all rights. Query w/ SASE. Photocopied, simultaneous OK. Reports in 3 wks. Accepts nonfiction. Catalog available. Index: 26, 46, 68.

Carefree Cooking Company, 1743 S.E. Spruce, Hillsboro, OR 97123. Publisher. No sub. info. Query w/SASE. Index: 38, 54, 67.

Carnot Press, PO Box 1544, Lake Oswego, OR 97034. No submission info. Query w/SASE. Index: 130.

Caronn's Town & Country with The Crib Sheet, 14109 N.E. 76th Street, Vancouver, WA 98662. Editor: Karen LaClergue. 206–892–3037. Monthly. Circ. 200. Sub. $10. Uses 15 mss per issue. Payment: Money and copies on publication. $5/500 wds and up; $2.50/below 500 wds. Photos & mss: $7.50. $2.50 inside cover. $5 cover photo. Byline given. Submit ms, SASE. Dot matrix, photocopies, simultaneous submissions, electronic OK. Reports in 5-6 wks. Nonfiction, fiction, poetry, photos, plays, cartoons. "For Town & Country portion: garden/plant tips & photos; decorating ideas & photos; remodeling ideas & photos. Crib Sheet portion: articles pertaining to childrearing. Also adult and juvenile fiction." Guidelines available; sample/$2. Index: 47, 51, 95.

Cascade Automotive Resources, 125 S.W. Wright Court, Troutdale, OR, 97060. Publisher. No submission info. Query w/SASE. Index: 130.

Cascade Farm Publishing Company, 21594 S. Springwater Road, Estacada, OR 97023. No submission info. Query w/SASE. Index: 130.

The Cascade Publishing Company, 3623 72nd Place S.E., Mercer Island, WA 98040. No submission info. Query w/SASE. Index: 130.

Cascades East, PO Box 5784, Bend, OR 97708. Editor/ads: Geoff Hill. 503–382–0127. Quarterly on recreation/general interest in Central Oregon. Circ. 9,000 (6,000 resort room copies). Sub. $8. Uses 6 mss per issue. Writers must be from the Central Oregon editorial area. Payment: $.03–.10 wd on publication. Byline given. Rights purchased: First. Submit ms, SASE. Photocopies OK. Reports in 6-8 wks. Nonfiction: 1,000–2,000 wds. Photos: B&W glossy/color prints or transparencies, $8 to $50. Guidelines available; sample/$2.50. Index: 33, 65, 92.

Cashmere Record, PO Box N, Cashmere, WA 98815. 509–782–3781. Weekly newspaper. No submission info. Query w/SASE. Index: 33.

Castalia Publishing Company, PO Box 1587, Eugene, OR 97440. 503–343–4433. Contact: Scot Patterson. Publisher of 2–3 hard/softcover books a year. Print run 2,000-5,000. No unsolicited mss. Pays royalties, advance. Rights purchased: All. Reports in 3 mo. Publishes in 1yr. Psychology textbooks & books on childrearing issues for parents. Materials are research-based. Catalog available. Index: 47, 100, 108.

CATALYST, McKettner Publishing, PO Box 85777, Seattle, WA 98145. Editors: M. & Kathleen Kettner. 206–523–4480. Literature magazine published 2-3 times a year; special issues of erotica. Subscription: $7 for 3 issues. 75% of each issue is freelance. Submit ms w/SASE. Buys one time rights. Byline given. Pays in copies. Accepts fiction, poetry, photos, cartoons and B&W art. "Open to all types of material, lean toward modern/experimental. Translations welcome. No length limits on poetry. Prose up to 10,000 wds." Samples available: *2nd Erotica*, $2, & *Mary Jane*, $3. Index: 51, 97, 111.

Catalytic Publications, 2711 E. Beaver Lake Drive S.E., Issaquah, WA 98027. 206–392–2723. Self-publisher of educational materials. Not a freelance market. Index: 43.

Catchline, Ski Business News, Drawer 5007, Bend, OR 97708. Trade periodical. No submission info. Query w/SASE. Index: 24, 115.

Catholic Sentinel, PO Box 18030, Portland, OR 97218. Newspaper. No submission info. Query w/SASE. Index: 105.

The Caxton Printers Ltd., 312 Main Street, Caldwell, ID 83605. 208–459–7421. Editor: Gordon Gipson. Publishes 6-10 nonfiction, hard/softcover original books a yr. on Western Americana only. Query, SASE. Accepts unsolicited submissions. Index: 5, 65.

CBA Bulletin, Citizen's Bar Association, PO Box 935, Medford, OR, 97501. Contact: Editor. Periodical. No submission info. Query w/SASE. Index: 74.

CCLAM Chowder, Shoreline Community College Library, 16101 Greenwood Ave. N., Seattle, WA, 98133. Contact: John Backes. Librarian newsletter. No submission info. Query w/SASE. Index: 31, 104.

CCW Publications, 3401 N.E. 11th Street, Renton, WA 98056. 206–228–8707. Publisher of 2 softcover books a year. Print run: 2,000. Not a freelance market. Catalog available. Index: 13, 43, 94.

Cedar Island Press, PO Box 113, West Linn, OR 97068. 503–636–7914. Self-publisher of 1 softcover original per year. Not a freelance market. Index: 54.

Celestial Gems, 404 State Street, Centralia, WA 98531. Contact: Gypsy Al Coolidge. Publisher. No submission info. Query w/SASE. Index: 130.

Center for East Asian Studies, Western Washington University, Bellingham, WA 98225. Publisher. No submission info. Query w/SASE. Index: 11, 31.

Center for Pacific Northwest Studies, Western Washington University, Bellingham, WA 98225. 206–647–4776. Contact: Dr. James W. Scott. Publisher of 1-2 softcover original books a yr. Print run: 750-1,000. Does not generally accept freelance material. Academic works on the Pacific NW, usually by resident faculty and graduate students. Catalog available. Index: 31, 89.

Center for Urban Education, 1135 S.E. Salmon, Portland, OR 97214-3628. Publisher of media directory & educational materials for non-profit groups. No submission info. Query w/SASE. Index: 43, 77, 80.

The Center Press, 14902 33rd Avenue N.W., Gig Harbor, WA 98335. 206–858–3064. No submission info. Query w/SASE. Index: 130.

Centerplace Publishing Co., PO Box 901, Lake Oswego, Or 97034. 503–636–8710 or 800–96–CHILD. Editor: Paul J. Lyons. Publisher of softcover parenting related/children's books. Accepts unsolicited mss. Pays on publication. Rights acquired: first. Query w/clips. Dot matrix,

For lists of abbreviations and the key to index numbers, see "How to Use this Section" on page 75.

Writer's Northwest Handbook 113

computer disc, OK. Reports in 2 wks. Publishes in 3 mo. Do all design/coordinate illustrations. "We focus on practical, how-to information for parents and children on self-improvement and improvement of relationships." Index: 29, 47, 100.

Central America Update, PO Box 6443, Portland, OR 97228. Editor: Millie Thayer. 503–227–5102. Periodical of "analytical feature articles on movements for social change and USA policy in Central America and on issues facing the solidarity movement." Circ. 1,500. Sub. $5/year. Uses 1 ms per issue. Payment: Copies. Byline given. Phone query, dot matrix, photocopies OK. Nonfiction, photos (B&W of local Central America related events). Sample $.25. Index: 84, 93, 98.

Central County Press, PO Box 1528, Silverdale, WA 98383. 206–692–9042. Weekly newspaper. No sub. info. Query w/SASE. Index: 33.

Central Idaho Magazine, Rt 2, Box 797, Grangeville, ID, 83530. Periodical. No submission info. Query w/SASE. Index: 69.

Central Kitsap Reporter, PO Box 1935, Silverdale, WA 98383. (PO Box 11651, Bainbridge Island, WA 98110.) 206–692–7008. Editor: James Busch. Ads: Jennie Cooley. Sub $12. Circ 17,000. Weekly newspaper. Accepts 2-3 freelance mss per issue. Pay: $5-$10 per story, depending; $10 per B&W print, any size; on acceptance. Byline given. Submit: ms, SASE. Reports in 1 mo. Accepts nonfiction, photos, cartoons. Index: 33.

Central Oregonian, 558 N. Main, Prineville, OR 97754. 503–447–6205. Semiweekly newspaper. No sub. info. Query w/SASE. Index: 33.

Centre Publications, 2000 W. 12th Avenue, Vancouver, BC, V6J 2G2. Contact: Editor. Publisher. No submission info. Query w/SASE. Index: 130.

Ceramic Scope, 3632 Ashworth N., Seattle, WA, 98103. Editor: Michael Scott. Periodical. Uses freelance material. Pays money on publication. Submit query w/clips, SASE. Accepts nonfiction. Index: 38.

"CETUS" The Journal of Whales, Porpoises & Dolphins, The Whale Museum, PO Box 945, Friday Harbor, WA 98250. Editor/ads: Jill Schropp. 206–378–4710. Semiannual journal which is "a peer-reviewed journal of cetology designed to give scientists and the public in-depth information." Circ. 2,000. Sub. membership. Uses 6 mss per issue. Payment: $.10 wd up to $250 on publication. Byline given. Rights purchased: First. Query w/ms, SASE. Dot matrix, photocopies, electronic OK. Nonfiction, photos, graphics, charts. Topics: biology, acoustics, behavior, ecology, politics, economics, history. 300-3,000 wds. Guidelines and sample available (for current newsstand price). Index: 6, 88, 109.

CGA Magazine, 1176 West Georgia, Suite 740, Vancouver, BC V6E 4A2. 604–669–3555. Monthly for accountants. No submission info. Query w/SASE. Index: 24.

Chain Saw Age, PO Box 13390, Portland, OR, 97213. 503–287–6115. Editor: Victor Graf. Ads: Ken Morrison. Monthly periodical. Sub. $9. Circ. 19,000. Uses 1-2 freelance mss per issue. Pays money on publication. Acquires 1st rights. Byline given. Submit ms. Photocopied OK. Accepts nonfiction, photos. Sample free. Index: 24, 92.

Channel Town Press, PO Box 575, LaConner, WA 98257. 206–466–3315. Weekly newspaper. No sub. info. Query w/SASE. Index: 33.

Chanticleer, Box 647, Lumby, BC V0E 2G0. Editor: Lynne Cormack. 604–547–6086. Published 10 times a year. Circ. 300. Sub. $5. Accepts freelance material. Payment: Copies. Submit ms, SASE. Dot matrix, photocopies, simultaneous submissions, electronic OK. Reports in 4 wks. Nonfiction, fiction, poetry. Topics: "General, good taste, suitable for family reading. Contemporary as well as material of traditional nature. Max 2,000 wds." Sample available/SASE. Index: 47, 51, 97.

Chelan Valley Mirror, PO Box 249, Chelan, WA 98816. 509–682–2213. Weekly newspaper. No submission info. Query w/SASE. Index: 33.

Chess International, 2905–B 10th St., Everett, WA, 98201-1462. 206–355–1816. Editor: Robert A. Karch. Chess correspondence dir., $15. No submission info. Query w/SASE. Index: 45.

The Chewalah Independent, PO Box 5, Chewalah, WA 99109. 509–935–8422. Weekly newspaper. No sub. info. Query w/SASE. Index: 33.

Childbirth Education Association, 14310 Greenwood Avenue N., Seattle, WA 98133-6813. Publisher. No submission info. Query w/SASE. Index: 29, 43, 47.

Chin Up Beacon, 9529 S.E. 32nd, Milwaukie, OR 97222. Monthly for the handicapped. No sub. info. Query w/SASE. Index: 126.

Chinkapin Press, Inc., PO Box 10565, Eugene, OR 97401. No submission info. Query w/SASE. Index: 130.

Chinook Observer, PO Box 427, Long Beach, WA 98631. 206–642–3131. Weekly newspaper. No submission info. Query w/SASE. Index: 33.

The Christ Foundation, PO Box 10, Port Angeles, WA 98362. Publisher. No submission info. Query w/SASE. Index: 105.

Christian Outlook, PO Box 1870, Hayden, ID 83835. 208–772–6184. Editor: Linda Hutton. Quarterly newsletter. Sub. $5. Circ. 300+. Uses 6-8 freelance mss per issue. Pays money, copies on acceptance. Acquires 1st rights. Byline given. Submit ms, SASE. Dot matrix, photocopied, simultaneous OK. Reports in 1 mo. Publishes in 6 mo. Accepts nonfiction, fiction, poetry. Tips: "Uplifting and spiritual material, but nothing preachy." Guidelines/sample SASE & 2 firstclass stamps. Index: 51, 97, 105.

Christian Update, 5431 S.E. Foster Road, Portland, OR 97206. Editor: Stephen Graham. Periodical. No submission info. Query w/SASE. Index: 105.

Christian Zion Advocate, PO Box 971, Port Angeles, WA 98362. Publisher. No submission info. Query w/SASE. Index: 105.

Chronicle, 195 S. 15th Street, Box 1153, St. Helens, OR 97051. 503–397–0116. Semiweekly newspaper. No submission info. Query w/SASE. Index: 33.

The Chronicle, PO Box 428, Creswell, OR 97426. 503–895–2197. Editor: Craig Hawkins. Ads: Gerri Hawkins. Sub: $15. Circ: 1,000. Weekly newspaper. Accepts freelance mss relating to Creswell only. Pay: Money, copies, on publication. Rights acquired: First. Byline given. Query, SASE. Dot matrix OK. Accepts: Nonfiction, photos. Topics: Individual arrangements. Sample/$.25. Index: 33.

The Chronicle, PO Box 88, , Aberdeen, WA, 98520. Contact: Editor. No submission info. Query w/SASE. Index: 130.

Circa Press, PO Box 482, Lake Oswego, OR 97034. 503–636–7241. Editor: Robert Brooks. Publisher of 3-5 hard/softcover original nonfiction books a yr. Accepts unsolicited mss. Pays royalties. Rights acquired: All. Submit SASE. Dot matrix, photocopies OK. Reports in 3-6 wks. Publishes in 6-9 mo. Catalog available. Index: 42, 98, 109.

Circinatum Press, Box 99309, Tacoma, WA 98499. No submission info. Query w/SASE. Index: 130.

Circle, Box 1682, Helena, MT, 59624. Editor: Christine Torgrimson. Periodical. No submission info. Query w/SASE. Index: 130.

For lists of abbreviations and the key to index numbers, see "How to Use this Section" on page 77.

114   Market Listings

Circle, Box 176, Portland, OR 97207. Periodical of poetry. No submission info. Query w/SASE. Index: 97.

CIRI-BETH Publishing Company, PO Box 1331, Tacoma, WA 98401-1331. No submission info. Query w/SASE. Index: 130.

Citizen Action, Oregon Public Employees Union, SEIU Local 503, 1127 25th Street, Salem, OR 97301. Bimonthly union publication. No submission info. Query w/SASE. Index: 71.

The City Collegian, Seattle Central Community College, 1718 Broadway Avenue, Seattle, WA 98122. Student newspaper. No submission info. Query w/SASE. Index: 31.

The City Open Press, Opus 2 Publications, 6332 S.E. Division St., Portland, OR 97206. Editor: T.C. Distel. 503–777–6121. Monthly tabloid for "Portland's progressive gay people." Tips: "We want to provide an outlet for the creative individuals among us. This includes poets, prose writers, artists, photographers. We are instituting a quarterly feature called 'Creatively Ours!' which will highlight the best of each item submitted to us." A prize will be offered. Index: 57 95, 97.

Clackamas County News, 224 S.W. Zobrist, Box 549, Estacada, OR 97023. 503–630–3241. Weekly newspaper. No submission info. Query w/SASE. Index: 33.

Clark Publishing, Inc., PO Box 11003, Tacoma, WA 98411. No submission info. Query w/SASE. Index: 130.

Clatskanie Chief, 90 Artsteele Street, Box 8, Clatskanie, OR 97016. 503–728–3350. Weekly newspaper. No submission info. Query w/SASE. Index: 33.

Classical Association of the Pacific NW Bulletin, University of Idaho, Moscow, ID 83843. Editor: C.A.E. Luschnig. Semiannual. No submission info. Query w/SASE. Index: 31.

Classics Unlimited, Inc., 2121 Arlington Avenue, Caldwell, ID 83605. Publisher. No submission info. Query w/SASE. Index: 130.

The Clatsop Common Sense, Clatsop Community College, Astoria, OR 97103. 503–325–0910 x311. Quarterly newspaper. No submission info. Query w/SASE. Index: 31.

Claustrophobia: Life-Expansion News, 1402 S.W. Upland Dr., Portland, OR, 97221-2649. 503–245–4763. Contact: Editor. Periodical. No submission info. Query w/SASE. Index:61.

Cleaning Consultant Services, Inc., 1512 Western Avenue, Seattle, WA 98101. Contact: William Griffin. 206–682–9748. Publisher of 4-6 trade softcover originals and reprints. References, directories, how-to and textbooks on cleaning and maintenance, health and self-employment and entrepreneurship. Query w/SASE for guidelines. Catalog available free. Index: 24, 43, 110.

Clear Water Journal, Eastern Oregon State College, La Grande, OR 97850. Editor: Tom Madden. Literary journal. No submission info. Query w/SASE. Index: 51, 76, 97.

Clients Council News, PO Box 342, Eugene, OR 97440. 503–342–5167. No submission info. Query w/SASE. Index: 130.

Clinton St. Quarterly, PO Box 3588, Portland, OR 97208. 503–222–6039. Editor: David Milholland. Ads: Rhonda Kennedy. Quarterly magazine, newspaper. Sub rate $8. Circ. 2 editions/50,000. Accepts freelance ms. Pays money on publication. Byline given. Query w/clips, ms, SASE. Simultaneous submissions OK. Reports in 1 mo. or less. Accepts nonfiction, fiction, cartoons. "CSQ covers a broad beat including Western American culture and U.S./international affairs. Specific topics covered in depth have included nuclear culture, US in Central America, sex roles and sexual identity, Western environmental concerns and art in its many forms. We print original fiction and exciting first-person accounts. Payment rates depend on story." Guidelines available.Sample $2.50. Index: 46, 51, 68.

Cloudburst Press, Box 90, Mayne Island, BC V0N 2J0. Publisher of books on holistic health. No submission info. Query w/SASE. Index: 61.

Cloudline, PO Box 462, Ketchum, ID 83340. Editor: Scott Preston. 208–788–3704. Biannual exploring "various themes relating to the conflict/impact of man's presence in the wilderness and natural environment." Circ. 300. Sub. $6. Rarely accepts freelance material, "but we are open." Payment: Copies on publication. Byline given. Rights purchased: First. Reports in 2-4 wks. Fiction, poetry, B&W graphics. Guidelines available w/SASE. Index: 46, 92, 97.

Coalition for Child Advocacy, PO Box 159, 314 E. Holly St., Bellingham, WA, 98227. 206–734–5121. Contact: Editor. Index: 29, 47, 61.

Coast Tidings, The News Guard, PO Box 848, Lincoln City, OR 97367. Editor: Duane C. Honsowetz. 503–994–2178. Periodical. No submission info. Query w/SASE. Index: 33, 103.

Coast to Coast Books, 2934 N.E. 16th, Portland, OR 97212. Contact: Mark Beach & Kathleen Ryan. Self-publisher of books on printing/publishing. No submission info. Query w/SASE. Index: 22, 102.

Coastal Press, Route 2, Box 3210, Lopez Island, WA 98261. No submission info. Query w/SASE. Index: 130.

Coeur d'Alene Homes Messenger, Coeur d'Alene Homes for the Aged, 704 W. Walnut, Coeur d'Alene, ID 83814. Quarterly directed to residents of local homes for the aged and their families. Circ. 4,000. No submission info. Query w/SASE. Index: 47, 100, 110.

Coffee Break, Box 248, Bandon, OR 97411. 503–347–2423. Newspaper. No submission info. Query w/SASE. Index: 130.

cold-drill Books, Department of English, Boise State University, Boise, ID 83725. 208–385–1999. Contact: Tom Trusky. Publisher of 1 softcover original book a yr. Print run: 500. No unsolicited mss. Publishes only authors whose work has appeared in *cold-drill Magazine*. Pay: Copies on publication. Rights acquired: First. Assignment only. Dot matrix, photocopies, simultaneous submissions OK. Accepts: Nonfiction, fiction, poetry, photos, plays, cartoons, other. Catalog available. Index: 14, 31, 77.

cold-drill Magazine, English Department, Boise State University, Boise, ID, 83725. 208–385–1999. Editor: Tom Trusky. Annual magazine. Sub rate $10. Circ. 500. Uses 3 freelance mss per issue. Pays copies on publication. Byline given. Rights purchased: first. Submit: ms, SASE. Dot matrix, photocopies, simultaneous submissions OK. Accepts nonfiction, fiction, poetry, photos, plays, cartoons, other. "Material must either be by an Idahoan or about Idaho; distant third: of interest to Idahoans (example: an essay on Chief Joseph's days in Oregon might be of interest, while an essay on Madonna would not be)." Tips: "Know the magazine; we're not your average literary magazine…Our format is boxed loose-leaf, which means we do 3-D comics, scratch 'n sniff poems, accordion-fold extravaganzas — plus traditional literary publishing (poems, short stories, plays, etc.)." Guidelines available. Sample $10. Index: 14, 31, 69.

For lists of abbreviations and the key to index numbers, see "How to Use this Section" on page 75.

Writer's Northwest Handbook   115

Collegian, Willamette University, 900 State Street, Salem, OR 97301. 503–370–6053. Periodical. No submission info. Query w/SASE. Index: 31.

Collegiate, City University, 16661 Northrup Way, Bellevue, WA 98008. Periodical. No submission info. Query w/SASE. Index: 31.

Colonygram, PO Box 15200, Portland, OR 97214. Editor: Susan Falk. 503–771–0428. Bimonthly newsletter of Oregon Writers Colony. Circ. 1,000. Sub. membership/$15. One or two short pieces per issue. Published by NW writers for NW writers. Payment: Copies on publication. Byline given. Submit ms w/SASE. Dot matrix, photocopies, simultaneous submissions, electronic OK. Nonfiction only, except December, special fiction issue. "Short pieces on marketing your writing: 250 wds, free copies on request. Book review on books about writing: 500 wds, $5. Strong interview with a published writer: 500-1,000 wds, query first, $10." Tip: "Read Colonygram first. Do you have something to contribute to other writers?" Sample/SASE. Index: 22, 102, 125.

Columbia Basin Herald, PO Box 910, Moses Lake, WA 98837. 509–765–4561. Daily newspaper. No submission info. Query/SASE. Index: 33.

Columbia Communicator, 4640 SW Macadam Ave., c/o W. Wharf, Portland, OR, 97201-4285. 503–236–7377. Editor: Donna Snyder. Monthly periodical. No submission info. Query w/SASE. Index: 130.

COLUMBIA The Magazine of Northwest History, Washington State Historical Society, 315 N. Stadium Way, Tacoma, WA 98403. 206–593–2830. Quarterly magazine. Editor: David L. Nicandri, 206–593–2830; Art Dwelley, 206–264–2500. Sub: Membership/single $4. Circ: 2,500. Accepts unsolicited mss. Pay: $25, copies, on publication. Rights acquired: First. Byline given. Submit: Query w/clips, ms, SASE. Reports in 2-4 wks. Publishes in 3 mos. Topics, NW history; preferred length 3,000 wds or less. Guidelines available. Sample, some. Index: 65, 76, 123.

The Columbia Press, 45 N.E. Harbor Court, Box 130, Warrenton, OR 97146. 503–861–3331. Weekly newspaper. No submission info. Query w/SASE. Index: 33.

The Columbian, 701 W. Eighth Street, PO Box 180, Vancouver, WA 98666. 206–694–3391. 503–224–0654. Daily newspaper. No submission info. Query w/SASE. Index: 33.

Columbiana, Chesaw Rt. Box 83F, Oroville, WA 98844. 509–485–3844. Editor: J. Payton. Ads: R. Gillespie. Quarterly bio-regional journal. Sub. $7.50. Circ. 4,000. Uses 10 freelance mss per issue. Pays money/copies on publication. Acquires 1st rights. Byline given. Query w/clips, SASE. Dot matrix, computer disc OK. Reports in 1 mo. Publishes in 1-6 mo. Accepts nonfiction, fiction, photos, cartoons. Topics: progressive, relevant to inland Northwest, Columbia River Drainage. Prefers features of 1,000 wds with accompanying illustrations. Pays $.01/word plus 6 mo. subscription. Photos: B&W prints only, $5+. Guidelines available. Sample $2. Index: 46, 89, 103.

Comic Relief, 264 E. Main St., Ashland, OR, 97520. 503–482–4669. Editor: Carole Fleming. Periodical. No submission info. Query w/SASE. Index: 68.

The Coming Revolution, Box A, , Livingston, MT, 59047. 406–222–8300. Contact: Editor. Periodical. No submission info. Query w/SASE. Index: 130.

Commercial Review, 1812 N.W. Kearney, Portland, OR, 97209. Weekly periodical on Portland business and commerce. Not a freelance market. Index: 24, 32.

Common Ground, Box 34090, Station D, Vancouver, BC V6J 4M1. Editor: Joseph Roberts. 604–733–2215. Ads: Phil Watson. Quarterly celebrating the art of living. Circ. 52,000. Sub. $10. Uses 6 mss per issue. Payment: $0-100, copies on publication. Byline given. Query w/ms, SASE. Nonfiction, fiction, photos, cartoons. Book reviews: 250-500 wds; interviews: 500-1,500 wds; topic article: 750-2,000 wds. Photos: B&W inside, $5-25; color cover only (usually from color transparency), $25-100. "Lots of highlights work best. Lots of mid-tone and good contrast." Tips: "We touch on a lot of subjects and are always looking for good editorials." Guidlines/sample available. Index: 45, 68, 95.

communiCAtion, Institute of Chartered Accountants of B.C., 1133 Melville Street, 6th Fl., Vancouver, BC V6E 4E5. Editor: Deborah L. Folka. 604–681–3264. Ads: Colin Campbell. Monthly. Circ. 6,500. Sub. $18 Cdn./$25 Foreign. Accepts freelance material. Writers must have business/finance/accounting knowledge. Payment: Copies on publication. Rights purchased: First. Submit ms, SASE. Phone query, photocopies OK. "We accept 1-2 page articles of interest to B.C. Chartered Accountants; human interest profiles on members of the profession, technical articles about accounting, auditing and taxation and pieces about related professions; all in the interest of keeping B.C. CAs informed about new technology, new events, progress and interesting features concerning their particular profession...We accept b/w photos that relate to an article." Sample available. Index: 24, 34, 42.

Communicator, SFCC, Rm 5-112, Communications Bldg., Spokane, WA, 99204. Contact: Editor. Weekly periodical. No submission info. Query w/SASE. Index: 31.

COMMUNICOM, 548 N.E. 43rd Avenue, Portland, OR 97213. 503–239–5141. Publisher of 1 softcover book for film/video/multi-image professionals. Print run: 5,000. Not a freelance market. Catalog available. Index: 24, 67, 80.

Community Digest Magazine, Suite 216, 1755 Robson Street, Vancouver, BC V6G 1C9. Editor: I. Popat. 604–875–8313. Ads: N. Ebrahim. 604–872–4749. Weekly to a multicultural audience. Circ. 20,000. Uses 2 mss per issue. No pay. Phone query, photocopies OK. Nonfiction. Index: 33, 39, 84.

Community Living Publications, PO Box 23305, Billings, MT, 59104. Editor: Cheryl Lane. Newspaper. No submission info. Query w/SASE. Index: 130.

Commuter, Linn-Benton Community College, 6500 S.W. Pacific Blvd., Albany, OR 97321. 503–928–2361x13. Newspaper. No submission info. Query w/SASE. Index: 31.

Comparative Literature, 223 Friendly Hall, University of Oregon, Eugene, OR 97403. Quarterly academic publication. Not a freelance market. Index: 31, 44, 76.

The Compass, Concordia Lutheran College, 2811 N.E. Holman, Portland, OR 97211. 503–288–9371. Newspaper. No submission info. Query w/SASE. Index: 31.

The Competitive Advantage, PO Box 10091, Portland, OR, 97210. 503–274–2953. Editor: Jim Moran. Monthly periodical. Sub. $96. Uses 1-2 freelance mss per issue. No pay. Byline given. Submit ms, phone. Dot matrix, photocopied OK. Accepts nonfiction, cartoons. Index: 130

For lists of abbreviations and the key to index numbers, see "How to Use this Section" on page 77.

116   Market Listings

C

Computer Able News, A Computing Magazine for Persons with Disabilities, PO Box 1706, Portland, OR 997207. Editor: Dennis Kviz. 503–644–2940. Ads: Kevin Mills. Monthly beginning 1/87. Circ. 10,000, internationally. Accepts freelance submissions of nonfiction (to 2,000 wds), photos and line art dealing with "computer applications for disabled persons." Also accepts reprints if informed of original source. Reports in 30 days. Gives byline and brief bio of author. Currently pays in copies, but will pay money ASAP, on publication. Query w/ms, SASE. Dot matrix, photocopies, simultaneous and electronic submissions OK. Index: 34, 126.

Computer Education News, PO Box 5182, #5 Harbor Mall, Bellingham, WA, 98227. Contact: Editor. Periodical. No submission info. Query w/ SASE. Index: 34.

Computer & Electronics News, 9513 S.W. Barbur Blvd., Suite 152, Portland, OR 97219. Magazine for computer users in Portland area. No submission info. Query w/SASE. Index: 34, 36.

Computer Innovations Desk Top Publishing, 360 Grand Dr., Bigfork, MT, 59911. Contact: Editor. Publisher. No submission info. Query w/ SASE. Index: 34.

Computer Learning Systems Inc., PO Box 70128, Bellevue, WA 98007. Publisher. No submission info. Query w/SASE. Index: 34, 43.

The Computing Teacher, University of Oregon, 1787 Agate Street, Eugene, OR 97403-1923. 503–686–4414. Editor: Anita Best. Ads: Sandi Lysne. Publishes 9 times a year. Circ. 12,000. Sub. $21.50. Uses 3-5 mss per issue. Writers must be well versed in computer education. "Submissions are reviewed anonymously by at least three qualified reviewers....TCT emphasizes teaching about computers, teaching using computer, teacher education, computer software programs and the general impact of computers in education today." Pays copies on publication. Query w/ ms, SASE. Dot matrix, simultaneous submissions, electronic OK. Reports in 10 wks. Nonfiction, photos. Approx. 600–3,000 wds. Guidelines available. Sample $3.50. Index: 34, 43.

Concerning Poetry, English Department, Western Washington University, Bellingham, WA 98225. Academic journal of literary criticism. No submission info. Query w/SASE. Index: 76, 97.

Concrete Herald, PO Box 407, Concrete, WA 98237. 206–853–8800. Weekly newspaper. No submission info. Query w/SASE. Index: 33.

Confluence Press, Inc., Lewis Clark State College, 8th Ave. & 6th St., Lewiston, ID 83501. 208–799–2336. Contact: James R. Hepworth. Publisher of 5 hard/softcover original books a yr. Press run 5,000. Accepts unsolicited submissions. Pays royalties, advance, on publication. Rights acquired: All. Submit query w/clips, SASE. Photocopies OK. Reports in 6-8 wks; publishes in 12-18 mo. Accepts nonfiction, fiction, poetry. "We're looking for the best writing in the Northwest. We have excellent national distribution." Catalog available/SASE. Index: 77, 89, 97.

Connections, 1991 Garfield Street, Eugene, OR 97405. 503–345–9599. Monthly. No submission info. Query w/SASE. Index: 130.

Connections Journal & Resource Directory, PO Box 10367, Eugene, OR 97440-2367. Editor/ads: Daniel D. Steinmetz. 503–683–1935. Quarterly "dedicated to exploring that which contributes toward better living in these changing times." Circ. 12,000. Sub. $8. Uses 2-5 mss per issue. Payment: Money, copies on publication. Byline given. Rights purchased: First. Query w/ms, SASE. Phone query, dot matrix, photocopies OK. Nonfiction, fiction, poetry, photos, cartoons, artwork. "Various topics are entertained. Style/content should in some way celebrate, or at least put forth, what brings value and purpose to our lives. Thoughtful, broadminded, probing articles on cultural and social phenomena which can build a sustainable society, are especially welcome." Photos: B&W glossies. Guidelines available; sample/$1. Index: 33, 94, 113.

Conscience & Military Tax Campaign, 4534 1/2 University Way N.E., #204, Seattle, WA, 98105. Editor: Katherine Bourdonnay. Quarterly periodical. No submission info. Query w/SASE. Index: 93, 101.

Conscious Living Foundation, PO Box 9, Drain, OR, 97435. 503–836–2358. Editor: Dr. Tim Lowenstein. Publishes 1-6 softcover books a yr. Accepts unsolicited submissions. Submit query w/clips. Dot matrix, photocopied, simultaneous, electronic subs OK. Reports in 3 wks. Publishes in 8 mos. Accepts nonfiction. Catalog available. Index: 130.

Construction Data & News, 925 N.W. 12th Avenue, Portland, OR, 97209. Contact: Editor. Periodical. No submission info. Query w/SASE. Index: 24, 119.

Constant Society, 4244 University Way N.E., PO Box 45513, Seattle, WA 98105. Publisher. No submission info. Query w/SASE. Index: 130.

Construction Sightlines, 124 W. 8th Street, North Vancouver, BC V7M 3H2. Editor: Vivian Rudd. 604–985–8711. Periodical. No submission info. Query w/SASE. Index: 119.

Consultant Services Northwest, Inc., 839 N.E. 96th St., Seattle, WA, 98115. 206–524–1950. Editor: Charna Klein. Publishes 1 softcover business book a yr. Does not accept unsolicited submissions. Index: 24.

Consumer Resource N.W., 1332 Grandridge Blvd. #200, Kennewick, WA 99336. 509–783–3337. Editor: Jo Hollier. Ads: Deb Layman. Monthly magazine. Circ 41,000. Uses 1-2 freelance mss per issue. Pays copies. Rights acquired: First. Byline given. Submit mss, SASE. Reports in 1 mo. Accepts nonfiction, poetry, photos. Topics: "Mature, retirement; 100-150 wds." PMT's on photos. Index; 36, 101, 110.

Contacts Influential, 140 S.W. Arthur, 3rd Fl., Portland, OR 97201. 503–227–1900. Monthly newsletter. Sub. $150. Circ. 400. Not a freelance market. Index: 24.

A Contemporary Theatre, 100 West Roy Street, Seattle, WA 98119. Contact: Barry Pritchard. Buys full-length scripts for the stage. No submission info. Query w/SASE. Index: 41.

Contemporary Issues Clearinghouse, 1410 S. Second, Pocatello, ID 83221. Publisher. No submission info. Query w/SASE. Index: 130.

Continuing Education Publications, Portland State University, PO Box 1383, Portland, OR, 97207. Contact: Tony Midson. 503–229–4890. Publisher of 1-2 hard/softcover books for "individuals with a desire for self-improvement or development of professional skills." Payment: Royalties. Submit outline, sample chapters and synopsis. "We're looking for materials for educators, students or professionals, especially items with a continuing education function or for self-instruction and improvement. Should be appropriate for academic review before acceptance. Writers should be established authorities, or have special insight." Index: 43.

Contractors Weekly, 1213 Valley, Seattle, WA 98109. 206–622–7053. Trade periodical. No submission info. Query w/SASE. Index: 24, 119.

Controversy in Review, PO Box 11408, Portland, OR, 97211. 503–282–0381. Editor: Richard E. Geis. Bimonthly periodical. Sub. $9. Circ. 1,000. Uses 1 freelance ms per issue. Pays copies on publication. Byline given. Submit ms, phone. Dot matrix, photocopied, simultaneous OK. Reports in 1-2 wks. Accepts nonfiction, cartoons. Index: 76, 98.

For lists of abbreviations and the key to index numbers, see "How to Use this Section" on page 75.

The Cookbook Factory, PO Box 11515, Eugene, OR 97440. Publisher. No submission info. Query w/SASE. Index: 38, 67.

Cooper Point Journal, Evergreen State College, Campus Activities Bldg., Rm 306A, Olympia, WA, 98505. Editor: Jennifer Seymore. Weekly periodical. No submission info. Query w/SASE. Index: 31.

Copper Canyon Press, Box 271, Port Townsend, WA 98368. Contact: Sam Hamill/Tree Swenson. 206–385–4925. Publisher of 7 hard/softcover originals, reprints a year; poetry and poetry in translation. Accepts no unsolicited material. Query w/SASE. Reports in 1 month. Publishes in 1 yr. Rights acquired: All. Catalog available. Index: 97.

Copyhook, 4416 134th Pl. S.E., Bellevue, WA, 98006. Editor: Helen Szablya. Periodical. No submission info. Query w/SASE. Index: 119.

Copyright Information Services, 440 Tucker Ave., PO Box 1460-A, Friday Harbor, WA 98250-1460. 206–378–5128. Contact: Jerome K. Miller. Publisher of 5 hardcover original books a yr. about USA copyright law. Accepts unsolicited submissions. Pays 15% net royalties. Submit query w/clips, SASE. Dot matrix, computer disc OK. Reports in 6 wks. Publishes promptly. Accepts nonfiction. Catalog available. Index: 74, 125.

Coquille Valley Sentinel, Box 519, Coquille, OR 97423. 503–396–3191, 503–572–2717. Weekly newspaper. No submission info. Query w/SASE. Index: 33.

Coriolis Publishing Company, 425 S.E. 3rd, Portland, OR 97214. No submission info. Query w/SASE. Index: 130.

Corvallis Gazette Times, 600 S.W. Jefferson Avenue, Box 368, Corvallis, OR 97339. 503–753–2641. Daily newspaper. No submission info. Query w/SASE. Index: 33.

Cottage Grove Sentinel, PO Box 31, Cottage Grove, OR 97424. 503–942–3325. Weekly newspaper. No submission info. Query w/SASE. Index: 33.

Coulee City News-Standard, PO Box 488, Coulee City, WA 99115. Editor/ads: Sue Poe. 509–632–5402. Weekly newspaper focusing on local agriculture and schools. Circ. 700. Sub. $10-12. Not a freelance market. Index: 3, 33, 43.

The Council for Human Rights in Latin America Newsletter, Kincaid Street, Eugene, OR 97401. No submission info. Query w/SASE. Index: 84, 98.

Council for Indian Education, 517 Rimrock Rd., Billings, MT 59102. 406–252–7451. Editor: Hap Gilliland. Ads: Marilyn Degel. Publishes 6 softcover books a yr. Accepts unsolicited mss. Pay: money, $.01 1/2 wd. on acceptance of short items, 10% of wholesale price royalty on books; copies. Rights acquired: First. Submit ms, SASE. Dot matrix, photocopies, simultaneous submissions OK. Reports in 1-6 mo. Publishes in 6 mo. Accepts nonfiction, fiction, poetry, on Native American life and culture, past or present. Also how-to books on Indian crafts. Must be true to Indian culture and thought, appropriate for use in schools with Indian students. Also short books on teaching. Catalog available. Index: 29, 43, 87.

Courier 4, Chemeketa Community College, PO Box 14007, Salem, OR 97309. 503–399–5134. Newspaper. No submission info. Query w/SASE. Index: 31.

The Courier, 174 N. 16th Street, Box 268, Reedsport, OR 97467. 503–271–3633. Weekly newspaper. No sub. info. Query w/SASE. Index: 33.

Courier-Herald, PO Box 157, Enumclaw, WA 98022. 206–825–2555. Weekly newspaper. No submission info. Query w/SASE. Index: 33.

Courier-Pioneer-Advertiser, PO Box 1091, Polson, MT, 59860. Newspaper. No submission info. Query w/SASE. Index: 130.

Courier-Times, PO Box 32, Sedro Woolley, WA 98284. 206–855–1641. Weekly newspaper. No submission info. Query w/SASE. Index: 33.

The Court Scribe, 2201 Friendly Street, Eugene, OR 97405. Publisher. No submission info. Query w/SASE. Index: 130.

Cove Press, 2125 Seal Cove Circle, Prince Rupert, BC V8J 2G4. No submission info. Query w/SASE. Index: 130.

Cowles Publishing Company, 927 Riverside, Spokane, WA 99210. No submission info. Query w/SASE. Index: 130.

Cowlitz County Advocate, PO Box 368, Castle Rock, WA 98611. 206–274–6663. Weekly newspaper. Editor: Terri Lee Grell. Ads: Barbara Thompson. Sub $20. Circ 5,000. Uses 1 freelance ms per issue, local slant. Pays copies, on publication. Rights acquired: First. Byline given. Submit: query w/clips, ms, SASE. Phone query, dot matrix, photocopies, electronic, computer disc OK. Accepts nonfiction, photos, news, features, columns. "We have a weekly column called 'Ad-libs' that is written by anyone who has a unique story to tell. We'd like it to be about the local area or Mt. St. Helens, but all submissions are considered. Keep it simple, and no more than 4 typewritten pgs." Sample $1. Index: 25, 33, 65.

Cowlitz-Wahkiakum Senior News, PO Box 2126, Longview, WA, 98632. Contact: Editor. Monthly periodical. No submission info. Query w/SASE. Index: 33, 110.

Crab Creek Review, 4462 Whitman Ave. N., Seattle, WA 98103. 206–633–1090. Editor: Linda Clifton/Carol Orlock, fiction. Literary magazine of poetry/fiction published 3 times a yr. Sub rate $8. Circ. 350-500. All articles freelance. Pays copies on publication. Rights purchased: First. Byline given. Submit ms, SASE. Dot matrix, photocopies OK. No simultaneous submissions. Reports in 6-8 wks. Publishes in 2-24 mo. Accepts fiction: up to 3,500 wds, strong voice, imagery; nonfiction: up to 3,500 wds; poetry: under 40 lines — ("free or formal, clear imagery, wit, voice that is interesting and energetic, accessible to the general reader rather than full of very private imagery and obscure literary allusion"); art: B&W, pen or brushwork. Tips: "Translations accepted — please accompany with copy of the work in the original language." Accepting work only by invitation until Sept. 1989. Guidelines available. Sample $3. Index: 51, 95, 97.

Crabtree Publishing, PO Box 3451, Federal Way, WA 98063. Contact: Catherine Crabtree. 206–927–3777. Publisher of 2 hard/softcover originals a year on cooking, home design, health/fitness, entertainment/restaurant guides. Print run: 5,000. Accepts freelance material with permission. "Send request letter stating type of material." Include SASE. Rights purchased: All. Guidelines/catalog available. Index: 45, 54, 61.

Craft Connection, PO Box 25124, Seattle, WA 98125. 206–367–7875. Editor: Cindy Salazar. Ads: Terrie Durkey. 206–746–6884. Sub $8.50. Press run 12,000. Accepts unsolicited mss. No pay. Rights acquired: First. Byline given. Photocopies, computer disc OK. Reports in 1 mo. Accepts nonfiction, fiction, photos (B&W), cartoons, graphics. "How-to's for any handcraft; general interest business, how to start, wholesale, marketing; history or topical story about any handcraft or artist; anything of general interest to women in crafts: selling, making, promoting." Sample $1.50. Index: 38, 67.

The Craft Network/The Craft Directory, PO Box 9945, Spokane, WA 99209-0945. 509–328–9330. Ads: Lynne Slaughter. Self-publisher of

For lists of abbreviations and the key to index numbers, see "How to Use this Section" on page 77.

118   Market Listings

softcover craft book. Not a freelance market. Index: 10, 38.

Crafts Report , 3632 Ashworth North, Seattle, WA, 98103. Periodical. No submission info. Query w/SASE. Index: 38.

Cranial Academy Newsletter, Cranial Academy, 1140 W. 8th Street, Meridian, ID 83642. Editor: Mrs. C.H. Rathjen. Quarterly. Circ. 300. No submission info. Query w/SASE. Index: 130.

Creative Children, c/o Keith McAlear, PO Box 1212, Polson, MT, 59860. Book Publisher. No submission info. Query w/SASE. Index: 29.

Creative News N' Views, Creative Employment for the Deaf Foundation, Inc., PO Box 1001, Tualatin, OR 97062. 503–624–0131(v) 503–624–0351(TDD). Editor: Paula Reuter-Dymeck. Ads: Don Carbone. Monthly newsletter for membership. No submission info. Query w/ SASE. Index: 71, 126.

The Crescent, George Fox College, Box A, Newberg, OR 97132. 503–538–8383. Newspaper. No submission info. Query w/SASE. Index: 31.

Crook County Historical Society Newsletter, 246 N. Main, Prineville, OR 97754. Irregular periodical. No submission info. Query w/SASE. Index: 65.

Crook Publishing, 106-235 Oliver Street, Williams Lake, BC V2G 1M2. No submission info. Query w/SASE. Index: 130.

Cross Cultural Press, 1166 S. 42nd St., Springfield, OR. 503–746–7401. Editor: Ken Fenter. Publisher of 1-2 hard/softcover original, subsidy books a yr. No unsolicited mss. Query 1st, SASE. Dot matrix, photocopies, computer disc OK. Reports in 1-4 wks. Publishes within 1 yr. Topics: Japanese/American experiences, Asian/American experiences. Index: 11, 12, 39.

Crosswind, PO Box 10, Oak Harbor, WA 98277. 206–675–6611. Weekly newspaper. No submission info. Query w/SASE. Index: 33.

Crow Publications, Inc., P.O. Box 25749, Portland, OR, 97225. 503–646–8075. Contact: Editor. Publisher. No submission info. Query w/ SASE. Index:130.

Crowdancing Quarterly, 570 W. 10th Ave., Eugene, OR, 97401. 503–485–3981. Editors: John Campbell & Holly V. Pink. Periodical. Sub. $7/ $12. Circ. 300. Uses 35+ freelance mss per issue. Pays copies. Byline given. Submit ms, SASE. Reports in 8-10 wks. Accepts fiction, poetry, other. Guidelines available. Sample $4. Index: 51, 97.

Crusader, Northwest Nazarene College, Nampa, ID 83651. 208–467–8556. Biweekly newspaper. No sub info. Query w/SASE. Index: 31.

Cruzzin Magazines, 878 Madrona St. S., PO Box 444, Twin Falls, ID, 83303. 208–734–1780. Free travel periodical. Circ. 15,000. No submission info. Query w/SASE. Index: 120.

Cryptogram Detective, 8137 S.E. Ash, Portland, OR, 97215. 503–256–2393. Editor: Joan Barton. Bimonthly periodical/membership. Uses 19 freelance mss per issue. Pays copies on publication. Byline given. Submit ms, SASE. Dot matrix, photocopied, simultaneous OK. Reports in 6 mo. Accepts fiction. Sample $1.25. Index: 45.

Crystal Musicworks, 2235 Willida Lane, Sedro Woolley, WA 98284. Publisher. No submission info. Query w/SASE. Index: 86.

Culinary Arts Ltd., PO Box 2157, Lake Oswego, OR 97035. 503–639–4549. Editor: Marjorie Guinn. Publishes 1-2 softcover books a year. Does not accept unsolicited submissions. Pays royalties. Query w/clips, SASE, phone. Index: 54.

Cumtux, Clatsop County Historical Society, 1618 Exchange Street, Astoria, OR 97103. Quarterly. No sub info. Query with/SASE. Index: 65.

Current, PO Box 247, Walla Walla, WA 99362. 509–529–1863. Editor/Ads: David Hiatt. Newspaper published 10 times a yr. Uses 10 freelance mss per issue. Pays in copies. Acquires 1st rights. Byline given. Submit SASE. Dot matrix, photocopied OK. Accepts nonfiction, fiction, poetry, photos, cartoons. Sample available. Index: 51, 95, 97.

Current Concepts in Oral & Maxillofacial Surgery, 407 N.E. 87th Avenue, Vancouver, WA 98664. Editor: Dr. Jack Stecher. 206–254–8540. Monthly. Also publishes *Current Concepts in Orthodontics* and *Current Concepts in Clinical Pathology — a Physician's Newsletter*. Circ. 12,000. Not a freelance market. Index: 61, 81.

Current Lit Publications, Inc., 1513 E. St., Bellingham, WA 98225. 206–671–6664. Publisher. No submission info. Query w/SASE. Index: 77.

The Current, North Coast Community Radio, PO Box 269, Astoria, OR, 97103. Contact: Editor. Monthly periodical. No submission info. Query w/SASE. Index: 33, 80.

Current News, Idaho Power Company, PO Box 70, Boise, ID 83707. Editor: Nikki B. Stilwell. Published 8 times a yr. Circ. 3,200. No submission info. Query with/SASE. Index: 24, 36, 101.

Currents, Idaho Department of Water Resources, Statehouse, Boise, ID 83720. Editor: Angela Neitzel. Monthly. Circ. 5,000. No submission info. Query with/SASE. Index: 35, 69, 101.

Curry Coastal Pilot, 507 Chetco Avenue, Box 700, Brookings, OR 97415. 503–469–3123. Weekly newspaper. No submission info. Query with/ SASE. Index: 33.

Curry County Echoes, Curry County Historical Society, 920 S. Ellensburg Avenue, Gold Beach, OR 97444. Editor: Virginia Fendrick. 503–247–6113. Monthly on local history. Sub. membership in historical society, $5. Not a freelance market. Index: 65.

Curry County Reporter, 510 N. Ellensburg Avenue, Box 766, Gold Beach, OR 97444. 503–247–6643. Weekly newspaper. No submission info. Query with/SASE. Index: 33.

CutBank, c/o English Department, University of Montana, Missoula, MT 59801. Editor: Paul S. Piper. Publishes 1 double issue a yr. Sub. $9. Circ. 450. Uses freelance material. Pays copies on publication. Byline given. Submit ms, SASE. Photocopied OK. Reports in 6-12 wks. Publishing time variable. Accepts fiction (to 40 ds pages), poetry (3-5), photos. "Work must be of high quality to be considered. No stylistic limitations." Samples $3-9. Index: 51, 76, 97.

The Cutting Edge, World Peace University, 35 S.E. 60th, Portland, OR 97215. Editor/ads: M. Boyd. 503–282–0280. Monthly on international peace education, global issues. Circ. 1,700. Sub. $15. Uses 5 mss per issue. Payment: Copies. Byline given. Submit ms, SASE. Dot matrix, photocopies, simultaneous submissions OK. "Newsbriefs: of peace 'events,' local USA, international. Essays: 300-500 wds; peace issues, inner development. Profile/interview: national, international figures in education, humanities, sociology. Book reviews: 200 wds; social psychological, education topics." Tips: Also needs essays/opinion for international shortwave broadcast. Sample: $1. Index: 84, 93, 114.

CVAS, Bellingham Public Library, Fairhaven Branch, Bellingham, WA, 98227. Periodical. No submission info. Query w/SASE. Index: 104.

Cybele Society, W. 1603 9th Avenue, Spokane, WA 99204-3406. Publisher. No submission info. Query with/SASE. Index: 130.

The Daily, 144 Communications, DS-20, University of Washington, Seattle, WA 98195. 206–543–2335. Newspaper. No submission info. Query with/SASE. Index: 31.

The Daily Astorian, Box 210, Astoria, OR 97103. 503–325–3211. Newspaper. No submission info. Query w/SASE. Index: 33.

Daily Barometer, Oregon State University, Memorial Union East 106, Corvallis, OR 97331. 503–754–2231. Newspaper. No submission info. Query w/SASE. Index: 31.

Daily Bulletin, PO Box 770, Colfax, WA 99111. 509–397–4333. Newspaper. No submission info. Query w/SASE. Index: 33.

The Daily Chronicle, 321 N. Pearl, PO Box 580, Centralia, WA 98531. 206–736–3311. Newspaper. No submission info. Query w/SASE. Index: 33.

Daily Emerald, University of Oregon, Box 3159, Eugene, OR 97403. 503–686–5511. Newspaper. No submission info. Query w/SASE. Index: 31.

Daily Evergreen, Room 113, Edward R. Murrow C.Cntr., PO Box 2008 C.S., Pullman , WA 99165-9986. Editor: Michael Strand. Newspaper. No submission info. Query w/SASE. Index: 31.

Daily Journal American, 1705 - 132nd N.E., PO Box 310, Bellevue, WA 98009. 206–455–2222. Newspaper. No submission info. Query w/ SASE. Index: 33.

Daily Journal of Commerce (see *Portland Business Today*).

The Daily News, Port Angeles, PO Box 1330, Port Angeles, WA 98362. Editor: Tony Wishik. 206–452–2345. Ads: Bob Blumhagen. 800–826–7714. Newspaper serving Clallam/Jefferson counties. Circ. 12,500. Sub. $6.75. Accepts freelance material. Payment: Money on publication. Byline given. Rights purchased: First. Query w/SASE. Dot matrix, photocopies, electronic OK. Nonfiction: up to 1,000 wds; $20-25. Photos: $5-35 per assignment. "Must be directly related to Clallam/Jefferson counties." Sample available. Index: 33.

The Daily Olympian, 1268 East Fourth Ave., PO Box 407, Olympia, WA 98507. 206–754–5400. Newspaper. No submission info. Query w/ SASE. Index: 33.

Daily Shipping News, 2014 NW 24th, Portland, OR, 97210. Periodical. No submission info. Query w/SASE. Index: 24.

The Daily Tidings, 1661 Siskiyou Blvd., Box 7, Ashland, OR 97520. 503–482–3456. Newspaper. No submission info. Query w/SASE. Index: 33.

Dairyline, United Dairymen of Idaho, 1365 N. Orchard, Boise, ID 83760. Bimonthly. Circ. 3,000. No submission info. Query w/SASE. Index: 3, 24.

Dalmo'ma, Empty Bowl Press, PO Box 646, Port Townsend, WA 98368. Editor: Michael Daley. 206–385–4943. Circ. 1,500. Sub. $7/issue. Irregularly published anthology of "literature and responsibility," and regional/rural quality of life, by NW writers. Accepts freelance submissions on themes. Nonfiction, fiction, poetry, photos, plays, cartoons — almost anything serious considered. Recent edition included a record. Rights revert to author. Pays in copies on publication. Reports in 2 mos. Query w/SASE. Dot matrix, photocopies and simultaneous submission OK. Guideline available; sample/$7. Index: 39, 51, 97.

Darvill Outdoor Publications, 1819 Hickox Road, Mt. Vernon, WA 98273. No submission info. Query w/SASE. Index: 92.

Davenport Times, PO Box 66, Davenport, WA 99122. 509–725–0101. Weekly newspaper. No submission info. Query w/SASE. Index: 33.

Dayton Chronicle, PO Box 6, Dayton, WA 99328. 509–382–2221. Weekly newspaper. No submission info. Query w/SASE. Index: 33.

Dayton Tribune, 408 4th, Box 68, Dayton, OR 97114. 503–864–2310. Weekly newspaper. No submission info. Query w/SASE. Index: 33.

Dead Mountain Echo, PO Box 900, Oakridge, OR 97463. 503–782–4241. Editor: John Nelson. Ads: Larry Roberts. Weekly newspaper. Sub: $25. Circ: 1,500. Accepts unsolicited submissions. Query w/SASE. Sample/$1. Index: 33.

Deals & Wheels, 2003 Todd Rd. #82, Vancouver, WA, 98661. Editor: Shelly Wilson. Periodical. No submission info. Query w/SASE. Index: 130.

Dee Publishing Company, 864 S. Commercial, Salem, OR 97302. No submission info. Query w/SASE. Index: 130.

Democrat, 517 E. Broadway #210, Vancouver, BC V5T 1X4. Editor: Stephen Brewer. 604–879–4601. Periodical. No submission info. Query w/ SASE. Index: 130.

Denali, Lane Community College, 4000 E. 30th Ave., Eugene, OR 97405. 503–747–4501 x2830. Editor: Karen Loche. College literary magazine. Editors could change yearly. SASE for guidelines. Index: 31, 51, 91.

The Denali Press, PO Box 021535, Juneau, AK 99802-1535. 907–586–6014. Editor: Alan Schorr. Publisher of 3 softcover original nonfiction books a yr. Accepts unsolicited mss. Pays royalties. Submit query w/clips, ms. Phone query, dot matrix, photocopies OK. Reports in 3 wks. Primarily publishers of reference books, but also travel guides and Alaskana, Hispanic, refugees/immigrants. Index: 4, 84, 104.

Desert Trails, Desert Trail Association, PO Box 589, Burns, OR, 97720. Editor: Jack Remington. Quarterly periodical. No submission info. Query w/SASE. Index: 130.

The Desktop Publishing Journal, 4027-C Rucker Ave. Suite 821, Everett, WA 98201. 206–568–2950. Editor: Linda Hanson. Ads: Jared Hays. Circ. 50,000. Sub. $10.99. Monthly journal. Uses 2-5 freelance mss per issue. Some technical expertise needed to write for us. Pays money on publication: $200 for feature articles of 4,000-7,000 wds., $100 for articles 1,000-4,000 wds., $25 for cartoons. Likes to trade articles for 1/4 page ads. Graphic req's: 85-line screen. Rights purchased: First. Reprints OK. Byline given. Query w/clips, SASE. All forms of submis. OK. Reports in 2 mos. Publishes in 2 mos. Accepts nonfiction, photos, cartoons. "We need articles written for all levels, but prefer beginner's level. How-to articles are preferred, but print anything and everything related to D.Pub." Guidelines. Sample $1.50. Index: 34, 102, 117.

DHA and Associates Publishing Company, PO Box 1861, Seattle, WA 98111. Contact: Don Alexander. No submission info. Query w/SASE. Index: 130.

For lists of abbreviations and the key to index numbers, see "How to Use this Section" on page 77.

120   Market Listings

Dialogue - Thoughtprints, Center Press, PO Box 675, Gig Harbor, WA 98335. Editor: E. J. Featherstone. 206–858–3964. Quarterly of "poetry with inspirational (nonreligious) — humourous — philosophical message." Circ. 2,000-3,000. Pays on publication. Byline given. Query w/ms, SASE. Dot matrix, simultaneous submissions OK. Publishes submissions in 3-12 mos. Nonfiction: on poetry and poetry markets, 250 wds, no pay. Poetry: 24 lines; pays in prizes/subs. Short rhymed humor: pays $1. Tips: "No 'sensational' morbid themes. Good imagery — meter will be edited if poem merits publication. Mankind's needs addressed, looking for upbeat material — no heavy religious or Pollyanna." Index: 94, 97.

The Digger, Oregon Association of Nurserymen, 224 S.W. Hamilton, Portland, OR 97201. Bimonthly agricultural trade magazine devoted to one of Oregon's largest, nationally important industries. No submission info. Query w/SASE. Index: 3, 24.

Dilithium Press & Portland House, 921 S.W. Washington, Portland, OR 97204. Contact: Gerald Spencer. 503–243–313 . Publisher of high level academic nonfiction related to science, business and economics. Not presently soliciting mss. Writers with book proposals they feel should be considered are requested to send a query w/SASE first. Index: 24, 42, 109.

Dillon Tribune-Examiner, 22 S. Montana, Dillon, MT, 59725. Contact: Editor. Newspaper. No submission info. Query w/SASE. Index: 33.

Dimi Press, 3820 Oak Hollow Lane S.E., Salem, OR 97302. 503–364–7698. Publisher of softcover/orig./reprint books and cassettes "dealing with relaxation and other self-help treatment methods for psychological problems." Accepts unsolicited/freelance mss. Query w/SASE. Pay: Royalties on publication. Byline given. Simultaneous submission OK. Reports in 4 wks. Catalog available. Index: 61, 67, 100.

Dioscoridus Press, Inc., 9999 S.W. Wilshire, Portland, OR 97225. 503–292–0961. Editor: Richard Abel. Ads: Michael Fox. Publishes 5 history-related hardcover originals, reprints per yr. Accepts unsolicited submissions. Acquires all rights. Submit query w/clips. Dot matrix, photocopied OK. Reports in 3-4 wks. Index: 62, 64.

The Direct Express, 1819 Grand Ave., Billings, MT, 59102-2939. Contact: Editor. Newspaper. No submission info. Query w/SASE. Index: 130.

Discovery, 1908 Second Street, Tillamook, OR 97141. 503–842–7535. Periodical. No submission info. Query w/SASE. Index: 130.

Discovery Press, Box 46295, Station G, Vancouver, BC V6R 4G1. Publisher of quality books on British Columbia. No submission info. Query w/SASE. Index: 23.

Dispatch, PO Box 248, Eatonville, WA 98328. 206–832–4411. Weekly newspaper. No submission info. Query w/SASE. Index: 33.

Diver Magazine, 8051 River Road, Richmond BC V6X 1X8. Editor: Neil McDaniel. 604–273–4333. Devoted to subjects of interest to divers. Published 9 times per yr. Accepts freelance material. Uses nonfiction articles, especially with photos. Query w/SASE. Index: 92, 103, 120.

Dog-Eared Publications, PO Box 814, Corvallis, OR, 97339. 503–753–4274. Editor: Nancy Field & Sally Machlis. Publisher. No submission info. Query w/SASE. Index: 130.

Dog River Review, PO Box 125, Parkdalee, OR 97041-0125. Editor: Laurence F. Hawkins, Jr. 503–352–6494. Semiannual of fiction, poetry, art. Circ. 200. Sub. $6. Accepts freelance material. Payment: Copies on publication. Rights purchased: First. Submit ms, SASE. Dot matrix, photocopies OK. Reports in 1-3 mos. Fiction: to 2,500 wds. Poetry: prefer verse to 30 lines but will consider longer, all forms. Also accepts plays, B&W art. "No pornography; eroticism OK. No sermonizing, self-indulgent material. No religious verse." Guidelines available; sample/$2. Index: 38, 51, 97.

Doll Mall, Paddlewheel Press, PO Box 230220, Tigard, OR, 97223. 503–292–8460. Contact: Editor. Quarterly. No submission info. Query w/SASE. Index: 130.

Douglas & McIntyre Publishers, 1615 Venables Street, Vancouver, BC V5L 2H1. Contact: Shaun Oakey. 604–254–7191. Publisher of hard and softcover originals and paperbacks, primarily by Canadian writers. Payment: Advances average $500; royalties 8-15%. Query or mss w/SASE. Nonfiction, fiction. Topics: ethnic, experimental, historical and women's literary fiction. Catalog available free. Index: 63, 98, 124.

Doves Publishing Company, PO Box 821, Newport, OR, 97365. Contact: Editor. Publisher. No submission info. Query w/SASE. Index: 130.

The Downtowner, PO Box 4227, Portland, OR 97208. Editor: Maggi White. 503–620–4121. Weekly focusing on Portland, entertainment, culture. Circ. 25,000. Sub. $13. Accepts freelance material. Payment: Money on publication. Byline given. Query w/SASE. Nonfiction, photos. "Short pieces, 2-3 pages typed. Buy very little not local." Index: 39, 45, 68.

Dragon Gate, Inc., 508 Lincoln Street, Port Townsend, WA, 98368. 206–783–8387. Editor: Marlene Blessing. Publishes 3-4 hard/softcover original, reprint books a yr. Press run: 2,000. Accepts unsolicited submissions. Submit query w/clips, SASE. Photocopied OK. Reports in 3 mo. Publishes in 1 yr. Accepts fiction, poetry. Catalog available. Index: 51, 97.

Dragonfly, 4120 N.E. 130th Place, Portland, OR 97230. Quarterly haiku journal. No submission info. Query w/SASE. Index: 97.

The Drain Enterprise, 309 1st Street, Drain, OR 97435. Newspaper. No submission info. Query w/SASE. Index: 33.

Dream Research, PO Box 1142, Tacoma, WA 98401. Editor: Adrienne Quinn. Publisher. No submission info. Query w/SASE. Index: 130.

Drelwood Publications, PO Box 10605, Portland, OR 97210. No submission info. Query w/SASE. Index: 130.

The Drift Group, 314 6th St. #8, Sidney, MT 59270. Editor: Suzanne Hackett. Periodical. No submission info. Query w/SASE. Index: 130.

Duane Shinn Publications, 5090 Dobrot, Central Point, OR 97501. No submission info. Query w/SASE. Index: 130.

The Duckabush Journal, PO Box 2228, Sequim, WA 98382-2228. 206–683–0647. Editor: Ken Crump. Literary regional periodical published 3 times a yr. Sub. $12. "A creative insight to the Olympic Peninsula and adjacent areas." Pays copies on publication. Submit ms, query w/SASE. Accepts poetry, short stories, historical studies, character sketches, other nonfiction, B&W art, photographs. Tips: Prose should have a tone or feeling of Olympic Peninsula. Guidelines available. Sample $4.50. Index: 51, 97, 122.

Duckburg Times, 400 Valleyview, Selah, WA 98942. Periodical. No submission info. Query w/SASE. Index: 130.

Eagle Signs, 1015 Hutson Road, Hood River, OR 97031. Publisher. No submission info. Query w/SASE. Index: 130.

Early Warning, Suite 1, EMU, Eugene, OR, 97403. Contact: Editor. Periodical. No submission info. Query w/SASE. Index: 130.

Earshot Jazz, PO Box 85851, Seattle, WA 98145-2858. 206–285–8893. Editors: P. de Barros/G. Bannister. Ads: Jeff Ferguson. Monthly magazine. Sub. $15. Uses 1 freelance ms per issue. Pays in copies. Byline given. Submit query w/clips. Reports in 1 mo. Accepts nonfiction. Sample free. Index: 86.

For lists of abbreviations and the key to index numbers, see "How to Use this Section" on page 75.

Writer's Northwest Handbook 121

Earth View, Inc., Star Route, Ashford, WA 98304. Publisher. No submission info. Query w/SASE. Index: 130.

The Earthling, Society of Separationists, Inc., PO Box 14054, Portland, OR, 97214. Editor: James Almblad. Periodical. No submission info. Query w/SASE. Index: 130.

Earthtone, PO Box 23383, Portland, OR 97223. Editor: Patricia Watters. 503–620–3917. Ads: Kathryn Beck. Bimonthly "'alternative' magazine aimed at college educated audience of the western U.S. who share an interest in country living, homesteading, animal husbandry, energy conservation, health, self-sufficiency, organic gardening." Accepts freelance material. Payment: $50-300 on publication. Byline given. Rights purchased: First. Submit ms, SASE. Electronic OK. Reports in 2 wks. Nonfiction, photos. Range from 500 wd fillers to 3,000 wd features. "Original artwork and 35mm or 120 B&W negatives or glossy B&W photographs...should be eye-catching and of sharp professional quality...an article's chances are greatly enhanced by superior graphics." Guidelines available. Sample $2. Index: 56, 61, 106.

Earthwatch Oregon, 2637 S.W. Water, Portland, OR 97210. Editor/ads: Heath Lynn Silberfeld. 503–222–1963. Quarterly on environmental issues of concern to Oregonians. Circ. 2,000. Sub. $25. Accepts freelance material. No pay. Byline given. Phone query, dot matrix, photocopies OK. Uses nonfiction, photos. "Environmental issues reporting/opinion pieces of 1-10 typewritten pages, with emphasis on legislative activity, lobbying, and enforcement of environmental law, statutes, rules." Photos: B&W prints. Sample available. Index: 46, 91, 98.

East is East, PO Box 95247, Seattle, WA 98145-2247. 206–522–1551. Contact: Editor. Periodical. No submission info. Query w/SASE. Index: 130.

East Oregonian, 211 S.E. Byers, Box 1089, Pendleton, OR 97801. 503–276–2211. Daily newspaper. No submission info. Query w/SASE. Index: 33.

East Washingtonian, PO Box 70, Pomeroy, WA 99347. 509–84–1313. Weekly newspaper. No submission info. Query w/SASE. Index: 33.

The Eastern Beacon, Eastern Oregon State College, Hoke College Center, La Grande, OR 97850. Editor: Liz Cobb. 503–963–1526. Bimonthly to college students, professors, staff and community. Circ. 1,500. Accepts freelance material. No pay. Byline given. Dot matrix, photocopies, simultaneous submission, electronic OK. Uses nonfiction, fiction, poetry, photos, cartoons. Sample available/SASE. Index: 31, 45, 115.

Eastern School Press, 146 Talent Avenue, PO Box 684, Talent, OR 97540. No submission info. Query w/SASE. Index: 130.

Eastern Washington State Historical Society, W. 2316 1st Avenue, Spokane, WA 99204. Publisher. No submission info. Query w/SASE. Index: 65.

Eastland Press, 611 Post Ave. Ste. #3, Seattle, WA 98104. 206–587–6013. Editor: Dan Bensky. Ads: Patricia O'Connor. Publishes 3 hardcover orig. books a yr. Accepts unsolicited mss. Pays royalties, advance on publication. Rights purchased: All. Submit: ms. Dot matrix, photocopy, computer disk OK. Reports in 1 mo. Publishing time varies. Accepts nonfiction, photos. "We publish only medical books, principally Oriental medicine and manual medicine (bodywork)." Guidelines/catalog available. Index: 61, 81.

Eastside a la Carte, 4231 135th Place S.E., Bellevue, WA 98006. Publisher. No submission info. Query w/SASE. Index: 130.

Eastside Courier-Review, c/o PO Box 716, Redmond, WA 98052. 206–885–4178. Weekly newspaper. No submission info. Query w/SASE. Index: 33.

Eastside Writers Newsletter, PO Box 8005, Totem Lake Post Office, Kirkland, WA 98034. Editor: Lyle Whitcomb. 206–821–7079. Monthly by and for members of Eastside Writers Association. Circ. 250. Sub. Membership. Not a freelance market. Index: 125.

Echo, PO Box 39, Leavenworth, WA 98826. 509–548–7911. Weekly newspaper. No submission info. Query w/SASE. Index: 33.

Echo Digest, 10300 S.W. Greenburg Road, #280, Portland, OR 97223. Editor: Owen R. Brown. Periodical. No submission info. Query w/SASE. Index: 130.

Echo Film Productions, Suite 200, 413 West Idaho Street, Boise, ID 83702. Freelance market for scripts. Query w/SASE. Index: 41, 122.

Economic Facts/Idaho Agriculture, University of Idaho Extension Service, College of Agriculture, Moscow, ID 83843. Editor: Neil Meyer. Quarterly. No submission info. Query w/SASE. Index: 3, 24, 69.

Ecotope Group, 2812 E. Madison, Seattle, WA 98112. Publisher. No submission info. Query w/SASE. Index: 130.

Edge Art Press, 154 N. 35, #204, Seattle, WA 98103. 206–547–4453. Contact: Editor. Publisher. No submission info. Query w/SASE. Index: 130.

Edmonds Arts Commission Books, 700 Main St., Edmonds, WA 98020. 206–775–2525. Editor: Ann Saling. Ads: Linda McCrystal. Press run 1,000. Self-publisher. Publishes 1 softcover orig. book a yr. Works on assignment only. Pays money, copies on acceptance. Rights purchased: First. Byline given. Dot matrix, photocopy OK. Reports in 1-2 mos. Publishes in 2-3 mos. Accepts nonfiction, fiction, poetry, cartoons, line drawings. Publication projects vary with contest subject. 500 word max. "Contest awards plus free copies." Sample $7.95+ hand. Index: 47, 65, 68.

The Edmonds View, 1827 160th Avenue N.E., Bellevue, WA 98008-2506. Weekly newspaper. No submission info. Query w/SASE. Index: 33.

Educational Digest, The Riggs Institute, 4185 S.W. 102nd Avenue, Beaverton, OR 97005. 503–646–9459. Periodical. No submission info. Query w/SASE. Index: 43.

Edwards Publishing Company, PO Box 42218, Tacoma, WA 98442. No submission info. Query w/SASE. Index: 130.

Ruth Edwins-Conley Publishing, 14600 51st N.E. #217, Marysville, WA 98270. 206–659–1229. Self-publisher of 1-2 softcover subsidy books a yr; "poems, fiction, diaries of literary merit, translations." Press run: 100. Not a freelance market. Index: 51, 97.

The Eighth Mountain Press, 642 SE 29th, Portland, OR 97214. 503–233–3936. Editor: Ruth Gundle. Press run 5,000. Publishes 2 softcover orig. books on feminist literary works a yr. Accepts unsolicited mss. Pays royalties. Query w/ clips & SASE. Photocopy OK. Reports in 1-2 mos. Accepts fiction, poetry. Index: 50, 57, 124.

Ekstasis Editions, PO Box 474, 1931 Ashgrove Street, Victoria, BC. Publisher. No submission info. Query w/SASE. Index: 130.

El Centinela, Pacific Press Publishing Association, 1350 Kings Road, Nampa, ID 83605. Editor: Tulio Peverini. Monthly. Circ. 113,000. No submission info. Query w/SASE. Index: 130.

For lists of abbreviations and the key to index numbers, see "How to Use this Section" on page 77.

122   Market Listings

Elan Northwest Publishers, PO Box 5442, Eugene, OR 97405. No submission info. Query w/SASE. Index: 130.

Elder Affairs, 315 Jones Bldg., 1331 3rd Ave., Seattle, WA 98101. Contact: Editor. Monthly periodical. No submission info. Query w/SASE. Index: 110.

The Elder Statesman, 301 - 1201 West Pender, Vancouver, BC V6E 2V2. Newspaper. No submission info. Query w/SASE. Index: 130.

Elegance Design Publications, 15431 S.E. 82nd Drive, Clackamas, OR 97015. Contact: Jean Pratt, Editor. 503–656–1988. No submission info. Query w/SASE. Index: 130.

Elephant Mountain Arts, PO Box 902, White Salmon, WA 98670. Contact: Chuck Williams. Publisher. No submission info. Query w/SASE. Index: 87, 88, 89.

Ellensburg Anthology, Four Winds Bookstore, 202 E. 4th, Ellensburg, WA 98926. Editor: Tom Lineham. 206–754–1708. Periodical of poetry and prose for emerging NW writers. Circ. 200-300. Sub. $3.50 + post. Uses 5 mss per issue. Payment: Copies. Byline given. Rights purchased: First. Submit ms, SASE. Dot matrix, photocopies, simultaneous submission, electronic OK. Reports in 2-4 mos. Fiction (2,000 wds), poetry (100 lines), plays (sections only), illustrations. "We are looking especially for new talent." Deadline: July 31 each yr. Guidelines available; sample/ $3.50/SASE. Index: 41, 51, 97.

Ellensburg Daily Record, Fourth & Main, PO Box 248, Ellensburg, WA 98926. 509–925–1414. Daily newspaper. No submission info. Query w/SASE. Index: 33.

Elliott Press, Pacific Lutheran University, Tacoma, WA 98447. 206–535–7387. Contact: Megan Benton. College "studio-laboratory" for the publishing arts. Limited editions. Not a freelance market. Index: 31.

EMC Retort, Eastern Montana College, Billings, MT 59101. Editor: Angela Enger. Newspaper. No submission info. Query w/SASE. Index: 31.

Em-Kayan, Morrison-Knudsen Corporation, PO Box 73, Boise, ID 83707. Editor: Vern Nelson. Monthly for employees, stockholders and customers of M-K. No submission info. Query w/SASE. Index: 24.

Emerald City Comix & Stories, P.O. Box 95402, Seattle, WA 98145-2402. 206–523–1201. Editor: Nils Osmar. Circ. 7,000. Sub. $3.50. Quarterly newspaper of fiction and comic strips. Uses 50 freelance mss/issue. Pays 2 copies on publication. Rights purchased: First. Byline given. Submit ms. "Must be accompanied by SASE!" Dot matrix, photocopy OK. Reports in 6 wks. Publishes in:3-6 mos. Accepts nonfiction, fiction, poetry, cartoons. "We publish short fiction up to 4,000 wds. Interested in thoughtful, well-crafted stories & poems, humorous & dramatic cartoons & comic strips." Guidelines available. Sample $1.50 in stamps. Index: 48, 51, 107.

Emerald House, PO Box 1769, Sand Point, ID 83864. Publisher. No submission info. Query w/SASE. Index: 130.

Emergency Librarian, P.O. Box C34069, Dept. 284, Seattle, WA 98124-1069. 604–734–0255. Editor: Ken Haycock. Ads: Dana Sheehan. Circ. 10,000. Sub. $40 prepaid. Publishes magazine 5 times a yr. Uses 3 freelance mss per issue. Request guidelines before writing. Pays money on publication. Rights purchased: All. Byline given. Query w/clips. Dot matrix, photocopy OK. Reports in 6 wks. Publishes within 1 yr. Accepts: Nonfiction, cartoons. Guidelines available. Index: 22, 43, 104.

Empire Press, PO Box 430, Waterville, WA 98858. 509–745–8782. Weekly newspaper. No submission info. Query w/SASE. Index: 33.

emPo Publications, 1002 E. Denny Way #202, Seattle, WA 98122. Editor: Trudy Mercer. Magazine of visual poetry and experimental writing. Sub $15 for 4 issues. Accepts freelance material. Pays copies on publication. Byline given. Submit: ms, SASE, IRC. Dot matrix, photocopies OK. No simultaneous submissions. Accepts: fiction under 1,000 wds, traditional poetry, photocopy art, B&W photos, graphics, letters to the editor. Soliciting visual poems for a series of postcards; planning a series of chapbooks and minibooks, 2-24 pgs. Sample $2. Index: 51, 97, 122.

Empress Publications, 635 Humboldt Street, No. 10, Victoria, BC V8W 1A7. No submission info. Query w/SASE. Index: 130.

Empty Bowl Press, PO Box 646, Port Townsend, WA 98386. Small press publisher of nonfiction, fiction, poetry and other material. No submission info. Query w/SASE. Index: 51, 97.

The Empty Space, 95 S. Jackson Street, Seattle, WA 98104. Contact: Tom Creamer. 206–587–3737. 225 seat, flexible stage theater accepts unsolicited full-length plays, one-acts, translations, adaptations, musicals, from regional playwrights (ID, MT, OR, WA, WY). Query w/SASE. Reports in 3 wks to query, 4 mos to scripts. Tips: "Holds N.W. Playwrights Conference where 3 playwrights are selected to work with director." Index: 41.

The Emshock Letter, Vongrutnorv Og Press, Inc., Randall Flat Rd., PO Box 411, Troy, ID 83871. 208–835–4902. Editor: Steven E. Erickson. Newsletter published 7-10 times per yr. Sub. $15. Submissions accepted only from subscribers. Pays in copies. Acquires 1st rights. Dot matrix, photocopied OK. Topics: "Widely variable: philosophical, metaphysical...represents a free-style form of expressive relation." Index: 13, 39, 68.

Enchantment Publishing of Oregon, Rt 1, Box 28H, Enterprise, OR, 97828. Editor: Irene Barklow. Publisher. No submission info. Query w/SASE. Index: 130.

Encore Arts in Performance Magazine, Encore Publishing, Inc. 1410 S.W. Morrison, Portland, OR 97205. Editor: Philbrook Heppner. 503–226–1468. Ads: Tom Brown. Published 60 times a season. Circ. 986,000. Not a freelance market. Sample: $.73. Index: 10, 41, 86.

Endeavor, Treasure Valley Community College, 650 College Blvd., Ontario, OR 97914. 503–889–6493. Biweekly newspaper "carrying campus news and nonfiction articles." Circ. 1,400. Payment: Copies. Byline given. Query wi/ms. Simultaneous submission OK. Nonfiction: 300-500 wds on experiences, problems of Eastern Oregon college students. Tips: "Query before submitting lengthy feature." Sample free. Index: 31.

Enfantaisie, 2603 SE 32nd Ave., Portland, OR 97202. 503–235–5304. Editor: Michael Gould. Published bimonthly for children learning French. Circ. 2,000. Not accepting submissions at this time. "We do not guarantee return of any unsolicited material." Index: 28, 29, 73.

Engineering Geology/Soils Engineering Symposium, Idaho Transportation Department, PO Box 7129, Boise, ID 83707. Annual periodical. Circ. 500. No submission info. Query w/SASE. Index: 69, 109.

Engineering News-Record, 6040 Fifth N.E., Seattle, WA 98115. 206–525–0433. Periodical. No submission info. Query w/SASE. Index: 24.

Ensemble Publications, Inc., 921 S.W. Morrison, Suite 530, Portland, OR 97205. No submission info. Query w/SASE. Index: 130.

Enterprise, c/o B. C. Central Credit Union, 1441 Creekside Drive, Vancouver, BC V6B 3R9. Editor: David Morton. Bimonthly concerning credit unions in B.C., aimed at managers and directors. Circ. 2,000. Payment: $200-300 on publication. Query w/SASE. Phone query, dot matrix

For lists of abbreviations and the key to index numbers, see "How to Use this Section" on page 75.

Writer's Northwest Handbook 123

OK. Publishes submissions in 1-2 mos. Nonfiction: 1,000-2,000 wds about credit unions and co-operatives. Photos: contact sheet and negatives w/article. Guidelines/ sample available. Index: 24.

Enterprise, PO Box 977, Lynnwood, WA 98046. 206–775–7521. Weekly newspaper. No submission info. Query w/SASE. Index: 33.

The Enterprise Courier, Box 471, Oregon City, OR 97045. 503–636–1911. Daily newspaper. No submission info. Query w/SASE. Index: 33.

Entertainment Publications, Inc., 8196 SW Hall Blvd., Beaverton, OR 97005. 503–646–8201. Contact: Editor. No submission info. Query w/ SASE. Index: 45.

Entreprenurial Workshops, 4000 Aurora Ave. N., Ste. 112, Seattle, WA, 98103. Editor: Fred Klein. Publisher. No submission info. Query w/ SASE. Index: 24.

Environmental Law, Northwestern School of Law, 10015 SW Terwilliger Blvd., Portland, OR 97219. 503–244–1181. Contact: Managing Editor. Sub. $20 (1 vol., 4 issues). Publishes journal on environmental law and natural resources only. Accepts unsolicited mss. No pay. Submit ms w/SASE. Photocopy OK. Reports in 2-3 wks. Accepts nonfiction. Sample $8-$10. Index: 46, 74.

Eotu, 1810 W. State #115, Boise, ID, 83702. Editor/Ads: Larry D. Dennis. Bimonthly magazine. Sub $18. Circ 200+. Uses 12-15 freelance mss per issue. Pays $5-25, 1 copy, on acceptance. Rights acquired: First. Byline given. Submit ms, SASE. Dot matrix, photocopies OK. Reports in 6-8 wks. Publishes in 2-6 mos. Accepts: fiction; cartoons; artwork, $5 for black ink or pen ("reproductions are great if the lines are clear"). "Experimental fiction. Try to write something that has never been written before. Genre unimportant. We've published everything from Romance to Western to SciFi (all in the same issue!). 5,000 wds maximum. Guidelines SASE. Sample $4. Index: 14, 48, 51.

Epicenter Press Inc., Box 60529, Fairbanks, AK 99706. 907–456–6853. Publishes 4-6 hard/softcover, originals, reprints a yr. Accepts unsolicited submissions w/SASE. Pays royalties. Acquires all rights. Submit ms, SASE. Reports in 4-6 wks. Accepts nonfiction. Index: 130.

Equinews, PO Box 1778, Vernon, BC V1T 8C3. 604–545–9896. Editor: Dr. B. J. White. Monthly newspaper. Sub. $15/Cdn, $20/US. Circ. 16,792. Uses freelance material. Pays $30-100/article on publication. Byline given. Submit ms, SASE. Dot matrix, photocopied OK. Reports in 2 mo. Publishes in 1-2 mo. Accepts nonfiction, photos, cartoons. Topics: all equine aspects. Photos, $5. Sample $2. Index: 6, 103.

ERGO! Bumbershoot's Literary Magazine, PO Box 21134, Seattle, WA 98111. Editor/ads: Louise DiLenge. 206–448–5233. Annual of "works by Bumbershoot literary arts program participants, book reviews, bookfair participant directory, articles of literary interest." Circ. 3,000. Accepts freelance material. Payment: Copies. Byline given. Query w/SASE. Phone query, dot matrix, photocopies, simultaneous submission, electronic OK. Uses nonfiction, fiction, poetry, photos, plays, cartoons. Photos: B&W glossy, no smaller than 3x5. Tips: "Reviews should be for small press publications. Articles should be of particular interest to the literary community. Make contact between the months of Feb./May." Sample: $1. Index: 51, 76, 97.

ERIC Clearinghouse on Educational Mgmt., 1787 Agate Street, Eugene, OR 97403. Contact: Stuart C. Smith. 503–686–5043. Publisher of softcover books on educational research. "The Educational Resources Information Center (ERIC) is a decentralized nationwide network, sponsored by the National Institute of Education, and designed to collect educational documents and to make them available to teachers, administrators, researchers, students." Query w/SASE. Photocopies OK. Education research. Guidelines/catalog available. Index: 1, 43.

ESQ, Washington State University Press, Pullman, WA 99164-5910. 509–335–3518. Quarterly. Sub. $15. No submission info. Query w/SASE. Index: 31.

Esquimalt Lookout, CFB, Esquimalt FMO, Victoria, BC V0S 1B0. Editor: A.C. Tassic. 604–385–0313. Periodical. No submission info. Query w/SASE. Index: 130.

Essence, Central Oregon Community College, NW College Way, Bend, OR 97701. 503–382–6112 X304. Editor: Bob Shotwol. College literary magazine. Editors could change yearly. SASE for guidelines. Index: 31, 51, 91.

Estrada Publications and Photography, 5228 Rambler Road, Victoria, BC V8Y 2H5. 604–658–8870. Self-publisher of 1 softcover book a yr for children, teachers. Not a freelance market. Index: 29, 67, 115.

Estrela Press, 2318 2nd Avenue, Box 23, Seattle, WA 98121. No submission info. Query w/SASE. Index: 130.

Et Cetera, King County Library System, 300 8th Ave. N., Seattle, WA 98109. Contact: Public Information Officer. Periodical. No submission info. Query w/SASE. Index: 104.

Eurock, PO Box 13718, Portland, OR 97213. Editor: Archie Patterson. 503–281–0247. Quarterly of new music by experimental musicians from around the world. Circ. 700. No pay. Byline given. Phone queries. "Interested in features, interviews, LP reviews. Knowledge necessary in this very specialized area of music...Familiarity with the publication's concept is necessary...Pre-arrangement of artists' material suggested." Sample: $1. Index: 86.

Europe Through the Back Door Travel Newsletter, 120 4th Ave. N., Edmonds, WA 98020. 206–771–8303. Editor: Eileen Owen. Sub. free. Circ. 12,000. Uses 2 freelance mss per issue. Pays copies on publication. Rights acquired: None. Byline given. Submit ms, SASE. Dot matrix, photocopies, simultaneous OK. Reports in 1 mo. Publishes within 1 yr. Accepts nonfiction, poetry, photos, cartoons. Budget European travel tips, unusual places, how-to, personal experiences, specific tips, keep it light, 500-700 wds. B&W photos, camera-ready. Guidelines available. Sample free. Index: 120.

Event, Kwantlen College, Box 9030, Surrey, BC V3T 5H8. Semiannual periodical. Not a freelance market. Index: 31.

Event, Douglas College, PO Box 2503, New Westminster, BC V3L 5B2. 604–520–5400. Editor: Vye Flindall. Literary journal published 3 times/yr. Sub. $17/2 yr. Circ. 1,000. Uses 6+ freelance mss per issue. Pays money ($25-100), copies on publication. Acquires 1st rights. Byline given. Submit ms, SASE. Photocopied OK. Reports in 3-4 mo. Publishes 10-15 mo. Accepts nonfiction, fiction, poetry, photos, plays, drama. Tips: invite involvement and present experiences; readers are sophisticated, open-minded. Usual fiction about 5,000 wds. Payment: $30/poem, $10/page for other. Prefer 5X7 glossy B&W prints. Guidelines/samples available. Index: 51, 76, 97.

Events Magazine, 7514 SW Barnes Rd. #B, Portland, OR 97225-6265. 503–224–6109. Editor: Greg Kroell. Monthly. Sub. $12. No submission info. Query w/SASE. Index: 45, 86.

The Everett Herald, PO Box 930, Everett, WA 98206. Newspaper. No submission info. Query w/SASE. Index: 33.

Evergreen Pacific Publs., 4535 Union Bay Pl. NE, Seattle, WA 98105. 206–524–7330. No submission info. Query w/SASE. Index: 130.

For lists of abbreviations and the key to index numbers, see "How to Use this Section" on page 77.

Evergreen Publishing, 901 Lenora, Seattle, WA 98121. 206–624–8400. Editor: Martin Rudow. Publisher. No submission info. Query w/SASE. Index: 130.

Ex Libris, Box 225, Sun Valley, ID 83353. Publisher. No submission info. Query w/SASE. Index: 130.

Exhibition, Bainbridge Island Arts Council, 261 Madison Ave. S., Bainbridge Island, WA 98110. 206–842–6017, 206–842–7901. Editors: Kari Berger, Art; John Willson, Margi Berger, literary. Ads: Kary Berger. Periodical. Sub. $15/yr. Circ. 1,000. Uses freelance material by Bainbridge Island residents and B.I. Arts Council Members ($15) wherever they may live. Pays in copies on publication. Byline given. Submit ms, SASE. Dot matrix, photocopied OK, no simultaneous. Reports in 2 mo. Accepts nonfiction, fiction, poetry. B&W line art, some half tones. Tips: Emphasis on design and production values in addition to literary and artistic standards. Sample $2. Index: 51, 97, 123.

Exponent, Montana State University, 330 Strand Union Building, Bozeman, MT 59717-0001. 406–994–2611. Semiweekly newspaper. No submission info. Query w/SASE. Index: 31.

The Extender, Jackson County Extension Service, 1301 Maple Grove Dr., Medford, OR 97501. 503–776–7371. Contact: Editor. Periodical. No submission info. Query w/SASE. Index: 3, 60.

Extension Service Publishers, Oregon State University, Corvallis, OR 97331. Agricultural and home economics publications for both commercial and home horticulture, farming and animal husbandry. No submission info. Query w/SASE. Index: 3, 36, 56.

Eye of the Raven, 91981 Taylor Road, McKenzie Bridge, OR 97401. Editor: Cheree Conrad. Monthly periodical. No submission info. Query w/SASE. Index: 130.

Facts Newspaper, 2765 East Cherry, Seattle, WA 98122. 206–324–0552. Weekly newspaper. No submission info. Query w/SASE. Index: 130.

Fade in Publications, 312 S. 6th, Bozeman, MT 59715. No submission info. Query w/SASE. Index: 130.

Fairbanks News-Miner, Box 710, Fairbanks, AK 99707. 907–456–6661. Daily newspaper. No submission info. Query w/SASE. Index: 33.

Fairchild Times, 1601 S. Flight Drive, Spokane, WA 99204-9767. 509–535–7089. Weekly newspaper. No submission info. Query w/SASE. Index: 33.

Fairhaven Communications, 810 N. State St., Bellingham, WA 98225. Contact: Editor. Publisher. No submission info. Query w/SASE. Index: 130.

Falcon Press Publishing Co., Inc., PO Box 731, Helena, MT 59624. 406–442–6597. Editor: Bill Scheider. Publishes 10-15 hard/softcover originals, reprints, subsidy books a yr. Payment & rights vary. Submit query, SASE. Dot matrix, photocopied, simultaneous OK. Reports in 2-3 wks. Publishing time varies. Accepts only for the "California Geographic Series" and recreational guide books for most Western states (hiking, fishing, hunting, river floating, etc.). Catalog available. Index: 53, 103.

Family Tree Pony Farm, Publications Division, 1708 Burwell, Bremerton, WA 98310. No submission info. Query w/SASE. Index: 130.

The Fanatic Reader, 9513 S.W. Barbur Blvd., Portland, OR 97219. Editor: Jim Burnett. 503–244–5468. Bimonthly that reviews the best of pop mags. Sub $30. Not a freelance market, but "a few reviewers may be needed. Contact first." Index: 76, 77, 80.

Fantasy Football, 18411 60th Pl. NE, Seattle, WA 98155. 206–525–6928. Editor: Bruce Taylor. New annual magazine. Newsstand $3.95. Circ. 37,000. Will use 3-4 freelance mss per issue. Pays copies. Byline given. Interested in columnist material on pro football, offensive play photographs, cartoons. Tips: football expertise and wit is important. Index: 115.

Fantasy and Terror, PO Box 20610, Seattle, WA 98102. Editor: Jessica A. Salmonson. An "octavo format magazine, payment in copies, uses macabre poems-in prose, themes covering ghosts and graves, morosity and fear, somewhat experimental, highly refined, dark, cruel, evil, jaded, darkly romantic. Not for everyone." Queries w/SASE. Sample: $2.50. Index: 48, 51, 97.

Fantasy Macabre, Box 20610, Seattle, WA 98102. Editor: Jessica A. Salmonson. Periodical. Payment: $.01 per wd., copies. Queries w/SASE. Fiction: under 3,000 wds, "supernatural literature with a slant towards translations from European authors. Translators always welcome...Lyric poetry (nothing experimental, no free verse)." Sample/$3.25. Index: 48, 51, 97.

Farah's, Inc., PO Box 66395, Portland, OR 97266. Contact: Dr. Madelain Farah. 503–236–1796. Self-publisher of softcover books: cooking, Mideast culture. Not a freelance market. Index: 54.

Farm & Ranch Chronicle, Box 157, Cottonwood, ID 83522. 208–962–3851. Monthly. No submission info. Query/SASE. Index: 3.

Farm Review, P.O. Box 153, Lynden, WA 98264. 206–354–4444. Monthly. No submission info. Query/SASE. Index: 3.

Fathom Publishing Company, PO Box 821, Cordova, AK 99574. No submission info. Query w/SASE. Index: 130.

Fax Collector's Editions, Inc., PO Box 851, Mercer Island, WA 98040. Publisher. No submission info. Query w/SASE. Index: 130.

Features Northwest, 5132 126th Place N.E., Marysville, WA 98270. Publisher. Contact John & Roberta Wolcott. 206–659–7559. No submission info. Query w/SASE. Index: 130.

Federal Way News, 1634 South 312th, Federal Way, WA 98003. 206–839–0700. Weekly newspaper. No submission info. Query w/SASE. Index: 33.

Fedora, PO Box 577, Siletz, OR 97380. Editor: John E. Hawkes. Periodical. No submission info. Query w/SASE. Index: 130.

Ferndale Record, 2008 Main St., Ferndale, WA 98248. 206–384–1411. Contact: Editor. Newspaper. No submission info. Query w/SASE. Index: 33.

Fernglen Press, 473 Sixth St., Lake Oswego, OR 97034. 503–635–4719. Self-publisher of 1 softcover book a yr. on hiking trails, Hawaii, nature. Index: 88, 92, 120.

The Fiction Review, Brick Lung Press, PO Box 12268, Seattle, WA 98102. Editor: S. P. Stressman. Ads: Stephanie Miskowski. Quarterly magazine. (Also publishes 1 chapbook a yr.) Sub. $15. Circ. 300. Uses 1-2 freelance mss per issue. Pays in copies on publication. Acquires 1st rights. Byline given. Submit ms, SASE. Reports in 2-8 wks. Publishes in 3-6 mos. Accepts nonfiction, fiction, other. "Essays on fiction. Reviews (500-750 wds) of collections & anthologies from small press or by writers needing more exposure. Stories any subject — prefer an edge to style —

For lists of abbreviations and the key to index numbers, see "How to Use this Section" on page 75.

Writer's Northwest Handbook   125

500-4,000 wds." Tips: "Do not follow trends in contemporary, published fiction. Be unique." B&W graphics, 6x6" max. Guidelines available. Sample $4. Index: 51, 76, 77.

N.H. Fieldstone Publishing, PO Box 22, Medina, WA 98039. No submission info. Query w/SASE. Index: 130.

Findhorn Publications, PO Box 57, Clinton, WA 98236. No submission info. Query w/SASE. Index: 130.

Fine Art & Auction Review, 2227 Granville Street, Vancouver, BC V6H 3G1. Editor: Anthony R. Westbridge. 604–734–4944. Tabloid devoted to auctions and fine art for collectors. Uses freelance material. Short nonfiction w/photos. No submission info. Query w/SASE. Index: 8, 10, 36.

Fine Madness, Box 15176, Seattle, WA 98115. Biannual journal of poetry, fiction reviews, essays. Circ. 600. Pays copies on publication. Byline given. Rights purchased: First. Accepts freelance mss. Typewritten or laser ms w/SASE only. Reports in 3 mos. Publishes in 1 yr. or less. Accepts fiction, poetry. "We discourage Victorian verse. No gratuitous sex/violence. Poetry, 10 poems max. Fiction, 20 pp. max. Annual awards for best of volume." Guidelines available. Sample $4.90. Index: 51, 76, 97.

FINNAM Newsletter, Finnish-American Historical Soc. of West, PO Box 5522, Portland, OR 97208. 503–654–0448. Editor: Gene A. Knapp. Quarterly, membership. Circ. 400. Uses freelance material. Byline given. Submit query w/clips, ms, phone, SASE. Dot matrix, photocopied OK. Accepts nonfiction, photos, other. Guidelines/sample available. Index: 65, 84.

Finnish American Literary Heritage Foundation, PO Box 1838, Portland, OR 97207. Publisher. No submission info. Query w/SASE. Index: 58, 73, 84.

Finnish Connection, PO Box 1531, Vancouver WA 98668-1531. Editor/ads: Eugene Messer. 206–254–8936. Sub. Assoc. $10/yr. Circ. 5,500. Published 6 times per yr. Accepts 2-3 freelance mss per issue pertaining to Scandinavians and Finns in the US and Canada: nonfiction, fiction, poetry and photos (B&W/color glossies) w/articles. Query w/clips, ms, SASE. Phone queries, photocopied & simultaneous submissions OK. Reports "promptly." Gives byline and pays $20-$50 on publication. Guidelines available; sample/$1. Index: 39, 73, 84.

Fins and Feathers (Idaho Edition), Fins & Feathers Publishing Company, 318 W. Franklin Avenue, Minneapolis, MN 55404. Editor: Bill Vogt. Monthly. No submission info. Query w/SASE. Index: 6, 92, 115.

FIR Report, 1301 Maple Grove Dr., Medford, OR 97501. 503–776–7116. Contact: Editor. Periodical. No submission info. Query w/SASE. Index: 130.

Firehouse Theater, 1436 S.W. Montgomery Street, Portland, OR 97201. Contact: Patricia Iron. 503–248–4737. Accepts scripts. Seeks new works by NW playwrights. Query w/SASE. Index: 41.

First Alternative Thymes, 1007 S.E. 3rd St., Corvallis, OR 97333. 503–929–4167. Editor: Christine Peterson. Monthly. Sub. $6. Circ. 1,000. Uses 10 freelance mss per issue. Pays in copies. Submit query w/clips, ms, phone, SASE. Dot matrix, photocopied, simultaneous OK. Reports in 1-2 wks. Accepts nonfiction, photos, cartoons. Sample available. Index: 2, 28, 45.

Firsthand Press, 137 Sixth Street, Juneau, AK 99801. No submission info. Query w/SASE. Index: 130.

Harriet U. Fish, PO Box 135, Carlsborg, WA 98324. 206–542–9195. Self-publisher of 1 softcover book, reprint a yr. on local history. Print run: 1,000. Not a freelance market. Catalog available. Index: 65.

The Fisherman's News, C-3 Building, Rm. 110, Fisherman's Terminal, Seattle, WA 98119. Bimonthly. No submission info. Query w/SASE. Index: 24.

Fishing Holes Magazine, PO Box 32, Sedro Woolley, WA 98284. Editor/Ads: Brad Stracener. Monthly. Sub. $15. Circ. 10,000. Uses 4-5 freelance mss per issue. Pays money on publication. Acquires 1st rights. Byline given. Submit query w/clips, SASE. Photocopied, electronic subs OK. Accepts nonfiction, photos. Guidelines/sample available. Index: 92, 103, 115.

Fishing and Hunting News, Outdoor Empire Publications Inc., Box C- 19000, 511 Eastlake E., Seattle, WA 98109. Weekly. No submission info. Query w/SASE. Index: 92, 103, 115.

Fishing Tackle Trade News, PO Box 2669, Vancouver, WA 98668-2669. Editor: John Kirk. 206–693–4721. Ads: Robert E. Wood. Published 10 times a yr. for retailers of fishing tackle, hunting gear, camping gear, marine equipment. Circ. 23,000. Sub. $35. Accepts freelance material. Payment: Money on acceptance. Byline given. Queries w/SASE. Phone queries, dot matrix, photocopies OK. Uses nonfiction, photos, cartoons, illustrations. "Stories cover management, merchandising, business topics, species slants (how retailers can use info on two particular species to assist their selling efforts). We also cover news of the resources, and publish success profiles, articles on to use products, and product round-ups." Approx. 1,000-1,500 wds. Photos: B&W, verticals, $25; $50 color transparencies; no Polaroid. Guidelines/sample available free, SASE. Index: 24.

Fjord Press, PO Box 16501, Seattle, WA 98116. 206–625–9363. Editor: Steve Murray. Publishes 4-6 hard/softcover originals, reprints a yr. Press run: 1,500-5,000. Accepts unsolicited submissions. Pays royalties, copies on publication. Submit query w/clips, SASE a must. Photocopied, simultaneous OK. Reports in 7-90 days. Publishes 18-24 mo. Accepts nonfiction, fiction. Topics: translations are main interest (include sample of original language text); "Also looking for top-notch fiction & nonfiction from western U.S. writers, preferably published ones, but we'll consider first-timers tif the literary quality is high — also thrillers (no murder mysteries)....95% of submissions are tdull for us, and we have yet to publish an unsolicited ms–but we have hope." Catalog available for 25-cent stamp. Index: 18, 51, 73.

Flashes, North Idaho Children, 321 22nd Avenue, PO Box 1288, Lewiston, ID 83501. Semiannual periodical. No submission info. Query w/ SASE. Index: 28.

Flight Press, 3630 W. Broadway, No. 2, Vancouver, BC V6R 2B7. Nonfiction publisher. No submission info. Query w/SASE. Index: 130.

The Florian Group, Astoria Building, 44 Hillshire Dr., Lake Oswego, OR 97034. 503–638–1972. Editor: F. Michael Sisavic. Publishes hard/softcover nonfiction travel books. Press run: 5,000-10,000. Accepts unsolicited submissions. Dot matrix, photocopied OK. Index: 120.

The Florist & Grower, 686 Honeysuckle N., Salem, OR 97203. 503–390–0766. Editor: Donald H. Johnson. Monthly periodical. No submission info. Query w/SASE. Index: 3, 24.

Flower of Truth Publishing Company, PO Box 3029, Forsyth, MT 59327. No submission info. Query w/SASE. Index: 130.

The Flyfisher, 1387 Cambridge Street, Idaho Falls, ID 83401. Editor: Dennis G. Bitton. 208–523–7300. Quarterly journal of the Federation of Fly Fishers. Circ. 10,000. Accepts nonfiction/fiction, to 2,000 wds, on flyfishing. Buys photos w/articles. Pays various rates on publication.

For lists of abbreviations and the key to index numbers, see "How to Use this Section" on page 77.

126   Market Listings

Query w/SASE. Guidelines available; samples $3 from Federation of Fly Fishers, PO Box 1088, West Yellowstone, MT 59758. Index: 38, 53, 115.

Flyfishing, Frank Amato Publications, PO Box 02112, Portland, OR 97202. 503–653–8108. Editor: Marty Sherman. Ads: Joyce Sherman. Magazine published 5 times a yr. Uses 15 freelance mss per issue. Pays money on publication. Acquires 1st rights. Byline given. Submit query w/clips, ms, SASE. Reports in 2 wks. Accepts nonfiction articles (approx. 1,500 wds) related to all aspects of flyfishing–location, water management, equipment, etc. "...buys ONLY stories which are accompanied by color transparencies, B&W glossies and/or original art work." Guidelines available. Index: 53.

Flyfishing News, Views & Reviews, 1387 Cambridge Drive, Idaho Falls, ID 83401. Editor: Dennis G. Bitton. 208–52–7300. Ads: Leigh Ann Stanger. Semimonthly. Circ. 4,000. Sub. $15. Uses 8 mss per issue. Payment: Money on publication. Byline given. Rights purchased: First. Query w/SASE. Reports in 2 wks. "Must have flyfishing as part of the article. Preferably something new and different. Fiction, essays and editorials welcomed." Photos: B&W and color slides w/article. If photos only, rates are for photos only. Cartoons accepted. Guidelines available; sample/$2. Index: 53, 92, 103.

The Flying Needle, 3165 S.W. Ridgewood Avenue, Portland, OR 97225. Editor: Glennis McNeal. Periodical. No submission info. Query w/SASE. Index: 130.

Flying Pencil Publications, P.O. Box 19062, Portland, OR 97219. 503–245–2314. Editor: Madelynne Diness. Press run: 5,000-40,000. Publishes 1 or more softcover original reprint books a yr. on Oregon sportfishing. Accepts unsolicited mss..Pay negotiable. Rights negotiable. Query w/clips & SASE. Reports in 2 wks. Accept nonfiction, photos ($100/cover quality photo; $10/BW photos illustrating Oregon sportfishing action or environments; wildlife photos also considered). "Publisher of *Fishing in Oregon, A Directory To Oregon Sportfishing Waters*." Index: 53, 92, 103.

Focus, Oregon Public Broadcasting, 7140 Macadam, Portland, OR 97219. Contact: Editor. Periodical. No submission info. Query w/SASE. Index: 80.

Focus on Books, PO Box 51103, Seattle, WA 98115. 206–527–2693. Editor: Ellen Hokanson. Quarterly newsletter. Sub. $12. Circ. 4,000. Promotes books for a fee. Not a freelance market. Index: 28, 89, 102.

Footnotes, Pacific Northwest Booksellers Assoc., PO Box 1931, Mount Vernon, WA, 98273. 206–336–3345. Editor: Kris Molesworth. Monthly. Circ. 500. Uses freelance material. Dot matrix, photocopied OK. Index: 22, 102.

Footprint Publishing Co. Ltd., PO Box 1830, Revelstoke, BC V0E 2S0. Published 3 hardcover original books in last 3 yrs. Does not accept unsolicited submissions. Index: 23, 63.

Judy Ford & Company, 11530 84th Ave. NE, Kirkland, WA 98034. 206–823–4421. Editor: Judy Ford. Publisher. No submission info. Query w/SASE. Index: 111.

Foreign Artists, Poets & Authors Review, 2921 E. Madison Ave., Ste. 7, Seattle, WA 98112. Quarterly. No submission info. Query w/SASE. Index: 73, 76.

Forelaws on Board, 320 S.W. Stark Street, Rm 517, Portland, OR 97204. Editor: Karen James. Periodical. No submission info. Query w/SASE. Index: 130.

Forest Industries Telecommunications, 3025 Hilyard, Eugene, OR 97405. Publisher. No submission info. Query w/SASE. Index: 24, 55, 78.

Forest Log, Department of Forestry, 2600 State St., Salem, OR 97310. 503–378–2562. Contact: Editor. Monthly, free. Does not use freelance material. Sample available. Index: 3, 55, 60.

Forest Planning, c/o Cascade Holistic Economic Consultant, PO Box 3479, Eugene, OR 97403. Editor: Dianne Weaver. Periodical. No submission info. Query w/SASE. Index: 55.

Forest Watch, CHEC Publications, PO Box 3479, Eugene, OR 97403. 503–686–2432. Editor: Anae Boulton. Monthly magazine of forestry concerns. Sub $20. Circ. 1,200. Unsolicited submissions OK. No pay. Byline given. Phone query OK. 1,500 to 3,000 wds.Topics: forest management, ecology, economics, wildlife habitat, recreation, pest management. Sample $2.50. Index: 46, 55, 103.

Forest World, World Forestry Center, 4033 S.W. Canyon Road, Portland, OR 97221. 503–228–1367. Editor: Anna Browne. Sub $25. Circ. 5,000. Quarterly published by the World Forestry Center in Portland, OR. Readers are located in 50 states and a dozen countries and are interested in forest conservation, forest recreation and related crafts and art forms. Uses 10 freelance mss per issue. Pays money, copies, on publication. Rights purchased: First. Byline given. Submit query w/clips, ms, SASE. Accepts nonfiction, photos. "We seldom buy mss without illustrative support. Payment for a story & photo package: $50-$250. Payment for photos or artwork purchased separately: $10-$100." Guidelines available. Sample $2.50. Index: 35, 38, 55.

The Foreword, 15455 65th Ave. S., Tukwila, WA 98188. Contact: Editor. Monthly periodical. No submission info. Query w/SASE. Index: 130.

Forks Forum & Peninsula Herald, PO Box 300, Forks, WA 98331. 206–374–2281. Weekly newspaper. No submission info. Query w/SASE. Index: 33.

Fort Lewis Ranger, PO Box 98801, Tacoma, WA 98499. 206–584–1212. Army base weekly newspaper. No submission info. Query w/SASE. Index: 83.

The Foundation Afield, Rocky Mountain Elk Foundation, Route 3, Wilderness Plateau, Troy, MT 59935. Periodical. No submission info. Query w/SASE. Index: 6, 35.

Fountain Books, 2475 W. 37th Avenue, Vancouver, BC V6M 1P4. Self-publisher of softcover books for lawyers and legal secretaries. Not a freelance market. Index: 74.

Fountain Publications, 3728 N.W. Thurman Street, Portland, OR 97210. No submission info. Query w/SASE. Index: 130.

Four Five One, PO Box 25426, Seattle, WA 98125-2328. Contact: Editor. Periodical. Submit ms, SASE. Accept fiction, poetry, essays. Index: 51, 97.

The Fox Hunt, 506 W. Crockett, Seattle, WA 98119. Publisher. No submission info. Query w/SASE. Index: 130.

For lists of abbreviations and the key to index numbers, see "How to Use this Section" on page 75.

Writer's Northwest Handbook 127

Fox Publishing Company, 320 S.W. Stark Street, Suite 519, Portland, OR 97204. Contact: Publishing Director. No submission info. Query w/ SASE. Index: 130.

Fox Reading Research Company, PO Box 1059, Coeur d'Alene, ID 83814. Publisher. No submission info. Query w/SASE. Index: 130.

Franklin County Graphic, PO Box 160, Connell, WA 99326. 509–234–3181. Weekly newspaper. No submission info. Query w/SASE. Index: 33.

The Charles Franklin Press, 7821 175th Street S.W., Edmonds, WA 98020. Contact: Linda Meyer or Denelle Peaker. 206–774–6979. Publisher of 3 nonfiction, hard/softcover, original books per yr.; self-help and booklets for national organizations. "We specialize in children's books which teach safety and common sense, especially sexual assault and abduction prevention skills. Most of our books are 25 to 40 pages. They must be written in a non-threatening style. We rely heavily on an organization's existing network to distribute our books. Print run: 5,000. Accepts freelance material. Payment: Money, 8% without split, 5 or 6% with split, or negotiable. Rights purchased: All. Query w/sample chapters or complete ms and SASE. Photocopies OK. Reports in 1 month. Publishes in 6 mos. Tips: "Author should indicate to publisher the market and extent of the market as well as organizations that might be interested in the book." Catalog available. Index: 29, 47, 124.

The Fraser Institute, 626 Bute Street, Vancouver, BC V6E1. 604–688–0221. Publisher of trade paperbacks. Not a freelance market. Index: 130.

Fredrickson/Kloepfel Publishing Company, 7748 17th S.W., Seattle, WA 98106. Contact: John Blair. 206–767–4915. Self-publisher of books on/of poetry for "drunks, weirdos, and other non-lit. types." Not a freelance market. Index: 39, 94, 97.

The Free Agent, PO Box 02008, Portland, OR 97202. 503–777–6428. Editors: Giraud, Kaushik, Lydgate. Ads: Matthew Giraud. Monthly. Sub. $15. Circ. 10,000. Uses 3-5 freelance mss per issue. Pays in copies. Byline given. Submit query w/clips, SASE. Dot matrix, photocopied OK. Reports in 1-2 wks. Accepts nonfiction, fiction, poetry, photos, plays, cartoons, other. Sample $1.50. Index: 51, 95, 97.

Free Press, PO Box 218, Cheney, WA 99004-0218. 509–235–6184. Weekly newspaper. No submission info. Query w/SASE. Index: 33.

Free! The Newsletter of Free Materials/Services, Department 284, Box C34069, Seattle, WA 98124-1069. Published 5 time a yr. Lists free materials which have been evaluated by professionals and are readily available. Short descriptions. Sub. $18. No submissions info. Query w/SASE. Index: 36, 43.

Free-Bass Press, Box 563, Eugene, OR 97440. No submission info. Query w/SASE. Index: 130.

Freedom Socialist, New Freeway Hall, 5018 Ranier Avenue S., Seattle, WA 98118. 206–722–2453. Political tabloid. No submission info. Query w/SASE. Index: 50, 98, 112.

Freighter Travel News, PO Box 12693, Salem, OR 97306. 503–399–8567. Editor: Leland Pledger. Monthly newsletter with firsthand reports of freighter voyages. Sub. $18. Freelance mss accepted. Pays copies. Byline given. Submit ms, SASE. Dot matrix, photocopies OK. Reports in 15 days. Publishes in 6 mo. Nonfiction. Tips: Wants articles on "recent travel experience aboard freighters, barges, or other unique water craft." Sample $1.50 Index: 120.

The Freighthoppers Manual, PO Box 191, Seattle, WA 98111. Editor: Dan Leen. Publisher. No submission info. Query w/SASE. Index: 120.

Friendly Press, 2744 Friendly Street, Eugene, OR 97405. No submission info. Query w/SASE. Index: 130.

Friends of the Trees Yearbook, Friends of the Trees Society, PO Box 1466, Chelan, WA 98816. Contact: Editor. Annual magazine. Sub. $5/$10. Circ. 8,000. Uses freelance material. Submit query w/clips, ms, phone, SASE. Dot matrix, photocopied, simultaneous, electronic subs OK. Accepts nonfiction. Sample $4. Index: 3, 19, 56.

Friendship Publications, Inc., PO Box 1472, Spokane, WA 99210. No submission info. Query w/SASE. Index: 130.

From The Woodpile, Matanuska-Susitna Community College, PO Box 899, Palmer, AK 99645. Contact: Barbara Mishler. 907–745–4255. Sub. $5/yr. Annual literary journal of poetry, short fiction, essays and photographs. "Designed to offer writers and photographers from remote Alaskan areas a market for their creative efforts. Though we come from University of Alaska's rural education system, we will consider mss from anywhere inside or outside Alaska." Query w/ms, SASE. Index: 51, 95, 97.

Front Row, PO Box 11438, Eugene, OR 97440. 503–683–8247. Editor: Jeremiah O'Brien. Monthly. Sub. $12.95. No submission info. Query w/ SASE. Index: 10, 41, 86..

Frontier Printing & Publishing, 322 Queen Anne Ave. N., Seattle, WA 98109. Editor: Jerry Russell. Publishes 4 books a yr. Press run: 3,000. Accepts unsolicited submissions. Pays royalties. Submit query. Reports in 1 mo. Publishes in 1 yr. Guidelines available. Index: 65, 67, 89..

Frontier Publications, 124 Ivy, Nampa, ID 83651. No submission info. Query w/SASE. Index: 130.

The Frontiersman, 1261 Seward Meridian Rd., Wasilla, AK 99687. 907–376–3288. Editors: Sean Hanlon/Duncan Frazier. Ads: Barb Stephl. Biweekly newspaper. Uses freelance material. Pays money on publication. Acquires 1st rights. Byline given. Submit query w/clips, SASE. Photocopied OK. Reports in 2 wks. Publishes in 2 wks. Accepts nonfiction about rural Alaska. Index: 4, 46, 65.

O.W. Frost Publisher, 2141 Lord Baranof Drive, Anchorage, AK 99503. No submission info. Query w/SASE. Index: 130.

Frostfox Magazine, North 626 Mullan, Suite 17, Spokane, WA, 99206. Editor: Michael Hargraves. Periodical. No submission info. Query w/ SASE. Index: 130.

Fryingpan, 7378 S.W. Pacific Coast Hwy, Waldport, OR 97394. Editors: Carol Alice/John Fry. Monthly magazine. No submission info. Query w/SASE. Index:130.

Function Industries Press, PO Box 9915, Seattle, WA 98109. Contact: Tom Grothus. 206–784–7685. Self-publisher. Helped the publication of two books by Invisible Seattle. "I cannot buy mss. I welcome correspondence from anyone interested in visual literature/graphic literature, but cannot return any ms without SASE." Operates computer bulletin board for writing. Index: 34, 80, 125.

Fur Bearers, 2235 Commercial Dr., Vancouver, BC, V5N 4B6. Contact: Editor. Periodical. No submission info. Query w/SASE. Index: 130.

Future in Our Hands, 120 4th Avenue N., Edmonds, WA 98020. Editor: Gene Openshaw, Rick Steves. 206–771–8303. Quarterly concerning world peace, hunger, simple lifestyles, nuclear arms race awareness. Circ. 5,000. Sub. free. Uses 4 mss per issue. Payment: Copies on publication. Byline given. Submit ms, SASE. Dot matrix, photocopies, simultaneous submission OK. Reports in 2 mos. Nonfiction (1,000 wds), poetry, cartoons. Sample free. Index: 93, 97.

For lists of abbreviations and the key to index numbers, see "How to Use this Section" on page 77.

128   Market Listings

Future Science Research Publishing Company, PO Box 06392, Portland, OR 97206-0020. 503–235–1971. Self-publisher of 1 softcover book, original; for new age science enthusiasts, alternate energy people, gravity researchers, physicists, space exploration enthusiasts. Not a freelance market. Catalog available. Index: 46, 109.

Gable & Gray Publishing, 1307 W. Main, Medford, OR 97501. 503–779–1353. Editor: Stephen Guettermann. Publishes 10-30 softcover books a yr. Avg. press run 10,000. Payment & rights negotiable. Submit outline, sample chapters, SASE. Dot matrix, photocopied, simultaneous OK. Reports in 2-3 mo. Publishes in 6 mo. Topics: health, sports & training, business manuals & how-to, New Age, environmental, others of a marketable nature. Tips: query should identify audience & why the ms is needed. "Controversial & provocative topics are great as long as the writer has the ability to present issues with strength & clarity." Guidelines available. Index: 24, 61, 115.

Gadfly Press, 8925 S.W. Homewood Street, Portland, OR 97225. Contact: Robert Lynott. 503–292–8890. Publisher of books on meteorology. No submission info. Query w/SASE. Index: 109.

Gahmken Press, PO Box 1467, Newport, OR 97365. 503–265–2965. Contact: Range D. Bayer. Publisher of 2 softcover nonfiction books a yr. Print run 75. Accepts unsolicited mss. Pays 4 copies. Rights purchased: First. Submit ms, SASE. Dot matrix, photocopies, computer disc OK. Reports in 3 wks. Publishes in 6 mo. "Monograph length mss dealing with detailed studies of OR ornithology or ornithologists are the only mss now desired." Guidelines available. Sample. Index: 88, 91, 108.

Gaining Ground, PO Box 9184, Portland, OR 97207. No submission info. Query w/SASE. Index: 130.

Galley Proofs, 131 W. 8th St., McMinnville, OR 97128. 503–472–8277. Editor: Jo McIntyre. Oregon Press Women membership newsletter. Circ. 200. Uses 2-3 freelance mss per issue. Pays in copies on publication. Byline given. Submit by phone query. Simultaneous OK. Reports in 1-4 wks. Publishes in 1-2 mo. Accepts nonfiction, photos. Topics: member profiles, organization news, First Amendment issues. Photos: B&W, prefer screened. Tips: "We are mainly interested in writing as a profession, newspaper people, public relations, freelance. Index: 80, 124, 125.

Galloway Publications, Inc., 2940 N.W. Circle Blvd., Corvallis, OR 97330. No submission info. Query w/SASE. Index: 130.

Garnet Publishing, PO Box 14713, Spokane, WA 99214. No submission info. Query w/SASE. Index: 130.

Garren Publishing, 1008 SW Comus, Portland, OR 97219. Contact: John H. Garren. 503–636–3506. Self-publisher of books on whitewater rivers. Not a freelance market. Index: 92.

Gasworks Press, 16292 37th N.E., Seattle, WA 98155. No submission info. Query w/SASE. Index: 130.

The Gated Wye, Office of State Fire Marshal, 3000 Market Street N.E. #534, Salem, OR 97310. 503–378–2884. Editor: Nancy Campbell. Monthly of "timely items and important features for the fire service." Sub $10. Circ. 1,150. Uses freelance mss. Pays copies on publication. Byline given. Query w/SASE. Phone queries, dot matrix, photocopies OK. Reports in 2 mo. Publishes in 2 mo. Accepts nonfiction, poetry; fire service related, training and education. Sample free. Index: 60, 71, 101.

Gazette, PO Box 770, Colfax, WA 99111. 509–397–4333. Weekly newspaper. No submission info. Query w/SASE. Index: 33.

Gazette-Tribune, PO Box 250, Oroville, WA 98844. 509–476–3602. Weekly newspaper. No submission info. Query w/SASE. Index: 33.

Gem Paperbacks, PO Box 1201, Burley, ID 83318. Publisher. No submission info. Query w/SASE. Index: 130.

Gem State Geological Review, Idaho Geological Survey, c/o University of Idaho, Moscow, ID 83843. Editor: Roger C. Stewart. Annual periodical. No submission info. Query w/SASE. Index: 59, 69, 109.

Gemaia Press, 209 Wilcox Lane, Sequim, WA 98382. No submission info. Query w/SASE. Index: 130.

Genealogical Forum of Portland Bulletin, Rm. 812, 1410 S.W. Morrison, Portland, OR 97205. Monthly. No submission info. Query w/SASE. Index: 58.

General Educational Development Institute, G Street N.W., Waterville, WA 98858. Publisher. No submission info. Query w/SASE. Index: 43.

Geo-Heat Center Bulletin, Oregon Institute of Technology, 3201 Campus Drive, Klamath Falls, OR 97603. 503–882–6321. Editor: Paul S. Lienau. Quarterly, free. Circ. 1,600. Uses freelance material. No pay. Submit ms. Photocopied OK. Accepts nonfiction. Sample free. Index: 31, 117.

Geologic Publications, Division of Geology & Earth Resources, Department of Natural Resources, Olympia, WA 98504. No submission info. Query w/SASE. Index: 59, 88, 109.

Geological News Letter, Geological Society of the Oregon Country, PO Box 8579, Portland, OR 97207. Monthly. No submission info. Query w/SASE. Index: 59, 88, 109.

Geophysical Institute, University of Alaska, 903 Koyukuk Avenue, Fairbanks, AK 99701. Publisher. No submission info. Query w/SASE. Index: 4, 88, 109.

Georgia Straight, 1135 W. 27th Avenue, Vancouver, BC V6K 1N6. Editor: Dan McLeod. 604–734–5520. Periodical. No submission info. Query w/SASE. Index: 130.

The Georgian Press Company, 2620 S.W. Georgian Place, Portland, OR 97201. Contact: E.K. MacColl. Publisher of Portland histories. Not a freelance market. Index: 65, 91.

Geriatric Press, Inc., PO Box 7291, Bend, OR 97708-7291. No submission info. Query w/SASE. Index: 110.

Getting Together Publications, 944 Hiawatha Place S., Seattle, WA 98144. 206–329–0172. No submission info. Query w/SASE before submitting. Index: 130.

Ghost Town Quarterly, Box 714, Philipsburg, MT 59858. 406–859–3736. Editor/Ads: Donna McLean. Quarterly magazine. Sub. $8. Circ. 5,000-7,000. Uses freelance material. Pays $.05/word on publication. Acquires first rights. Byline given. Submit ms, SASE. Dot matrix, photocopied OK. Reports in 2-3 mo. Publishes 1-12 mo. Accepts nonfiction, fiction, poetry, photos, cartoons, historical documents (letters, diary pages). Features a "Students' Corner" for K-12 writers. Topics: traditions, history & heritage of ghost towns in North America; events of a his-

For lists of abbreviations and the key to index numbers, see "How to Use this Section" on page 75.

Writer's Northwest Handbook 129

torical nature; unique places to visit; unusual museums. Tips: use extreme care with factual information. Guidelines available. Sample $3.50. Index: 28, 90, 120.

Daniel W. Giboney, PO Box 5432, Spokane, WA 99205. 509-926-3338. Self-publisher of a book on divorce. Not a freelance market. 74.

Gilgal Publications, PO Box 3386, Sunriver, OR 97707. 503–593–8639. Editor: Judy Osgood. Periodical. No submission info. Query w/SASE. Index: 130.

GIS/CAD Mapping Solutions, Venture Communications, Inc., P.O. Box 02332, Portland, OR 97202. 503–236–5810. Fax 503–245–1110. Editor: Michael J. Carey. Sub. $99. Publishes monthly newsletter & manuals. No unsolicited mss on manuals. Freelance accepted for newsletter. Needs technical knowledge on subject to write for us. Pay negotiable on publication. Rights purchased: All. No byline in newsletter. Phone query OK. Dot matrix, photocopy OK. Accepts nonfiction. "Technology, mapping, training for public sector and vendors. Key = applications, not product literature." Sample: $8 end-users. Copies for interested writers. Index: 34, 101, 117.

Glacier Natural History Association, Inc., Glacier National Park, West Glacier, MT 59963. Publisher. No submission info. Query w/SASE. Index: 88.

Glass Studio Magazine, Box 23383, Portland, OR 97223. Editor: Jim Wilson. 503–620–3917. Monthly for professional glass artists, studios, museums. Payment: $100-300 on publication. Rights purchased: First. Submit ms, SASE. Dot matrix, simultaneous submissions OK. Reports in 3 wks. Publishes in 2 mos. Nonfiction: 1,500-2,500 wds dealing with glass art, business for artists, hazards in industry. Photos: Slides or B&W glossy with article. Guidelines available; sample/$2. Index: 10, 24.

Globe, PO Box 145, Marysville, WA 98270. 206–659–1300. Weekly newspaper. No submission info. Query w/SASE. Index: 33.

Globe & Mail, 920-1200 Burrard St., Vancouver, BC V6Z 2C7. Contact: Editor. Periodical. No submission info. Query w/SASE. Index: 130.

The Globe Pequot Press - Western Office, 9553 Palatine Ave. N., Seattle, WA 98103. 206–782–6083. Carolyn J. Threadgill. Press run 3,000+. Publishes 60-80 books a yr. on popular topics ranging from business to outdoor recreation. Accepts unsolicited mss. Pays royalties, advance on acceptance & publication. Rights purchased: All. Submit query w/clips, ms w/SASE. Dot matrix, photocopy OK. Reports in 2 mo's. Publishes in 1 yr. Tips: typed, ds with ample margins required. Catalog available. Index: 24, 38, 115.

Globe Publishing Co., 3625 Greenwood N., Seattle, WA 98103. Publishes poetry and prose on love. No submissions info. Query w/SASE. Index: 51, 97.

Glover Publications, PO Box 21745, Seattle, WA 98111. No submission info. Query w/SASE. Index: 130.

Gluten Intolerance Group of North America, PO Box 23053, Seattle, WA 98102. Publisher. No submission info. Query w/SASE. Index: 61.

Goal Lines, The Oregon Youth Soccer Association, 1750 Skyline Boulevard #25, Portland, OR 97221. 503–292–5542. Editor: Judy Davidson. Ads: Don Patch. Newspaper published 5 times/yr. Sub. $6. Circ. 25,000. Uses freelance material. Byline given. Query w/clips, SASE. Dot matrix, computer disc OK. Reports in 2 wks. Publishes in next issue. Accepts nonfiction, photos. Guidelines available. Sample $1. Index: 25, 115.

Golden Eagle, Audubon Society, Golden Eagle Chapter, PO Box 8261, Boise, ID 83707. Editor: Scott Tuthill. Monthly. No submission info. Query w/SASE. Index: 35, 88, 92.

Golden Adler Books, PO Box 641, Issaquah, WA 98027-0641. Editor: Miriam Klemer. Publisher. No submission info. Query w/SASE. Index: 130.

The Golden Eagle, Autobody Craftsman of America, 1904 N.E. 45th Avenue, Portland, OR 97213. 503–284–7762. Editor: Jim Warinner. Monthly magazine. No submission info. Query w/SASE. Index: 119.

Golden Horizons, Inc., 2724 NE 45th St., Ste. 645, Seattle, WA 98105. 206–525–8160. Publishes 2 softcover original books a yr. Not a freelance market. Index: 110.

Golden Messenger, 3025 Lombard, Everett, WA 98201. Contact: Editor. Monthly. No submission info. Query w/SASE. Index: 130.

Goldermood Rainbow, 331 W. Bonneville Street, Pasco, WA 99301. Publisher. No submission info. Query w/SASE. Index: 130.

Golf Sports Publishing, PO Box 3687, Lacey, WA 98503. Self-publisher of 1 softcover book a yr. for golfers. Print run: 10,000. Not a freelance market. Index: 115.

Goliards Press, 3515 18th Street, Bellingham, WA 98225. No submission info. Query w/SASE. Index: 130.

Gonzaga University Press, Gonzaga University, Spokane, WA 99202. No submission info. Query w/SASE. Index: 31.

Good Medicine Books, Box 844, Invermere, BC V0A 1K0. Publisher of books on history and nature. No submission info. Query w/SASE. Index: 64, 88.

Goodfruit Grower, PO Box 9219, Yakima, WA 98909. 509-457-8188. Editor: Phil Shelton. Ads: Randy Morrison.Sub $18. Circ. 13,000. Trade magazine published 21 times a yr. Uses 4-6 freelance mss per issue. Pay: $2 column inch, $5 pictures, more for color or cover material; on publication. Rights acquired: First. Byline given. Submit query w/clips. Phone query, dot matrix OK. Reports in 4 wks. Publishes in 4-12 wks. Accepts nonfiction, photos. "...the official trade publication of the Washington State tree fruit industry, but circulates far beyond the boundaries of the state and is a respected source of information for orchardists everywhere, including overseas. Subject matter includes growing and marketing of commercial tree fruit. Grower profiles, too." Index: 3, 24.

Gorge Current, 209 Oak St. #206, Hood River, OR 97031. 503–386–6223. Editor: Mike Worral. Periodical. No submission info. Query w/SASE. Index: 130.

Gospel Tract Distributors, 8036 N. Interstate Avenue, Portland, OR, 97217. 503–283–5985. Contact: President. Publisher. No submission info. Query w/SASE. Index: 105.

Bruce Gould Publications, PO Box 16, Seattle, WA 98111. No submission info. Query w/SASE. Index: 130.

The Grange News, 3104 Western Avenue, Seattle, WA 98121-1073. Editor: Dave Howard. 206–284–1750. Monthly for rural WA audience on agricultural news/information about the Grange. Circ. 48,000. Payment: Money on acceptance. Byline given. Query w/SASE. Publishes submissions in 1 month. Nonfiction: 600-800 wds on agriculture, personal finances, home economics. Index: 3.

For lists of abbreviations and the key to index numbers, see "How to Use this Section" on page 75.

130   Market Listings

Granny Soot Publications, 1871 E. Pender Street, Vancouver, BC V5L 1W6. No submission info. Query w/SASE. Index: 130.

Grant County Journal, PO Box 998, Ephrata, WA 98823. 509–754–4636. Weekly newspaper. No submission info. Query w/SASE. Index: 33.

Grants Pass Daily Courier, 409 S.E. Seventh Street, Box 1468, Grants Pass, OR 97526. 503–474–3200. Daily newspaper. No submission info. Query w/SASE. Index: 33.

Grapevine Publications, Inc., PO Box 118, Corvallis, OR 97339. Contact: Chris Coffin. 503–754–0583. Publisher of 2-5 nonfiction, softcover books a yr., mainly technically oriented for calculator & computer owners. Print run: 3,000-10,000. Accepts freelance material. Rights purchased: First. Query with outline, sample chapters and SASE. Dot matrix, photocopies OK. Reports in 4 wks. Publishes in 6-12 mos. Presents "technical material to readers in a non-intimidating, friendly manner. We like to use humor, illustrations, etc. We're interested in what you have if it fits into our upbeat, understandable, uniquely different style. We're into teaching through no-jargon, straightforward, conversational writing." Index: 34, 118.

Graphic Arts Center Publishing Company, 3019 N.W. Yeon Avenue, Box 10306, Portland, OR 97210. Accepts no submissions. Index: 130.

Gray Beard Publishing, 107 W. John Street, Seattle, WA 98119. No submission info. Query w/SASE. Index: 130.

Gray Power, 6112 S.E. Division, Portland, OR 97206. Semiannual. No submission info. Query w/SASE. Index: 110.

Herbi Gray, Handweaver, PO Box 2343, Olympia, WA 98507. 206–491–4138. Self-publisher of softcover originals books on handweaving. Accepts no submissions. Catalog available. Index: 38, 67.

Grayfellows, Inc., 1221 N.E. 51 Street #106, Hillsboro, OR 97124-6080. Publisher. No submission info. Query w/SASE. Index: 130.

Grays Harbor County Vidette, PO Box 671, Montesano, WA 98563. 206–249–3311. Weekly newspaper. No submission info. Query w/SASE. Index: 33.

Gray's Publishing, Ltd., Box 2160, Sidney, BC V8L 3S6. Contact: Marilyn Horsdal. 604–652–5911. Publisher of hard/softcover originals and reprints on Canadiana, biography, history. No submission info. Query w/SASE. Index: 18, 26, 64.

Great Blue Graphics, 416 West C St., Moscow, ID 83843. 208–882–8245. Editor: Rae Ellen Moore. Publisher. No submission info. Query w/SASE. Index: 130.

Great Expectations, PO Box 8000-411, Sumas, WA 98295. Bi-monthly periodical. No submission info. Query w/SASE. Index: 130.

Great Expeditions Magazine, Box 8000-411, Sumas, WA 98295-8000 (or Box 8000-411, Abbotsford, B.C. V2S 6H1). 604-852-6170. Editor: Craig Henderson. Bimonthly magazine. Sub $18. Circ. 3,500. Uses 36 freelance mss per issue. Pays $20-35 for first or second rights, copies, on publication. Byline given. Submit query w/clips, SASE. Dot matrix, photocopies, simultaneous subs OK. Reports in 6 wks. Publishes in 1-6 mos. Accepts nonfiction: "Unusual, off-the-beaten path travel, budget travel outside of North America. Articles 800-2,500 wds." Guidelines available. Sample $2. Index: 120.

Great Falls Montana Catholic Register, PO Box 2107, Great Falls, MT 59403. Newspaper. No submission info. Query w/SASE. Index: 105.

Great Falls Tribune, 205 River Drive S., PO Box 5468, Great Falls, MT 59403. Editor: Terry Dwyer. 406–761–6666. Daily newspaper. No submission info. Query w/SASE. Index: 33.

Great Northwest Publishing & Distributing Company, PO Box 103902, Anchorage, AK 99510. No submission info. Query w/SASE. Index: 130.

Green Bough Press, 3156 W. Laurelhurst Drive N.E., Seattle, WA 98105. 206–523–0022. Self-publisher of 1 softcover book a yr. for children on animals and writing. Not a freelance market. Catalog available. Index: 6, 29, 125.

Greener Pastures Gazette, Relocation Research, Box 864, Bend, OR 97709. Editor: Bill Seavey. Periodical dealing with return to the countryside. No submission info. Query w/SASE. Index: 106.

Greenwood Publications, 12324 25th N.E., Seattle, WA 98125. No submission info. Query w/SASE. Index: 130.

Greer Gardens, 1280 Goodpasture Island Rd., Eugene, OR 97401. 503–686–8266. Editor: Harold Greer. Publisher. No submission info. Query w/SASE. Index: 130.

Gresham Outlook, 1190 N.E. Division Street, PO Box 880, Gresham, OR 97030. 503–665–2181. Semiweekly newspaper. No submission info. Query w/SASE. Index: 33.

Grey Whale Press, 4820 S.E. Boise, Portland, OR 97206. Publisher of poetry from new women writers. No submission info. Query w/SASE. Index: 97, 124.

Greycliff Publishing Co., Box 1273, Helena, MT 59624. Publisher. No submission info. Query w/SASE. Index: 130.

The Griffin Press, PO Box 85, Netarts, OR 97143. 503–842–2356. No submission info. Query w/SASE. Index: 130.

Griggs Printing & Publishing, 426 1st Avenue, Box 1351, Havre, MT 59526. No submission info. Query w/SASE. Index: 130.

Gros Ventre Treaty Committee, Ft. Belknap Agency, Harlem, MT 59526. Publisher. No submission info. Query w/SASE. Index: 87.

Group 1 Journal, 45 W. Broadway, Ste. 205, Eugene, OR 97401. 503–344–7813. No submission info. Query w/SASE. Index: 130.

The Group Theatre Company, 3940 Brooklyn Avenue N.E., Seattle, WA 98105. Contact: Tim Bond. Uses full length comedies and dramas. No submission info. Query w/SASE. Index: 41.

Gryphon West Publishers, PO Box 12096, Seattle, WA 98102. Publisher of 1 hard/softcover original a yr. Query w/SASE. Index: 130.

Guide Magazine, One in Ten Publishing Co., PO Box 23070, Seattle, WA 98102. 206–323–7343. Editor: Bill Swigart. Ads: Lee Johnson. Monthly magazine, gay-lesbian oriented issues, social info. Sub. $12.95. Circ. 12,000. Uses 3 freelance mss per issue. Pays money on publication, $5 for photos. Rights acquired: First. Byline given. Submit query w/clips, SASE. Dot matrix, photocopies, simultaneous, computer disc OK. Reports in 4 wks. Publishes in 2 mos. Accepts nonfiction, fiction, photos, cartoons. Sample $1. Index: 57, 60, 84.

H.B. Publications, 38 Cloverview, Helena, MT 50601. Contact: Editor. Publisher. No submission info. Query w/SASE. Index: 130.

For lists of abbreviations and the key to index numbers, see "How to Use this Section" on page 75.

H.T.C. Publishing Company (Hot Tub Cooks), 21915 N.E. 24th Court, Redmond, WA 98052. No submission info. Query w/SASE. Index: 130.

Hack'd, PO Box 17640, Portland, OR 97217. 503-289-5220. Editor: Jim Dodson. Ads: Chris Dodson. Quarterly for those whose interests include motorcycle sidecars as an unequaled form of transportation. Sub rate. $10. Circ. 3,000. Accepts freelance mss. Pays copies. Rights acquired: None. Byline given. Query, SASE. Dot matrix, photocopies, simultaneous submission, electronic, computer disc OK. Accepts nonfiction, fiction, poetry, photos, plays, cartoons. Sample available. Index: 67, 103, 120.

Had We But, Inc., 305 Bellevue Avenue E. #304, Seattle, WA 98102. 206–328–2523. Publisher. No submission info. Query w/SASE. Index: 130.

Haiku Zasshi Zo, 3026 N.W. 65th, Seattle, WA 98117. Editor: George Klacsanzky. 206–784–3111. Biannual journal. "...a liberal forum for haiku poets...to encourage the art of haiku writing in the English language." Circ. 500-700. Payment: Copies on publication. Submit mss, SASE. Dot matrix, simultaneous submission OK. Reports in 1-3 mos. Publishes in 1-6 mos. Nonfiction: 300-1,500 wds, book reviews on subjects relating to haiku. Columns: 20-40 wds on contests, events. Poetry: 1,500 wds, haiku or haibun. Tips: Encourages amateurs. "We like to see at least 6 haiku per submission." Sample: $3. Index: 97.

Haker Books, 2707 1st Avenue N., Great Falls, MT 59401. Publisher. No submission info. Query w/SASE. Index: 130.

Hampshire Pacific Press, 3043 S.W. Hampshire Street, Portland, OR 97201. No submission info. Query w/SASE. Index: 130.

Hancock House Publishers Ltd., 1431 Harrison Ave., Blaine, WA 98230. 206–354–6953. Editor: Herb Bryce. Ads: Ray Brown. Publishes 13 hard/softcover, originals, reprints a yr. Accepts unsolicited submissions. Pays royalties on publication. Submit query w/clips. Photocopied, computer disc OK. Reports rejects immediately, others in 2-6 mos. Publishing time varies, 2-yr. max. Accepts nonfiction: "Guide books, Indian titles, Northern biographies." Tips: "All subjects must be approached with professional/academic standards." Catalog available. Index: 87, 88, 89.

Hand Voltage Publications, 7362 Woodlawn Ave. NE, Seattle, WA 98115. 206–525–3923. Editors: Rody Nikitins, Judith Young. Publisher. No submission info. Query w/SASE. Index: 130.

Hands Off, PO Box 68, Tacoma, WA 98401. Publisher. No submission info. Query w/SASE. Index: 130.

Hapi Press, 512 S.W. Maplecrest Drive, Portland, OR 97219. Contact: Joe E. Pierce. 503–246–9632. Self-publisher of 3 softcover, originals, reprints, subsidy books a yr. "Most of our publications are either textbooks for university classes or reference books. Lengths vary and slant is up to author." Print run: 350. Accepts freelance material. Payment: Money. Rights purchased: All. Query w/SASE. Dot matrix, simultaneous submission OK. Reports in 2 mos. Publishes in within 1 yr. Accepts nonfiction, poetry. Tips: "We need some sort of reasonably guaranteed market, because we have little or no advertising budget. We send copies out for review and rely on people to find us." Catalog available. Index: 77, 118.

Haralson Enterprises, PO Box 31, Yarrow, BC V0X 2A0. Self-publisher of softcover nonfiction & fiction books. Not a freelance market. Index: 26, 63, 87.

Harbor Features, PO Box 1368, Friday Harbor, WA 98250. Publisher. No submission info. Query w/SASE. Index: 130.

Harbor Press, 1602 Lucille Parkway, N.W., Gig Harbor, WA 98335. 206–851–9598. Contact: Editor. Publisher. No submission info. Query w/SASE. Index: 130.

Harbour Publishing, Box 219, Madeira Park, BC V0N 2H0. Contact: Editor. Publisher. No submission info. Query w/SASE. Index: 130.

Harbour & Shipping, 355 Burrard Street, C310, Vancouver, BC V6C 3G6. Contact: Liz Bennett. Periodical magazine. No submission information. Query w/SASE. Index: 24.

Hard Row to Hoe, Seven Buffaloes Press, PO Box 249, Big Timber, MT 59011. Editor: Art Cuelho. Published 3 times a yr. "Mostly regional reviews of Rural America that librarians, individuals, and the general public can use as a guide to purchasing books and mags about the common people who still work the land." Sub. $3. No submission info. Query w/SASE. Sample/$1 SASE. Index: 76, 106.

Harstine House, 1005 E. Roy, Seattle, WA 98102. Publisher. No submission info. Query w/SASE. Index: 130.

Hartley & Marks, Inc., Box 147, Point Roberts, WA 98281. Publisher of 4 hard/softcover original books per yr. Accepts freelance submissions. Pays royalties on publication. Submit query w/clips, ms, SASE. Photocopied OK. Reports in 3 mo. Accepts nonfiction. Topics: agriculture/farming, architecture, gardening, health, how-to, medical, psychology, senior citizens, technical. Catalog available. Index: 3, 67, 100.

Harvest House Publishers, 1075 Arrowsmith, Eugene, OR 97402. 503–343–0123. Editor: LaRae Weikert. Publishes 50 hard/softcover originals, reprints books a yr. Accepts unsolicited submissions. Pays royalties on publication. Submit query w/clips, ms, SASE. Photocopied, simultaneous OK. Reports in 2-8 wks. Accepts nonfiction, fiction. Topics: "...we have a specialty–books that 'help the hurts of people.' We publish Bible-study-oriented books and fiction with a Christian theme or message consistent with Scripture." Catalog available. Index: 105.

Harvest/The Reader's Hearth, 2322 Latona Dr. NE, Salem, OR 97303. 503–393–9131. Editor: William Michaelian, Jay Thomas Collins. Bimonthly magazine. Sub. $10. Circ. 3,000. Uses 6-8 freelance mss per issue from senior writers 50 yr.+. Pays copies, on publication. Rights acquired: First. Byline given. Submit query w/clips, ms, SASE. Dot matrix, photocopies OK. Reports in 4-6 wks. Publishes in 2-4 mos. Accept nonfiction, fiction, poetry (prefer free verse), photos/B&W. "Reminiscences, short stories, poetry, personal and family histories, as well as regional histories. 100-5,000 wds. Will excerpt from larger works...Write directly and with honesty, speaking in your own voice." Sample $2. Index: 47, 65, 110.

Havin' Fun, Inc., PO Box 70468, Eugene, OR 97401. 503–344–6207. Publisher of 2 softcover original books a yr. for children. Accepts unsolicited submissions w/SASE. Catalog available. Index: 29.

Headlight Herald, Pacific Coast Newspapers, Inc., 1908 Second Street, Tillamook, OR 97141. Editor: Mark H. Dickson. 503–842–7535. Newspaper. No submission info. Query w/SASE. Index: 130.

Health Education League of Portland, 9242 S.W. Terwilliger Blvd., Portland, OR 97219. Periodical. No submission info. Query w/SASE. Index: 61.

Health News and Notes, NW Portland Area Indian Health Board, 520 S.W. Harrison, #440, Portland, OR 97201-5258. Editor: Sheila Weinmann. Quarterly. No submission info. Query w/SASE. Index: 61, 87.

Healthview, Corporate Communications Department, Good Samaritan Hospital, 1015 N.W. 22nd Avenue, Portland, OR 97210. Editor: Dick Baltus. 503–229–7711. Quarterly for patients and hospital staff. No submission info. Query w/SASE. Index: 61.

For lists of abbreviations and the key to index numbers, see "How to Use this Section" on page 75.

HearSay Press, PO Box 42265, Portland, OR 97242. Contact: Cliff Martin. 503–233–2637. Publisher of 4-6 hard/softcover, originals, reprints a yr. on: social sciences, especially oral history, sociology, anthropology; music, criticism, reference works, contemporary themes/subjects; literature, esp. local (Pacific NW themes and authors). Print run: 2,000-5,000. Accepts freelance material. Payment: Advance, royalties. Rights purchased: All. Query, outline, table of contents w/SASE. Dot matrix, photocopies, simultaneous submissions OK. Reports in 2 wks. Publishes in 6-12 mos. Accepts nonfiction, fiction. Index: 76, 86, 114.

Heartland Magazine, Fairbanks News Miner, Fairbanks, AK 99701. Editor: Dave Stark. Weekly. No submission info. Query w/SASE. Index: 4.

Heartwood, Box 90, Manson's Landing, Cortes Island, BC V0P 1K0. Quarterly journal for professional care givers. Uses short fiction and nonfiction relating to physical and mental health and philosophy. Also uses some poetry and illustrative material. Query w/SASE. Index: 51, 61, 114.

Heated Closet, 1202 W. Franklin St., Boise, ID 83702. New periodical looking for poetry, short stories & essays. Less than 2,000 wds. Submit ms, SASE. Index: 51, 97.

Heliworld Press, 3229 Sunset Wy, Bellingham, WA 98226. 206–758–7396. Editor: George Hayden. Publisher. No submission info. Query w/SASE. Index: 130.

Helstrom Publications, 3121 S.E. 167th Avenue, Portland, OR 97236. No submission info. Query w/SASE. Index: 130.

Hemingway Western Studies Series, c/o Research Center, Boise State University, Boise, ID 83725. Contact: Jim Baker. 208–385–1572. Publisher of nonfiction, softcover originals on Western American culture. Print run: 2,000. Accepts freelance material. Payment: Copies; royalties after expenses met. Rights purchased: First. Query with outline, sample chapters, SASE. Dot matrix, photocopies, simultaneous submissions OK. Reports in 6 mos. Publishes in 1 yr. Catalog available. Index: 31, 39, 89.

Henry Art Gallery, DE-15, University of Washington, Seattle, WA 98195. Publisher. No sub. info. Query w/SASE. Index: 10, 31.

Heppner Gazette-Times, 147 W. Willow, Box 337, Heppner, OR 97836. 503–676–9228 or 503–676–9492. Weekly newspaper. No submission info. Query w/SASE. Index: 33.

Herald, 107 Division, Grandview, WA 98930. 509–882–3712. Weekly newspaper. No submission info. Query w/SASE. Index: 133.

Herald & News, 1301 Esplanade, Box 788, Klamath Falls, OR 97601. 503–883–4000. Daily newspaper. No submission info. Query w/SASE. Index: 33.

The Herb Market Report, O.A.K., Inc., 1305 Vista Drive, Grants Pass, OR 97527. 503–476–5588. Editor: Richard Alan Miller. Ads: Iona Miller. Monthly newsletter. Sub. $12. Circ. 2,000+. Uses 1 freelance ms per issue. Payment is through trade only. Acquires 1st rights. Submit by phone query. Photocopied OK. Reports in 1 wk. Publishes in 3 mo. Nonfiction. Topics: alternative agriculture, herbs & spices, marketing, cottage industry, rural economic development, processing, small farming, foraging, secondary timber products. Tips: 2,000-4,000 wds. Artwork. Sample $1.50. Index: 3, 55, 67.

Heritage Music Review, 4217 Fremont N., Apt 5, Seattle, WA 98103. Contact: Editor. Periodical. No submission info. Query w/SASE. Index: 86.

Heritage Quest, PO Box 40, Orting, WA 98360. 206–893–2029. Editor: Leland K. Meitzler. Bimonthly with articles on genealogy and local history, all geared toward helping researchers. Sub rate $30. Circ. 10, 000. Uses 8 freelance mss per issue from historians or genealogists. Pays from $.75 to $1.25 per column inch, on publication. Byline given. Rights purchased: All. Submit ms, SASE. Reports in 1 mo. Publishes in 2-6 mos. Guidelines available. Sample $6. Index: 58, 62, 64.

The Hermiston Herald, 158 E. Main, Box 46, Hermiston, OR 97838. 503–567–6457. Weekly newspaper. No submission info. Query w/SASE. Index: 33.

Heron Books, Inc., PO Box 1230, McMinnville, OR 97128. Contact: Jay Nunley. Publisher of softcover, nonfiction books for educators, parents. Print run: 5,000. Not a freelance market. Index: 29, 43, 114.

Heron's Quill, 10511 S.E. Crystal Lake Lane, Milwaukie, OR 97222. Publisher. No submission info. Query w/SASE. Index: 130.

Hewitt Research Foundation, PO Box 9, Washougal, WA 98671. Periodical. No submission info. Query w/SASE. Index: 130.

Hi Baller Forest Magazine, 117-543 Seymour Street, North Vancouver, BC V6B 3H6. Editor: Paul Young. 604–669–7833. No submission info. Query w/SASE. Index: 130.

Hidden Assets, PO Box 22011, Seattle, WA 98122. Publisher. No submission info. Query w/SASE. Index: 130.

Shaun Higgins, Publisher, W 428 27th Avenue, Spokane, WA 99203. No submission info. Query w/SASE. Index: 130.

High & Leslie Press, 490 Leslie St. S.E., Salem, OR 97301. 503–363–7220. Publishes softcover original books. Does not accept unsolicited submissions. Index: 130.

Highline Times & Des Moines News, PO Box 518, Burien, WA 98166. 206–242–0100. Weekly newspaper. No submission info. Query w/SASE. Index: 33.

Highway Information, Idaho Transportation Department, PO Box 7129, Boise, ID 83707. Editor: Pat Youngblood. Bimonthly. Circ. 1,200. No submission info. Query w/SASE. Index: 69, 101.

Hillsboro Argus, 150 S.E. Third, Hillsboro, OR 97123. 503–684–1131. Semiweekly newspaper. No submission info. Query w/SASE. Index: 33.

Janice McClure Hindman, PO Box 208, Durke, OR 97905. Contact: Editor. Publisher. No submission info. Query w/SASE. Index: 130.

The Hispanic News, 2318 Second Avenue, Seattle, WA 98121. Editor: Rick Garza. 206–441–4537. Newspaper "dedicated to serving the more than 127,000 Chicano/Latinos in Washington State." No submission info. Query w/SASE. Index: 27, 84.

Historic Preservation League of Oregon Newsletter, PO Box 40053, Portland, OR 97240. Contact: Editor. Quarterly. No submission info. Query w/SASE. Index: 9, 65, 91.

Historical Gazette, PO Box 527, Vashon, WA 98070. 206–463–5656. Editor: Roger Snowden. Ads: Don King. Monthly. Sub. $10. Circ. 10,000. Uses freelance material. Pays money on publication. Byline given. Submit query w/clips, ms, phone. Dot matrix, photocopied OK. Accepts nonfiction, photos, other. Guidelines available. Sample $.50. Index: 65.

For lists of abbreviations and the key to index numbers, see "How to Use this Section" on page 75.

Writer's Northwest Handbook 133

Historical Perspectives, Oregon State Archives, 1005 Broadway NE, Salem, OR 97310. 503–378–4241. Editor: John Lazuk. Free semiannual newsletter. Circ: 2,500. No freelance mss accepted. Sample. Index: 58, 60, 65.

Historical Society of Seattle & King County, 2161 E. Hamlin Street, Seattle, WA 98112. Publisher. No submission info. Query w/SASE. Index: 65.

Holden Pacific, Inc., 814 35th Avenue, Seattle, WA 98122. 206–325–4324. Self-publisher of 1 wine/travel book a yr. Not a freelance market. Index: 54, 120.

Holistic Resources, PO Box 3653, Seattle, WA 98124. 206–523–2101. Editor: Susan James. Periodical. No submission info. Query w/SASE. Index: 61.

The Hollywood Star, 2000 N.E. 42nd Avenue, Portland, OR 97213. Periodical. No submission info. Query w/SASE. Index: 130.

Opal Laurel Holmes Publisher, PO Box 2535, Boise, ID 83701. No submission info. Query w/SASE. Index: 130.

Holtz-Carter Publications, 4326 Dyes Inlet Road N.W., Bremerton, WA 98312. Contact: Nancy Holtz-Carter. 206–377–2432. Publisher of 1 softcover book a yr. on cottage crafts for consumers and crafters. Print run: 5,000. Accepts freelance material. Unspecified payment schedule. Query w/SASE. Photocopies OK. Nonfiction, poetry, photos. Guidelines available. Index: 38, 97.

Home Education Magazine, PO Box 1083, Tonasket, WA 98855. Editor/Ads: Helen Hegener. Semimonthly magazine. Sub. $24. Circ. 5,200. Uses 12-15 freelance mss per issue. Writers must know about home schooling or alternative education. Pays money/copies (about $10 per 750 wds) on publication. Byline given. Submit query w/clips, ms, SASE. Dot matrix, photocopied, simultaneous, electronic, computer disc OK. Accepts nonfiction, poetry, photos, cartoons, artwork. Photos: clear B&W, rates negotiable. Guidelines/catalog available. Sample $4.50. Index: 28, 43, 47.

Home Education Press, PO Box 1083, Tonasket, WA 98855. Editor: Helen Hegener. Self-publisher of 3-4 softcover original, reprint books per yr. relating to home schooling or alternative education. Submit query, SASE. Dot matrix, photocopied, simultaneous, electronic/modem, computer disc OK. Catalog available. Index: 28, 43, 47.

Homer News, 162 W. Pioneer Ave., Homer, AK 99603. 907–235–7767. Weekly newspaper. No submission info. Query w/SASE. Index: 33.

Homes & Land Magazine, 910 N.E. Minnehaha, Vancouver, WA 98665. Editor: Alicia Ord. Periodical. No submission info. Query w/SASE. Index: 130.

Homestead Book Company, P.O. Box 31608, Seattle, WA 98103. 206–782–4532. Editor: David Tatelman. Publisher of 2-3 softcover, original books a yr. Accepts unsolicited submissions. Pays royalties. Rights acquired: All. Byline given. Query w/clips, SASE. Dot matrix, photocopies OK. Reports in 3 mos. Publishes: 6 mos. Accepts nonfiction, cartoons. Topics: restaurants, drugs, music, food, counter-culture. Index: 37, 54, 86.

Honeybrook Press, PO Box 883, Rexburg, ID 83440. 208–356–5133. Editor: Donnell Hunter. Publishes 3 books a yr., poetry chapbooks, and some subsidy printing. Accepts unsolicited mss only on a subsidy basis. Reports in 2 wks. Publishes in 2 mos. "Except for subsidy printing, I publish only those authors I am interested in who are already established." Index: 97.

Hood River News, 409 Oak Street, Box 390, Hood River, OR 97301. 503–386–1234. Weekly newspaper. No submission info. Query w/SASE. Index: 33.

Hook & Needle Times, Wild & Woolie Yarns, Marysville, WA 98270. 206–659–7577. Editor: Mildred Koop. Monthly. No submission info. Query w/SASE. Index: 38.

Horizons Alaska Magazine, PO Box 110306, Anchorage, AK 99511. Editor: Pat Glenham. 907–563–4673. Ads: John Tullis. Monthly on business, travel. Circ. 250,000. Sub. $20. Accepts freelance material. Byline given. Rights purchased: First. Submit ms, SASE. Dot matrix, photocopies, simultaneous sub. OK. Reports in 1-2 mos. Uses nonfiction, fiction, poetry, photos, cartoons. Topical Alaskan: 800 wds. General business: 800 wds. Pacific Rim business: 900 wds. Book reviews: 600 wds. Travel: (AK and worldwide) 800 wds. Lifestyle: 900-1,000 wds. Outdoor: 900-1,000 wds. Photos: B&W prints/color slides. Sample free. Index: 4, 24, 120.

Horizons SF, Box 75, Student Union Bldg., UBC, Vancouver, BC V6T 1W5. Biannual science fiction & fact publication which showcases unpublished Canadian writers. Query w/SASE. Index: 31, 48, 109.

Horsdal & Schubart Publishers, Ltd., Box 1, Ganges, BC V0S 1E0. 604–537–4334. Editor: Marlyn Horsdal. Publishes 1-2 hard/softcover, original books a yr. Does not accept unsolicited mss. Query w/SASE first. Reports in 2 wks. Publishes in 6-9 mos. Accepts nonfiction, Canadian histories and biographies. Catalog available. Index: 18, 26, 63.

Horse Times, Rt. 7, Box 7195, Nampa, ID 83651. Editor: Jo O'Connor. Periodical. No submission info. Query w/SASE. Index: 6, 103.

Horsemanship, 105 Old Oak Circle, Grants Pass, OR 97526. 503–476–8902. Self-publisher of 1 hardcover book a year for horse owners. Print run: 6,000. Not a freelance market. Index: 6

Hot Off The Press, 7212 S. Seven Oaks, Canby, OR 97013. Publisher. No submission info. Query w/SASE. Index: 130.

Hot Springs Gazette, 12 S. Benton, Helena, MT 59601-6219. 406–482–5766. Editor: Suzanne Hackett. Periodical. Sub. $12. Circ. 1,000. Uses 12 freelance mss per issue. Pays copies on publication. Acquires 1st rights. Byline given. Submit ms. Dot matrix, photocopied OK. Reports in 2 mo. Accepts nonfiction, fiction, poetry, cartoons. Guidelines available. Sample $4. Index: 45, 66, 76.

Hound Dog Press, 10705 Woodland Ave., Puyallup, WA 98373. 206–845–8039. Self-publisher of 1 hardcover book on bloodhounds for search & rescue work. Not a freelance market. Index: 6, 99.

House by the Sea Publishing Company, 8610 Hwy. 101, Waldport, OR 97394. No submission info. Query w/SASE. Index: 130.

House of Charles, 4833 N.E. 238th Avenue, Vancouver, WA 98662. Publisher. No submission info. Query w/SASE. Index: 130.

House of Humor, PO Box 7302, Salem, OR 97303. 503–585–6030. Editor: Paul Everett. Publisher. No submission info. Query w/SASE. Index: 68.

Housewares Canada, 2000 W. 12th Avenue, Vancouver, BC V6J 2G2. Contact: Editor. Periodical. No submission info. Query w/SASE. Index: 130.

For lists of abbreviations and the key to index numbers, see "How to Use this Section" on page 75.

134   Market Listings

How To Travel Inexpensively, Nomadic Books, 201 N.E. 45th, Seattle, WA 98105. Periodical. No submission info. Query w/SASE. Index: 36, 120.

The Howe Street Press, 212 E. Howe Street, Seattle, WA 98102. No submission info. Query w/SASE. Index: 130.

Howell Publishing Company, Inc., PO Box 104139, Anchorage, AK 99510. No submission info. Query w/SASE. Index: 130.

Howlet Press, 2741 S.W. Fairview Blvd., Portland, OR 97201. 503–227–6919. Contact: Doris Avshalomov. Fine letterpress self-publisher of limited editions of poetry and other literary works. Query w/SASE. "I will publish chapbooks (letterpress) or print full-length books for self-publishing (upon acceptance)." Index: 77, 97.

HTH Publishers, PO Box 468, Freeland, WA 98249. No submission info. Query w/SASE. Index: 130.

Hubbub, A Poetry Magazine, Trask House Books, Inc., 2754 S.E 27th, Portland, OR 97202. Editor: Carlos Reyes. 503–235–1898. Nationally circulated biannual magazine of poetry. No editorial strictures. Circ. 350. Submit 3-5 poems w/SASE. Pays in copies. Index: 97.

Hulogos'i Cooperative Publishers, Box 1188, Eugene, OR 97440. 503–343– 0606. Publisher of 8 softcover originals a year on NW region, environment, political activism, co-operatives and New Age consciousness. Print run: 5,000. Accepts freelance material. Payment: 8-10 % of retail, every 6 mo. Rights purchased: first; can be individually negotiated. Submit ms, SASE. Dot matrix, photocopies, simultaneous submissions, electronic OK. Reports in 1 month. Publishes in 6-12 mos. Uses nonfiction, poetry, photos, cartoons. Index: 46, 89, 112.

Hundman Publishing, 5115 Montecello Dr., Edmonds, WA 98037. 206–743–2607. Editor: Cathy Hundman Lee. Publisher. No submission info. Query w/SASE. Index: 130.

Hungry Horse News, 926 Nucleus Ave., PO Box 189, Columbia Falls, MT 59912. 406–862–2151. Contact: Editor. Newspaper. No submission info. Query w/SASE. Index: 33.

Hunt Magazine, PO Box 58069, Renton, WA 98058. 206–226–4534. Editor: Bill Boylon. No submission info. Query w/SASE. Index: 130.

Hyde Park Press, PO Box 2009, Boise, ID 83701. No submission info. Query w/SASE. Index: 130.

Hydrazine, Northwest Science Fiction Society, PO Box 24207, Seattle, WA 98124. Contact: Editor. Periodical. No submission info. Query w/SASE. Index: 48.

Hyperlink, PO Box 7723, Eugene, OR 97401. Contact: Editor. No submission info. Query w/SASE. Index: 130.

I Can See Clearly Now, 262 W. Beach Lane, Coupeville, WA 98239. Publisher. No submission info. Query w/SASE. Index: 130.

Ice River, 953 N. Gale, Union, OR 97883. 503–562–5638. Editor: David Memmott. Quarterly. Circ. 300/1,000. Quarterly tabloid/semiannual journal. Sub. $10. "Special interest is in speculative writing, i.e., SF, modern fantasy, experimental, modernism, futurism, surrealism.... we are always looking for reviews of books and magazines in our field of interest, also poetry and short-short fiction for the tabloid." Tips: fiction up to 1,500 wds; only publishes one each issue of tabloid. B/W art for tabloid: fantastic art, SF, surrealistic, etc. "Please be familiar with the magazine & our interests." Guidelines available. Samples $2.50/magazine, $.75/tabloid. Index: 48, 51, 97.

Iconoclast, Foundation of Human Understanding, 111 Evelyn, Grants Pass, OR, 97526. Contact: Editor. Monthly. No submission info. Query w/SASE. Index: 130.

Idaho, Boise State University, College of Business, Department of Economics, Boise, ID 83725. Editor: Charles L. Skoro. Quarterly. No submission info. Query w/SASE. Index: 24, 31, 69.

The Idaho, Dept. of English, University of Idaho, Moscow, ID 83843. Editor: Tina Foriyes. Periodical. No submission info. Query w/SASE. Index: 31.

Idaho Archaeologist, Idaho Archaeological Society, PO Box 7532, Boise, ID 83707. Editor: Mark G. Plew. Semiannual. Circ. 100. No submission info. Query w/SASE. Index: 7, 69.

Idaho Argonaut, Student Union Building, University of Idaho, Moscow, ID 83843. 208–885–7825. Semiweekly newspaper written & published by students. Sub. $18/yr. Circ. 7,000. Not a freelance market. Index: 31, 69, 116.

Idaho Arts Journal, PO Box 1644, Sandpoint, ID 83864. 208–263–1020. Editor: Jane Fritz. Bi-monthly tabloid. Sub. $10. Circ. 20,000. Uses freelance material. Pays money ($20-40) or ads on publication. Acquires 1st rights. Submit query w/clips. Dot matrix, photocopied OK. Accepts nonfiction, fiction, poetry, photos, plays, cartoons. Tips: 800-word reviews, vignettes; 1,200 word features, creative writing. Photos: B&W, 5x7 or 8x10, $25 for publication. No payment at this time for poetry. SASE for themes and guidelines. Sample $1.50. Index: 10, 69, 97.

Idaho Business Review, 4218 Emerald Street, Suite B, Boise, ID 83706. Editor: Carl A. Miller. Weekly periodical. Circ. 2,000. No submission info. Query w/SASE. Index: 24, 69.

Idaho Cities, Association of Idaho Cities, 3314 Grace Street, Boise, ID 83707. Editor: Ray Holly. Monthly. Circ. 2,200. No submission info. Query w/SASE. Index: 69, 101.

Idaho Citizen, PO Box 9303, Boise, ID 83707. Editor: Kenneth L. Robinson. Monthly. Circ. 1,200. No submission info. Query w/SASE. Index: 69, 101.

Idaho Clean Water, Division of Environment/IDHW, 450 West State Street, Boise, ID 83720. Editor: Tom Aucutt. 208–334–5867. Quarterly focusing on improving Idaho's water quality. Circ. 2,000. Sub. free. No submission info. Query w/SASE. Guidelines/sample available free. Index: 35, 46, 69.

Idaho Conservation League Newsletter, PO Box 844, Boise, ID 83701. Editor: Renee Guillierie. Monthly. Circ. 1,300. No submission info. Query w/SASE. Index: 35, 69.

Idaho Council on Economic Education Newsletter, 1910 University Drive, Boise, ID 83725. Editor: Dr. Gerald Drayer. Semiannual periodical. Circ. 7,000. No submission info. Query w/SASE. Index: 42, 43, 69.

Idaho County Free Press, 318 Main, Grangeville, ID 83530. Contact: Editor. Periodical. No submission info. Query w/SASE. Index: 130.

Idaho English Journal, English Dept., Boise State University, Boise, ID 83725. Editor: Driek Zirinsky. Semiannual. No submission info. Query w/SASE. Index: 43, 44, 69.

For lists of abbreviations and the key to index numbers, see "How to Use this Section" on page 75.

Idaho Farm Bureau News, Idaho Farm Bureau Federation, PO Box 4848, Pocatello, ID 83205. 208–232–7914. Editor: Mike Tracy. Monthly newspaper. Circ. 29,000. Does not accept freelance material. Index: 3.

Idaho Farmer-Stockman, 910 Main Street, Sonna Building, Suite 310, Boise, ID 83702. Biweekly agricultural periodical. Circ. 18,000. Uses news and farmer profiles. Guidelines available w/SASE. Index: 3, 69.

Idaho Fish & Game News, PO Box 25, Boise, ID 83807. Editor: Jack Trueblood. Bimonthly newspaper. No submission info. Query w/SASE. Index: 53, 92.

Idaho Forester, College of Forestry/Wildlife/Range Sc., University of Idaho, Moscow, ID 83843. Annual. Circ. 1,200. No submission info. Query w/SASE. Index: 3, 55, 69.

Idaho Foxfire Network, c/o Reva Luvaas, PO Box 1207, Wallace, ID 83873. 208–752–6978. Periodical. No submission info. Query w/SASE. Index: 130.

Idaho Genealogical Society Quarterly, Idaho Genealogical Society, 325 W. State, Boise, ID 83702. Editor: Lois Hamilton. Circ. 500. No submission info. Query w/SASE. Index: 58.

Idaho Grange News, PO Box 367, Meridian, ID 83642. Editor/ads: Glen Deweese. 208–888–4495. Bimonthly of agriculture and fraternal news. Circ. 8,000. Sub. membership. Not a freelance market. Index: 3, 69.

Idaho Humanities Council Newsletter, Len B. Jordan Building, 650 W. State St., Rm 300, Boise, ID 83720. 208–345–5346. Editor: Sharron Bittich. Circ: 5,200. Index: 69, 75.

Idaho Law Review, University of Idaho, College of Law, Moscow, ID 83843. Editor: Nancy M. Morris. Published 3 times a year. Circ. 1,000. No submission info. Query w/SASE. Index: 69, 74.

Idaho Librarian, Idaho Library Association, c/o University of Idaho, Library, Moscow, ID 83843. Editor: Donna M. Hanson. Quarterly. Circ. 600. No submission info. Query w/SASE. Index: 22, 69, 104.

Idaho Motorist, Idaho Automobile Association, PO Box 917, Boise, ID 83701. Editor: Grant C. Jones. Irregular periodical. No submission info. Query w/SASE. Index: 36, 69, 120.

Idaho Museum of Natural History, PO Box 8183, Idaho State University, Pocatello, ID 83209. Editor: B. Robert Butler. 208–236–3717. Periodical of primitive pottery/ceramics. Circ. 250. Uses 2-5 mss per issue. Byline given. Submit ms, SASE. Phone query, photocopies OK. "Notes on replication of experiments in primitive pottery manufacture, processes, techniques, etc. Observations, discoveries, tips, materials, techniques, especially as they relate to prehistoric or folk pottery, but also as they can be applied to contemporary ceramics." Photos: glossy. Tips: "Good, straight forward writing; first person, present tense." Index: 7, 69, 88.

Idaho Pharmacist, Idaho State Pharmaceutical Association, 1365 N. Orchard, Rm 103, Boise, ID 83706. Editor: JoAn Condie. Monthly. Circ. 350. No submission info. Query w/SASE. Index: 24, 61, 69.

Idaho Potato Commission Report, Idaho Potato Commission, PO Box 1068, Boise, ID 83701. Bimonthly. No submission info. Query w/SASE. Index: 3, 24, 69.

Idaho Power Bulletin, Idaho Power Company, PO Box 70, Boise, ID 83707. Editor: Jim Taney. Quarterly. Circ. 60,000. No submission info. Query w/SASE. Index: 24.

Idaho Press-Tribune, PO Box 9399, Nampa, ID 83652-9399. Editor: Richard Coffman. 208–467–9251. Daily newspaper. No submission info. Query w/SASE. Index: 33.

Idaho Register, Box 2835, Boise, ID 83701. Editor: Colette Cowman. 208–342–2997. Weekly periodical. Circ. 14,300. No submission info. Query w/SASE. Index: 33.

Idaho Senior Citizen News, Bee Enterprises, PO Box 6662, Boise, ID 83707. Editor: Kendall Bauer. Monthly. No submission info. Query w/ SASE. Index: 110.

Idaho State Historical Society, 610 N. Julia Davis Drive, Boise, ID 83706. Publisher. No submission info. Query w/SASE. Index: 65, 69.

Idaho State Journal, 305 S. Arthur, Pocatello, ID 83204. 208–232–4161. Contact: Editor. Newspaper. No submission info. Query w/SASE. Index: 69.

Idaho State University Press, c/o University Bookstore, Box 8013, Pocatello, ID 83209. No submission info. Query w/SASE. Index: 31, 102.

The Idaho Statesman, Box 40, Boise, ID 83707. 208–377–6200. Daily newspaper. No submission info. Query w/SASE. Index: 33.

Idaho, The University, University of Idaho, Office of University Info., Moscow, ID 83843. Editor: Beth Grubb. Periodical. No submission info. Query w/SASE. Index: 31.

Idaho Thoroughbred Quarterly, Idaho Thoroughbred Breeders Association, PO Box 841, Meridian, ID 83642. No submission info. Query w/ SASE. Index: 3, 6, 24.

Idaho Voice, Idaho Fair Share, Inc., 817 W. Franklin Street, Boise, ID 83702. Editor: Ralph Blount. 208–343–1432. Quarterly to membership of Idaho Fair Share. Circ. 10,000. Sub. $15. 90% of magazine freelance material. Byline given. Uses nonfiction, poetry, photos, cartoons. Photos: B&W, 3x5 preferred. Index: 36, 42, 98.

Idaho Voter, League of Women Voters of Idaho, 1507 E. Lander, Pocatello, ID 83201. Editor: Sally M. Gibson. Quarterly. No submission info. Query w/SASE. Index: 69, 98, 101.

Idaho Wheat, Idaho Wheat Growers Association, Suite M, Owyhee Plaza, Boise, ID 83702. Editor: Vicki Higgins. Bimonthly. Circ. 13,850. No submission info. Query w/SASE. Index: 3, 24, 69.

Idaho Wildlife, Idaho Department of Fish & Game, PO Box 25, Boise, ID 83707. 208–334–3748. Editor: Diane Ronayne. Bimonthly magazine with widespread readership (40% outside ID, 60% inside), interested in outdoor activities, including but not limited to fishing and hunting, with strong ties to Idaho. Sub. $10. Circ. 14,000. Accepts only photographs. "Only photographers with substantial files of subjects photographed in

For lists of abbreviations and the key to index numbers, see "How to Use this Section" on page 75.

136   Market Listings

Idaho are placed on the want list mailing list." Send sample sleeve of slides. Pays $20 per photo for 1 time rights, cover $60 plus 2 copies and byline. Guidelines available. Sample $1.50. Index: 46, 53, 69.

Idaho Wool Growers Bulletin, Idaho Wool Growers Association, PO Box 2596, Boise, ID 83701. Editor: Stan Boyd. Monthly. Circ. 1,800. No submission info. Query w/SASE. Index: 3, 24, 69.

Idaho Yesterdays, Idaho State Historical Society, 610 N. Julia Davis Drive, Boise, ID 83706. Editor: Judith Austin. Quarterly. Circ. 1,500. No submission info. Query w/SASE. Index: 65, 69.

Idahoan, National Railroad Historical Society, PO Box 8795, Boise, ID 83707. Editor: Milt Sorensen. Monthly. Circ. 60. No submission info. Query w/SASE. Index: 38, 62, 65.

Idahobeef, Idaho Cattle Association, 2120 Airport, Boise, ID 83705. Editor: Tom Hovenden. Monthly. Circ. 900. No submission info. Query w/ SASE. Index: 3, 24, 69.

Idahoan/Palouse Empire News, PO Box 8197, Moscow, ID 83843. 208–882–5561. Daily newspaper. No submission info. Query w/SASE. Index: 33.

Idaho's Economy, College of Business, Boise State University, Boise, ID 83725. 208–385–1158. Editor: C. Skoro. Quarterly magazine. Sub. free. Circ. 4,500. Uses freelance material. Pays in copies. Byline given. Submit ms, SASE. Dot matrix, photocopied, computer disc. Reports in 2 mo. Publishes in 6 mo. Accepts nonfiction. Sample available. Index: 24, 42, 69.

IEA Reporter, Idaho Educational Association, PO Box 238, Boise, ID 83701. Editor: Gayle Moore. Monthly. Circ. 9,000. No submission info. Query w/SASE. Index: 43, 69, 71.

IFCC News, PO Box 17569, 5340 N. Interstate Avenue, Portland, OR 97217. 503–243–7930. Periodical. No submission info. Query w/SASE. Index: 130.

IHSA News, Idaho Health Systems Agency, 1412 W. Washington, Suite B, Boise, ID 83707. Editor: Jan Ioset. Quarterly. Circ. 4,000. No submission info. Query w/SASE. Index: 61, 69.

Il Centro, Italian Cultural Centre Society, 3075 Slocan St., Vancouver, B.C. V5M 3E4. 604–430–3337. Editor: Anna Terrana. Newsletter of the Italian Canadian community published 3-4 times a yr. Sub. $12. Circ. 4,000. Accepts no freelance mss. Sample free. Index: 26, 33, 84.

Illinois Valley News, 319 Redwood Highway, Box M, Cave Junction, OR 97523. Editor/ads: Robert R. Rodriquez. 503–592–2541. Weekly newspaper. Circ. 3,300. Sub. $9. Uses 2 mss per issue. Payment: Average $.20 per column inch on publication. $3 per photo. Byline given. Photocopies, simultaneous submissions OK. Reports in 2 wks. Nonfiction, photos (B&W). "News & general interest for Illinois Valley." Sample: $.35/SASE. Index: 33.

Illuminator, PO Box 3727, Spokane, WA 99203. Editor: Steve Blewett. 509–489–0500. Monthly of the Washington Water Power Company. Circ. 3,150. Uses 0-5 mss per issue. Pymt: $.05-15 wd, depending on quality, on publication. Byline given. Rights purchased: All. Dot matrix, photocopies, simultaneous submissions, electronic OK. Reports in 2 wks. Uses nonfiction, photos. "Primarily assignments; editor gives editorial direction. 95% is human interest, employee involvement, etc." Sample available. Index: 24, 36.

Image Imprints, PO Box 2764, Eugene, OR 97402. Contact: Marje Blood. Publisher. No submission info. Query w/SASE. Index: 130.

Image West Press, PO Box 5511, Eugene, OR 97405. No submission info. Query w/SASE. Index: 130.

Images, Lane County ESD, PO Box 2680, Eugene, OR 97402. Editor: Dr. Marilyn Olson. Publication of poetry and art by students in Lane County. No submission info. Query w/SASE. Index: 10, 29, 97.

Imagesmith, PO Box 1524, Bellevue, WA 98009. Publisher. No submission info. Query w/SASE. Index: 130.

Imaginationary Books, 1917 Warren Avenue N., Seattle, WA 98109. Publisher. No submission info. Query w/SASE. Index: 130.

Impact, OSPIRG, 027 S.W. Arthur, Portland, OR 97201. Periodical. No submission info. Query w/SASE. Index: 91, 101, 116.

Impressions Publishing Company, PO Box 3286, Boise, ID 83703. No submission info. Query w/SASE. Index: 130.

In Common, Tsunami Publications, Box 104004, Anchorage, AK 99510. Editor/Ads: Jay Brause. 907–337–0872. Gay/lesbian monthly. Accepts freelance material. Byline given. Submit ms, SASE. Dot matrix, photocopies OK. Uses nonfiction, fiction, poetry, photos, cartoons. "Must be gay/lesbian oriented material, preferably with an Alaska or Pacific NW slant." Photos: B&W glossy news/documentation photos, as well as artistic photos suitable for a general public audience. Index: 57.

In Context, PO Box 215, Sequim, WA 98382. Periodical. No submission info. Query w/SASE. Index: 130.

In Focus, 5000 Deer Park Dr. S.E., Salem, OR 97301. 503–581–8600. Newspaper. No submission info. Query w/SASE. Index: 130.

In.S.Omnia, PO Box 9915 Seattle, WA 98109. Editor: Tom Grothus. 206–784–7685. *In.S.Omnia* magazine is "an electronic (computer) bulletin board, a public writing lab if you will. It is publicly accessible by telephone at (206) RUG-SOUL. It is free. If any writer (amateur or professional, licensed or self-proclaimed) wishes to share texts, discuss literature, engage in word games and/or collaborative writing projects, and so forth, and has access to a computer with modem, then please feel free to call." Index: 34, 76, 125.

In Stride Magazine, 12675 S.W. 1st, Portland, OR 97005. Contact: Editor. Periodical. No submission info. Query w/SASE. Index: 130.

IN–SIGHTS, PO Box 1338, Coeur d'Alene, ID 83814. 208–667–4019. Editor/Ads: Pearl Ko Fleck/Paulette Bethel. Quarterly. Sub. $8/yr. Circ. 1,200. Accepts freelance material. No pay. Byline given. Submit ms, SASE. Dot matrix, photocopied OK. Reports in 2-6 wks. Topics: alternative life styles concerning physical, mental, emotional and spiritual; "nurture the awakening consciousness of life universal." Tips: length, column or more as needed (column is 325 wds); "say what you need to say." Photos: B&W only, no payment at this time. Sample $1. Index: 13, 61, 94.

INCTE Newsletter, Inland NW Council Teachers of English, PO Box 9261, Moscow, ID 83843-1761. Quarterly. No submission info. Query w/ SASE. Index: 43.

Incredible Idaho, Division of Tourism & Industrial Development, Room 108 Capitol Bldg., Boise, ID 83720. Quarterly. No submission info. Query w/SASE. Index: 24, 69, 120.

Incunabula Press, 310 N.W. Brynwood Lane, Portland, OR 97229. No submission info. Query w/SASE. Index: 130.

For lists of abbreviations and the key to index numbers, see "How to Use this Section" on page 75.

Independent, PO Box 27, Port Orchard, WA 98366. 206–876–4414. Weekly newspaper. No submission info. Query w/SASE. Index: 33.

Independent, PO Box D, Tenino, WA 98589. 206–264–2500. Weekly newspaper. No submission info. Query w/SASE. Index: 33.

Independent, PO Box 67, Wapato, WA 98951. 509–879–2262. Weekly newspaper. No submission info. Query w/SASE. Index: 33.

The Independent Record, PO Box 4249, Helena, MT 59604. 406–442–7190. Daily newspaper. No sub. info. Query w/SASE. Index: 33.

Indian Feather Publishing, 7218 S.W. Oak, Portland, OR 97223. No submission info. Query w/SASE. Index: 130.

Info, International Sled Dog Racing Assoc., PO Box 446, Nordman, ID 83848. Editor: Nancy Molburg. Bimonthly. Circ. 2,000. No submission info. Query w/SASE. Index: 6, 92, 115.

Info Alternatives, 121 5th Avenue N., Suite 201, Edmonds, WA 98020. Publisher. No submission info. Query w/SASE. Index: 130.

Infoletter, International Plant Protection Center, Oregon State University, Corvallis, OR, 97331. 503–754–3541. Editor: A.E. Deutsch. Free quarterly. Circ. 8,600. Not a freelance market. Sample free. Index: 3, 31, 56.

Information Center, Northwest Regional Educational Lab, 101 S.W. Main Street, Portland, OR 97204. 503–275–9555. Editor: M. Margaret Rogers. Publisher. No submission info. Query w/SASE. Index: 43.

Information Press, PO Box 957, Sisters, OR 97759. Contact: Richard Yates. 503–549–5181. Annually publishes 3-4 hard/softcover "reference books related to government, business — mostly in-house production." Accepts freelance material. No submission info. Query w/SASE. Index: 24, 60, 104.

Inky Trails Publications, Box 345, Middletown, ID 83644. Editor: Pearl Kirk. Literary magazine published 3 times a year. Circ. 300. "Uses 90% freelance poems. Non-subscribers must buy issue in which their efforts appear. Does not pay." Submit ms, SASE. Reports in 2-8 wks. Publishes in 2-3 yrs. Uses nonfiction, fiction, poetry, illustrations. "Adventure, fantasy, historical, humorous, mystery, religious (not preachy), romance, western and animals. We prefer unpublished material...and do not want to receive: horror, make fun of, porno or gay/lesbian material." Offers periodic cash awards for best subscriber efforts. Guidelines available w/SASE/$.44. Sample for 9x12 SASE/$.70. Index: 48, 51, 68.

Inland Country, Inland Power & Light Company, E. 320 Second Ave., Spokane, WA 99202. Editor: Chuck Bandel. Monthly. Index: 33, 36, 47.

Inland Register, PO Box 48, Spokane, WA 99210. 509–456–7140. Ads: Margaret Nevers. Regional Catholic news magazine. Sub. $15. Circ. 10,000. Accepts freelance mss. Freelance qualification: Roman Catholic. Pays money on publication. Byline given. Submit ms, SASE. Photocopies OK. Reports in 1 mo. Publishes in 1 mo. Accepts nonfiction, $.10/wd; photos, $10 (negotiable). Sample $1. Index: 105.

Inner Growth Books, Box 520, Chiloquin, OR 97624. Self-publisher of 2 softcover original books. Index: 94, 100, 105.

Innkeeping World, PO Box 84108, Seattle, WA 98124. Editor: Charles Nolte. Trade publication. 10 times a year. Circ. 2,000. Not a freelance market. Index: 24.

Inscriptions, Creative Writing Program Newsletter, Department of English, GN-30, University of Washington, Seattle, WA 98195. Periodical. No submission info. Query w/SASE. 31, 125.

Insight Northwest, PO Box 95341, Seattle, WA 98145-2341. Bimonthly on human potential. From statement of philosophy: "We create our own reality. We can heal ourselves. Synergy works better." No submission info. Query w/SASE. Sample/free. Index: 61, 94, 100.

Institute for Quality in Human Life, 6335 N. Delaware Avenue, Portland, OR 97217. Publisher. No submission info. Query w/SASE. Index: 130.

Institute for the Study of Traditional American Indian Arts, PO Box 66124, Portland, OR 97266. Publisher. No submission info. Query w/SASE. Index: 10, 87.

Institute of Marine Science, University of Alaska, Fairbanks, AK 99701. Publisher. No info. Query w/SASE. Index: 6, 19, 109.

Institute of Social & Economic Research, University of Alaska, 707 A Street, Anchorage, AK 99501. Publisher. No submission info. Query w/SASE. Index: 4, 42, 114.

Insurance Adjuster, 2322 Seattle-First National, Seattle, WA 98154. 206–624–6965. Monthly. No submission info. Query w/SASE. Index: 24.

Insurance Week, 2322 Seattle-First National, Seattle, WA 98154. 206–624–6965. No submission info. Query w/SASE. Index: 24.

The Insurgent Sociologist, University of Oregon Sociology Dept., Eugene, OR 97403. Quarterly journal of radical analysis in sociology. No submission info. Query w/SASE. Index: 31, 112, 114.

Integrity Publications, PO Box 9, 100 Mile House, Yarrow, BC V0K 2E0. No submission info. Query w/SASE. Index: 130.

Interact, Special Education Department, PSU, PO Box 751, Portland, OR, 97207-0751. Editor: Susan Wapnick. Periodical. No submission info. Query w/SASE. Index: 31, 43.

Interface, 1910 Fairview Ave. E., Seattle, WA 98102-3699. Contact: Editor. Periodical. No submission info. Query w/SASE. Index: 130.

Interior Voice, Box 117, Kelowna, BC V1Y 7N3. Quarterly devoted to human consciousness, environment and related topics. Uses fiction, nonfiction, poetry, cartoons, etc. No submission info. Query w/SASE. Index: 46, 51, 97.

Intermountain Logging News, Statesman-Examiner, Inc., Box 271, Colville, WA 99114. 509–684–4567. Monthly. No submission info. Query w/SASE. Index: 24, 78.

International Communication Center, School of Communications DS-40, University of Washington, Seattle, WA 98195. Publisher. No submission info. Query w/SASE. Index: 31, 80.

International Examiner, 318 6th Avenue S., Suite 127, Seattle, WA 98104. Editor: Ron Chew. 206–624–3925. Ads: Xandria LaForga. Bimonthly for Asian American communities of Seattle/King County. Circ. 17,500. Sub. $12. Accepts freelance material. Payment: $10 on publication. Byline given. Query w/SASE. Dot matrix, photocopies OK. "Topics of interest and significance to Asian Americans, particularly in the NW. Historical articles, feature interviews, investigative journalism, straight news, analysis." Sample/$.50. Index: 11, 12, 84.

International Prospector & Developer, 621-602 W. Hastings Street, Vancouver, BC V6B 1P2. Editor: David O'Keefe. 604–684–8032. Periodical. No submission info. Query w/SASE. Index: 24, 59.

For lists of abbreviations and the key to index numbers, see "How to Use this Section" on page 75.

Interport USA, Inc., PO Box 02009, Portland, OR 97202. Editor: George Cervantes, 503–771–6804. Self-publisher of 1 softcover, indoor gardening book a year. Press run: 10,000. Accepts freelance material. Outline w/SASE. Dot matrix, photocopies, simultaneous, electronic OK. Reports in 60 days. Pay: 5-10% every 6 mos. Index: 56.

Intertext, 2633 E. 17th Avenue, Anchorage, AK 99508. Contact: Sharon Ann Jaeger. Publisher of 1-4 hard/softcover original books a year. Press run: 1,000. Accepts freelance material. Payment: 10% royalty after costs of production, promotion, and distribution. Rights purchased: first; option on second printing. Query w/sample chapters, SASE. Phone queries OK. No simultaneous ms submissions. Reports in 2-9 mos. Publishes in 1-2 yrs. Uses fiction, poetry, translations, literary criticism and theory. "Query first, poets sending 3-5 poems, fiction writers sending sample chapter to show the quality of language, w/SASE and by first-class mail. Authors already selected for publication represent a range of orientations; vivid use of imagery and strong, alchemical use of language are essential. Topics are entirely the authors' choices, but we cannot really use religious poetry or light verse. We are no longer looking for chapbook mss; poetry collections should be powerful, sustained groups of 48-80 poems; fiction mss may be either aggregates of short stories or novellas — a novel would have to be extremely remarkable to be considered at this time." Guidelines available w/SASE. Index: 51, 76, 97.

Interwest Applied Research, 4875 SW Griffith Dr., Beaverton, OR 97005. 503–641–2100. Editor: Mary L. Lewis. Publisher of hard/softcover education materials & videos, 30-60 topics per yr. in 2-4 subject areas. Pay: Money, on acceptance. Rights acquired: All. Byline depends on extent of contribution. Phone query, computer disc OK. Reports in 1 month. Publishes in 3-12 mos. "Actively soliciting writers for development of textbooks, study guides, examination questions and video scripts for production/distribution as college-level course materials. Topics include math, music, geography, law, child development, philosophy, and others. Payment by assignment; assignments vary from 2 days to 6 mos. Call for Writer Information Form describing current needs and soliciting information on writer's qualifications. Writers are interviewed after selection based on this form." Index: 43, 108, 118.

Intuition Trainings, 7800 185th Place SW, Edmonds, WA 98020. 206–775–8365. Editor: Janet V. Burr. Publisher. No submission info. Query w/SASE. Index: 130.

InUnison, InUnison Publications, Inc., PO Box 48, Salem, OR 97308. 503–581–2888. Editor: Jean Fuller Anderson. Ads: Greg Johnson. Quarterly magazine examining issues important to Oregon's thinking women. Circ. 15,000. Uses 3 freelance mss per issue. Negotiated payment for feature articles on publication. Byline given. Submit query w/clips, SASE. Dot matrix, WP computer disc. Reports in 4 wks. Publishes to fit format. Accepts nonfiction. Topics: social & community issues, business, art, education, families, politics and economics; theme is equity for women. Tips: interested in informative, thought-provoking, entertaining articles about women, their jobs and families; buys some humor relating to women's lives; no fashion or food articles. "We want insightful, substantive writing about women who set their goals and accomplish them." Guidelines available. Sample $3. Index: 47, 124.

Investor's Clinic, 12 Greenridge Court, Lake Oswego, OR, 97034-1429. 503–636–5720. Contact: Editor. Monthly. Sub. $60. Circ. 6,000. Uses freelance material. Submit query w/clips, ms, phone, SASE. Dot matrix, photocopied, simultaneous OK. Accepts nonfiction. Sample if available. Index: 24, 42.

IPEA News, Idaho Public Employees Association, 1434 W. Bannock, Boise, ID 83702. Editor: Jim Vineyard. Quarterly. Circ. 4,700. No submission info. Query w/SASE. Index: 69, 71.

ISBS, Inc., 5602 N.E. Hassalo St., Portland, OR 97213. Editor: Jeanette Bokma. Publisher. No submission info. Query w/SASE. Index: 130.

Island Books, 3089 Gibbons Road, Duncan, BC V9L 1E9. Publisher. No submission info. Query w/SASE. Index: 130.

Island Spring, PO Box 747, Vashon, WA 98070. Publisher. No submission info. Query w/SASE. Index: 130.

Island Publishers, Box 201, Anacortes, WA 98221-0201. Contact: Editor. Publisher. No submission info. Query w/SASE. Index: 130.

Issaquah Press, PO Box 1328, Issaquah, WA 98027. 206–392–6434. Weekly newspaper. No submission info. Query w/SASE. Index: 33.

IWA, International Woodworkers of America, 25 Cornell Ave., Gladstone, OR 97027-2547. Contact: Editor. Membership newsletter. No submission info. Query w/SASE. Index: 71.

IWUA Alert, Idaho Water Users Association, 410 S. Orchard, Suite 144, Boise, ID 83705. Editor: Sherl L. Chapman. Quarterly devoted to water resource management issues. Circ. 1,250. Not a freelance market. Index: 3, 35, 69.

IYE Magazine (in your ear magazine) , 5111 S. Mayflower, Seattle, WA 98118. 206–722–3331. Editor: Jim Hollis. Audio literary magazine. No submission info. Query w/SASE. Poetry, short stories, avant garde writing. "We will set up recording for audio publication." Index: 14, 51, 97.

Jacada Publishing Company, PO Box 30651, Seattle, WA 98103. No submission info. Query w/SASE. Index: 130.

Jackson Creek Press, 2150 Jackson Creek Dr., Corvallis, OR 97330. 503–752–4666. Editor/Ads: Cheryl McLean. Publishes 1 softcover original book a yr. on travel, outdoor recreation; focus on NW. Accepts unsolicited mss. Pays copies, royalties. Submit prospectus and sample chapters. Photocopies, simultaneous submissions OK. Reports in 2 mos. "Looking to fill gaps in NW travel/outdoor recreation book publishing field. Want new ideas, thoroughly researched mss in accessible, easy-to-read style. General audience. Call for guidelines. Index: 89, 92, 120.

Jackson Mountain Press, Box 2652, Renton, WA 98056. Contact: Carole Goodsett. 206–255–6635. Annually publishes 3-4 popular geology books, and local interest cookbooks. Print run: 5,000. Accepts freelance material. Rights purchased: First. Query w/outlines, SASE. Dot matrix, photocopies OK. Reports in 1 month. Publishes in 6-12 mos. Geology: state field guides, 48-200 pg; general popular geology subjects up to 100 pg. Food: local interest cookbooks, to 100 pg; guides to best of area, best of type, to 200 pg. Tips: "Our expertise is in marketing local guides to specific areas, i.e., specific city, half a state, or NW." Catalog available. Index: 54, 59, 89.

Jalapeno Press, PO Box 12345, Portland, OR 97212-0345. No submission info. Query w/SASE. Index: 130.

The Jason, Willamette University - D248, 900 State St., Salem, OR 97301. 503–370–6905. Editor: Margaret Jester. Annual for students writers only. No pay. Byline given. Submit ms. Dot matrix, photocopied OK. Accepts fiction, poetry, photos, plays, cartoons, other. Sample $2. Index: 31, 51, 97.

Jennifer James, Inc., 3903 E. James, Seattle, WA 98122. No submission info. Query w/SASE. Index: 100.

Janes Publishing, 25671 Fleck Rd., Veneta, OR 97487-9510. Contact: Bobbi Corcoran. 503–343–2408. No submission info. Query w/SASE. Index: 130.

For lists of abbreviations and the key to index numbers, see "How to Use this Section" on page 75.

Writer's Northwest Handbook   139

Janus Press, PO Box 578, Rogue River, OR 97537. No submission info. Query w/SASE. Index: 130.

Jawbone Press, Waldron Island, WA 98297. No submission info. Query w/SASE. Index: 130.

JC/DC Cartoons Ink, 5536 Fruitland Road N.E., Salem, OR 97301. Publisher. No submission info. Query w/SASE. Index: 68.

Jean's Oregon Collections, Route 1, Box 764, No. 3, Astoria, OR 97103. Publisher. No submission info. Query w/SASE. Index: 130.

Jefferson Review, 145 S. Main Street, Box 330, Jefferson, OR 97352. 503–327–2241. Weekly newspaper. No submission info. Query w/SASE. Index: 33.

Jeopardy, Western Washington University, 350 Humanities Bldg., Bellingham, WA 98225. 206 676 3118. Editor: Lori L. Fox. Annual literary magazine. Sub. $3. Circ. 4,000. Accepts unsolicited mss. Pays copies, on publication. Rights acquired: First. Byline given. Submit: ms, SASE. Dot matrix, photocopies, simultaneous OK. Accepts fiction, poetry, photos (slides if color or B&W prints), art work. No over-long stories or poems. Index: 51, 97, 122.

Jesuit Books, Seattle University, Seattle, WA 98122. No submission info. Query w/SASE. Index: 105.

Jewell-Johnson & Company, Inc., 502 Benton Street, Port Townsend, WA 98368. Publisher. No submission info. Query w/SASE. Index: 130.

Jewish Review, PO Box 40728, Portland, OR 97240. Editor: Elaine Cogan. 503–226–3701. Ads: Dru Duniway. Monthly. Circ. 5,000. Sub. free. Uses 1-3 mss per issue. Writers must have "good writing, knowledge or interest of Oregon Jewish community." Payment: $.10/wd on publication. Byline given. Rights purchased: First. Query w/SASE. Reports in 1 month. News: 150-250 wds; features: to 1,000 wds. Cartoons. Photos: $25, B&W. Sample/SASE. Index: 39, 91, 105.

Jewish Transcript, 609 Securities Bldg., Seattle, WA 98101. 206–624–0136. Weekly newspaper. No submission info. Query w/SASE. Index: 105.

Jimmy Come Lately Gazette, PO Box 1750, Sequim, WA 98382. Editor: JoAnne Booth. 206–683–7238. Ads: Dianne Christensen. Weekly community newspaper. Circ. 10,500. Sub. $15. Infrequently accepts freelance material. Writers must have "very strong local emphasis." Payment: Usually $25. Byline given. Query w/SASE. Dot matrix, photocopies OK. Uses nonfiction, poetry, photos, cartoons. "Emphasis on local people, events and issues. Our 3 person news staff provides about all the material we have space for, although we do work with some freelancers for historical pieces, etc." Sample/$1. Index: 25, 33, 95.

Henry John & Company, PO Box 10235, Dillingham, AK 99576. Publisher. No submission info. Query w/SASE. Index: 130.

Joint Development Trading Company Ltd., R.R. 3, 1970 Nicholas Place, Victoria, BC V8X 3X1. Publisher. No submission info. Query w/SASE. Index: 130.

Jomac Publishing Inc., 621 S.W. Morrison, #1450, Portland, OR 97205. Editor: Jo Ann Lippert. Publisher. No submission info. Query w/SASE. Index: 130.

Edward-Lynn Jones & Associates, 5517 17th Avenue N.E., Seattle, WA 98105. Publisher. No submission info. Query w/SASE. Index: 130.

Stan Jones Publishing Co., 3421 E. Mercer St., Seattle, WA 98112. 206–323–3970. Editor: Stan Jones. Self-publisher of 1-2 softcover fishing, outdoor-oriented books a yr. Average print run 15,000. Not a freelance market. Catalog available. Index: 53, 54, 89.

Jordan Valley Heritage House, 43592 Hwy 226, Stayton, OR 97383. Publisher. No submission info. Query w/SASE. Index: 130.

Journal, PO Box 519, Friday Harbor, WA 98250. 206–378–4191. Weekly newspaper. No submission info. Query w/SASE. Index: 33.

The Journal, 278 Main St., Morton, WA 98356. 206–496–5993. Contact: Editor. No submission info. Query w/SASE. Index: 130.

Journal of B.C. English Teachers' Association, c/o Pat Curtis, Port Coquitlam Secondary, 3550 Wellington Street, Port Coquitlam, BC V3B 3Y5. No submission info. Query w/SASE. Index: 23, 43, 44.

Journal of Business, S. 104 Division St., Spokane, WA 99202. 509–456–5257. Editors: Norman Thorpe. Ads: Dick Zarowny. Biweekly newspaper published by Northwest Business Press Inc. Sub. $18. Circ. 15,500. Uses 2-3 freelance mss per issue, looking for high quality writing. Pays $20–75 per piece, "depending on quality, work put into it, and amount of work we have to do on it." Pays on publication. Rights purchased: First in this market. Byline given. Phone query, dot matrix OK. Reports in 2-3 wks. Publishes in 2-3 mos. Accepts news or columns, business news about the Spokane-Coeur d'Alene market and surrounding area. Sample $2.00. Index: 24, 32.

Journal of Computer Based Instruction, Miller Hall 409, Western Washington University, Bellingham, WA 98225. No submission info. Query w/SASE. Index: 31, 34, 43.

The Journal of Ethnic Studies, Western Washington University, Bellingham, WA 98225. No submission info. Query w/SASE. Index: 31, 84, 114.

Journal of Everett & Snohomish County History, Everett Public Library, 2702 Hoyt, Everett, WA 98201. Biannual. No submission info. Query w/SASE. Index: 65.

Journal of Financial & Quantitative Analysis, University of Washington, School of Business, 127 Mackenzie Hall, DJ-10, Seattle, WA 98105. 206–543–4660. Published 5 times a yr. No submission info. Query w/SASE. Index: 24, 31, 42.

Journal of Health, Physical Education, Recreation, Dance & Athletics, Dept. of Health, Physical Ed, University of Idaho, Moscow, ID 83843. Editor: Sharon Stoll & Frank Pettigrew. Published semiannually. No submission info. Query w/SASE. Index: 40, 43, 61.

Journal of the Idaho Academy of Science, Idaho Academy of Science, c/o Dept. of Biochemistry, University of Idaho, Moscow, ID 83843. Editor: Duane LeTourneau. Semiannual. Circ. 200. No submission info. Query w/SASE. Index: 31, 43, 109.

Journal of the Nez Perce County Historical Society, Nez Perce Historical Society, 3rd & C Streets, Lewiston, ID 83501. Editor: Bea Davis. Semiannual. Circ. 130. No submission info. Query w/SASE. Index: 65, 87.

The Journal of the Oregon Dental Association, 17898 S.W. McEwan Road, Portland, OR 97224. Editor: Howard F. Curtis, DMD. 503–620–3230. Quarterly. No submission info. Query w/SASE. Index: 24, 61.

Journal of Personality Assessment, Society for Personality Assessment, Inc., 2814 S.W. Labbe, Portland, OR 97221. Bimonthly journal. No submission info. Query w/SASE. Index: 100.

For lists of abbreviations and the key to index numbers, see "How to Use this Section" on page 75.

Journal of Pesticide Reform, Northwest Coalition for Alternatives to Pesticides, PO Box 1393, Eugene, OR 97440. 503–344–5044. Editors: Mary O'Brien, Caroline Cox. Sub. $15. Circ. 2,500. Occasionally accepts unsolicited mss. Uses some freelance mss from specialists in the field. Pay negotiable, 1 copy or more. Byline given. Phone query OK, and assignment. Dot matrix, photocopies, computer disc OK. Uses illustrations. Topics: scientific or public interest, material on pesticides, pesticide reform, sustainable forestry & agriculture, pesticide policies & alternatives. "Call first to get approval, guidelines. Prefer experienced specialists in field. Occasional research papers, interviews with specialists." Sample $3. Index: 3, 46, 117.

Journal of the Seattle-King County Dental Society, PO Box 10249, Bainbridge Island, WA 98110. 206–682–7813. Monthly. No submission info. Query w/SASE. Index: 24, 61.

Junction City News, 4466 Pawnee, Boise, ID 83704. 208–323–9611. Editor: Ron Atencio. Newspaper. No submission info. Query w/SASE. Index: 33.

Junior League of Eugene Publishers, 2839 Willamette Street, Eugene, OR 97405. No submission info. Query w/SASE. Index: 130.

Juniper Ridge Press, Box 338, Ashland, OR 97520. 503–482–9585. Editor: Rosana Hart. Self- publisher of 1-3 softcover original books, and 3-5 videotapes, a yr., for llama owners. Print run 2,000. Accepts no unsolicited mss. Pays copies, royalities. Submit any way — dot matrix, photocopies, simultaneous OK. Accepts: Nonfiction "primarily related to llamas. Will consider submissions from writers knowledgeable about the animals. Most of our products are created in house." Catalog available. Index: 3, 6, 103.

Jupiter Publications, 7527 Lake City Way N.E., Seattle, WA 98115. No submission info. Query w/SASE. Index: 130.

Just in Time Publishing, 401 Olson Road, Longview, WA 98632. No submission info. Query w/SASE. Index: 130.

Just Out, PO Box 15117, Portland, OR 97215. Editor: Jay Brown. 503–236–1252. Tabloid for the gay/lesbian community. No submission info. Query w/SASE. Index: 57.

K.B.S. Press, PO Box 665, Kenmore, WA 98028. No submission info. Query w/SASE. Index: 130.

Kabalarian Philosophy, 908 W. 7th Avenue, Vancouver, BC V5Z 1C3. Publisher. No submission info. Query w/SASE. Index: 94.

Kalispell Inter-Lake, PO Box 8, Kalispell, MT 59901. Editor: Dan Black. 406–755–7000. Daily newspaper. No submission info. Query w/SASE. Index: 33.

Kalispell News, PO Box 669, Kalispell, MT 59901. Editor: JoAnn Speelman. 406–755–6767. Weekly newspaper. No submission info. Query w/SASE. Index: 33.

Kamloops Museum & Archives, 207 Seymour Street, Kamloops, BC V2C 2E7. Publisher. No submission info. Query w/SASE. Index: 23, 63, 88.

Karanda Books, PO Box 3098, Gresham, OR 97030. Publisher. No submission info. Query w/SASE. Index: 130.

Karwyn Enterprises, 17227 17th Avenue W., Lynnwood, WA 98036. Publisher. No submission info. Query w/SASE. Index: 130.

KBProgram Guide, 20 S.E. 8th, Portland, OR 97214. Editor/ads: Tony Hansen. 503–231–8032. Accepts freelance material. No pay. Byline given. Uses nonfiction, fiction, poetry. Index: 39, 80, 86.

Joan Keil Enterprises, PO Box 205, Medina, WA 98039. Contact: Editor. Publisher. No submission info. Query w/SASE. Index: 130.

Keizertimes, 4817 River Road N., Keizer, OR 97303. 503–390–1051. Weekly newspaper. No submission info. Query w/SASE. Index: 33.

Kenmore Northlake News, PO Box 582, Woodinville, WA 98072. 206–483–0606. Weekly newspaper. No submission info. Query w/SASE. Index: 33.

Ketch Pen, Washington Cattlemen's Association, Inc., PO Box 96, Ellensburg, WA 98926. Editor: Ann E. George. Monthly. No submission info. Query w/SASE. Index: 3.

Ketchikan News, PO Box 7900, Ketchikan, AK 99901. 907–225–3157. Biweekly newspaper. No submission info. Query w/SASE. Index: 33.

Key to Victoria, #10 - 635 Humboldt Street, Victoria, BC V8W 1A7. Editor: Janice Strong. 604–388–4342. Periodical. No submission info. Query w/SASE. Index:130.

Key Word, 115 Grandview Terrace, Longview, WA 98632. Publisher. No submission info. Query w/SASE. Index: 130.

Keyboard Workshop, P.O. Box 700, Medford, OR 97501. 503–664–6751. Self-publisher of 50 new cassettes, videos or softcover original books a yr. Accepts no freelance material. Index: 67, 86.

Ki2 Enterprises, PO Box 13322, Portland, OR 97213. Editor: K. Canniff. Publisher of 2 originals per yr., "totally unique nonfiction about OR/WA." Average print run 5,000. Accepts freelance material. Payment negotiated at time of purchase. Rights purchased: All. Submit outline, sample chapter, SASE. "Tell me why readers need this book too." Dot matrix, photocopies, simultaneous OK. Reports in 4-6 wks. Publishes in 1 yr. Accepts nonfiction, 80-160 pg., B&W artwork and photos. Tips: "We don't do 'coffee table' books." Index: 89, 120.

KID Broadcasting Corporation, PO Box 2008, Idaho Falls, ID 83401. Publisher. No submission info. Query w/SASE. Index: 80.

Kid Care Magazine, PO Box 1058, Clackamas, OR 97015. 503–239–2334. Editor: Margaret Ramsom. Ads: Clay Sheldon. Quarterly. Sub. $5. Circ. 10,000+. Uses freelance material. Writers must be knowledgeable about the topic. Pays copies. Acquires first rights. Byline given. Query w/clips, ms, SASE. Dot matrix, photocopied OK. Reports in 2-4 wks. Publishes within 12 mo. Accepts nonfiction, fiction, poetry, photos, cartoons, tips & ideas. Topics: infants through teens; adults taking care of/living with children; day care; how to. Tips: 100-650 wds length, short, easy to read. Photos: B&W, children & adults in everyday action. Guidelines available. Sample $3. Index: 28, 29, 61.

Kids Lib: Oness Press, PO Box 11141, Portland, OR, 97211. Contact: Editor. Newsletter. No submission info. Query w/SASE. Index: 28, 29.

KILSA News, Shoreline Community College Library, 16101 Greenwood Ave. N., Seattle, WA 98133. Contact: Editor. Periodical. No submission info. Query w/SASE. Index: 31.

Kindred Joy Publications, 554 Ⓥ 4th, Coquille, OR 97423. 503–396–4154. Contact: Marilee Miller. Self-publisher of 1-4 softcover original, subsidy books on regional/natural history. Press run 1,000. Not a freelance market. Catalog available. Index: 65, 88.

For lists of abbreviations and the key to index numbers, see "How to Use this Section" on page 75.

Kinesis, 400A West 5th Avenue, Vancouver, BC V5Y 1J8. Periodical 10 times a yr. No submission info. Query/SASE. Index: 124.

King Books, 817 S. 265th Street, Kent, WA 98032. Publisher. No submission info. Query w/SASE. Index: 130.

Kiowa Press, PO Box 555, Woodburn, OR 97071. 503–981–3017. Self-publisher of 1 hardcover book a year. Press run: 1,100. Not a freelance market. Catalog available. Index: 51, 83, 97.

Kitsap County Herald, PO Box 278, Poulsbo, WA 98370. 206–779–4464. Weekly newspaper. No submission info. Query w/SASE. Index: 33.

Klamath Falls Publishing Co., PO Box 788, Klamath Falls, OR 97801. 503–883–4000. Publishes *Cascade Cattleman, Cascade Horseman, Polled Hereford Journal.* Uses freelance features focusing on people in the trades. Include photos. Index: 3, 6.

Klamath Pioneer Publishing, 132 S. 7th Street, Klamath Falls, OR 97601. No submission info. Query w/SASE. Index: 130.

Klassen & Foster Publications, PO Box 18, Barriere, BC V0E 1E0. No submission info. Query w/SASE. Index: 130.

KMG Publications, 290 E. Ashland Lane, PO Box 1055, Ashland, OR 97520. No submission info. Query w/SASE. Index: 130.

Kodiak Mirror, 216 W. Rezanoff, Kodiak, AK 99615. 907–486–3227. Daily newspaper. No submission info. Query w/SASE. Index: 33.

Korea Times, 7320 20th N.E., Seattle, WA 98115. 206–525–9222. Weekly newspaper. No submission info. Query w/SASE. Index: 11, 12, 33.

Krause House, Inc., PO Box 880, Oregon City, OR 97045. Publisher. No submission info. Query w/SASE. Index: 130.

KSOR Guide to the Arts, 1250 Siskiyou Boulevard, Ashland, OR 97520. Periodical. No submission info. Query w/SASE. Index: 10, 80.

The Kutenai Press, 515 Stephens Ave., Missoula, MT 59801. 406–549–6383. Editor: Emily Strayer. Publisher of 2-3 chapbooks a yr. Press run 150-300. Generally doesn't accept unsolicited mss. Pays copies, 10% of run. Rights acquired: First. Byline given. Photocopies OK. Accepts fiction, poetry. Tips: limited editions made by hand, occasional trade editions; prices vary — $25 and up. Catalog available. Index: 77, 97.

La Posta: A Journal of American Postal History, PO Box 135, Lake Oswego, OR, 97034. 503–657–5685. Editor: Richard W. Helbock. Ads: Cathy R. Clark. Bi-monthly magazine. Sub. $10. Circ. 1,200. Uses 5-6 freelance mss per issue. Byline given. Submit ms. Dot matrix, electronic subs OK. Accepts nonfiction. Sample $3. Index: 38, 65.

Lacon Publishers, Route 1, PO Box 15, Harrison, ID 83833. No submission info. Query w/SASE. Index: 130.

Lacoz Chicana, Idaho Migrant Council, 317 Happy Day Blvd., Caldwell, ID 83606. Editor: Victor D. Munoz. Monthly. Circ. 1,500. No submission info. Query w/SASE. Index: 27, 69, 84.

Lake County Examiner, 101 N. "F" Street, Box 271, Lakeview, OR 97630. 503–947–3370. Weekly newspaper. No submission info. Query w/SASE. Index: 33.

Lake Oswego Review, 111 A Street, PO Box 548, Lake Oswego, OR 97034. 503–635–8811. Semiweekly newspaper. No submission info. Query w/SASE. Index: 33.

Lakewood Press, 8190 Gravelly Lake Drive, Tacoma, WA 98499. 206–581–5321. Weekly newspaper. No submission info. Query w/SASE. Index: 33.

Lambrecht Publications, RR #5, Duncan, BC V9L 4T6. 604–748–8722. Self-publisher of 1 softcover health/cookbook a year. Print run 500+5,000. Not a freelance market. Catalog available. Index: 23, 54, 61.

J.G. Lampkin Publishing, 15346 Stone Avenue N., Seattle, WA 98133. No submission info. Query w/SASE. Index: 130.

The Lamron, Western Oregon State College, WOSC College Center, Monmouth, OR 97361. 503–838–1171. Newspaper. No submission info. Query w/SASE. Index: 31.

Lance Publications, PO Box 61189, Seattle, WA 98121. 206–442–4613. Cookbooks. No submission info. Query w/SASE before submitting. Index: 54.

LAND, "Bill Anderson's Trap and Farm Journal", 4466 Ike Mooney Rd., Silverton, OR 97381. Editor: Bill Anderson. A.K.A. *Living Among Nature Daringly.* Seeks freelance material, vernacular writing style, how-to's. No submission info. Query w/SASE. Index: 3.

Landmark, 1000 Friends of Oregon, 300 Willamette Building, 534 S.W. 3rd Avenue, Portland, OR 97204. Editor: Marie Reeder. 503–223–4396. Quarterly on land use planning. Circ: 15,000. Sub. membership in 1,000 Friends of OR./$3 single issue. Uses 2 mss per issue. Payment: Copies on publication. Byline given. Rights purchased: First. Submit ms, SASE. Phone queries, dot matrix, photocopies, simultaneous submissions OK. Reports in 2 wks. Nonfiction: 500-2,500 wds on farm/forest land conservation; efficient, environmentally sound development. For educated, professional readership, interested in concrete examples or research/economic facts. Photos: B&W glossy. Sample available. Index: 35, 42, 72.

Landmarks, 835 Securities Building, Seattle, WA 98101. Editor: Barbara Krohn. 206–622–3538. Quarterly on NW history, archaeology, historic preservation. Circ. 12,000. Sub. $10. Accepts freelance material. No pay. Byline given. Rights purchased: First. Query w/ms, SASE. Phone queries, dot matrix, photocopies OK. Reports in 1-3 mos. Uses nonfiction, photos (B&W, no preferred size). Guidelines available, sample/free. Index: 7, 65, 89.

Lane County Living, PO Box 2686, Eugene, OR 97402. Bimonthly. No submission info. Query w/SASE. Index: 130.

Lane Regional Air Pollution, 225 N. 5th #501, Springfield, OR 97477. Editor: Marty Douglass. Periodical. No submission info. Query w/SASE. Index: 46.

Lang Publications, 490 N. 31st Street, Suite 100, Billings, MT 59101. No submission info. Query w/SASE. Index: 130.

Larry Langdon Publications, 34735 Perkins Road, Cottage Grove, OR 97424. No submission info. Query w/SASE. Index: 130.

The Lariat, 12675 S.W. First St., Beaverton, OR 97005. Editor: Barbara Zellner. 503–644–2233. Monthly devoted to horses and related subjects. No submission info. Query w/SASE. Index: 6, 103.

J. Larsen Publishing, PO Box 586, Deer Lodge, MT 59722. No submission info. Query w/SASE. Index: 103.

Latah County Genealogical Society Newsletter, 110 S. Adams, Moscow, ID 83843. Editor: Dorothy Viets Schell. 208–882–5943. Quarterly. Circ. 80. Sub. membership of $8. Not a freelance market. Sample: $2. Index: 58, 69.

For lists of abbreviations and the key to index numbers, see "How to Use this Section" on page 75.

Latah County Historical Society, 110 S. Adams, Moscow, ID 83843. Publisher. No submission info. Query w/SASE. Index: 65.

Latah Legacy, 110 S. Adams, Moscow, ID 83843. Editor: Stan Shepard. 208–882–1004. Quarterly on local historical subjects. Circ. 550. Sub. membership. Sometimes accepts freelance material if of interest. Payment: Copies. Byline given. Submit ms, SASE. Phone queries, dot matrix, photocopies OK. Nonfiction, photos (related to article). Sample: $2. Index: 65, 69.

Laughing Dog Press, PO Box 1622, Vashon, WA 98070. 206–463–3153 or 463–3153. Published 1 hard/softcover original book of poetry a year. Print run: 500. Uses freelance material. Query w/SASE. Dot matrix, photocopies OK. reports in 6 mos. Publishes in 1-2 yrs. Pays in copies. Rights purchased: first. "Poetry by women, including broadsides, chapbooks, book length, and anthologies. Will consider work by men, but main focus is women and women's issues." Tips: "Our books are handmade and limited to first edition runs of 500 copies," both cloth and paper bound. Index: 22, 97, 124.

The Lavender Network, PO Box 5421, Eugene, OR 97405. 503–485–7285. Editor: Ronald B. Zahn. Ads: Sally Sheklow. Monthly magazine published by an all-volunteer non-profit corporation. Sub. $12. Circ. 4,000. Uses freelance material. Pays copies on publication. Acquires 1st rights. Byline given. Submit ms., SASE. Dot matrix, photocopied OK. Reports in 1 mo. Accepts nonfiction, fiction, poetry, photos, cartoons. Topics: any gay and lesbian, feminist related topics, especially those expressing wellness themes." Photos: B&W prints only. Sample for postage. Index: 50, 57, 61.

LaVoz Newsmagazine, 157 Yesler Way #209, Seattle, WA 98104. 206–461–4891. Editor: Bob Marvel. Ads: Raquel Orbegoso. Bilingual/Spanish tabloid published 10 times a yr. Sub. $10. Circ. 15,000 statewide. Accepts freelance material. Payment on publication negotiable. Acquires 1st rights. Byline given. Submit phone query. Dot matrix, photocopied OK. Accepts nonfiction, cartoons. Topics: subjects of interest to Latinos. Sample available. Index: 27, 33, 73.

LC Review, Lewis & Clark College, 0615 S.W. Palatine Hill Road, Portland, OR 97219. 503–244–6161. Periodical. No submission info. Query w/SASE. Index: 31.

Le Beacon Presse, 2921 E. Madison Avenue, Seattle, WA 98112. Contact: Keith Gormazano. 206–328–8109. Publisher. No submission info. Query w/SASE. Index: 130.

Le Beacon Review, 2921 E. Madison Ave., Suite 7, Seattle, WA 98112. Quarterly. No submission info. Query w/SASE. Index: 130.

Leader, c/o Port Townsend Publishing, PO Box 552, Port Townsend, WA 98368-552. 206–385–2900. Weekly newspaper. No submission info. Query w/SASE. Index: 33.

Lebanon Express, 90 E. Grant Street, Box 459, Lebanon, OR 97355. 503–258–3151. Semiweekly newspaper. No submission info. Query w/ SASE. Index: 33.

Left Coast Review, PO Box 19825, Seattle, WA 98109. 206–284–6323 206–789–1884. Contact: Editor. Monthly magazine. No submission info. Query w/SASE. Index: 130.

Legacy House, Inc., PO Box 786, 139 Johnson Avenue, Orofino, ID 83544. 208–476–5632. Self-publisher of 4 hard/softcover original books a year for animal lovers, children, history buffs. Print run: 1,000. Not a freelance market. Index: 6, 29, 62.

L'Epervier Press, 4522 Sunnyside N., Seattle, WA 98103. 206–547–8306. No submission info. Query w/SASE. Index: 130.

Lesbian Contradiction: A Journal of Irreverent Feminism, 1007 N. 47, Seattle, WA 98103. Editor: Betty Johanna, Jane Meyerding. Quarterly newspaper format with journal content. Sub. $6. Circ. 2,000. Uses 4-6 freelance mss per issue. Pays copies on publication. Rights acquired: None. Byline given. Submit ms, SASE. Readable dot matrix, photocopies OK. Reports in 2-8 wks. Publishes within 1 yr. Accepts: nonfiction, B&W photos, cartoons, B&W line drawings; "Anything of interest to feminist (&/or lesbian feminist) women. Emphasis on non-academic material, with analysis or commentary based on personal experience." Uses essays, interviews, commentaries (10 pp. or less); book, movie, music reviews (3 pp. or less), queries, testimonies. Guidelines available. Sample $1-$2. Index: 50, 57.

Letter to Libraries, Oregon State Library, State Library Building, Salem, OR 97310. 503–378–2112. Editor: Jo Ann Sipple. Newsletter. No submission info. Query w/SASE. Index: 31, 104.

Lewis County News, PO Box 10, Winlock, WA 98596. 206–785–3151. Weekly newspaper. No submission info. Query w/SASE. Index: 33.

Lewis River News & Kalama Bulletin, PO Box 39, Woodland, WA 98674. 206–225–8287. Weekly newspaper. No submission info. Query w/ SASE. Index: 33.

Lewiston Morning Tribune, Box 957, Lewiston, ID 83501. 208–743–9411. Editor: John McCarthy. Daily newspaper, art section once a wk. Circ. 25,000. Accepts freelance book reviews. Pays in copies. Byline given. Submit ms. Dot matrix, photocopied, simultaneous OK. Publishes within a mo. Book reviews on Northwest writers or nonfiction with subjects centered in the NW & Rocky Mountains (Washington, Oregon, Idaho & Montana). Index: 33, 76, 89.

Lewistown News-Argus, PO Box 900, Lewistown, MT 59457. Editor: Vonnie Jacobson. Newspaper. No submission info. Query w/SASE. Index: 33.

LFL Associates, 52 Condolea Court, Lake Oswego, OR 97034-1002. Publisher. No submission info. Query w/SASE. Index: 130.

Library & Information Resources, 2125 S.W. 4th Ave., Suite #202, Portland, OR 97201. Contact: Editor. Periodical. No submission info. Query w/SASE. Index: 104.

Life Messengers Inc., 3530 Bagley Avenue N., Seattle, WA 98111. Publisher. No submission info. Query w/SASE. Index: 130.

Life Press, PO Box 17142, Portland, OR 97217. 503–285–3906. No submission info. Query w/SASE. Index: 130.

Life Scribes, Box 848, Livingston, MT 59047. 406–222–6433. Editor. Quarterly newsletter. Sub. $15. Accepts freelance material. Pays copies. Rights acquired: First. Byline given. Submit ms., SASE. Dot matrix, photocopies, simultaneous, electronic OK. Reports in 6 mo. Publishes in 2-3 mo. "We like short articles dealing with the journaling process or journal entries with date and name." Guidelines, sample available. Index: 125.

Lifecraft, PO Box 1, Heisson, WA 98622. Contact: Editor. Publisher. No submission info. Query w/SASE. Index: 130.

Lifeline America, 4035 Aurora Ave. N., Seattle, WA 98103. 206–633–0494. Editor: Jerry Miller. Periodical dealing with substance addictions and recovery issues for families. No submission info. Query w/SASE. Index: 47, 61.

For lists of abbreviations and the key to index numbers, see "How to Use this Section" on page 75.

Lifeline Magazine, 352 Halladay, Seattle, WA 98109. Editor: Alison Leary. Periodical. No submission info. Query w/SASE. Index: 130.

Lifeprints, Blindskills, Inc., PO Box 5181, Salem, OR 97304. Published 5 times a year. No submission info. Query w/SASE. Index: 126.

Lifeworks Letter, Woodland Park Hospital, 10300 N.E. Hancock, Portland, OR 97220. 503–257–5128. Editor: Sharon Wood. Bimonthly newsletter. Sub. free. Circ. 14,000. Uses 2 freelance mss per issue. Pays money on acceptance. Acquires first rights. Byline given. Submit by assignment only, SASE. Dot matrix OK. Publishes in 2-6 mo. Accepts poetry, photos. Tips: short poetry; photos: shots/captions about women's issues. "Limited freelance opportunity." Sample $.55. Index: 61 124.

Light-House Publications, 1721 Wallace, Vancouver, BC V6R 4J7. No submission info. Query w/SASE. Index: 130.

The Light Spectrum, Box 215-mp, Kootenai, ID 83840. Contact: Editor. Periodical. No submission info. Query w/SASE. Index: 130.

Lighthouse Magazine, Lighthouse Publications, PO Box 1377, Auburn, WA 98071-1377. Editor: Tom Clinton. Bimonthly. Uses fiction, poetry; children's stories and poetry. Pays money on publication. Reports in 1 mo. Index: 28, 51, 97.

Lightship Press Ltd., 2736 Quadra Street, Victoria, BC V8T 4E7. No submission info. Query w/SASE. Index: 130.

Limberlost Press, PO Box 1563, Boise, ID 83701. Contact: Richard Ardinger. Query/SASE. Nonfiction, poetry. Index: 39, 76, 97.

Limousin West, Box 5027, Salem, OR 97304. 503–362–8987. Editor: Tim Hinshaw. Ads: Tommy Badley. Bimonthly. Sub. $6. Circ. 4,200. Uses 6 freelance mss per issue. Pays money, copies on publication. Acquires 1st rights. Byline given. Phone. Dot matrix, photocopied OK. Reports in 2 wks. Accepts nonfiction, photos. Guidelines available. Sample $1/SASE. Index: 3, 6.

Lincoln County Historical Society, 545 S.W. 9th Street, Newport, OR 97365. Publisher. No submission info. Query w/SASE. Index: 65.

Line, c/o English Dept., Simon Fraser University, Burnaby, B.C. V5A 1S6. 604–291–3124. Editor: R. Miki. Ads: I. Niechoda. Semiannual journal. Sub. $12. Circ. 300. Uses 5 freelance mss per issue. Pays money, copies on publication. Acquires all rights. Submit query w/clips. Dot matrix, photocopied OK. Reports in 3-4 mos. Publishes in 5-12 mos. Accepts nonfiction: literary criticism, reviews; "Contemporary (Canadian & American) writing & its modernist sources; 30 pp. max.; payment rate yet to be determined. Sample $8. Index: 76, 77, 125.

Line Rider, Idaho Cattle Association, PO Box 15397, Boise, ID 83705. Editor: Carol Reynolds. Published 10 times a year. Circ. 1,600. No submission info. Query w/SASE. Index: 3, 6, 69.

The Linews, Linfield College, PO Box 395, McMinnville, OR 97128. 503–472–1157. Newspaper. No submission info. Query w/SASE. Index: 31.

Listen: Journal of Better Living, Pacific Press Publishing Association, 1350 Kings Road, Nampa, ID 83605. Editor: Gary Swanson. Monthly magazine of the Seventh-Day Adventist Church. Circ. 185,000. No submission info. Query w/SASE. Index: 47, 105.

Listen To Your Beer, Box 546, Portland, OR 97207. Periodical. No submission info. Query w/SASE. Index: 36, 38.

Listening Post - KUOW FM, Box 9595, Seattle, WA 98195. Editor: Anna Manildi. 206–543–9595. Monthly of public radio station. Circ. 12,000. Sub. membership. Uses 1 mss per issue. Byline given. Phone queries OK. Nonfiction, fiction, photos, cartoons. "Short articles of interest to KUOW listener supported radio. Classical music, news and info, arts, theater." Index: 10, 80, 101.

Literary Markets, PO Drawer 1310, Point Roberts, WA 98281-1310. 604–277–4829. Editor: Bill Marles. Bimonthly newsletter. Sub. $12/yr. Circ. 1,000. Uses freelance material. Pays in copies on publication. Submit ms, SASE. Dot matrix, photocopied, simultaneous OK. Reports in 2 mo. Publishes immediately after acceptance. "Wants poems/editorials about writing & the writing life. Length limit–250 wds or 30 lines. Pays a one-year subscription." Guidelines available. Sample. Index: 97, 125.

Lithiagraph Classifieds, 278 Idaho St., Ashland, OR 97520. Contact: Editor. Periodical. No submission info. Query w/SASE. Index: 33.

Litmus, Inc., 350 S. Palouse, Walla Walla, WA 99362. Publisher. No submission info. Query w/SASE. Index: 130.

Little Red Hen, Inc., PO Box 4260, Pocatello, ID 83201. Publisher. No submission info. Query w/SASE. Index: 130.

Little Wooden Books, 1890 Road 24 SW, Matawa, WA 99344. Contact: Editor. Book Publisher. No submission info. Query w/SASE. Index: 130.

Littleman Press, Box 7262, Seattle, WA 98133. No submission info. Query w/SASE. Index: 130.

Livestock Express, 4346 S.E. Division, Portland, OR 97206. Monthly. No submission info. Query w/SASE. Index: 3, 6, 24.

Livingston Enterprise, PO Box 665, Livingston, MT 59047. Editor: John Sullivan. Newspaper. No submission info. Query w/SASE. Index: 33.

Llama World, PO Box 300, Athena, OR 97813. Quarterly. No submission info. Query w/SASE. Index: 6.

The Lockhart Press, Box 1207, Port Townsend, WA 98368. No submission info. Query w/SASE. Index: 130.

Log House Publishing Company Ltd., Box 1205, Prince George, BC V2L 4V3. Publisher of nonfiction books on modern log building construction. No submission info. Query w/SASE. Index: 67, 118.

The Log, Rogue Community College, 3345 Redwood Highway, Grants Pass, OR 97526. 503–479–5541 x201. Weekly newspaper. No submission info. Query w/SASE. Index: 31.

Loggers World, 4206 Jackson Hwy., Chehalis, WA 98532. Periodical. No submission info. Query w/SASE. Index: 24, 71, 78.

Logging & Sawmill Journal, 1111 Melville Street, Suite 700, Vancouver, BC V6E 3V6. Editor: Tony Whitney. No submission info. Query w/SASE. Index: 3, 24, 78.

Logistics & Transportation Review, University of British Columbia, 1924 West Mall, Vancouver, BC V6T 1W5. Editor: W.G. Waters, II. 604–228–5922. Periodical. No submission info. Query w/SASE. Index: 23, 24, 31.

London Northwest, 929 S. Bay Road, Olympia, WA 98506. Publisher. No submission info. Query w/SASE. Index: 130.

Lone Star Press, PO Box 165, Laconner, WA 98257. No submission info. Query w/SASE. Index: 130.

Long House Printcrafters & Publishers, 2387 Mitchell Bay Road, Friday Harbor, WA 98250 No submission info. Query w/SASE. Index: 130.

Longanecker Books, PO Box 127, Brewster, WA 98812. Publisher. No submission info. Query w/SASE. Index: 130.

For lists of abbreviations and the key to index numbers, see "How to Use this Section" on page 75.

144   Market Listings

Longview Daily News, 770 11th Avenue, PO Box 189, Longview, WA 98632. 206–577–2500. Daily newspaper. No submission info. Query w/ SASE. Index: 33.

Loompanics Unlimited, Box 1197, Port Townsend, WA 98368. Contact: Michael Hoy. Publisher of nonfiction how-to, reference and self-help of esoteric nature. Counter cultural and political subjects. No submission info. Query w/SASE. Index: 37, 112.

Lord Byron Stamps, PO Box 4586, Portland, OR 97208. Editor: Tom Current. 503–254–7093. Self-publisher of softcover "occasional monographs, catalogs or other books on British philately." No submission info. Query w/SASE. Index: 30, 38.

Loud Pedal, Oregon Region, S.C.C.A., 154 Idylwood Dr. S.E., Salem, OR 97302. Editor: Margie Swanson. Monthly. No submission info. Query w/SASE. Index: 130.

Louis Foundation, Main Street, PO Box 210, Eastsound, WA 98245. Publisher. No submission info. Query w/SASE. Index: 130.

Love Line Books, 790 Commercial Avenue, Coos Bay, OR 97420. Contact: Editor. Publisher. No submission info. Query w/SASE. Index: 130.

Lumby Historians, c/o Rosemary Deuling, R.R. 2, Lumby, BC V0E 2G0. Publisher. No submission info. Query w/SASE. Index: 63.

LUNO: Learning Unlimited Network of Oregon, 31960 SE Chin St., Boring, OR 97009. 503–663–5153. Newsletter published 9 times a yr. Sub. $10. Circ. 100. Accepts unsolicited mss. Pays copies. Byline given. Submit w/SASE. Photocopies OK. Accepts nonfiction, poetry, cartoons. Topics: "Education, especially family/home schooling, education alternatives, learning styles, related politics." Index: 29, 37, 43.

Lynx House Press, 9305 SE Salmon Ct., Portland, OR 97216. 503–253–0669. Editor: Christopher Howell. Publishes 8 hard/softcover original books a year. Does not accept unsolicited submissions. Pays small advance plus 10% of cloth & paper press run on publication. Submit ms, SASE. Photocopied OK. Reports in 3 mo. Publishes in 6-18 mo. Accepts fiction, poetry, plays. "We are an ambitious and highly selective literary press." Catalog available. Index: 41, 51, 97.

MAAE Rhythm, Montana Alliance for Arts Education, PO Box 9116, Helena, MT 59604. Contact: Editor. Quarterly journal. No submission info. Query w/SASE. Index: 10.

M/T/M Publishing Company, PO Box 245, Washougal, WA 98671. No submission info. Query w/SASE. Index: 130.

MacManiman, Inc., PO Box 546, Fall City, WA 98024. Publisher. No submission info. Query w/SASE. Index: 130.

Madison County History Association, PO Box 228, 207 Mill Street, Sheridan, MT 59749. Publisher. No submission info. Query w/SASE. Index: 65, 85.

Madison Park Press, 3816 E. Madison Street, Seattle, WA 98112. No submission info. Query w/SASE. Index: 130.

Madisonian, 122 W. Wallace, Virginia City, MT, 59755. Contact: Editor. Periodical. No submission info. Query w/SASE. Index: 130.

The Madras Pioneer, 452 Sixth Street, Box W, Madras, OR 97741. 503–475–2275. Weekly newspaper. No submission info. Query w/SASE. Index: 33.

Madrona Publishers, Inc., PO Box 22667, Seattle, WA 98122. Contact: Sara Levant. 206–325–3973. Publisher of 10 hard/softcover originals & subsidy s a year. Print run: 7,500. Accepts freelance material. Payment: Royalties. Rights purchased: First. Query with outline, sample chapter, SASE. Dot matrix, photocopies, simultaneous submissions OK. Reports in 6-8 wks. Publishes in 1 year. Nonfiction: At least 150 typewritten pgs. "Since we do not specialize, we will consider almost any topic of interest to a broad adult market. Particular interests are alcoholism (especially alcoholism as a physical, not mental, disease); feminist issues; and small business, especially the business side of crafts. No novels, poetry, drama, children's books." Guidelines/catalog $.39. Index: 24, 38, 50.

Magnolia House Publishing, 2843 Thorndyke Ave, Seattle, WA 98199. No submission info. Query w/SASE. Index: 130.

Magnolia News, 225 West Galer, Seattle, WA 98119. 206–282–900. Weekly newspaper. No submission info. Query w/SASE. Index: 33.

Magpie, PO Box 127, Salem, OR 97308. 503–588–3705. Editor: John W. Wilkerson. Periodical. No submission info. Query w/SASE. Index: 37.

Sal Magundi Enterprises, 12960 S.W. Carmel Street, Portland, OR 97224-2032. Publisher. No submission info. Query w/SASE. Index: 130.

The Mail Tribune, 33 N. Fir Street, Box 1108, Medford, OR 97501. 503–776–4411. Daily newspaper. No submission info. Query w/SASE. Index: 33.

The Malahat Review, University of Victoria, PO Box 1700, Victoria, BC V8W 2Y2. Editor: Constance Rooke. 604–721–8524. Quarterly of fiction/poetry. Circ. 1,200. Sub. $15. Uses 20-25 mss per issue. Payment: Fiction – $35 per 1,000 wds + one year sub on acceptance. Poetry – $15 per pg + one year sub. Rights purchased: First. Reports in 6-8 wks. Fiction, poetry, plays. No restrictions on topic, slant or length. Tips: "Send one story at a time, or 6-10 pgs of poetry." Sample: $6. Index: 31, 51, 97.

Malheur Enterprise, 263 "A" Street W, Box 310, Vale, OR 97918. 503–473–3377. Weekly newspaper. No submission info. Query w/SASE. Index: 33.

Management Information Source Inc., 1107 N.W. 14th Avenue, Portland, OR 97209-2802. Publisher. No submission info. Query w/SASE. Index: 24.

Management/Marketing Associates, Inc., 707 S.W. Washington Street, Bank of California Tower, Portland, OR 97205. Publisher. No submission info. Query w/SASE. Index: 24.

Manna Publications, Inc., PO Box 1111, Camas, WA 98607. No submission info. Query w/SASE. Index: 130.

Manufactured Homes Magazine, POBox 354, Bremerton, WA 98310. Editor: Sandra Haven. 206–377–1590. Ads: Dennis Haven. Published 10 times a year with information on selection, purchase, protection, maintenance, and enjoyment of living in mobile, modular and panelized homes. Circ. 12,000. Sub. $12. Uses 1-3 mss per issue. Payment: Up to $.10/wd on acceptance. Byline given. Rights purchased: First. Query w/mss, SASE. Photocopies OK. Reports in 2 wks to query; 4-6 wks on mss. Nonfiction: Need "humorous reflections, 'Reader Projects', a 200-500 word description of how a homeowner customized a manufactured home after purchase, and cartoons." Photos: B&W, color photos. Guidelines available, sample: $1.50. Index: 36, 66, 67.

Manx Publishing Co., 429 S. Montana, Helena, MT 59601. Contact: Editor. Publisher. No submission info. Query w/SASE. Index: 130.

The Marijuana Report, PO Box 8698, Portland, OR 97207. Editor: John Sajo. 503–239–5134. Bimonthly tabloid on marijuana issues, politics,

For lists of abbreviations and the key to index numbers, see "How to Use this Section" on page 75.

Writer's Northwest Handbook 145

special initiatives, drug education; published by the Oregon Marijuana Initiative. Circ. 50,000. Payment: $.10 wd on publication. Submit ms, SASE. Phone queries, dot matrix, simultaneous submissions OK. Reports in 1 month. Nonfiction: 500-3,000 wds; any subject. Fiction, poetry: Inquire. Photos: B&W, preferably screened, $25-50. Tips: "Need well researched articles on impact of marijuana laws, i.e., who is in prison for marijuana. Also urinalysis." Sample available. Index: 51, 97, 101.

Marine Digest, 1732 Fourth S., Seattle, WA 98124. 206–682–2484. Periodical. No submission info. Query w/SASE. Index: 24, 79.

Maritime Publications, PO Box 527, Everson, WA 98247. Self-publisher. Not a freelance market. Index: 24, 79.

Market Times, Pike Place #12, Seattle, WA 98101. Contact: Editor. Monthly. No submission info. Query w/SASE. Index: 130.

Marketing Index International Pub., PO Box 19031, Portland, OR 97219. Contact: Editor. Bimonthly. No submission info. Query w/SASE. Index: 24.

Marketing Reports & Trade Leads, USA Dry Pea & Lentil Council, PO Box 8566, Moscow, ID 83843. Editor: Don Walker. Published 18 times a year. No submission info. Query w/SASE. Index: 3, 24.

Markins Enterprises, 2039 S.E. 45, Portland, OR 97215. Contact: Myrna Perkins. 503–235–1036. Self-publisher of 4 softcover children's picture books per year – educational, science oriented, entertaining. Press run: 500. Index: 29, 45, 109.

The Martlet, University of Victoria, Box 1700, Victoria, BC V8W 2Y2. Editors: Mike O'Brian/Kim Balfour. 604–721–8359. Periodical. No submission info. Query w/SASE. Index: 31.

The Mason Clinic, 1100 9th Avenue, PO Box 900, Seattle, WA 98111. Publisher. No submission info. Query w/SASE. Index: 130.

Mason County Journal & Belfair Herald, PO Box 430, Shelton, WA 98584. 206–426–4412. Weekly newspaper. No submission info. Query w/SASE. Index: 33.

Masonic Tribune, 2314 Third Avenue, Seattle, WA 98121. 206–285–1505. Editor: Ruth Todahl. Ads: Sid Worbass. Weekly newspaper. Sub: $15. Circ: 5,500. Material supplied by fraternal members. No pay. Byline given. Uses B&W glossy photos. Guidelines available. Sample $.50. Index: 126.

The Mast, Pacific Lutheran University, Tacoma, WA 98447. 206–535–7387. Contact: Editor. Weekly student newspaper. Index: 31.

Master Gardener Notes, OSU Extension, Multnomah County Office, 211 S.E. 80th Avenue, Portland, OR 97215. Editor: Enid Larsen. Monthly. No submission info. Query w/SASE. Index: 56.

Master Press, PO Box 432, Dayton, OR 97114. No submission info. Query w/SASE. Index: 130.

Masterstream, PO Box 1523, Longview, WA 98632. Contact: Editor. Periodical. No submission info. Query w/SASE. Index: 130.

Masterworks, Inc., General Delivery, Lopez, WA 98261-9999. Contact: Editor. Publisher. No submission info. Query w/SASE. Index: 130.

Math Counseling Institute Press, 4518 Corliss Avenue N., Seattle, WA 98103. No submission info. Query w/SASE. Index: 43.

Matrix, c/o The Daily, 132 Communications DS/20, University of Washington, Seattle, WA 98195. 206–543–2700. Monthly literary supplement of poetry and short fiction in the UW paper, The Daily. Circ. 25,000. No pay. Byline given. Simultaneous submissions OK. Publishes submissions in 1-2 mos. Fiction: 1,500 wds, any subject. Poetry: Varies. Photos: B&W. Tips "We prefer to print the work of UW students, but on occasion have published non-student works. We receive about 100 submissions a month but have space for about 20-25." Index: 31, 51, 97.

Maverick Publications, Drawer 5007, Bend, OR 97708. Contact: Ken Asher. 503–382–6978. Publisher of 10 hard/softcover originals per year for the general trade. Print run: 2,000. Accepts freelance material. Payment: Money. Rights acquired: Book rights plus 50% of subsidiary. Query w/outline, sample chapters, SASE. Dot matrix, photocopies, simultaneous submissions, electronic OK. Reports in 6 wks. Publishes in 6 mos. Nonfiction, fiction. Catalog available. Index: 41, 51, 89.

Mazama, 909 N.W. 19th, Portland, OR 97209. Periodical on rock and mountain climbing and related subjects for club members. Sub. membership. No submission info. Query w/SASE. Index: 92, 103, 115.

McKenzie River Reflections, PO Box 12, McKenzie Bridge, OR 97413. Editors/ads: Ken & Louise Engelman. 503–896–3448. Weekly of local news, tourist, recreation. Circ. 1,000. Sub. $11. Uses 1 ms per issue. Payment: Copies. Byline given. Query w/SASE. Dot matrix, photocopies OK. Nonfiction, fiction, poetry, photos (B&W), plays, cartoons. Sample: Free. Index: 33, 89, 103.

MCS Enterprises, PO Box 30160, Eugene, OR 97403. Publisher. No submission info. Query w/SASE. Index: 130.

MCSA-Medical Committee & Service Association, 10223 N.E. 58th Street, Kirkland, WA 98033. Publisher. No submission info. Query w/SASE. Index: 61, 81.

Media Weavers, Rt 3, Box 376, Hillsboro, OR 97124. 503–621–3911. Contact: Dennis Stovall, Linny Stovall. An imprint of Blue Heron Publishing, Media Weavers publishes books on writing, publishing. Query w/SASE. Reports in 1 mo.. Payment & rights negotiable. Gives byline. Dot matrix, photocopies, simultaneous, electronic, computer disc OK. Index: 89, 102, 125.

Mediaor Company, Box 631, Prineville, OR 97754. Publisher. No submission info. Query w/SASE. Index: 130.

Medic Publishing Company, PO Box 89, Redmond, WA 98073. 206–881–2883. Editor: Murray Swanson. Publisher of 4 softcover booklets a yr. Circ: 30,000. Accepts unsolicited mss. Pay: Royalties. Query w/clips, SASE. Dot matrix, photocopies OK. Reports in 30 days. Topics: Bereavement, medical — patient instruction. All are booklets, typically 24 pgs, 9,000 wds. "We are the country's leading publisher of grief literature, with some titles exceeding 1 million copies." Catalog available. Index: 61, 81, 100.

Medium, PO Box 22047, Seattle, WA 98122. 206–323–3070. Weekly newspaper. No submission info. Query w/SASE. Index: 33.

The Medium, 711 Hoyt Ave., Everett, WA 98201. Contact: Editor. Periodical. No submission info. Query w/SASE. Index: 130.

Melior Publications, PO Box 1905, Spokane, WA 99210-1905. 509–455–9617. Editor: Barbara Chamberlain. Ads: Michael McGagin. Press run: 2,000-20,000. Publisher of 4-5 hard/softcover, original books a yr. Unsolicited mss accepted. Submit ms, SASE. Dot matrix, photocopies, simultaneous OK. Reports in 6 mos. Publishes in 12-18 mos. Topics: historical works for general audience; well illustrated, well researched. Pacific NW focus, but expanding into Southwest, West Coast. New series: "Contemporary American Voices" — looking for thoughtful essays by people who are newsmakers or who have something significant to say. "We look for something that can be presented attractively that will enter-

For lists of abbreviations and the key to index numbers, see "How to Use this Section" on page 75.

tain as it educates and enlightens. Heritage, history topics, regional or national in scope, are considered carefully. Doing our first historical novel — may look at more." Catalog available. Index: 62, 65, 89.

Memory Publishing, 316 219th Avenue N.E., Redmond, WA 98053. No submission info. Query w/SASE. Index: 130.

Mercury Services, Inc., PO Box 1523, Longview, WA 98632-0144. 206–577–8598. Ads: Bruce Grimm. Bi-monthly newsletter. Sub. $6/yr. Circ. 2,500. Uses 1 freelance ms per issue. Pays on publication in copies. Acquires 1st rights. Byline given. Submit query w/clips, SASE. Dot matrix, photocopies, simultaneous, computer disc subs OK. Reports in 4-6 wks. Publishes 45-50 days. Accepts nonfiction: transportation related; safety issues. B&W photos. Index: 32, 60, 74.

Merril Press, PO Box 1682, Bellevue, WA 98009. 206–454–7009. Editor: Ron Arnold. Ads: Julie Versnel. Publishes 4-6 hard/softcover originals, reprints, subsidy books/yr. Accepts unsolicited mss. Pays money, royalties. Acquires all rights. Prefers phone query. Dot matrix, photocopies, simultaneous, electronic/modem, computer disc OK. Publishes in 3-6 mo. Accepts nonfiction: how-to, politics, special interest, hobby material, economics. Index: 38, 42, 67.

Message, Montana Info, Box 229, Condon, MT 59826. Contact: Editor. Quarterly. No submission info. Query w/SASE. Index: 130.

Message Post: Portable Dwelling Info-Letter, PO Box 190-MW, Philomath, OR 97370. Editor: Holly Davis. Newsletter published 3 times a yr. Subs. $5/6 issues. Circ. 1,000. Uses 20 freelance mss per issue. Pays subscription or ad on acceptance. Submit w/SASE. Dot matrix, photocopied, simultaneous, electronic/modem, computer disc OK. Accepts nonfiction: Information useful for camping for long periods or living in tipis, vans, trailers, boats, remote cabins, etc. No photos, line drawings & screens only. Want candid reports from those doing what they are writing about. Polish not important. Guidelines available. Sample $1. Index: 67, 92.

The Messenger, PO Box 1995, Vancouver, WA 98668. Editor: Marilyn Forbes. 206–696–8171. Ads: John Castile. Monthly for senior citizens. Circ. 14,000. Sub. $5. Uses 1-2 mss per issue. Payment: Free sub. Byline given. Rights purchased: First. Query w/SASE. Phone queries, photocopies OK. Nonfiction, photos (B&W glossy, any size, not prescreened), cartoons. "All material must relate directly to senior citizens. Strong preference for upbeat informational or feature articles from NW writers. 250 wds preferred maximum. Deadline, 12th of each month for following month's issue." Tips: "All material for this non-profit publication must be non-promotional. I encourage novice freelancers to submit pieces." Sample: Free. Index: 36, 65, 110.

Metamorphous Press, Inc., PO Box 10616, Portland, OR 97210-0616. 503–228–4972. Editor: Anita Sullivan. Publishes 6 hard/softcover, originals, reprints, subsidy books/yr. Accepts unsolicited mss. Submit query w/clips, SASE. Dot matrix, photocopied OK. Reports in 3-4 mo. Accepts nonfiction. Topics: self-help, psychology, health & fitness, business and sales, education, and children. Catalog available. Index: 43, 61, 100.

Methow Valley News, PO Box 97, Twisp, WA 98856. 509–997–7011. Weekly newspaper . No submission info. Query w/SASE. Index: 33.

Metrocenter YMCA, PO Box 85334, Seattle, WA 98145. Editor: Jack C. Thompson. 206–547–4003. Quarterly on pop culture, music, politics. Circ. 500. Accepts freelance material. Byline given. Query w/SASE. Phone queries, simultaneous submissions, electronic OK. Nonfiction, cartoons, essays, analysis. Guidelines and sample available. Index: 39, 86, 98.

M'Godolim, The Jewish Literary Magazine, 2921 E. Madison Avenue, Suite 7, Seattle, WA 98112. Quarterly ethnic periodical. No submission info. Query w/SASE. Index: 84, 105.

Mica Publishing Company, PO Box 14931, Portland, OR 97214. Contact: Joanne Stevens Sullivan. 503–230–2903. Self-publisher of 1 hard/softcover book of poetry per year. Print run: 2,000. Not a freelance market. Catalog available. Index: 97.

Micro Cornucopia, 155 N.W. Hawthorne, Bend, OR 97701. Editor: David S. Thompson. Periodical. No submission info. Query w/SASE. Index: 34.

Microconsulting Press, PO Box 15075, Portland, OR 97214. No submission info. Query w/SASE. Index: 34.

Microsoft Press, PO Box 97200, Bellevue, WA 98009. Contact: Salley Oberlin. Publisher of 25-50 hard/softcover nonfiction books on software, aimed at "people interested in computers, science and people." Query, w/ms, outline, sample chapters, SASE. Dot matrix, photocopies, simultaneous submissions, electronic OK. Publishes submissions in 6-9 mos. Catalog available. Index: 34.

MIDCO Enterprises, PO Box 1266, Gresham, OR 97030. Editor: Lynette M. Middleton. Publisher. No submission info. Query w/SASE. Index: 130.

Midgard Press, 4214 Midway Avenue, Grants Pass, OR 97527. 503–476–3603. Self-publisher of hardcover books for dairy goat owners. Print run: 5,000. Not a freelance market. Index: 3, 6.

Midnight Shambler, 1595 Saginaw St. S., Salem, OR 97302. Contact: Editor. Magazine. Uses freelance material. No submission info. Query w/SASE. Index: 10, 48.

Midwifery Today, PO Box 2672, Eugene, OR 97402. Editor: Jan Tritten. 503–345–1979. Ads: Bobbi Corcoran. 503–343–2408. Quarterly for midwifery practitioners and consumers. Sub. $18. Uses 13 mss per issue. Payment: Copies on publication. Byline given. Rights purchased: First. Query w/ms, SASE. Phone queries, dot matrix, photocopies, simultaneous submissions OK. Reports in 6 wks. Nonfiction, fiction, poetry, photos, cartoons. "Articles to help birth practitioners do their work well. We have 20 different columns and take a variety of articles, both scientific and spiritual. We always need good research articles. Biographical sketch of writer included." Guidelines available, sample: $5. Index: 61, 124.

Migrant Education News, PO Box 901, Sunnyside, WA 98944. 509–839–0440. Editor: Larry Ashby. Ads: Donna Allec. Newspaper published 10 times/yr. Sub. $10. Circ. 7,500. Uses 3-5 freelance mss per issue. No pay. Acquires 1st rights. Byline given. Submit query w/clips, SASE. Dot matrix, photocoped, electronic, MAC computer disc OK. Reports in 1 wk. Publishes in 1 mo. Accepts nonfiction, photos. Topics: migrant farmworker students, problems and successes; migrant teachers in WA public schools. Use original research gleaned from local, state & federal records via public information laws. Research concerning program audits, budgets, etc. welcome; other factual investigative reporting; interviews with elected officials. Prefer hard, factual stories with documentation. Photos: 8x10 B&W glossy, $15 on acceptance; $5/head & shoulder shots. Index: 27, 43, 84.

Milco Publishing, 18910 37th S., Seattle, WA 98188. No submission info. Query w/SASE. Index: 130.

The Milepost, Alaska N.W. Publishing Company, Box 4-EEE, Anchorage, AK 99509. Periodical. No submission info. Query w/SASE. Index: 4.

The Miler, Oregon Institute of Technology, Klamath Falls, OR 97601. 503–822–6321 x189. Contact: Editor. No submission info. Query w/SASE. Index: 31.

For lists of abbreviations and the key to index numbers, see "How to Use this Section" on page 75.

Writer's Northwest Handbook 147

Miles City Star, PO Box 1216, Miles City, MT 59301. Editor: Gerald Anglum. Newspaper. No submission info. Query w/SASE. Index: 33.

Milestone Publications, Box 2248, Sidney, BC V8L 3S8. No submission info. Query w/SASE. Index: 130.

The Mill City Enterprise, 117 N.E. Wall, Box 348, Mill City, OR 97360. 503–897–2772. Weekly newspaper. No submission info. Query w/ SASE. Index: 33.

Merl Miller & Associates, PO Box 539, Rockaway, OR 97136-0539. Publisher. No submission info. Query w/SASE. Index: 130.

Robert Miller Productions, 12051 S.W. Orchard Hill Way, Lake Oswego, OR 97034. Publisher. No submission info. Query w/SASE. Index: 130.

Minds Ink Publishing, PO Box 2701, Eugene, OR 97402. 503–689–4785. Editor: Phillip Hennin. Publishes 10 softcover books/yr. Accepts unsolicited mss. Submit query w/clips, SASE. Dot matrix, photocopied, simultaneous, electronic, computer disc (IBM) OK. Reports in 6 wks. Business, success stories, business resource material. Photos: graphics preferred, price negotiable. Index: 24, 25, 67.

Miner & Gem State Miner, PO Box 349, Newport, WA 99156. 509–447–2433. Weekly newspaper. No submission info. Query w/SASE. Index: 38, 59, 103.

Mineral Land Publications, PO Box 1186, Boise, ID 83701. Contact: Editor. Publisher. No submission info. Query w/SASE. Index: 130.

Mining Review, 124 W. 8th Street, North Vancouver, BC V7M 3H2. Editor: Vivian Rudd. 604–985–8711. Periodical. No submission info. Query w/SASE. Index: 24, 109.

The Minnesota Review, Department of English, Oregon State University, Corvallis, OR 97331. Editor: Fred Pfeil. Literary review. No submission info. Query w/SASE. Index: 31, 76, 97.

Minutes Magazine, 50 S.W. Second Ave., Suite 416, Portland, OR 97204. 503–243–2616. Editor: Len Rothbaum. Periodical. No submission info. Query w/SASE. Index: 130.

MIR Publication Society, PO Box 730, Grand Forks, BC V0H 1H0. Publisher. No submission info. Query w/SASE. Index: 130.

The Mirror, Marylhurst College for Lifetime Learning, Marylhurst, OR 97036. Editor: Courtney Rojas. Periodical. No submission info. Query w/SASE. Index: 31.

MIS:Press, PO Box 5277, Portland, OR 97208. Editor: Kim Anne Thomas. Publishes 24 hard/softcover computer/business books a yr. Pays royalities, advance. Rights acquired: All. Submit query w/clips, ms, SASE. Reports in 2-3 wks. Publishes in 3-6 mos. In-depth books on PC/MAC topics/products or business topics (management-oriented). Catalog available. Index: 24, 34, 117.

Mississippi Mud, 1336 S.E. Marion Street, Portland, OR 97202. Editor: Joel Weinstein. Literary/arts magazine published 2-3 times a year. Circ. 1,500. Uses 4-5 stories, 15-20 poems per issue. Payment: Money, copies on publication. Byline given. Rights purchased: First. Submit ms, SASE. Dot matrix, simultaneous submissions OK. Reports in 2-4 mos. Publishes in 3-12 mos. Fiction: 2,500-5,000 wds; $0-25 or copies. Poetry: no restrictions; $0-15 or copies. Sample: $3.50. Index: 51, 97.

Missoulian, PO Box 8029, Missoula, MT 59807. 406–721–5200. Daily newspaper. No submission info. Query w/SASE. Index: 33.

The Mobile/Manufactured Homeowner, PO Box 354, Bremerton, WA 98210. Periodical. No submission info. Query w/SASE. Index: 36, 66.

Modern & Contemporary Poetry of the West, Boise State University, Department of English, 1910 University Drive, Boise, ID 83725. Editor: Tom Trusky. Periodical 3 times a year. Circ. 500. No submission info. Query w/SASE. Index: Index: 31, 97.

Modern Language Quarterly, 4045 Brooklyn Ave. N.E., Seattle, WA 98105. No submission info. Query w/SASE. Index: 44, 73.

Molalla Pioneer, 217 E. Main Street, Box 168, Molalla, OR 97038. Weekly newspaper. No submission info. Query w/SASE. Index: 33.

Mole Publishing Company, Route 1, Box 618, Bonners Ferry, ID 83805. No submission info. Query w/SASE. Index: 130.

Monday Magazine, 1609 Blanshard St., Victoria, BC V8W 2J5. 604–382–6188. Editor: Richard VanDine. Weekly alternate news magazine. Sub. $30. Circ. 40,000. Accepts unsolicited submissions. Uses 1-2 freelance mss per issue. Payment: usually $.12-.15/wd on publication. Rights acquired: First. Byline given. Submit ms, SASE. Reports in 1-4 wks. Publishes in 1-4 wks. Accepts nonfiction: 1,000-2,000 wds; features of local or regional interest about politics, government, social issues, arts & entertainment. Guidelines available. Index: 26, 45, 121.

Monroe Monitor/Valley News, PO Box 399, Monroe, WA 98272. Editor: Fred Willenbrock. 206–794–7116. Ads: Pat Oliffeer. Weekly newspaper. Circ. 3,500. Sub. $17 out of county. Not a freelance market. Index: 33.

Montana Artpaper, PO Box 1456, Billings, MT 59103. Editor: Renee Sherrer. Periodical. No submission info. Query w/SASE. Index: 10.

Montana Arts Council, 35 S. Last Chance Gulch, Helena, MT 59620. 406–444–6430. Editor: Julie Cook. Publishes 1 softcover book a yr. Accepts unsolicited submissions. Submit query w/clips, SASE. Dot matrix, photocopied, simultaneous, electronic subs OK. Accepts fiction, poetry, other. Guidelines available. Index: 10, 51, 97.

Montana Books Publishers, Inc., PO Box 30017, 1716 N. 45th Street, Seattle, WA 98103. No submission info. Query w/SASE. Index: 130.

Montana Business Quarterly, Bureau of Business & Economic Research, University of Montana, Missoula, MT 59812. No submission info. Query w/SASE. Index: 24, 42, 85.

Montana Crafters Inc. Review, PO Box 1254, Helena, MT 59624. Contact: Editor. Monthly. No submission info. Query w/SASE. Index: 38.

Montana Crop & Livestock Reporting Service, PO Box 4369, Helena, MT 59604. Publisher. No submission info. Query w/SASE. Index: 3, 6, 85.

Montana Department of Labor & Industry, PO Box 1728, Helena, OR 59604. Publisher. No submission info. Query w/SASE. Index: 24, 71, 85.

Montana English Journal, Montana State University, Department of English, Bozeman, MT 59717. 406–586–2686. Editor: Sharon Beehler. Periodical. No submission info. Query w/SASE. Index: 31.

Montana Farmer-Stockman, NW Unit Farms Magazines, PO Box 2160, Spokane, WA 99210. 509–459–5361. Semimonthly farm magazine. Also see listing for OR, WA, ID editions. No submission info. Query w/SASE. Index: 3, 24, 85.

For lists of abbreviations and the key to index numbers, see "How to Use this Section" on page 75.

148 Market Listings

Montana Historical Society Press, 225 N. Roberts, Helena, MT 59620. 406–444–4708. Editor: W. Lang, M. Keddington. Publisher of nonfiction hard/softcover original, reprint books. Does not accept unsolicited submissions. Index: 65, 85, 87.

Montana Kaimin, University of Montana, Missoula, MT 59812. Contact: Editor. Student newspaper. No submission info. Query w/SASE. Index: 31.

Montana Magazine, PO Box 5630, Helena, MT 59604. Editor: Carolyn Cunningham. 406–443–2842. Bimonthly devoted to Montana, "outdoor, history, places to go, geology, hunting, wildlife, personality profiles, travel." Circ. 85,000 to college educated, under 50, $25,000 & above bracket. Payment: $100-150 on publication. Byline given. Query w/ms, SASE. Phone queries, dot matrix, simultaneous submissions OK. Reports in 4-6 wks. Publishes within 1 year. Nonfiction: 2,000 wds, where to go items; "turning more and more to assigned writers for the longer features." Photos: Write for guidelines; $75 cover, $50 center section. Tips: "...Need items for our 'Over the Weekend' column. Must be Montana travel pieces. B&W prints accompanying. Although we do not accept as much freelance material as previously, are still open to good features, so it's worth submitting major features for consideration." Guidelines available. Index: 85, 120.

Montana the Magazine of Western History, Montana Historical Society, 225 N. Roberts, Helena, MT 59620. 406–444–4708. Editor: M. Keddington. Ads: Chris Eby. Quarterly on history of MT and the West. Sub. $18. Circ. 11,000. Accepts unsolicited submissions. Pays copies. Byline given. Submit query w/clips, ms,SASE. Dot matrix, photocopies OK. Accepts nonfiction. Guidelines and sample available. Index: 62, 85, 87.

Montana Newsletter, Montana State Library, 1515 E. 6th Ave., Helena, MT 59620. Contact: Editor. Periodical. No submission info. Query w/ SASE. Index: 31, 104.

The Montana Poet, PO Box 269, Gallatin Gateway, MT 59730. 406–586–6023. Editor: Don "Cheese" Akerlow. Quarterly. Sub. $10. Circ. 1,000. 100% freelance mss. Pays 1 copy on publication. Rights acquired: 1st. Byline given. Dot matrix, photocopied, simutaneous OK. Reports usually in 4 wks. Publishes in 1-4 issues. Accepts: poetry on any subject, any style, no more than 5 submissions at a time; short stories, 500-1,000 wds; and cartoons. Submissions must be neatly printed or typed, include legal size SASE. Payment is copy of the magazine. Guidelines available. Sample $2. Index: 85, 90, 97.

Montana Review, 1620 N. 45th Street, Seattle, WA 98103. 206–633–5929. Editor: Rich Ives. Ads: Rich Ives. Semiannual literary periodical. Circ. 500. Sub. $9. Accepts freelance material. Payment: Money, copies on publication. Byline given. Rights purchased: First. Submit ms, SASE. Dot matrix, photocopies OK. Reports in 2-8 wks. Nonfiction, fiction, poetry, translations, book reviews. "Any length, subject. Literary quality is our only criteria. Pay varies according to current grant status." Index: 51, 76, 97.

Montana Senior Citizens News, PO Box 3363, Great Falls, MT 59403. 406–761–0305, 800–672–8477 (in Montana). Editor: Jack W. Love, Jr. Ads: Jane Basta. Bimonthly tabloid. Sub. $6. Circ. 14,000. Uses 5 freelance mss per issue. Pays $.04/word on publication. Acquires 1st rights. Byline given. Submit ms, SASE, phone query. Dot matrix, photocopied, electronic/modem OK. Reports in 10 days. Accepts nonfiction, fiction, poetry, photos, cartoons. Topics: stories and articles of interest to seniors, particularly colorful, unique biographical sketches. Photos required with personality profiles; submit contact sheet or negatives, pay $5. Tips: length generally 500-1,000 wds; positive, upbeat, focus on the value of life experiences; humor/satire preferred for political topics. Sample $2. Index: 85, 110.

Montana Standard, PO Box 627, Butte, MT 59703-0627. 406–782–8301. Daily newspaper. No submission info. Query w/SASE. Index: 33.

Monte Publishing Company, PO Box 361, Underwood, WA 98651. 509–493–2396. Self-publisher of 1 softcover book a year for juveniles. Print run: 2,000. Not a freelance market. Catalog available. Index: 29, 65, 105.

Montevista Press, 5041 Meridian Road, Bellingham, WA 98226. 206–734–4279. Editor: J. Burkhart. Publisher of 1 hard/softcover book a yr. Freelance material not accepted. Catalog available. Index: 6, 62, 65.

Monthly, The, Wine Bros. Publishing, 603 Stewart Street, Suite 1020, Seattle, WA 98101. 206–682–3565. Editor: David Hooper. Ads: Todd Bitts. Monthly for media professionals. Sub. $29.50/yr. Circ. 10,000. Uses two freelance mss per issue. Pays on publication. First rights. Byline given. Submit query w/clips, SASE, may be computer disc. Reports 2 wks. Publishes 1 mo. Topics: news and features, media and marketing in the NW (advertising, print & broadcast media, film & video, etc.). Sample $2.50. Index: 24, 80, 102.

Mooncircles, Circles of Exchange, PO Box 021703, Juneau, AK 99802-1703. Editor. Nan Hawthorne. Monthly. No submission info. Query w/ SASE. Index: 130.

Moonstone Press, 15712 S.E. 4th Street, Bellevue, WA 98008. Editor: Gayle Vogel Thomsen. 206–746–9201. Publisher of "poetry, prose and mythological illustrations about the Goddess and other literary, amusing and mystical subjects." No submissions info. Query w/SASE. Index: 13, 45, 50.

Moore Publications, PO Box 2530, Redmond, WA 98052. No submission info. Query w/SASE. Index: 130.

Mooseyard Press, PO Box 6462, Kent, WA 98064. 206–631–9013. Editors: Olga Joanow, Katherine Speed, L. Pagliaro. Magazine published once or twice a year. Subs. $7. Circ. 500+. Accepts unsolicited mss. Pays in copies. Byline given. Submit ms, SASE. Dot Matrix, photocopies, electronic/modem, computer disk (MAC only) OK. Reports in 2 mo. Publishes in 3-4 mo. Accepts nonfiction, fiction, poetry. Guidelines available. Sample $3. Index: 51, 94, 97.

Morgan Notes, 3128 Penny Creek Rd., Bothell, WA, 98012, 206–743–6098. Contact: Jeanette Schouer. Periodical. No submission info. Query w/SASE. Index: 130.

The Morning Side/Network, Eastern Oregon Regional Arts Council, Eastern Oregon State College, La Grande, OR 97850. Contact: Editor. Quarterly. No submission info. Query w/SASE. Index: 10.

Morse Press, PO Box 24947, Seattle, WA 98124. Contact: Ronn Talbot Pelley. 206–282–9988. Publisher of 4 softcover books, originals, reprints annually. "Confirmation materials, chancel dramas, Lenten programs, counseling guides." Print run: 5,000. Accepts freelance material. Payment: Money, royalties. Rights purchased: All. Sample chapters w/SASE. Photocopies, simultaneous submissions OK. Reports in 6 wks. Publishes in 1 year. Nonfiction, plays. Catalog available. Index: 43, 105.

Morton Journal, PO Drawer M, Morton, WA 98356. 206–496–5993. Weekly newspaper. No submission info. Query w/SASE. Index: 33.

Mosaic Enterprises, Ltd., 1420 St. Paul Street, Kelowna, BC V1Y 2E6. Publisher. No submission info. Query w/SASE. Index: 130.

Mother of Ashes, PO Box 135, Harrison, ID 83833-0135. Contact: Judith Shannon Paine. Small publisher. Query w/SASE. Index: 51, 96, 97.

For lists of abbreviations and the key to index numbers, see "How to Use this Section" on page 75.

Writer's Northwest Handbook   149

Mt. Tabor Bulletin, 12311 N.E. Glisan #103, Portland, OR 97230. 503–256–2833. Editor: Shelli Smith. Periodical. No submission info. Query w/SASE. Index: 33.

Mount Vernon Press, 1121 112th N.E., Bellevue, WA 98004. No submission info. Query w/SASE. Index: 130.

The Mountain Guide, Blue Mountain Community College, Box 100, Pendleton, OR 97801. 503–276–1260. Periodical. No submission info. Query w/SASE. Index: 31.

Mountain Light, Idaho Historical Society, 610 N. Julia Davis Drive, Boise, ID 83702. Editor: Judith Austin. Quarterly. No submission info. Query w/SASE. Index: 65, 69.

Mountain Meadow Press, PO Box 447, Kooskia, ID 83539. 208–926–4526. Publishes 2-3 "parent-participatory education" softcover books a year. Does not accept unsolicited submissions. Index: 43, 47, 116.

Mountain Mist Lending Library, 23561 Vaughn Road, Veneta, OR 97487. 503–935–7701. Contact: Editor. Publisher. No submission info. Query w/SASE. Index: 130.

Mountain News, 1615 W. 4th Avenue, Vancouver, BC V6J 1L8. 604–732–1351. Nationally circulated magazine published 5 times per year. Uses nonfiction articles on natural enjoyment and awareness of the outdoors. Uses photos with articles. No submissions info. Query w/SASE. Index: 35, 92, 103.

Mountain Press Publishing Company, 1600 North Avenue W., Missoula, MT 59806. Publisher. Titles/yr: 12. No submission info. Query w/SASE. Index: 130.

Mountain View Publishing Company, Tin Cup Road, Darby, MT 59829. No submission info. Query w/SASE. Index: 130.

The Mountaineers, 306 2nd Ave. W., Seattle, WA 98119. 206–285–2665. Editor: Stephen Whitney. Ads: Priscilla Johnston. Publishes 20 hard/softcover, originals, reprints a yr. Accepts unsolicited mss. Pays money, royalties, advance. Acquires 1st rights. Submit query w/clips, ms, Dot matrix, photocopies, sumultaneous OK. Reports in 2-8 wks. Publishes 1 yr. plus. Accepts nonfiction: how-tos, guidebooks and adventure narratives for non-motorized, non-competitive outdoor sports (skiing, biking, hiking, climbing, mountaineering, kayaking, walking, etc.). Also works on conservation, mountaineering history. Book-length, payment varies. Guidelines available. Index: 88, 92, 103.

Mr. Cogito, Mr. Cogito Press, PO Box 627, Pacific University, Forest Grove, OR 97116. Editors: Robert Davies/John Gogol. Irregular magazine of "poems in English and translated into English, various themes, eg. Central America." Dot matrix, mss OK. Reports in 2-8 wks. Infrequently pays. Purchases 1st anthology and publishing rights. Poetry: 1 pg; image and sound and diction important; pays in copies. Sample copies $.75. Index: 31, 97.

Mr. Cogito Press, PO Box 627, Pacific University, Forest Grove, OR 97116. Editors: Robert Davies/John Gogol. Publishes 2-3 softcover books per year. Submit ms, SASE. Dot matrix, photocopies, simultaneous submissions, electronic OK. Publishes in 3-4 mos. Poetry: translations, and English. Tips: "We are a very small press, highly selective; our magazine submissions are our source for selecting authors." Index: 31, 97.

Ms. Leroy Press, 3511 S. 172nd, Seattle, WA 98188. 206–243–3687. Self-publisher of softcover originals. Print run: 5,000. Not a freelance market. Catalog available. Index: 107, 111.

MSU Exponent, Montana State University, Bozeman, MT 59717. Contact: Editor. Student Newspaper. No submission info. Query w/SASE. Index: 31.

Mukluks Hemcunga, PO Box 1257, Klamath Falls, OR 97601. Monthly. No submission info. Query w/SASE. Index: 130.

Multiples Press, 1821 S. 4th W., Missoula, MT 59801-2229. Contact: Editor. Publisher. No submission info. Query w/SASE. Index: 130.

Multnomah Press, 10209 S.E. Division, Portland, OR 97266. Contact: Georgene Hayley. 503–257–0526. Publisher of 25-40 books per year of "Christian literature that is contemporary while faithful to the Scriptures." Print run: 8,000. Accepts freelance material. Query w/SASE. Dot matrix, photocopies, simultaneous submissions, electronic OK. Publishes in 9 mos. Guidelines/catalog. Index: 51, 105.

Murkwood Enterprises, PO Box 244, Leavenworth, WA 98826. Publisher. No submission info. Query w/SASE. Index: 130.

Murray Publishing Company, 2312 3rd Avenue, Seattle, WA 98121. Contact: John Murray. Publisher of textbooks and other non-fiction. No submission info. Query w/SASE. Index: 118.

Museum of History & Industry, 2700 24th Avenue E., Seattle, WA 98112. Publisher. No submission info. Query w/SASE. Index: 64, 65, 70.

Mushroom, The Journal, Box 3156, University Station, Moscow, ID 83843. 208–882–8720. Editor: Don Coombs. Quarterly. Sub. $16. Circ. 2,000. Uses 4 freelance mss per issue. Pays money/copies on publication. Acquires 1st rights. Byline given. Submit query w/clips, ms. Dot matrix, photocopied, computer disc (DOS/ASCII) OK. Reports in 1 mo. Publishes in 2-6 mo. Accepts non-fiction, poetry, photos, cartoons. "Material should be relevant in some way to what's going on outdoors with plants, animals and insects." Personal experience okay if it includes valuable learning for the reader. B&W prints or color negatives. Guidelines available. Sample $4 (3 or more $3 ea.). Index: 67, 88, 92.

Musings, 1235 Island Highway, Campbell River, BC V9W 2K4. 604–287–8043. Published 3 times a year on local history, Campbell River Museum activities. Circ. 250. Sub. $10. Not a freelance market. Sample: $1.25/SASE. Index: 65.

The Mustard Seed Faith, Inc., PO Box 3, St. Helens, OR 97051. Contact: Editor. Publisher. No submission info. Query w/SASE. Index: 105.

My Awe/Zine Orgy, 1501 N.E. 102 St., Seattle, WA 98125. Contact: Editor. Periodical. No submission info. Query w/SASE. Index: 130.

My Little Salesman, My Little Salesman, Inc. Publications, PO Box 2328, Eugene, OR 97402. Monthly. No submission info. Query w/SASE. Index: 130.

Myrtle Point Herald, 410 Spruce Street, Myrtle Point, OR 97458. 503–572–2717. Weekly newspaper. No submission info. Query w/SASE. Index: 33.

Mystery Time, PO Box 1870, Hayden, ID 83835. 208–772–6184. Editor: Linda Hutton. Annually published collection. Price $5. Uses freelance material. Pays $.0025-.01 per word for 1st rights, 1 copy for reprint rights. Submit short story (to 1,500 wds) w/SASE. Photocopied, simultaneous OK. Tips: short stories, suspense/mystery theme only, avoid present tense; poetry about mysteries or mystery writers. "Six authors are nominated annually for the Pushcart Prize in Fiction." Index: 51, 97.

For lists of abbreviations and the key to index numbers, see "How to Use this Section" on page 75.

150 Market Listings

Nanaimo Historical Society, PO Box 933, Nanaimo, BC V9R 5N2. Contact: Mrs. Mar. 604–758–2828. Self-publisher of historical hard/softcover originals — 1 every 2-3 year. Print run: 3,000. Not a freelance market. Index: 23, 58, 63.

National Book Company, PO Box 8795, Portland, OR 97207-8795. 503–228–6345. Publishes hard/softcover books. Accepts unsolicited submissions. Reports in 1-2 mo. Publishes in 6-12 mo. Accepts non-fiction. Publisher of textbooks and multimedia instructional programs and computer software in Jr. High –Jr. College range, although some publications include library and business reference books, educational policy studies, ethnic issues, or computer software whose market may be broader. Catalog available. Index: 34, 75, 118.

National Boycott Newsletter, 6506 28th Avenue N.E., Seattle, WA 98115. Editor: Todd Putnam. 206–523–0421. Quarterly on consumer action in the market place, boycotts and socially responsible investing. Circ. 4,000-5,000. Sub. $3. Uses 1-2 mss per issue. Payment: Money, copies on publication. Byline given. Query w/ms, SASE. Phone queries, dot matrix, photocopies, electronic OK. Non-fiction, photos, cartoons. "Corporations/multinationals and their environmental, social, economic impacts; boycotts and consumer action; boycotts called by human rights, peace, labor, environmental, and civil, women's and animal rights organizations." Sample available. Index: 36, 71, 93.

National Fisherman Magazine, 4215 21st W., Seattle, WA 98199. 206–283–1150. Periodical. No submission info. Query w/SASE. Index: 53.

National Home Education Guild, 515 N.E. 8th St., Grants Pass, OR 97256. Contact: Editor. Periodical. No submission info. Query w/SASE. Index: 43.

National Percent for Art Newsletter, 311 E. 17th, Spokane, WA 99203. Editor: Richard Twedt. Quarterly of news on state, regional and local public art commissions and % for art programs. Sub. $24. Index: 10.

National Seafood Educators, PO Box 60006, Richmond Beach, WA 98160. Contact: Editor. No submission info. Query w/SASE. Index: 53, 54, 61.

Native American Education Newsletter, 517 Rimrock Rd., Billings, MT 59102. 406–252–7451. Editor: Hap Gilliland. Ads: Marilyn Degel. Newsletter issued 3 times a year. Circ. 2,000. Uses 1-2 freelance mss per issue. Pays copies. Acquires 1st rights. Byline given. Submit ms, SASE. Dot matrix, photocopied, simultaneous OK. Reports in 2 mo. Accepts non-fiction, fiction, poetry, cartoons. Topics: American Indian education. Tips: short, up to 1,000 wds; audience is teachers, librarians and others interested in Indian education. Guidelines available. Sample SASE. Index: 43, 87.

Native Plant Society of Oregon Bulletin, c/o Jan Anderson, 1960 N.W. Lovejoy #2, Portland, OR 97209. Monthly newsletter. Circ. 600. Submit ms, SASE. Dot matrix OK. No pay. Non-fiction: "Writers contribute articles about ecology, horticulture, conservation of natural history of native plants. Contributors are usually NPSO members, but do not have to be. Botanical accuracy is essential. Material is not copyrighted." Guidelines available. Index: 19, 56, 89.

Natural Living, 611 Market Street, Kirkland, WA 98033. Periodical. No submission info. Query w/SASE. Index: 61.

Nature Conservancy-Oregon Chapter Newsletter, 1234 N.W. 25th, Portland, OR 97210. Editor: Katharine Snouffer. No submission info. Query w/SASE. Index: 35, 92.

Naturopath and the Natural Health World, 1920 N. Kilpatrick, Portland, OR 97217. Editor: Dr. John W. Noble. Monthly. No submission info. Query w/SASE. Index: 61, 81.

Navillus Press, 1135 Waller SE, Salem, OR, 97302. Contact: Editor. Publisher. No submission info. Query w/SASE. Index: 130.

NBS West, PO Box 1039, Vashon, WA 98070. Publisher. No submission info. Query w/SASE. Index: 130.

NC Publishing, 103-1548 Johnston Road, White Rock, BC V4B 3Z8. No submission info. Query w/SASE. Index: 130.

Nechako Valley Historical Society, PO Box 1318, Vanderhoof, BC V0J 3A0. Publisher. No submission info. Query w/SASE. Index: 63.

The Neighbor, 2812 N.W. Thurman, Portland, OR 97210. Monthly tabloid with neighborhood news for NW Portland residents and workers. Circ. 14,000. Payment: Money on publication. Byline given. Rights purchased: First serial. Query w/ms, SASE. Phone queries, dot matrix, simultaneous submissions OK. Reports in 1-2 wks. Non-fiction. Index: 33.

Nerve Press, 5875 Elm Street, Vancouver, BC V6N 1A6. Publisher of children's fiction & sci-fi. No submission info. Query w/SASE. Index: 29, 48, 51.

Nesbitt Enterprises, 5220 N.E. Roselawn, Portland, OR 97218. Publisher. No submission info. Query w/SASE. Index: 130.

Nettle Creek Publishing, 600 1st Avenue, Suite 310, Seattle, WA 98104. No submission info. Query w/SASE. Index: 130.

Network News, OCADSV, 2336 S.E. Belmont, Portland, OR 97214. Bimonthly. No submission info. Query w/SASE. Index: 130.

Network News, Senior Writers Network, E. 1419 Marietta Ave., Spokane, WA 99207. 509–487–3383. Editor: Elinor Nuxoll. Quarterly newsletter. Sub. $6. Circ. 200+. Uses 3 freelance ms per issue from writers age 50+. Submit ms, SASE. Dot matrix, photocopied OK. Reports in 2-3 mo. Acquires 1st rights. Byline given. 350-500 word contest (specified topic) in each issue. Pays prizes (books on writing) for members, sub. for non-members. "Main purpose...is to put senior writers in touch with others with similar writing backgrounds and interests." Sample $1. Index: 51, 110, 125.

New Breed News, North American Indian League, Box 7309, Boise, ID 83707. No submission info. Query w/SASE. Index: 87.

New Capernaum Works, 4615 N.E. Emerson Street, Portland, OR 97218. Publisher. No submission info. Query w/SASE. Index: 130.

The New Era Newspaper, 1200 Long Street, Box 38, Sweet Home, OR 97386. 503–367–2135. Weekly newspaper. No submission info. Query w/SASE. Index: 33.

New Horizons Publishers, 737 10th Avenue, PO Box 20744, Seattle, WA 98102. Contact: Lewis Green. 206–323–1102. No submission info. Query w/SASE. Index: 130.

New Leaf Books of Oregon, 1450 NE A St., Grants Pass, OR 97526. 503–474–0139. Publishes 2-3 softcover books a yr. Rights acquired vary. Submit ms, SASE. Dot matrix, photocopied, simultaneous subs. OK. Reports in 1 mo. Accepts non-fiction. Books mostly about Southern Oregon and/or the California far north. Focus is on nature, history, outdoor recreation. Some books about the Pacific Northwest or Far West. Mostly self-publishing, some titles in partnership with other writers. Generally require some financial interest by the writer. Catalog available. Index: 88, 89, 103.

For lists of abbreviations and the key to index numbers, see "How to Use this Section" on page 75.

Writer's Northwest Handbook   151

New Moon Publishing Co., PO Box 2046, Corvallis, OR 97339. Editor: Thomas Alexander. Publisher. No submission info. Query w/SASE. Index: 130.

New River Times, 310 1/2 First Avenue, Fairbanks, AK 99701. Periodical. No submission info. Query w/SASE. Index: 130.

New Star Books, 2504 York Avenue, Vancouver, BC V6K 1E3. 604–738–9429. Publisher of 8 non-fiction softcover originals a year for left-wing readers. Query, manuscript, outline, sample chapters w/SASE. Publishes in 1 year. Non-fiction: labour, social history, feminism, gay liberation, ethnic studies. Catalog available. Index: 50, 71, 112.

The New Times, PO Box 51186, Seattle, WA 98115-1186. 206–524–9071. Editor: Krysta Gibson. Monthly newspaper. Sub. $8.50/yr. Circ. 16,000. Uses 10 freelance mss per issue. Pays on acceptance in subs. Acquires 1st rights. Byline given. Submit photocopied ms, SASE. Reports in 30-60 days. Publishes in 30-60 days. Accepts non-fiction, cartoons. Topics: "New Age" : spirituality, human potential, psychology/therapeutic, holistic health, philosophical, interviews with New Age people. Photos B&W, 5x7 or larger, nature or human interest; 1 yr. subs. for payment. "We're looking for positive information which will help our readers grow spiritually, emotionally & physically." Guidelines SASE. Sample $1. Index: 13, 94, 105.

New Woman Press, 2000 Mountain Trail, Wolf Creek, OR 97497. Literary press. No submission info. Query w/SASE. Index: 51, 124.

Newberg Graphic, 109 N. School, Box 110, Newberg, OR 97132. 503–538–2181. Weekly newspaper. No submission info. Query w/SASE. Index: 33.

Newberg Times, PO Box 370, Beaverton, OR 97075-0370. Weekly newspaper. No submission info. Query w/SASE. Index: 33.

Newport News-Times/Lincoln County Leader, 831 N.E. Avery, Box 965, Newport, OR 97365. 503–265–8571. Weekly newspaper. No submission info. Query w/SASE. Index: 33.

News Bulletin, Salem Area Seniors, Inc., 1055 Erixon N.E., Salem, OR 97303. Monthly. No submission info. Query w/SASE. Index: 110.

The News Examiner, PO Box 278, Montpelier, ID 83254. Editor: Therese Stamm. Newspaper. No submission info. Query w/SASE. Index: 33.

The News Guard, 930 S.E. Highway 101, Box 848, Lincoln City, OR 97367. 503–994–2178. Weekly newspaper. No submission info. Query w/SASE. Index: 33.

News-Journal, 600 S. Washington, Kent, WA 98031. 206–872–6600. Daily newspaper. No submission info. Query w/SASE. Index: 33.

News-Miner, PO Box 438, Republic, WA 99166. 509–775–3558. Weekly newspaper. No submission info. Query w/SASE. Index: 33.

News Register, 611 E. Third, Box 727, McMinnville, OR 97128. 503–472–5114. Daily newspaper. No submission info. Query w/SASE. Index: 33.

News & Reports, Idaho Department of Education, Len B. Jordan Building, Boise, ID 83720. Editor: Helen J. Williams. Monthly. Circ. 20,000. No submission info. Query w/SASE. Index: 43, 69.

The News-Review, 345 N.E. Winchester, Box 1248, Roseburg, OR 97470. 503–672–3321. Daily newspaper. No submission info. Query w/SASE. Index: 33.

News-Times, P.O. 408, Forest Grove, OR 97116. 503–357–3181. Contact: Editor. Weekly newspaper. No submission info. Query w/SASE. Index: 33.

News Tribune, PO Box 596, Everett, WA 98206. 206–258–9396. Weekly newspaper. No submission info. Query w/SASE. Index: 33.

News & Views, 1133 Melville Street, 6th floor, Vancouver, BC V6E 4E5. Editor: Maureen McCandless. 604–681–3264. Periodical. No submission info. Query w/SASE. Index: 33.

Newscast, PO Box 998, Ephrata, WA 98823. 509–754–4636. Weekly newspaper. No submission info. Query w/SASE. Index: 33.

Newsletter, Portland Friends/Cast Iron Architecture, 213 S.W. Ash, Rm 210, Portland, OR 97204. Editor: William J. Hawkins. Semiannual. No submission info. Query w/SASE. Index: 9.

Newsletter-Portland Soc. for Calligraphy, PO Box 4621, Portland, OR, 97208. Editor: Lillian Pierce. Quarterly. No submission info. Query w/SASE. Index: 38.

The Newspoke, Anchorage School District, 1800 Hillcrest, Anchorage, AK 99503. Contact: Editor. Periodical. No submission info. Query w/SASE. Index: 43.

The Next War, Pressing America, PO Box 201672, Anchorage, AK 99520. 907–561–4622. Editor: Michael Meyers. Quarterly. Sub. $3.95 ea. Circ. 200. Uses 4 freelance mss per issue. Pays money, copies on publication. Acquires 1st rights. Byline given. Submit ms, SASE. Dot matrix, photocopied, simultaneous OK. Reports in 4-8 wks. Accepts fiction, poetry, photos, plays, cartoons. Guidelines available. Sample $3.95. Index: 5, 51, 97.

Nexus Press, 13032 N.E. 73rd, Kirkland, WA 98033. No submission info. Query w/SASE. Index: 130.

Niche Press, 600 E. Pine St. #692, Seattle, WA 98122. 206–281–8540. Editor: Mark Jaroslaw. Publisher of 2 softcover original books per year. Does not accept unsolicited mss. Regional information and guidebooks. Index: 62, 89, 125.

Nike Times, Nike, Inc., 3900 S.W. Murray Road, Beaverton, OR 97005. Editor: Chris Van Dyke. Company publication. No submission info. Query w/SASE. Index: 24.

Nisqually Valley News, PO Box 597, Yelm, WA 98597. 206–458–2681. Weekly newspaper. No submission info. Query w/SASE. Index: 33.

Nobility Press, PO Box 17603, Portland, OR 97217. 503–289–5216. Editor: Kelly Osmont. Publisher. No submission info. Query w/SASE. Index: 130.

Nomadic Newsletter, Nomadic Books, 201 N.E. 45th, Seattle, WA, 98105. Contact: Editor. Periodical. No submission info. Query w/SASE. Index: 130.

Nordic West, PO Box 7077, Bend, OR 97708. Editor: Richard Coons. Monthly magazine devoted to cross-country skiing in the western USA. Query w/SASE. Index: 92, 103, 115.

For lists of abbreviations and the key to index numbers, see "How to Use this Section" on page 75.

152   Market Listings

North American Post, 662 1/2 S. Jackson Street, Seattle, WA 98104. Editor: Shiro Masaki. 206–623–0100. Japanese language newspaper, published 3 times a week, with an English section once a week. Circ. 2,000. Sub. $55. Accepts freelance material very infrequently. No pay. Byline given. Submit ms, SASE. Non-fiction, poetry, photos. Sample available. Index: 12, 73.

North Beach Beacon, PO Box 1207, Ocean Shores, WA 98569. 206–289–3359. Weekly newspaper. No submission info. Query w/SASE. Index: 33.

North Bend News, 2067 Sherman Avenue, Box 507, North Bend, OR 97459. 503–756–5134. Weekly newspaper. No submission info. Query w/ SASE. Index: 33.

The North Coast Times Eagle, 286 Bond St. #4, Astoria, OR 97103. Editor: Michael Paul McCusker. No submission info. Query w/SASE. Index: 33.

North Country Press, PO Box 12223, Seattle, WA 98105. No submission info. Query w/SASE. Index: 130.

North Island Gazette Printers & Publishers, PO Box 458, Port Hardy, BC V0N 2P0. No submission info. Query w/SASE. Index: 130.

North Pacific Publishers, PO Box 13255, Portland, OR 97213. No submission info. Query w/SASE. Index: 130.

North Publishing, 3030 14th Avenue W., #205, Seattle, WA 98119. No submission info. Query w/SASE. Index: 130.

North Seattle Press, 4128 Fremont N., Seattle, WA 98103. 206–547–9660. Editor: Clayton Park. Ads: Karina Erickson. Biweekly. Sub. free. No submission info. Query w/SASE. Index: 33.

Northern Kittitas County Tribune, PO Box 287, Cle Elum, WA 98922. 509–674–2511. Weekly newspaper. No submission info. Query w/ SASE. Index: 33.

Northern Lights, Northern Lights Institute, PO Box 8084, Missoula, MT 59807-8084. Editor/Ads: Debra Clow. 406–721–7415. Quarterly about ID, WY, MT and the NW, public policy issues. Circ. 4,000. Sub. minimum donation $15. Uses 5-10 freelance mss per issue. Payment $.10/wd and copies on publication. Byline given. Rights purchased: First. Query w/clips, ms, SASE. Dot matrix, photocopies OK. Reports in 6-8 wks. Publishes in 3-6 mos. Accepts non-fiction, photos, cartoons. Encourage writers & artists to send SASE for guidelines. "We want articles that capture not only the facts, but also the mood, landscape, humor and personalities of the subject in question…we are interested in problems in the West that need solutions, but we are also interested in writing about the things in the West that make it such a wonderful place to live." Sample $5. Index: 46, 68, 89.

Northern Times Press, PO Box 880, Terrace, BC V8G 4R1. No submission info. Query w/SASE. Index: 130.

Northland Publications, PO Box 12157, Seattle, WA 98102. No submission info. Query w/SASE. Index: 130.

Northshore Citizen, PO Box 706, Bothell, WA 98041. 206–486–1231. Weekly newspaper. No submission info. Query w/SASE. Index: 33.

Northwest Airlifter, PO Box 98801, Tacoma, WA 98499. 206–584–1212. Weekly newspaper. No submission info. Query w/SASE. Index: 15.

Northwest Aluminum News, 910 Lloyd Center Tower, 825 N.E. Multnomah Street, Portland, OR 97232-2150. No submission info. Query w/ SASE. Index: 24.

Northwest Anthropological Research Notes, University of Idaho, Laboratory of Anthropology, Moscow, ID 83843. Editor: Roderick Sprague. Semiannual. Circ. 300. No submission info. Query w/SASE. Guidelines available. Index: 7.

Northwest Arctic NUNA, Maniilaq Assoc., PO Box 256, Kotzebue, AK 99752. 907–442–3311. Contact: Editor. Free monthly. Circ. 3,000. Uses 2 freelances mss per issue. Pays copies. Byline given. Submit by phone, SASE. Dot matrix, photocopied OK. Report and publishing time varies. Accepts non-fiction, fiction, poetry, photos. Sample free. Index: 4, 87.

Northwest Arts, Box 75297, Seattle, WA 98125-0297. Editor: Maxine Cushing Gray. 206–524–2146. Biwkly with emphasis on criticism and news; regional coverage. Circ. 750. Sub. $15. Uses 2-3 freelance mss per issue. Pymt: $15/article, $5/poem, $10/photo; copies; sub, if desired; on pub. Byline given. Rights purchased: First. Query w/ SASE. Reviews: only after consultation; two ds typed pgs. Photos: B&W, any size. Poems. Tips: "Special interest in work by Native Americans." Sample: $.50. Index: 10, 39, 87.

Northwest Beachcomber, 200 W. Highland Drive, #101, Seattle, WA 98119. Contact: Eloise Holman. Publisher. No submission info. Query w/ SASE. Index: 38, 103.

Northwest Bed & Breakfast Travel Unlimited, 610 S.W. Broadway, Ste. 609, Portland, OR 97205. 503–243–7616. Self-publisher of 1 softcover book per year. Bed & breakfast directory, western US, western Canada, Hawaii, UK & France. Not a freelance market. Index: 25, 89,120.

Northwest Boat Travel, PO Box 220, Anacortes, WA 98221. Editor: Gwen Cole. Quarterly magazine on boat travel from Olympia, WA to Skagway, AK: sites, resorts, cruises, anchorages. Uses 6 mss for the May and June issues only. Payment: $75-100 on publication. Byline given. Submit ms, SASE. Photocopies OK. Non-fiction: 2-4 pgs; "cruises, history of boating sites, anchorages, towns, sea life." Photos: B&W 3 1/2x5 or larger; parks, landmarks, city scenes; $5-10; color slides for cover/$100. Index: 79, 120.

Northwest Chess, PO Box 84746, Seattle, WA 98124-6046. Periodical. No submission info. Query w/SASE. Index: 45, 103.

Northwest Construction News, 109 W. Mercer, Seattle, WA 98119. 206–285–2050. Trade periodical. No submission info. Query w/SASE. Index: 24, 42.

Northwest Discovery, Journal of NW History & Natural History, 1439 E. Prospect Street, Seattle, WA 98112. Editor: Harry Majors. Not accepting mss. Index: 65, 88.

The Northwest Dispatch, 913 S. 11th Street, Box 5637, Tacoma, WA 98405. 206–272–7587. Periodical. No submission info. Query w/SASE. Index: 33.

Northwest Edition, 130 2nd Avenue S., Edmonds, WA 98020 3588. Editor: Archy Satterfield. 206–774–4411. Monthly magazine on "natural resources, use and enjoyment of 4 NW states, AK and W. Canada." Circ. 22,000 to college educated, 35 and over, love NW and outdoors. Uses 95% freelance, 12-15 mss per issue. Payment: $50-400 on publication. Byline given. Rights purchased: First. Query w/SASE. Simultaneous submissions OK. Reports in 2-4 wks. Non-fiction: 800 wds on home, foods, gardens, outdoor recreation, farms. Photos: 35 mm, prefer color; $25-200 cover. Index: 56, 89, 103.

For lists of abbreviations and the key to index numbers, see "How to Use this Section" on page 75.

Writer's Northwest Handbook 153

Northwest Energy News, 850 S.W. Broadway, Suite 1100, Portland, OR 97205. Editor: Carlotta Collette. 503–222–5161. Bimonthly magazine reporting on power planning, fish, wildlife restoration activities in OR, WA, ID, MT. Published by NW Power Planning Council. Circ. 15,000 to electric energy professionals, fisheries managers, NW Indian tribes. Generally does not accept freelance, but will entertain story ideas. Photos: B&W, "salmon (live, not on hooks) and other NW wildlife"; pay varies. Tips: "Not responsible for unsolicited photos or mss. We have in-house writers, but an occasional story idea, w/clips, may make it." SASE. Index: 35, 89, 92.

The Northwest Environmental Journal, FM-12, University of Washington, Seattle, WA 98195. 206–543–1812. Semiannual of NW environmental research and policy. Sub. $16. Uses 1-2 freelance mss per issue. Payment: Reprints; no pay. Byline given. Submit ms, SASE. Phone queries OK. "Scholarly articles written for a broad audience, sans jargon...All NW environmental topics may be relevant (NW= AK, BC, WA, OR, ID, Western MT). Usual length 20-25 pgs (top length of 50). Ours is a refereed journal; 3 scholarly reviewers read each ms." Photos: as needed to make a point. Guidelines available, sample/$9. Index: 46, 89, 101.

Northwest Ethnic News, 1107 N.E. 45th, Ste. 315A, Seattle, WA 98105. 206–633–3239. Editor: Allegra Askman. Monthly. Sub. $10. Circ. 10,000. Uses 3-9 freelance mss per issue. Pays copies. Acquires 1st rights. Byline given. Submit query w/clips. Dot matrix, photocopied OK. Accepts non-fiction, photos, cartoons. Sample, SASE. Index: 39, 84.

Northwest Examiner, PO Box 10673, Portland, OR 97229. Editor: Bob Chieger. Ads: Allan Classen. 503–241–2353. Monthly newspaper for NW Portland and adjacent area on neighborhood news, events, features. Circ. 16,000. Sub. $15. Uses 2-4 freelance mss per issue. Pays money, on publication. Byline given. Rights purchased: First. Query w/clips, ms, SASE. Phone queries, dot matrix, photocopies, simultaneous submissions, computer disc OK. Reports in 2 wks. Publishes in 2 mos. Accepts non-fiction, fiction, poetry, photos (B&W prints), cartoons. Features: 1,500 wds. One poetry/prose page per issue. Interested in contributions from NW Portland residents on NW Portland. Sample $1. Index: 33, 95, 101.

Northwest Foodservice & Hospitality, 3826 SW 339th St., Federal Way, WA 98023. 206–838–1901. Editor: Beverly L. Adams-Gordon. Quarterly. No submission info. Query w/SASE. Index: 119.

Northwest Golfer, 920 108th N.E., Bellevue, WA 98004. 206–455–5545. Periodical. No submission info. Query w/SASE. Index: 89, 103.

Northwest Gourmet, PO Box 23129, Seattle, WA 98102. Editor: Mary C. Wright. 206–325–2587. Monthly tabloid magazine of NW regional food/wine. Circ. 15,000 to educated, affluent, urban audience. Uses 36 mss year. Payment: $50 plus on publication. Byline given. Query w/ms, SASE. Phone queries, dot matrix, simultaneous submissions OK. Publishes submissions in 1-2 mos. Non-fiction: 1,500 wds; NW products, industry pieces, recipes, winery/brewery news. Tips: "Recipes (3-5 per article) must be original." Guidelines and sample available. Index: 45, 54, 89.

Northwest Historical Consultants, 2780 26th Street, Clarkston, WA 99403. Publisher. No submission info. Query w/SASE. Index: 65.

Northwest-Idaho Beverage Analyst, Bell Publishers, 2403 Champa Street, Denver, CO 80205. Editor: Mariette Bell. Monthly. Circ. 150. No submission info. Query w/SASE. Index: 24, 69.

Northwest Inland Writing Project Newsletter, c/o Elinor Michel, College of Education, University of Idaho, Moscow, ID 83843. 208–885–6586. Submissions editor: Duane Pitts, Box 385, Odessa, WA 99159. 509–982–0171. Quarterly. Sub. $5/$10/$25. Circ. 300. Uses freelance material. Pays copies on publication. Byline given. Submit query w/clips., ms, SASE. Dot matrix, photocopied, simultaneous OK. Reports in 3 wks. Publishes next issue usually. Accepts non-fiction, fiction, poetry, cartoons, other (student/teacher work). Topics: elementary, jr./sr. high, college writing; reading-writing connections; teaching ideas/techniques about writing; classroom research in reading/writing. Tips: length may vary: 50-300+ wds, depends on subject. Tips: practical ideas for use in classroom stressed; limited amounts of student work produced in writing workshops accepted. Index: 43, 44, 125.

Northwest Living, 130 Second Avenue S., Edmonds, WA 98020. 206–774–4111. Editor: Terry W. Sheely. Ads: Rick Paul. Monthly of NW people doing NW things. Sub. $14.95. Circ. 25,000. Uses 12 freelance mss per issue. Pays money on publication. Rights acquired: 1 time NA. Byline given. Query w/clips, SASE. Photocopies OK. Reports in 6 wks. Publishes in 6-12 mos. Accepts non-fiction: "Emphasize suburban and rural subjects; major interests in natural science, natural history, homes, foods, gardening, outdoor recreation, regional travel, cottage industries, crops, and related subjects;" and photos. Request guidelines & free sample. Back issues $2.50. Index: 88, 92, 120.

Northwest Lookout, PO Box 3366, Salem, OR 97302. Editor: Dennis L. Tomkins. 503–364–2942. Trade publication of Northwest Christmas Tree Association published 3 times a year. Circ. 2,000 to Christmas tree growers, wholesalers, retailers, related product mfgs and sellers. Byline given. Query w/SASE to editor at 324 Sumner Avenue, Sumner, WA 98390. Guidelines available. Index: 3, 24, 89.

Northwest Magazine, 1320 S.W. Broadway, Portland, OR 97201. 503–221–8228. Editor: Jack Hart. Ads: Marsha Davis. 503–221–8229. Weekly included with Sunday Oregonian. Circ. 400,000 to "25-49 year old readers, affluent, sophisticated." Uses 4-5 mss per issue. Pays money, copies, on acceptance. Byline given. Rights purchased: First. Query w/SASE. Dot matrix, photocopies, electronic OK. Accepts non-fiction, fiction, poetry, photos. $500+ for major cover stories; $150-350 for inside stories (1,500-4,000 wds); $75-125 for shorter personal essays and similar material. Photos: submit either color slides (preferably Kodachrome) or B&W contact prints with negatives. Guidelines available. Sample free. Index: 51, 103, 120.

Northwest Matrix, 2266 Alder, Eugene, OR 97405. Publisher. No submission info. Query w/SASE. Index: 130.

NORTHWEST MOTOR Journal for Automotive Industry, 1710 S. Norman Street, Seattle, WA 98144-2819. Editor/ads: J.B. Smith. 206–324–5619. Monthly for the automotive parts and service industry. Circ. 6,000. Sub. $10. Accepts freelance material. Writers must have industry documentation. Payment: Copies on publication. Byline given. Rights purchased: All. Query w/SASE. Sample: $1. Index: 24, 89.

Northwest Notes, St. Peter Hospital Library, 415 Lilly Rd., Olympia, WA 98506. Contact: Editor. Periodical. No submission info. Query w/SASE. Index: 61, 104.

Northwest Nurserystock Report, 10041 N.E. 132nd St., Kirkland, WA 98034. 206–821–2535. Editor: John Bjork. Periodical. No submission info. Query w/SASE. Index: 3, 24.

Northwest Oil Report, 4204 S.W. Condor Ave., Portland, OR 97201. Editor: C.J. Newhouse. Periodical. No submission info. Query w/SASE. Index: 24.

Northwest Outpost, Northwest Chapter, Paralyzed Veterans of America, 901 S.W. 152nd Street, Seattle, WA 98166. 206–241–1843. Periodical. No submission info. Query w/SASE. Index: 83, 89, 126.

For lists of abbreviations and the key to index numbers, see "How to Use this Section" on page 75.

Northwest Pace, 3845 Old Stage Rd., Central Point, OR 97502. 503–826–7700. Editor: Mark Flint, 503–826–7700. Periodical. No submission info. Query w/SASE. Index: 130.

The Northwest Palate, PO Box 10860, Portland, OR 97210. 503–228–4897. Editor: Judy Peterson-Nedry. Bi-monthly newsletter featuring wines from OR, WA, & ID. Pays on publication. Submit query, ms, or phone. Accepts non-fiction, photos. Topics: food & wine, breweries, distilleries, travel, lodging, lifestyles by NW writers. Sample $3.50. Index: 3, 54, 120.

Northwest Panorama Publishing, Inc., PO Box 1858, Bozeman, MT 59771. 800–547–2525. No submission info. Query w/SASE. Index: 130.

Northwest Passage, Western Oregon State College, English Dept., 345 N. Monmouth Ave., Monmouth, OR 97361. 503–838–1220 X249/281. Editor: Donald J. Weis. College literary magazine. Editors could change yearly. SASE for guidelines. Index: 31, 51, 91.

Northwest Passage, Western Oregon State College/English Dept., 345 N. Monmouth Ave., Monmouth, OR, 97361. 503–838–1220 x249. Magazine. No submission info. Query w/SASE. Index: 31, 51, 91.

Northwest Passages Historical Newsletter, 27006 Gap Road, Brownsville, OR 97327. 503–466–5208 or 503–369–2835. Editors: Pat Hamline or Margaret Carey. Bimonthly newsletter. Sub. $12. Uses 1 or 2 freelance mss per issue. Pays 5 copies on publication. Acquires 1st rights. Byline given. Submit query w/clips, photocopied ms, SASE, or phone. Reports in 1 mo. Publishes within 6 mo. Accepts non-fiction. Topics: short historical articles about the Northwest, 250-750 wds. Material must be well-researched and historically accurate. Encourages reminiscences within word limit. "Our publication is an informal one, containing articles and bits about people and events of early days in the Northwest. We also like to accept obscure but interesting material from old newspapers and out-of-print books." Can use good photo's with articles, pay in copies. Guidelines available. Sample $2. Index: 65, 89.

Northwest Public Power Bulletin, PO Box 4576, Vancouver, WA 98662. Editor: Rick Kellogg. 206–254–0109. Ads: Tina Nelson. Monthly periodical on public power issues in the NW. Circ. 4,000. Sub. $18. Accepts freelance material. Payment: Generally $100-300 for major articles with photos, on publication. Byline given. Rights purchased: First. Query w/SASE. Phone queries OK. Reports in 1 month. Non-fiction: "People, issues, activities relating to public power entities, regional electrical issues. Area covered: OR, WA, ID, Western MT, Northern CA, B.C. and AK." Photos: B&W glossies. Rates negotiable. Tips: "Not interested in investor owned utilities, counter-culture energy schemes, anti-nuke propaganda." Sample available. Index: 89, 101.

Northwest Recreation, 1917 S.E. 7th, Portland, OR 97214. Editor: William H. MacKenzie. 503–643–0679. Ads: R. Eppinger. Quarterly on "NW recreation/urban upscale." Circ. 5,000. Free to members of Profile One; distributed to prospective members free. Uses 4 mss per issue. Payment for new writers starts at $.10/wd on acceptance. Byline given. Rights purchased: First. Query w/SASE. Photocopies OK. Reports in 4 wks. Non-fiction: "3 articles per issue on recreational opportunities offered by Profile One. Topics assigned. Average length 1,200 wds. One topic chosen from freelance submissions for 1,200 word article focusing on NW lifestyle, history, etc." Photos: Color transparencies with all pieces; $20 for inside photos, $75 for cover. Tips: "No telephone queries. We want lively first person articles that draw the reader into the recreational experience." Guidelines available. Index: 89, 92, 103.

Northwest Report, 300 S.W. Sixth Avenue, Portland, OR 97204. 503–248–6800. Periodical. No submission info. Query w/SASE. Index: 130.

Northwest Review, 369 PLC, University of Oregon, Eugene, OR 97403. Editor: John Witte, poetry; Cecelia Hagen, fiction. 503–686–3957. Ads: Bev Trump. Sub. $11. Press run 1,100. Literary triannual published in March, July and November. Subscribers in 50 states and 38 foreign countries. Receives approx. 4,000 submissions annually; publishes 90. Accepts unsolicited submissions. Pays in copies on publication. Rights acquired: first. Byline given. Submit complete mss, SASE. Dot matrix, photocopies OK. No simultaneous submissions are considered. Reports in 4-8 wks. Publishes in 1-4 mos. Accepts non-fiction, fiction, poetry, plays, interviews, essays, artwork. Guidelines available. Sample $3. Index: 51, 76, 77.

The Northwest Review of Books, PO Box 45593, Seattle, WA 98145-0593. Editor: Jane Friedman. 206–323–3597. Quarterly magazine focusing on NW authors and publishers. Circ. 5,000. Uses 16-20 mss a year. Payment: Money on publication. Byline given. Submit ms, SASE. Phone queries, dot matrix, simultaneous submissions OK. Reports in 1 month. Publishes in 1-3 mos. Non-fiction: 600-900 wds; history, biography, photography, science; $15. Columns: 100 wds; brief review section, $5. Photos: 85 line screen. Tips: "Lively writing for our wide audience." Index: 22, 76, 102.

Northwest Roadapple, The Newspaper for Horsemen, 4346 S.E. Division, Portland, OR 97206. Editor: John Jangula. 503–238–7071. Monthly tabloid for horse people. Circ. 24,000. Submit ms, SASE. Phone queries, dot matrix, simultaneous submissions OK. Publishes in 2 mos. Non-fiction, poetry, photos (80 lines, 3x5). Index: 6, 103.

Northwest Runner, 1231 N.E. 94th, Seattle, WA 98115. Editor/ads: Jim Whiting. 206–526–9000. Monthly. Circ. 7,000. Sub. $13.97. Uses 10 mss per issue. Payment: Money on publication. Byline given. Rights purchased: First. Reports in 2-4 wks. "Columns/short articles: 700-1,000 wds; $25-50. Features: 1,000 wds to whatever length will keep readers' interest; $35-75. Readers of NWR range from beginners to 20+ year veterans, though most have been running for at least a couple of yrs. We like training articles, how-to, personal experiences, and especially humor. Photos: B&W glossy; $15." Sample: $3. Index: 115.

Northwest Sailboard, P.O. Box 75685, Seattle, WA 98125. Contact: Editor. Periodical. No submission info. Query w/SASE. Index: 115.

Northwest Sailor, 2611 NW Market, Seattle, WA 98107. 206–789–8116. Editor: Daniel Schworer. Monthly tabloid. Pays money. Submit phone query. Accepts non-fiction, photos. Topics: news, activities, and information related to sailboating through the Northwest and Southwest Canada. Index: 21, 115.

Northwest Science, Washington State University Press, Pullman, WA 99164-5910. 509–335–3518. Quarterly. Sub. $25. No submission info. Query w/SASE. Index: 31, 89, 109.

Northwest Seasonal Worker, Northwest Seasonal Workers Association, 145 N. Oakdale St., Medford, OR 97501. Editor: Jana Clark. Monthly. Sub. $12.50. No submission info. Query w/SASE. Index: 3, 27, 84.

Northwest Silver Press, 88 Cascade Key, Bellevue, WA 98006. No submission info. Query w/SASE. Index: 130.

Northwest Skier & Northwest Sports, PO Box 5029, Seattle, WA 98105. Periodical. No submission info. Query w/SASE. Index: 92, 115.

Northwest Stylist and Salon, PO Box 1117, Portland, OR 97207. Editor: David Porter. 503–226–2461. Monthly trade magazine. Circ. 26,000. Sub. $12/free to salons. Accepts freelance material. Payment: $1.50/column inch (when assigned) on publication. Byline given. Query w/SASE.

For lists of abbreviations and the key to index numbers, see "How to Use this Section" on page 75.

Writer's Northwest Handbook 155

Phone queries OK. Articles: deadline the 1st of month; 500-750 wds with photo. "Query first. I prefer to give a writer the slant I want, and I would like to talk to people to give them hints on things I'd like covered in their area...Anything to do with hair and beauty for the industry, professional beauty salons, schools and supply houses." Photos: B&W; $5 or $15-20 for cover. Tips: needs stringers in OR/WA. Index: 24, 49.

The Northwest Technocrat, Technocracy Inc., 7513 Greenwood Avenue N., Seattle, WA 98103-4690. Periodical. No submission info. Query w/ SASE. Index: 94.

Northwest Unit Farm Magazines, PO Box 2160, Spokane, WA 99210-1615. 509–459–5361. Semimonthly periodicals on farming in the NW states. Circ. 17,245. No submission info. Query w/SASE. Index: 3.

Northwest Wine Almanac, First Nocl Publishing Co., PO Box 85595, Seattle, WA 98145-1595. Contact: Editor. Periodical. No submission info. Query w/SASE. Index: 54.

Northwest Women in Business, PO Box 82, Corvallis, OR 97339. Periodical. Byline given. Rights purchased: First. Query w/ms, SASE. Reports in 6 wks. Publishes in 2 mos. Non-fiction, photos. Guidelines available, sample: $2. Index: 24, 124.

Northwest Wool Gatherer's Quarterly, 2058 14th Avenue W., Seattle, WA 98119. Editor/ads: Nancy Swenson. 206–284–4860. Circ. 1,000. Sub. $8. Uses 3 mss a issue. Payment: Money, copies on publication. Byline given. Rights purchased: First. Query w/ms or outline, SASE. Photocopies OK. Reports in 2 mos. Publishes in 3-6 mos. Non-fiction, fiction: 1-3 pgs. ds; on spinners, weavers, fiber artists, fiber growers, teachers, travel, book reviews, gallery reviews, how-to articles. Slant: articles which inspire, inform everyone involved with fiber; emphasis on celebrating NW fiber community so one end of the spectrum (fiber artists) can appreciate and understand the other end of the spectrum (fiber growers) and all areas between. Beginners to expert level. Sample: $2. Index: 6, 10, 38.

Nor'westing, PO Box 375, Edmonds, WA 98020. Editor: Thomas F. Kincaid. 206–776–3138. Ads: Wendelborg Hansen. Monthly for NW boaters. Circ. 11,000. Sub. $12. Uses 4-8 mss per issue. Payment: $100 on publication. Byline given. Rights purchased: First. Query w/SASE. Phone queries, dot matrix, photocopies, simultaneous submissions, electronic OK. Reports in 1 month. Nonfiction: 1,500-3,000 wds. Photos: covers/ $75. Guidelines available. Index: 21, 92, 103.

Noted, 919 N.W. 63rd St., Seattle, WA 98107. Contact: Editor. Periodical. No submission info. Query w/SASE. Index: 130.

NRG Magazine, 6735 S.E. 78th, Portland, OR 97206. Editor: Dan Raphael. Biannual magazine of nonfiction, fiction, poetry, photos and graphics. Circ. 1,000. Sub. $4/year, $7/two yrs. "Any form or genre, but it should be work with energy — work that doesn't add up — open ended." Payment: Copies. Acquires no rights. Gives byline. Reports in 1 month. Submit mss w/SASE. Dot matrix, photocopied and simultaneous submissions OK. Sample: $1 & up. Index: 14, 51, 97.

Nuclear News Bureau, CALS, 454 Willamette, Eugene, OR 97401. Periodical. No submission info. Query w/SASE. Index: 130.

Nugget, Box 610, Nome, AK 99762. 907–443–5235. Weekly newspaper. No submission info. Query w/SASE. Index: 33.

Nugget Enterprises, PO Box 184, Enumclaw, WA 98022. Contact: Roy F. Mayo. 206–825–3855. Self-publisher of 1-2 softcover originals on gold and gold mining. Print run: 1,000. Not a freelance market. Catalog available. Index: 59, 65, 103.

The Nurse Practitioner: The American Journal of Primary Health Care, 109 W. Mercer, Seattle, WA 98119. Editor: Linda J. Pearson. 206–285–2050. Ads: Barton Vernon. Monthly for nurses in advanced primary care practice. Circ. 11,600. Sub. $27. Accepts freelance material. Writers must be nurse practitioners. No pay. Byline given. Query w/SASE. Phone queries, dot matrix, photocopies OK. Clinical articles; reports of appropriate research; role, legal and political issues. Guidelines available; sample/$3. Index: 61, 81.

Nursery Trades BC, 101A-15290-103A Avenue, Surrey, BC V3R 7A2. Editor: J.C. Crocco. 604–585–2225. Periodical. No submission info. Query w/SASE. Index: 3, 24.

Nutrition Notebook, Idaho Dairy Council, 1365 N. Orchard, Boise, ID 83706. Editor: Mary Pittam. Semiannual. Circ. 3,000. No submission info. Query w/SASE. Index: 3, 6, 61.

Nyssa Gate City Journal, 112 Main Street, Box 1785, Nyssa, OR 97913. 503–372–2233. Weekly newspaper. No submission info. Query w/ SASE. Index: 33.

O&B Books, Inc., 1215 N.W. Kline Place, Corvallis, OR 97330. Publisher. No submission info. Query w/SASE. Index: 130.

Observer, Oregon State Council on Alcoholism, PO Box 12547, Salem, OR 97309. Monthly. No submission info. Query w/SASE. Index: 61.

The Observer, 1710 6th Street, Box 3170, La Grande, OR 97850. 503–963–3161. Daily newspaper. No submission info. Query w/SASE. Index: 33.

OCLC PAC-NEWS, PO Box 03376, Portland, OR 97203. Editor: Bruce Preslan. 503–283–4794. Periodical. No submission info. Query w/ SASE. Index: 130.

Ocotillo Press, 215 N. 51st Street, Seattle, WA 98103. No submission info. Query w/SASE. Index: 130.

OCTE Chalkboard, Portland State University, PO Box 751, Portland, OR 97207. Editor: U.H. Hardt. Periodical. No submission info. Query w/ SASE. Index: 31.

ODOT News, Oregon Department of Transportation, 140 Transportation Building, Salem, OR 97310. 503–378–6546. Editor: Andy Booz. Periodical. No submission info. Query w/SASE. Index: 60, 101.

Odyssey Publishing, 301 Lynn Street, Seattle, WA 98109. No submission info. Query w/SASE. Index: 130.

Offshoot Publications, 1280 Goodpasture Island Road, Eugene, OR 97401-1794. Self-publisher of 1 hard/softcover book a yr. Index: 56.

Old Bottle Magazine/Popular Archaeology, Drawer 5007, Bend, OR 97708. Editor: Shirley Asher. 503–382–6978. Monthly. Circ. 3,000. Sub. $12. Uses 10 mss per issue. Payment: $10 published pg. on publication. Byline given. Rights purchased: All. Query w/ms, SASE. Dot matrix, photocopies, simultaneous submissions, electric OK. Reports in 6 wks. Nonfiction: "Dedicated to the discovery, research and preservation of relics of the industrial age in general and the establishment of specialized, representative collection by individuals." Photos: $50 color cover. Sample/$1. Index: 7, 8, 30.

Old Farm Kennels, N.E. 5451 Eastside Hwy., Florence, MT 59833. Publisher. No submission info. Query w/SASE. Index: 6.

For lists of abbreviations and the key to index numbers, see "How to Use this Section" on page 75.

156   Market Listings

Old Harbor Press, PO Box 97, Sitka, AK 99835. 907–747–3584. Publisher of 1 hard/softcover original, reprint a year. Press run: 3,000. Does not accept unsolicited submissions. Index: 4, 54, 65.

Old News, Clatsop County Historical Society, 1618 Exchange St., Astoria, OR 97103. Contact: Editor. Irregular periodical. No submission info. Query w/SASE. Index: 65, 89, 91.

Old Oregon, 101 Chapman Hall, University of Oregon, Eugene, OR 97403. Editor: Tom Hager. 503–686–5047. Quarterly for graduates. Circ. 90,000. No unsolicited submissions. Uses 6 freelance mss per issue. Pays $.10/wd on acceptance + 2 copies. Byline given. Query w/clips, SASE. Photocopies, electronic, computer disc OK. Reports in 3 wks. Publishes in 3-6 mos. Nonfiction: features 2,500-3,000 wds; columns 1,500 wds. Photos: 8x10 B&W glossy. All topics relate to UO issues, people, ideas. Sample available. Index: 31.

Old Stuff, The Paddlewheel Press, PO Box 230220, Tigard, OR 97223. Editor: Marge Davenport. 503–639–5637. Periodical. No submission info. Query w/SASE. Index: 64.

Old Time Bottle Publishing, 611 Lancaster Drive N.E., Salem, OR 97301. No submission info. Query w/SASE. Index: 130.

Old Violin-Art Publishing, Box 500, 225 S. Cooke, Helena, MT 59624. No submission info. Query w/SASE. Index: 102.

Older Kid News, PO Box 1602, Pendleton, OR 97801. 503–276–9035. Editor: John Brenne. Periodical. No submission info. Query w/SASE. Index: 33, 45, 110.

Olive Press, 333 S.E. 3rd, Portland, OR 97214. No submission info. Query w/SASE. Index: 130.

Olympia News, PO Box 487, Olympia, WA 98507. 206–943–2950. Contact: Editor. Weekly newspaper. No submission info. Query w/SASE. Index: 33.

Olympic Magazine, Olympic Publishing Company, Box 353, Port Ludlow, WA 98365. Editor: Dan Youra. 206–437–9172. Published 3 times a year. Circ. 100,000. Byline given. Query w/SASE. Simultaneous submissions OK. Nonfiction. Sample available. Index: 89, 120, 123.

Olympic Publishing Company, PO Box 353, Port Ludlow, WA 98365. Publisher of 2 nonfiction books a year: local history/travel, boating, other. Query, outline, sample chapters w/SASE. Reports in 2 mos. Catalog available. Index: 21, 65, 120.

Omak-Okanogan County Chronicle, PO Box 553, Omak, WA 98841. 509–826–1110. Weekly newspaper. No submission info. Query w/SASE. Index: 33.

Omega Publications, PO Box 4130, Medford, OR 97501. No submission info. Query w/SASE. Index: 130.

OMGA Northwest Newsletter, Oregon Master Gardener Association, Linn County Extension Service, PO Box 756, Albany, OR 97321. Periodical. No submission info. Query w/SASE. Index: 56.

Onion World, Columbia Publishing, PO Box 1467, Yakima, WA 98907-1467. Editor: D. Brent Clement. Periodical. No submission info. Query w/SASE. Index: 3.

Onset Publications, 692 Elkader Street, Ashland, OR 97520. No submission info. Query w/SASE. Index: 130.

Ontario, PO Box 130, Ontario, OR 97914. Editor: Fran McLean. Quarterly. No submission info. Query w/SASE. Index: 130.

Oolichan Books, PO Box 10, Lantzville, BC V0R 2H0. 604–390–4839. Editor: Ron Smith, Rhonda Bailey. Ads: R. Smith. Circ. 1,000. Publisher of 8 hard/softcover, original books a year. Accepts unsolicited submissions. Payment: 10% royalty on number of copies sold, twice a yr. Six free copies on publication. Rights acquired: Profits from sale of rights shared with author on % basis as specified in our contract. Query w/ SASE. Reports in 2 mos. Publishes within 1 yr. Nonfiction, fiction, poetry. Topics: literary press, primarily interested in high quality fiction and poetry. Also publishes B.C. history and a few general titles of specific interest to western Canadians. Length can vary from 48 pp. for poetry title to 448 pp. for regional history. Catalog available SASE. Index: 51, 63, 97.

Open Hand Publishing, Inc., 600 E. Pine, Suite 565, Seattle, WA 98122. 206–323–3868. Editor: P. Anna Rodielk. Publishes 2 hard/softcover, originals, reprints a yr. Press run 5,000. Does not accept unsolicited mss. Pays royalties, advance. No rights acquired. Phone Query. Dot matrix, photocopied OK. Accepts nonfiction, Afro-American issues, bilingual children's books. Catalog available. Index: 17, 20, 29.

Open Path Publishing, Box 3064, Boise, ID 83703-0064. Contact: Editor. Publisher. No submission info. Query w/SASE. Index: 130.

Open Road Publishers, PO Box 46598, Station G, Vancouver, BC V6R 4G8. 604–736–0070. Self-publisher, softcover. Not a freelance market. Index: 120.

Opening Up, 3819 S.E. Belmont, Portland, OR 97214. Periodical. No submission info. Query w/SASE. Index: 130.

Opinion Rag, PO Box 20307, Seattle, WA 98102. Contact: Debbie Lester. Periodical. No submission info. Query w/SASE. Index: 130.

Optical Engineering, PO Box 10, Bellingham, WA 98225. 206–676–3290. Bimonthly. No submission info. Query w/SASE. Index: 130.

The Optimist, Idaho State School for the Deaf & Blind, 202 14th Avenue E., Gooding, ID 83330. Editor: Edward Born. Monthly. No submission info. Query w/SASE. Index: 126.

ORC Enterprises Ltd., 7031 Westminster Highway, Suite 305, Richmond, BC V6X 1A3. Publisher. No submission info. Query w/SASE. Index: 130.

Orcas Publishing Company, Route 1, Box 81, Eastsound, WA 98245. No submission info. Query w/SASE. Index: 130.

Oregon Administrator, ASPA, Oregon Chapter, PO Box 73, Portland, OR 97207. Monthly. No submission info. Query w/SASE. Index: 119.

Oregon Arts News, Oregon Arts Commission, 835 Summer N.E., Salem, OR 97301. 503–378–3625. Monthly. No submission info. Query w/ SASE. Sample available. Index: 10, 39, 91.

Oregon Association of Christian Writers Newsletter, 2495 Maple Avenue N.E., Salem, OR 97303. 503–364–9570. Published 3 times a year. Sub. $5. Not a freelance market. Index: 105, 125.

Oregon Association of Nurserymen, 2780 S.E. Harrison, Milwaukie, OR 97222. Publisher. No submission info. Query w/SASE. Index: 3, 24.

Oregon Authors, The Information Place, State Library Bldg., Salem, OR 97310. Annual publication listing those authors who had books published during the preceding year which were written while they lived in Oregon. Works by corporate authors and editors are excluded unless of

For lists of abbreviations and the key to index numbers, see "How to Use this Section" on page 75.

Writer's Northwest Handbook   157

local interest; textbooks and technical works, unless of timely or regional significance, are excluded. Inclusion depends upon notification of the library of publication, either by the author or by some other means. Authors wishing to ensure their inclusion should provide documentation to the library. The Oregon State Library is interested in maintaining its collection of works by regional writers, and encourages them to make sure the library knows of their books. No submission info. Query w/SASE. Index: 77, 91, 104.

Oregon Birds, S. Willamette Ornithological Society, PO Box 3082, Eugene, OR 97403. Quarterly devoted to the study and enjoyment of Oregon's birds. No submission info. Query w/SASE. Index: 6, 91, 103.

Oregon Business Magazine, 208 S.W. Stark, Suite 404, Portland, OR 97204. Editor: Robert Hill. 503–233–0304. Monthly on the business and economy in OR. Circ. 23,000 business owners, executives. Uses 4 mss an issue. Payment: $.10/wd on publication. Byline given. Rights purchased: First. Query w/ms, SASE. Simultaneous submissions OK. Reports in 1-2 mos. Publishes in 1-8 mos. Nonfiction: 1,000-2,000 wds on business topics; departments, 500-1,000 wds. Guidelines available; sample/SASE with $1.05 post. Index: 24, 91.

Oregon Business Review, 264 Gilbert Hall, University of Oregon, Eugene, OR 97403. Contact: Editor. Periodical. No submission info. Query w/SASE. Index: 24, 31.

Oregon Business Women, 29353 SE Church Rd., Boring, OR 97009. Editor: Lani Staab. Quarterly. No submission info. Query w/SASE. Index: 24, 124.

Oregon Catholic Press, PO Box 18030, Portland, OR 97218. Contact: Editor. Publisher. No submission info. Query w/SASE. Index: 105

Oregon Central News, Oregon Central Credit Union, 336 N.E. 20th, Portland, OR 97232. Editor: Arleen Payne. Periodical. No submission info. Query w/SASE. Index: 24.

Oregon Chinese News, The Chinese Cons. Benevolent Association, 1941 S.E. 31st Avenue, Portland, OR 97214. Periodical. No submission info. Query w/SASE. Index: 12, 84, 91.

Oregon Coast Magazine, PO Box 18000, Florence, OR 97439. Editors: Rob Spooner, Alicia Spooner. Bimonthly covering the entire Oregon coast. Circ. 30,000. Payment: $20-150 on publication. Accepts freelance material. Byline given. Rights purchased: First. Query w/ms, SASE. Dot matrix OK. Reports in 3 mos. Nonfiction: any length on OR coast topics. Photos: B&W prints or color slides with article. Tips: "Study an issue and understand our style before submitting articles." Guidelines/sample available. Index: 91,120.

Oregon Commentator, Box 11533, Eugene, OR 97440. Editor: Thomas W. Mann. 503–686–3721. Periodical. No submission info. Query w/SASE. Index: 130.

Oregon Committee for the Humanities, 418 SW Washington, Rm. 410, Portland, OR 97204. 503–241–0543. Semi-annual humanities magazine. Circ. 10,000. Uses 2-3 freelance mss per issue. Payment rates vary, on acceptance. Acquires 1st rights. Byline given. Submit SASE. Dot matrix, photocopies OK. Reports in 3 mo. Publishes in 6 mo. Accepts nonfiction, essays in any area of the humanities; audience is educated general public. Length varies. Guidelines/samples available. Index: 64, 75, 76.

Oregon Computer News, 16562 SW 72nd Ave., Portland, OR 97224. Contact: Editor. Periodical. No submission info. Query w/SASE. Index: 34.

Oregon Conifer, Sierra Club, 2637 S.W. Water Avenue, Portland, OR 97201. Editor: Teresa A. Kennedy. 503–224–1538. Bimonthly journal for the OR chapter of the Sierra Club; covers local wildernesses, current legislation on the environment, chapter club outings. Circ. 6,000. Sub. membership. Accepts freelance material. Payment: Copies. Byline given. Rights purchased: First. Query w/ms, SASE. Phone query, photocopies OK. Nonfiction, fiction, poetry, cartoons. "Pro-environmental reports, essays, book reviews, map reviews. Articles of outdoor activity interests." Photos: B&W and color prints; no slides; 4x5 prints preferred; screened photos must be 85 lines. Index: 46, 91, 92.

Oregon Contractor, Oregon State Association of PHC, Inc., 3000 Market Street Plaza N.E., Suite 508, Salem, OR 97301. 503–399–7344. Bimonthly trade journal for member contractors. No submission info. Query w/SASE. Index: 24, 119.

Oregon Council on Alcoholism, and Drug Abuse Newsletter, 4506 S.E. Belmont Street, Suite 220, Portland, OR 97215. Editor: Doreen Thomas. 503–232–8083. Bimonthly providing info on alcoholism and drug abuse, issues pertaining to families. Query w/ms, SASE. Phone query OK. No pay. Nonfiction. Tips: "Interested in current topics on alcoholism and drug treatment, legislative issues, and family therapy." Sample available. Index: 47, 61, 101.

Oregon Cycling, 23750 S.W. Gage Road, Wilsonville, OR 97070. Editor: Maryjane Keep. 503–638–6306. Published 8 times a year. Circ. 8,000. Sub. $4.50. Accepts freelance material. Byline given. Dot matrix, photocopies, simultaneous submissions, electronic OK. Nonfiction, poetry, photos, cartoons. Tips: "O.C. appeals mainly to well-heeled middle class. Health, fitness, personal experiences, personal opinions, anything related to cycling." Sample/free. Index: 16, 103, 115.

Oregon East Magazine, Eastern Oregon State College, Hoke Hall, La Grande, OR 97850. Editor/ads: Kathy Gilmore. 503–963–1787. Annual of creative literature and visual art. Circ. 800-1,000. Sub. $5. 50% of each issue freelance material. Payment: Copies on publication. Byline given. "We reserve the right to print piece in specified issue and maybe again in future anthology, nothing more." Query w/ms, SASE. Dot matrix, photocopies, simultaneous submissions, electronic OK. Deadline: March. Reports by June. Publication: Sept. Fiction: short stories, max of 4,700 wds. Poetry: no line max; accepts haiku. Photos, plays, essays, criticism, interviews, any art medium. Guidelines available; sample/$4. Index: 41, 97, 122.

Oregon Economic Development Department, International Trade Division, 595 Cottage Street N.E., Salem, OR 97310. Publisher. No submission info. Query w/SASE. Index: 24, 42, 91.

Oregon Education, Oregon Education Association, 1 Plaza Southwest, 6900 S.W. Hanes Road, Tigard, OR 97223. Monthly. No submission info. Query w/SASE. Index: 43.

Oregon English, Oregon Council of Teachers of English, PO Box 1305, Lake Oswego, OR 97034. Editor: Robert Hamm. 503–229–4677. Semi-annual magazine on education, teaching ideas, literature, short stories, poetry, usually by educators. Circ. 1,000. Accepts freelance material. Byline given. Query w/ms, SASE. Dot matrix, simultaneous submissions OK. Reports in 1-3 mos. Publishes in 6 mos. Nonfiction: 2,000 wds on education and literature. Fiction: 2,000 wds on any subject. Departments: 100-500 wds on poetry and educational teaching ideas. Poetry: 12-30 lines, any style. No photos. Sample available. Index: 43, 51, 97.

For lists of abbreviations and the key to index numbers, see "How to Use this Section" on page 75.

158 Market Listings

Oregon Episcopal Churchman, PO Box 467, Lake Oswego, OR 97034. 503–636–5613. Editor: Annette Ross. Monthly. Sub. $2. No submission info. Query w/SASE. Index: 105.

Oregon Farm Bureau News, 1730 Commercial S.E., Salem, OR 97308. Monthly. No submission info. Query w/SASE. Index: 3.

Oregon Farmer-Stockman, 6910 S.W. Lake Road, Portland, OR 97222. Editor: Dick Yost. 503–653–2885. Ads: Eric Bosler. Semimonthly periodical of farming, ranching. Circ. 20,000. Sub. $9. Uses 1 ms per issue. Writer must have intimate knowledge of agriculture. Payment: Up to $50 on acceptance. Byline given. Rights purchased: First. Query w/ms, SASE. Dot matrix OK. Reports in 1 month. Nonfiction; photos: color prints with negatives. Tips: "Will consider all submissions, but majority of copy is staff produced." Sample available. Index: 3.

Oregon Focus, City of Roses Publishing Co. for Oregon Public Broadcasting, 7140 SW Macadam Ave., Portland, OR 97219. 503–293–1904. Editor: Marjorie Floren, Ads: Ann Romano. Monthly magazine for membership. Sub. $35. Circ. 65,000. Rarely accepts freelance material, very specific to TV programs. Pays money on publication. Byline given. Submissions by assignment only. Dot matrix, photocopied, simultaneous, computer disc OK. Reports in 30 days. Publishes in 30-60 days. Accepts nonfiction on assignment, background material on a new public TV series, occasionally on a personality connected to public TV. Index: 18, 52, 80.

Oregon Freemason, 709 S.W. 15th Ave., Portland, OR 97205. 503–228–3446. Editor: Sally Spohn. Monthly. No submission info. Query w/SASE. Index: 119.

Oregon Future Farmer, Agricultural Education, OBE, 700 Pringle Parkway S.E., Salem, OR 97310. Quarterly. No submission info. Query w/SASE. Index: 3.

Oregon Gay News, PO Box 2206, Portland, OR 97208. 503–222–0017. Editor: Christopher L. Smith. Weekly. No submission info. Query w/SASE. Index: 57.

Oregon Geology, Oregon Dept. of Geology/Mineral Industries, 910 State Office Building, Portland, OR 97201. 503–229–5580. Editor: Beverly F. Vogt. Monthly for audience ranging from professional geologists to amateur geologists to planners and politicians. Sub: $6. Circ. 2,000-3,000. Accepts freelance material from writers qualified to write about geology. No pay. Rights acquired: All. Byline given. Submit ms, SASE. Dot matrix, photocopies, computer disc OK. Reports in 1 month. Accepts nonfiction: geology, mining, mining history, field trip guides, anything related to geology in OR; 40 ds typed pages max length. Also: cartoons; photos: B&W glossy. Guidelines available; sample. Index: 59, 91 .

Oregon Grange Bulletin, Oregon State Grange, 1313 S.E. 12th, Portland, OR 97214. Semimonthly publication of Oregon State Grange, concerning news and issues of importance to agriculture. No submission info. Query w/SASE. Index: 3.

Oregon Health Sciences University, Center Foundation, 3181 S.W. Sam Jackson Park, Portland, OR 97201. Contact: Editor. Publisher. No submission info. Query w/SASE. Index: 31, 61, 109.

Oregon Historical Quarterly, 1230 S.W. Park Avenue, Portland, OR 97205. 503–222–1741. Editor: Rick Harmon. Quarterly. Sub rate. $25. Circ. 8,600. Uses 3-4 freelance mss per issue. Pays copies. Rights acquired: All. Byline given. Phone query OK. Reports in 8 wks. Publishes in 2 1/2 yr. Accepts nonfiction — history and culture of Pacific Northwest. Photos used. Sample $2.50. Index: 64, 89, 91.

Oregon Historical Society News, 1230 S.W. Park Avenue, Portland, OR 97205. Editor: Marguerite W. Wright. 503–222–1741. Periodical. No submission info. Query w/SASE. Index: 65, 89, 91.

Oregon Historical Society Press, 1230 S.W. Park, Portland, OR 97205. Contact: Bruce Taylor Hamilton. 503–222–1741. Publisher of 8-12 hard/softcover originals, reprints a year. Print run: 2,000. Accepts freelance material. Rights purchased: All; negotiable on all contracts. Query w/ outline, sample chapters, SASE. Photocopies OK. Reports in 2-6 wks. Publishes in 2-3 yrs. Nonfiction, fiction, photos. "All nonfiction works based on firm scholarship or experience in Pacific NW history and allied subjects. Will review article-length (for *Oregon Historical Quarterly*) to book length mss. Material must be new or new interpretation." Guidelines/catalog available. Index: 65, 87, 89.

The Oregon Horse, PO Box 17248, Portland, OR 97217. Editor: Jim Burnett. 503–285–0658. Ads: Rich Weinstein. Bimonthly trade magazine on thoroughbred racing and breeding industry. Circ. 3,000. Sub. $12. Uses 1-3 mss per issue. Payment: $75-150 (for feature) on publication. Byline given. Rights purchased: First. Query w/ms, SASE. Phone query, photocopies OK. Reports in 2 wks. "Particularly need profiles of Oregon breeders, owners, trainers." Sample available. Index: 6, 91, 115.

Oregon Humanities, Oregon Committee for the Humanities, 418 S.W. Washington, Portland, OR 97204. Bimonthly. No submission info. Query w/SASE. Index: 39, 91.

Oregon Independent Grocer, Oregon Independent Retail Grocers Assoc., 310 S.W. 4th, Portland, OR 97204. Bimonthly trade. No submission info. Query w/SASE. Index: 24, 91.

Oregon Jersey Review, 993 Rafael Street N., Salem, OR 97303. Quarterly. No submission info. Query w/SASE. Index: 3, 6, 91.

Oregon Law Review, School of Law, University of Oregon, Eugene, OR 97403. Quarterly. No submission info. Query w/SASE. Index: 74, 91.

Oregon Legionnaire, 421 S.W. 5th, Portland, OR 97204. Bimonthly. No submission info. Query w/SASE. Index: 83.

Oregon Libertarian, PO Box 1250, McMinnville, OR 97128. 503–472–8277. Editor/Ads: Jo McIntyre. Monthly newsletter. Sub. $12. Circ. 200/250. Accepts unsolicited freelance material. Uses 1-5 mss per issue. Pays money ($5-10 per 250-500 wds) or copies on publication. Acquires first rights. Byline given. Submit query w/SASE, phone query. Dot matrix, photocopies OK. Reports in 1-6 wks. Publishes in 1-2 mo. Accepts nonfiction, photos, cartoons. Topics: victims of government, beating city hall, grassroots freedom fighting, benefits of freedom, how personal liberty stimulates creativity, etc. "Would like articles from Greens, bioregionalists, decentralists, anarchists, feminists, tax protesters and others interested in networking with fellow freedom lovers." B/W prints only, pays $10 if screened, $5 if not. Free sample. Index: 60, 91, 98.

Oregon Library Foundation Newsletter, Oregon Library Foundation, State Library Building, Salem, OR 97310-0642. Editor: Wesley A. Doak. Quarterly. No submission info. Query w/SASE. Index: 104.

Oregon Library News, Oregon Library Association, Hood River County Library, 502 State Street, Hood River, OR 97031. Editor: June Knudson, President. Periodical. No submission info. Query w/SASE. Index: 43, 104.

Oregon Masonic News, PO Box 96, Forest Grove, OR 97116. Contact: Editor. Periodical. No submission info. Query w/SASE. Index: 119.

Oregon Motorist, 600 S.W. Market, Portland, OR 97201. Editor: Doug Peeples. Monthly for members of Oregon AAA. Circ. 225,000. Accepts

For lists of abbreviations and the key to index numbers, see "How to Use this Section" on page 75.

Writer's Northwest Handbook   159

freelance material "on limited basis." Query w/ms, SASE. Dot matrix, simultaneous submissions OK. Pay and rights purchased are negotiable. Nonfiction: 2 ds pages. Fillers: no pay. Guidelines/sample available. Index: 91, 120.

Oregon Music Educator, 337 W. Riverside Drive, Roseburg, OR 97470. Quarterly. No submission info. Query w/SASE. Index: 43, 86.

Oregon Optometry, College of Optometry, Pacific University, Forest Grove, OR 97116. Quarterly. No submission info. Query w/SASE. Index: 31, 61.

Oregon Outdoors, Oregon Trails Publications, PO Box 644, Hillsboro, OR 97123. Monthly. No submission info. Query w/SASE. Index: 91, 92, 103.

Oregon Outlook, State School for the Deaf, 999 Locust N.E., Salem, OR 97310. Published 8 times a year. No submission info. Query w/SASE. Index: 43, 91, 126.

Oregon Public Employee, 1127 25th S.E., PO Box 12159, Salem, OR 97309. Monthly. No submission info. Query w/SASE. Index: 71, 91, 101.

Oregon Publisher, Oregon Newspaper Publishers Association, 7150 SW Hampton Street, Suite 232, Portland, OR 97223. Editor: Caroline Hopfner. Monthly trade. No submission info. Query w/SASE. Index: 24, 91, 102.

Oregon Realtor, Oregon Association of Realtors, PO Box 351, Salem, OR 97308. Editor: Max Chapman. Monthly. No submission info. Query w/SASE. Index: 24, 91, 119.

Oregon Restaurateur, PO Box 2427, Portland, OR 97208. Editor: Keith Pfohl. 503–282–4284. Bimonthly trade magazine for "Oregon restaurateurs, food service industry operations, and Restaurants of Oregon Association members...All editorial content is commissioned on a 'work-for-hire' basis; writing and photography guidelines are given with each assignment...The editor is not responsible for unsolicited contributions which must include a SASE if return is requested." Index: 24, 119.

Oregon Scholastic Press, 201 Allen Hall, University of Oregon, Eugene, OR 97403. Contact: Editor. Publisher. No submission info. Query w/SASE. Index: 43, 118.

Oregon School of Design Newsletter, 734 N.W. 14th Avenue, Portland, OR 97209. 503–222–3727. No submission info. Query w/SASE. Index: 9, 10, 43.

Oregon School Study Council Bulletin, 1787 Agate Street, University of Oregon, Eugene, OR 97403. 503–686–5045. Monthly offers an in depth description of effective programs in the state's schools. Each issue focuses on topics of significance to administrators and lay board members. Sub. membership. No submission info. Query w/SASE. Index: 43, 91.

Oregon Science Teacher, Rt. 1 Box 148, Hillsboro, OR 97123. Quarterly. No submission info. Query w/SASE. Index: 43, 91, 109.

The Oregon Scientist, PO Box 230220, Tigard, OR 97223. 503–292–8460. Editor: L. B. Cady. Uses freelance material, varies per issue. Requires research/science or technology expertise. Acquires 1st rights. Byline given. Submit phone query. Sample available. Index: 109, 117.

Oregon Snowmobile News, PO Box 6328, Bend, OR 97708. Editor: Larry Lancaster. Monthly of the Oregon State Snowmobiling Assoc. No submission info. Query w/SASE. Index: 91, 92, 103.

Oregon Sportsman & Conservationist, 1177 Pearl Street, PO Box 1376, Eugene, OR 97440. Bimonthly on outdoor non-competitive sports, conservation and related issues in OR. No submission info. Query w/SASE. Index: 35, 91, 103.

Oregon State Parks Quarterly, 525 Trade Street N.E., Salem, OR 97310. 503–378–2796. No submission info. Query w/SASE. Index: 91, 92, 103.

Oregon State Trooper, PO Box 717, Tualatin, OR 97062. 503–639–9651. Editor: Ralph Springer. Magazine published 3 times a yr. Sub. $8/4 issues. Circ. 2,000. Accepts freelance material. Pays money or copies. Byline given. Submit query w/clips. Dot matrix OK. Reports in 4 wks. Publishing time varies. Accepts nonfiction, photos. "Seeking photos, mss covering OSP officers at work, off-duty, etc., accident scenes w/OSP slant, etc., features on OSP troopers, hobbies, etc." B&W photo's preferred, usually pays $7.50 per photo. Index: 71, 91, 119.

Oregon State Poetry Association Newsletter, 2915 S.E. 58th Avenue, Portland, OR 97206. Editor: Helen Klopfenstein. 503–777–8209. Quarterly. Circ. 300. Sub. membership. Uses 4 mss per issue from OSPA members. Payment: Copies on request. Byline given on longer pieces. Query w/ms, SASE. Phone query, dot matrix, photocopies, simultaneous submissions (if writer indicates where) OK. Reports in 2 wks. Nonfiction; poetry, 3-8 lines, related to writing poetry or poets; cartoons, poetry related. Photos: assignment only. "Opinion pieces on trends in poetry. Market updates. Book reviews. Short articles on poetry groups state-wide, individual poets who enjoy remarkable success, poetry and its role in political and social issues, projects in poetry by OSPA members (special exhibits, children's contests, readings, etc.) — Oregon poetry news almost exclusively, unless of national or international importance. Items must be very short, 100-500 wds." Index: 76, 91, 97.

Oregon State University Press, 101 Waldo Hall, Corvallis, OR 97331. 503–754–3166. Editor: Jo Alexander. Publishes 6 nonfiction, hard/softcover original & reprint books a year. Print run varies. Accepts unsolicited submissions. Pays royalties. Rights purchased: negotiable. Submit query, ms, SASE. Dot matrix, photocopies OK. Reports in 1 mo. Publishes in approx. 1 yr. "We publish only scholarly book-length manuscripts in a limited range of disciplines, with a special emphasis on the Pacific Northwest." Tips: "Query with sample chapter & table of contents. Acceptance process is lengthy & involves outside reviews & editorial board." Catalog available. Index: 65, 89, 108.

Oregon Stater, OSU Alumni Assoc., 104 Memorial Union Bldg., Corvallis, OR 97331. 503–754–4611. Published 7 times a year. Circulation 96,000. Uses 4 freelance mss per issue. Pays money on publication. Rights acquired: first. Byline given. Submit query w/clips. Dot matrix, photocopies, computer disc OK. Index: 31, 43, 91.

Oregon Teamster, 1020 N.E. 3rd, Portland, OR 97232. Semimonthly union publication. No submission info. Query w/SASE. Index: 71, 91.

Oregon Veterans Forum, 1412 S.E. 25th, Portland, OR 97214. Monthly. No submission info. Query w/SASE. Index: 83, 91.

Oregon Wheat, 305 S.W. 10th, PO Box 400, Pendleton, OR 97801. Editors: Wesley Grilley/Bruce Andrews. 503–276–7330. Bimonthly magazine dedicated to the "improvement of wheat farming in OR." Circ. 9,000. Interested in general trade mss by industry professionals only. Byline given. Query w/SASE. Dot matrix, simultaneous submissions OK. Reports in 1 mos. Publishes in 2 mos. Nonfiction: 3 typewritten, ds pgs on issues pertaining to wheat farming. "Rarely print anything outside of technical wheat farming subjects." Guidelines available; sample/free. Index: 3, 24, 91.

For lists of abbreviations and the key to index numbers, see "How to Use this Section" on page 75.

Oregon Wildlife, Oregon State Department of Fish/Wildlife, 506 S.W. Mill, Portland, OR 97201. Bimonthly. No submission info. Query w/SASE. Index: 6, 91, 92.

Oregon Wine Calendar, 644 S.E. 20th Avenue, Portland, OR 97214. Editor: Richard Hopkins. 503–232–7607. Periodical. No submission info. Query w/SASE. Index: 36, 91, 103.

Oregon/Washington Labor Press, 1902 S.E. Morrison, Portland, OR 97214. Editor: Mary Lyons. 503–231–4990. Monthly newspaper of the Oregon & Washington AFL-CIO organizations. Sub. $10/yr. No submission info. Query w/SASE. Index: 71, 91.

The Oregonian, 1320 S.W. Broadway, Portland, OR 97201. 503–221–8327. Daily newspaper. No submission info. Query w/SASE. Index: 121.

Oregon's Agricultural Progress, Agricultural Experiment Station, Oregon State University, Corvallis, OR 97331. Editor: Robert E. Witters. Periodical. No submission info. Query w/SASE. Index: 3, 31, 91.

Oriel Press, 2020 S.W. Kanan Street, Portland, OR 97201-2039. No submission info. Query w/SASE. Index: 130.

Ornamentals Northwest, Department of Horticulture, Oregon State University, Corvallis, OR 97331. Editor: James L. Green. Quarterly. No submission info. Query w/SASE. Index: 3, 31, 56.

Oscillator, Oregon State Correctional Institution, 3405 Deer Park Drive S.E., Salem, OR 97310. Weekly. No submission info. Query w/SASE. Index: 91, 99.

Merle Osgood Productions, 720 11th Street, Bellingham, WA 98225. Publisher. No submission info. Query w/SASE. Index: 130.

Osprey Press, PO Box 499, Snohomish, WA 98290-0499. No submission info. Query w/SASE. Index: 130.

Othello Outlook, PO Box "O", Othello, WA 99344. 509–488–3342. Weekly newspaper. No submission info. Query w/SASE. Index: 33.

Other Press, Douglas College, PO Box 2503, New Westminster, BC V3L 5B2. 604–525–3830. Periodical. No submission info. Query w/SASE. Index: 31.

Our Little Friend, PO Box 7000, Boise, ID 83707. Editor: Louis Schutter. Weekly magazine for children published by Seventh-Day Adventist Church. Circ. 65,785. No submission info. Query w/SASE. Index: 29, 105.

Out North Arts & Humanities, Inc., Box 100140, Anchorage, AK 99510-0140. 907–279–9916. Contact: Gene Dugan. Theatre company. Accepts scripts "that reflect the experiences of Lesbians and gay men." Submit ms, SASE. Index: 41, 52, 57.

Out of the Ashes Press, PO Box 42384, Portland, OR 97242. No submission info. Query w/SASE. Index: 130.

Outdoor Empire Publishing, Inc., PO Box C-19000, Seattle, WA 98109. Editor: William Farden. No submission info. Query w/SASE. Index: 130.

Outdoor Pictures, PO Box 277, Anacortes, WA 98221. Publisher. No submission info. Query w/SASE. Index: 92, 95.

Outdoors West, Federation of Western Outdoor Clubs, 512 Boylston Avenue E., #106, Seattle, WA 98102. Semiannual tabloid concerning use and protection of wilderness and recreation resources.. No submission info. Query w/SASE. Index: 35, 46, 92.

Outlaw Newsletter, PO Box 4466, Bozeman, MT 59772. 406–586–7248. Editor: Jeri Walton. Quarterly newsletter of Western happenings, cowboy poetry & book reviews. Sub. $7. Does not accept unsolicited submissions. Submit query w/clips. Index: 51, 89, 97.

Outlook, PO Box 455, Sedro Woolley, WA 98284. 206–855–1306. Weekly newspaper. No submission info. Query w/SASE. Index: 33.

Outlook, Canadian Jewish Outlook Society, 6184 Ash Street, #3, Vancouver, BC V5Z 3G9. 604–324–5101. Editors: Ben Chud/Henry Rosenthal. Periodical. No submission info. Query w/SASE. Index: 84, 105.

Outpost, Pacific Quest Publications, Pouch 112010, Anchorage, AK 99511. Editor: Wayne Adair. Monthly. No submission info. Query w/SASE. Index: 130.

Overland West Press, PO Box 17507, Portland, OR 97217. No submission info. Query w/SASE. Index: 102.

Overlook, Sierra Club, 2637 S.W. Water Avenue, Portland, OR 97201. Periodical. No submission info. Query w/SASE. Index: 35, 46.

The Overseas Times, PO Box 442, Surrey, BC V3T 5B6. Editor: Ben P. Sharma. 604–588–8666. Periodical. No submission info. Query w/SASE. Index: 130.

The Ovulation Method Newsletter, Ovulation Method Teachers Association, PO Box 10-1780, Anchorage, AK 99501. Contact: Editor. Quarterly. Sub. $10. Circ. 500. Uses freelance material. Pays in copies. Byline given. Submit ms, SASE. Dot matrix, photocopied OK. Accepts nonfiction, cartoons. Sample available. Index: 47, 61, 124.

Owl Creek Press, 1620 N. 45th Street, Seattle, WA 98103. Contact: Rich Ives. 206–633–5929. Publisher of 6-10 hard/softcover, original, reprint books a year. Print run: 1,000. Accepts freelance material. Payment: 10% in copies to 20% in cash. Rights purchased: All. Sample chapters w/SASE. Dot matrix, photocopies OK. Reports in 2-12 wks. Nonfiction, fiction, poetry. "Any length, subject. Literary quality is our only criteria." 2 annual contests. Poetry Chapbook contest: under 40 pgs, $5 entry fee, July 1 deadline. Poetry Book Contest: over 50 pgs, $8 entry fee, Dec. 31 deadline. Prize: publication with 10% payment in copies of the first printing and additional pay in cash or copies for additional printing. Catalog available. Index: 51, 76, 97.

Owyhee Historical Society Bulletin, Owyhee County Historical Society, Murphy, ID 83650. Editor: Vivian Gottsch. Monthly. Circ. 400. No submission info. Query w/SASE. Index: 65, 69.

Owyhee Outpost, PO Box 67, Murphy, ID 83650. Editor: Linda Morton. 208–495–2319. Annual. Circ. 500. Sub. $5. Uses 2-4 mss per issue. Payment: Copies on publication. Byline given. Rights purchased: First. Query w/ms, SASE. Dot matrix, photocopies OK. Reports in January. Nonfiction: only articles on Owyhee County history, 3-10 typed, ds pgs. Photos: 5x7 or 8x10 B&W. Tip: "Articles must include bibliography or source of information." Sample/$5. Index: 62, 65, 69.

The Oz Press, PO Box 33088, Seattle, WA 98133. No submission info. Query w/SASE. Index: 130.

P.R.O. Newsletter of Oregon, PO Box 06801, Portland, OR 97206. 503–775–2974. Editor: S. Alexander. Ads: Michelle Tennesen. Bimonthly. Sub. $15. Circ. 500. Uses 2-3 freelance mss per issue. Pays copies. Acquires 1st rights. Byline given. Submit query w/clips, ms, phone, SASE.

For lists of abbreviations and the key to index numbers, see "How to Use this Section" on page 75.

Writer's Northwest Handbook   161

Dot matrix, photocopied, simultaneous OK. Reports in 1 mo. Accepts nonfiction. Topics: children, family. Sample, SASE. Index: 28, 47.

Pacific, The Seattle Times, PO Box 70, Seattle, WA 98111. 206–464–2283. Weekly Sunday supplement to the Seattle Times. Accepts very little freelance material. Query w/SASE. Index: 39, 89, 123.

Pacific Affairs, University of British Columbia, 2021 West Mall, Vancouver, BC V6T 1W5. Scholarly journal of UBC. No submission info. Query w/SASE. Index: 23, 31, 101.

Pacific Bakers News, Star Route 2, PO Box 310, Belfair, WA 98119. 206–275–6421. Monthly trade journal. No submission info. Query w/ SASE. Index: 24, 119.

Pacific Banker, 3000 Northrup Way, Ste. 200, Bellevue, WA 98004. 206–827–9900. Editor: Richard Rambeck. Ads: Box Pluss. Monthly. Sub. $15. Circ. 8,900. Accepts freelance material, usage varies. Pays 2 copies. Acquires first rights. Byline given. Submit ms w/SASE, phone query. Dot matrix, computer disc OK. Reports only if accepted. Publishing time varies. Accepts nonfiction, photos. Topics: issues germane to bank and thrift executives in the 10 Western states, minus Wyoming, Colorado & New Mexico. 500-1,000 wds. Editorial calendar available. Sample $2. Index: 24, 42, 119.

Pacific Builder & Engineer, 3000 Northrup Way #200, Bellevue, WA 98004–1407. 206–827–9900. Trade journal. Accepts freelance material. Pays money on publication. Acquires first rights. Byline given. Submit query w/clips, SASE. Dot matrix, photocopied, computer disc OK. Reports in 1 mo. Accepts nonfiction stories on non-residential construction, about 1,500-2,000 wds, must include art. Photos: color transparencies or B&W negatives & contact sheet. Index: 24, 89, 119.

Pacific Coast Nurseryman Magazine, 303 N.W. Murray Road, Suite 6A, Portland, OR 97229. Editor: John Humes. 503–643–9380. Monthly trade magazine of the nursery, horticulture industry. Circ. 10,000. Byline given. "Seldom purchase because we have more info than can usually use...Minimal fee of $25." Query w/ms, SASE. Phone query, dot matrix, simultaneous submissions OK. Publishes in 2-12 mos. Nonfiction: 300-1,200 wds. Photos: B&W glossies; reimburse cost. Tips: "All submissions subject to editing. Small business retailing, new horticulture research, new agricultural breakthroughs. Not interested in articles aimed at home gardener." Sample/$2. Index: 3, 24, 119.

Pacific Educational Press, Faculty of Education, UBC, Vancouver, B.C. V6T 1Z5. 604–228–5385. Editor/Ads: Sharon Radcliffe. Publishes 12 quarterly journals and 5 hard/softcover original books a year. Accepts unsolicited book submissions. Pays royalties/advance on publication. Rights acquired vary. Submit query w/clips, SASE. Photocopies OK. Reports in 1 mo. Accepts educational & academic nonfiction. Catalog/sample available. Index: 31, 35, 43.

Pacific Fast Mail, PO Box 57, Edmonds, WA 98020. Contact: Donald Drew. Publisher. No submission info. Query w/SASE. Index: 130.

Pacific Fisheries Enhancement, PO Box 5829, Charleston, OR, 97420. Contact: Editor. Periodical. No submission info. Query w/SASE. Index: 24, 53.

Pacific Fishing, 1515 N.W. 51st, Seattle, WA 98107. 206–789–5333. Monthly. No submission info. Query w/SASE. Index: 24, 53.

Pacific Gallery Publishers, PO Box 19494, Portland, OR 97219. No submission info. Query w/SASE. Index: 130.

Pacific House Enterprises, 65 W. 26th Ave., Eugene, OR 97405. 503–344–0395. Contact: Editor. Publisher. No submission info. Query w/ SASE. Index: 130.

Pacific Index, Pacific University, U.C. Box 695, Forest Grove, OR 97116. 503–357–6151. Newspaper. No submission info. Query w/SASE. Index: 31.

Pacific Institute, 100 W. Harrison, Seattle, WA 98119. Publisher. No submission info. Query w/SASE. Index: 130.

Pacific International Publishing Company, PO Box 1596, Friday Harbor, WA 98250-1596. No submission info. Query w/SASE. Index: 130.

Pacific Marketer, Northwest Furniture Retailer, 121 Borea N., Seattle, WA 98109. Monthly. No submission info. Query w/SASE. Index: 24.

Pacific Meridian Publishing, 13540 Lake City Way N.E., Seattle, WA 98125. No submission info. Query w/SASE. Index: 130.

Pacific Northwest Agencies Inc., Plainsman Publications, 1437 129-A Street, Ocean Park, Surrey, BC V4A 3Y8. Publisher. No submission info. Query w/SASE. Index: 130.

Pacific Northwest Executive, Graduate School of Bus. Administration, 336 Lewis Hall, DJ-10, University of Washington, Seattle, WA 98195. Editor: Jerry Sullivan. 206–543–1819. Quarterly of business management/economics. Circ. 25,000. Sub. free. Uses 1-2 mss per issue. Payment: $250-500 on acceptance. Byline given. Rights purchased: First. Query w/SASE. Dot matrix, photocopies, simultaneous submissions, electronic OK. Nonfiction: 1,500-3,000 wds. "Our typical issue will be read at the workplace by people who are keeping themselves informed as part of their jobs. Thus, we serve an educational, not an entertainment function. In recent issues we have featured a debate on comparable worth, a series on Japanese business, a story on the implications for managers of an employee with a life-threatening illness, and an overview on wheat in a changing marketplace." Guidelines/sample available. Index: 24, 42, 89.

Pacific Northwest Forum, Eastern Washington University, Cheney, WA 99004. Quarterly. No submission info. Query w/SASE. Index: 31.

Pacific Northwest Labor History Association, 1018 N. 96th, Seattle, WA 98115. Publisher. No submission info. Query w/SASE. Index: 24, 65, 71.

Pacific Northwest Magazine, 222 Dexter Avenue N., Seattle, WA 98109. 206–682–2704. Published 9 times a year. Query w/SASE. Index: 39, 45, 89.

Pacific NW National Parks & Forests Association, 2001 6th Avenue, Room 1840, Seattle, WA 98121. Publisher. No submission info. Query w/ SASE. Index: 35, 89, 92.

Pacific Northwest Quarterly, University of Washington, 4045 Brooklyn N.E., JA-15, Seattle, WA 98105. 206–543–2992. No submission info. Query w/SASE. Index: 31.

Pacific Press Publishing Association, Seventh-Day Adventist Church, PO Box 7000, Boise, ID 83707. 208–467–7400. Publisher of 50 books a year. Query w/SASE. Index: 105.

The Pacific Review, Pacific University, U.C. Box 607, Forest Grove, OR 97116. 503–357–6151 X2406. Editor: Michael Steele. College literary magazine. Editors could change yearly. SASE for guidelines. Index: 31, 51, 91.

For lists of abbreviations and the key to index numbers, see "How to Use this Section" on page 75.

162   Market Listings

Pacific Rim Press, PO Box 2148, Lake Oswego, OR 97035. 503–244–8462. Self-publisher only. Not a freelance market. Index: 54, 120.

Pacific Soccer School, 1721 22nd Avenue, Forest Grove, OR 97116. Publisher. No submission info. Query w/SASE. Index: 103, 115.

Pacific Yachting, 1132 Hamilton Street, #202, Vancouver, BC V6B 2S2. Monthly magazine about yachting in the Pacific region. Industry news and features on people, places and events. No submission info. Query w/SASE. Index: 21, 24, 103.

Pacifica International, 9406 Little River, Glide, OR 97443. 503–496–0431. Editor: Steve Serrao. Publisher. Uses some freelance material. Submit query, outline, sample chap., ms, SASE. Accepts nonfiction. Guidelines available. Index: 130.

Packrat Press, 4366 N. Diana Lane, Oak Harbor, WA 98277. 206–675–6016. Self-publisher of 2 hard/softcover, originals, reprints a year. Print run: 500. Not a freelance market. Catalog available. Index: 98, 114, 120.

Packrat Press Books, PO Box 74, Cambridge, ID 83610. Publisher. No submission info. Query w/SASE. Index: 130.

Painted Smiles, 1105 W. Idaho St., Boise, ID 83702. Contact: Editor. Publisher. No submission info. Query w/SASE. Index: 130.

Pair-o'-Dice Press, 525 S.E. 16th Avenue, Portland, OR 97214. No submission info. Query w/SASE. Index: 130.

Paladin Publishing Corp., 2575 NE Kathryn, Ste. 28, Hillsboro, OR, 97124. 503–648–3303. Editor: Suzann Laudenslager. Publisher. No submission info. Query w/SASE. Index: 130.

Pallas Communications, 4226 NE 23rd Ave., Portland, OR 97211. 503–284–2848. Editor: Douglas Bloch. Publisher of 2-3 New Age softcover original books per year. Accepts unsolicited submissions. Pays royalties. Submit query, sample chapter, outline w/SASE. Dot matrix, photocopied, simultaneous, computer disc OK. Reports in 4-6 wks. Publishes within 1 yr. Accepts nonfiction. Topics: self-help, psychology, astrology, metaphysics, holistic health, women's spirituality, and inspirational writing; "any path that leads to personal or planetary transformation." Catalog available. Index: 13, 61, 100.

Palmer-Pletsch Associates, PO Box 8422, Portland, OR 97207. Publisher. No submission info. Query w/SASE. Index: 130.

Palouse Journal, PO Box 9632, Moscow, ID 83843. 208–882–6704. Editor: Tim Steury. Ads: Opal Gerwig. Magazine published 5 times/yr. Sub. $10/yr. Circ. 10,000. All freelance-written (5-8 mss per issue). Pays money on publication. Acquires 1st rights. Byline given. Submit query w/clips, SASE. Dot matrix, photocopied OK. Reports in 1 mo. Publishing time varies. Accepts very little fiction. Topics: local history, natural history, politics, environment issues, sports, food, science, business, regional travel, arts, people, "just about anything–but must be of interest to regional readers." Study sample before querying. Guidelines, sample available. Index: 33, 89, 103.

Panda Press Publications, Richards Road, Roberts Creek, BC V0N 2W0. Contact: L.R. Davidson. 604–885–3985. Publisher of 1 softcover original a year. Print run: 300. Accepts freelance material. Payment: Copies. Rights purchased: First. Query, sample chapters w/SASE. Photocopies, simultaneous submissions OK. Reports in 3-4 wks. Publishes in 1-3 yrs. Fiction: "Stories of any kind with excellent, three-dimensional characters interacting with each other and the plot in a logical and interesting way." Index: 14, 48, 107.

Pandora Publishing Ltd., 1999 Lansdowne Road, Victoria, BC V8P 1B1. No submission info. Query w/SASE. Index: 130.

Pandora's Treasures, 1609 Eastover Terrace, Boise, ID 83706. Publisher. No submission info. Query w/SASE. Index: 130.

Panegyria, Aquarian Tabernacle Church, PO Box 85507, Seattle, WA 98145. Contact: Editor. Periodical. No submission info. Query w/SASE. Index: 105.

Panoply Press, Inc., PO Box 1885, Lake Oswego, OR 97035. 503–620–7239. Publisher of 2-5 softcover original books a year. Accepts unsolicited queries. Pays royalties. Submit query w/clips, SASE. Dot matrix, photocopied OK. Nonfiction. Topic: real estate. Index: 24.

Panorama Publication Ltd., #210 - 1807 Maritime Mews, Granville Island, Vancouver, BC V6H 3W7. No submission info. Query w/SASE. Index: 130.

Paper Radio, PO Box 85302, Seattle, WA 98145. 206–524–7434. Editor: N. S. Knvern/Dagmar Howard. Three issues annually. Sub. $6/yr. Circ. 200. Fully freelance written. Pays in copies on publication. No rights acquired. Byline given. Submit ms, SASE. Dot matrix, photocopied, simultaneous OK. Reports in 2-3 wks. Publishes in 1-6 mo. Accepts nonfiction, fiction, poetry, photos, plays, cartoons, B&W art. Topics: publishes mostly short stories, poetry, visual art. Short stories tend to be under 3,000 wds, poems under 20 lines, & visual pieces 8X11 or smaller. Prefers things which are radical, experimental, political (that which is oblique rather than direct). "We have published humor, erotica & essays." See an issue before sending anything. Sample $2.50. Index: 14, 77, 122.

Paralog, Oregon Paralyzed Veterans of America, 5611 S.E. Powell Blvd., Portland, OR 97206. Contact: Editor . 503–775–0938. Periodical. Circ. 600. Sub. free to members. Payment: Copies on publication if requested. Byline given. Query w/ms, SASE. Phone query, dot matrix, photocopies, simultaneous submissions OK. Reports in 2 mos. Nonfiction: subjects of interest to paralyzed veterans. Sample available. Index: 83, 126.

Paradise Creek Journal, Brink Hall, Room 220, University of Idaho, Moscow, ID 83843. 208–885–6156. Editor: Erik Ruthruff. Semi-annual journal. Sub. $4. Circ. 200-400. Accepts submissions by U of I or Lewis Clark St. College students only. Pays copies on publication. Byline given. Query w/SASE. Photocopied, computer disc OK. Reports in 3 mo. Accepts nonfiction, fiction, poetry, plays. B&W photos. Guidelines available. Sample $2. Index: 31, 69, 116.

Paradise Publications, 8110 S.W. Wareham, Portland, OR 97223. 503–246–1555. Publisher of 2 softcover books/yr. & 4 quarterly newletters on travel. Press run 1,000. Catalog available. Newsletter sample available. Index: 120.

Paragon, 1332 Grandridge Blvd., Ste. 200, Kennewick, WA 99336. 509–783–3337. Editor: Kismet Kechejian. Bimonthly for seniors. No submission info. Query w/SASE. Index: 110.

Paragon Publishing Company, Central Way Plaza, 15 Central Way, #163, Kirkland, WA 98033. No submission info. Query w/SASE. Index: 130.

Parallel Publishers Ltd., PO Box 3677, Main Post Office, 349 W. Georgia Street, Vancouver, BC V6B 3Y8. No submission info. Query w/SASE. Index: 130.

Parenting Press, Inc., 7744 31st Ave. NE, Seattle, WA 98115. 206–527–2900. Editor: Shari Steelsmith. Publishes 4 books/yr. Accepts unsolicited submissions. Submit query w/clips. Dot matrix, photocopied, simultaneous OK. Reports in 2-3 mo. Publishes in 9-24 mo. Accepts nonfic-

For lists of abbreviations and the key to index numbers, see "How to Use this Section" on page 75.

Writer's Northwest Handbook   163

tion. Topics: child guidance/parenting, social skills building books for children. Payment: royalties 5-8% of list. Write for submission guidelines before submitting material. Catalog available. Index: 28, 43, 47.

Parkside Press, 2026 Parkside Court, West Linn, OR 97068. No submission info. Query w/SASE. Index: 130.

Parlie Publications, 6283 Tack Court, West Linn, OR 97068. Publisher of books on parliamentary procedure. No submission info. Query w/ SASE. Index: 104.

Parsley, Sage & Time, Pike Market Senior Center, 1931 1st Ave., Seattle, WA 98101. Contact: Editor. Periodical. No submission info. Query w/ SASE. Index: 110.

Passage, Seattle Arts Commission, 305 Harrison, Seattle, WA 98109. Editor: Diane Shamash. 206–625–4223. Periodical. No submission info. Query w/SASE. Index: 10, 39, 122.

Passages Travel Magazine, 1110 Tower Bldg., Seattle, WA 98101. 206–467–1149. Editor: Pat Glenham. Ads: John Tullis. Bimonthly magazine. Sub. $20. Circ. 85,000. Uses freelance material. Byline given. Submit ms, SASE. Dot matrix, photocopied OK. Reports in 2 mo. Accepts nonfiction, fiction, photos, cartoons. "No pay, family magazine in business 5 yrs, comp. subscr. & copies." Article length 1,000 wds. Topics: travel in U.S., Mexico, Hawaii, Caribbean. Photos: 4-color slides or transparencies, B&W prints. "Are willing to publish works from unpublished authors if up to standard. Emphasis on pictorial with good text." Guidelines available. Index: 51, 92, 120.

Pathways, Inky Trails Publications, PO Box 345, Middleton, ID 83644. Editor: Pearl Kirk. Published 3 times a year. Circ. 300. Query w/ms, SASE. Reports in 2-8 wks. Publishes in 2-3 yrs. Nonfiction, fiction, poetry. "Fantasy, animals, essays, humor, travels, historical and children's own ideas. 500-1,200 wds. Encourage new writers, especially children. Do not want horror or porn." Guidelines: SASE/$.44 post. Sample: $7 w/ 9x12 SASE. Index: 28, 48, 68.

The Patriot, Runaway Publications, PO Box 1172, Ashland, OR 97520–0040. 503–482–2578. Self-publisher only. Sub. $10/5 issues, approx. 1 every other mo. Circ. 100-200. Not a freelance market. Catalog available. Sample $2. Index: 5, 97.

PAWS, Progressive Animal Welfare Society, PO Box 1037, Lynnwood, WA 98046. Contact: Editor. Periodical. No submission info. Query w/ SASE. Index: 6.

Paws IV Publishing Co., PO Box 2364, Homer, AK 99603. 907–235–7697. Contact: Shelley Gill. Publisher of 2 hard/softcover originals a year. Accepts unsolicited submissions. Submit ms, SASE. Photocopied, simultaneous OK. Reports in 1 mo. Accepts nonfiction, fiction. Topics: Alaska, children's. Index: 2, 4, 29.

Pea & Lentil News, PO Box 8566, Moscow, ID 83843. Editor: Tracy Bier. 208–882–3023. Quarterly. Circ. 4,500. Not a freelance market. Index: 3, 24.

The Peak, Peak Trailers, Simon Fraser University, Burnaby, BC V5A 1S6. 604–291–3598. Student newspaper published 39 times a year. Circ. 8,000. Sub. $28. Accepts freelance material typed ds. Byline given. No pay. Nonfiction, student issues. Index: 31, 39, 43.

Peak Media, Box 925, Hailey, ID 83333-0925. 208–726–9494. Editor: Colleen Daly. Monthly. No submission info. Query w/SASE. Index: 130.

Peanut Butter Publishing, 911 Western Avenue, Suite 401, Seattle, WA 98104. 206–628–6200. Publisher of 40 hard/softcover, original, re-prints, subsidy books a year. Print run: 5-10,000. Accepts freelance material. Rights purchased: First, all. Outline, sample chapters, ms w/SASE. Dot matrix, photocopies OK. Nonfiction: Food cooking, dining. Catalog available. Index: 45, 54, 103.

Peavine Publications, PO Box 1264, McMinnville, OR 97128–1264. 503–472–1933. Editor: W. P. Lowry. Publishes 1 or 2 softcover books/yr. Accepts unsolicited mss. Submit query w/clips, SASE. Reports in 1 mo. Accepts fiction. Topics: weather and climate, ecology. Index: 59, 109, 118.

The Pedersens, PO Box 128, Sterling, AK 99672. Self-publisher of 0-4 softcover, original, reprint books a year. Print run: 1,000. Not a freelance market. Index: 4, 29, 62.

Peel Productions, Rt. 4, Box 396, Sherwood, OR 97140. 503–639–9747. Editor: Susan Joyce. Publishes 2-3 hard/softcover, original books/yr. Accepts unsolicited mss. Pays in copies, royalties on publication. Acquires first rights. Submit query w/clips, SASE. Photocopies OK. Reports in 5-6 wks. Publishes in 1 yr. Accepts nonfiction, fiction. Children's picture, story books. "Write for guidelines if you are interested in submitting work." Catalog available. Index: 6, 29, 96.

Pelican Publications, Box 773, Pelican, AK 99832. 907–735–2243. No submission info. Query w/SASE. Index: 130.

Pemberton Pioneer Women, R.R. 1, Pemberton, BC V0N 2L0. Publisher. No submission info. Query w/SASE. Index: 23, 63, 124.

Pen Print, Inc., 114 S. Lincoln Street, Port Angeles, WA 98362. Publisher. No submission info. Query w/SASE. Index: 130.

Pendleton Record, 809 S.E. Court, Box 69, Pendleton, OR 97801. 503–276–2853. Weekly newspaper. No submission info. Query w/SASE. In-dex: 33.

Peninsula Gateway, PO Box 407, Gig Harbor, WA 98335. 206–858–9921. Weekly newspaper. No submission info. Query w/SASE. Index: 33.

Peninsula Magazine, PO Box 2259, Sequim, WA 98382. 206–683–5421. Editor: Rachel Bard. Quarterly magazine devoted to the Olympic Peninsula. Uses freelance material. Pays $.10/wd. on publication. Acquires 1st rights. Submit query, SASE. Dot matrix, photocopied, simultaneous, electronic/modem OK. Reports in 1 mo. Publishes next issue. Accepts nonfiction, photos. Topics: Olympic Peninsula — outdoor activities, history, sports events, archaeology, culinary adventures, festivals/celebrations, unique business enterprises, craftspeople. Tips: avg. length 400-1,700 wds; feature articles related to Olympic National Park, 2,500 wds. Guidelines available. Index: 92, 120, 123.

Pennypress, Inc., 1100 23rd Avenue E., Seattle, WA 98112. Contact: Penny Simkin. 206–324–1419. Publisher of 1 nonfiction, softcover original a year. Print run: 3,000. Rarely accepts freelance material. Query w/SASE. Dot matrix, photocopies, simultaneous submissions, electronic OK. Reports in 1-5 mos. Publishes in up to 2 yrs. "Our publications deal with controversial issues in childbearing and topics of interest to young families. They are accurate, up-to-date and encourage decision making by informed consumers in matters relating to maternity care and parenting…I am very selective and usually invite authors to write for Pennypress." Write w/query and ask for guidelines; they vary according to audience targeted. Catalog available. Index: 47, 61, 124.

People's Law Books, PO Box 14223, Portland, OR 97214. Publisher. No submission info. Query w/SASE. Index: 43, 74.

For lists of abbreviations and the key to index numbers, see "How to Use this Section" on page 75.

164   Market Listings

Perceptions, 525 Cottonwood #1, Missoula, MT 59801. 406–543–5875. Editor: Temi Rose. Chapbook journal of mostly women's poetry published 3 times a year. Uses 25 freelance mss per issue. Pays copies on publication. Byline given. Submit ms. Accepts nonfiction, fiction, poetry, photos, cartoons. Sample $2. Index: 97, 124.

Perceptions, Literature/Composition Division, Mt. Hood Community College, Gresham, OR 97030. Contact: Editor. Periodical. No submission info. Query w/SASE. Index: 31.

Performance Press, PO Box 7307, Everett, WA 98201-0307. 206–252–7660. Self-publisher of 3 softcover books a year on Catholic charismatics. Print run: 10,000. Not a freelance market. Catalog available. Index: 47, 68, 105.

Peridot Press, 1463 Marion St. NE, Salem, OR 97301. Contact: Editor. Publisher. No submission info. Query w/SASE. Index: 130.

The Permaculture Activist, 4649 Sunnyside Ave. N., Seattle, WA 98103. 206–547–6838. Editor: Guy Baldwin. Quarterly. Sub. $16. Circ. 1,000-5,000. Uses freelance material. No pay. Byline given. Phone query. Dot matrix, photocopied OK. Accepts nonfiction, photos. Free sample. Index: 3, 56.

Permaculture with Native Plants, Box 38, Lorane, OR 97451. Editor: Curtin Mitchell. Periodical. No submission info. Query w/SASE. Index: 3, 56.

Permafrost, University of Alaska-Fairbanks, Department of English, Fairbanks, AK 99775-0640. 907–474–5247. Editors: Robin Lewis, Natalie Kusz. Periodical. Sub. $4. Circ. 500. Uses freelance material. Pays copies. Submit ms, SASE. Dot matrix, photocopied OK. Reports in 1-3 mo. Accepts nonfiction, fiction, poetry, photos, other. Guidelines available. Sample $2. Index: 31, 51, 97.

Perseverance Theatre, 914 Third Street, Douglas, AK 99824. Interested in scripts. No submission info. Query w/SASE. Index: 41.

Pet Gazette, PO Box 1369, Vancouver, WA 98666. 206–696–3197. Monthly. No submission info. Query w/SASE. Index: 6, 38.

Pharmaceutical Technology, 320 N. "A" Street, Springfield, OR 97477. Publisher. No submission info. Query w/SASE. Index: 24, 109.

Phelps Enterprises, 3838 Kendra, Eugene, OR 97404. Publisher. No submission info. Query w/SASE. Index: 130.

Philam Books, Inc., 2101-2077 Nelson Street, Vancouver, BC V6G 2Y2. Publisher. No submission info. Query w/SASE. Index: 130.

Henry Philips Publishing, 19316 3rd Avenue N.W., Seattle, WA 98177. No submission info. Query w/SASE. Index: 130.

Phinney Ridge Review, Phinney Neighborhood Association, 6532 Phinney Ave. N., Seattle, WA 98103. Editor: Ed Medeiros. Quarterly. No submission info. Query w/SASE. Index: 33, 47, 61.

Phoenix Publishing Company, PO Box 10, Custer, WA 98240. No submission info. Query w/SASE. Index: 130.

Photography at Open-Space, 510 Fort Street, Victoria, BC V8W 1E6. Publisher. No submission info. Query w/SASE. Index: 95.

Pictorial Histories Publishing Company, 713 S. 3rd, Missoula, MT 59801. 406–549–8488. Contact: Stan Cohen. Publishes 12 hard/softcover books/yr. Accepts unsolicited submissions. No submission info given. Query w/SASE. Index: 64, 83, 95.

Pierce County Business Examiner, 5007 Pacific Hwy East, Ste. 22, Tacoma, WA 98424. 206–922–1522. Editor: Jeff Rhodes. Ads: Jeff Rounce. Biweekly newspaper of business news for Tacoma-Pierce County. Circ. 17,000. Sub. $15. Uses 4 freelance mss per issue. Payment: $2/column inch and copies on publication. Byline given. Purchases 1st rights. Query w/SASE. Phone query, dot matrix, photocopies OK. Nonfiction: 2.5 pages ds. "Articles on business topics primarily for Pierce Co., but applicable to all of WA considered. Photos: B&W 5x7 or larger. $2/inch. Sample, SASE. Index: 24, 123.

Pierce County Herald, PO Box 517, Puyallup, WA 98371. 206–841–2481. Weekly newspaper. No submission info. Query w/SASE. Index: 33.

Pika Press, PO Box 457, Enterprise, OR 97828. 503–426–3623. Editor: Rich Wandschneider. Publishes 3-5 hard/softcover originals, reprints a year. Press run: 1,500-3,000. Pays royalties. Submit query w/clips, phone. Accepts: books of special interest to the inland Northwest. "Chances for an outside manuscript now are very slim. A year from now we should be better able to evaluate manuscripts." Index: 65, 89, 92.

Pike Place Market Craft Catalog, 1916 Pike Place, Box 12-234, Seattle, WA 98101-1013. 206–587–5767. Editor: Paul Dunn. Quarterly. No submission info. Query w/SASE. Index: 38.

Pill Enterprises, N22790, Hwy 101, Shelton, WA 98584. 206–877–5825. Self-publisher only. Not a freelance market. Index: 54.

Pilot Rock News, 169 N.W. Alder Place, Box J, Pilot Rock, OR 97868. 503–443–2321. Weekly newspaper. No submission info. Query w/SASE. Index: 33.

Pinstripe Publishing, PO Box 711, Sedro-Woolley, WA 98284. 206–855–1416. Editor: Helen Gregory. Publishes 1-2 softcover original books/yr. Query only w/outline & SASE. How-to, small business & crafts. Booklist available. Index: 24, 38, 67.

Pioneer Log, Lewis and Clark College, LC Box 21, Portland, OR 97219. 503–244–6161. Student newspaper. No submission info. Query w/SASE. Index: 31, 43, 45.

Pioneer News, Bank of British Columbia, 1165 - 555 Burrard Street, Vancouver, BC V7X 1K1. Periodical. No submission info. Query w/SASE. Index: 24.

Pioneer Press Books, 37 S. Palouse, Walla Walla, WA 99362. 509–522–2075. Editor: Robert A. Bennett. Publisher of 3-5 hard/softcover, books/yr. Pays royalties. Query, SASE. Report time varies. Nonfiction: Western history. Index: 65, 89, 90.

Pioneer Trails, Umatilla County Historical Society, PO Box 253, Pendleton, OR 97801. Irregularly published. No submission info. Query w/SASE. Index: 65, 91.

Pioneer Publishing Company, Box 190, Big Timber, MT 59011. Contact: Editor. Publisher. No submission info. Query w/SASE. Index: 130.

Pioneer Square Gazette, Pioneer Square Association, PO Box 4006, Seattle, WA 98104. Editor: Lori Kinnear. Periodical, 3 times per yr. No submission info. Query w/SASE. Index: 130.

Planned Parenthood Association of Idaho, 4301 Franklin Road, Boise, ID 83705. Publisher. No submission info. Query w/SASE. Index: 43, 47.

For lists of abbreviations and the key to index numbers, see "How to Use this Section" on page 75.

Writer's Northwest Handbook   165

Playboard Magazine, 7560 Lawrence Drive, Burnaby, BC V5A 1T6. Editor: Mick Maloney. 604–738–5287. Mass circulation monthly magazine of entertainment and arts. No submission info. Query w/SASE. Index: 10, 45.

Playful Wisdom Press, PO Box 834, Kirkland, WA 98083-0834. 206–823–4421. Editor: William Ross. Ads: Neil Sorenson. Publishes 3 softcover, original books/yr. Accepts unsolicited submissions, send a few pages w/SASE before the whole ms. "Playfully instructive insights about the human condition. Our books are for and by grownups who delight in childlike enthusiasm and celebrate being alive. We love love." Index: 13, 47, 100.

Pleneurethic International, Earth Light Bookstore, 113 E. Main, Walla Walla, WA 99362. Publisher. No submission info. Query w/SASE. Index: 130.

Plugging In, Columbia Education Center, 11325 SE Lexington, Portland, OR 97266. 503–760–2346. Editor: Dr. Ralph Nelsen. Periodical. No submission info. Query w/SASE. Index: 43.

Plus, Suite 410, 550 Burrard St., Vancouver, BC V6C 2J6. Editor: Don Stanley. Periodical. No submission info. Query w/SASE. Index: 130.

PMUG Mouse Tracks, PO Box 8895, Portland, OR 97207. 503–254–2111. Editor: Michael Pearce. Ads: Jim Lyle, 503–641–1587 or 255–5718. Monthly. Sub. $24. Circ. 900. Uses 7-10 freelance mss per issue. Written by Mac users. No pay. Acquires 1st rights. Byline given. Submit ms, SASE, phone. Electronic sub OK. Accepts nonfiction, cartoons. Guidelines available. Sample $4. Index: 34.

PNLA Quarterly, 1631 E. 24th Ave., Eugene, OR 97403. 503–344–2027. Editor: Katherine G. Eaton. Quarterly. Sub. $15. Circ. 1,100. Uses freelance material. Byline given. Phone query. Photocopied OK. Accepts nonfiction, cartoons. Sample. $6.50. Index: 22, 73, 102.

Poe Studies, Washington State University Press, Pullman, WA 99164-5910. 509–335–3518. Semiannual. Sub. $8. Nonfiction. No submission info. Query w/SASE. Index: 31, 51, 76.

Poetic Space, PO Box 11157, Eugene, OR 97440. Editor: Thomas Strand. Magazine published 3-4 times a year. Sub. $10. Circ. 600. Uses 10-15 freelance mss per issue. Pays copies on publication. Byline given. Submit ms w/SASE. Dot matrix, photocopied OK. Reports in 1-3 mo. Publishes in 1-2 mo. Accepts nonfiction, short (1,200-1,500 wds) fiction, contemporary poetry, literary essays (1,200-1,500 wds), line drawings, simple graphics, book reviews (600-1,000 wds). Guidelines available. Sample $2. Index: 14, 51, 97.

Poeticus Obscuritant Publications, PO Box 85817, Seattle, WA 98145. Contact: Patrick McCabe. No submission info. Query w/SASE. Index: 97.

Poetry Exchange, c/o Horizon Books, 425 15th Avenue E., Seattle, WA 98112. Editor: Staff. Ads: Staff. Monthly. Circ. 1,400. Sub. $10/year. Assignment only. "We are a community newsletter. The Poetry Exchange includes a calendar of literary readings, announcements about small press books, workshops, and a mss wanted column. Also contains reviews and articles (query 1st — unsolicited material is not accepted.)" Index: 51, 97, 102.

Poetry Northwest, 4045 Brooklyn Avenue N.E., University of Washington, Ja-15, Seattle, WA 98105. Periodical. No submission info. Query w/ SASE. Index: 31, 89, 97.

Poetry Today, Box 20822, Portland, OR 97220. Periodical. No submission info. Query w/SASE. Index: 76, 97.

Poets. Painters. Composers., 10254 35th Avenue S.W., Seattle, WA 98146. Contact: Joseph Keppler. 206–937–8155. Publisher of 1-2 softcover original books. Print run: 300. Accepts freelance material. Payment: Copies (negotiable). Query w/ms, SASE. Photocopies OK. Reports in 1-2 mos. Publishes in 3 mos. Poetry, art, music, essays; experimental, short works, original in concept and design, provocative, ingenious, knowledgeable, beautiful. Index: 10, 14, 97.

Point of View, Aperture Northwest, Inc., PO Box 12065, Broadway Station, Seattle, WA 98102. 206–382–9220. Editor: Richard K. Woltjer. Monthly. No submission info. Query w/SASE. Index: 80, 88, 122.

The Pointed Circle, Portland Community College, Cascade Campus, 708 N. Killingsworth, Portland, OR 97217. 403–244–6111 x5405. Contact: M. McNeill, M. Dembrow. Annual (mid-May) student literary magazine. Submit ms/SASE. Dot matrix, photocopied OK. Accepts nonfiction, fiction, poetry, photos, plays, cartoons. Sample free. Index: 31, 51, 97.

Points Northwest, Washington State University, Owen Science & Engineering Library, Pullman, WA 99164-3200. Contact: Editor. Periodical. No submission info. Query w/SASE. Index: 31.

Points & Picas Magazine, 422 N. Grant St., Moscow, ID 83843. 208–882–3373. Editor: Gary Lundgren. Periodical, 3 times a yr. No submission info. Query w/SASE. Index: 130.

Polestar Press, R.R. 1, Winlaw, BC V0G 2J0. No submission info. Query w/SASE. Index: 130.

Polk County Itemizer-Observer, 147 S.E. Court Street, Box 108, Dallas, OR 97338. 503–623–6364. Weekly newspaper. No submission info. Query w/SASE. Index: 33.

Poltergeist Press, 706 S. Morain Street, Kennewick, WA 99336. No submission info. Query w/SASE. Index: 130.

POME News, Home Orchard Society, PO Box 776, Clackamas, OR 97015. 503–630–3392. Editors: Winnifred and Ken Fisher. Quarterly newsletter. Sub. $10. Circ. 1,200. Uses freelance material. Byline given. Phone query. Photocopied, computer disc OK. Reports in 8 wks. Publishes in 1 yr. Accepts nonfiction articles on home-growing of fruits and nuts and recipes. Sample available. Index: 3, 54, 56.

Ponderosa Publishers, Route 1, Box 68, Saint Ignatius, MT 59865. No submission info. Query w/SASE. Index: 130.

Pope International Publications, PO Box 203, Abbotsford, BC V2S 4N8. No submission info. Query w/SASE. Index: 130.

Poptart, 3505 Commercial Dr., Vancouver, BC V5N 4E8. Contact: Editor. Periodical. Accepts fiction, poetry, drawings. No submission info. Query w/SASE. Index: 51, 97.

Port Orford News, 519 W. 10th, Box 5, Port Orford, OR 97465. 503–332–2361. Weekly newspaper. No submission info. Query w/SASE. Index: 33.

Port Side: The Port of Portland Magazine, PO Box 3529, Portland, OR 97208. Quarterly with news and economic facts relating to shipping and cargo handling. No submission info. Query w/SASE. Index: 24, 79.

For lists of abbreviations and the key to index numbers, see "How to Use this Section" on page 75.

166   Market Listings

Port/Manhattan Publishers, 6406 N. Maryland Avenue, Portland, OR 97217. No submission info. Query w/SASE. Index: 130.

The Portable Wall, Basement Press, c/o Dan Struckman, 215 Burlington, Billings, MT 59101. 406–256–3588. Editor: Gray Harris. Journal published 1 or 2 times a yr. Sub. $5. Circ. 200-500. Accepts freelance material. Pays copies on acceptance. Byline given. Submit ms, SASE. Dot matrix, photocopied OK. Publishes in 6-12 mo. Accepts nonfiction, fiction, poetry, cartoons. "This magazine is highest quality hand-set type on fine paper — articles and stories must be short, terse...can reproduce almost any line drawing...." Sample $5. Index: 68, 85, 96.

Portfolio, College of Business, Boise State University, Boise, ID 83725. Semiannual. Circ. 2,500. No submission info. Query w/SASE. Index: 24, 31.

Portland and Area Events, 26 S.W. Salmon Street, Portland, OR 97204. 503–222–2223. Monthly newspaper. No submission info. Query w/SASE. Index: 25, 45.

Portland Atari Club Computer News, PO Box 1692, Beaverton, OR 97005. 503–667–3306. Editor: Teri Williams. Monthly. No submission info. Query w/SASE. Index: 34.

Portland Business Today, PO Box 10127, Portland, OR 97210. Editor: Jeff McIvor. 503–226–1311. Ads: Bob Smith. Newspaper, general business with emphasis on local news. Circ. 4,000. Sub. $105/year. Uses 1 mss per issue. Payment: Negotiable; on publication. Byline given. Query w/ms, SASE. Makes assignments. Phone query, dot matrix, photocopies, simultaneous submissions (if noncompeting) OK. Reports in 1-2 wks. Nonfiction: 600-700 wds. Photos: B&W 5x7 or larger. Sample/$.75. Index: 24, 42.

Portland Family Calendar, 1714 NW Overton, Portland, OR 97209. 503–220–0459. Editor: Bonnie Martin Fazio. Ads: Greg Hudson. Monthly. Sub. $10. Circ. 10,000. Accepts freelance material, uses 3-4 per issue. Pays $20-40 on publication. Acquires first rights. Byline given. Submit query w/clips, ms, SASE, phone query. Dot matrix, photocopied OK. Report time varies. Publishing time varies. Accepts nonfiction, original artwork. Topics: resources, activities and events for families in the Portland Metro area; also welcome are informative articles about parents' concerns, such as health issues, nutrition, emotional health and education, and how-to articles describing things to make and projects to do with kids. Strive for the tone of one parent talking to another. Length varies from 2-7 ds pages. Pay $5-10 for original artwork, usually to accompany articles; content from children involved in various activities to pictures of toys, food, pets and other theme-related illustrations. Query leading to specific assignment preferred for artwork. Sample free if picked up. Index: 28, 47, 66.

Portland Gray Panther Pulse, 1819 NW Everett, Portland, OR 97209. 503–224–5190. Contact: Editor. Monthly. No info. Query w/SASE. Index: 110.

The Portland Guide, 4475 S.W. Scholls Ferry Road, Suite 256, Portland, OR 97225. Monthly visitor's guide for Portland. Focuses on events and directories. No submission info. Query w/SASE. Index: 25, 45, 120.

Portland Magazine, 816 SW First Ave., Portland, OR 97204. 503–274–7640. Editor: David Gemma. Ads: George Lee. Monthly magazine. Sub. $18/yr. Circ. 20,000. Uses 5-9 freelance mss per issue. Writers must live in Greater Portland vicinity. Pays 10-15 cents/word on acceptance or publication. Acquires at least 1st rights. Byline given. Submit query w/clips, ms, SASE, or phone. Dot matrix, photocopied, computer disc OK. Reports in 3 mo. Publishes in 3 mo. Accepts nonfiction, fiction, photos. Topics: what makes Portland such a special place to live — architecture & design; restaurants; recreation & leisure; arts, music & celebrations; citizens of note; issues & development. Tips: major spreads, 2,000-3,000 wds; shorter, 1,000-2,000 wds; fiction, 1,500-4,000 wds, prefer 2,500, no vulgar language, sex or violence. "...pleased to be a regular outlet for creative writing by local authors." Guidelines available. Sample $1. Index: 33, 51, 68.

Portland Media Review, University of Portland, 5000 N. Williamette Blvd., Portland, OR 97203. Editor: Frank King. Periodical. No submission info. Query w/SASE. Index: 31, 80.

Portland News of the Portland Chamber of Commerce, 221 N.W. 2nd, Portland, OR 97209. Contact: Editor. Periodical. No submission info. Query w/SASE. Index: 119, 121.

Portland Observer, 2201 N. Killingsworth, Box 3137, Portland, OR 97208. Weekly. No submission info. Query w/SASE. Index: 33.

Portland Review, PO Box 751, Portland, OR 97207. 503–464–4531. Editor: Jim Carr. Semiannual magazine. Sub. $10. Uses freelance material. Pays copies on publication. Submit ms, SASE. Dot matrix, photocopied, simultaneous OK. Accepts nonfiction, fiction, poetry, photos, plays, cartoons. Photos: B&W only. Guidelines available. Sample $3. Index: 14, 77, 95.

Portland Scribe, 4540 S.W. Kelly Ave., Portland, OR 97201. Editor: Rob Delt. Monthly. No submission info. Query w/SASE. Index: 22, 45.

Positively Entertainment & Dining, PO Box 16009, Portland, OR 97233. 503–253–0513. Editor: Bonnie Carter. Monthly. Sub. $14. Circ. 10,000. Uses freelance material. Byline given. Submit query w/clips, phone. Photocopied OK. Accepts nonfiction, photos, plays, cartoons. Sample available. Index: 45, 54, 115.

Post Register, 333 Northgate Mile, Idaho Falls, ID 83401. Contact: Editor. Newspaper. No submission info. Query w/SASE. Index: 33.

Postcard/Paper Club Newsletter, Box 814, E. Helena, MT 59635. Editor: Tom Mulvaney. Quarterly. No submission info. Query w/SASE. Index: 38.

Postliterate Press, 6027 1st Avenue N.W., Seattle, WA 98107. No submission info. Query w/SASE. Index: 130.

Potato Country, Box 1467, Yakima, WA 98907. Editor: D. Brent Clement. 509–248–2452. Published 9 times a year featuring potato industry of OR, WA, ID. Circ. 6,000. Payment: $100 on publication. Byline given. Rights purchased: All. Query w/ms, SASE. Dot matrix OK. Reports immediately. Nonfiction: 5-6 ds pages on features and news. Photos: W/mss, B&W. Guidelines available. Index: 3, 24.

Potato Grower of Idaho, Harris Publishing, Inc., PO Box 981, Idaho Falls, ID 83402. Editor: Steve Janes. 208–522–5187. Monthly. No submission info. Query w/SASE. Index: 3, 24, 69.

Potboiler Magazine, Richards Road, Roberts Creek, BC V0N 2W0. Editor/ads: L.R. Davidson. 604–885–3985. Semiannual. Circ. 250-300. Sub. $5. Uses 7-12 mss per issue. Payment: Copies on publication. Byline given. Rights purchased: First. Query w/ms, SASE. Photocopies OK. Reports in 6-8 wks. Fiction, cartoons, comics. "Science fiction, fantasy, horror, weird, unusual, mainstream, graphic stories, fumetti, comics, collage pieces." Guidelines and sample available. Index: 14, 48, 107.

For lists of abbreviations and the key to index numbers, see "How to Use this Section" on page 75.

Writer's Northwest Handbook 167

Potlatch Times, Potlatch Corporation, Western Division, PO Box 1016, Lewiston, ID 83501. Editor: Bea Davis. Monthly for employees and business community. Circ. 6,500. No submission info. Query w/SASE. Index: 24.

Poverty Bay Publishing Company, 529 S.W. 294th Street, Federal Way, WA 98003. No submission info. Query w/SASE. Index: 130.

Poverty Hill Press, PO Box 519, Leavenworth, WA 98826. No submission info. Query w/SASE. Index: 130.

Powell's Books, 1005 W. Burnside Street, Portland, OR 97209. Editor: Terry Naito. 503–228–4651. Periodical. "This publication will be about books and more books...to provide a 'behind the scenes' look at Powell's Books itself...how and why we choose the used books that we do, and offer tips on selling us your own used books." No submission info. Query w/SASE. Index: 22, 76, 102.

Prensa Samizdat, Publishers Research Service, PO Box 21094, Seattle, WA 98111. Contact: Maria Abdin. Publishes saddle-stitched booklets, corner-stapled mss. Submit abstract and/or outline, SASE. Reports "ASAP." Accepts nonfiction. Topics: monographs furthering individual, family and public strength and well-being; public health/sanitation, appropriate technology, alternative health and education, preventive health care, medical subjects for laymen. Tips: particularly interested in environmental health. Guidelines available. Index: 61, 81, 87.

Prescott Street Press, PO Box 40312, Portland, OR 97240-0312. 503–254–2922. Publisher of hard/softcover originals. Accepts freelance material. Payment negotiated. Rights purchased: First, all. Reports in 1 mo. Publishing time varies. Topics: poetry, art. "PSP arranges artwork and pays artist. Please query if possible." Catalog available. Index: 10, 97.

PreSeminar Press, Inc., 3330 N.E. 135th Avenue, Portland, OR 97230. No submission info. Query w/SASE. Index: 130.

Press Gang Publishers Ltd., 603 Powell Street, Vancouver, BC V6A 1H2. 604–253–2537. Editor: Barbara Kuhne. Publishes 2-3 softcover originals, reprints/yr. Press run 1,000-1,500. Accepts unsolicited submissions. Pays royalties. Acquires all rights. Submit query w/clips, SASE. Dot matrix, photocopied, computer disc OK. Reports in 2-4 mo. Publishes within 12 mo. Accepts nonfiction, fiction. "We give priority to Canadian women's writing. Submissions sought by Native women. No longer accepting children's books. We are a feminist collective interested in publishing fiction and nonfiction that challenges traditional assumptions about women and provides a feminist framework for understanding our experience. We look for work that is not homophobic, racist, classist or sexist." Catalog available. Index: 50, 57, 87.

Press Porcepic Ltd., 235 - 560 Johnson Street, Victoria, BC V8W 3C6. Contact: Terri Jack. 604–381–5502. Publisher of 7 softcover trade books a year. Print run: 1,500. Accepts freelance material. Payment: Royalties; advance negotiable. Rights purchased: All. Query w/outline, sample chapters, SASE. Dot matrix, photocopies OK. Include cover letter. Reports in 10-12 wks. Publishes in fall. Fiction, poetry, science fiction, children's literature. "We publish Canadian authors only." Guidelines/catalog available. Index: 29, 48, 51.

Pressing America, PO Box 201672, Anchorage, AK 99520. Contact: Michael Meyers. 907–272–4257. Publisher. Query w/SASE. Index: 51, 76, 98.

Preston & Betts, c/o Camosun College, Victoria, BC V8P 5J2. Publisher. No submission info. Query w/SASE. Index: 31.

Price Guide Publishers, PO Box 525, Kenmore, WA 98028. No submission info. Query w/SASE. Index: 24, 36.

Primary Treasure, PO Box 7000, Boise, ID 83707. Editor: Louis Schutter. Periodical. No submission info. Query w/SASE. Index: 28, 105.

Primavera Productions, PO Box 669, Union, OR 97883. Publisher. No submission info. Query w/SASE. Index: 130.

Prime Time, North Bend Publishing Co., PO Box 507, North Bend, OR 97459. 503–756–5134. Editor: Gail Snyder. Ads: Bruce Root. Monthly newspaper. Sub. free to seniors. Circ. 12,000. Uses 5 freelance mss/issue. Pays $25 on publication. Byline given. Submit query for assignment only, SASE. Simultaneous OK. Reports in 2-3 mo. Publishes in 1-2 mo. Accepts nonfiction senior issues and features with a local slant (Coos County), 500-600 wds (w/B&W negatives. $25). Guidelines available. Sample $.50. Index 106, 110.

Prime Times, 2819 1st Ave., #240, Seattle, WA 98121. 206–282–3499. Editor: A.E. Thein. Monthly for seniors. Sub. $5. Circ. 50,000. Uses freelance material. Pays money on publication. Byline given. Submit w/SASE. Accepts nonfiction, photos. Index: 76, 110.

Princess Publishing, PO Box 386, Beaverton, OR 97075. 503–646–1234. Publishes 5-7 hard/softcover originals, subsidy books a year. Accepts unsolicited submissions. Phone query. Reports in 2-3 wks. Accepts nonfiction, poetry. Topics: self-help, new age, sales, management, business. Index: 13, 24, 100.

The Print, Clackamas Community College, 19600 S. Molalla Avenue, Oregon City, OR 97045. 503–657–8400. Newspaper. No submission info. Query w/SASE. Index: 31.

Printed Matter, PO Box 2008, Portland, OR 97208. 503–223–5335. Editor/Ads: Brigette Sarabi. Quarterly newsletter. Sub. $10/yr. Circ. 1,000. Pays in copies. Acquires first rights. Byline given. Submit phone query. Dot matrix, photocopied OK. Reports in 1-2 mo. Publishes 1-3 mo. Accepts nonfiction, photos, cartoons. Topics: must be film-related, generally 500-1,500 wds, oriented toward media artists. Photos: B&W prints, line drawings, no payment. Sample available. Index: 52, 80.

Printed Word Publishing, 23561 Vaughn Road, Veneta, OR 97487. No submission info. Query w/SASE. Index: 130.

The Printer's Devil, PO Box 135, Harrison, ID 83833-0135. 208–689–3738. Semi-annual newsletter. Sub. rates on request. Circ. 500. Uses 1 freelance ms per issue. May pay ad space on publication. Submit w/SASE. Photocopies, simultaneous OK. Reports in 1 mo. Publishes within 6 mo. Accepts nonfiction, poetry, photos, cartoons, other. Topics: "Graphic arts for the small press. To 1,500 wds. B&W glossy prints. Line art not flatted — quality photocopies OK. Payment by private arrangement. Request a copy of the newsletter." Guidelines available. Sample for postage. Index: 67, 102, 122.

The Printer's Northwest Trader, Rocky Mountain Printer's Trader, 736 S.E. Ankeny Street, Portland, OR 97214. Editor/ads: Frank Schmuck. 503–234–5792. Monthly for graphic arts industry. Circ. 4,000. Sub. $5. Uses 2 mss per issue. Payment: Copies. Byline given. Dot matrix, photocopies OK. Nonfiction: New product releases, new tech., activity within the printing ind. Index: 10, 102, 119.

Printery Farm, 153 Benson Road, Port Angeles, WA 98362. 206–457–0248. Self-publisher of 2-3 softcover originals a year. Press run: 200. Not a freelance market. Index: 18, 47.

Prism, University Student Media Committee, Oregon State University, Corvallis, OR 97331. Editor: David Fowler. Quarterly magazine. No submission info. Query w/SASE. Index: 31.

PRISM International, Department of Creative Writing, University of British Columbia, Buch E462-1866 Main Mall, Vancouver, B.C. V6T 1W5. 604–255–9332. Editor: Janis McKenzie. Quarterly magazine. Sub. $12/yr. Circ. 1,200. Uses freelance material. Pays $25/page on publica-

For lists of abbreviations and the key to index numbers, see "How to Use this Section" on page 75.

168 Market Listings

tion. Acquires 1st rights. Byline given. Submit ms, SASE. Dot matrix, photocopied OK. Reports & publishes up to 3 mo. Accepts fiction, poetry, plays, cover art, imaginative nonfiction (as opposed to reviews, articles). "We like to see imaginative, fresh & new work." U.S. contributors use SAE w/IRCs. Tips: "...read one or two back issues before submitting...always looking for new and exciting writers." Guidelines available. Sample $4. Index: 41, 51, 97.

Products for Peace, 822 N.E. 90th Street, Seattle, WA 98115-3040. Publisher. No submission info. Query w/SASE. Index: 36, 93.

Programmer's Journal, PO Box 30160, Eugene, OR 97403. Contact: Editor. Periodical. No submission info. Query w/SASE. Index: 130.

Progress, Clark College, 1800 E. McLoughlin, Vancouver, WA 98663. 206–699–0159. Weekly newspaper. No submission info. Query w/SASE. Index: 31.

The Progress, 910 Marion, Seattle, WA 98104. Editor: Bill Dodds. Monthly. No submission info. Query w/SASE. Index: 130.

Progressive Woman, 2035 SW 58th St., Portland, OR 97221. 503–292–2922. Editor: Bobbie Hasselbring. Ads: Donna-Rose Pappas. Bi-monthly newspaper. Sub. $12. Circ. 15,000. Uses 4 freelance mss per issue. Pays money on acceptance & publication. Acquires 1st rights. Byline given. Submit query w/clips, SASE, phone query. Dot matrix, photocopied, simultaneous OK. Reports in 1 mo. Publishes in 1-2 mo. Accepts nonfiction, cartoons. Topics: articles of interest to Oregon women in business; fashion, travel; food pieces possible, but all must have business-woman slant, e.g., best business lunch restaurants, packing for business travel. Photo's required for profile pieces, encouraged for others. Index: 24, 124.

Property Tax Charges, Associated Taxpayers of Idaho, PO Box 1665, Boise, ID 83701. Editor: Sue Fowler. Annual. No submission info. Query w/SASE. Index: 36, 69, 101.

Prosser Record-Bulletin, PO Box 750, Prosser, WA 99350. 509–786–1711 Weekly newspaper. No submission info. Query w/SASE. Index: 33.

The Province, 2250 Granville St., Vancouver, BC V6H 3G2. Contact: Editor. No info. Query w/SASE. Index: 130.

Provincial Archives of British Columbia, Sound and Moving Image Division, Victoria, BC V8V 1X4. Publisher. No submission info. Query w/SASE. Index: 23, 63, 122.

PSU Perspective, Portland State University Alumni News, PO Box 751, Portland, OR 97207. Periodical. No submission info. Query w/SASE. Index: 31, 43, 45.

Ptarmigan Press, 3609 N.E. 45th, Seattle, WA 98105. No submission info. Query w/SASE. Index: 130.

Publication Development Inc., Box 23383, Portland, OR 97223. Editor:Jim Wilson. Publisher. No submission info. Query w/SASE. Index: 130.

Publishers' Press, 1935 S.E. 59th Avenue, Portland, OR 97215. No submission info. Query w/SASE. Index: 130.

Publishing Enterprises, Inc., 3636 S. 334th, Auburn, WA 98002. Publisher. No submission info. Query w/SASE. Index: 130.

Publishing Northwest Newsletter, 5770 Franson, North Bend, OR 97459. 503–756–5757. Editor: Frank Walsh. Bimonthly. Sub. $9.50. Circ. 300. Not a freelance market. "We print contributions from subscribers, who should query first. No payment, but byline and publicity are given to contributor." Index: 102.

Puffin Press, 6738 Wing Point Road N.E., Bainbridge Island, WA 98110. No submission info. Query w/SASE. Index: 130.

Puget Sound Business Journal, 1008 Western Ave., Suite 515, Seattle, WA 98104. Editor: David Suffia. 206–583–0701. Ads: Steven Maris. Weekly of local and regional business news and business features. Circ. 20,000. Sub. $26. Uses 1 ms per issue. Payment: $75-150 on acceptance. Byline given. Rights purchased: First. Phone query, dot matrix OK. Reports in 1 week. Nonfiction: up to four ds pages. Cartoons. Photos: on assignment only. Sample/free SASE. Index: 24, 42, 123.

The Pullman Herald, PO Box 609, Pullman, WA 99163. Editor: Guy Pace. 509–334–4500. Ads: Linda Jordan. Semiweekly. Circ. 2,500. Sub. $22. Uses 3 mss per issue. Payment: Average $15-20 for 20-30 column inches; on acceptance. Byline given. Rights purchased: All. Query w/ms, SASE. Photocopies OK. Nonfiction, poetry, photos, cartoons. "Topics open to general interest subjects." Photos: B&W, 85 line screens preferred (not required); pay approx. $5. Sample/$.50. Index: 3, 33, 43.

Pulphouse, Box 1227, Eugene, OR 97440. Editor: Kristine Kathryn Rusch. Periodical. No submission info. Query w/SASE. Index: 48.

Pulphouse Reports, 212 Pearl #2, Eugene, OR 97401. 503–342–7486. Editor: Dean Wesley Smith. Irregular periodical, free. Circ. 100. No submission info. Query w/SASE. Index: 130.

Push Pull Press, PO Box 21701, Seattle, WA 98111. No submission info. Query w/SASE. Index: 130.

Quaint Canoe, 4055 9th Ave. N.E. #301, Seattle, WA 98105. Editor: Ron Swanson. Periodical. No submission info. Query w/SASE. Index: 130.

Quality Publications, 12180 S.W. 127th, Tigard, OR 97223. Self-publisher. No submission info. Query w/SASE. Index: 130.

The Quarterdeck Review, Columbia River Maritime Museum, 1792 Marine Drive, Astoria, OR 97103. Editor: Larry Gilmore. 503–325–2323. Quarterly for museum members on museum news and maritime history. Circ. 2,000. Sub. membership. Not a freelance market. Sample available. Index: 65, 79.

Quarterly Review, Center for the Study of Women in Society, University of Oregon, Eugene, OR, 97403. Contact: Editor. Quarterly. No submission info. Query w/SASE. Index: 31, 124.

The Quartz Press, PO Box 465, Ashland, OR 97520. 503–482–8119. Publisher of 2 softcover books a year. Print run: 100. Accepts freelance material. Payment: Royalties negotiated. Dot matrix, photocopies OK. Reports in 6 mos. Publishes in 1-2 yrs. Nonfiction, fiction, poetry, plays. "We seek revolutionary material with no known market, and hence not publishable commercially." Index: 39, 51, 97.

The Quartz Theatre, Box 465, Ashland, OR 97520. Interested in scripts. No submission info. Query w/SASE. Index: 41.

Queen Anne News, 225 West Galer, Seattle, WA 98119. 206–282–0900. Weekly newspaper. No submission info. Query w/SASE. Index: 33.

Quest, Reed College, 3203 S.W. Woodstock Blvd., Portland, OR 97202. 503–771–1112. Weekly newspaper. No submission info. Query w/SASE. Index: 31.

For lists of abbreviations and the key to index numbers, see "How to Use this Section" on page 75.

Writer's Northwest Handbook 169

Quest for Excellence, St. Luke's Regional Medical Center, 190 E. Bannock, Boise, ID 83712. Editor: Rita Ryan. Quarterly magazine for patients, staff and friends of the hospital. Circ. 17,000. No submission info. Query w/SASE. Index: 61.

Quest Northwest, PO Box 200, Salkum, WA 98582. Contact: Dean Marshall. 206–985–2999. Publisher. No submission info. Query w/SASE. Index: 130.

Quicksilver Productions, Box 340, Ashland, OR 97520. 503–482–5343. Publisher of 4 books a year. No submission info. Query w/SASE. Index: 130.

Quiet Canoe, 4055 9th Ave. N.E. #301, Seattle, WA 98105. Editors: Ron Swanson, Bryan McPeak. Poetry periodical. No submission info. Query w/SASE. Index: 97.

Quimper Press, c/o Port Townsend Publishing, PO Box 552, Port Townsend, WA 98368-0552. No submission info. Query w/SASE. Index: 130.

Quincy Valley Post-Register, PO Box 217, Quincy, WA 98848. 509–787–4511. Weekly newspaper. No submission info. Query w/SASE. Index: 33.

R.C. Publications, 1828 N.E. Stanton, Portland, OR 97212. 503–287–1009. Self-publisher of 1 softcover book a year. Print run 5,000. Not a freelance market. Catalog available. Index: 38, 67.

R.N. Idaho, Idaho State Nurses Association, 1134 N. Orchard, #8, Boise, ID 83706. Periodical 6 times a year. Circ. 750. No submission info. Query w/SASE. Index: 24, 61, 71.

Racer West Magazine, PO Box 675, Maple Falls, WA 98266. 503–620–4108. Editor: Mary C. Harris. Quarterly. Sub. $6.95. Circ. 40,000. Uses 8 freelance mss per issue. Submit query w/clips, phone. Dot matrix, photocopied OK. Accepts nonfiction, fiction, photos. Guidelines available. Sample $2.95. Index: 16, 115.

Racing Wheels, 7502 N.E. 133rd Avenue, Vancouver, WA 98662. 206–892–5590. Periodical. No submission info. Query w/SASE. Index: 130.

the raddle moon, 9060 Ardmore Dr., Sidney, BC V8L 3S1. 604–656–4045. Editor: Susan Clark. Semiannual literary journal. Sub. $8. Circ. 700. Uses freelance material. Submit ms, SASE. Photocopied OK. Reports in 2 mo. Accepts nonfiction, fiction, poetry, photos, plays, other. "...publishing language-centered and 'new lyric' poetry, essays, fiction, photographs and graphics." Index: 76, 97

Radiance Herbs & Massage Newsletter, 113 E. Fifth, Olympia, WA 98501. 206–357–9470. Editor: Barbara Park. Ads: Carolyn McIntyre. Bimonthly periodical. Sub. Free/$5. Circ. 10,000. Uses 1-2 freelance mss per issue. Byline given. Phone assignment, SASE. Accepts nonfiction, poetry, photos, cartoons. Sample $.50. Index: 56, 61, 97.

Railway Milepost Books, 4398 Valencia Avenue, North Vancouver, BC V7N 4B1. Publisher. No submission info. Query w/SASE. Index: 130.

Rain, Clatsop Community College, Astoria, OR 97103. College literary magazine. SASE for guidelines. Index: 31, 51.

Rain Belt Publications, Inc., 18806 40th Avenue W., Lynnwood, WA 98036. No submission info. Query w/SASE. Index: 130.

Rain Country Press, PO Box 2030, Port Angeles, WA 98392. Contact: Editor. Publisher. No submission info. Query w/SASE. Index: 130.

Rain: Resources for Building Community, 1135 S.E. Salmon, Portland, OR 97214. Editor/ads: F. Lansing Scott. 503–231–1285. Quarterly magazine devoted to "articles & book/periodical/organization reviews on subjects relating to community-based responses to social & ecological problems." Circ. 2,000. Sub. $18 or $12 to low income (under $7,500). Uses 5-10 mss a year. Payment in-kind from magazine; write for details. Byline given. Query w/ms, SASE. Phone query, dot matrix, simultaneous submissions OK. Publishes in 1-4 mos. Nonfiction: 800-3,000 wds on "community economics, sustainable agriculture, organizational development, bioregionalism, socially responsible uses of computers, renewable energy." Reviews: 50-400 wds related to themes. Photos: B&W, returned w/SASE. Guidelines available for SASE; samples "with next bulk mailing." Index: 33, 34, 42.

Rainbow News, Oregon Rainbow Coalition, PO Box 6797, Portland, OR 97228-6797. Periodical of political news. No submission info. Query w/SASE. Index: 74, 84, 98.

Rainbow Press, PO Box 855, Clackamas, OR 97015. Contact: Jo Ann Blanchard & Victoria Fairham. 503–657–9838. Publisher of 3-5 softcover books a year. Print run: 3,000. Accepts freelance material. Byline given. Rights purchased: All. Query w/SASE. Dot matrix, photocopies, simultaneous submissions, electronic OK. Reports in 3 wks. Publishes in 6-9 mos. Nonfiction: health/nutrition; business; children/parenting; crafts; travel. 96-160 pgs. "Need outstanding children's books and travel guides." Guidelines/catalog available. Index: 24, 29, 120.

Rainbow Publications, 9520 NE 120th #A-2, Kirkland, WA 98033-2662. Editors: Barbara/Donald Fletcher. Publisher. No submission info. Query w/SASE. Index: 130.

Raincoast Books, 112 E. 3rd Avenue, Vancouver, BC V5T 1C8. Publisher. No submission info. Query w/SASE. Index: 130.

Rainforest Publishing, PO Box 101251, Anchorage, AK 99510. 907–274–8687. Editor: Duncan Frazier. Publishes 1-3 softcover books a year. Press run 3,000. Payment negotiated. Acquires 1st rights. Submit query. Photocopied, simultaneous OK. Reports in 1 mo. Publishes in 6 mo. Accepts nonfiction on any Alaska-related topic. Catalog available. Index: 4.

Rainy Day Press, 1147 E. 26th Street, Eugene, OR 97403. Contact: Mike Helm. 503–484–4626. Publisher of 1-2 books a year of NW folklore, history, poetry. Has not published for others yet, but would "listen to a good idea." Index: 65, 89, 97.

Rainy Day Publishing, 13222 S.E. 57th Street, Bellevue, WA 98006. Contact: Renae R. Knapp. 206–746–0802. No submission info. Query w/ SASE. Index: 130.

Ralmar Press, 3623 S.W. Nevada Street, Portland, OR 97219. No submission info. Query w/SASE. Index: 130.

Ramalo Publications, 8652 Swiss Place, Anchorage, AK 99507. Editor: Marie Fish. Publisher. No submission info. Query w/SASE. Index: 130.

Random Lengths, PO Box 867, Eugene, OR 97440-0867. 503–686–9925. Weekly periodical with reports on N. American forest products marketing. Print run: 12,300. Sub. rate: $145. Not a freelance market. Sample/$2.50. Index: 24, 78.

Random Lengths Publications, Inc., PO Box 867, Eugene, OR 97440-0867. 503–686–9925. Self-publisher weekly, bi-weekly newsletters, 3 hard/softcover books/yr. Not a freelance market. Index: 24.

Randy Stapilus Ridenbaugh Press, 2020 N. 20th St., Boise, ID 83702. Publisher. No submission info. Query w/SASE. Index: 130.

For lists of abbreviations and the key to index numbers, see "How to Use this Section" on page 75.

RAP Press, 2917 N.E. Alameda, Portland, OR 97212. No submission info. Query w/SASE. Index: 130.

Rational Island Publishers, 719 2nd Ave. N., Seattle, WA 98109. 206–284–0311. Self-publisher of 5-6 hard/softcover originals, reprints a year. Not a freelance market. Catalog available. Index: 130.

Raven Press, PO Box 135, Lake Oswego, OR 97034. Editor: Richard W. Helbock. Publisher. No submission info. Query w/SASE. Index: 130.

Raxas Books, 207 W. Hastings Street #1103, Vancouver, BC V6B 1H7. Publisher of cookbooks and guides. No submission info. Query w/SASE. Index: 38, 54, 67.

Re-Entry, PO Box 13535, Portland, OR 97213. Publisher. No submission info. Query w/SASE. Index: 130.

Read Me, 1118 Hoyt Ave., Everett, WA 98201. 206–259–0804. Editor: Ron Fleshman; Linda McMichael/Kay Nelson, Fiction; Robert R. Ward, Poetry. Ads: Pete Young. Quarterly magazine. Sub. $5/yr. Circ. 2,000. Uses 20+ freelance mss per issue. Pays $1-20 and 2 copies (1/2 price for more) on publication. Byline given. Submit ms w/SASE only. Dot matrix, photocopied, simultaneous, computer disc OK. Accepts nonfiction, fiction, poetry, cartoons, puzzles, filler. "A grass roots publication for regular folks. Access and vitality are key wds." Tips: 1,000-3,000 wds, best under 2,000, entertain, fresh perspectives, inform. Contests each issue, no fees. No erotica, no overt didactic works, no academic. No photo's. Graphics/cartoons, $1-20. Guidelines available. Sample $1.50. Index: 2, 51, 68.

The Reader, 1751 W. Second Ave., Vancouver, BC V6J 1H7. 604–681–0041. Editor: Kevin Dale McKeown. Bimonthly magazine of book reviews. Sub. free. No submission info. Query w/SASE. Index: 22, 76.

The Real Comet Press, 3131 Western Ave. #410, Seattle, WA 98121-1028. 206–283–7827. Editor: Ann Ross or Catherine Hillenbrand. Ads: Suzanne Albright. Publishes 6-8 hard/softcover, originals, reprints/yr. Accepts unsolicited submissions. Pays royalties, advance. Submit query w/ clips, SASE. Accepts nonfiction, comics. Topics: contemporary culture, especially where art, humor and social commentary intertwine. Catalog available. Index: 10, 39, 68.

Record, PO Box 1338, Odessa, WA 99159. 509–982–2632. Weekly newspaper. No submission info. Query w/SASE. Index: 33.

The Record, A.S.U.O. Publications, Suite 4 EMU, University of Oregon, Eugene, OR 97403. Periodical. No submission info. Query w/SASE. Index: 31.

The Record-Courier, 1718 Main, Box 70, Baker, OR 97814. 503–523–5353. Weekly newspaper. No submission info. Query w/SASE. Index: 33.

Recovery Life, PO Box 31329, Seattle, WA 98103. 206–547–2217 or 800–252–6624. Editor: Neil Scott. Bi-monthly inserted into *Alcoholism & Addiction Magazine*. Uses freelance material. Pays in copies. Byline given. Submit ms, SASE. Dot matrix, photocopied OK. Accepts nonfiction, fiction, poetry. Topics: principles of addiction recovery, first-person stories, physical fitness/nutrition, humor, tips, recipes. Tips: upbeat poetry, tips on planning a sober vacation, holiday season, etc. Guidelines available. Sample $5. Index: 61, 100.

Recreation Consultants, Box 842, Seattle, WA 98111. 206–329–7894. Self-publisher. Not a freelance market. Index: 130.

Red Cedar Press, 606 First St., Nanaimo, B.C. V9R1Y9. 604–753–8417. Editor: W. & A. Baker, L. McLeod. Ads: A. Baker. Publishes 2 softcover books/yr. Press run 500-1,000. Does not accept unsolicited submissions at the present time. Index: 26, 65, 76.

Red Lyon Publications, 1975 Minda, Eugene, OR 97401-1935. No submission info. Query w/SASE. Index: 130.

Red Octopus Theatre Company, PO Box 1403, Newport, OR 97365. "Invites original, one-act scripts for its annual Original Scripts workshop. Performances by professional actors are provided of selected plays. Scripts are solicited during June for fall performance. The playwrights have workshop time with actors and a director to develop the scripts. Professional critique and honorariums are provided." Query w/SASE. Index: 41.

Redmond Spokesman, 226 N.W. Sixth, Box 788, Redmond, OR 97756. 503–548–2184. Weekly newspaper. No submission info. Query w/SASE. Index: 33.

The Redneck Review of Literature, PO Box 730, Twin Falls, ID 83301. Semi-annual magazine of literature from the contemporary American West. Sub. $14. Query w/SASE. Sample $6. Index: 51, 77, 97.

Reed, The Quarterly Magazine of Reed College, Reed College, 3203 S.E. Woodstock, Portland, OR 97202. Editor: S. Eugene Thompson. Periodical. No submission info. Query w/SASE. Index: 31, 43.

The Reel Scoop, 1410 31st Ave., Seattle, WA 98122. 206–329–8034. Contact: Editor. Monthly. No submission info. Query w/SASE. Index: 130.

Reference & Research Book News, 5606 N.E. Hassalo, Portland, OR 97213-3640. Editor/ads: Jane Erskine. 503–281–9230. Quarterly reviews reference books. Circ. 5,400. Sub. $18. Assigned only. "Consider assigning book reviews to specially qualified librarians." Payment: Money on acceptance. Possible byline. "This publication lists and reviews 100-300 newly published reference books each issue for the benefit of librarians who buy books. Reviews are 80-150 wds. Payment varies according to qualifications of the reviewer." Sample/$5. Index: 1, 104.

Reflections Directory, PO Box 13070, Portland, OR 97213. Editor: Beth Howell. 503–281–4486. Ads: John Ivy. Quarterly on holistic health. Circ. 35,000. Sub. $8. Accepts freelance material. Byline given. Rights purchased: First. Phone query, dot matrix, photocopies, electronic OK. Nonfiction (max 700 wds), poetry, photos (B&W glossy), cartoons. Topics: holistic health, thinking; people doing business in a holistic manner. Sample available. Index: 61, 93, 100.

Reflector, 603 W. Main, Battle Ground, WA 98604. 206–687–5151. Weekly newspaper. No submission info. Query w/SASE. Index: 33.

Register, PO Box 68, Warden, WA 98857. 509–349–2357. Weekly newspaper. No submission info. Query w/SASE. Index: 33.

The Register-Guard, 975 High Street, Box 10188, Eugene, OR 97440. Editor: Bob Keefer. 503–485–1234. Daily newspaper. No submission info. Query w/SASE. Index: 33.

Reidmore Books, Inc., PO Box 2598, Eugene, OR 97402. Publisher. No submission info. Query w/SASE. Index: 130.

Reliance Press, 4127 Phinney N., Seattle, WA 98103. No submission info. Query w/SASE. Index: 130.

Reliant Marketing & Publishing, PO Box 17456, Portland, OR 97127. Contact: Florence K. Riddle. Publisher of 1 softcover original book a year. Print run: 4,000. Accepts freelance material. Query w/outline, SASE. Dot matrix, photocopies OK. Reports in 3 wks. Nonfiction: "how-to, self-help, money making, for the general public." Guidelines available. Index: 38, 61, 67.

For lists of abbreviations and the key to index numbers, see "How to Use this Section" on page 75.

Rendezvous, Idaho State University, Department of English, PO Box 8113, Pocatello, ID 83209. Annual. No submission info. Query w/SASE. Index: 31, 43, 44.

Reporter, PO Box 38, Mercer Island, WA 98040. 206–232–1215. Weekly newspaper. No submission info. Query w/SASE. Index: 33.

Repository Press, RR 7, RMD 35, Buckhorn Road, Prince George, BC V2N 2J5. Contact: John Harris. Publisher of 2 softcover books a year. Print run: 200. Not a freelance market. Catalog available. Index: 51, 96, 97.

Researcher Publications, Inc., 18806 40th Avenue W., Lynnwood, WA 98036. No submission info. Query w/SASE. Index: 130.

Resource Development, Box 91760, West Vancouver, BC V7V 4S1. Periodical. No submission info. Query w/SASE. Index: 130.

Resource Recycling, PO Box 10540, Portland, OR 97210. 503–227–1319. Editor: Jerry Powell. Ads: Jean Hamilla. Trade journal published 7 times a year. Sub. $27. Circ. 3,600-4,800. Uses 1-3 freelance mss per issue. Pays money/copies on publication. Acquires first rights. Byline given. Submit query w/clips. Photocopied, electronic, computer disc OK. Reports in 6-8 wks. Publishes 6+ mo. Accepts nonfiction articles on multi-material recycling topics. B&W glossy photo's preferred, rates variable. Guidelines & sample available. Index: 35, 46.

The Retort, Idaho Academy of Science, c/o Department of Chemistry, Boise State University, Boise, ID 83725. Editors: Edward Matjeka & Richard Banks. Published 3 times a year. No submission info. Query w/SASE. Index: 31, 43, 109.

Review, Seattle Community College, 1718 Broadway Avenue, Seattle, WA 98122. Periodical. No submission info. Query w/SASE. Index: 31.

Review, PO Box 511, Toppenish, WA 98948. 509–865–4055. Weekly newspaper. No submission info. Query w/SASE. Index: 33.

Review of Social & Economic Conditions, Institute of Social & Economic Research, University of Alaska, 3211 Providence Dr., Anchorage, AK 99508. 907–786–7710. Editor: Linda Leask. Irregularly published magazine. Sub. free except Canada & foreign. Circ. 1,800-2,500. Not a freelance market. Catalog & sample available. Index: 4, 32, 42.

Revolution Books/Banner Press, 5232 University Way N.E., Seattle, WA 98105. 206–527–8558. Radical and socialist books. Index: 34, 74, 112.

Reynard House, 5706 30th N.E., Seattle, WA 98105. Publisher. No submission info. Query w/SASE. Index: 130.

Rhapsody!, Clackamas Community College, 19600 S. Molalla, Oregon City, OR 97045. 503–657–8400. Semiannual literary magazine. Circ. 500. Query w/ms, SASE. Phone query, dot matrix OK. Fiction: 3-5 ds typed pages on any subject. Fillers: 3-4 ds typed pages on "people in the arts (writing, photo, art, music, etc.). Poetry: 4-25 lines. Photos: "good, creative photographs." Tips: "We accept submissions from Clackamas County residents or students of Clackamas C.C. only." Index: 51, 76, 95.

Rhino Press, PO Box 5207, Sta. B, Victoria, BC V8R 6N4. No submission info. Query w/SASE. Index: 130.

Rhyme Time Poetry Newsletter, PO Box 1870, Hayden, ID 83835. 208–772–6184. Editor: Linda Hutton. Bimonthly. Pays 1 copy on publication. Submit ms, SASE. Photocopied, simultaneous OK. Accepts "quality poetry, preferably rhymed, and fewer than 16 lines. We aim to encourage beginning poets, as well as...published professionals." Six poets nominated annually for Pushcart Prize in Poetry. Also publishes an annual anthology of contest winners & best poetry. Guidelines/sample, SASE + 2 first-class stamps. Index: 97.

Richmond Review, 5811 A Cedarbridge Way, Richmond, BC V6K 1W6. Contact: Editor. Periodical. No submission info. Query w/SASE. Index: 130.

Rickreall Creek House, PO Box 13, Rickreall, OR 97371. 503–623–6889. Editor: Susan Henry. Publishes 2 softcover original books/yr. Submit proposal w/SASE. Reports in 2-3 wks. Publishes within year. Accepts nonfiction, fiction. Topics: open. Catalog available. Index: 51.

Ricwalt Publishing Company, Fisherman's Terminal, C-3 Bldg., Seattle, WA 98119. No submission info. Query w/SASE. Index: 130.

Right White Line, 531 N. Inlet, Lincoln City, OR 97367. Publisher. No submission info. Query w/SASE. Index: 130.

The Ritzville Adams County Journal, PO Box 288, Ritzville, WA 99169. 509–659–1020. Weekly newspaper. No submission info. Query w/ SASE. Index: 33.

Rival Publishers, PO Box 5628, Everett, WA 98206. No submission info. Query w/SASE. Index: 130.

River City Press, PO Box 1128, Tualatin, OR 97062. 503–692–5381. Editors: Ed Maggi/Kathy Leach. Ads: Cheri Galloway. Bi-weekly local newspaper. Accepts freelance material. Acquires 1st rights. Byline given. Submit ms. Accepts nonfiction (local news). Sample $2. Index: 25, 33.

River West Books, 663 S. 11th Street, Coos Bay, OR 97420. Publisher. No submission info. Query w/SASE. Index: 130.

RNABC News, Registered Nurses' Association, 2855 Arbutus Street, Vancouver, BC V6J 3Y8. Editor: Bruce Wells. 604–736–7331. Periodical. No submission info. Query w/SASE. Index: 23, 61, 71.

Robinson Publishing Company, Inc., 207 S.W. 150th, Seattle, WA 98166. No submission info. Query w/SASE. Index: 130.

Rock Rag, 13879 S.E. Foster Road, Dayton, OR 97114. Editors Toby & Troy. Ads: Bryce Van Patten. Periodical. No submission info. Query w/ SASE. Index: 37, 86.

The Rocket/Murder, Inc., 2028 5th St., Seattle, WA 98121. 206–728–7625. Editor: Charles R. Cross. Ads: Courtney Miller. Monthly magazine. Sub. $12. Circ. 65,000. Accepts freelance material, usage varies. Freelance qualifications require knowledge of popular music. Pays money on publication. Byline given. Submit query w/clips, ms w/SASE. Dot matrix, photocopies OK. Reports in 1 mo. Accepts nonfiction, photos, cartoons. Tips: record review — 1-2 paragraphs; features — 500-1,000 wds. B&W photos preferred. Guidelines available. Sample cost varies. Index: 86.

Rocketlab, PO Box 1139, Florence, OR 97439. Publisher. No submission info. Query w/SASE. Index: 130.

Rockhound Rumblings, 3450 Crestview Drive S., Salem, OR 97302. Editor: G. Goetzelman. Monthly. No submission info. Query w/SASE. Index: 30, 38, 103.

Rocky Butte Publishers, 5635 N.E. Alameda, Portland, OR 97213. No submission info. Query w/SASE. Index: 130.

Rolling Drum Press, Box 2101, Boise, ID 83701. Editor: Kirk Garber. Publisher. No submission info. Query w/SASE. Index: 130.

Romar Books, 18002 15th Ave. NE, Ste. B, Seattle, WA 98155-3838. 206–368–8157. Editor: Larry Reynolds. Publishes 6 soft/hardcover books

For lists of abbreviations and the key to index numbers, see "How to Use this Section" on page 75.

172   Market Listings

nnually. Accepts unsolicited submissions. Submit query w/SASE. Dot matrix, photocopied, simultaneous OK. Reports in 8 wks. Publishes in 1 r. Specializes in mail order books for targeted audiences. Index: 102.

Room of One's Own, PO Box 46160, Station G, Vancouver, BC V6R 4G5. Feminist literary quarterly. Sub. $10. Circ. 2,000. Uses freelance material. Pays money on publication. Acquires 1st rights. Byline given. Submit ms. Photocopied OK. Reports in 3-4 mo. Publishes in 3-6 mo. Accepts nonfiction, fiction, poetry, photos. Sample $3. Index: 41, 97, 124.

The Rose, Publication of the Portland Jaycees, University Station, PO Box 622, Portland, OR 97207. 503–231–2800. Editor: Keeya Prowell. Periodical. No submission info. Query w/SASE. Index: 24, 119, 121.

The Rose Arts Magazine, 336 SE 32nd Ave., Portland, OR 97214. 503–231–0644. Editor/Ads: Terry Hammond. Bimonthly dedicated to the promotion of art and artists. Sub. $6. Circ. 10,000 in metro Portland. Uses 5 freelance mss per issue. Pays 2 1/2 cents a word on publication. Acquires 1st rights. Byline given. Submit ms, SASE. Dot matrix, photocopied, electronic, PC computer disc OK. Reports in 6 wks. Publishes in 1-5 mo. Accepts nonfiction, fiction, photos, cartoons, rarely poetry. Topics: the arts, humanities, history, "any scholarly focus rendered in a bright style might be acceptable." No reviews. Tips: articles up to 3,000 wds; fiction, 3,500. Guidelines available. Sample $1. Index: 10, 39, 51.

Rose Press, 6531 S.E. Ivon Street, Portland, OR 97206. No submission info. Query w/SASE. Index: 130.

Roseburg Woodsman, c/o Hugh Dwight Advertising, Inc., 4905 SW Griffith Dr. Ste. 101, Beaverton, OR 97005. Editor: Shirley P. Rogers. 503–646–1384. Monthly on wood & wood products to customers and friends of Roseburg Forest Products Co. Circ. 7,500. Sub. free. Uses 2-3 mss per issue. Payment: $50-100 on publication. Rights acquired: One time. Query with ms, SASE. Photocopies OK. Reports in 2 wks. Nonfiction: with photos; must be wood-related; 500-1,000 wds. Photos: Color transparencies only (35mm OK) accompanying ms only. No single photos. $25 per printed photo, $125 cover. Tips: Only buy mss & photos together. Assignments occasionally available at higher rate. Guidelines available; sample/free. Index: 5, 9, 78.

Rosewood Press, PO Box 10304, Olympia, WA 98502. Contact: Mark Schwebke. Publisher: poetry, underground posters, network artwork/poetry broadsides, some experimental prose. Pays copies. Byline given. Query w/clips, SASE. Dot matrix OK. Index: 14, 97, 122.

Royal Banner, PO Box 516, Royal City, WA 99357. 509–346–9456. Weekly newspaper. No submission info. Query w/SASE. Index: 130.

Ruah, Sacred Art Society, 0245 S.W. Bancroft, Portland, OR 97201. 503–236–2145. Editor: LaVaun Maier. Quarterly. Sub. $12. No submission info. Query w/SASE. Index: 130.

The Rude Girl Press, Box 331, Reed College, 3203 S.E. Woodstock Boulevard, Portland, OR 97202. Periodical. No submission info. Query w/ SASE. Index: 31, 50.

Rumors & Raggs, PO Box 33231, Seattle, WA 98133. 206–742–4FUN. Editor: Seaun Richards. Monthly. No submission info. Query w/SASE. Index: 130.

Runaway Publications, PO Box 1172, Ashland, OR 97520-0040. 503–482–2578. Self-publisher of 1 softcover book a year. Print run: 200. Not a freelance market. Catalog available. Index: 5, 14, 97.

Rural Property Bulletin, PO Box 2042, Sandpoint, ID 83864. 208–263–1177. Editor: Sandy Weaver. Monthly. Sub. $12. Circ. 12,000. Not a freelance market. Sample $1. Index: 36, 69.

Ruralite, Box 558, Forest Grove, OR 97116. Editor: Walt Wentz. 503–357–2105. Ads: Paula Barclay. Monthly. Circ. 222,000. Sub. $5. Accepts freelance material. Payment: $30-110 on acceptance. Byline given. Purchases first rights. Query with ms, SASE. Dot matrix, photocopies, simultaneous submissions OK. Reports in 1 week. Nonfiction: "Max length 1,000 wds, general family interest stories slanted to Pacific NW; oddities in history, admirable or unusual characters, humor, community improvement, self-help, rural electrification, unusual events or interesting places, etc. We do not purchase fiction, poetry, sentimental nostalgia, or articles set outside NW. Appropriate photos add greatly to chances of acceptance. Photos: B&W, preferably with 35 or 120mm negatives. Pay usually included with story. Tips: "*Ruralite* has a 'string' of local contributors, from whom most of our stories are purchased. However, we also purchase from 15-20 freelance stories a year." Guidelines available; sample/$1. Index: 47, 68, 106.

Ryder Press, 424 N.W. 14th, Portland, OR 97209. No submission info. Query w/SASE. Index: 130.

S.O.L.E. Publications, PO Box 2063, Beaverton, OR 97075. No submission info. Query w/SASE. Index: 130.

Sachett Publications, 100 Waverly Drive, Grants Pass, OR 97526. 503–476–6404. Self-publisher of 1 softcover original book a year. Print run: 1,000-2,500. Not a freelance market. Catalog available. Index: 30, 43, 120.

Sagittarius Press, 930 Taylor, Port Townsend, WA 98368. 206–385–0277. No submission info. Query w/SASE. Query w/SASE. Index: 38, 65.

St. Alphonsus Today, St. Alphonsus Regional Medical Center, 1055 N. Curtis Road, Boise, ID 83706. Editor: Bob Hieronymus. Quarterly. Circ. 12,500. Not a freelance market. Index: 61, 81.

Sakura Press, 36787 Sakura Lane, Pleasant Hill, OR 97455-9727. 503–747–5817. Self-publisher of 1-3 softcover originals a year and tapes & cards. Print run: 500. Not a freelance market. Assignment only. Guidelines available, SASE. Index: 11, 73.

Salmon Trout Steelheader, Frank Amato Publications, PO Box 02112, Portland, OR 97202. 503–653–8108. Editor: Frank Amato. Ads: Joyce Sherman. Bimonthly magazine. Sub. $12.95. Circ. 37,000. Uses 15 freelance mss per issue. Pays money on publication. Acquires 1st rights. Byline given. Submit query w/clips, ms, SASE. Reports in 2 wks. Accepts nonfiction related to fishing and conservation. Topics: how to — salmon, steelhead, trout fishing. Articles should be accompanied by B&W or color (35 mm or 5x7 prints). Guidelines available. Index: 53, 67.

Salud de la Familia News, PO Box 66, Woodburn, OR 97071. Contact: Editor. Quarterly. No submission info. Query w/SASE. Index: 84.

Sammamish Valley News, PO Box 716, Redmond, WA 98052. 206–885–4178. Weekly newspaper. No submission info. Query w/SASE. Index: 33.

Sandhill Publishing, Box 197 Sta A, Kelowna, BC V1Y 7N5. 604–763–1406. Editor: Nancy Wise. Publisher. No submission info. Query w/ SASE. Index: 130.

Sandpiper Press, PO Box 286, Brookings, OR 97415. Contact: Marilyn Riddle. 503–469–5588. Publisher of 1 softcover book year printed for vision-impaired (18 pt. large print books). Print run: 1,000-1,500. Accepts freelance material. Query w/SASE. Photocopies, simultaneous sub-

For lists of abbreviations and the key to index numbers, see "How to Use this Section" on page 75.

Writer's Northwest Handbook   173

missions OK. Reports in 2 mos. Nonfiction, fiction, poetry, cartoons. "Peace, brotherhood, one God seen from many angles individually, The Holy Spirit or Great Spirit our constant companion, verified Native American legends, healing plants, first-person experiences of rising above physical handicaps to find what we CAN do instead of settling for what we can't (no bragging or preaching). Rod Serling type short stories; no horror; want irony and moral and surprise ending." Guidelines/catalog available. Index: 48, 93, 126.

The Sandy Post, 17270 Bluff Road, Box 68, Sandy, OR 97055. 503–668–5548. Weekly newspaper. No submission info. Query w/SASE. Index: 33.

Santiam Books, 744 Mader Avenue S.E., Salem, OR 97302. Publisher. No submission info. Query w/SASE. Index: 130.

Sasquatch Publishing Company, 1931 2nd Avenue, Seattle, WA 98101. Contact: David Brewster. Publisher of 2-4 softcover nonfiction originals, "mostly guidebooks and reprints of *Weekly* material." Payment: Royalties. Query with outline, sample chapters, SASE. Nonfiction: "Travel in the NW." Tips: "Most of our books are produced totally by in-house staff of writers and researchers, though we have purchased material from other writers on occasion." Index: 89, 120.

Satellite Dealer Magazine, PO Box 53, Boise, ID 83707. Editor: Howard Shippey. 208–322–2800. Ads: Pam Waite. Monthly. Circ. 15,000. Uses 5-6 mss per issue. Writers "must be familiar with satellite technology or small business management." Payment: $200-500 on average, on acceptance. Byline given. Query w/SASE. Dot matrix, photocopies, electronic OK. Reports in 2-4 wks. Nonfiction, 1,500 wds. Topics: small business management, TVRO electronics, political developments affecting the satellite TV industry. Photos by assignment only. Guidelines/sample available. Index: 24, 80.

Satellite Guide, CommTek, 9440 Fairview Avenue, Boise, ID 83704. Editor: Fran Fuller. Monthly satellite reception guide. Circ. 10,000. No submission info. Query w/SASE. Index: 1, 104.

Satellite World, CommTek, 9440 Fairview Avenue, Boise, ID 83704. Editor: Bruce Kinnaird. Monthly. Circ. 15,000. No submission info. Query w/SASE. Index: 1, 104.

Saturday's Child, PO Box 148, Cloverdale, OR 97112. Publisher. No submission info. Query w/SASE. Index: 29, 47.

Sauvie Island Press, 14745 N.W. Gillihand Road, Portland, OR 97231. No submission info. Query w/SASE. Index: 130.

Saving Energy, 5411 117 Avenue S.E., Bellevue, WA 98006. Periodical. No submission info. Query w/SASE. Index: 36.

Saxifrage, Pacific Lutheran University, Tacoma, WA 98447. 206–535–7387. Contact: Editor. Annual student creative arts magazine. Index: 31.

Scappoose Spotlight, 52644 N.E. First, Box C, Chinook Plaza, Scappoose, OR 97056. 503–543–6387. Weekly newspaper. No submission info. Query w/SASE. Index: 33.

School Media Services, Dept. of Education, Public Office Bldg., Salem, OR, 97310. Contact: Editor. Periodical. No submission info. Query w/SASE. Index: 43.

The School Paper, Eugene Public Schools, 200 N. Monroe, Eugene, OR 97402. Periodical. No submission info. Query w/SASE. Index: 43.

Schpitfeir Publishing, 911 Western Avenue, Suite 327, Seattle, WA 98104. 206–622–7222. No submission info. Query w/SASE. Index: 130.

Science Fiction Review, PO Box 11408, Portland, OR 97211. Editor: Richard E. Geis. Quarterly. No submission info. Query w/SASE. Index: 48.

Scitech Book News, 5600 N.E. Hassalo, Portland, OR 97213-3640. Editor: Mary Hart. 503–281–9230. Monthly list/reviews 350-400 newly published scientific/technical books for librarians primarily. Circ. 5,400. Sub. $28. Not a freelance market. Assignment only. "We will consider assigning book reviews to specially qualified scientific and technical people." Payment: Money on acceptance. Sample/$3. Index: 104, 109.

Screenings, Oregon Archaeological Society, PO Box 13293, Portland, OR 97213. Monthly. No submission info. Query w/SASE. Index: 7, 88, 109.

Script, Northwest Playwrights' Guild, PO Box 95292, Seattle, WA 98145. 206–365–6026. Editors: Z. Sharon Glantz/Carl Sander. Quarterly for membership. Circ. 400-500. Uses 2 freelance mss per issue. Pays copies on publication. Byline given. Submit query w/clips, phone. Dot matrix, photocopied OK. Reports in 1 mo. Accepts nonfiction. Sample $.50. Index: 10, 41.

Sea Grant Program, University of Alaska, 303 Tanaka Drive, Bunnell Bldg. Rm. 3, Fairbanks, AK 99701. Publisher. No submission info. Query w/SASE. Index: 31, 88, 109.

Sea Kayaker, Sea Kayaker, Inc., 1670 Duranleau Street, Vancouver, BC V6H 3S4. 604–263–1471. (6327 Seaview Ave. NW, Seattle, WA 98107) Editor: Beatrice Dowd. Ads: Shirl Bayer. Quarterly magazine. Sub. $12US. Circ. 12,000. Uses 2-3 freelance mss per issue. Requires sea kayaking expertise. Pays $.05-10/word on publication. Acquires 1st rights. Byline given. Submit query w/clips, ms w/SASE. Dot matrix OK. Reports in 2-3 mo. Publishes in 6-9 mo. Accepts nonfiction, fiction, photos, cartoons. Material must be related to sea kayaking. B&W prints preferred, $15-35. "Best guidelines contained in our back issues." Guidelines available. Sample $4.05. Index: 2, 21, 120.

Sea Pen Press & Paper Mill, 2228 N.E. 46th Street, Seattle, WA 98105. Publisher. No submission info. Query w/SASE. Index: 130.

Seablom Design Books, 2106 2nd Avenue N., Seattle, WA 98109. Publisher. No submission info. Query w/SASE. Index: 130.

Seafood Leader Magazine, 4016 Ashworth N., Seattle, WA 98103. 206–633–2840. Periodical. No submission info. Query w/SASE. Index: 24.

Seagull Publishing, 2628 W. Crockett, Seattle, WA 98199. No submission info. Query w/SASE. Index: 130.

The Seal Press, 3131 Western Ave. #410, Seattle, WA 98121. 206–283–7844. Editor: Faith Conlon. Ads: Deborah Kaufmann. Publishes 10 softcover originals, reprints, a year. Press run 4,000-5,000. Query w/clips, SASE. Dot matrix, photocopied OK. Reports in 4-8 wks. Accepts nonfiction, fiction. "We are a feminist publisher specializing in works by women writers." Catalog available. Index: 50, 57, 124.

Searchers Publications, 4314 Island Crest Way, Mercer Island, WA 98040. No submission info. Query w/SASE. Index: 130.

Seaside Signal, 113 N. Holladay, Box 848, Seaside, OR 97138. 503–738–5561. Weekly newspaper. No submission info. Query w/SASE. Index: 33.

Seattle, PO Box 22578, Seattle, WA 98122. Monthly. No submission info. Query w/SASE. Index: 33.

Seattle Airplane Press, 6727 Glen Echo Lane, Tacoma, WA 98499. No submission info. Query w/SASE. Index: 130.

For lists of abbreviations and the key to index numbers, see "How to Use this Section" on page 75.

174   Market Listings

Seattle Aquarium, Pier 59, Waterfront Park, Seattle, WA 98101. Publisher. No submission info. Query w/SASE. Index: 6, 88.

Seattle Art Museum Program Guide, Volunteer Park, 14th E. and E. Park, Seattle, WA 98112. Periodical. No submission info. Query w/SASE. Index: 10, 39.

Seattle Arts, Seattle Arts Commission, 305 Harrison, Seattle, WA 98109. Editor: Linda Knudsen. 206–625–4223. Monthly relating to SAC concerns. Circ. 5,000. Accepts freelance material if material relevant to arts in Seattle by competent author. Payment: Depends on budget, on publication. Byline given. Phone queries OK. Assignments only. "We have a literary supplement to the newsletter 2 times per year. Authors are accepted only if they respond to the call for submissions (published in the newsletter). Those accepted are selected by jury process." Sample available. Index: 10.

Seattle Audubon Society, 619 Joshua Green Bldg., Seattle, WA 98101. Publisher. No submission info. Query w/SASE. Index: 6, 35, 92.

Seattle Business, 109 W. Mercer Street, Seattle, WA 98119. Editor: Tim Healy. 206–285–2050. Monthly of the Greater Seattle Chamber of Commerce. "Serves business executives in the Puget sound area with analysis, how-to and feature articles, plus economic tables and business data." Circ. 8,200. Buys 1-2 mss per issue. Payment: Money on publication. Byline given. Query w/SASE. Dot matrix, simultaneous submissions OK. Nonfiction: 1,500-2,000 wds on "business topics related to Seattle area." Pay negotiable. Departments: 1,000 wds on "personal experience of business people." No pay. Photos: Query first — payment negotiable. Guidelines available; sample/$2. Index: 24, 123.

Seattle Business, Vernon Publications, 3000 Northrup Way, Ste. 200, Bellevue, WA 98004. 206–827–9900. Editor: Michele Andrus Dill. Ads: Ruth Schubert. Monthly magazine. Sub. $18/yr. Circ. 8,400. Uses freelance material. Pays money per length, copies. Acquires 1st, all rights. Byline given. Submit ms, SASE. Dot matrix OK, computer disc if agreed on. Reports only if accepted. Publishing time varies. Accepts nonfiction, photos. Topics: business issues germane to Greater Seattle area. 500-2,000 wds. Editorial calendar available. Sample $3.50. Index: 15, 42, 60.

Seattle Business Magazine, 1200 One Union Square, Seattle, WA 98101. 206–477–7214. No submissions info. Query w/SASE. Index: 24.

Seattle Chinese Post, 409 Maynard S., Rm 16, Seattle, WA 98104. 206–223–0623. Weekly newspaper. No submission info. Query w/SASE. Index: 12, 33, 39.

Seattle Gay News, 704 E. Pike Street, Seattle, WA 98122. Editor: George Bakan. 206–324–4297. Weekly for gay/lesbian audience. Circ. 20,000. Sub. $35. Accepts freelance material. Payment: Money, copies, on publication. Dot matrix OK. Nonfiction, fiction, photos ($5), cartoons. Sample available. Index: 37, 57.

The Seattle Medium, 2600 S. Jackson, Seattle, WA 98144. Editor: Connie Bennett Cameron. 206–323–3070. "Pacific Northwest's largest Black-owned newspaper." No submission info. Query w/SASE. Index: 20.

Seattle Monthly, 1932 First Ave., Ste. 218, Seattle, WA 98101. 206–441–4215. Editor: Charles E. Harris. Ads: Susan Crowell. Monthly magazine. Circ. 15,000. Uses 1-4 freelance mss per issue. Pays $1/column inch on publication plus 1 mo. Acquires 1st rights. Byline given. Submit query w/clips, SASE. Photocopied, simultaneous, electronic, computer disc OK. Reports in 2 wks. Publishes in 1-6 mo. Accepts nonfiction, poetry, photos, cartoons. Topics: urban issues, Northwest personalities, travel, cultural events. Sample $.65. Index: 39, 121, 123.

Seattle Post-Intelligencer, 6th & Wall Streets, Seattle, WA 98121. Editor: John Reistrup. Daily newspaper. No submission info. Query w/SASE. Index: 121.

The Seattle Review, Padelford Hall GN-30, University of Washington, Seattle, WA 98195. Editor: Nelson Bentley, Poetry/Charles Johnson, Fiction. Ads: Janie Smith. 206–543–9865. Semiannual literary magazine. Circ. 1,000. Sub. $7/year. Uses 2-4 stories, 20 poems per issue. Payment: $5-20, 2 copies, 1 year sub, on publication. Byline given. Rights purchased: First, reverts to author. Submit ms, SASE. Dot matrix, photocopies OK. Reports in 3-6 mos. Nonfiction, fiction, poetry. Will consider most topics and length varies, limited only by issue requirements. No photos. Sample: 1/2 price. Index: 31, 51, 97.

Seattle Star, PO Box 30044, Seattle, WA 98103. 206–547–1753. Editor: Michael Dowers. Bi-monthly cartoon tabloid. Accepts freelance material. Pays copies/advertising trade. Submit w/SASE. Photocopied OK. "Looking for humorous cartoons." Sample $1. Index: 68.

Seattle Times, Fairview Ave. N. & John Street, PO Box 70, Seattle, WA 98111. 206–464–2111. Daily newspaper . No submission info. Query w/SASE. Index: 121.

Seattle Weekly, 1931 Second Avenue, Seattle, WA 98101. Editor: David Brewster. Weekly. Circ. 30,000. Payment: Money on publication. Byline given. Query, outline w/SASE. Nonfiction. Guidelines available; sample $.75. Index: 39, 76.

Seattle's Child/Eastside Project, PO Box 22578, Seattle, WA 98122. 206–322–2594. Editor: Ann Bergman. Ads: Alzyne Sulkin. Monthly magazine. Sub. $15. Circ. 20,000. Uses 3 freelance mss per issue. Pays $.10/word on publication. Acquires 1st rights. Byline given. Submit query w/clips, ms, SASE. Dot matrix, photocopied, simultaneous OK. Reports in 3 mo. Publishes in 6-24 mo. Accepts nonfiction. Topics: directed to parents and professionals working with kids. Audience well-read, sophisticated. Tips: 400-2,500 wds. Guidelines available. Index: 29, 33, 47.

Seattle's Child Publishing, PO Box 22578, Seattle, WA 98122. Contact: Ann Bergman. Publisher of 1-2 softcover, nonfiction originals on same subjects and for same audience as above. Payment: Money, royalties. Query, manuscript, outline, sample chapters w/SASE. Dot matrix, photocopies, electronic OK. Reports in 3 mos. Publishes in 2 yrs. Tips: "Issues relevant to parent, educators, professionals working with children 12 or under." Index: 29.

Second Amendment Foundation, James Madison Bldg., 12500 N.E. 10th Place, Bellevue, WA 98005. Publisher. No submission info. Query w/SASE. Index: 130.

Second Language Publications, PO Box 1700, Blaine, WA 98230. Also, PO Box 82370, Burnaby, BC V5C 5P8. No submission info. Query w/SASE. Index: 73.

Second Thoughts Press, PO Box 10741, Eugene, OR 97440. 503–344–3491. Self-publisher of 1 softcover book a year for travelers. Print run: 500-1,000. Not a freelance market. Catalog available. Index: 120.

Select Homes, 4250 Dawson Street, Vancouver, BC V5C 4B1. Editor: Pam Withers. 604–293–1275. Ads: Allen Barnett. Published 8 time year. Circ. 175,000. Sub. $14.97. Uses 4-6 mss per issue. Payment: Money, copies, on acceptance. Byline given. Rights purchased: First Canadian. Query w/SASE. No phone queries. Assignment only. Photocopies, simultaneous submissions (if explained) OK. Reports in 3 wks. Nonfiction,

For lists of abbreviations and the key to index numbers, see "How to Use this Section" on page 75.

Writer's Northwest Handbook 175

cartoons, humor essays. "House maintenance, house renovation, house finance, house decorating, news of interest to homeowner, architecture, energy issues as related to homeowning, humor essay." Photos: $50-100 per stock photo, on publication; negotiable day-rates for shoots ($450 per day average). Tips: Use mostly Canadian material. See guidelines before querying. Send clips. Guidelines available; sample $2. Index: 9, 66, 67.

Self-Counsel Press, Inc., Subsidiary of International Self-Counsel Press, Ltd., 1303 N. Northgate Way, Seattle, WA 98133. 206–522–8383. Publisher of softcover original, nonfiction. No submission info. Query w/SASE. Guidelines/catalog available. Index: 67.

Sellwood Bee, 8113 S.E. 13th Avenue, Portland, OR 97202. 503–235–8335. Weekly newspaper. No submission info. Query w/SASE. Index: 33.

Charles Seluzicki, Fine Press Series, Fine and Rare Books, 3733 N.E. 24th Avenue, Portland, OR 97212. Contact: Charles Seluzicki. 503–284–4749. Publisher of 2-4 hard/softcover originals, reprints a year. Print run: 50-300. Accepts freelance material with strict qualifications. Payment: Copies, small cash payment at times. Rights purchased: First. Submit ms, SASE. Photocopies OK. Reports in 1 month. Publishes in 6-24 mos. Book arts, fiction, poetry, plays. "We are interested in the best possible writing for fine press formats. Such publishing requires materials that suggest the strong graphic and tactile expression. Primarily mss are solicited. Our authors have included Ted Hughes, William Stafford, Tess Gallagher, Seannes Heaney and Charles Simic (among others)." Catalog available. Index: 22, 51, 97.

The Senior Citizen News, 10211 S.W. Barbur Blvd., Suite 109 A, Portland, OR 97219. 503–245–6442. Editor: Carl Olson. Monthly. Sub. $7.50. No submission info. Query w/SASE. Index: 33, 110.

Senior News of Island County, 2845 E. Hwy 525, Langley, WA 98260. 206–321–1600. Editor: Claudia Fuller. Monthly, free. Circ. 3,600. Uses freelance material. No pay. Submit ms, SASE. Dot matrix, photocopied OK. Accepts nonfiction, poetry, photos, cartoons. Index: 95, 97, 110.

Senior News, PAMI Publications, PO Box 229, Salem, OR 97308. Editor: Robert Webb. 503–299–8478. Monthly. No submission info. Query w/SASE. Index: 110.

Senior Scene, 223 N. Yakima, Tacoma, WA 98403. 206–272–2278. Periodical. No submission info. Query w/SASE. Index: 110.

Senior Times, 7802 E. Mission, Spokane, WA, 99206. Contact: Editor. Periodical. No submission info. Query w/SASE. Index: 110.

Senior Tribune, PO Box 29018, Portland, OR 97229. Editor: Greg Johnson. 503–223–9054. Monthly tabloid serving residents 55 and older in Multnomah, Clackamas and Washington counties. "Distributed free to banks and savings and loan institutions, senior and community centers, retirement complexes, medical clinics, Social Security offices." Tips: "Individuals and organizations are encouraged to submit articles of interest to older persons. The deadline for all copy is the 15th of each month." Index: 110.

The Senior Voice, 325 E. 3rd Avenue, Anchorage, AK 99501. Editor: Liz Lauzen. 907–277–0787. Ads: Pat Bressett. Monthly, senior advocate for legislative, health, consumer affairs. Sub. $10 for Alaskans over 55/others $20. Seldom accepts freelance material. "Source should be well versed in Alaskan concerns." Byline given. Index: 4, 110.

Sentinel, Box 799, Sitka, AK 99835. 907–747–3219. Daily newspaper. No submission info. Query w/SASE. Index: 33.

Sentinel, 117 W. Main Street, Goldendale, WA 98620. 509–773–4212. Weekly newspaper. No submission info. Query w/SASE. Index: 33.

Service Business, 1512 Western Ave., Seattle, WA 98101. 206–622–4241. Editor: Martha Ireland. Ads: Betty Saunders. Quarterly magazine. Sub. $20. Circ. 5,000. Uses 5-10 freelance mss per issue. Requires knowledge in field or good research ability. Pays $10-90 up to 1,500 wds on publication. Acquires 1st rights. Byline given. Submit query w/clips, ms w/SASE, phone query. Good dot matrix, photocopied, computer disc OK. Accepts nonfiction, photos, cartoons. Topics: cleaning & maintenance for self-employed professionals in this field, interviews with successful cleaning business operators, business management advice geared to on-site cleaning. Positive slant, helpful, friendly, polished ms only. Photos B&W or color, not over 5X7, $10 per shot, plus film & developing. Guidelines $.25, SASE. Sample $3. Index: 24, 71, 117.

Sesame, Windyridge Press, PO Box 327, Medford, OR 97501. Editor: Gene Olson. 503–772–5399. Monthly newsletter for writers. Sub. $26. No submission info. Query w/SASE. Index: 76, 125.

Seven Buffaloes Press, PO Box 249, Big Timber, MT 59011. Contact: Art Cuelho. Publisher of a newsletter series, poetry, fiction, essays; devoted to the rural heritage, farmers, workers, the land, and to regionalism. The role of the small press is "at best...the seedbed of this country's best potential writers and poets...You can pick up 50 to over 100 magazines in this country and find the same poets in all of them. You don't see that in magazines or presses where strong focus is on regionalism." No submission info. Query w/SASE. Catalog/free. Index: 3, 51, 97.

Shalom, Oregon, c/o NCCJ, 506 S.W. 6th, Suite 414, Portland, OR 97204. Quarterly of the Oregon chapter of the National Council of Christians and Jews. No submission info. Query w/SASE. Index: 105.

Shane Press, 4719 S.E. Woodstock, Portland, OR 97206. No submission info. Query w/SASE. Index: 130.

R.L. Shep, PO Box C-20, Lopez Island, WA 98261. 206–468–2023. Publisher hard/softcover, originals, reprints. Not a freelance market. Catalog available. Index: 130.

Sherman County For The Record, Sherman County Historical Society, Moro, OR 97039. Editor: Sherry Kaseberg & Patty Moore. Semiannual magazine of local history. Prints 1,000 copies, mainly for residents of Sherman County. No pay. Submit ms, SASE. Phone queries OK. Nonfiction: "Our authors are mostly local people. No one is paid. Profit is for the historical society." Sample available. Index: 65.

Sherman County Journal, 107 W. 1st, Box 284, Moro, OR 97039. 503–565–3515. Weekly newspaper. No submission info. Query w/SASE. Index: 33.

Shiloh Publishing House, 1490 Greenview Ct., Woodburn, OR 97071. 503–981–4328. Editor: Carol Robeson. Publisher. No submission info. Query w/SASE. Index: 130.

Shining Knight Press, PO Box 1030, Waldport, OR 97394. 503–563–5327. Editor: Diana Gregory. Publishes 2-3 books/yr. Pays royalties. Submit query w/clips, SASE, include publishing record. Fine dot matrix, photocopied, computer disc OK. Reports in 4-6 wks. Publishes in 1 yr. Accepts nonfiction. Topics: reference & help books for writers only. "Non-pedantic writing preferred. No rehash of *Writer's Digest* books. Fresh, specific topics on writing. No 'how to make a living freelancing.' Topic may be old if slant is fresh." Catalog available. Index: 104, 125.

Duane Shinn Publications, 5090 Dobrot, Central, OR 97502. No submission info. Query w/SASE. Index: 130.

Shires Books, R.R. 3, Site 1, Nanaimo, BC V9R 5K3. Publisher. No submission info. Query w/SASE. Index: 130.

For lists of abbreviations and the key to index numbers, see "How to Use this Section" on page 75.

176   Market Listings

Shoban News, Box 427, Fort Hall, ID 83203. Weekly periodical. Circ. 1,500. No submission info. Query w/SASE. Index: 33.

Shorey Publications, 110 Union Street, PO Box 21626, Seattle, WA 98111. No submission info. Query w/SASE. Index: 130.

Signal Elm Press, 1300 E. Denny #205, Seattle, WA 98122. Publisher: psychology, religion, metaphysics, New Age. Query w/outline. Index: 13, 100, 105.

Sign of the Times, A Chronicle of Decadence, PO Box 70672, Seattle, WA 98107-0672. 206–323–6779. Editor: Mark Souder. Biannual. Sub. $15/2 yrs. Circ. 750. Uses 11 freelance mss per issue. Acquires first rights. Pays copies on publication. Byline given. Submit ms w/SASE. Dot matrix, photocopied, electronic OK. Reports in 6 wks. Accepts fiction, photographs, drama, cartoons. Guidelines available. Index: 51, 68, 95.

Signature, 22912 102nd Place W., Edmonds, WA 98020. Editor: Charla Reid. 206–774–0800. Ads: Susan Henning. Monthly on the visual arts. Circ. 10,000. Sub. $12. Accepts freelance material, assignment only. Byline given. Rights purchased: First. Dot matrix OK. Nonfiction: "Visual arts. Very people paper. We like the personal touch during an interview, i.e. special effects or new ways of creating. Also expect photos. Payment, if agreement with editor beforehand, is $1.50 published inch." Photos: B&W, 8x10 glossy. Tips: "We are a smaller paper, so the editorial department must know beforehand about an article you'd like to submit." Guidelines/sample available. Index: 9, 95, 122.

Signmaker Press, PO Box 967, Ashland, OR 97520. No submission info. Query w/SASE. Index: 130.

Signpost Books, 8912 192nd S.W., Edmonds, WA 98020. Contact: Cliff Cameron. 206–776–0370. Publisher of 2-3 softcover originals a year on NW outdoor recreation, with emphasis on hiking, bicycling, canoeing/kayaking, and cross country skiing. Print run: 3-5,000. Accepts freelance material. Pay negotiated. Query, sample chapters w/SASE. Dot matrix, photocopies, simultaneous submissions, electronic (call first) OK. Reports in 3-4 wks. Nonfiction: "We focus on self-propelled outdoor recreation activities in the Pacific NW." Length 100-250 published pgs, including text, photos, maps. Tips: "In addition to showing knowledge of a subject, it is impressive when the author shows that he/she has considered the whole book, including artwork, appendices, promotional material for covers, potential markets, and other details of the finished book." Index: 16, 92, 103.

SIGNPOST for Northwest Trails, 16812 36th Avenue W., Lynnwood, WA 98037. Editor: Ann Marshall. 206–743–3947. Ads: Jim Eychaner. Monthly for lovers of the outdoors, written primarily for hikers, backpackers, ski tourers and snowshoers, but also including climbing and paddling. Circ. 3,300. Sub. $20. Uses 0-5 mss per issue. Payment: $10-15, copies, on publication. Byline given. Rights purchased: First. Submit ms, SASE. Dot matrix, photocopies, simultaneous submissions OK. Reports in 6 wks. Nonfiction: features 750-1,500. Photos: B&W glossy, 5x7 minimum size. Cover photo, 8x10 B&W glossy, $20, must show a scene from WA or OR, and include a person or people. Illustrations. Guidelines available; sample/$2. Index: 92, 103.

Signpost Press, Inc., 412 N. State Street, Bellingham, WA 98225. No submission info. Query w/SASE. Index: 130.

Signs of the Times, PO Box 7000, Boise, ID 83707. Editor: Kenneth J. Holland. 208–465–2577. Monthly magazine, "shows how *Bible* principles are relevant in today's world." Circ. 325,000. Payment: Money on acceptance. Byline given. Rights purchased: First. Submit ms, SASE. Phone queries, simultaneous submissions OK. Reports in 2-3 wks. Publishes in 3-6 mos. Nonfiction: 500-3,000 wds on "home, marriage, health, inspirational human interest articles that highlight a Biblical principle, and personal experiences solving problems with God's help." Photos: B&W contact sheets, 5x7 & 8x10 prints, 35mm color transparencies. Buys photos with or without articles. Guidelines, sample available. Index: 105.

The Silver Apple Branch, 1036 Hampshire Road, Victoria, BC V8S 4S9. Editor: Janet P. Reedman. Periodical of Irish myths and legends. Accepts freelance material. Payment: Copies. Byline given. Query w/SASE. Reports in 3-6 wks. Fiction, poetry. Max story length 1,500. Original fiction featuring Irish heroes. Index: 39, 51, 97.

Silver Bay Herb Farm, 9151 Tracyton Blvd., Bremerton, WA 98310. Contact: Mary Preus. 206–692–1340. Publisher. No submission info. Query w/SASE. Index: 56.

Silver Fox Connections, Emilie Johnson, 1244 S.W. 301st Street, Federal Way, WA 98003. Publisher. No submission info. Query w/SASE. Index: 130.

Silver Owl Publications, Inc., PO Box 51186, Seattle, WA 98115. 206–524–9071. Publisher. New Age books. Query w/SASE. Index: 93, 94, 105.

Silver Pennies Press, 1365 E. 30th Avenue, Eugene, OR 97405. No submission info. Query w/SASE. Index: 130.

Silver Seal Books, PO Box 106, Fox Island, WA 98333. Publisher. No submission info. Query w/SASE. Index: 130.

Silverfish Review, PO Box 3541, Eugene, OR 97403. Poetry review published 3 times a year. Accepts freelance material. Sponsors a poetry chapbook competition. Query w/SASE. Index: 97.

Silverleaf Press, PO Box 70189, Seattle, WA 98107. Editor: Ann E. Larson. Publishes 1-2 softcover original books a year. Accepts unsolicited submissions. Pays royalties on publication. Submit ms, SASE. Dot matrix, photocopied OK. Reports in 1-3 mo. Publishes in 6-12 mo. Accepts fiction, cartoons. Topics: feminist writing, "...does not have to be political, but should contain strong women (including Lesbian) characters." Currently accepting novels and short story collections. Catalog available. Index: 51, 57, 124.

The Silverton Appeal-Tribune, Mt. Angel News, 399 S. Water, Box 35, Silverton, OR 97381. 503–873–8385. Weekly newspaper. No submission info. Query w/SASE. Index: 33.

Single Scene, PO Box 248, Silverton, OR 97381. Contact: Editor. Monthly. No submission info. Query w/SASE. Index: 130.

Single Vision Publications, PO Box 804, Lebanon, OR 97335. 503–258–5888. Self-publisher 1 softcover book/yr. inspirational prose/poetry. Press run: 1,000. Not a freelance market. Index: 97, 105.

Singles Northwest Magazine, Box 458/618, The Parkway, Richland, WA 99352. Editor: B. Taliferro Hall. Monthly. No submission info. Query w/SASE. Index: 45.

Sinsemilla Tips Magazine, PO Box 2046, Corvallis, OR 97339. 503–757–8477. Editor: Don Parker. Ads: Tom Alexander. Quarterly magazine. Sub. $20. Circ. 15,000. Uses 4-5 freelance mss per issue. Pays $25-100 on publication. Acquires all rights. Byline given. Submit query w/clips, SASE. Dot matrix, photocopied, electronic, computer disc OK. Reports in 1 mo. Publishes in 3-6 mo. Accepts nonfiction, fiction, photos, car-

For lists of abbreviations and the key to index numbers, see "How to Use this Section" on page 75.

Writer's Northwest Handbook   177

toons. Prefer articles on cultivation of marijuana, i.e., interviews with growers, tips on cultivation, political reports. Shorts: 500-1,000 wds. Features: 1,000-2,000 wds. Photos: color or B&W, $10-50 per photo. Sample $6.50. Index: 3, 56, 98.

Siskiyou, Southern Oregon State College, Stevenson Union, Ashland, OR 97520. 503–482–6306. Newspaper. No submission info. Query w/ SASE. Index: 31, 39, 43.

Siskiyou Journal, The Siskiyou Regional Education Project, PO Box 741, Ashland, OR 97520. 503–482–5969. Editors: Marc Prevost & Jim Kelly. Ads: Susan Brock. Bimonthly. Sub. $16/$25. Circ. 5,000. Uses 4-6 freelance mss per issue. Pays money, copies on publication. Submit query w/clips, ms, SASE, phone. Dot matrix, photocopied, simultaneous, electronic subs OK. Reports in 2-4 mo. Accepts nonfiction, fiction, poetry, photos, cartoons, other. Sample $2. Index: 42, 61, 98.

The Siuslaw News, PO Box 10, 148 Maple Street, Florence, OR 97439. Editor: Robert Serra. 503–997–3441. Ads: Bruce Waterbury. Weekly newspaper. Circ. 5,000. Sub. Lane County $10/other $15. Accepts freelance material. Byline given. Query with ms, SASE. Phone queries, dot matrix, photocopies OK. Nonfiction, photos. Index: 33.

Skagit Argus, PO Box 739, Mount Vernon, WA 98273. 206–336–6555. Weekly newspaper. No submission info. Query w/SASE. Index: 33.

Skagit County Historical Society, PO Box 424, Mount Vernon, WA 98273. Publisher. No submission info. Query w/SASE. Index: 65, 123.

Skagit Farmer and Tribune, PO Box 153, Lynden, WA 98264. 206–354–4444. Weekly newspaper. No submission info. Query w/SASE. Index: 33.

Skagit Valley Herald, PO Box 578, Mount Vernon, WA 98273-0739. 206–336–5751. Daily newspaper. No submission info. Query w/SASE. Index: 33.

Skamania County Pioneer, PO Box 250, Stevenson, WA 98648. 509–427–8444. Weekly newspaper. No submission info. Query w/SASE. Index: 33.

The Skanner, 2337 N. Williams, PO Box 5455, Portland, OR 97228. Weekly tabloid of the Portland Black community. No submission info. Query w/SASE. Index: 20, 33.

Skein Publications, PO Box 5326, Eugene, OR 97405. No submission info. Query w/SASE. Index: 130.

Skies America, Plaza West, Suite 310, 9600 S.W. Oak Street, Portland, OR 97223. Editor: Robert Patterson. 503–244–2299. Inflight magazine. Accepts freelance material. Payment: $100-300 for feature articles, on publication. Query w/SASE. Nonfiction: features 1,200-1,500 wds; departments 500-700 wds, $50-100. Prefer photos with article, B&W prints and color transparencies. "Timely, original material in the fields of business, investing, travel, humor, health/medicine, sports, city features, geographical features." Guidelines available; sample/$3. Index: 24, 120.

Skipping Stones, c/o Aprovecho Institute, 80574 Hazelton Rd., Cottage Grove, OR 97424. 503–942–9434. Editor: Arun N. Toke. New quarterly magazine by and for children (multi-ethnic children's forum). Uses freelance mss. Pays in copies. Acquires 1st rights. Submit ms w/SASE. Accepts nonfiction, fiction, poetry, photos, cartoons. Topics: "Environmental awareness, cultural diversity, multi-ethnic literature." Pen-pal letters, children's activities, project reports welcome. Tips: Shorter items preferred (1-2 ds pages). If writing is other than English, submit translation if possible. Guidelines available. Sample $4. Index: 29, 39, 84.

Skookum Publications, Site 176 Comp 4, 1275 Riddle Road, Penticton, BC V2A 6J6. 604–492–3228. Editor: Doug Cox. Publisher of 2-3 softcover books a year. Does not accept freelance submissions. Index: 63, 65.

Skribent Press, 9700 S.W. Lakeside Drive, Tigard, OR 97223. No submission info. Query w/SASE. Index: 130.

Sky River Press, 236 E. Main, Ashland, OR 97520. Contact: Steve Bohlert/Asha Anderson. 503–488–0645. Publisher of 2 hard/softcover originals, reprints, subsidy books a year "which contribute to the development of a sustainable culture." Accepts freelance material. Rights purchased: First, all. Query, with outline, sample chapters, ms, SASE. Dot matrix, photocopies, simultaneous submissions OK. Nonfiction, fiction, poetry, photos, plays, cartoons. Index: 13, 35, 36.

Skydog Press, 6735 S.E. 78th, Portland, OR 97206. Contact: Dan Raphael. Publisher of fiction and poetry books. Submissions are through announced contests or by invitation. Payment: Copies on publication. Byline given. Dot matrix, photocopies, simultaneous submissions OK. Fiction, poetry. "More conventional poetry" than NRG. See NRG Magazine. Index: 51, 97.

Skyline West Press, PO Box 85171, Seattle, WA 98145-2171. Publisher. No submission info. Query w/SASE. Index: 130.

Skyviews, PO Box 2473, Seattle, WA, 98111. 206–323–6779. Editor: Jim Maloney. Periodical. No submission info. Query w/SASE. Index: 130.

Skyword, 1334 Seymour Street, Vancouver, BC V6B 3P3. Airline magazine. No submission info. Query w/SASE. Index: 120.

SL Publishers, Box F110-223, Blaine, WA 98230. No submission info. Query w/SASE. Index: 130.

Slightly West, The Evergreen State College, CAB 305, Olympia, WA 98505. 206–866–6000. Editor: Christie Eikeberg. Biannual. $2. Circ. 1,500. Uses freelance material. Pays in copies. Byline given. Submit ms, SASE. Dot matrix, photocopied OK. Reports in 1 mo. Accepts nonfiction, fiction, poetry, photos, cartoons. Guidelines available. Index: 31, 51, 97.

Slo-Pitch News, Varsity Publications, 2300 N.E. 65th St., Seattle, WA 98115. Monthly. No submission info. Query w/SASE. Index: 115.

Slug Press, 128 E. 23rd Avenue, Vancouver, BC V5V 1X2. No submission info. Query w/SASE. Index: 130.

Small Farmer's Journal, PO Box 68, Reedsport, OR 97467. Farmer's literary quarterly, including poetry. No submission info. Query w/SASE. Index: 3.

Small Pleasures Press, 88 Virginia Street #29, Seattle, WA 98101. No submission info. Query w/SASE. Index: 130.

Small World Publications, PO Box 305, Corvallis, OR 97339. 503–757–8231. Editors: Rick & Suzannah Cooper. Self-publisher. Not a freelance market. Index: 61, 67, 68.

The Smallholder Publishing Collective, Argenta, B.C. V0G 1B0. 604–366–4283. Editor: Betty Tillotson. Magazine published approx. 4 times a year. Sub. $14/6 issues. Circ. 750. Uses freelance material. No pay. Acquires all rights. Byline given. Submit query, SASE. Photocopies OK. "We're a group of volunteers putting together a magazine for country people regarding rural living (all aspects) & our copy is largely made up of letters and articles from readers...non-profit." Index: 33, 56, 106.

For lists of abbreviations and the key to index numbers, see "How to Use this Section" on page 75.

178 Market Listings

Smith, Smith & Smith Publishing Company, 17515 S.W. Blue Heron Road, Lake Oswego, OR 97034. No submission info. Query w/SASE. Index: 130.

Smith-Western, Inc., 1133 N.W. Glisan Street, Portland, OR 97209. Publisher. No submission info. Query w/SASE. Index: 130.

Smoke Signals, Pacific Press Publishing Association, 1350 Kings Road, Nampa, ID 83605. Editor: Francis A. Soper. Monthly of the Seventh-Day Adventist Church. No submission info. Query w/SASE. Index: 105.

SmokeRoot, University of Montana, Department of English, Missoula, MT 59812. University literary publication. No submission info. Query w/SASE. Index: 31, 76.

Smuggler's Cove Publishing, 107 W. John Street, Seattle, WA 98119. No submission info. Query w/SASE. Index: 130.

Smurfs In Hell, 2210 N. 9th, Boise, ID 83702. Contact: Editor. Periodical. No submission info. Query w/SASE. Index: 130.

Snake River Alliance Newsletter, PO Box 1731, Boise, ID 83701. Monthly. Circ. 1,200. No submission info. Query w/SASE. Index: 130.

Snake River Echoes, PO Box 244, Rexburg, ID 83440. Editors: Louis Clements/Ralph Thompson. 208–356–9101. Quarterly on Snake River history. Circ. 700. Sub. $10. Uses 6 mss per issue. Byline given. Submit ms, SASE. Photocopies OK. Nonfiction, photos (B&W). "We print history of Snake River area of Eastern Idaho, Eastern Wyoming." Sample/$1. Index: 65, 69, 89.

The Sneak Preview, PO Box 639, Grants Pass, OR 97526. 503–474–3044. Editor: Curtis Hayden. Ads: Les Addison. Biweekly. Sub. $10. Circ. 10,000. Uses 1-2 freelance mss per issue. Pays money on publication. Byline given. Submit ms. Photocopied OK. Accepts nonfiction, fiction, poetry, photos, cartoons. Sample $.50. Index: 33, 39, 45.

Snohomish County Tribune, PO Box 71, Snohomish, WA 98290. 206–776–7546. Weekly newspaper. No submission info. Query w/SASE. Index: 33.

Snohomish Publishing Company, PO Box 499, Snohomish, WA 98290. Contact: David Mach. 206–568–4121. Publisher of 50 softcover, reprint books a year. Accepts freelance material. Rights purchased: First. Query with outline, SASE. Photocopies, electronic OK. Nonfiction, fiction, poetry, photos, plays, cartoons. Guidelines available. Index: 77, 80, 102.

The Snow Man Press, 1765 Rockland Avenue, Victoria, BC V8S 1X1. No submission info. Query w/SASE. Index: 130.

Snowmobile West, Harris Publishing Company, 520 Park Avenue, Idaho Falls, ID 83402. Editor: Darryl Harris. Bimonthly. Circ. 95,000. No submission info. Query w/SASE. Index: 38, 92, 103.

Socialist Party of Canada, PO Box 4280, Sta. A, Victoria, BC V8X 3X8. Publisher. No submission info. Query w/SASE. Index: 98, 112.

Society for Industrial Archeology, Dept. of History/Social Sciences, Northern Montana College, Havre, MT 59501. Contact: Editor. Quarterly. No submission info. Query w/SASE. Index: 7, 31.

Society of Photo-Optical Instrumentation Engineers, PO Box 10, 1022 19th Street, Bellingham, WA 98227. Publisher. No submission info. Query w/SASE. Index: 24, 109, 117.

Society of Professors of Education, Portland State University, School of Education, PO Box 751, Portland, OR 97207. Publisher. No submission info. Query w/SASE. Index: 31, 43.

Solo Magazine, Box 1231, Sisters, OR 97759. Quarterly. No submission info. Query w/SASE. Index: 130.

Solstice Books, PO Box 76, Winlaw, BC V0G 2J0. Publisher. No submission info. Query w/SASE. Index: 130.

Solstice Press, Box 111272, Anchorage, AK 99511. Contact: Director. No submission info. Query w/SASE. Index: 130.

Solstice Press, PO Box 9223, 112 S. 4th Street, Moscow, ID 83843. Contact: Ivar Nelson or Pat Hart. 208–882–0888. Publisher of 3-4 softcover originals a year on camping, local history and travel in the NW. Payment: Royalties. Query with ms, outline, sample chapters, SASE. "We cater to Pacific Northwesterners and will consider anything which would be of interest to these people. We focus particularly on local history and outdoor recreation (camping series: *Rainy Day Guides*)." Index: 65, 103, 120.

Solus Impress, PO Box 22, Sirdar, BC V0B 2C0. Publisher. No submission info. Query w/SASE. Index: 130.

Solus Impress, Porthill, ID 83853. Publisher. No submission info. Query w/SASE. Index: 130.

SONCAP News, Southern Oregon Northwest Coalition for Alternatives to Pesticides, PO Box 402, Grants Pass, OR 97526. 503–474–6034. Editor: Louise Nicholson. Quarterly newsletter. Sub. $10. Circ. 700. Accepts freelance material. Submit ms. Dot matrix, photocopied, simultaneous, electronic/modem OK. Accepts nonfiction, poetry, cartoons. Topics: forestry & environmental ecology, pesticides & herbicides alternatives; air, soil, water, visual quality; worker right-to-know; roadside vegetation management, organic gardening, clearcutting, etc. Sample available. Index: 46, 55, 56.

Sono Nis Press, 1745 Blanshard Street, Victoria, BC V8W 2J8. 604–382–1024. Editor: Patricia M. Sloan. Publishes 10 hard/softcover originals per yr. Accepts unsolicited submissions. Pays royalties. Submit query w/clips, SASE. Dot matrix, photocopied, simultaneous OK. Reports in 3 wks. Accepts nonfiction, poetry. Index: 23, 65, 97.

SOS Publishing, Box 68290, Oak Grove, OR 97268. No submission info. Query w/SASE. Index: 130.

Gordon Soules Books Publishers Ltd., 1352-B Marine Dr., West Vancouver, BC V7T 15B. 604–922–6588. Editor: Gordon Soules. Publishes 4 hard/softcover nonfiction books a yr. Accepts unsolicited submissions. Query w/clips, SASE. Index: 2, 23, 103.

The Source, 2575 NE Kathryn, Ste. 28, Hillsboro, OR 97124. 503–693–1390. Editor: Suzann Laudenslager. Periodical. No infor. Query w/ SASE. Index: 126.

Source Publishing, 6105 S.W. Bonita Road #K305, Lake Oswego, OR 97034-3227. Contact: Jan Kennedy. 503–224–5529. No submission info. Query w/SASE. Index: 130.

The Sourdough, Fairbanks Law Library, 604 Barnette St., Fairbanks, AK 99701. Contact: Editor. Periodical. No submission info. Query w/ SASE. Index: 74, 104.

Sourdough Enterprises, 16401 3rd Avenue S.W., Seattle, WA 98166. Contact: Howard Clifford. 206–244–8115. Publisher of 2-3 softcover

For lists of abbreviations and the key to index numbers, see "How to Use this Section" on page 75.

Writer's Northwest Handbook   179

originals, reprints a year for an audience of travel, history, rail fans. Press run: 500-20,000. Accepts freelance material. Rights purchased: First. Query w/SASE. Photocopies, simultaneous submissions OK. Reports in 2-3 wks. Nonfiction. Index: 4, 64, 120.

South County Citizen, c/o Northshore Citizen, PO Box 706, Bothell, Wa 98041. 206–486–1231. Weekly newspaper. No submission info. Query w/SASE. Index: 33.

South District Journal, 2720 Hanford Street, Seattle, WA 98144. 206–723–1300. Weekly newspaper. No submission info. Query w/SASE. Index: 33.

South Pierce County Dispatch, 115 Center St. E., Eatonville, WA 98328. 206–832 4411. Newspaper. No submission info. Query w/SASE. Index: 33.

South Whidbey Record, c/o Box 10, Oak Harbor, WA 98277. 206–321–5300. Weekly newspaper. No submission info. Query w/SASE. Index: 33.

Southeastern Log, Box 7900, Ketchikan, AK 99901. Editor: Nikki Murray Jones. 907–225–3157. Periodical. No submission info. Query w/SASE. Index: 130.

Southern Oregon Historical Society, PO Box 480, Jacksonville, OR 97530. Publisher. No submission info. Query w/SASE. Index: 64, 91.

Southern Willamette Alliance/Eugene Peace Works, 454 Willamette, Eugene, OR 97403. 503–484–1665. Editors: Jeff Land/Freda London. Ads: Dave Zupan. Monthly newspaper. Sub. $15/yr. Circ. 10,000. Uses 1-3 freelance mss per issue. Pay varies. Byline given. Submit by phone query, SASE. Electronic, computer disc OK. Accepts nonfiction, photos, cartoons. Art work for cover and cartoons especially desired. "Excellent exposure to 20,000 or more." Index: 37, 46, 98.

The Southwestern, Southwestern Oregon Community College, Coos Bay, OR 97420. 503–888–2525. Biweekly newspaper. No submission info. Query w/SASE. Index: 31, 39, 43.

Southwestern Oregon Publishing Co., 350 Commercial, Coos Bay, OR 97420. 503–269–1222. Publisher. No submission info. Query w/SASE. Index: 130.

Sovereign Press, 326 Harris Road, Rochester, WA 98579. Publisher of 5 books a year. No submission info. Query w/SASE. Index: 130.

Sovereignty, Inc., PO Box 909, Eastsound, WA 98245. Contact: Robin Weischedel. 206–376–2177. Self-publisher of 4 hardcover books a year for laymen and professionals, New age and metaphysical. Print run: 30,000. Not a freelance market. Catalog available. Index: 13, 94, 100.

Speaking of Taxes, Associated Taxpayers of Idaho, PO Box 1665, Boise, ID 83701. Editor: Russell Westerberg. Irregular periodical. Circ. 1,500. No submission info. Query w/SASE. Index: 42, 69, 101.

Special Child Publications, J.B. Preston, Editor & Publisher, PO Box 33548, Seattle, WA 98133. 206—771–5711. Publisher of 5-10 softcover originals, subsidy (rarely) books a year. Print run: 500-2,000. Rarely accepts freelance material. Payment: 10% of cash received, payable 6 mos after close of royalty period. Rights purchased: All. Query with outline, SASE. Photocopies OK. Reports in 1 month. Publishes in 1-3 yrs. Professional books, college texts, curriculum guides, assessment instruments. Tips: "Mss must be neatly typed, following *Chicago Manual*. Authorial style should approximate *Psychology Today* or *Omni*. Guidelines, catalog available. Index: 43, 100, 118.

Special Interest Publications, 202-1132 Hamilton Street, Vancouver, BC V6B 2S2. No submission info. Query w/SASE. Index: 130.

The Spectator, Seattle University, Seattle, WA 98122. Contact: Editor. Periodical. No submission info. Query w/SASE. Index: 31, 43.

Spencer Butte Press, 84889 Harry Taylor Road, Eugene, OR 97405. 503–345–3962. Self-publisher of softcover books. Not a freelance market. Index: 62, 97.

Spice West Publishing Company, PO Box 2044, Pocatello, ID 83201. No submission info. Query w/SASE. Index: 130.

Spilyay Tymoo, PO Box 870, Warm Springs, OR 97761. 503–553–1644. Editor: Sid Miller. Sub. $9. Biweekly newspaper for tribal membership. Uses local news, Native American issues. Sample $1. Index: 33, 84, 87.

Spindrift, Shoreline Community College, 16101 Greenwood Ave. N., Seattle, WA 98133. 206–546–4785. Editor/Ads: Sheila Bender. Annual magazine. Sub. $6-7. Circ. 500. Accepts freelance material. Pays copy on publication. Byline given. Submit ms, SASE. Dot matrix, photocopied OK. Reports in 3 mo. Accepts nonfiction, fiction, poetry, photos, plays, cartoons, B&W drawings. Tips: 4,500 wds on prose, 6 poems, 15 pages dialogue. Photos & art: B&W, 24x24 max. Audience includes essay, fiction & poetry lovers, art enthusiasts. "Genuine work that avoids greeting card sentiment." Sample $6. Index: 31, 51, 97.

Spirit Mountain Press, PO Box 1214, Fairbanks, AK 99707. Contact: Larry Laraby. 907–452–7585. Self-publisher of 3-6 softcover books about AK. Print run: 1,500. Accepts freelance material. Rights purchased: First. Submit ms, SASE. Dot matrix, photocopies OK. Reports in 1-6 mos. Publishes in 6-12 mos. Nonfiction, fiction, poetry. "We are looking for material from or about Alaska primarily." Catalog available. Index: 4, 18, 97.

Spiritual Women's Times, PO Box 51186, Seattle, WA 98115-1186. 206–524–9071. Editor: Krysta Gibson. Quarterly newspaper. Sub. $7.50/yr. Circ. 15,000. Uses 5-10 freelance mss per issue. Pays by subscription on acceptance. Acquires 1st rights. Byline given. Submit ms w/SASE. Photocopies OK. Reports in 30-60 days. Accepts nonfiction, poetry, photos, cartoons. Topics: women's issues dealing with empowering women from within; healing, spirituality, psychology, redefining the feminine in our society. Photos 5X7 or larger B&W glossy. Pictures of women which give us images inspiring growth. Guidelines available SASE. Sample $1. Index: 50, 105, 124.

Spit in the Ocean, 85829 Ridgeway Road, Pleasant Hill, OR 97401. Editor: Ken Kesey. Periodical. No submission info. Query w/SASE. Index: 130.

Spokane Area Economic Development Council, PO Box 2147, W. 1020 Riverside, Spokane, WA 99210. Publisher. No submission info. Query w/SASE. Index: 42, 123.

Spokane Chronicle, PO Box 2160, Spokane, WA 99210. 509–455–7010. Daily newspaper. No submission info. Query w/SASE. Index: 33.

Spokane House Enterprises, Box 4, Nine Mile Falls, WA 99026. Contact: Editor. Publisher. No submission info. Query w/SASE. Index: 130.

Spokane Interplayers Ensemble, PO Box 1691, Spokane, WA 99210. Interested in scripts. No submission info. Query w/SASE. Index: 41.

For lists of abbreviations and the key to index numbers, see "How to Use this Section" on page 75.

180   Market Listings

Spokes, Rotary Club of Portland, Penthouse Floor, Hotel Benson, Portland, OR 97205. Weekly periodical. No submission info. Query w/SASE. Index: 119.

The Spokesman-Review, PO Box 2160, Spokane, WA 99210. 509–455–7010. Daily newspaper. No submission information. Query w/SASE. Index: 33.

Sport Flyer, PO Box 98786, Tacoma, WA 98499. Editor: Bruce Williams. 206–588–1743. Monthly tabloid devoted to recreational aviation. Circ. 10,000. Rights purchased: One time rights, 1st or 2nd. Query w/SASE. Phone queries, dot matrix, simultaneous submissions OK. Reports in 2-3 wks. Publishes in 2-3 mos. Nonfiction: 1,500-3,500 wds on "news related to aviation, safety, pilot reports." Departments/columns/fillers, query. Photos: B&W prints $10, color slides or prints $25-50. Guidelines available; sample/$2. Index: 15, 103, 115.

Sports Digest, The Enterprise Courier, PO Box 471, Oregon City, OR 97045. 503–656–1911. Editor: Dick Mezejewski. Monthly. No submission info. Query w/SASE. Index: 103, 115.

Sports Northwest Magazine, 4556 University Way, Seattle, WA 98105. Editor: John Erben. 206–547–9709. Monthly tabloid on "participant sports: running, bicycling, hiking, skiing, triathletics, and lesser known sports such as ultimate frisbee, lacrosse, etc." Circ. 25,000. Payment: $1.50 column inch, on publication. Byline given. Query w/SASE. Phone queries, simultaneous submissions OK, modem preferred. Nonfiction: up to 2,000 wds. Fiction: up to 2,000 wds (humor, a personal account or satire." Photos: color slide for cover pays $85, interior B&W action shots, pay varies. Guidelines available. Sample/SASE. Index: 95, 103, 115.

Spotlight, PO Box 51103, Seattle, WA 98115. 206–527–2693. Editor: Ellen Hokanson. Newsletter published 3-4 times a year. Sub. free. Circ. 5,000. Promotes books for a fee. Not a freelance market. Catalog & sample free. Index: 89, 102.

Spotlight Northwest, PO Box 51103, Seattle, WA 98115. 206–527–2693. Editor: Ellen Hokanson. Semiannual newsletter. Sub. free. Circ. 200. Promotes books for a fee. Not a freelance market. Catalog & sample free. Index: 89, 102.'

The Sprague Advocate, PO Box 327, Sprague, WA 99032. 509–257–2311. Editor/Ads: Kim Nolt. Weekly newspaper. Sub. $17/yr. instate. Circ. 600. Accepts freelance material. Byline given. Submit query w/clips, SASE. Dot matrix, photocopied OK. Accepts nonfiction. Must be info relevant to area, and only on space-available basis. No payment for unsolicited copy. Sample $1. Index: 33, 39, 45.

Springfield Historical Commission, Planning Department, Springfield City Hall, Springfield, OR 97477. Publisher. No submission info. Query w/SASE. Index: 65, 91.

The Springfield News, 1887 Laura Street, Box 139, Springfield, OR 97477. 503–746–1671. Daily newspaper. No submission info. Query w/SASE. Index: 33.

The Sproutletter, Sprouting Publications, Box 62, Ashland, OR 97520. Editor: Ann Roberts. 503–535–2469. Ads: same. Bimonthly devoted to holistic health through live and raw foods, sprouting and indoor gardens. Query w/SASE. Nonfiction, photos. Index: 56, 61.

ST 2 Publishing, 203 Si Town Road, Castle Rock, WA 98611. No submission info. Query w/SASE. Index: 130.

St. Johns Review, 8410 N. Lombard Street, Portland, OR 97203. 503–286–0321. Weekly newspaper. No submission info. Query w/SASE. Index: 33.

St. Nectarios Press, 10300 Ashworth Avenue N., Seattle, WA 98133-9410. 206–522–4471. Self-publisher of 3-4 softcover originals, reprints a year for Eastern Orthodox Christian audience. Print run: 2,000. Not a freelance market. Catalog available. Index: 105.

St. Paul's Press, PO Box 100, Sandy, OR 97055. No submission info. Query w/SASE. Index: 130.

Stamp Collector, PO Box 10, Albany, OR 97321. 503–928–3569. Editor: Kyle Johnson. Ads: Joan Hanten. Weekly newspaper. Sub. $19.95. Circ. 22,000. Uses 8 freelance mss per issue. Pays $20+ on publication. Acquires 1st rights. Byline given. Submit query w/SASE, phone query. Dot matrix OK. Reports in 14 days. Publishing time variable. Accepts nonfiction geared toward stamp collectors, including beginner and advanced collectors and their interests. B&W photos preferred. Guidelines available. Sample $1. Index: 30, 38.

The Stamp Wholesaler, PO Box 706, Albany, OR 97321. 503–928–4484. Editor: Sherrie Steward. Ads: Joan Hanten. Newspaper published 28 times a yr. Sub. $16.95. Circ. 6,000. Uses 4 freelance mss per issue. Pays money on publication. Acquires 1st rights. Byline given. Submit phone query, SASE. Dot matrix OK. Accepts nonfiction. Topics: "Dedicated to promoting the growth and prosperity of the philatelic industry through the exchange of information and ideas." Includes feature articles about stamp dealers and other news of the stamp industry. Sample available. Index: 24, 30, 38.

Standard-Register, PO Box 988, Tekoa, WA 99033. 509–284–5782. Editor: Bonita Lawhead. Ads: Barbara Schweiter. Weekly newspaper. Sub. $17/yr. in-county. Circ. 1,800. Uses one freelance mss per issue. Pays $.50 per col. inch on publication. Byline given. Submit query w/clips, SASE, phone query. Dot matrix, photocopied. Reports in 2 wks. Publishes in 30-60 days. Accepts nonfiction of local human interest, local recreation, agriculture. B&W photos or negatives, color photos, $3 on publication. Sample $.35. Index: 3, 33, 103.

Stanwood/Camano News, PO Box 999, Stanwood, WA 98292. 206–629–2155. Weekly newspaper. No submission info. Query w/SASE. Index: 33.

The Star, PO Box 150, Grand Coulee, WA 99133. 509–633–1350. Weekly newspaper. No submission info. Query w/SASE. Index: 33.

Star Press, Box 835, Friday Harbor, WA 98250. No submission info. Query w/SASE. Index: 130.

Star System Press, PO Box 15202, Wedgewood Station, Seattle, WA 98115. No submission info. Query w/SASE. Index: 130.

Star Valley Publications, PO Box 421, Noti, OR 97461. No submission info. Query w/SASE. Index: 130.

Starbright Books, 1611 E. Dow Road, Freeland, WA 98249. Publisher. No submission info. Query w/SASE. Index: 130.

Starmont House, PO Box 851, Mercer Island, WA 98040. Publisher. No submission info. Query w/SASE. Index: 130.

Starwind Press, 507 3rd Avenue #547, Seattle, WA 98104. 206–523–1201. No submission info. Query w/SASE. Query w/SASE. Index: 130.

Stat, Oregon Medical Association, 5210 S.W. Corbett, Portland, OR 97201. Monthly. No submission info. Query w/SASE. Index: 61, 81, 119.

Statesman-Examiner, PO Box 271, Colville, WA 99114. 509–684–4567. Weekly newspaper. No submission info. Query w/SASE. Index: 33.

For lists of abbreviations and the key to index numbers, see "How to Use this Section" on page 75.

Writer's Northwest Handbook   **181**

Statesman-Journal, 280 Church Street N.E., Box 13009, Salem, OR 97309. 503–399–6611. Daily newspaper. No submission info. Query w/ SASE. Index: 33.

Stay Away Joe Publishers, Box 2054, Great Falls, MT 59401. No submission info. Query w/SASE. Index: 130.

Stay Smart Shoppers, 2729 S. Marylhurst Drive, West Lynn, OR 97068. Publisher. No submission info. Query w/SASE. Index: 36.

Stayton Mail, PO Box 400, Stayton, OR 97383. 503–769–6338. Weekly newspaper. No submission info. Query w/SASE. Index: 33.

Stephens Press, Drawer 1441, Spokane, WA 99210. No submission info. Query w/SASE. Index: 130.

Stepping Out Magazine, PO Box 113, Lake Oswego, OR 97034. Editor: Lucinda Wagenblast. 503–774–5151. Ads: Leslie Jones. Semiannual of creative endeavors in the arts, business and living. Circ. 180,000. Sub. $14/2 year. Accepts freelance material. Payment: Money, varies upon article requirements, on publication. Byline given. Rights purchased: All. Query w/SASE. Photocopies OK. Nonfiction: "Articles on the arts, business and travel. This magazine is intended to inform and enlighten readers about the creative undertakings and achievements on the West coast." Guidelines available; sample/$2.50. Index: 10, 24, 120.

Steppingstone Magazine, Canby High School, 721 S.W. 4th Street, Canby, OR 97013. 503–266–5811. Editor: Paul Dage. Annual. $1. Circ. 300. Not a freelance market. Index: 24, 25.

Steppingstone Press, PO Box 2757, Boise, ID 83701. 208–384–1577. Editors: Martha Miller, Dorris Murdock. Publisher. No submission info. Query w/SASE. Index: 116.

Sterling Travel Publications, 12616 12th Avenue, Seattle, WA 98168. No submission info. Query w/SASE. Index: 120.

The Steward, Erb Memorial Union, University of Oregon, Eugene, OR 97403. Periodical. No submission info. Query w/SASE. Index: 31.

The Stoma Press, 13231 42nd Avenue N.E., Seattle, WA 98125. No submission info. Query w/SASE. Index: 130.

M.J. Stone Publishers, 1808 Seattle Tower, Seattle, WA 98125. No submission info. Query w/SASE. Index: 130.

Stonechild Press, PO Box 2469, Havre, MT 59501. Editor: Paul Fussette. Publisher. No submission info. Query w/SASE. Index: 130.

Stonehouse Publications, Timber Butte Road, Box 390, Sweet, ID 83670. No submission info. Query w/SASE. Index: 130.

Stoneydale Press Publishing Company, 295 Kootenai Creek Road, Stevensville, MT 59890. No submission info. Query w/SASE. Index: 130.

Stories & Letters Digest, 801 S. Puget Sound Ave., Tacoma, WA 98405. 206–752–9434. Editor: James R. Humphreys. Quarterly magazine. Sub. $9. Circ. 300. Uses 4-8 freelance mss per issue. Pays 1/4-1/2 cent/word on acceptance. Acquires 1st rights. Byline given. Submit ms, SASE. Dot matrix, photocopied OK. Reports in 2-4 wks. Publishes in 3-6 mos. Accepts fiction, other. "Literate, entertaining and wholesome short stories. No restrictions on subject matter as long as it is not pornographic...also publishes letters." Guidelines available. Sample $2.50. Index: 45, 51.

Storypole Press, 11015 Bingham Avenue E., Tacoma, WA 98446. No submission info. Query w/SASE. Index: 130.

Straub Printing & Publishing Company, 4535 Union Bay Place N.E., Seattle, WA 98105. No submission info. Query w/SASE. Index: 130.

Strawberry Fields, PO Box 33786, Seattle, WA 98133-0786 Editor: Ken Boisse. Bimonthly. No submission info. Query w/SASE. Index: 130.

Street Times, 1236 S.W. Salmon, Portland, OR 97205. 503–223–4121. Editor: Laura Williams. Bimonthly. Circ. 1,500. Uses freelance material. No submission info. Query w/SASE. Accepts nonfiction, fiction, poetry, photos, cartoons. Sample available. Index: 29.

Studio 403, PO Box 70672, Seattle, WA 98107-0672. Contact: Editor. Publisher (fiction, photos, cartoons, other). No submission info. Query w/ SASE. Index: 51, 68, 95.

Studio Solstone, PO Box 4304, Pioneer Sq. Station, Seattle, WA 98110. Contact: Michael Yaeger. 206–624–9102. Self-publisher of 2 softcover books a year. Print run: 5,000. No submission info. Query w/SASE. Index: 130.

Subterranean Company, PO Box 10233, Eugene, OR 97440. Publisher. No submission info. Query w/SASE. Index: 130.

Sugar Producer, Harris Publishing Company, 520 Park Avenue, Idaho Falls, ID 83402. Editor: Darryl Harris. Semiannual periodical. Circ. 20,000. No submission info. Query w/SASE. Index: 3, 24.

Sumner House Press, 2527 W. Kennewick Ave., Suite 190, Kennewick, WA 99336. 509–783–7800. Editor: R. F. Hill. Publisher. No submission info. Query w/SASE. Index: 130

Sun, PO Box 689, Sunnyside, WA 98944. 509–837–3701. Weekly newspaper. No submission info. Query w/SASE. Index: 33.

The Sun, 248 S. Bridge, Box 68, Sheridan, OR 97378. 503–843–2312. Weekly newspaper. No submission info. Query w/SASE. Index: 33.

The Sun—Editorial, 2250 Granville St., Vancouver, BC V6H 3G2. Contact: Editor. Periodical. No submission info. Query w/SASE. Index: 130.

Sun-Enterprise, 1697 Monmouth Street, Box 26, Independence, OR 97351. 503–838–3467. Weekly newspaper. No submission info. Query w/ SASE. Index: 33.

Sun King Publishing Company, PO Box 68503, Seattle, WA 98168-0503. No submission info. Query w/SASE. Index: Index: 130.

Sun Magic, 911 N.E. 45th, Seattle, WA 98105. Publisher. No submission info. Query w/SASE. Index: 130.

Sun Moon Press, PO Box 1516, Eugene, OR 97440. No submission info. Query w/SASE. Index: 130.

The Sun Tribune, 104 E. Central, Box 430, Sutherlin, OR 97479. 503–459–2261. Weekly newspaper. No submission info. Query w/SASE. Index: 33.

Sun Valley Books, Box 1688, Sun Valley, ID 83358. Self-publisher. No submission info. Query w/SASE. Index: 130.

Sun Valley Center for Arts & Humanities, Dollar Road, Sun Valley, ID 83353. Contact: Director. No submission info. Query w/SASE. Index: 10.

Sun Valley Magazine, PO Box 2950, Ketchum, ID 83340. Editor: Mike Riedel. Published 3 times a year. Circ. 2,600. No submission info. Query w/SASE. Index: 45, 69, 103.

For lists of abbreviations and the key to index numbers, see "How to Use this Section" on page 75.

Sunburst, 1322 Coral Drive W., Tacoma, WA 98466-5832. Publisher. No submission info. Query w/SASE. Index: 130.

Sunburst Press, PO Box 14205, Portland, OR 97214. Editor: Johnny Baranski. Ads: Grace Jewett. Self-publisher of 1 softcover original book a year. Press run: 300-1,000. Not a freelance market. Catalog available. Index: 93, 97, 105.

Sundance Publishing Company, 1270 Colgan Court S.E., Salem, OR 97302. No submission info. Query w/SASE. Index: 130.

Sunfire Publications, PO Box 3399, Langley, BC V3A 4R7. 604–576–6561. Contact: Garnet Basque. Publisher of hard/softcover originals, reprints on "historical subjects from British Columbia, Alberta and the Yukon." Catalog available. Index: 23, 63, 90.

Sunnyside Daily News, PO Box 878, Sunnyside, WA 98944. 509–837–4500. Daily newspaper. No submission info. Query w/SASE. Index: 33.

Sunrise Publishing, PO Box 38, Lincoln City, OR 97367. No submission info. Query w/SASE. Index: 130.

Sunrise Tortoise Books, Box 61, Sandpoint, ID 83864. Publisher. No submission info. Query w/SASE. Index: 130.

Survival Education Association, 9035 Golden Givens Road, Tacoma, WA 98445. Publisher. No submission info. Query w/SASE. Index: 130.

Swale Publications, 4003 Airport Way S., Seattle, WA 98108. Editor: Roberto Valenze/Phoebe Bosche. Periodical. No submission info. Query w/SASE. Index: 130.

Swedish Press, 1661 Duranleau Street, Vancouver, BC V6H 3S3. Editor/ads: Anders Neumueller. 604–682–3404. Monthly of Swedish interest. Sub. $12. Uses 2 mss per issue. Payment: Copies. Byline given. Rights purchased: First. Submit ms, SASE. Photocopies OK. Nonfiction. "Swedes, Swedish descendants and topics interesting to them as well as Swedish slants on general stories are welcomed by *Swedish Press* — North America's only Swedish monthly magazine — published since 1929." Photos: B&W and color landscapes for cover. Swedes & Swedish interest B&W on inside. Sample/$1 w/SASE. Index: 84, 95.

Sweet Forever Publishing, PO Box 1000, Eastsound, WA 98245. Contact: Editor. Publisher. No submission info. Query w/SASE. Index: 130.

Sweet Reason: A Journal of Ideas, History/Culture, Oregon Committee for the Humanities, 418 S.W. Washington, Rm 410, Portland, OR 97204. Editor: Charles Deemer. 503–241–0543. Annual. Circ. 7,000. Accepts freelance material. Writers need humanities expertise. Payment: Up to $.07 wd, on publication. Byline given. Rights purchased: First. Query w/ms, SASE. Dot matrix, photocopies OK. Reports in 4-8 mos. Nonfiction & essays on topics relevant to the humanities, 2,000-5,000 wds. Tips: "Specialized journal; read recent issue, query editor." Guidelines/sample available. Index: 39, 44, 64.

Syringa Publishing, 1340 Eldorado #D, Boise, ID 83704. Editor: Susan A. Lewis. Publisher. No submission info. Query w/SASE. Index: 130.

Table Rock Sentinel, Southern Oregon Historical Society, PO Box 480, Jacksonville, OR 97530-0480. 503–899–1847. Editor: Natalie Brown. Ads: Ted Lawson. Self-publisher of membership magazine & newsletter. Circ. 2,000. Uses one freelance ms per issue. Requires historical accuracy & expertise. Pays money ($10-100) on acceptance (30-60 days). Byline given. Submit query w/clips, SASE. Dot matrix, photocopied OK. Reports in 30 days. Publishing time varies. Accepts nonfiction feature articles, poetry, book reviews. Topics: relating to the history of the southern Oregon region. Photos 8X10 glossy, professional ($5-10). Guidelines available. Sample $2.50. Index: 65, 91.

Tacoma Daily Index, PO Box 1303, Tacoma, WA 98401. 206–627–4853. Daily newspaper. No submission info. Query w/SASE. Index: 33.

Tacoma News Tribune, PO Box 11000, Tacoma, WA 98411-0008. Editor: Al Gibbs. 206–597–8551. Daily newspaper. "The only freelance writing currently being accepted by our newspaper is for the travel section." Query w/SASE. Index: 33, 120.

Tahana Whitecrow Foundation, PO Box 18181, Salem, OR 97305. Editor: Melanie Smith. Publisher. No submission info. Query w/SASE. Index: 130.

Tahlkie Books, Landing Road, Skamania, WA 98648. Publisher. No submission info. Query w/SASE. Index: 130.

Tai Chi School, PO Box 2424, Bellingham, WA 98227. Contact: Editor. Publisher. No submission info. Query w/SASE. Index: 115.

Talonbooks, 201 - 1019 E. Cordova Street, Vancouver, BC V6A 1M8. Publisher of books on drama, fiction, poetry. No submission info. Query w/SASE. Index: 41, 51, 97.

Tao of Wing Chun Do, 11023 N.E. 131st, Kirkland, WA 98033. Publisher. No submission info. Query w/SASE. Index: 130.

TAPJOE: The Anaprocrustean Poetry Journal of Enumclaw, PO Box 5. Roslyn, WA 98941. Editor: Lisa Therrell. Ads: Steve McConnell. Journal/chapbook published 2-3 times a year. Sub. $6.50/4 issues. Circ. 250. Accepts freelance material. Pays in copies. Acquires 1st rights. Submit ms, SASE. Photocopies OK. Reports in 1-3 mo. Publishes in 2-6 mo. Accepts poetry only. Guidelines available. Sample $1.50. Index: 97.

Target Seattle, 909 4th Avenue, Seattle, WA 98104. Publisher. No submission info. Query w/SASE. Index: 130.

Tari Book Publishers, 146 E. 34th Avenue, Eugene, OR 97405. No submission info. Query w/SASE. Index: 130.

TASH (The Association for Persons with Severe Handicaps), 7010 Roosevelt Way, NE, Seattle, WA 98115. Publisher. No submission info. Query w/SASE. Index: 126.

Tass Graphics, 2727 Front Street, Klamath Falls, OR 97601. Publisher. No submission info. Query w/SASE. Index: 130.

Tax Fax Publishing Co., PO Box 84275, Vancouver, WA 98684. Contact: Editor. Publisher. No submission info. Query w/SASE. Index: 130.

Teaching Home, P.O. Box 20219, Portland, OR 97220-0219. Editor: Sue Welch. Periodical. No submission info. Query w/SASE. Index: 28, 29, 43.

Teaching Research Infant and Child Center, Monmouth, OR 97361. Contact: Editor. Periodical. No submission info. Query w/SASE. Index: 28, 29, 43.

Tech Talk, Oregon Institute of Technology, Klamath Falls, OR 97601. 503–882–6321. Weekly newspaper. No submission info. Query w/SASE. Index: 31.

Technical Analysis of Stocks & Commodities, 9131 California Avenue S.W., Seattle, WA 98136-2551. 206–938–0570. Editor: John Sweeney. Ads: Lou Knoll Kemper. Monthly magazine. Sub. $69/yr. Circ. 15,000. Uses 2-3 freelance mss per issue. Writers should be knowledgeable about trading. Pays $2.75/col. inch, $50 min. on publication; cartoons, small items, flat $15. Acquires 1st rights. Byline given. Submit ms, SASE. Dot matrix, photocopied, electronic, computer disc OK. Reports in 1 day. Publishes in 3-6 mo. Accepts nonfiction, fiction, how-to articles on trading.

For lists of abbreviations and the key to index numbers, see "How to Use this Section" on page 75.

Writer's Northwest Handbook   183

Topics/theme blocks: psychology of trading, technical vs. fundamental, using statistics, chart work & technical analysis, new technical methods (charting, computer use), trading techniques, basics, reviews (books, articles, software, hardware), humor (incidents, cartoons, photos). Guidelines available. Sample, "nothing if related to article." Index: 32, 34, 67.

Technocracy Digest, 3642 Kingsway, Vancouver, BC V5R 5M2. Editor: E. McBurnie. 604–434–1134. No submission info. Query w/SASE. Index: 94.

Temporal Acuity Press, 1535 121st Avenue S.E., Bellevue, WA 98005. No submission info. Query w/SASE. Index: 130.

Ten Bridges, PO Box 14891, Portland, OR 97214. Editor: Jo Amberman. Periodical. No submission info. Query w/SASE. Index: 130.

Eddie Tern Press, 430 S.W. 206th Street, Seattle, WA 98166. No submission info. Query w/SASE. Index: 130.

Tertiumquid Press, 312 Sunset Drive, Longview, WA 98632. No submission info. Query w/SASE. Index: 130.

Testmarketed Downpour, Linfield College, Box 414, McMinnville, OR 97128. 503–472–4121. Editor: Barbara Drake. College literary magazine. Editor could change yearly. SASE for guidelines. Index: 31, 51, 91.

The Textile Booklist, PO Box C-20, Lopez Island, WA 98261. Contact: Editor. Quarterly. No submission info. Query w/SASE. Index: 38.

TGNW Press, 2429 E. Aloha, Seattle, WA 98112. 206–328–9856. Editor: Roger Herz. Publishes 2 books/yr. Accepts unsolicited submissions. Submit ms, SASE. May be dot matrix. Accepts nonfiction: humorous children's, humor, baseball. Index: 29, 68, 115.

That New Publishing Company, 1525 Eielson Street, Fairbanks, AK 99701. No submission info. Query w/SASE. Index: 130.

That Patchwork Place, Inc., 18800 142nd Avenue N.E., Suite 2A, Woodinville, WA 98072. Contact: Nancy Martin. 206–483–3313. Publisher of 6 softcover books a year on quilting, creative sewing. Print run: 10,000. Accepts freelance material. Rights purchased: All. Pay: varies. Query w/outline, SASE. Dot matrix, photocopies OK. Reports in 1 month. "Quilting techniques or quilt history; new techniques or speed techniques for patchwork; creative sewing especially that related to folk art, quilting, Christmas and other holidays." Guidelines/catalog available. Index: 38, 122.

The Dalles Chronicle, 414 Federal Street, The Dalles, OR 97508. 503–296–2141. Daily newspaper. No submission info. Query w/SASE.

The Dalles Weekly Reminder, PO Box 984, The Dalles, OR 97508. Editor: Gerald Ericksen. 503–298–4725. Ads: Saundra Bernards. Weekly newspaper. Circ. 4,000. Sub. $18. Almost never accepts freelance material, but "I'll look at anything of local interest." Byline given. No pay: "If something were exclusive and really good, we could possibly negotiate a small payment." Submit ms, SASE. Phone queries, dot matrix, photocopies, simultaneous submission OK. Reports immediately. "Local means Wasco or Sherman counties only." Photos: B&W photos or negatives preferred. Index: 3, 65, 101.

These Homeless Times, Burnside Community Council, 313 E. Burnside St., Portland, OR 97214. 503–231–7158. Editor: Susan Elwood. Quarterly. Sub. $10. Uses freelance material. No submission info. Query w/SASE. Index: 121.

Theytus Books, Box 218, Penticton, BC V2A 6K3. Publisher. No submission info. Query w/SASE. Index: 87.

Thin Power, PO Box 2206, Seattle, WA 98111. Publisher. No submission info. Query w/SASE. Index: 130.

The Third Age Newspaper, 3402 112th St. SW, Everett, WA 98204. Contact: Editor. Periodical. No submission info. Query w/SASE. Index: 130.

This is Alaska, 1041 E. 76th, Suite C, Anchorage, AK 99502. Editor: Frank Martone. 907–349–7506. Periodical. No submission info. Query w/SASE. Index: 4.

This Week, Box 4227, Portland, OR 97208. Editor: Maggi White. Weekly newspaper. Circ. 500,000 mailed to homes. 2-3 mss used per issue. Pays money on publication. Byline given. Query w/SASE. Phone queries OK. Nonfiction: 600-1,800 wds. Tips: "Most is local by assignment. If writer's clips show a lot of style, might give assignments." Index: 33, 36, 54.

Thorn Creek Press, Route 2 Box 160, Genesee, ID 83832. No submission info. Query w/SASE. Index: 130.

Thunderchief Corporation, 18460 S.E. Stephens Street, Portland, OR 97233-5537. Contact: Editor. Publisher. No submission info. Query w/SASE. Index: 130.

The Thurston-Mason Senior News, 529 W. 4th Ave., Olympia, WA 98501. 206–786–5595. Editor: Rick Crawford. Ads: Don Hellum. Monthly tabloid free to senior citizens. Circ. 15,000. Uses freelance material. May pay copies on publication. Byline given. Submit ms, SASE. Dot matrix, photocopied OK. Accepts nonfiction, cartoons. Topics: local news, health, nutrition, leisure, travel, finance, legislation for retirees. Sample for postage. Index: 33, 110.

Tidepools, Peninsula College, Port Angeles, WA 98362. 206–452–9277. Editor: Alice Derry. Periodical. No submission info. Query w/SASE. Index: 31.

Tidewater, 322-10th Ave. E. C5, Seattle, WA 98102. Contact: Editor. Quarterly (fiction, poetry, reviews). No submission info. Query w/SASE. Index: 51, 76, 97.

Timber!, Willamette Timbermen Association, Inc., 589 S. 72nd St., Springfield, OR 97478. 503–726–7918. Editor: Ted Ferrioli. Monthly. No submission info. Query w/SASE. Index: 55, 78.

Timber Press, 9999 S.W. Wilshire, Portland, OR 97225. 503–292–0961. Editor: Richard Abel. Ads: Michael Fox. Publishes 30 agriculture/farming/forestry/gardening hardcover original, reprints per year. Accepts unsolicited submissions. Acquires all rights. Submit query w/clips. Dot matrix, photocopied OK. Reports in 3-4 wks. Accepts nonfiction. Index: 3, 55, 56.

Timberbeast, PO Box 3695, Eugene, OR 97403. 503–686–8416. Editor/Ads: Bill Roy. Journal. Sub. $12 yr. Circ. 1,200+. Uses 2-3 freelance mss per issue. Pays copies. Byline given. Submit query w/clips, ms, SASE, phone. Dot matrix, photocopied, computer disc OK. Reports in 3 wks. Publishes in 6 mo. Accepts nonfiction, photos, cartoons. Topics: Pacific NW historical logging — individuals, companies, equipment, methods; "Reviews of relevant materials, 'great loggers I have known.'" Sample available. Index: 55, 65, 78.

Timber/West Magazine, PO Box 610, Edmonds, WA 98020. 206–778–3388. Monthly periodical. No submission info. Query w/SASE. Index: 130.

For lists of abbreviations and the key to index numbers, see "How to Use this Section" on page 75.

184   Market Listings

Timberline Press, PO Box 70071, Eugene, OR 97401. Self-publisher. Not a freelance market. Index: 130.

Timberman Times, Umpqua Community College, PO Box 967, Roseburg, OR 97470. 503–440–4600. Newspaper. No submission info. Query w/SASE. Index: 31.

Time Designs, Colton, OR 97017. Editor: T. Woods. Periodical. No submission info. Query w/SASE. Index: 130.

Time to Pause, Inky Trails Publications, PO Box 345, Middleton, ID 83644. Editor: Pearl Kirk. Semiannual literary magazine featuring poetry, fiction, nonfiction, and art. Circ. 200. Submit ms, SASE. Reports in 2-8 wks. Nonfiction: 3,500-5,500 wds on book reviews, essays, historical or nostalgic humor, inspirational, personal experience and travel. Fiction: 3,500-5,500 wds on fantasy, historical, humorous, mystery, romance, suspense, and western. Poetry: 4-70 lines of verse, free verse, light verse, or traditional. Tips: "Do not want horror, porno, etc." Sample: SASE. Index: 48, 68, 120.

Timeless Books, PO Box 160, Porthill, ID 83853. Contact: Terence Buie. 604–227–9224. Self-publisher of 2 nonfiction, softcover original books a year. Print run: 2-3,000. Not a freelance market. Catalog available. Index: 94, 105.

Times, PO Box 97, Waitsburg, WA 99361. 509–337–6631. Weekly newspaper. No submission info. Query w/SASE. Index: 33.

The Times, 109 Spalding Avenue, Box 278, Brownville, OR 97327. 503–466–5311. Weekly newspaper. No submission info. Query w/SASE. Index: 33.

The Times-Journal, 319 S. Main, Box 746, Condon, OR 97823. 503–384–2421. Weekly newspaper. No submission info. Query w/SASE. Index: 33.

The Times Journal Publishing Co., 7476 U.S. Hwy #12, Morton, WA 98356. Publisher. No submission info. Query w/SASE. Index: 130.

The Times News, 132 3rd St. W., Twin Falls, ID 83301. Contact: Editor. Newspaper. No submission info. Query w/SASE. Index: 33.

Tin Man Press, Box 219, Stanwood, WA 98292. No submission info. Query w/SASE. Index: 130.

Tiptoe Literary Service, PO Box 206-H, Naselle, WA 98638-0206. 206–484–7722. Self-publisher of 4 softcover originals, reprints a year. Rarely uses freelance material. Query w/clips., SASE. Topic: writer guide pamphlets. Index: 34, 48, 125.

Titania Publications, PO Box 30160, Eugene, OR 97403. No submission info. Query w/SASE. Index: 29, 34.

Tolemac, Inc., PO Box 418, Ashland, OR 97520. Contact: Editor. Publisher. No submission info. Query w/SASE. Index: 130.

Tomorrow's Forest, Oregon Forest Industries Council, PO Box 12519, Salem, OR 97309. Editor: Al Wilson. Periodical. No submission info. Query w/SASE. Index: 46, 55.

Topping International Institute, 1419 N. State, Bellingham, WA 98226. 206–647–2703. Editor: Bernie Topping. Publisher. No submission info. Query w/SASE. Index: 130.

Tops Learning Systems, 10978 S. Mulino Road, Canby, OR 97013. Publisher. No submission info. Query w/SASE. Index: 130.

The Torch, Lane Community College, 205 Center Bldg., 4000 E. 30th Avenue, Eugene, OR 97405. 503–747–4501. Weekly newspaper. No submission info. Query w/SASE. Index: 31.

Totline, 17909 Bothell Way S.E., Ste. 101, Bothell, WA 98012. 206–485–3335. Editor: Jean Warren. Ads: Sharon Schumacher. Bi-monthly newsletter. Sub. $15. Circ. 6,500. Uses freelance material from writers with early childhood educational experience. Pays money on acceptance. Acquires all rights. Byline given. Submit ms, SASE. Dot matrix, photocopied OK. Reports in 10-12 wks. Accepts nonfiction poetry. Topics: activity ideas, i.e., craft, art, educational, games, cultural awareness; articles with activities around a central theme, inspirational poetry for adults. Tips: sketches encouraged for clarification. Guidelines available. Sample $2. Index: 29, 43.

Touch the Heart Press, PO Box 373, Eastsound, WA 98245. No submission info. Query w/SASE. Index: 130.

The Touchstone Press, PO Box 81, Beaverton, OR 97075. Contact: Oral Bullard. 503–646–8081. Publisher of 2-3 softcover originals a year for outdoor people. Print run: 3,000. Accepts freelance material. Payment: Royalties. Rights purchased: All. Query, sample chapters w/SASE. Photocopies OK. Reports in 15-45 days. Publishes in 1 year. Trail guides, wildflower books, wilderness guides, local history (OR, WA, CA, ID, MT, NV). Catalog available. Index: 65, 88, 92.

Towers Club, USA Newsletter, Box 2038, Vancouver, WA 98668. Editor: Jerry Buchanan. 206–574–3084. Monthly "covers the field of selling info in printed or taped format directly to the consumer. Advertising tips, sources, news of the industry." Sub. $46. Not a freelance market. Index: 24, 102.

Town Forum, Inc., Cerro Gordo Ranch, PO Box 569, Cottage Grove, OR 97424. Publisher. No submission info. Query w/SASE. Index: 130.

Toy Investments, Inc., 19428 66th Ave. S., Building Q-111, Kent, WA 98032-2123. Contact: Editor. Publisher. No submission info. Query w/SASE. Index: 130.

Trace Editions, Fine and Rare Books, 3733 N.E. 24th Avenue, Portland, OR 97212. Contact: Charles Seluzicki. 503–284–4749. Publisher of 2 hard/softcover books a year. Print run: 500. Accepts freelance material. Payment: Copies; small cash payment at times. Rights purchased: First. Submit ms, SASE. Photocopies OK. Reports in 1 month. Publishes in 6-12 mos. Nonfiction, fiction, poetry, plays. "Quality writing in well-designed offset formats produced to high standards. Primarily, mss are solicited. Our authors include Sandra McPherson, Vasko Popa, Charles Wright, Charles Simic and Z. Herbert." Catalog available. Index: 22, 51, 97.

Trail Breakers, Clark County Genealogical Society. PO Box 2728, Vancouver, WA 98668. 206–256–0977. Editor: Rose Marie Harshman. Quarterly newsletter. Sub. $12. Circ. 500. Accepts freelance material. Byline given. Submit query, ms, SASE. Nonfiction, photos: how-to articles, research articles, Clark County genealogy. Sample $3. Index: 58, 65.

Trail City Archives, 1394 Pine Avenue, Trail, BC V1R 4E6. Publisher. No submission info. Query w/SASE. Index: 23, 63.

Training Associates Ltd., 2665 W. 42nd Avenue, Vancouver, BC V6N 3G4. Contact: Peter Renner. 604–263–7091. Publisher of 2 softcover, how-to books a year. Print run: 2,500. Accepts freelance material. Pays biannually; 10–18%; advance to be negotiated. Negotiates rights purchased. Outline, sample chapters w/SASE. Dot matrix, photocopies OK. Reports in 4 wks. Publishes in 6 mos. Nonfiction: how-to, business and training. Catalog available. Index: 24, 43, 67.

For lists of abbreviations and the key to index numbers, see "How to Use this Section" on page 75.

Writer's Northwest Handbook   185

The Trainmaster, PNC-National Railway Historical Society, 800 N.W. 6th Ave., Portland, OR 97209. 503–226–6747. Contact: Editor. Monthly. Sub. $5. Circ. 500. Not a freelance market. Index: 64, 120.

Trainsheet, c/o Tacoma Chapter NRHS Inc., PO Box 340, Tacoma, WA 98401-0340. Editor: Art Hamilton. 206–537–2169. Published 10 times a year. Circ. 300. Sub. $17. Uses 1 ms per issue. No pay. Submit ms, SASE. Phone queries, dot matrix, photocopies OK. Nonfiction: railroad history; max 2 pgs (1,000 + wds) typed 3 1/2" wide max. Photos: 5x7, B&W; no pay. Index: 64, 120.

Transformation Times, PO Box 425, Beavercreek, OR 97004. 503–632–7141. Editor: Connie L. Faubel. Ads: E. James Faubel. Published 10 times a year. Sub. $8/yr. Circ. 8,000. Uses 4-5 freelance ms per issue. Pays ads on publication. Acquires 1st rights. Byline given. Submit ms, SASE. Dot matrix, photocopied, computer disc (*Word Star*) OK. Reports in 15 days. Publishes in 1-2 mo. Accepts nonfiction, fiction. Topics: metaphysical, holistic, human potential, occult sciences, environmental quality, socially responsible issues, book and video reviews. No longer than 1,500 wds. Guidelines available. Sample $1. Index: 13, 25, 61.

Transonic Hacker, 1402 S.W. Upland Dr., Portland, OR 97221-2649. Editor: Eric Geislinger. Periodical. No submission info. Query w/SASE. Index: 130.

Trask House Press, 2754 S.E. 27th, Portland, OR 97202. Contact: Carlos Reyes. 503–235–1898. Irregular publisher of poetry books. Print run: 500. Accepts freelance material. No submission info. Query w/SASE. Reports in 30-60 days. Poetry. Index: 97.

Travel Oregon Magazine, 1131 Fairfield, Eugene, OR 97402. 503–688–7134. Contact: Editor. Periodical. No submission info. Query w/SASE. Index: 91, 120.

Traveller's Bed & Breakfast, PO Box 492, Mercer Island, WA 98040. Contact: Editor. Publisher. Index: 120.

Treasure Valley Good News, 5353 Franklin Rd., Boise, ID 83705. 208–344–7788. Editor: Hal Neale Glanville. Newspaper. No submission info. Query w/SASE. Index: 33.

Treasure Valley This Week, 5225 Irving, Boise, ID 83705. 208–327–1000. Editor: Ken Burrows. Weekly newspaper. Sub. $10. No submission info. Query w/SASE. Index: 33.

Tremaine Publishing, 2727 Front Street, Klamath Falls, OR 97601. No submission info. Query w/SASE. Index: 130.

Trestle Creek Review, N. Idaho College, 1000 W. Garden Ave., Couer d'Alene, ID 83814. Editor: Fay Wright. Periodical. No submission info. Query w/SASE. Index: 31.

Triad Ensemble, PO Box 61006, Seattle, WA 98121. 206–322–1398. Contact: Victor Janusz. "A relatively young Seattle theater company with a strong interest in new regional works." No submission info. Query w/SASE. Index: 41.

Tri-County News, 231 W. Sixth, Box 394, Junction City, OR 97448. 503–998–3877. Weekly newspaper. No submission info. Query w/SASE. Index: 33.

Tri-County Bulletin, 3033 S.W. 174th, Portland, OR 97236. Editor: Quentin Smith, Jr. 503–760–6566. Monthly tabloid distributed free in Portland-metro area. Community news. Circ. 26,000. No submission info. Query w/SASE. Index: 33.

Tri County Special Services, 48 E. 1st North, St. Anthony, ID 83445. Contact: Editor. Publisher. No submission info. Query w/SASE. Index: 130.

Tribune, PO Box 400, Deer Park, Wa 99006. 509–276–5043. Weekly newspaper. No submission info. Query w/SASE. Index: 33.

The Trolley Park News, 1836 N. Emerson, Portland, OR 97321. Editor/ads: Richard Thompson. 503–285–7936. Semimonthly on historic electric railway preservation. Circ. 200. Sub. membership $10-25. Uses 1 ms per issue. Payment: negotiable; on publication. Byline given. Rights purchased: First. Phone queries, dot matrix, photocopies, simultaneous submission, electronic OK. Reports in 1-2 mos. Nonfiction: "Historic articles on NW, particularly OR, street and interurban railways (including where vehicles are now, tracing abandoned rights-of-way; how-to restore streetcars; and memories of lines ridden)." Photos: 8x10, 5x7, 3x5; B&W glossy preferred. Maps & car body plans also useful. Sample/SASE. Index: 30, 65, 120.

Trout, PO Box 6255, Bend, OR 97708. Editor: Thomas R. Pero. 503–382–2327. 503–382–9177. Periodical. No submission info. Query w/SASE. Index: 3, 35, 92.

Trout Creek Press, 5976 Billings Road, Parkdale, OR 97041. Contact: Laurence F. Hawkins, Jr.. 503–352–6494. Publisher of 2 softcover poetry books a year. Print run: 400. Accepts freelance material. Pay: % of receipts after material costs recovered. Rights purchased: First. Query w/SASE. Dot matrix, photocopies OK. Reports in 1-3 mos. Publishes in 6-12 mos. "Open to any poetic project with artistic merit. Probably favor experimental work, provided it is not tesoteric." Guidelines available. Index: 14, 97.

Truck Art, 158 S. 297th Place, Federal Way, WA 98003. Publisher. No submission info. Query w/SASE. Index: 130.

Truck Logger, 124 W. 8th Street, North Vancouver, BC V7M 3H2. Editor: Vivian Rudd. 604–985–7811. Periodical. No submission info. Query w/SASE. Index: 24, 71, 78.

Trucking Canada - Western Edition, 4250 Dawson Street, Burnaby, BC V5C 4BL. Editor: Heather Conn. 604–293–1275. Monthly consumer magazine for Canada's owners and operators of small fleets. Circ. 13,500. Payment: $.20/wd max, on publication. Byline given. Query w/ms, SASE. Phone queries, dot matrix OK. Reports ASAP. Publishes in 3-4 mos. Nonfiction: to 2,000 wds on new truck technology, new truck models, unique trucks, industry news, legislation, and travel news. Fiction: to 1,000 wds on humorous trucking anecdotes and anything involving trucking on and off the road. Departments: to 800 wds on trucking humor, maintenance, technology, cartoons. Photos: $150 for color cover, $40 inside color, $25 B&W. Tips: "We're looking for hard hitting investigative pieces within trucking industry, eg., union representation of owners and operators, effects of deregulation, truckers' working conditions, treatment by companies, etc." Sample available. Index: 24, 71, 119.

True North/Down Under, Box 55, Lantzville, BC V0R 2H0. Annual. No submission info. Query w/SASE. Index: 130.

Truth on Fire (Hallelujah), PO Box 223, Postal Sta. A, Vancouver, BC V6C 2M3. 604–498–3895. Editor: Wesley H. Wakefield. Bimonthly evangelical magazine. Sub. $5. Circ. 1,000-10,000. Uses freelance material. Pays $15 & up on acceptance. Byline given. Submit query w/clips. Dot matrix, photocopied, simultaneous OK. Reports in 6 wks. Publishing time varies. Accepts nonfiction, photos. "Biblically oriented to evangelical & Wesleyan viewpoint." Topics: peace, anti-nuclear, racial equality & justice, religious liberty, etc. Tips: "prefer action or solution-oriented articles; must understand evangelical viewpoint & life style." Guidelines/sample available. Index: 105.

For lists of abbreviations and the key to index numbers, see "How to Use this Section" on page 75.

186   Market Listings

Truth on Fire (Hallelujah), Same as preceding. Also publishes 2-3 softcover assigned originals, reprints a year. Will consider queries. Rates vary on assignment. Index: 105.

Tumwater Action Committee Newsletter, 500 Tyee Drive, Tumwater, WA 98502. No submission info. Query w/SASE. Index: 101, 123.

Tundra Drums, PO Box 868, Bethel, AK 99559. Weekly newspaper. No submission info. Query w/SASE. Index: 33.

Tundra Times, 411 W. 4th Avenue, Anchorage, AK 99510. 907–274–2512. Periodical of Eskimo, Indian and Aleut news. No submission info. Query w/SASE. Index: 4, 87.

Turman Publishing Company, Queen Anne Square No. 508, 200 W. Mercer Street, Seattle, WA 98119. No submission info. Query w/SASE. Index: 130.

Turock Fitness Publishers, PO Box 19257, Seattle, WA 98119. No submission info. Query w/SASE. Index: 61.

TV Week, 320 - 9940 Lougheed Highway, Burnaby, BC V3J 1N3. Weekly periodical. No submission info. Query w/SASE. Index: 45, 77.

Twin Peaks Press, PO Box 129, Vancouver, WA 98666. 206–694–2462. Contact: Helen Hecker. Publisher of 4-5 hard/softcover reprints a year. Accepts unsolicited submissions. Submit query, SASE. Pays on publication. Dot matrix, photocopied, simultaneous OK. Accepts nonfiction. Catalog available. Index: 61, 81, 120.

Two Louies Magazine, 2745 NE 34th Ave., Portland, OR 97212. Editor: Buck Munger. Periodical. No submission info. Query w/SASE. Index: 130.

Two Magpie Press, PO Box 177, Kendrick, ID 83537. 208–276–4130. Not a freelance market. Query w/SASE. Index: 130.

Two Rivers Press, 28070 S. Meridian Road, Aurora, OR 97002. No submission info. Query w/SASE. Index: 130.

U.S. Department of Agriculture, Forest Service, Pacific Northwest & Range Experiment, Station, PO Box 3890, Portland, OR 97208. Publisher. No submission info. Query w/SASE. Index: 3, 35, 88.

Umatilla County Historical Society News, PO Box 253, Pendleton, OR 97801. Quarterly. No submission info. Query w/SASE. Index: 65, 91.

Umbrella Books, Div. of Harbor View Publications Group, PO Box 1460–A, Friday Harbor, WA 98250-1460. 206–378–5128. Editor: Jerome K. Miller. Publishes 4 softcover original books a year. Accepts unsolicited submissions. Pays 10% royalty plus payment for photos. Submit query w/ clips, SASE. Dot matrix, computer disc OK. Reports in 6 wks. Publishes very promptly. Accepts nonfiction. Topics: tour guides to the Pacific Northwest. Guidelines available. Index: 89, 120.

Umpqua Free Press, 425 N.W. Second Avenue, Box 729, Myrtle Creek, OR 97457. 503–863–5233. Weekly newspaper. No submission info. Query w/SASE. Index: 33.

Umpqua Trapper, Douglas County Historical Society, 10176 Garden Valley Road, Roseburg, OR 97470. 503–459–2864. Quarterly historical journal to county residents. Circ. 300. Accepts freelance material. No pay. Byline given. Nonfiction: historical relating to Douglas County or family stories. Index: 65.

Underground Express, National Speleological Society, 853 Fairview Ave. SE, Salem, OR 97302. Editor: Clay Patrick. Quarterly. No submission info. Query w/SASE. Index: 103, 115.

Unicorn Rising Ltd., Route 2, PO Box 360, Sheridan, OR 97378. Publisher. No submission info. Query w/SASE. Index: 130.

Unicornucopia, 2536 N.W. Overton, Portland, OR 97210-2441. No submission info. Query w/SASE. Index: 130.

Union-Bulletin, PO Box 1358, Walla Walla, WA 99362. 509–525–3300. Daily newspaper. No submission info. Query w/SASE. Index: 33.

Uniquest Publications, 120 SE Everett Mall Way #1328, Everett, WA 98208. Contact: Editor. Publisher. No submission info. Query w/SASE. Index: 130.

United Press International, 1320 S.W. Broadway, Portland, OR 97201. 503–226–2644. News Bureau. No submission info. Query w/SASE. Index: 130.

U of A, Institute of Marine Science, University of Alaska, Fairbanks, AK 99701. Publisher. No submission info. Query w/SASE. Index: 31, 88, 109.

University of Alaska Library, Elmer E. Rasmuson Library, Fairbanks, AK 99701. Publisher. No submission info. Query w/SASE. Index: 31, 104.

University of Alaska Museum, 907 Yukon Drive, Fairbanks, AK 99701. Publisher. No submission info. Query w/SASE. Index: 4, 7, 88.

University of Alaska Press, Signers' Hall, U of A, Fairbanks, AK 99776-1580. 907–474–6389. Editor: Carla Helfferich. Ads: Debbie Van Stone. Publishes 3-8 hard/softcover original, reprint books a yr. Accepts unsolicited submissions. Submit ms, SASE. Nonfiction: emphasis on scholarly and nonfiction works related to Alaska, the circum-polar north, and the North Pacific rim. Index: 4, 31, 108.

University of British Columbia Press, 6344 Memorial Road, Vancouver, BC V6T IW5. 604–228–3259, 228–4161, 228–4545. Editors: Jane Fredeman (humanities), Karen Morgan (social sciences). Ads: Marie Stephen. Publishes hard/softcover originals, reprints, subsidy books. Accepts unsolicited submissions. Pays royalties. Acquires all rights. Submit query w/clips. Photocopied OK. Accepts nonfiction. Topics: humanities and social sciences: monographs and upper level textbooks. Catalog available. Index: 63, 76, 118.

University Herald, 1225 N. 43rd, Seattle, WA 98103. 206–522–9505. Weekly newspaper. No submission info. Query w/SASE. Index: 33.

U of I, Center for Business Development/Research, College of Business/Economics, University of Idaho, Moscow, ID 83843. Publisher. No submission info. Query w/SASE. Index: 24, 42, 69.

University of Idaho Press, U of I, Moscow, ID 83843. 208–885–6245. Editor: James J. Heaney. Ads: Rebecca Rd. Publishes 6-8 hard/softcover, original, reprint, subsidy books a year. Accepts unsolicited submissions. Pays 8-12% net royalties, advance on publication. Submit ms, SASE. Photocopied, computer disc OK. Reports in 3 mo. Publishes in 9 mo. Accepts nonfiction, fiction: scholarly and regional, including Native American studies, resource and policy studies, Pacific Northwest history and natural history, literature and criticism. Ms between 25,000-100,000 wds. Catalog available. Index: 77, 87, 188.

For lists of abbreviations and the key to index numbers, see "How to Use this Section" on page 75.

U of M, Publications in History, University of Montana, Missoula, MT 59812. No submission info. Query w/SASE. Index: 62, 65, 85.

The University News, Boise State University, 1910 University Drive, Boise, ID 83725. 208–385–1464. Weekly newspaper. Circ. 15,000. No submission info. Query w/SASE. Index: 31.

U of O, Bureau of Governmental Research/Service, PO Box 3177, Eugene, OR 97403. Publisher. No submission info. Query w/SASE. Index: 101.

U of O, Center for Educational Policy & Management, College of Education, University of Oregon, Eugene, OR 97403. Publisher. No submission info. Query w/SASE. Index: 43.

U of O, Center of Leisure Studies, Dept. of Recreation/Parks, Rm. 138, University of Oregon, Eugene, OR 97403. Publisher. No submission info. Query w/SASE. Index: 103.

U of O, Forest Industries Management Center, College of Business Administration, University of Oregon, Eugene, OR 97405. Publisher. No submission info. Query w/SASE. Index: 24, 55, 88.

University of Portland Review, 5000 N. Portland Blvd., Portland, OR 97203. Editor: Dr. Thompson Faller. 503–283–7144. Semiannual tabloid magazine for college educated laymen. Circ. 1,000. Accepts 200 mss per year. Payment: 5 copies. Byline given. Phone queries OK. Reports in 6 mos. Publishes in 1 year. Nonfiction: to 2,000 wds on any subject. Fiction: to 2,000 wds on any subject. Poetry: any length and style. Tips: "Its purpose is to comment on the human condition and to present information on expanding knowledge in different fields. With regard to fiction, only that which makes a significant statement about the contemporary scene will be employed." Sample/$.50. Index: 39, 43, 51.

University of Portland Writers, English Department, U. of Portland, 5000 N. Willamette Blvd, Portland, OR 97203-5798. Contact: Editor. Periodical. No submission info. Query w/SASE. Index: 31, 125.

University Press of the Pacific, Box 66129, Seattle, WA 98166. Not a freelance market. Index: 130.

U of V, English Literature Studies Monograph Series, Department of English, PO Box 1700, Victoria, BC V8W 2Y2. Publisher. No submission info. Query w/SASE. Index: 31, 43, 76.

U of V, Western Geographical Series, Department of Geography, PO Box 1700, Victoria, BC V8W 2Y2. Publisher. No submission info. Query w/SASE. Index: 31, 59.

U of W, Graduate School of Business, MacKenzie Hall, D-J 10, Seattle, WA 98195. Publisher. No submission info. Query w/SASE. Index: 24, 31.

U of W, Office of Publications, G-16 Communications Bldg., University of Washington, Seattle, WA 98195. No submission info. Query w/ SASE. Index: 31, 43, 102.

University of Washington Press, Box 50096, Seattle, WA 98105. No submission info. Query w/SASE. Index: 31.

Update, B.C. Teachers' Federation, 2235 Burrard Street, Vancouver, BC V6T 3H9. Publisher. No submission info. Query w/SASE. Index: 23, 43, 71.

Upper Snake River Valley Historical Society, Box 244, Rexburg, ID 83440. Editor: Louis Clements. 208–356–9101. Periodical. No submission info. Query w/SASE. Index: 65, 69.

Upword Press, PO Box 1106, Yelm, WA 98597. 206–458–3619. Editor: Lyn Evans. Ads: Warren Evans. Publishes 4-6 hard/softcover originals a year. Accepts unsolicited submissions. Submit query w/clips, ms, SASE. Dot matrix, photocopied OK. Reports in 6 wks. Nonfiction, fiction: New Age, metaphysical. Index: 13, 14.

Urban Design Centre Society, 1630 E. Georgia St., Vancouver, BC V5L 2B2. Publisher. No submission info. Query w/ SASE. Index: 9, 39, 113.

The Urban Naturalist, Audubon Soc. of Portland, 5151 NW Cornell Rd., Portland, OR 97210. 503–292–6855. Editor/Ads: Mike Houck. Quarterly journal. Sub. $20/yr. Circ. 1,500. Uses 4-6 freelance mss per issue. No pay. Byline given. Submit by assignment only. Publishes in 2 mo. Topics: "Volunteer only, articles & illustrations on Portland area natural history topics." Volunteer authors and artists, decisions by entire group. Guidelines available. Sample $5. Index: 35, 46, 88.

Urquhart Associates, Inc., 3811 Seattle First Bank Bldg., PO Box 75092, Northgate Station, Seattle, WA 98154. Contact: Edward F. Urquhart. 206–523–3200. Publisher of 2 softcover books a year. Print run: 2,000. Accepts freelance material. Pay negotiable. Rights purchased: First. Query w/outline, sample chapters, SASE. Reports in 1 month. Publishes in 3 mos. Nonfiction, photos. Index: 24, 36, 120.

User-Friendly Press, 6552 Lakeway Dr., Anchorage, AK 99502. 907–263–9172. Contact: Ann Chandonnet. Self-publisher of 1 or less softcover book a year on Alaskan history and poetry. Does not accept unsolicited submissions. Back list available $7.95. Index: 4, 62, 87.

VA Practitioner, Aster Publishing Corp., PO Box 10460, Eugene, OR 97470-2460. Editor: James McCloskey. Monthly. No submission info. Query w/SASE. Index: 130.

Vagabond Press, PO Box 395, Ellensburg, WA 98926. 509–962–8471. Editor: John Bennett. Publishes 3 softcover books/yr. Press run 1,000. Accepts unsolicited submissions. Pays on publication. Acquires 1st rights. Submit query, SASE. Photocopies OK. Reports in 1 mo. Accepts nonfiction, fiction. Catalog available. Index: 51.

Vail Publishing, 8285 S.W. Brookridge, Portland, OR 97225. 503–292–9964. Self-publisher of 1 softcover book a year. Print run: 2,000. Not a freelance market. Catalog available. Index: 43, 118.

Valentine Publishing Company, PO Box 1378, Ashland, OR 97504. Contact: James L. Rodgers. 503–773–7035. Self-publisher. No submission info. Query w/SASE. Index: 130.

Valley American, 932 1/2 6th Street, Clarkston, WA 99403. 509–758–9797. Weekly newspaper. No submission info. Query w/SASE. Index: 33.

Valley Farms, 250 Mill Road, Helena, MT 59601. No submission info. Query w/SASE. Index: 130.

Valley Herald, 205 N. Main, Box 230, Milton-Freewater, OR 97862. 503–938–3361. Weekly newspaper. No submission info. Query w/SASE. Index: 33.

For lists of abbreviations and the key to index numbers, see "How to Use this Section" on page 75.

Valley Herald, PO Box 14027, Spokane, WA 99214. 509–924–2440. Weekly newspaper. No submission info. Query w/SASE. Index: 33.

Valley Optimist, PO Box 98, Selah, WA 98942. 509–697–8505. Weekly newspaper. No submission info. Query w/SASE. Index: 33.

Valley Record & North Bend Record, PO Box 300, Snoqualmie, WA 98065. 206–888–2311. Weekly newspaper. No submission info. Query w/SASE. Index: 33.

Valley Times, 9730 S.W. Cascade Blvd., Box 370, Beaverton, OR 97075. Weekly newspaper. No submission info. Query w/SASE. Index: 33.

Valley View Blueberry Press, 21717 N.E. 68th Street, Vancouver, WA 98662. No submission info. Query w/SASE. Index: 130.

Van Dahl Publications, PO Box 10, Albany, OR 97321. 503–928–3569. Editor: Kyle Jansson. Publisher of 1-2 books per year for stamp collectors. Does not accept unsolicited submissions. Index: 30, 38.

Vancouver Columbian, 701 West Eighth, PO Box 180, Vancouver, Wa 98668. 206–694–3391. Daily newspaper. No submission info. Query w/SASE. Index: 33.

Vancouver Courier, 2094 West 43rd Ave., Vancouver, BC V6M 2C9. Contact: Editor. No submission info. Query w/SASE. Index: 130.

Vancouver History, Vancouver Historical Society, PO Box 3071, Vancouver, BC V6B 3X6. Quarterly. No submission info. Query w/SASE. Index: 23, 63, 65.

Vancouver Magazine, 1205 Richard Street, Vancouver, BC V6B 3G3. Editor: Malcolm F. Parry. 604–685–5374. Mass market monthly of local entertainment & culture. No submission info. Query w/SASE. Index: 39, 45.

Vancouver Symphony, 400 E. Broadway, Vancouver, BC V5T 1X2. Editor: Marilyn Johnson. 604–875–1661. Periodical. No submission info. Query w/SASE. Index: 39, 86.

Vandina Press, PO Box 1551, Mercer Island, WA 98040. 206–232–3239. Editor: Francine Porad. Publishes 1-2 softcover poetry chapbooks a year. Also publishes a poetry journal, Brussels Sprout, 3 times a year. No submission info. Query w/SASE. Index: 97.

Vanessapress, PO Box 81335, Fairbanks, AK 99708. No submission info. Query w/SASE. Index: 130.

Vanguard, Portland State University, PO Box 751, Portland, OR 97207. 503–229–4539. Semiweekly newspaper. No submission info. Query w/SASE. Index: 31.

Vanguard, Multnomah School of the Bible, 8435 N.E. Glisan, Portland, OR 97220. Monthly newspaper. No submission info. Query w/SASE. Index: 31, 105.

Vardaman Press, 2720 E. 176th Street, Tacoma, WA 98445. No submission info. Query w/SASE. Index: 130.

Vashon Point Productions, Rt 1 Box 432, Vashon, WA 98070. 206–567–4829. Editor: Joyce Delbridge. Publisher of 1 softcover book per 2 yrs. Accepts unsolicited submissions "when needed." Pays in copies on publication. Byline given. Submit ms, SASE, phone. Dot matrix, photocopied, simultaneous OK. Accepts nonfiction, fiction, poetry, photos, cartoons, line drawings relating to incidents on Northwest ferries. Tips: slant toward humor/realistic stories/cartoons, some fantasy. Sample $8.95. Index: 5, 77, 89.

Vashon-Maury Island Beachcomber, PO Box 447, Vashon, WA 98070. Editor: Jay Becker. 206–463–9195. Ads: Judy Scott. Weekly. Circ. 3,800. Sub. $20. Uses 1 per issue. Payment: Money on publication. Byline given. Rights purchased: First. Query w/SASE. Nonfiction: "Will consider anything relating to the Island and Islanders; nothing else. $50 for package of 450 wds about interesting Islander with picture (send 35mm negs and we'll develop). Does not need to live on Island now, could be Peace Corp volunteer someplace else, but must have a point, theme, reason for being in article that is different or so typical it hurts." Guidelines available; sample/SASE. Index: 33.

VCC, Vancouver Community College, 100 W. 49th Avenue, Vancouver, BC V5Y 2Z6. 604–324–5415. Periodical. No submission info. Query w/SASE. Index: 31.

Vector Associates, PO Box 6215, Bellevue, WA 98008. Publisher. No submission info. Query w/SASE. Index: 130.

Vector Publishing, PO Box 1271, Mount Vernon, WA 98273. No submission info. Query w/SASE. Index: 130.

Veda News, PO Box 802, Bandon, OR 97411. Editor: Mildred Robinson. Bimonthly. No submission info. Query w/SASE. Index: 130.

Velosport Press, 1100 E. Pike, Seattle, WA 98122. Contact: Denise de la Rosa. 206–329–2453. Publisher of 1 softcover book a year on cycling. Print run: 6,000. Accepts freelance material. Pay negotiable. Sample chapters w/SASE. Photocopies OK. Reports in 1 month. Publishes in varies. Index: 16.

Venture Communications, Inc., PO Box 02332, Portland, OR 97202. 503–236–5810. Editor: Michael J. Carey. Publishes original books related to technology (GIS/CAD, RFP), mapping, training for public sector and vendors. Accepts freelance material. Payment negotiable. Acquires all rights. Submit phone query. Dot matrix, photocopied OK. Reports in 1 wk. Publishes in 1-2 mo. Tips: applications, not product literature. Index: 34, 101, 117.

Vernier Software, 2920 S.W. 89th St., Portland, OR 97225. 503–297–5317. Editor: Chris Vernier. Publisher. No submission info. Query w/SASE. Index: 34.

Vernon Publications, Inc., 3000 Northrup Way, Ste. 200, Seattle. 206–827–9900. Daily/weekly newsletter. No freelance accepted. 24, 42.

Vet's Newsletter, 700 Summer Street NE, Salem, OR 97310-1201. 503–373–2000. Editor: Barb Nobles. Bimonthly. No submission info. Query w/SASE. Index: 83.

Victory Music Review, PO Box 7515, Bonney Lake, WA 98390. Editor: Diane Schulstad. 206–863–6617. Ads: Chris Lunn. Monthly. Sub. $15/yr. Circ. 6,000. Uses freelance material. Pays copies/nothing. Phone query. Dot matrix OK. Publishes in 15-90 days. Topics: folk, jazz record reviews — 125 wds; local concert reviews — 200 wds. Sample $1. Index: 25, 45, 86.

Video Librarian, PO Box 2725, Bremerton, WA 98310. 206–377–2231. Editor/Ads: Randy Pitman. Monthly. Sub. $35. Circ. 350. Uses 1 freelance ms per issue. Pays copies on publication. Byline given. Dot matrix, photocopied OK. Reports in 2 wks. Accepts nonfiction. Free sample. Index: 52, 80.

Videosat News, CommTek, 9440 Fairview Avenue, Boise, ID 83704. Editor: Tom Woolf. Monthly. Circ. 24,500. No submission info. Query w/SASE. Index: 36, 45, 52.

For lists of abbreviations and the key to index numbers, see "How to Use this Section" on page 75.

Writer's Northwest Handbook   189

Vidiot Enterprises, 501 N. M Street, Tacoma, WA 98403. Publisher. No submission info. Query w/SASE. Index: 130.

Views, Sexual Minorities Center, Western Washington University, Viking Union 217, Bellingham, WA 98225. Periodical. No submission info. Query w/SASE. Index: 57, 124.

The Village Idiot, Mother of Ashes Press, PO Box 66, Harrison, ID 83833-0066. 208–689–3738. Editor: Judith Shannon Paine. Magazine, approx. twice a year. Sub. $15. Circ. 300. Accepts unsolicited submissions. Pays in copies on publication. Acquires 1st rights. Byline given. Submit ms, SASE. Reports in 1-3 mo. Publishes in 6-12 mo. Accepts fiction, poetry, photos, art. Guidelines available. Sample $4. Index 51, 96, 97.

The Villager, PO Box 516, Wilsonville, OR 97070-0516. Editor: K.C. Swan. Monthly. No submission info. Query w/SASE. Index: 130.

Vincentury, St. Vincent Hospital & Medical Center, 9205 S.W. Barnes Road, Portland, OR 97225. Periodical for patients, relatives, employees and community. No submission info. Query w/SASE. Index: 61.

Vintage Northwest, (King's Press), PO Box 193, Bothell, WA 98041. 206–487–1201. Editor: Margie Brons. Ads: Ruth Murphy. 206–486–6180. Semi-annual. No sub. Circ. 450 distr. at local senior centers. Accepts freelance mss only from age 55+. Pays in copies on publication. Submit ms, SASE, no more than 1,000 wds. Photocopies OK. Reports in 6 mo. Publishes 1-6 mo. Accepts nonfiction, fiction, poetry, illustrations. Topics: variety. "We like senior's experiences, humorous stories or poems; we object to sexist language, sermonic types or political." Guidelines available. Sample $2. Index: 51, 97, 110.

Virtue, PO Box 850, Sisters, OR 97759. Editor: Becky Durost. Non-denominational Christian women's magazine. No submission info. Query w/SASE. Index: 105, 124.

Vision Books, 790 Commercial Avenue, Coos Bay, OR 97420. Publisher. No submission info. Query w/SASE. Index: 130.

Visions, 19600 NW Von Neumann Drive, Beaverton, OR 97006. 503–690–1121. FAX 503–690–1029. Editor: Steve Dodge. Ads: Norman Elder. Quarterly magazine. Free. Circ. 15,000. Uses 2 freelance mss per issue. Pays money on acceptance. Acquires at least 1st rights. Byline given. Submit query w/clips, 9x12 SASE. Dot matrix, photocopied, simultaneous, computer disc OK. Reports in 2-4 wks. Publishes 1-4 mo. Accepts nonfiction, photos, cartoons. Topics: science and technology, from computer advances and high technology to biology and environment. Length: 1,000-3,000 wds. Science briefs (250 wds) with emphasis on the unusual. Personality profiles of scientists (1,000 wds). Photos: photomicrographs, B&W and color, needed; photos that reveal the unusual or relatively unseen, $50-350. Tips: "Science with an emphasis on people and non-technical explanations of technology especially welcome. Would like to see clips from experienced NW writers willing to work on assignment." Guidelines & free sample for 9x12 SASE. Index: 34, 46, 109.

Vitamin Supplement, 260 SW Marine Dr., Vancouver, BC V5X 2R5. Editor: Tracey Cochrane. Quarterly. No submission info. Query w/SASE. Index: 61.

Leo F. Vogel, 2526 Dilling Road, Connell, WA 99326. 509–234–5112. Self-publisher of hard/softcover original books. Print run: 2,000. Not a freelance market. Index: 65, 68.

The Voice, Ore-Ida Foods, PO Box 10, Boise, ID 83707. Editor: Susan C. Gerhart. Company journal published 3 x per year for employees, management and business contacts. Circ. 6,000. No submission info. Query w/SASE. Index: 24.

The Voice, Oregon Advocates for the Arts, 1313 Mill Street S.E., Salem, OR 97301-6307. Contact: Editor. Periodical. No submission info. Query w/SASE. Index: 10, 39, 91.

Void Press, Box 45125, Seattle, WA 98145. 206–522–8055. Editor: John Stehman. Publisher, small press runs, personal invitation. Poetry, other. Catalog $1. Index: 97.

W.H. 1, 21349 N.W. St. Helens Road, Portland, OR 97231. Publisher. No submission info. Query w/SASE. Index: 130.

W.S. Productions, 6597 Faber Crescent, Delta, BC V4E 1K1. Publisher. No submission info. Query w/SASE. Index: 130.

Wahkiakum County Eagle, PO Box 368, Cathlamet, WA 98612. 206–795–3391. Weekly newspaper. No submission info. Query w/SASE. Index: 33.

Donald E. Waite Photographer & Publisher Company, 35-22374 Lougheed Hwy., Maple Ridge, BC V2X 2T5. No submission info. Query w/SASE. Index: 130.

Walking Bird Publishing, 340 N. Grand Street, Eugene, OR 97402. Contact: Editor. Publisher. No submission info. Query w/SASE. Index: 130.

Wallowa County Chieftain, 106 N.W. First Street, Box 338, Enterprise, OR 97828. 503–426–4567. Weekly newspaper. No submission info. Query w/SASE. Index: 33.

Warner Pacific College Art & Literature Magazine, Warner Pacific College, 2219 S.E. 68th Ave., Portland, OR 97215. College literary magazine. SASE for guidelines. Index: 31, 51, 91.

Warner World, Warner Pacific College, 2219 S.E. 68th, Portland, OR 97215. 503–775–4366. Newspaper. No submission info. Query w/SASE. Index: 31.

Warren Publishing House, PO Box 2253, Alderwood Manor, WA 98036. No submission info. Query w/SASE. Index: 130.

Wash 'n Press, 5210 NE 16th, Seattle, WA 98105. 206–523–5529. Contact: Marilyn Stablein. Publisher. No submission info. Query w/SASE. Index: 51, 97.

The Washington Alumnus, University of Washington Alumni Assoc., 1415 N.E. 45th, Seattle, WA 98105. Editor: Judy Thorne. 206–543–0540. Periodical. No submission info. Query w/SASE. Index: 31, 123.

Washington Arts, Mail Stop GH-11, Olympia, WA 98504-4111. Periodical. No submission info. Query w/SASE. Index: 10, 39, 123.

Washington Cattleman, Box 2027, Wenatchee, WA 98801. 509–662–5167. Monthly. No submission info. Query w/SASE. Index: 3, 6, 24.

Washington Clubwoman, 11404 N.E. 97th Street, Vancouver, WA 98662. Monthly. No submission info. Query w/SASE. Index: 130.

Washington Cookbook, PO Box 923, Spokane, WA 99210. Publisher. No submission info. Query w/SASE. Index: 38, 123.

Washington Crop & Livestock Reporting Service, 417 W. Fourth Avenue, Olympia, WA 98501. Publisher. No submission info. Query w/SASE. Index: 3, 6, 123.

For lists of abbreviations and the key to index numbers, see "How to Use this Section" on page 75.

190   Market Listings

Washington Farmer Stockman, 211 Review Building, Spokane, WA 99210. 509–455–7057. Semimonthly ag business publication. No submission info. Query w/SASE. Index: 3, 24, 123.

Washington Food Dealer, 8288 Lake City Way N.E., Box 15300, Seattle, WA 98115-0030. 206–522–4474. Editor/Ads: Arden D. Gremmert. Grocery trade magazine published 11 times per year. Sub. $20/yr. Circ. 4,000. Accepts freelance material. Pays in copies. Acquires 1st rights. Byline given. Query w/clips, SASE, phone query on ideas. Dot matrix, photocopies, simultaneous, computer disc OK. Reports in 1 mo. Publishing time varies. Accepts nonfiction, grocery related only, particularly focusing on Northwest. Length variable. Photos B&W or color, originals, (no-pre-screened), no payment. Sample free. Index: 24, 54, 119.

The Washington Grange News, 3104 Western Avenue, Seattle, WA 98121. 206–284–1753. Semimonthly. No submission info. Query w/SASE. Index: 3, 101, 123.

The Washington Horse, PO Box 88258, Seattle, WA 98188. Editor: Joe LaDuca/Bruce Batson. 206–226–2620. Ads: Joe LaDuca. 206–772–2381. Monthly periodical on thoroughbred horse racing & breeding. Circ. 3,400. Sub. $30. Uses 2 mss per issue. Payment: $100 on publication. Byline given. Assignment only. Photocopies OK. Nonfiction, B&W photos. Sample/free.

Index: 6, 24, 115.

Washington Insurance Commissioner, Insurance Bldg., Olympia, WA 98504. Publisher. No submission info. Query w/SASE. Index: 24, 36, 123.

Washington Library News, Washington State Library AJ-11, Olympia, WA 98504. Contact: Editor. Periodical. No submission info. Query w/SASE. Index: 104.

Washington Magazine, 901 Lenora, Seattle, WA 98121. 206–624–8400. Editor: David W. Fuller. Bimonthly. Sub. $15. Circ. 71,000. Uses freelance material. Pays money on publication. Acquires 1st rights. Byline given. Submit query w/clips, SASE. Dot matrix, electronic subs OK. Reports in 2 wks. Accepts nonfiction, photos. Guidelines/sample, SASE. Index: 39, 45, 123.

Washington Newspaper, 3838 Stone Way North, Seattle, WA 98103. 206–643–3838. Monthly periodical. No submission info. Query w/SASE. Index: 130.

Washington Professional Publications, PO Box 1147, Bellevue, WA 98009. 206–643–3147. Self-publisher of real estate books. Not a freelance market. Index: 24, 36, 123.

Washington Sea Grant Program, University of Washington, 3716 Brooklyn Avenue N.E., Seattle, WA 98105. Contact: Louie Echols. 206–543–6600. Publisher. No submission info. Query w/SASE. Index: 88, 109.

Washington State Bar CLE, 5050 Madison, Seattle, WA 98104. Publisher. No submission info. Query w/SASE. Index: 74, 113, 123.

Washington State Historical Society, 315 N. Stadium Way, Tacoma, WA 98403. Publisher. No submission info. Query w/SASE. Index: 65, 123.

Washington State Library, Washington 1 Northwest Room, WS Library AJ-11, Olympia, WA 98504. 206–753–4024. Editor: Gayle Palmer. Publishes 1 softcover list of Washington author books per year. Not a freelance market. Catalog available. Index: 104, 123, 125.

Washington State Migrant Ed News, PO Box 901, Sunnyside, WA 98944. Editor: Larry Ashby. Monthly. No submission info. Query w/SASE. Index: 27, 43, 123.

Washington State University Press, Washington State University, Cooper Publications Bldg., Pullman, WA 99164-5910. 509–335–3518. Editor: Fred C. Bohm. Publishes 10 hard/softcover originals, reprints per year. Press run: 2,000 normal. Accepts unsolicited submissions. Pays copies/royalties. Rights acquired vary. Submit ms. Dot matrix, photocopied, computer disc OK. Reports in 8-12 wks. Publishes in 12-18 mo. Accepts nonfiction. Topics: regional studies (history, political science, literature, science); Western Americana; Asian American, Black, Women's Studies; Pacific NW art, natural sciences. Publishes 7 scholarly journals: *Poe Studies; ESQ: A Journal of the American Renaissance; Western Journal of Speech Communication; Communication Reports; Northwest Science; Western Journal of Black Studies; Journal of International Education Administrator.* Catalog available. Index: 5, 62, 84.

Washington Stylist and Salon, PO Box 1117, Portland, OR 97207. Editor: David Porter. 503–226–2461. Monthly trade. Circ. 36,000. Sub. free to licensed salons; others $12. Accepts freelance material. Pays only when assigned at $1.50 inch, on publication. Byline given. Query w/SASE. Phone queries OK. Assignment. Nonfiction: 500-750 wds w/photos. "Anything to do with hair and beauty for the industry, professional beauty salons, schools and supply houses." Photos: B&W, $5, or $15-20 for cover. Tips: needs stringers in OR/WA. "Query first. I prefer to give a writer the slant I want, and I would like to talk to people to give them hints on things I'd like covered in their area." Index: 24.

Washington Teamster Newspaper, 552 Denny Way, Seattle, WA 98109. 206–622–0483. Weekly union newspaper. No submission info. Query w/SASE. Index: 71, 123.

Washington Thoroughbred, WA Thoroughbred Breeders Assn., PO Box 88258, Seattle, WA 98138. 206–226–2620. Editor: Sue Van Dyke. Ads: Joe LaDuca. Monthly. Sub. $40/yr. Uses one freelance article per issue. Assignment only. Pays money on publication. Byline given. Photocopy OK. Reports in 1 wk. Publishes in 2-4 mo. Accepts nonfiction, fiction: thoroughbred horse racing and breeding, local angle preferred. Photos: B&W, color acceptable with good lighting. Index: 6, 115.

Washington Trails Association, 16812 36th Avenue W., Lynnwood, WA 98037. Contact: Jim Eychaner. 206–743–3947. Self-publisher of 1-3 softcover original books a year. Print run: 1,000. Not a freelance market at this time. Index: 92, 103.

The Washington Trooper, PO Box 1525, Husum, WA 98623. Editor: Ron Collins. Quarterly. Accepts freelance material. Payment: $5-75 on publication. Query w/SASE. Nonfiction: Wants mss on "legislation, traffic and highway safety for members of WA State Patrol Troopers Assoc. as well as for state legislators, educators, court officials and like-minded folks in the state of WA." 500-3,500 wds. Tips: Contributors must be "familiar with goals and objectives of the WA State Patrol and with law enforcement in general in the Pacific NW." Index: 101, 123.

Washington Water News, Washington State University, Pullman, WA 99164. Periodical. No submission info. Query w/SASE. Index: 3, 35, 101.

Washington Wildfire, PO Box 45187, Seattle, WA 98145-0187. Editor: Nancy Boulton. 206–633–1992. Periodical. No submission info. Query w/SASE. Index: 130.

For lists of abbreviations and the key to index numbers, see "How to Use this Section" on page 75.

Washington Wildlife, 600 N. Capitol Way, Olympia, WA 98504. Editor: Janet O'Mara. Quarterly wildlife recreation magazine. Circ. 13,000. Payment: Copies on publication. Byline given. Submit ms, SASE. Phone queries, dot matrix, simultaneous submission OK. Reports in 1 month. Publishes in 3-9 mos. Nonfiction: 1,500-2,500 wds. Photos: wildlife in WA. Index: 6, 95, 103.

Washington Women, Dawn Publishing, PO Box 6254, Federal Way, WA 98003. 206–941–2148. Editor: Sue McStravic. Ads: Marilyn Salter. Monthly newspaper. Sub. $12/yr. Circ. 25,000. Uses 4-5 freelance articles per issue. No pay. Acquires all rights. Byline given. Submit: phone query. Dot matrix, photocopied, electronic, computer disc OK. Reports in 2 wks. Publishes 1-2 issues. Accepts nonfiction, fiction, poetry. No longer than 500 wds. Topics: items of interest to business & professional women. Index: 24, 102, 124.

Washington's Land & People, College of Agriculture & Home Ec., Washington State University, Pullman, WA 99164. Contact: Editor. Semiannual. No submission info. Query w/SASE. Index: 3, 31, 123.

WashPIRG Reports, 5628 University Way N.E., Seattle, WA 98105. Editor: Beth Helstien. 206–526–8843. Published 3 times a year on environmental and consumer issues. Circ. 20,000. Sub. $15. Uses 1 ms per issue. Query w/ms, SASE. Dot matrix, photocopies, simultaneous submission, electronic OK. Nonfiction: nuclear waste, environment, consumer issues, good government. Sample/free. Index: 36, 46, 101.

Waterfront Press Company, 1115 N.W. 45th, Seattle, WA 98107. No submission info. Query w/SASE. Index: 130.

Waterlines Magazine, 4917 Leary Ave. NW, Seattle, WA 98107. Editor: Kay Walsh. Periodical. No submission info. Query w/SASE. Index: 130.

Watermark, Oregon State Library, State Library Building, Salem, OR 97310. Monthly. No submission info. Query w/SASE. Index: 22, 104.

Watermark Press, 6909 58th N.E., Seattle, WA 98115. No submission info. Query w/SASE. Index: 130.

Wavefront, PO Box 22070, Postal Station B, Vancouver, BC, V6A 3Y2. 604–254–3521. Editors/Ads: Carolyn McLuskie/Al Razutis. Periodical published 3 times a yr. Sub. $18/$20 US. Circ. 200. Uses 6 freelance mss per issue. Pays copies. Byline given. Submit ms, SASE. Photocopied OK. Reports immediately. Accepts nonfiction, fiction, poetry, photos. Sample $6. Index: 51, 97, 109.

Waves, c/o Eridani Prod, P.O. Box 47111, Seattle, WA 98146-7111. 206–325–8037. Contact: Editor. Periodical. No submission info. Query w/ SASE. Index: 130.

We Alaskans, c/o The Anchorage Daily News, PO Box 6616, Anchorage, AK 99502. Editor: Kathleen McCoy. Periodical. No submission info. Query w/SASE. Index: 4, 33.

We Proceeded On, Lewis/Clark Trail Heritage Foundation, 5054 S.W. 26th Place, Portland, OR 97201. Editor: Robert E. Lange. Quarterly. No submission info. Query w/SASE. Index: 62.

Weather Workbook Company, 827 N.W. 31st Street, Corvallis, OR 97330. Publisher. No submission info. Query w/SASE. Index: 130.

R.M. Weatherford Press, 10902 Woods Creek Road, Monroe, WA 98272. No submission info. Query w/SASE. Index: 130.

Webb Research Group, PO Box 314, Medford, OR 97501. 503–664–4442. Editor: Mr. B. Webber. Publishes 5 hard/softcover subsidy books a year. Does not accept unsolicited submissions. Nonfiction only: subjects on Pacific Northwest (OR, WA, ID) and Oregon Trail. Must be library reference quality, but readable by 8th graders for use in schools. Require biblio., index, ISBN mandatory, CIP almost mandatory. Must have photos. Query w/SASE. Index: 87, 89, 90.

Wednesday Magazine, 19044 Jensen Way, Poulsbo, WA 98370. 206–697–2225. Editor: Paul Goheen. Community newspaper. Index: 33.

Weekly, PO Box 587, Woodinville, WA 98072. 206–483–0606. Weekly newspaper. No submission info. Query w/SASE. Index: 33.

Welcome Press, 2701 Queen Anne N., Seattle, WA 98109. 206–282–5336. Self-publisher of 1-2 softcover originals, reprint books a year. of Scandinavian interest. Print run: 2,500. Not a freelance market. Index: 39, 84.

Welcome to Planet Earth, Great Bear Publishers, PO Box 5164, Eugene, OR 97405. Editor: Mark Lerner. Monthly. No submission info. Query w/SASE. Index: 130.

Wells & West Publishers, 1166 Winsor Street, North Bend, OR 97459. No submission info. Query w/SASE. Index: 130.

Wenatchee Daily World, PO Box 1511, Wenatchee, WA 98801. 509–663–5161. Daily newspaper. No submission info. Query w/SASE. Index: 33.

Wenatchee News Agency Inc., 814 S. Wenatchee Avenue, Wenatchee, WA 98801. Publisher. No submission info. Query w/SASE. Index: 130.

West Coast Baby Magazine, 1920 Broadway Street, Vancouver, WA 98663. Editor: Mike Weber. 206–696–1150. Ads: Francis Fisher. Monthly magazine for new parents. Circ. 25,000. Uses 2-3 mss per issue. Payment: Money on publication. Byline given. Rights purchased: First. Query w/SASE. Dot matrix, photocopies, simultaneous submissions (with notification) OK. Nonfiction: "Serious 'how-to' or medical articles, humor/ fiction regarding new parenthood. Fiction (very seldom). Photos: need 4-color cover and feature photography. Rates negotiable. Guidelines available. Index: 29, 47, 124.

West Coast Review, Department of English, Simon Fraser University, Burnaby, BC V5A 1S6. Editor: Tom Martin. 604–291–4287. Quarterly. Circ. 700. Sub. $12. Uses 20 mss per issue. Payment: $10-15/pg for unsolicited mss, on acceptance. Byline given. Rights purchased: First. Submit ms, SASE. Dot matrix OK. Reports in 2 mos. Nonfiction. Fiction and poetry, no restriction on theme, style. Tips: "Read at least 1 issue before submitting (sample copy of current issue available for $3.50). American contributors enclose sufficient Canadian postage or IRC." Guidelines available; sample/$2.50. Index: 31, 51, 97.

West Hills Bulletin/Mt. Tabor Bulletin, 12311 NE 122nd #103, Portland, OR 97230. 503–256–2833. Editor: Shelli Smith. Ads: Quentin Smith. Monthly newspaper. Sub. $5/yr. Circ. 31,000. Uses 8-15 freelance mss per issue. Pay "other" on publication. Byline given. Submit ms, SASE, phone query. Dot matrix, photocopied, simultaneous, electronic, computer disc OK. Reports in 3-4 wks. Accepts nonfiction, local human interest, cartoons. Sample for postage. Index: 25, 33, 101.

West Lane News, 25027 Dunham, Box 188, Veneta, OR 97487. 503–935–1882. Weekly newspaper. No submission info. Query w/SASE. Index: 33.

Mark West Publishers, PO Box 1914, Sandpoint, ID 83864. No submission info. Query w/SASE. Index: 130.

For lists of abbreviations and the key to index numbers, see "How to Use this Section" on page 75.

192 Market Listings

West Side, Box 5027, Salem, OR 97304. 503–362–8987. Editor/Ads: Tim Hinshaw. Monthly. Sub. $6. Circ. 7,500. Uses 3 freelance mss per issue. Requires journalism/photo experience. Pays money, copies on publication. Acquires 1st rights. Byline given. Phone query. Dot matrix, photocopied OK. Reports in 1 wk. Accepts nonfiction, photos. Free sample. Index: 95.

Western Aluminum News, Western Aluminum Producers, PO Box 8484, Portland, OR 97207. Monthly. No submission info. Query w/SASE. Index: 24.

Western Banker Magazine, Western Banker Publications, 824 W. Franklin, Boise, ID 83702. Monthly. Circ. 5,500. No submission info. Query w/SASE. Index: 24.

Western Business, PO Box 31678, Billings, MT 59107. Editor: James Strauss. 406–252–4788. Monthly. No submission info. Query w/SASE. Index: 24.

Western Cascade Tree Fruit Association Quarterly, 9210 131st N.E., Lake Stevens, WA 98258. No submission info. Query w/SASE. Index: 3, 24.

Western Doll Collector, PO Box 2061, Portland, OR 97208-2061. 503–284–4062. Editor/Ads: Richard Schiessl. Monthly. Sub. $20. Uses freelance. Byline given. Accepts nonfiction, fiction, poetry, photos. No submission info. Sample available. Index: 38.

Western Engines, PO Box 192, Woodburn, OR 97071. Monthly. No submission info. Query w/SASE. Index: 130.

Western Fisheries, Ste. 202-1132 Hamilton Street, Vancouver, BC V6B 2S2. Editor: Henry L. Frew. 604–687–1581. Periodical. No submission info. Query w/SASE. Index: 24, 35, 53.

The Western Flyer, PO Box 98786, Tacoma, WA 98499-0786. Editor: Bruce Williams. 206–588–1743. Biweekly tabloid of aviation news and features. Circ. 19,000. Uses 2-3 freelance mss per issue. Payment: $3 an inch, on publication. Byline given. Rights purchased: First. Submit ms, SASE. Phone queries, dot matrix, simultaneous submission OK. Reports in 2-3 wks. Publishes in 1-3 mos. Nonfiction: 1,500-3,500 wds; aviation news, pilot reports, safety, business. Query on fiction, columns, poetry. Photos: B&W prints, color slides, prints. Guidelines available; sample/$2. Index: 15, 24, 103.

Western Horizons Books, PO Box 4068, Helena, MT 59604. 406–442–7795. Publishes 1 softcover original book a year. Does not accept unsolicited submissions. Query w/clips, SASE. Photocopied OK. Accepts nonfiction, fiction. Topics: sports-boxing, historical-Montana/Upper Rocky Mountain Region. Index: 65, 85, 115.

Western Horizons Press, 15890 S.E. Wallace Rd., Milwaukie, OR 97222. 503–654–1626. Editor: Leonard Delano. Publisher. No submission info. Query w/SASE. Index: 130.

Western Investor, Willamette Publishing, Inc., 400 S.W. 6th, Portland, OR 97204. Quarterly. No submission info. Query w/SASE. Index: 24.

Western Journal of Black Studies, Washington State University Press, Pullman, WA 99164-5910. 509–335–3518. Quarterly. Sub. $15. No submission info. Query w/SASE. Index: 20, 65, 114.

Western Livestock News, PO Box 30755, Billings, MT 59107. 406–259–2457. Editor: Marcia Cranes. Publishes both a weekly newspaper and an annual book covering related news and issues in the state. Query w/SASE. Index: 3, 6.

Western Living, 504 Davie Street, Vancouver, BC V6B 2G4. Editor: Andrew Scott. 604–669–7525. Monthly of western Canadian living, with emphasis on home design. Sub. free. Accepts freelance material. Payment: Averages $.30/wd, on acceptance. Rights purchased: First. Query first with typed, single pg outline w/SASE. Nonfiction, fiction, poetry. "...Seeks to provide the reader with authoritative coverage of its subject areas, which include cuisine, fashion, recreation, the arts, foreign and local travel, architecture and interior design. We want only the best writing, photography and illustration available...the editorial is geared to the interests of homeowners with disposable income. We want to be a showcase of all the good things in the WEST. Stories should have a stimulating or off-beat angle that will capture the attention of educated readers, both male and female. Whenever possible, we want a regional, Western angle." Photos with story: $25-200, B&W 8x10 glossies preferred; prefer 2 1/4 or 4x5 slides. Guidelines avail. Index: 9, 23, 103.

Western News, PO Box M, Libby, MT 59923. Editor: June McMahon. 406–293–4124. Weekly newspaper. No submission info. Query w/SASE. Index: 33.

Western Newsletter, The Book Shop, 908 Main Street, Boise, ID 83702. Editor: Jean Wilson & Lori Benton. Published 3 times a year. Circ. 350. No submission info. Query w/SASE. Index: 76, 77.

Western Publishing, PO Box 61031, Seattle, WA 98121. Contact: Robert D. Ewbank. Periodical. Accepts freelance material. Query w/SASE. Topics: Music, performing arts, poetry, painting. Index: 10, 86, 97.

Western Trailer & Mobile Home News, 362 Pittock Block, Portland, OR 97205. Editor: Robert Kyle. 503–222–1255. Monthly. No submission info. Query w/SASE. Index: 24.

Western Trucking, 4250 Dawson Street, Burnaby, BC V5C 4B1. Periodical. No submission info. Query w/SASE. Index: 24, 36.

Western Viking, 2040 N.W. Market Street, Seattle, WA 98107. 206–784–4617. Weekly newspaper. No submission info. Query w/SASE. Index: 33.

Western Wood Products Association, 1500 Yeon Building, Portland, OR 97204. Publisher. No submission info. Query w/SASE. Index: 24.

Westgate Press, 15050 SW Koll Pkwy. Ste. G2, Beaverton, OR 97006. 503–646–0820. Editor: Dr. Pam Munter. Self-publisher of 1 hardcover psychology book a year. Not a freelance market. Index: 100.

Westridge Press, 1090 Southridge Pl. S., Salem, OR 97302. Contact: Editor. Publisher. No submission info. Query w/SASE. Index: 130.

Westside Record Journal, PO Box 38, Ferndale, WA 98248. 206–384–1411. Weekly newspaper. No submission info. Query w/SASE. Index: 33.

Westwind, Northwest Science Fiction Society, PO Box 24207, Seattle, WA 98124. Editor: Bob Suryan. Periodical. No submission info. Query w/SASE. Index: 48.

Westwind Publishing, Box 3586, Boise, ID 83703. Contact: Editor. Publisher. No submission info. Query w/SASE. Index: 130.

For lists of abbreviations and the key to index numbers, see "How to Use this Section" on page 75.

Westwind Review, Southern Oregon State College, Ashland, OR 97520. Editor: Herman H. Schmeling. Annual. No submission info. Query w/ SASE. Index: 31.

Westworld Magazine/Canada Wide Magazines, 401-4180 Lougheed Highway, Burnaby, BC V5C 6A7. 604–299–7311. Editor: Robin Roberts. Ads: Pat Meyers. Periodicals published 4-6 times a year. Circ. 96,000-420,000. Not a freelance market. Index: 26.

What's Happening, 335 W. 20th, Eugene, OR 97405. Editor: Songa Ungemach. 503–484–0519. Weekly tabloid on the arts, events, entertainment. Circ. 15,000-20,000. Uses 2 mss per issue. Payment: $.03/wd, on publication. Byline given. Dot matrix, simultaneous submission OK. Nonfiction/fiction: 500-1,500 wds. Columns: 500-1,00 wds. Poetry. Photos: B&W. Guidelines available; sample w/SASE. Index: 10, 45.

Wheat Life, 109 E. First, Ritzville, WA 99169. 509–659–0611. Editor/Ads: Sherrye Wyatt Phillips. Publishes 11 issues per year. Sub. $12/yr. Circ. 14,000. Uses 2 freelance mss per year. Pays in copies. Acquires 1st rights. Byline given. Submit ms, SASE. Nonfiction only: agriculture — wheat & barley, but with warmth. Recipes/cooking profiles, or features using barley or wheat in a unique way. B&W prints. Sample $.50. Index: 3, 54.

Wheatherstone Press, 20 Wheatherstone, Lake Oswego, OR 97034. No submission info. Query w/SASE. Index: 130.

Wheel Press, 9203 S.E. Mitchell Street, Portland, OR 97266. Contact: Arthur Honeyman. 503–777–6659. Self-publisher of 2 softcover, original, reprint, subsidy books a year. Audience: "Students, educators, sensitive readers of all ages interested in social issues with emphasis on (but not limited to) handicapped people." Print run: 500. Sometimes accepts freelance material. Submit ms, SASE. Reports in 1 month. Nonfiction, fiction, poetry, plays, cartoons. No photographs or multi-colored pictures. Topics: "Almost any subject." Catalog available. Index: 29, 51, 126.

Whidbey News Times & Whidbey Today, PO Box 10, Oak Harbor, WA 98277. 206–675–6611. Weekly newspaper. No submission info. Query w/SASE. Index: 33.

Whistler Publishing, Box 3641, Courtenay, BC V9N 6Z8. Contact: K. Ben Buss. 604–334–2852. Publisher of 10 nonfiction, softcover originals per year to outdoor recreation enthusiasts, environmentally aware. Accepts freelance material. Payment: Money, royalties. Ms outline, sample chapters w/SASE. Nonfiction: "Any material applicable to the outdoors from handicrafts to hiking and from cottage industries to flora & fauna...should be of a practical nature easily illustrated or photographed." Index: 46, 92, 103.

G.M. White, PO Box 365, Ronan, MT 59864. 406–676–3766. Self-publisher of softcover Indian and Eskimo culture and history books. Not a freelance market. Index: 38, 87, 89.

White Mammoth, 2183 Nottingham Dr., Fairbanks, AK 99709. 907–479–6034. Contact: M. L. Guthrie. Publishes 2-3 softcover books a year. Not a freelance market. Index: 4, 88.

White Ribbon Review, Oregon Women Temperance Union, 1171 F. Street, Springfield, OR 97477. Bimonthly. No submission info. Query w/ SASE. Index: 105, 113, 124.

White Salmon Enterprise, PO Box 21, White Salmon, WA 98627. 206–493–2112. Weekly newspaper. No submission info. Query w/SASE. Index: 33.

Whitefish Pilot, 312 2nd St., Whitefish, MT 59937. 406–862–3505. Contact: Editor. Newspaper. No submission info. Query w/SASE. Index: 130.

Whitehall Ledger, 15 W. Legion, Whitehall, MT 59759. Contact: Editor. Periodical. No submission info. Query w/SASE. Index: 130.

Whitehouse Publishing, Box 1778, Vernon, B.C. V1T 8C3. 604–545–9896. Editor/Ads: Dr. B. J. White. Monthly newspaper. Sub. $15/Can., $20/USA. Circ. 16,792. Uses freelance material. Pays $30-100 per article on publication. Acquires 1st rights. Byline given. Submit ms, SASE. Dot matrix, photocopied OK. Reports in 2 mo. Publishes in 1-2 mo. Accepts nonfiction, photos, cartoons. Topics: Equine-oriented only, all aspects. Photos $5 B&W, good color. Sample $2. Index: 6, 103.

Whitman College Press, Office of Publications, Whitman College, Walla Walla, WA 99362. No submission info. Query w/SASE. Index: 31, 43.

Whitman-Latah Republic, PO Box 8307, Moscow, ID 83843. Weekly newspaper. No submission info. Query w/SASE. Index: 33.

Whole Air, PO Box 98786, Tacoma, WA 98499-0786. Editor: Bruce Williams. 206–588–1743. Periodical on hang gliding. Uses 2-3 freelance mss per issue. Payment: $3 an inch, 1 month after publication. Byline given. Rights purchased: First. Submit ms, SASE. Phone queries, dot matrix, simultaneous submission OK. Reports in 2-3 wks. Publishes in 1-3 mos. Nonfiction: 1,500-3,500 wds. Query on fiction, poetry, columns. Photos: B&W prints, color slides, prints. Guidelines available; sample/$2. Index: 15, 103, 115.

Wicazo Sea Review, Eastern Washington University, English & Indian Studies, Cheney, WA 99004. 509–359–2871. Editor: Elizabeth Cook-Lynn. Biannual. Sub. $8/15. Circ. 300. Uses freelance material. Pays copies. Acquires 1st rights. Byline given. Submit query w/clips, ms, SASE. Photocopied OK. Reports in 3 mo. Accepts nonfiction, fiction, poetry, photos. Sample $4. Index: 7, 62, 87.

Wiggansnatch, PO Box 20061, Seattle, WA 98102. Editor/ads: James Moore. Quarterly journal on neo-paganism. Circ. 500. Sub. $6. Uses 10 mss per issue. Payment: Copies on publication. Byline given. Rights purchased: First, non-exclusive reprint. Submit ms, SASE. Dot matrix, photocopies, simultaneous submission OK. Reports in 1 month. Nonfiction, fiction, cartoons. "We emphasize personal experiences in magick, ritual, ecology, etc. Anything of interest to a neo-pagan audience. Departments include: real magic, myth, dreams, spirit, politics, shamanism, wicca, tarot." Guidelines available; sample/$2. Index: 13, 37, 57.

Wilbur Register, PO Box 186, Wilbur, WA 99185. 509–647–5551. Weekly newspaper. No submission info. Query w/SASE. Index: 33.

Wild Oregon, Oregon Natural Resources Council, 1161 Lincoln Street, Eugene, OR 97401. Editor: Jeff Schier. Periodical. No submission info. Query w/SASE. Index: 35, 88, 91.

Wilderness House, 11129 Caves Hwy., Cave Junction, OR 97523. Publisher. No submission info. Query w/SASE. Index: 130.

Wildfire, Bear Tribe Medicine Society, PO Box 9167, Spokane, WA 99209-9167. Editor: Matthew Ryan. Ads: Joseph LaZenka.. Quarterly magazine. Sub. $10. Circ. 10,000. Uses freelance material. Pays money. Acquires 1st rights. Submit ms/SASE. Photocopied Apple/Mac computer disc OK. Accepts nonfiction, fiction, poetry, photos, cartoons. Topics: New Age, permaculture, Native American, philosophy, UFOs. Tip: "No sensationalism." Guidelines available. Sample $2.95. Index: 13, 46, 87.

Wildlife Safari Newsletter, Safari Game Search Foundation, PO Box 600, Winston, OR 97496. Editor: Bonnie Riggs. 503–679–6761. Periodical. No submission info. Query w/SASE. Index: 6.

For lists of abbreviations and the key to index numbers, see "How to Use this Section" on page 75.

Wildlife-Wildlands Institute, 5200 Upper Miller Creek Road, Missoula, MT 59803. Publisher. No submission info. Query w/SASE. Index: 6, 35, 88.

Wildwood Press, 209 S.W. Wildwood Ave., Grants Pass, OR 97526. 503–479–3434. Self-publisher of 1 softcover original book. Does not accept unsolicited submissions. Index: 2, 92.

Willamette Collegian, 900 State Street, Salem, OR 97301. 503–370–6053. Bimonthly student newspaper of Willamette University. No submission info. Query w/SASE. Index: 31.

The Willamette Journal of the Liberal Arts, Willamette University D-180, Salem, OR 97301. 503–370–6272. Editor: Lane McGaughy. Ads: Elsa Struble. Sub. $5/issue. Circ. 700. Journal published 1-2 times a year. Uses freelance material. Pays in copies. Acquires all rights. Byline given. Submit ms, SASE. Photocopied, computer disc OK. Accepts nonfiction, fiction, poetry, photos. Topics: any scholarly essays in the liberal arts. Guidelines available. Sample $3.75. Index: 31, 75, 108.

Willamette Kayak & Canoe Club, PO Box 1062, Corvallis, OR 97339. Publisher. No sub. info. Query w/ SASE. Index: 103, 115.

Willamette Law Review, College of Law, Willamette University, Salem, OR 97301. Quarterly. No submission info. Query w/SASE. Index: 74, 113.

Willamette Press, PO Box 2065, Beaverton, OR 97075. No submission info. Query w/SASE. Index: 130.

Willamette Week, 2 N.W. 2nd Avenue, Portland, OR 97209. Editor: Mark Zusman. 503–243–2122. Weekly alternative news, art and regional living magazine. Circ. 50,000. Uses 60% freelance mss per copy. Payment: $.02-04/wd. Query w/ms, SASE. Dot matrix, simultaneous submission (if informed) OK. Publishes in 1 month. Nonfiction: to 5,000 wds; art, entertainment, politics, Portland based subjects. Guidelines and sample available w/SASE. Index: 10, 45, 98.

The Willamette Writer, PO Box 2485, Portland, OR 97208. 503–293–5616. Monthly newsletter for the membership of Willamette Writers. Circ. 750. Sub. membership. Not a freelance market. Index: 22, 102, 125.

The Willapa Harbor Herald, PO Box 627, Raymond, WA 98577. 206–942–3466. Weekly newspaper. No submission info. Query w/SASE. Index: 33.

William & Allen, PO Box 6147, Olympia, WA 98502. Publisher. No submission info. Query w/SASE. Index: 130.

Willoughby Wessington Publishing Company, PO Box 911, Mercer Island, WA 98040. No submission info. Query w/SASE. Index: 130.

Willow Springs, Eastern Washington University, PO Box 1063, M5-1, Cheney, WA 99201. 509–458–6429. Editor: Gillian Conoley. Ads: Jan Strever. Semiannual magazine. Sub. $7. Circ. 800-1,000. Uses 10-15 freelance mss per issue. Pays copies on publication. Acquires N.A. serial rights. Byline given. Submit ms, SASE. Photocopied OK. Reports in 1-2 mo. Publishes in 1-6 mo. Accepts nonfiction, fiction, fine poetry, photos, cartoons, translations. "We have a bias toward work that uses fresh language and tests the boundaries of the imagination." Guidelines & samples available. Index: 51, 76, 97.

Wilson Publications, PO Box 712, Yakima, WA 98907. 509–457–8275. Self-publisher. Not a freelance market. Index: 62, 120.

Wind Row, Washington State University, English Dept., Pullman, WA 99164. Contact: Editor. Periodical. No submission info. Query w/SASE. Index: 31.

Wind Vein Press, PO Box 462, Ketchum, ID 83340. Contact: Scott Preston. 208–788–3704. Self-publisher of high quality limited editions. "All of the books published by Wind Vein will be privately arranged." Not a freelance market. Index: 22, 69, 97.

Windham Bay Press, PO Box 34283, Juneau, AK 99803. 907–789–4362. Editor: Ellen Searby. Publishes 3 softcover originals a year. Travel guidebooks on assignment only, to fit established series. Catalog available. Index: 115, 120.

Windsor Publications, Inc., 1425 Oak, Eugene, OR 97405. Contact: Ed Lusch. Publishes wildlife artwork & prints, specifically gamefish & birds. Query SASE. Index: 6, 53, 122.

Windyridge Press, PO Box 591, Rogue River, OR 97537. No submission info. Query w/SASE. Index: 130.

Winn Book Publishers, PO Box 80096, Seattle, WA 98108. Contact: Larry Winn. 206–763–9544. Not a freelance mkt at this time. Index: 130.

The Wire Harp, Building 5, MS-3050, W. 3410 Fort George Wright Dr., Spokane, WA 99204. Contact: Editor. Annual. No submission info. Query w/SASE. Index: 130.

Wise Buys, 511 NW 74th St., Vancouver, WA 98665-8414. Editor: Pat Stenback. Periodical. No submission info. Query w/SASE. Index: 36.

Wistaria Press, 4373 N.E. Wistaria Drive, Portland, OR 97213. No submission info. Query w/SASE. Index: 130.

WLA Highlights, Washington Library Assoc., 1232 143rd Ave. S.E., Bellevue, WA 98007. Contact: Editor. Periodical. No submission info. Query w/SASE. Index: 104.

Woman to Woman Magazine, 535 W. 10th, 2nd Fl., Vancouver, B.C. V52 1K9. 604–736–0218. Editor: S. Massingham-Pearce. Ads: Megan Abbott. Monthly tabloid. Sub. $11.88/. Circ. 60,000. Uses 8-10 freelance mss per issue. Pays $.15-.25/wd., half on acceptance, half on publication. Acquires 1st rights. Byline depends on size. Submit query w/clips, SASE. Dot matrix, photocopied OK. Reports in 4-6 wks. Publishes in 2-4 mo. average. Accepts fiction, nonfiction, photos. Topics: health, beauty, human interest, business profiles, crafts. Tips: 200-1,200 wds, entertaining, BC oriented, tabloid style writing — fast, informal, plenty of quotes, personal accounts & anecdotes; aim to stimulate interest & entertain. Pictures must be accompanied by negatives, no slides, original only. Guidelines available. Sample $.99. Index: 49, 54, 124.

Womanshare Books, PO Box 681, Grants Pass, OR 97526. Publisher. No submission info. Query w/SASE. Index: 124.

Womanspirit, PO Box 263, Wolf Creek, OR 97497. Quarterly. No submission info. Query w/SASE. Index: 13, 50, 124.

The Women's Yellow Pages, PO Box 3975, Portland, OR 97208. 503–644–7913. Annual business and professional women's directory with edition for Seattle & Portland. Circ. 50,000. Sub. free. Uses 10 mss per issue. Payment: Copies on publication. Byline given. Query w/SASE. Phone queries, dot matrix, photocopies, simultaneous sub., electronic OK. Reports in 2-6 wks. Nonfiction, 1-6 pgs, typed ds. Women in bus. or professions, and related women's issues. Sample free. Index: 24, 124.

For lists of abbreviations and the key to index numbers, see "How to Use this Section" on page 75.

Womyn's Press, PO Box 562, Eugene, OR 97440. 503–485–3207. Editor: Betsy Brown, Kaseja O., Jessica Jenkins. Ads: Gail Elber. Bi-monthly newspaper. Sub. $5-15/yr. Circ. 1,000. Uses freelance material from women only. Pays in copies. Byline given. Query, SASE. Dot matrix, photocopied OK. Reports ASAP. Publishes within 2 mo. Accepts nonfiction, fiction, poetry, photos, cartoons. Tips: poetry, not more than a page; articles 2,000 wds. Sample $1. Index: 50, 57, 124.

Wood Bone Fire, 6809 27th NE, Seattle, WA 98115. Contact: Editor. Magazine. Uses freelance material. Submit ms, SASE. Accepts fiction, poetry, other. Index: 10, 51, 97.

Wood Lake Books, Inc., S-6, C-9, R.R. 1, Winfield, BC V0H 2C0. Publisher. No submission info. Query w/SASE. Index: 130.

Woodburn Drag Script, 7730 State Hwy. 214 N.E., Woodburn, OR 97071. Periodical. No sub. info. Query w/SASE. Index: 103, 115.

Woodburn Independent, 650 N. 1st Street, Box 96, Woodburn, OR 97071. 503–981–3441. Weekly newspaper. No submission info. Query w/SASE. Index: 33.

Woodford Memorial Editions, Inc., PO Box 55085, Seattle, WA 98155. Publisher. No submission info. Query w/SASE. Index: 130.

Woodstock Independent News, PO Box 2354h Avenue, Portland, OR 97202. Editor: Jerry Schmidt. 503–233–1797. Ads: same. Monthly newspaper. Circ. 20,000. Sub. free. No submission info. Query w/SASE. Index: 33.

Tom Worcester, 11678 S.E. Capps Road, Clackamas, OR, 97015. Publisher. No submission info. Query w/SASE. Index: 130.

Word Power, Inc., PO Box 17034, Seattle, WA 98107. Publisher. No submission info. Query w/SASE. Index: 130.

Word Works, PO Box 2206, Main Post Office, Vancouver, BC, V6B 3W2. Contact: Editor. Monthly. No submission info. Query w/SASE. Index: 130.

Words & Pictures Unlimited, 1257 NW Van Buren Ave., Corvallis, OR 97330. Contact: Editor. Publisher. No submission info. Query w/SASE. Index: 130.

Words Press, PO Box 1935, Beaverton, OR 97075. No submission info. Query w/SASE. Index: 130.

Wordware, PO Box 14300, Seattle, WA 98114. Contact: Marguerite Russell. 206–328–9393. Publisher. No submission info. Query w/SASE. Index: 130.

Work Abroad Newsletter, 2515 Rainier Ave. S., Suite 307, Seattle, WA 98144. Editor: Robert Velick. Monthly. Sub. $5. Circ. 5,000. Uses freelance material. Pays money on publication. Byline given. Submit query w/clips, SASE. Photocopied OK. Nonfiction. Sample $5. Index: 71, 120.

Workingman's Press, PO Box 12486, Seattle, WA 98111. No submission info. Query w/SASE. Index: 130.

The World, Box 1840, Coos Bay, OR 97420. 503–269–0238. Daily newspaper. No submission info. Query w/SASE. Index: 33.

World Peace University, 35 S.E. 60th, Portland, OR 97215. Contact: Susan Henry. 503–282–0280. Publisher of 4 softcover originals per year. Print run: 3,000. Not a freelance market; submissions are by invitation. "We plan to sponsor and host International Conference of writers for peace in 1988. Writers, editors, and publishers wishing to receive information about this should write to request a place on our mailing list." Index: 43, 93, 105.

World Wide Publishing Corporation, PO Box 105, Ashland, OR 97520. No submission info. Query w/SASE. Index: 130.

World Without War Council, 1512 N.E. 45th, Seattle, WA 98102. Publisher. No sub. info. Query w/SASE. Index: 93, 101, 113.

Writer's Chapbook, Rolling Drum Press, Box 2101, Boise, ID 83701. Editor: Kirk Garber. Periodical. No submission info. Query w/SASE. Index: 125.

Writer's Info, PO Box 1870, Hayden, ID 83835. 208–772–6184. Editor: Linda Hutton. Monthly with advice for beginning freelancers. Sub. $12. Uses freelance material. Payment "starts at $1" on acceptance. Byline given. Acquires 1st rights. Submit ms, SASE. Photocopies, simultaneous submission OK. Reports in 1 mo. Nonfiction, poetry. To 300 word on any aspect of freelancing, short poems and riddles related to writing. Guidelines available/sample, SASE, 2 first-class stamps. Index: 50, 97, 125.

Writers-In-Waiting Newsletter, 837 Archie St., Eugene, OR 97402. 503–688–5400. Editor/Ads: Bjo Ashwill. Bimonthly. Sub. $10/yr. Uses 3-4 freelance mss per issue. Pays in copies on publication. Acquires 1st rights. Byline given. Submit ms, SASE. Dot matrix, photocopied, simultaneous OK. Reports in 2 mo. Publishes in 2-6 mo. Accepts nonfiction, fiction, poetry. Topics: how-to articles for beginning writers. "Please, no more how-to-cope-with-rejection! Be specific with craft techniques." Tips: special feature, Works-in-Progress column–fiction or poetry is critiqued. Guidelines available. Sample $2.50. Index: 51, 97, 125.

Writers Information Network, PO Box 11337, Bainbridge Island, WA 98110. 206–842–9103. Contact: Elaine Wright Colvin. Bi-monthly newsletter. Sub. $10/yr. Not a freelance market. Index: 22, 105, 125.

Writer's NW, Media Weavers, Rt. 3, Box 376, Hillsboro, OR 97124. 503–621–3911. Editors: Linny Stovall, Dennis Stovall. Quarterly publication from Media Weavers (imprint of Blue Heron Publishing, Inc.) for writers, teachers, publishers, librarians, students. Uses freelance material. Query w/SASE first. Pays in copies. Tips: 500–1,000 wd articles on all aspects of writing and publishing; regular columns include book reviews, profiles of publishers, and technical reviews (software, how-to). Welcomes news from writers, teachers, publishers and librarians for items in "Calendar" and "News & Notes" sections. Free in U.S. if sent with bulk mailing. Single copy $2.50. Index: 89, 102, 125.

Writer's Publishing Service Company, 1512 Western Ave., Seattle, WA 98101. 206–284–9954. Contact: Jeff Mosely. Publishes 15-20 hard/softcover originals, reprints, subsidy books a year. Accepts unsolicited submissions. Pays money/royalties/advance on acceptance/publication. Acquires first/all rights. Submit query w/clips, ms, phone, SASE. Dot matrix, photocopied, simultaneous, computer disc OK. Reports in 6 wks. Accepts nonfiction, fiction, poetry, photos, plays, cartoons, other. "We are specialists in self-publishing. However, we do purchase or co-publish 3-5 projects a year." Index: 51, 58, 97.

Writing Magazine, Box 69609, Sta. K., Vancouver, BC V5K 4W7. 604–738–2032. Editor: Colin Browne. Published 3 times a yr. Circ. 650. Accepts freelance submissions. Pays money and subscription. Submit several poems, a long poem, 1-2 stories, a chapter, SASE. Photocopied OK. Reports in 2 mo. Accepts fiction, poetry. Sample $3. Index: 51, 97, 125.

For lists of abbreviations and the key to index numbers, see "How to Use this Section" on page 75.

Writing Pursuits, 1863 Bitterroot Dr., Twin Falls, ID 83301. 208–734–0746. Newsletter, 10 issues/yr. Sub. $4.50/10. Uses 2-3 freelance mss per issue. Pays copies on acceptance. Byline given. Query, SASE. Dot matrix, photocopied OK. Reports in 2 wks. Publishes in 1-2 mo. Accepts nonfiction, short-short stories, poetry, cartoons. Guidelines available. Sample $.25 & #10 SASE. Index: 51, 125.

The Written ARTS, Room 828 Alaska Building, Second & Cherry, Seattle, WA 98104. Editor: Joan Mann. 206–344–7580. Literary magazine of the King County Arts Commission. Uses 30 mss per issue. Byline given. Rights revert to author on publication. Query w/SASE. Nonfiction, fiction, poetry. Guidelines and sample available. Index: 51, 97.

WSEO Dispatch, Washington State Energy Office, 400 E. Union, 1st Floor, ER-11, Olympia, WA 98504. Editor: Linda Waring. Bimonthly. No submission info. Query w/SASE. Index: 60, 123.

Wynkyn Press, R.R. 3, Wildwood Crescent, Ganges, BC VOS 1E0. No submission info. Query w/SASE. Index: 130.

X-Press, 3905 W. 12th Avenue, Vancouver, BC V6R 2P1. 604–224–0886. Contact: Editor. Publishes 1+ softcover books a year. Press run: 3,000. Does not accept unsolicited submissions. Index: 130.

Michael Yaeger, PO Box 4304, Pioneer Square, Seattle, WA 98104. 206–624–9102. Self-publisher. Not a freelance market. Index: 14, 68, 89.

Yakima Herald-Republic, 114 North Fourth Street, PO Box 9668, Yakima, WA 98909. 509–248–1251. Daily newspaper. No submission info. Query w/SASE. Index: 33.

Yakima Nation Review, PO Box 386, Toppenish, WA 98948. 509–865–5121. Newspaper. No submission info. Query w/SASE. Index: 87, 89.

Yakima Valley Genealogical Society Bulletin, PO Box 445, Yakima, WA 98907. 509–248–1328. Editor: Ellen Brzoska. Quarterly journal. Sub. $11/yr. Uses freelance material. No pay. Submit ms, SASE. Photocopied, computer disc OK. Accepts articles related to family history. Sample available. Index: 58, 123.

Ye Galleon Press, PO Box 287, Fairfield, WA 99012. 509–283–2422. Publisher of hard/softcover originals, reprints, books per year. Print run: 100-3,500. Accepts freelance material. Rights purchased: varies. Reports in 1 mo. Nonfiction, poetry. Northwest Coast voyage books; "I publish (at my expense) Pacific NW and rare western U.S. history. Modern books with living authors are nearly all paid for by authors, but editions are sometimes split." Catalog available. Index: 5, 62, 97.

Yellow Hat Press, PO Box 34337, Sta. D, Vancouver, BC V6J 4P3. Editor: Beverly D. Chiu. Publisher. No submission info. Query w/SASE. Index: 130.

Yellow Jacket Press, Rt 4, Box 7464, Twin Falls, ID 83301. Editor: Bill Studebaker. Publisher. No submission info. Query w/SASE. Index: 130.

YIPE, Washington Poets Association, Box 71213, Rainier, OR 97048. Editor: Carolyn Norred. Periodical. No submission info. Query w/SASE. Index: 97.

Young American, America's Newspaper for Kids, PO Box 12409, Portland, OR 97212. 503–230–1895. Editor: Kristina Linden. Monthly. Sub. $15/yr. Circ. 4 million. Uses 3 mss per issue. Payment: $.07/wd, on publication. Byline given. Rights purchased: First. Submit ms, SASE. Dot matrix, photocopies OK. Reports in 4 mos. Publishes within year. Nonfiction to 500 wds. Fiction to 1,000 wds. Poetry, photos (B&W/$5), plays, cartoons. Guidelines available. Sample $1.50. Index: 29, 68, 109.

Young Pine Press, c/o International Examiner, 318 6th Avenue S., #123, Seattle, WA 98104. No submission info. Query w/SASE. Index: 130.

Young Voices, PO Box 2321, Olympia, WA 98507. 206–357–4683. Contact: Editor. Sub. $14. No submission info. Query w/SASE. Index: 28, 29.

Your Public Schools, Superintendent of Public Instruction, Old Capitol Bldg. FG-11, Olympia, WA 98504. Contact: Editor. Periodical. No submission info. Query w/SASE. Index: 43.

Zap News, Box 1994, Eugene, OR 97440. Periodical. No submission info. Query w/SASE. Index: 130.

The Zig Zag Papers, PO Box 247, Zig Zag, OR 97049. 503–622–3425. Self-publisher of 1 book per year on science & technology. Print run: 3,000. Not a freelance market. Index: 109.

For lists of abbreviations and the key to index numbers, see "How to Use this Section" on page 75.

Writer's Northwest Handbook   197

Resources

The following lists include over 500 Northwest resources for writers, publishers, teachers, librarians, artists, and researchers. We have excluded the names of all the schools which have writing classes, although many of their special programs for writers are listed. Almost every community college, college, university, and extension program offers classes in creative writing, journalism and photography. There are too many to include them all. Also, we have not listed the many "for profit" private classes and workshops available throughout the region. Information about these can be found by contacting local schools and writers' groups.

If you send us information about events, organizations, classes, contests, or other resources which we overlooked (or corrections), we'll include it in the updates section of our quarterly tabloid, *Writer's NW*.

Organizations

Adventist Composers, Arrangers and Poets, Inc., PO Box 11, Days Creek, OR 97429. Contact: Eleanor B. Davis.

Adventist Writers' Association of Western Washington, 18115 116th Ave. S.E., Renton, WA 98058. 206–235–1435. How-to newsletter on writing and marketing to Seventh-day Adventist publications. Meetings held 6 times a yr. to critique and/or hear speakers. Annual week-long writing class in June. Anyone may join.

Alaska Arts Southeast, Box 2133, Sitka, AK 99835.

Alaska Arts-in-Prisons, 540 W. 10th Street, Juneau, AK 99801.

Alaska Association of Small Presses, PO Box 821, Cordova, AK 99574. Contact: M. Constance Taylor. 907–424–3116.

Alaska Historical Society, Box 10355, Anchorage, AK 99511.

Alaska Press Women, PO Box 104056, Anchorage, AK 99510. Purposes are: "to promote the highest ideals of journalism; to provide exchange of journalistic ideas and experiences of men and women in commuications; and to coordinate efforts on matters of national interest to women." There are active chapters in Juneau, Anchorage, Mat-Su and Fairbanks. There is an annual competition for work performed the previous year.

Alaska State Council on the Arts, 619 Warehouse Avenue, Suite 220, Anchorage, AK 99501. Contact: Chris D'Arcy. 907–279–1558. For resident writers, they offer a fellowship program every other year of $5,000. Write for grant guidelines. Next application deadline, early Fall, 1990.

Alaska Theatre of Youth, Box 104036, Anchorage, AK 99510.

The Alcuin Society, PO Box 3216, Vancouver, BC V6B 3X8. Contact: Doreen Eddy. Formed in the mid-sixties, supports book arts and fine printing with publications and events. For more information, check in the listings for their publication, *Amphora*.

Allied Arts Council N. Central Washington, PO Box 573, Wenatchee, WA 98801. Contact: Margie Jones. 509–662–1213.

Allied Arts Council Walla Walla Valley, PO Box 68, Walla Walla, WA 99362. Contact: R.L. Friese. 509–529–0089.

Allied Arts Council Yakima Valley, 5000 W. Lincoln Ave., Yakima, WA 98908. 509–966–0930. Contact: Ann Byerrum. Annual spring writers workshop.

Allied Arts Literary Guild, PO Box 5182, Bellingham, WA 98227. 206–671–1155. Contact: Carol Anderson. Support group for writers, published authors, photographers, anyone interested in book publishing.

Allied Arts of Seattle, 107 S. Main Street, Seattle, WA 98104. Contact: Francis Van Ausdal. 206–624–0432.

Allied Arts of Tacoma/Pierce County, 901 Broadway Plaza, Pantages Centre 5th Floor, Tacoma, WA 98402. Contact: Jane Matsch. 206–272–3141.

Allied Arts of Whatcom County, PO Box 2584, Bellingham, WA 98227. 206–676–8548. Contact: Miriam Barnett. Literary guild and nonprofit arts council, meets monthly.

American Pen Women, Rt. 1, Box 53, Reardon, WA 99029. 509–796–5872. Contact: Charlotte Chester. State newsletter, *Branch Pen Points*, sponsors contest, meets monthly.

American Society of Magazine Photographers, Washington Chapter, Aperture PhotoBank, Inc., 1530 Westlake Ave. N., Seattle, WA 98109. Contact: Marty Lokins. 206–282–8166.

Amniote Egg Writers Group, 1123 F Street, Anchorage, AK 99501.

Arts at Menucha, PO Box 4958, Portland, OR 97208. Annual artists summer camp/workshops in fine and applied arts and literature sponsored by Creative Arts Community.

Arts Council Mid-Columbia Region, PO Box 3069, Richland, WA 99302-3069. Contact: Chris Dow. 509–943–0524.

Arts Council of Pendleton, PO Box 573, Pendleton, OR 97801. 503–276–8826. Contact: Carolyn Wallace.

Arts Council of Snohomish, PO Box 5038, Everett, WA 98206. Contact: Nelda Coxley. 206–252–7469.

Arts Council of the Grand Coulee, PO Box 405, Grand Coulee, WA 99133. Contact: Jerry Rumberg.

Arts & Crafts Guild of Oregon, PO Box 601, Oakridge, OR 97463. 503–782–4431. Contact: Clara Bailey.

Associated Arts of Ocean Shores, PO Box 241, Ocean Shores, WA 98569. Contact: Margie McBride.

Association for the Multi-Image/Idaho Chapter, c/o Paul Franklin, Custom Recording & Sound, 3907 Custer Drive, Boise, ID 83705. Photographers organziation.

Association for the Multi-Image/Montana Chapter, c/o Doug Brekke, PO Box 1295, Big Timber, MT 59011. Photographers organization.

Association for the Multi-Image/Oregon Chapter, PO Box 6098, Portland, OR 97228. Contact: David P. Knippel. 503–224–3660. Photographers organization.

Association for the Multi-Image/Washington Chapter, Pacific Northwest Bell, 800 Stewart St., Rm. 401, Seattle, WA 98101. Contact: Tony Beck. Photographers organization.

Association of Book Publishers of British Columbia, 1622 W. 7th Avenue, Vancouver, BC V6J 1S5. Contact: Tony Gregson. 604–734–1611.

Auburn Arts Commission, 25 W. Main, Auburn, WA 98001. 206–931–3043. Contact: Josie Emmons Vine. Writers' Conference last weekend in October.

Bainbridge Island Arts Council, c/o Nancy Rekow, Executive Director, 8489 Fletcher Bay Road, Bainbridge Island, WA 98110. 206–842–7901. In addition to other activities, they publish a *Poets & Artists Calendar* from their annual Poets & Artists Competition (See Contests.)

Bainbridge Writer's Guild, c/o Nancy Rekow, 8489 Fletcher Bay Road N.E., Bainbridge, WA 98110. 206–842–4855. Formed in 1986 to serve writers of all levels in Bainbridge Island area. Sponsors poetry readings. Publishes local work. Query with SASE, phone OK. (See Events.)

Ballard Arts Council, c/o Ballard Chamber of Commerce, 2208 N.W. Market Street #204, Seattle, WA 98107. Contact: Larry L. Jones. 206–523–8280.

Bay Area Arts Council/South Coast Tourism Assn., 886 S. 4th Street, Coos Bay, OR 97420. Contact: Lionel Youst. 503–267–6500.

Beaverton Arts Commission, PO Box 4755, Beaverton, OR 97076. 503–526–2222. Contact: Jayne Bruno Scott.

Bellevue Allied Arts Council, 9509 N.E. 30th, Bellevue, WA 98004-1741. Contact: Gigi Mauritzen. 206–455–2589.

Bellevue Arts Commission, PO Box 90012, Bellevue, WA 98009. Contact: Mary Pat Byrne. 206–455–6881.

Bellingham Arts Commission, City Hall, 210 Lottie Street, Bellingham, WA 98225. Contact: Susann Schwiesow. 206–734–3410.

Bend-in-the-River Writers Guild, c/o Doris M. Hall, 62340 Powell Butte Road, Bend, OR 97701. 503–389–5845. "A writers support group, largely poets, but some other kinds of writing are represented. We meet for mutual enrichment, support, and critiques; and to share information about markets, workshops, readings." (See Events.)

Billings Arts Association, 2714 Beartooth, Billings, MT 59101. 406–652–4698. Contact: Robert Cushing, Writers Chair.

Billings Arts Association Writers, 3706 Duck Creek Rd., Billings, MT 59101. 406–656–2524. Contact: Alice Madsen. Branch interest group of Montana Institute of the Arts. Offers criticism, support, workshops and state-level writing contest for poetry and prose. Meets monthly.

Book Publicists Northwest, PO Box 19786, Seattle, WA 98109. 206–285–2665. Contact: Anne Damron. Professional group of in-house and freelance book publicists. Anyone actively engaged in promoting books, authors and publishing in the NW is eligible for membership. Meets monthly.

British Columbia Arts Council, Cultural Services Branches, Parliament Building, Victoria, BC V8V 1X4. 604–387–1241.

Burnaby Writers, 6450 Gilpin Street, Burnaby, BC V5G 2J3.

Canadian Authors Association (B.C. Branch), 15066 - 98th Avenue, Surrey, BC V3R 5W8. Contact: Margaret Moffatt.

Canadian Book Information Centre, 1622 W. 7th Avenue, Vancouver, BC V6J 1S5. Contact: Natalie Chapman.

Cannon Beach Arts Association, PO Box 684, Cannon Beach, OR 97110. 503–436–1204. Contact: Rainmar Bartle.

Capital Writers Circle, PO Box 549, Juneau, AK 99802. 907–586–1266. Contact: Mike Macy. "Organization devoted to the enjoyment of literature and the development of writers of all genres." Meets every other week.

Caribou Writers Group, c/o Williams Lake Library, 110 Oliver Street, Williams Lake, BC V2G 1G0.

Cascade Poets, 6123 N. Commercial, Portland, OR 97217. Contact: Wilma Erwin. 503–283–3682. "We meet on the last Monday of the month at Cascade Center, 705 N. Killingsworth, Portland, OR 97217. We welcome all poets. Poets should bring 12 copies of a poem they'd like to have critiqued. Free. We're looking forward to seeing you."

Center for the Book in the Oregon State Library, State Library Building, Salem, OR 97310. 503–378–4367. Contact: Wes Doak. "A statewide program including exhibits, special collections designed to increase awareness and appreciation of books and reading."

Center for Pacific Northwest Studies, Western Washington University, Bellingham, WA 98225. 206–676–3125, James D. Moore, Regional Archives, 206–647–4776, James W. Scott, Director. "Collections include manuscript materials, business records, maps, photographs, etc. on the PNW, especially NW Washington. Phone ahead of visit."

Central Curry Council for the Arts & Humanities, PO Box 374, Gold Beach, OR 97444. 503–247–6854. Contact: Robert E. Simons.

Central Oregon Arts Society, PO Box 45, Bend, OR 97709. 503–382–1372. Contact: Lyn Comini.

Central Oregon Coast Writers, Mary Esther Miller, Rt 1 Box 59X, Otis, OR 97368. 503–994–5476.

Centrum Foundation, PO Box 1158, Port Townsend, WA 98368. Contact: Carol Jane Bangs. 206–385–3102. "Centrum is a multipurpose arts and education foundation, designing, implementing, and administering a variety of programs and festivals throughout the year. Among the various activities are programs in music, visual arts, gifted education, and literary activities. Residencies are provided for visual artists, writers and a literary press and art press." Literary activities include: "Publications, including anthologies of high school writing and, for several years, the periodical *Crosscut*, a *Foxfire* type oral literature project. Centrum also provides references and information for the northwest literary community, acts as a clearinghouse for literary information, and participates in a number of national literary projects and programs." (See Events, Classes.)

Children's Book Writers of the Eastside, c/o Carol Krefting Youngberg, 6133 111th Avenue N.E., Kirkland, WA 98033. 206–822–1170.

Christian Scribes, 9340 S.E. Morrison, Portland, OR 97216. Contact: Shirley Cody.

Christian Writers, c/o Mrs. Carl T. Jones, 207 N.E. "A" Steet, College Place, WA 99324. 509–525–4350.

Citizen's Council for the Arts, 307 S. 19th Street, Coeur d'Alene, ID 83814.

Clackamas County Arts Council, Clackamas Community College, 19600 S. Molalla Ave., Oregon City, OR 97045. 503–656–9543. Contact: Harriet Jorgenson.

Coastal Fellowship of Christian Writers, 7784 Hwy 20, Toledo, OR 97391. Contact: Beth Dickinson. 503–336–3410. "Coastal Fellowship of Christian Writers meet at the Toledo Public Library. Group focus — encouragement and critique."

Coeur d'Alene City Arts Commission, City Hall, Coeur d'Alene, ID 83814.

Columbia Basin Allied Arts, 28th & Chanute, Moses Lake, WA 98837. Contact: Brenda Teals. 509–762–5351.

Columbia Gorge Arts Council of Washington & Oregon, PO Box 211, Corbett, OR 97019. 503–248–0232. Contact: Ed Bonham.

Columbia Gorge Showcase, PO Box 825, Hood River, OR 97031. 503–386–5113. Contact: Kate Mills.

Comox Writers Group, 319 Church Street, Comox, BC V9N 5G6.

Composers, Authors and Artists of America, Inc., Rt. 1, Box 53, Reardan, WA 99029. Contact: David Chester. "To promote all of the arts." State poetry contest, elementary school workshop. (See Contests.)

Coquille Valley Art Association, HC 83, Box 625, Coquille, OR 97423. 503–396–2866. Contact: Yvonne Marineau.

Cornucopia Project, Rt. 1, Box 189A, Halfway, OR 97834. Contact: Alice Covey.

Corvallis Arts Center, 700 SW Madison, Corvallis, OR 97330. 503–754–1551. Contact: Susan Johnson.

Creative Arts Guild, 520 SW 5th, Albany, OR 97321. 503–926–2211 or 928–7924. Contact: Connie Petty.

Creative People Support Group, Supportletter, 2905 Mayfair Avenue N., Seattle, WA 98109. Contact: Beth Bauer. 206–283–0505. "Informal pot luck dinner; encouragement, emotional support, positive critique of works in progress — to promote creativity; writers, artists, musicians, song writers, poets, needle workers, cooks, photographers, craftpersons — we encourage and enjoy creativity and creative people. *Supportletter* mailed to those showing continuing interest in group (by attendance, or by verbal contact with editor)."

Creston Writers League, Box 2807, Creston, BC V0B 1G0.

Crossroads Arts Center, PO Box 235, Baker, OR 97814. 503–523–3704. Contact: Peter Decius.

Dallas Arts Association, PO Box 192, Dallas, OR 97338. 503–623–5594. Contact: LaVonne Wilson or Janet Burton, 623–5700/623–5567.

Des Moines Arts Commission, 22513 Marine View Drive, Des Moines, WA 98188. Contact: Jack Kniskern.

Desert Arts Council, Blue Mountain CC, 405 N. 1st, Suite 107, Hermiston, OR 97838. 503–567–1800. Contact: Karen Bounds.

Dillon Authors Association, PO BOx 212, Dillon, MT 59725. Contact: Sally Garrett Dingley. 406–683–4539. "Monthly writers meetings on 2nd Tuesday from Sept. through May of each year. Six meetings have guests with special expertise, three meetings are critiquing sessions. A diverse membership of local and regional writers, published and aspiring.... Newsletter published approximately ten times a year. 55+ members, 12 newsletter exchanges." (See Classes.)

Eastern Oregon Regional Arts Council, RSI House, Eastern Oregon State College, La Grande, OR 97850. 503–963–1624. Contact: Anne Bell.

Eastside Writers Association, PO Box 8005, Totem Lake Post Office, Kirkland, WA 98034. Contact: Pat Ahern, Pres. 206–747–5368. Writers group meets the 2nd Tuedsay of each month, Sept. through May, from 7:30 to 9:00 pm at First Congregational Church in Bellevue. Off I-405 at N.E. 8th and 108th. Dues $10 to pay for church, newsletter and speakers for each meeting. Meetings are open to non-members, donation of $2. Eastside Writers is for "anyone who writes, or wants to write. We have members who have been writing for years, and we have outright beginners. Some of our members have sold everything they've written, and some don't even want to sell." (See Classes.)

Edmonds Arts Commission, Anderson Cultural Center, 700 Main Street, Edmonds, WA 98020. Contact: Linda McCrystal. 206–775–2525.

Elgin Arts Council, Rt. 1, Box 1A, Elgin, OR 97827. 503–437–7772. Contact: Pamela Davis or Christine McLaughlin.

El-Wyhee Arts Council, 1520 E. 8th N., Mt. Home, ID 83647.

Ellensburg Arts Commission, 420 North Pearl, Ellensburg, WA 98926. Contact: Phyllis Stamm. 509–986–3065.

Entheos, Seabeck, WA 98380-0370. Contact: Karen C. Hayden. 206–830–4758. Writers and photographers organization.

Enumclaw Arts Commission, 1339 Griffin, Enumclaw, WA 98022. Contact: Evelyn Lercher. 206–825–1038.

Esquimalt Writers Group, 527 Fraser Street, Victoria, BC V9A 6H6.

Everett Cultural Commission, 3002 Wetmore, Everett, WA 98201. Contact: Lynda Vanderberg. 206–259–8701.

The Federation of British Columbia Writers, Box 24624, Sta. C, Vancouver, BC V5T 4E2. Contact: J. Drabek/T. Carolan. 604–683–2057. "A non-profit society of professional and aspiring writers, the Federation acts as an umbrella organization for writers of all genres.... Similar organizations in other provinces and in many European countries exist because writers need to unite to achieve their common goals. Unlike writers groups representing specific genres, such as ACTRA, the Writers' Union or PWAC, the Federation's broadly-based membership allows it to direct its voice to larger concerns vital to every B.C. writer." To this end, the Federation publishes a quarterly newsletter, works with other writers' organizations to promote: photocopying & copyright legislation, establishment of a provincial Writers' Centre and Archives, payment for public use of written material, public readings, and wider funding and support for writers. (See Classes, Events.)

Fictioneers, 13211 39th Avenue N.E., Seattle, WA 98125. Contact: Beth Casey. 206–282–2729. Monthly meetings for writers, held at Seattle Downtown Public Library, 3rd Saturday of the month at 10:30 am. Group has been in existence for over 40 years, and is not sponsored by the Library. Meetings include manuscript reading, critiques, discussions. (See Classes, Contests.)

Florence Arts & Crafts Association, PO Box 305, Florence, OR 97349.

Fort St. John Writers, #310 9215-94A Street, Fort St. John, BC V1J 6E4.

Friends of Mystery, c/o Jay Margulies, 2421 N.W. Pettygrove, Portland, OR 97210. 503–241–0759.

Friends of the Library, c/o Dianne Sichel, 3057 S.W. Fairview, Portland, OR 97201. 503–228–0841. Organizes readings by nationally known writers.

Grants Pass Arts Council, 201 Barbara Dr., Grants Pass, OR 97526. 503–479–5541. Contact: Doug Norby.

Grants Pass Writers Workshop, 114 Espey Rd., Grants Pass, OR 97526. Contact: Dorothy Francis, 503–476–2038. (See Classes.)

Greater Condon Arts Association, PO Box 165, Condon, OR 97823. 503–384–5114. Contact: Darla Ceale.

Harney County Arts & Crafts, PO Box 602, Burns, OR 97720. 503–573–7693. Contact: Royaline Oltman.

Hillsboro Community Arts, PO Box 1026, Hillsboro, OR 97123. 503–648–4019. Contact: Marilyn Helzerman.

Idaho City Arts Council, PO Box 219, Idaho City, ID 83631.

Idaho Commission on the Arts, 304 W. State Street, Boise, ID 83720. Contact: John Shelton. 208–334–2119. Grants, fellowships/apprenticeships, artists-in-education program residencies.

Idaho Falls Diary Workshop, PO Box 50953, Idaho Falls, ID 83405. 208–524–2569. Contact: Joan Juskie-Nellis. Diary writers meet monthly to read and discuss members' entries, publication possibilities. "Very informal group—doesn't advertise, word of mouth to stay small—looking for serious diary writers."

Idaho Falls Poetry Workshop, PO Box 50953. Idaho Falls, ID 83405. 208–524–2569. Contact: Joan Juskie-Nellis. Monthly meetings to read and critique poetry, share marketing information, and exchange information.

Idaho State Library, 325 W. State Street, Boise, ID 83720.

Idaho Writers, 619 N. 12th Ave., Pocatello, ID 83201.

Idaho Writers' League, c/o Bernadette McMonigle, 423–16th St., Pocatello, ID 83201. 208–232–3038.

Idaho Writers' League, Coeur d'Alene Chapter, N. 950 Highland Ct. Post Falls, ID 83854. 208–773–2513. Contact: Robin Bruce. "...to encourage novice and veteran writers alike in their writing endeavors. Manuscripts are read and critiqued at meetings and workshops, and market strategies are discussed. New writers are always welcome." Meets monthly. (See Contests.)

Idaho Writers' League, Twin Falls Chapter, 1863 Bitterroot Dr., Twin Falls, ID 83301. 208–734–0746. Contact: Bill White. Meets monthly.

International Association of Scholarly Publishers, c/o University of Washington Press, PO Box C50096, Seattle, WA 98195. Contact: Dorothy Anthony. 206–543–8870.

Interurban Center for the Arts, 12401 S.E. 320th Street, Auburn, WA 98002. Contact: Helen S. Smith. 206–833–9111.

Island County Arts Council, PO Box 131, Langley, WA 98260. Contact: Linda Good. 206–321–6439.

Kent Arts Commission, 220 S. 4th Avenue, Kent, WA 98031. Contact: Patrice Thorell. 206–872–3350.

Ketchikan Area Arts & Humanities Council, 338 Main Street, Ketchikan, AK 99901.

King County Arts Commission, The Alaska Building, 506 2nd Ave. #1115,, Seattle, WA 98104. Contact: Susan T. Hoare. 206–344–7580. The Commission has a Literary Arts Committee; publishes *The Written Arts*, a literary magazine and *The Arts*, a newsletter; it funds and sponsors writing related events and projects. Contact them to get on their mailing list for publications.

Kitsap Writers Club, c/o Phil Kirschner, 916 Hull Avenue, Port Orchard, WA 98366. 206–876–3622.

Klamath Arts Council, PO Box 1706, Klamath Falls, OR 97601. Contact: Anita Ward.

Klamath Falls Arts Association, 2310 Marina Dr., Klamath Falls, OR 97601.

La Grande Arts Commission, 1605 Walnut, La Grande, OR 97850. 503–963–6963. Contact: Michael Frasier.

Lake Arts Council, 307 S. 'E', Lakeview, OR 97630. 503–947–2931. Contact: Stanley Wonderly.

Lane Literary Guild, c/o Lane Regional Arts Council, 411 High Street, Eugene, OR 97401. Contact: Henry Alley. 503–484–6259. "The Lane Literary Guild is a non-profit organization representing the professional interests of poets, fiction writers and dramatists living in Lane County. Our goals are to foster the development of a writing community, to provide information and support for individual writers and to increase the audience for literature in Lane County." Membership benefits include: "Reduced rates for monthly readings and workshops; free admission at open readings; 10% discount on purchases at The Literary Lion Bookstore; regular notification of all Guild-sponsored events." (See Classes, Events.)

Lane Regional Arts Council, 411 High St., Eugene, OR 97401. 503–485–2278. Contact: Douglas Beauchamp. Provides education, information, and services to the professional arts community: *Artists Notes*, a monthly publication listing professional opportunities for writers & artists; consulting for projects.

Langley Literary Guild, 9582 - 132A Street, Surrey, BC V3V 5R2.

The League of Canadian Poets, 15097 Victoria Avenue, White Rock, BC V4B 1G4. Contact: Allen Safarik.

Lebanon Fine Arts & Crafts Center, 472 F St., Lebanon, OR 97355. Contact: Donna Garrett. 503–259–2514.

The Literary Center, PO Box 85116, Seattle, WA 98145-1116. Contact: Marilyn Stablein. 206–524–5514. "The Literary Center, 1716 N. 45th Street, is a writer's resource organization — to help writers help themselves. It includes: a small press gallery (containing small press books, magazines, broadsides, tapes, etc.); a resource library (containing foundation directories, information about local readings and workshops, national markets, etc.); Literary Hotline (524–5514), a 24-hour pre-recorded listing of local literary events." Funded in part by a grant from King County Arts Commission and support of the Allied Arts Foundation. (See Classes, Events.)

Lost River Community Arts Council, Box B, Arco, ID 83213

Lynnwood Arts Commission, City Hall, 19100-44th Avenue W., Lynnwood, WA 98036. Contact: Judith Nebot. 206–775–1971.

Magic Valley Arts Council, PO Box 1158, Twin Falls, ID 83301.

Mercer Island Arts Council, Community Center at Mercer View, 8236 S.E. 24th Street, Mercer Island, WA 98040. Contact: Judith Clibborn. 206–233–3545.

Metropolitan Arts Commission, 1120 SW 5th, Portland, OR 97204. 503–796–5111. Contact: Selina Ottum. "Grants to artists and arts organizations (including small presses) for public, non-profit projects (no fellowship program). Bimonthly newsletter listing MAC programs, other deadlines, competitions."

Mid-Valley Arts Council, 265 Court NE, Salem, OR 97301. 503–364–7474. Contact: Catherine Leedy.

Monmouth/Independence Community Arts Association, PO Box 114, Monmouth, OR 97361. 503–838–4141 Contact: Deb Curtis.

Montana Arts Council, 35 S. Last Chance Gulch, Helena, MT 59620. Contact: Julie Cook. 406–444–6430. State arts organization, publishes *Artistsearch*, a monthly newsletter. Also publishes 1 book annually as part of their First Book Award for MT residents. Send for guidelines for grant applications, and to get on mailing list for newsletter.

Montana Institute of the Arts, PO Box 1456, Billings, MT 59103. Contact: Ron Paulick. 406–245–3688. "The Montana Institute of the Arts was founded in 1948 by members of the academic and professional community across Montana. It has been effective in helping to establish art centers and museums in the state and continues to stimulate enthusiam and acceptance of the arts." There are branches in many cities, with various interest groups, writing being one of them. The organization offers workshops, visiting artists, contests, festivals. The monthly newsletter has a special section for writers. For more information, contact Aline Moore, 11333 Gooch Hill Rd., Gallatin Gateway, MT 59730. (See Contests, Events.)

Moscow City Arts Commission, 122 E. 4th Street, Moscow, ID 83843.

Moscow Moffia Writers' Workshop, 621 East 'F' St., Moscow, ID 83343. Contact: Jon Gustafson. Weekly writers' discussion groups. Sponsors workshops throughout the Northwest. (See Classes.)

Mountlake Terrace Arts Commission, Parks & Recreation Department, 228th Street S.W., Mountlake Terrace, WA 98043. Contact: David Fair. 206–776–9173.

Mystery Writers of America – Northwest, c/o Frank Denton, 14654 8th Avenue S.W., Seattle, WA 98166.

Nanaimo Writers, 3413 Littleford Street, Nanaimo, BC V9T 4C4.

National League of Penwomen, Seattle Branch, c/o Dorothy Croman, 1000 N.E. 82nd Avenue #121, Vancouver, WA 98664-1839.

National League of American Pen Women, Spokane, c/o Thalia Kleinoeder, E. 1020 Bedivere Dr., Spokane, WA 99218.

National League of American Pen Women, Tacoma, c/o Jane Keffler, 7606 37th W., Unit 3d, Tacoma, WA 98466. 206–564–5542.

National Writers Club, Jefferson Chapter, 3431 S. Pacific Hwy. #49, Medford, OR 97501. Contact: Herbert Wood.

National Writers Club, Seattle Chapter, PO Box 55522, Seattle, WA 98155. 206–783–3401. Contact: Leon Billig. "Monthly programs, special workshops and symposia, social events, critique groups, networking, special interest activities, professional visibility."

Nightwriters, Rt 1, Box 432, Vashon, WA 98070. 206–567–4829. Contact: Joyce Delbridge. Regular meetings at Vashon Library, open invitation, small fee, critique group.

No Frills, 1118 Hoyt Ave., Everett, WA 98201. 206–259–0804. "Active working writers meet Tuesdays for critiques. Share brags, moans, and dues for space rental." Meets weekly.

North Olympic Arts Council, 114 W. Front Street, Odyssey Book Shop, Port Angeles, WA 98362. Contact: Craig Whalley. 206–457–1045.

North Santiam Arts League, Inc., PO Box 424, Stayton, OR 97383. 503–769–7268 or 769–7321. Contact: Anita Riter.

Northwest Association of Book Publishers, PO Box 3363, Salem, OR 97302. 503–364–7698. Contact: Dick Lutz. "A networking group of small publishers. Monthly meetings with guest speakers & newsletter. Welcomes the beginning self-publisher who wants to learn." Monthly meetings at Marylhurst College, Lake Oswego.

Northwest Outdoor Writers' Association, 3421 E. Mercer St., Seattle, WA 98112. 206–323–3970. Contact: Stan Jones. Association of professional outdoor writers, editors, artists and photographers in Western U.S. and Canada.

Northwest Playwrights' Guild, PO Box 95292, Seattle, WA 98145. Contact: Sharon Glantz. 206–545–4500. Their goal is to satisfy needs of NW playwrights and individuals or organizations interested in supporting the new works of Northwest playwrights. There is a membership fee of $10, plus $10 per year dues. This includes a newsletter; information brochures on copywriting, submission procedures, etc.; a play bank; workshops and readings of new works; referral network of actors and directors; writing critiques; visiting playwrights. (See Classes, Events.)

Northwest Renaissance, 13021 10th Ave. S., Seattle, WA 98168. Contact: Michael Spence. Puget Sound area poetry organization. (See Classes, Events.)

Northwest Writers, Inc., PO Box 3437, Portland, OR 97208. Organization of professional writers intended to offer support, pool resources and share information and job opportunities.

Nyssa Fine Arts Council, Inc., PO Box 2356, Nyssa, OR 97913. 503–372–2981. Contact: Marie Wilson.

O-Ya-Ka Story League, Multnomah County Central Library, Room E, 801 S.W. 10th Avenue, Portland, OR 97205. Contact: Lois Abeling. 503–244–9415. Meets monthly. Affiliated with National Story League, Western District. Story workshop sponsored by Western District held at Marylhurst alternate summers.

Oakley Valley Arts Council, PO Box 176, Oakley, ID 83346.

Oregon Arts Commission, 835 Summer Street N.E., Salem, OR 97301. 503–378–3625. Individual, non-repeating, fellowships granted annually. A writer can suggest any project to a non-profit organization, and apply to OAC for a project grant four times a year. Write for guidelines or check with local arts councils in Oregon.

Oregon Association of Christian Writers, 2495 Maple N.E., Salem, OR 97303. 503–364–9570. Contact: Marion Duckworth. Organized for "the purpose of promoting higher standards of craftsmanship in the field of Christian journalism and encouraging a greater sense of spiritual responsibility in the Christian writer." The group hold writer's seminars 3 times a year, in Salem, in Eugene and in Portland. (See Classes.)

Oregon Coast Council for the Arts, PO Box 1315, Newport, OR 97365. 503–265–9231. Contact: Sharon Morgan. "We are a regional arts council with a strong history of literary programs and support for emerging writers." (See Events.)

Oregon Coast Performing Arts Society, PO Box 546, Cannon Beach, OR 97110. 503–436–1227.

Oregon Committee for the Humanities, 418 S.W. Washington Street, Room 410, Portland, OR 97204. 503–241–0543. Write to the Committee for grant guidelines and information on their Chautauqua series

Oregon Council of Teachers of English, (OCTE), PO Box 2515, Portland, OR 97208. 503–238–1208. Contact: Joe Fitzgibbon. For teachers of English, language arts, literature and creative writing at all levels. Publishes , *Oregon English* and *Chalkboard*. Sponsors "Teachers-as-Writers," (See Contests.)

Oregon East Poets & Writers Group, Oma Miller, Rt 4 Box 4050, Sp. #75, La Grande, OR 97850. 503–963–4354.

Oregon Press Women, PO Box 25354, Portland, OR 97225. 503–292–4945. Contact: Glennis McNeal. Professional group for broadcasters, journalists, public relations practitioners, freelancers, photographers, journalism educators. Meets twice yearly. Sponsors contests for members, high school students. (See Events, Contests.)

Oregon State Poetry Association, 1645 S.E. Spokane Street, Portland, OR 97202. Contact: Leona Ward. 503–777–8209. Founded in 1956 to "promote the appreciation and creation of poetry," OSPA has units active in Ashland, Bend, the Central Oregon Coast, Grants Pass, La Grande, Medford, Roseburg, and Salem. Other groups meet informally in other cities. "Members are provided with occasions to showcase and sell their books, and are kept informed of poetry events through the quarterly *OSPA Newsletter*. For information about the *OSPA Newsletter*, contact Helen Klopfenstein, 2915 S.E. 58th Avenue, Portland, OR 97206 or call 503–233–0766. (Also see publications listings.) A membership directory is published annually. Dues are $10, with a special discount for seniors over 75 and students under 21." (See Contests, Events.)

Oregon Students Writing & Art Foundation, PO Box 2100, Portland, OR 97208-2100. Contact: Chris Weber. 503–232–7737. An organization of students and teachers involved in publishing an anthology of student writing compiled from the winners of the Starfire Contest. Students are involved in all aspects of the book, editing, design, publicity, etc. (See Contests.)

Oregon Writers Alliance, 4950 SW Hall Blvd., Beaverton, OR 97005. Writers' support group meets twice a month.

Oregon Writers Colony, PO Box 15200, Portland, OR 97215. Contact: Marlene Howard. 503–771–0428. "The Oregon Writers' Colony is a support group for writers, the purpose of which is to create an atmosphere encouraging creative growth. It is a non-profit corporation which works to help writers with education in their craft, information for marketing, and communication with their peers." The group has available for writers a retreat house on the Coast and publishes a newsletter, *Colonygram*, which shares information on markets, contests, workshops and member news. It publishes an annual anthology, *In Our Own Voices*. Accepting mss after May, 1987. (See Contests, Events.)

Pacific Northwest Book Publishers Association, PO Box 1931, Mt. Vernon, WA 98273.

Pacific Northwest Booksellers Association, Rt. 1, Box 219B, Banks, OR 97106. 503–324–8180. Contact: Debby Garman.

Pend Oreille Arts Council, c/o Eve's Leaves, 326 N. 1st Avenue, Sandpoint, ID 83864.

Peninsula Cultural Arts Center, 533 N. Sequim Avenue, Sequim, WA 98382. Contact: Patricia Gallup. 206–683–8364.

Periodical Writers Association, 3782 W. 22nd Avenue, Vancouver, BC V6S 1J6.

Periodical Writers Association of Canada (PWAC), PWAC National Office, 24 Ryerson Ave., Toronto, Ontario M5T 2P3. 461–868–6913. Contact: Paulette Pelletier-Kelly. Professional association of freelancers in Canada. Chapters in Victoria, Vancouver, Calgary.

Playwrights-In-Progress, 3047 NE 182nd, Seattle, WA 98155. 206–363–5905. Contact: Nikki Louis. Weekly meetings for readings of members' plays. PIP also sponsors workshops.

Poetry Publishers Association, 5136 NE Glisan, Portland, OR 97213. 503–231–7628. Contact: Bert Lybrand. "The promotion of the use of poetry in print."

Poetry Scribes of Spokane, 3328 E. 36th, Spokane, WA 99223. 509–448–8292. Contact: Betty Egbert. Poetry critique group, meets monthly. Publishes *Turquoise Lanterns*, an annual anthology.

Port Alberni Writers, #38 4467 Wallace Street, Port Alberni, BC V9Y 3Y4.

Port Orford Arts Council, PO Box 771, Port Orford, OR 97465.

Port Townsend Arts Commission, City Hall, 607 Water Street, Port Townsend, WA 98368.

Portland Freelancers. 503–288–3856. Contact: Agnes Kempton. A workshop on the second Monday of every month.

Portland Science Fiction Society, PO Box 4602, Portland, OR 97208. 503–283–0802. Contact: John Lorentz.

Pro Poets of Salem, 2285 Rogers Lane NW, Salem, OR 97304. Contact: Winifred Layton. "Poetry writers invited to monthly meetings at Salem Public Library."

Progressive Fine Arts Association, 2637 SE Tibbetts, Portland, OR 97202. 503–232–0330. Contact: Kathryn Bogle.

Prose & Poetry, c/o Pansy Rapp, W. 2203 1st, Spokane, WA 99204 or c/o Lora Carman, N. 4210 Maringo Dr., Spokane, WA 99212. Writing club meets once a month at N. Argonne Library.

Publishing Industry Group, PO Box 2701, Eugene, OR 97402. 503–689–4785. Contact: Phil Hennin. (Tentative—not yet formally organized.) Publishers, graphic artists, printers, writers welcome. Group may be formally organized in 1989, specific to Oregon, especially Southern Oregon from Eugene south.

Pulphouse Gang, 212 Pearl #2, Eugene, OR 97401. 503–342–7486. Contact: Dean Wesley Smith. Serious writing support group. "Most of the writers are in the field of science fiction and horror, but not all." Meets every other week.

Red-Wood Writer's Workshop, 24309 47th Ave. SE, Woodinville, WA 98072. 206–481–3240. Contact: Linda Foss. Support group for area writers. Meetings include readings, creative exercises, sharing ideas and information.

Reedsport Arts Council, 310 Fir St., Reedsport, OR 97467. Contact: Donna Fulhart.

Regional Arts Council of Central Oregon, 25 NW Minnesota #11, Bend, OR 97701. 503–382–5055. Contact: Rebecca Sario.

Renton Municipal Arts Commission, 200 Mill Avenue S., Renton, WA 98055. Contact: Harriette Hilder. 206–235–2580.

Renton Writers Workshop, c/o Beth Cole, 18618 S.E. 128th Street, Renton, WA 98056. Contact: Beth Cole/Marilyn Kamcheff. 206–255–5711. An 11 year old writers organization meets in the Administrative Center of the Renton School District, 435 Main Avenue South, Renton. "We try to improve our craft by pursuing regular writing habits, giving constructive criticism, and sharing publishing information. Annual dues are $5." Meets twice a month from 9:30 a.m. to 12:30 p.m.

Romance Writers of America, c/o Sally Fozoft, 1065 Cherry, Anchorage, AK 99504.

Romance Writers of America, c/o Sally Garett Dingley, PO Box 212, Dillion, MT 59725.

Romance Writers of America, Portland/Vancouver Chapter, 7000 S.E. Thiessen Rd., Milwaukie, OR 97267. 503–659–2559. Contact: Iona Lockwood. "To give encouragement and support to writers, published and unpublished, who are interested in the romance genre via monthly meetings, newsletters, workshops, etc. Meets monthly.

Romance Writers of America, c/o Darlene Layman, 7270 Thasof Avenue N.E., Bremerton, WA 98310.

Romance Writers of America, c/o Jackie Taylor, 5032 Crary Avenue, Fort Lewis, WA 98433.

Romance Writers of America, c/o Margo McIntosh, 1810 Amick Road, Mt. Vernon, WA 98273.

Romance Writers of America, c/o Selwyn Young, 620 N. 202, Seattle, WA 98133.

Romance Writers of America, c/o Joan Overfield, PO Box 875, Spokane, WA 99210.

Romance Writers & Readers Group, Langara Campus, Vancouver Community College, Vancouver, BC V5Y 2Z6. Contact: President.

Roseburg Writers Group, c/o Pat Banta, 548 Echo Bend Drive, Roseburg, OR 97470. 503–673–6486.

Salmon Arts Council, PO Box 2500, Salmon, ID 83467.

Sandpoint Writer's Project, 5706 E. Dufort Rd., Sagle, ID 83860. 208–263–8223. Contact: Tom Birdseye. "Informal discussions and critique sessions."

Scribe's Forum, 1810 Ameck Rd., Mt. Vernon, WA 98273. Contact: Margo McIntosh.

Sea-Tac Arts Council, 1809 S. 140th, Seattle, WA 98168. Contact: Dorothy Harper. 206–241–5960.

Seahurst Writers, c/o Frances Mangan, 14700 6th S.W., Seattle, WA 98146.

Seannchae, c/o Willo Davis Roberts, 12020 Engebretson Road, Granite Falls, WA 98252. 206–691–6159.

Seaside Guild of Artists, Inc., PO Box 1122, Seaside, OR 97138.

Seattle Arts Commission, Seattle Center House, 305 Harrison Street, Seattle, WA 98109. Contact: Barbara Thomas. 206–625–4223. Send for their guidelines for grants, and get on their newsletter mailing list for information on area events.

Silver Sage Art Council, Rt. 5, Box 314, Blackfoot, ID 83321.

Skagit Valley Writer's League, c/o Linda Griffin, 1315 Cedar Lane, Mount Vernon, WA 98273.

Snohomish Arts Commission, 116 Union Avenue, Snohomish, WA 98290-2943. Contact: Volkert Volkersz. 206–568–3115.

Society of Children's Book Writers/Washington Chapter, 186320 NE 202nd St., Woodinville, WA 98072. 206–481–4091. Contact: Linda Wagner. Group provides "encouragement and information for published and non-published writers or illustrators of all types of childrens' literature." Meets monthly.

The Society of Children's Book Writers, NW Chapter, 12180 SW Ann Pl., Tigard, OR 97223. 503–639–5754. Contact: Margaret Bechard.

Society of Professional Journalists, Sigma Delta Chi, Willamette Valley Professional Chapter, PO Box 1717, Portland, OR 97207. 503–244–6111 x4181. Contact: Oren Campbell. "Association representing all areas of journalism and all levels of experience." Meets monthly September through May.

South Coast Council for the Arts and Humanities, c/o Coos-Curry Council of Governments, 170 S. Second Street, Suite 204, Coos Bay, OR 97420. 503–267–6500. Contact: Lionel Youst.

Southcoast Tourism Assn/Bay Area Arts Council, PO Box 1641, Coos Bay, OR 97420. 503–756–2900. Contact: Judith Kobrin.

Speakers and Writers, Inc., PO Box 5804, Aloha, OR 97006-0804.

Spindrift Writers, Box 151, Parksville, BC V0R 2S0. Contact: President, Julia K. Ogilvie.

Spokane Arts Commission, City Hall - 4th Floor, W. 808 Spokane Falls Blvd., Spokane, WA 99201-3333. Contact: Sue Ellen Heflin. 509–456–3857.

Spokane Christian Writers, 1405 E. 54th, Spokane, WA 99223. 509–448–6622. Contact: Niki Anderson. Christian writers critique group. Meets monthly.

Spokane Writers, c/o Kay Sandberg, E. 128 Hawthorne #223, Spokane, WA 99218.

Springfield Arts Commission, City of Springfield, Office of Community & Economic Development, 225 N. 5th St., Springfield, OR 97477. 503–726–3783. Contact: Bruce Newhouse.

Tacoma Arts Commission, Tacoma Municipal Bldg., 747 Market Street, Rm 134, Tacoma, WA 98402-3768. Contact: Zia Gipson. 206–591–5191.

Tacoma Writer's Club, c/o Wilma LaFavor, Secy., 1122 N. 6th St. #1, Tacoma, WA 98403. Weekly/monthly workshops including poetry, articles and fiction. "Members study marketing their work, and discuss ideas about illustrating, query letters, etc." The group publishes a monthly newsletter.

Tiimutla Arts Council, Rt. 3, Box 7, Pendleton, OR 97801. 503–276–1881. Contact: Leah Conner.

Tillamook Arts Association, 910 Main St., Tillamook, OR 97141. Contact: Ed Sharples.

Umpqua Valley Arts Association, PO Box 1105, Roseburg, OR 97470. 503–672–2532. Contact: Heidi Land.

Upper Valley Arts, 321 9th Street, Leavenworth, WA 98826. Contact: R. J. Ritz. 509–548–5202.

Valley Art Association, PO Box 333, Forest Grove, OR 97116. 503–357–3703. Contact: Merrie French.

The Valley Center for the Arts, PO Box 2183, Mount Vernon, WA 98273. Contact: Lynn Jacobs. 206–428–2865.

Valley Poets of Medford, c/o Leona Williams, 2300 Barnett Road #12, Medford, OR 97504. 503–773–8329.

Vancouver Island Literary Society, 2610 Lynburn Crescent, Nanaimo, BC V9S 3T6.

Vashon Allied Arts Inc., PO Box 576, Vashon, WA 98070. Contact: Jeffery Basom. 206–463–5131.

Vernon Writers Group, Box 647, Lumby, BC V0E 2G0.

Wallowa Valley Arts Council, PO Box 306, Enterprise, OR 97828. 503–426–4775. Contact: Michael Kurtz or Terri Barnett, 432–5911.

Washington Christian Writers Fellowship. See Writers Information Network.

Washington Poets Association, 6002 S. Fife Street, Tacoma, WA 98409. Contact: Amelia Haller. Organization to raise awareness and appreciation of poetry; publishes a newsletter 4 times a year, holds an annual meeting/banquet in May, and workshops/events across the state. Refer to Poetry in Vancouver USA (See Contests), A Poetry Event at Longview (See Events) and Rattlesnake Mountain (See Classes).

Washington Press Association, Inc., 217 9th Ave. N., Seattle, WA 98109. 206–623–8632. Contact: Diane Bevins. Communications professionals: broadcasting, publishing, advertising, public relations, education, freelancing.

Washington State Arts Commission, 110–9th & Columbia Bldg., Mail Stop GH-11, Olympia, WA 98504-4111. Contact: Michael A. Croman. Send for guidelines for grants and get on mailing list for their newsletter of information on the arts.

Washington Volunteer Lawyers for the Arts, 1402 3rd Avenue, Seattle, WA 98101. Contact: Clare M. Grause. 206–223–0502. "WVLA provides free and low cost legal services to artists and arts organizations throughout Washington state. Our services include: an attorney referral service for artists with specific legal problems related to their work; seminars and workshops on legal topics of critical interest to artists; and publications on legal topics of interest to artists and attorneys interested in art law."

Wenatchee Arts Commission, PO Box 519, Wenatchee, WA 98801. Contact: Peggy Mead.

Wenatchee Christian Writers Fellowship, 211 Ridgemont Drive, E. Wenatchee, WA 98801. Contact: Millie Hynes. 509–884–3279.

West Coast Women and Words Society, Box 65563, Sta. F, Vancouver, BC V5N 4B0. 604–872–8014. Contact: President. A coalition of women from all aspects of "the creation and distribution of the written word.... Our goal is to make the words of women a more pervasive and influential force in Canadian society."

Western Screenplay Development Society, 1804 – 13 W. 4th Avenue, Vancouver, BC V6J 1M3.

Western World Haiku Society, 4102 N.E. 130th Place, Portland, OR 97230-1499. Contact: Lorraine Ellis Harr.

Whatcom Writers, c/o Margot Rowe, 1237 W. Racine Street, Bellingham, WA 98226. 206–734–9818. "A group of published and unpublished writers of adult age. Members' manuscripts are read aloud followed by constructive criticism aimed at helping the author to produce a saleable piece of work. Market news, contests, workshops, etc. are brought to the attention of members. We share success and failure with equal interest. Meetings held the 3rd Tuesday of each month."

White Rock & Surrey Writers Club, 13245 Marine Drive, Surrey, BC V4A 1E6. Contact: Lynda James. 604–531–8879. "We are a group of professional and non-professional writers. Meeting every third Wednesday of each month at Centennial Arena, White Rock, B.C. Criticising and exchanging ideas, and markets available for manuscripts in process.... Also publication of book 150 pages — *Gems of Poetry & Prose*." (See Contests.)

Willamette Writers, PO Box 2485, Portland, OR 97208. 503–233–1877. Contact: Al Siebert. "Serves the literary communities of Oregon, Washington and Idaho." Monthly programs, newsletter, annual conference and contest, small critique groups. (See Contests, Events.)

Willapa Writers Circle, PO Box 336, Ocean Park, WA 98640. 206–665–4725. Contact: Lila Scheer. Twice-monthly meetings during summer to read and critique. The group self-published *Willapa Review*, "excellent sample of what a small group can do."

Women's Arts Productions, 1908 Ladysmith Lane, Juneau, AK 99801.

Wordsmiths of Battle Ground, 13210 NE 199th St., Battle Ground, WA 98604. 206–687–3767. Contact: Pat Redjoa. "Writers of mid-to high-level skill banding together to share critiques of ongoing work, writing exercises, market and educational information, and encouragement."

Writers Information Network, PO Box 11337, Bainbridge Island, WA 98110. 206–842–9103. Contact: Elaine Wright Colvin. Also known as Washington Christian Writers Fellowship. Meets at Seattle Pacific University bimonthly.

Writer's Support Group, 411 Winger Rd., Williams Lake, BC V2G 3S6. Contact: Ann Walsh.

Yakima Arts Council, 5000 W. Lincoln, Yakima, WA 98908. Contact: Anne Byerrun. 509–966–0930.

Young Audiences of Oregon, Inc., 418 SW Washington, Rm. 202, Portland, OR 97204. 503–224–1412. Non-profit educational organization sponsors professional performing artists (e.g., storytelling, poetry) in schools.

Classes

Centrum Foundation, PO Box 1158, Port Townsend, WA 98368. Contact: Carol Jane Bangs. 206–385–3102. Activities include: "A residency program for 3-4 writers each year; a press-in- residence, Copper Canyon Press, with press tours, and in some years Letterpress workshops with Tree Swenson, Copper Canyon co-publisher and designer of books for several Northwest presses; special workshops featuring writers and experts in other fields, convened to address major societal issues; writing workshops for high school students from Washington State." (See Organizations, Events.)

Clarion West, 340 15th Ave. E., Ste. 350, Seattle, WA 98112. 206–322–9083. Contact: Richard Terra. Summer science fiction and fantasy writing workshop ("emphasis on science fiction and fantasy, but is not exclusive of other genres and forms"), six weeks, late June to early August. (See Events.)

Confluence Press, Inc., 8th Ave. & 6th St., LCSC, Lewiston, ID 83501. 208–799–2336. Contact: James R. Hepworth. Courses in the publishing arts at Lewis Clark State College are available through Confluence Press. Offers on-the-job training to student interns at the Press; and occasional half-day workshops in publishing for junior high, high school and college editors. Sponsor of Writers-in-the-Schools Projects. Also sponsors The Visiting Writers Series, offering 5 residencies to writers a year. They regularly meet with classes. (See Contests, Events, Miscellaneous.)

Dillon Authors Association, PO Box 212, Dillon, MT 59725. Contact: Sally Garrett Dingley. 406–683–4539. Holds an annual Saturday workshop each fall. (See Organizations.)

Eagle River Fine Arts Academy, Box 773989, Eagle River, AK 99577.

Eastside Writers Association, PO Box 8005, Totem Lake Post Office, Kirkland, WA 98034. Contact: Pat Ahern. 206–747–5368. Holds seminars. (See Organizations.)

The Federation of British Columbia Writers, Box 24624, Sta. C, Vancouver, BC V5T 4E2. Contact: J. Drabek/T. Carolan. 604–683–2057. "It organizes Outreach Workshops, taking professional development weekends with established writers to communities throughout the province." (See Organizations, Events.)

Fictioneer's, 13211 39th Avenue N.E., Seattle, WA 98125. Contact: Beth Casey 206–282–2729. Holds workshops. (See Contests, Organizations.)

Grants Pass Writers Workshop, Dorothy Francis, 114 Espey Road, Grants Pass, OR 97526. 503–476–2038. (See Organizations.)

Haystack, Division of Continuing Education, Portland State University, PO Box 1491, Portland, OR 97207. Contact: Steve Reischman. 503–229–4812. Offers writing classes during summer conference at Cannon Beach.

Kootenay School of Writing, 105–1045 West Broadway, Vancouver, BC V6B 2W7. 604–732–1013. Write for more information on future events, their literary publication, *Writing*, the Vancouver Literary Calendar, and KSW Writers' Club.

Lane Literary Guild, c/o Lane Regional Arts Council, 411 High Street, Eugene, OR 97401. Contact: Henry Alley. 503–484–6259. Offers workshops. (See Events, Organizations.)

The Literary Center, PO Box 85116, Seattle, WA 98145-1116. Contact: Marilyn Stablein. 206–524–5514. Contact the Center about workshops, seminars. (See Events, Organizations.)

Media Weavers, Rt. 3, Box 376, Hillsboro, OR 97124. 503–621–3911. Contact: Linny Stovall. Offers workshops in writing, publishing, marketing.

Moscow Moffia Writers' Workshop, 621 East 'F' St., Moscow, ID 83343. Contact: Jon Gustafson. Sponsors workshops throughout the Northwest. (See Organizations.)

Northwest Inland Writing Project, College of Education, University of Idaho, Moscow, ID 83843. 208–885–6586. Contact: Elinor Michel. "NIWP can provide writing workshops and/or in-services to teachers, school districts, and teacher organizations on a variety of topics related to teaching writing.... Can be scheduled with individual or district."

Northwest Playwrights Guild, PO Box 95292, Seattle, WA 98145. Contact: Sharon Glantz. 206–545–4500. Holds workshops. (See Organizations, Events.)

Northwest Renaissance, 13021–10th Ave. S., Seattle, WA 98168. Contact: Michael Spence. Poetry organization. (See Organizations, Events.)

Northwest Writing Institute, Campus Box 100, Lewis & Clark College, Portland, OR 97219. Contact: Kim Stafford, Director. 503–293–2757. "The Northwest Writing Institute at Lewis & Clark College supports campus writing programs, and seeks to assist writers and the literary community in the region through workshops and other programs." Coordinates Oregon Writing Project; Writer to Writer (a seminar for high school students to work with professional writers of fiction, poetry, nonfiction, journalism and script- writing); Young Writers.

Oregon Association of Christian Writers, 2495 Maple N.E., Salem, OR 97303. 503–364–9570. Contact: Marion Duckworth. "We hold 3 writer's seminars a year: January in Salem, May in Eugene, October in Portland. Each includes a variety of workshops and activities to help writers." (See Organizations.)

Oregon Writers Workshop, Pacific Northwest College of Art, 1219 S.W. Park, Portland, OR 97205. 503–226–4396. Contact: Kathy Budas. Graduate level workshops in poetry writing, fiction, nonfiction and drama.

Oregon Writing Project, Department of English, University of Oregon, Eugene, OR 97403. Contact: Nathaniel Teich, Director. 503–686–3911.

Rattlesnake Mountain Writers' Workshop, Rt 1 Box 5240, West Richland, WA 99352. Contact: Nancy Girvin. 509–967–9324. Sponsored by Washington Poets' Association (See Organizations). The workshop "is a full-scale writer's conference with emphasis on Contemporary Poetry. Our program includes workshops for participants (writers) and auditors, those who wish to be part of the writing process from the sidelines. We offer craft lectures staged by our conference poets and critic Charles Altieri. We also feature a teachers' workshop as a regular part of our program, led by experienced teachers who are also published writers." As the Tri-Cities area is fairly isolated, a goal is to integrate the community by inviting the public to lectures, readings, autograph parties, and attend classes as auditors. "Another goal of this project is fostering and promoting a love of language in our children by providing our teachers and those from surrounding communities professional guidance and inspiration in creative writing."

Sitka Summer Writers Symposium, Box 1827, Sitka, AK 99835. 907–747–8808.

Summer Writing Workshop, c/o James McAuley, Creative Writing Program, Eastern Washington University, Cheney, WA 99004. 509–359–2829. Program is held in Ireland.

Writers of the Pacific Northwest Workshop, Tillamook Bay Community College, 2510 First Street, Tillamook, OR 97141. Contact: Director. 503–842–2503. Annual summer workshops with working writers and media professionals as teachers. Usually held in June.

Writing, Department of English, Pacific Lutheran University, Tacoma, WA 98447. Summer writing program designed to serve educators, scientists and writers. "Professional skills are honed in small classes, and through much individual attention from instructors."

A Poetry Event at Longview, Lower Columbia College, Box 68, Longview, WA 98632. Contact: Judith Irwin. 206–577–2083. Or contact Amelia Haller from the Washington Poets Association at 206–472–4787. Put on by Washington Poets Association in January. (See Organizations.)

Alaska Humanities Forum, 943 W. 6th Ave. N. #120, Anchorage, AK 99501.

ARS Poetica, Eastern Oregon State College, La Grande, OR 97850. Contact: George Venn. Poetry and fiction readings series.

Arts at Menucha, PO Box 4958, Portland, OR 97208. Summer workshop/art camp held in Corbett, Oregon overlooking the Columbia Gorge. Includes writing workshops sponsored by Creative Arts Community.

Authors' & Artisans' Fair, Allegory Bookshop, Box 255, Gleneden Beach, OR 97388. Contact: Veronica Johnson. 503–764–2020.

Bainbridge Writer's Guild, c/o Nancy Rekow, 8489 Fletcher Bay Road N.E., Bainbridge, WA 98110. 206–842–4855. Sponsors poetry readings. (See Organizations, Contests.)

Bend-in-the-River Writers Guild, c/o Doris M. Hall, 62340 Powell Butte Road, Bend, OR 97701. 503–389–5845. "Occasional public poetry readings take place in conjunction with Central Oregon Art Society." (See Organizations.)

Bloomsbury Books, 266 E. Main, Ashland, OR 97520. 503–488–0029. Autograph parties.

Bookloft, 107 E. Main St., Enterprise, OR 97828. 503–426–3351. Bookstore, coffee shop and art gallery; acts as cultural center of the Wallowa Valley. Sponsors readings and welcomes meetings of local cultural organizations.

Bumbershoot, PO Box 9750, Seattle, WA 98109-0750. 206–622–5123. Contact: Judith Roche. Bumbershoot Literary Arts is a four-day literary Festival each Labor Day weekend, as part of Bumbershoot, Seattle's Arts Festival. There are readings, literary panel discussions, mixed media performances, other literary displays and performances, and the largest Small Press Bookfair in the Northwest. (See Contests.)

Castalia Series, 239 Savery, University of Washington, Seattle, WA 98105.

Catbird Seat Bookstore, 1231 SW Washington, Portland, OR 97205. 503–222–5817. Contact: Deborah Robboy. Autograph parties.

Centrum Foundation, PO Box 1158, Port Townsend, WA 98368. Contact: Carol Jane Bangs. 206–385–3102. The annual Port Townsend Writers' Conference serves over 200 writers each July and features a faculty distinguished for excellence both in writing and teaching. (See Classes, Organizations.)

Christian Writers Conference, Warner Pacific College, 2219 S.E. 68th, Portland, OR 97215. Contact: George Ivan Smith. 503–775–4366.

Clarion West, 340 15th Ave. E., Ste. 350, Seattle, WA 98112. 206–322–9083. Contact: Richard Terra. "Will be sponsoring the World Fantasy Convention in Seattle in 1989." (See Classes.)

Confluence Press, Inc., 8th Ave. & 6th St., LCSC, Lewiston, ID 83501. 208–799–2336. Contact: James R. Hepworth. Confluence Press and Lewis Clark State College sponsor the Visiting Writers Series which includes lectures free to the public. They sponsor The Stegner Lecture, also free to the public, featuring a prominent fiction writer. The Annual Young Author's Conference takes place in November. During the Conference teachers and student participants meet with faculty and guest instructors. Students work on drafting, revising and editing their projects and submit their work for judging in March. Four year $1,000 scholarships are then awarded. (See Classes, Contests, Misc.)

Crab Creek Review Association, 4462 Whitman Ave. N., Seattle, WA 98103. 206–633–1090. Contact: Linda Clifton. Sponsors readings in the Seattle and Northshore areas by artists published in *Crab Creek Review*.

Christian Writers Conference, c/o Humanities Dept., Seattle Pacific University, Seattle, WA 98119. 206–281–2036. Contact: Rose Beynoldson or Linda Wagner. "Offers information, inspiration, and instruction for writers for both inspirational markets and secular with major focus on the inspirational markets." Conference is held the last week of June each year, includes opportunity for appointments with editors.

Edmonds Arts Commission, 700 Main St., Edmonds, WA 98020. 206–775–2525. Contact: Linda McCrystal. Spring quarter: half day seminar for writers. Fall quarter: full day writers conference, "Write on the Sound." Write for information.

Elliott Bay Book Store, 1st Street & S. Main, Seattle, WA 98104. 206–624–6600. Offers readings.

The Federation of British Columbia Writers, Box 24624, Sta. C, Vancouver, BC V5T 4E2. Contact: J. Drabek/T. Carolan. 604–683–2057. "The Federation promotes public readings by B.C. writers, and hosts readings by visiting writers.... It seeks Foundation and Provincial and National government funding for projects such as writing competitions, National Book Week presentations, membership directories, a rural Writers' Retreat, and Writers' Awards." (See Classes, Organizations.)

The Festival of the Written Arts, Box 2299, Sechelt, BC V0N 3A0. 604–885–9631. Contact: Betty Keller. Annual 3-day program of readings and discussions by Canadian writers. Writers-in-Residence programs, small workshop groups with professional instruction. Write for information.

Foothills Poetry Series, Peninsula College, Port Angeles, WA 98362. Contact: Alice Derry or Jack Estes. 206–452–9277.

Keizer Artfair, 4748 Lowell Ave. NE, Keizer, OR 97303. 503–393–2457 or 393–6144. Third weekend in September each year. Writers can contact Keizer Art Association for an application.

Lane Literary Guild, c/o Lane Regional Arts Council, 411 High Street, Eugene, OR 97401. Contact: Henry Alley. 503–484–6259. Sponsors the "Writers at the Hult — an annual series emphasizing poets and novelists who are both locally and nationally known." (See Classes, Organizations.)

Laughing Horse Book Collective, 1322 NW 23rd, Portland, OR 97210. 503–227–5440. Holds readings every other Friday at 8 pm.

Let's Talk About It (Book/Discussion Programs), Oregon State Library, State Library Bldg., Salem, OR 97310. Contact: Kathryn Prather/Mary Ginnane. 503–378–2112. "The Oregon State Library (through grants made to the Oregon Library Association) supports libraries in setting up 'Let's Talk About It' book discussion programs. Each library hosts a series of five programs, each program is centered around a book title. The audience has read the book. A scholar gives a short lecture on the work and then the audience breaks into discussion groups. The programs were originally funded nationwide by the National Endowment for the Humanities and sponsored by the American Library Assoc."

The Literary Center, PO Box 85116, Seattle, WA 98145-1116. Contact: Marilyn Stablein. 206–524–5514. The Center sponsors readings, seminars. (See Classes, Organizations.)

Literuption, Sponsored by Northwest Writers, Inc., PO Box 3437, Portland, OR 97208. A spring book fair and celebration in Portland with readings, booths, films and exhibits.

Meet the Author Program Series, Rainier Beach Library, 9125 Rainier Avenue S., Seattle, WA 98118. 206–386–1906. Fall & winter scheduling.

Montana Institute of the Arts, PO Box 1456, Billings, MT 59103. Contact: Ron Paulick. 406–245–3688. Sponsors a 2-day annual summer festival. Location changes each year. (See Organizations, Contests.)

Mountain Writers Series, Mt. Hood Community College, 26000 S.E. Stark, Gresham, OR 97030. Contact: Sandra Williams. 503–232–7337. "The Mountain Writers Series presents regular poetry readings, each preceded by a brief musical performance, featuring artists of local, regional and national reputation, at noon on scheduled Fridays during the academic year (Oct.-June) on the MHCC campus. The public is welcome at all performances, and those wishing to receive announcements of events should write to be included on the mailing list. Artists wishing to perform in the Series should apply by August 15 with a sample of their work, phone number, and brief statement of biographical/publication/performance history."

Northwest Artists Workshop, 522 N.W. 12th Avenue, Portland, OR 97209. 503–220–0435. Alternative space sponsoring visual arts, exhibits, performance art, plays, poetry readings. Also artist books.

Northwest Playwrights Guild, PO Box 95292, Seattle, WA 98145. Contact: Sharon Glantz. 206–545–4500. Holds workshops and readings of new works. (See Organizations, Classes.)

Northwest Renaissance, 13021 10th Ave. S., Seattle, WA 98168. Contact: Michael Spence. Puget Sound area poetry organization, presents poetry in the schools and other readings. (See Classes, Organizations.)

Oregon Press Women, PO Box 25354, Portland, OR 97225. 503–292–4945. Contact: Glennis McNeal. Sponsors Spring and Fall workshops for writers, editors, photographers, graphics artists on professionalism stress management, career development, personal growth. Open to non-members. Fall 88, Kah-Nee-Tah; Spring 89, Ashland; Fall 89, Oregon Coast; Spring 90, Timberline; Fall 90, Bend. Write to be added to conference mailing list. (See Organizations, Contests.)

Oregon State Fair, 437 Mildred Lane S., Salem, OR 97306. 503–363–3793. Contact: Mary Kay Callaghan. Oregon authors table space at the State Fair. Application forms available in February each year.

Oregon State Poetry Association, 1645 S.E. Spokane Street, Portland, OR 97202. Contact: Leona Ward. 503–777–8209. "OSPA originated the observance of Poetry Day in the state, and continues this tradition with a conference in October. OSPA sponsors a second conference in the spring." It also hosts readings throughout the year, and acts as coordinator for member poets who want to give readings. (See Contests, Organizations.)

Oregon Writers Colony, PO Box 15200, Portland, OR 97215. Contact: Marlene Howard. 503–771–0428. "Spring and Fall: sponsors Weekend Writing Conferences; conferences feature local published writers speaking on various aspects of writing and professional and practical solutions to technical and marketing problems. Conferences feature group housing and meals, and informal, friendly atmosphere where writers can get to know their peers. July: week long writing workshops in fiction and nonfiction. Students stay together in group housing, bring their typewriters and computers, and work on specific projects. (See Contests, Organizations.)

Oregon Writing Project, Department of English, University of Oregon, Eugene, OR 97403. Nathaniel Teich, Project Director. 503–686–3911. "The Oregon Writing Project at the University of Oregon is affiliated with the National Writing Project network. It now includes more than 140 projects in 44 states and abroad which have adopted the successful model of the University of California, Berkeley/Bay Area Writing Project. This model has achieved national recognition for improving students' writing by increasing teachers' knowledge and instructional skills in composition." Experienced teachers are eligible for the 4-week summer institute.

Pacific Northwest Poets, PO Box 45637, Seattle, WA 98145. 206–545–8302. Contact: Robert R. Ward. Poetry reading series put on by the Bellowing Ark Society, October–May, Seattle Public Library, Downtown Branch.

Pacific Northwest Writers Conference, 1811 N.E. 199th Street, Seattle, WA 98155. Contact: Gladys Johnson. 206–364–1293. Sponsors summer conference program, as well as winter workshops. (See Contests.)

Performing Arts Series, 1520 E. 8th N., Mountain Home, ID 83647.

Poetic Space, PO Box 11157, Eugene, OR 97440. Contact: Donald Hildenbrand. Poetry readings in local art gallery, 3-4 readings a year.

Poetry in Vancouver USA, Eugene Messer, PO Box 5182, Vancouver, WA 98668-5128. An event in August sponsored by the Washington Poets Association (See Organizations), which includes workshops, open mike, guest poets and contest.

Poets & Composers Performance Series, 10254 35th Avenue S.W., Seattle WA 98146. Contact: Joseph Keppler. 206–937–8155. "Readings, concerts, lectures, performances."

Portland Poetry Festival, Northwest Service Center, 1819 N.W. Everett, Portland, OR 97209. 503–285–4451.

Powell's Book Store, 1005 W. Burnside, Portland, OR 97209. Regular autograph parties and readings.

Red Sky Poetry Theatre, Five-0 Tavern, 507 15th Avenue E., Seattle, WA 98112. 206–322–9693.

Salem Art Fair, Mission Mill Museum Assn., 1313 Mill St. SE, Salem, OR 97301. 503–585–7012. Contact: Patti Wilbrecht. Oregon Authors' Table at annual July art fair.

Satyricon, 125 NW 6th, Portland, OR 97209. 503–243–2380. Evening poetry readings, usually weekly.

Seattle Group Theatre, 3940 Brooklyn Ave. NE, Seattle, WA 98105. 206–545–4969. Contact: Tim Band. Presents annual 3-week Multicultural Playwrights' Festival. (See Contests.)

Sitka Summer Writers Symposium, Box 2420, Sitka, AK 99835. 907–747–3794. Contact: Carolyn Service. Annual week-long conference in June. Faculty of 5-7, enrollment limited to 55. "Themes vary from year to year, but usually encompass ideas of social and cultural importance.... Emphasis on discussion of ideas; manuscript critiques done on an individual basis."

Warm Beach Christian Writers & Speakers Conference, Warm Beach Camp & Conference Center, 20800 Marine Drive N.W., Stanwood, WA 98292.

Events

Western Montana Writers Conference, Office of Continuing Education, Western Montana College, Dillon, MT 59725. 406–683–7537. Contact: Sally Garrett-Dingley or Susan K. Jones. Annual conference featuring a writer-in-residence with expertise on a specific writing genre. Info for July, 1989 conference will be available in May, 1989.

Willamette Writers, PO Box 2485, Portland, OR 97208. 503–233–1877. Contact: Al Siebert. Sponsors Annual Writers Conference in August. (See Contest, Organization.)

Yellowstone Art Center's Regional Writers Project, 401 N. 27th Street, Billings, MT 59101. 406–256–6804. Contact: Adrea Sukin/Jet Holoubek. The Project sponsors a lecture series in connection with its role as distributor of fine regional literature. (See Distributors.)

Contests

Aardvark Literary Services Annual Poetry Contest, 192 Balsam Place, Penticton, BC V2A 7V3. Contact: J. Alvin Speers. 604–492–0272. Publishers of *Breakthrough! Magazine* offer prizes dependent on number of entries. Fee: $3 per poem, by money order. No checks outside BC due to processing cost. Three entries per contestant, maximum 40 lines, subjects open. Prefer rhyme, but author's choice. Submit on 8 1/2 x 11 sheets with name, address and signed permission for 1 time publication in Contest Anthology. Include SASE with Canadian stamp or IRC.

Bainbridge Island Arts Council. (See Northwest Poets & Artists Calendar.)

Benton County Fair Poetry Contest for Youngsters, 471 N.W. Hemlock, Corvallis, OR 97330. Contact: Linda Smith. 503–753–3335. Poetry contest for children; also exhibits adult poems at the fair.

Bumbershoot, PO Box 9750, Seattle, WA 98109-0750. 206–622–5123. Contact: Judith Roche. Written works competition included at their Labor Day arts festival. Write for more information. (See Events.)

Clark College Open Contest and Workshop, 4312 NE 40th St., Vancouver, WA 98661. 206–695–2777. Contact: Arlene Paul. Poetry contest (reading fee required), poetry workshop and writing craft lectures — March, 1989. Write for more information.

Composers, Authors and Artists of America, Inc., Rt. 1, Box 53, Reardan, WA 99029. Contact: David Chester. Sponsors a state poetry contest. Write for info. (See organizations.)

Confluence Press, Inc., Lewis Clark State College, 8th Avenue & 6th Street, Lewiston, ID 83501. 208–799–2336. Contact: James R. Hepworth. Four-year $1,000 scholarships in writing are given annually via the Young Author's Conference. (See Classes, Events, Misc.)

CutBank Competition, c/o English Department, University of Montana, Missoula, MT 59812. 406–243–5231. A.B. Guthrie, Jr. Short Fiction Award & Richard Hugo Memorial Poetry Award. CutBank holds an annual competition for the best short story and best poem published each year in CutBank. First Prize: $100 each category. Honorable Mention: $50 each category. Write for more information.

The Eighth Mt. Poetry Prize, 624 SE 29, Portland, OR 97214. 503–233–3936. Contact: Ruth Gundle. "Annual $1,000 prize and publication for poetry manuscript selected by judges. Submissions accepted January & February. Winner announced beginning of May. Publication w/standard royalty contract the following Fall. SASE for details."

Fiction Contest, Northwest Magazine, The Oregonian, 1320 S.W. Broadway, Portland, OR 97201. Northwest Magazine has held several fiction contests for young writers with cash awards and publication of winners' stories. Contests are for those age 30 and under, and residents of the Pacific NW (OR, WA, ID, BC). Inquire for information on future contests.

Fictioneers, 13211 39th Avenue N.E., Seattle, WA 98125. Contact: Beth Casey. 206–282–2729. A writer's organization which holds three annual contests: short story, article, poetry. Write for more information. (See Classes, Organizations.)

Great Expeditions, PO Box 46499, Station G, Vancouver, BC V6R 4G7. Contact: Marilyn Marshall.

Idaho Writers League, Coeur d'Alene Chapter, N. 950 Highland Ct., Post Falls, ID 83854. 208–773–2513. Contact: Robin Bruce. Conducts a nationally-advertised poetry contest. Members eligible for state semiannual writing competition. Write for guidelines. (See Organizations.)

Literary Lights, PO Box 25809, Seattle, WA 98125. Annual literary short story contests. Send SASE for guidelines.

Montana Arts Council, New York Block, 48 North Last Chance Gulch, Helena, MT 59620. 406–763–4437. Contact: Julie Cook. First Book Award, Individual Artist Fellowship—available to Montana residents only. Deadline late April.

Montana Institute of the Arts, PO Box 1456, Billings, MT 59103. 406–245–3688. Contact: Aline Moore, 11333 Gooch Hill Rd., Gallatin Gateway, MT 59730. Annual writers contest including categories for unpublished novels, short stories, articles, poetry. Contact by February each year. (See Events, Organizations.)

National League of American Pen Women, Washington State Branches, 4909 Whitman Ave. N, Seattle, WA 98103. 206–485–7607. Contact: Jean Immerwahr. Centennial writers contest open to all women. Deadline postmark Feb. 1, 1989. Nonfiction only, must relate to Washington State. Entry fee $3 each ms, limit two. Prizes: First, $150; second, $100; third, $75; five honorable mentions. Do not send originals. Complete rules, send SASE.

Northwest Poets & Artists Calendar, Bainbridge Island Arts Council, c/o Nancy Rekow, Executive Director, 8489 Fletcher Bay Road, Bainbridge Island, WA 98110. Contact: Nancy Rekow. 206–842–7901. Material for the annual Calendar is jury selected from entries in Annual Poets & Artists Competition, which is open to residents of AK, ID, MT, OR, WA or BC (1989 deadline for 1990 calendar will be February 15). The calendar is a full-color, 12 month wall calendar, 12 x 12, with large squares to write in. Each month features a full color photo of an original piece of art, placed together with a poem. For info on 1989 calendar or on competition for 1990 calendar, write to the above address.

Oregon Book Awards, Oregon Institute of Literary Arts, PO Box 42598, Portland, OR 97242. 503–223–3604. Contact: Karen Reyes. Recognizes and promotes Oregon writers and publishers. Write for information. (See Miscellaneous.)

Oregon Press Women High School Contest, PO Box 25354, Portland, OR 97225. 503–292–4945. Contact: Glennis McNeal. Spring contest for high school journalists. Categories for features, photography, news, editorial. Judged by professional journalists. Entry forms available from journalism teachers or OPW Contest Committee. (See Events, Organizations.)

Oregon State Poetry Association, 1645 S.E. Spokane Street, Portland, OR 97202. Contact: Leona Ward. 503–777–8209. "OSPA contests are held spring and fall and offer cash prizes in several categories ($300 total, April 1986). The number and theme of categories vary from year to year. Guidelines are published in the spring and fall issues of the OSPA Newsletter. Non-members may request them in March and August by sending SASE to above address." No entry fee to members. (See Event, Organizations.)

Oregon Students Writing & Art Foundation, PO Box 2100, Portland, OR 97208-2100. Contact: Chris Weber. 503–232–7737. Writing & Art contest for students grades K-12. Winners are published in an anthology created by students. Winners receive a free copy of the book. The teacher cited on the entry receives a free copy also. Enter in either or both categories: write a true story in the first person; make one or more pictures with any materials and of any size. (See also Organizations.)

Oregon Writers Colony, PO Box 15200, Portland, OR 97215. Contact: Marlene Howard. 503–771–0428. Writing contests in April, July and October. Winners are awarded full tuition scholarships to the writing conferences. See Colonygram for details. (February, April, August issues). (See Events, Organizations.)

Owl Creek Press Contests, c/o Rich Ives, 1620 N. 45 Street, Seattle, WA 98103. Two annual poetry contests offer publication with 10% payment in copies of the first printing and additional payment in cash or copies for any additional printing.

Pacific Northwest Writers Conference, 1811 N.E. 199th Street, Seattle, WA 98155. Contact: Gladys Johnson. 206–364–1293. Organization sponsoring two annual writers' conferences — one in the summer and one in the winter in the Seattle-Tacoma area — with associated contests. (See Events.)

Pacific Northwest Young Reader's Choice Award, Pacific Northwest Library Association, University of Washington, 133 Suzzallo Library, FM-30, Seattle, WA 98195. Contact: Mae Benne. 206–543–1794.

Poetry in Vancouver USA, Eugene Messer, PO Box 5182, Vancouver, WA 98668-5128. Contest offered as part of Poetry In Vancouver USA, an annual event held in August by the Washington Poets Association. (See Organizations.)

PRISM International Short Fiction Contest, Department of Creative Writing, University of British Columbia, Vancouver, BC V6T 1W5. Contact: Wayne Hughes. 604–228–2514. Annual short fiction contest. Deadline each year on Dec. 1. Prizes: $1,000 first, $500 second, $250 third. Send an SASE for guidelines.

Pulp Press International 3-Day Novel Competition, PO Box 3868, Vancouver, BC V6B 3Z3. Contact: F.H. Eger. 604–687–4233. "A Contest for Normal People." Annual 3-day novel writing contest is just that. "Completed manuscripts must be accompanied by an affidavit signed by at least one living witness and no manuscripts can be over 716 pages long." Send SASE. No registration fee. Register with one of the sponsoring bookstores. Prize is a publishing offer from Pulp Press Book Publishers. Write for more information.

Rhyme Time Poetry Newsletter, PO Box 1870, Hayden, ID 83835. 208–772–6184. Contact: Linda Hutton. "Monthly contests, some with no entry fees."

Seattle Group Theatre, 3940 Brooklyn Ave. NE, Seattle, WA 98105. 206–545–4969. Contact: Tim Band. Annual 3-week Multicultural Playwrights' Festival and cash/travel awards — 8 winners (6 readings, 2 workshops). (See Events.)

Shorelines Poetry Contest, Edith Modlin, Route 2 Box 42, Otis, OR 97368.

Signpost Press – 49th Parallel Poetry Contest, PO Box 4065, Bellingham, WA 98227. 206–734–9781. Contact: Knute Skinner. Cash awards poetry contest, entry fee, submissions must be postmarked between October 1, 1988 and January 3, 1989. Write for guidelines.

Silverfish Review, PO Box 3541, Eugene, OR 97403. Poetry Chapbook Competition.

Teachers as Writers Competition, Chemeketa Community College, PO Box 14007, Salem, OR 97309. Sponsored by the Oregon Council of Teachers of English. Prose and poetry contest open to Oregon teachers of kindergarten through college. (See OCTE, Organizations.)

Valentine's Poetry Contest, Washington Park Zoo, 4001 S.W. Canyon Road, Portland, OR 97221. Contact: Anne Brown. 503–226–1561. Annual contest for preschool through high school age students. Entries are about favorite animals at the Washington Park Zoo. Each winner receives a copy of the anthology of winning poems.

Washington State Library, Northwest Room AJ-11, Olympia, WA 98504. 206–753–4024. Contact: Gayle Palmer. In conjunction with the Washington Author collection, the library holds an annual award ceremony honoring the best books written by Washington Authors published the previous year. (See Misc.)

Western States Book Awards, Western States Art Foundation, 207 Shelby Street, Suite 200, Santa Fe, NM 87501. Contact: Cheryl Alters Jamison. 505–988–1166. "Presented biennially in even-numbered years to publisher & author in 3 categories: fiction, nonfiction, poetry." Cash award to publisher and author and promotional aid.

White Rock & Surrey Writers Club, 13245 Marine Drive, Surrey, BC V4A 1E6. Contact: Lynda James. 604–531–8879. Annual literary contest. Write for guidelines. (See Organizations.)

Willamette Writers, PO Box 2485, Portland, OR 97208. 503–233–1877. Contact: Al Siebert. Annual Kay Snow Writing Contest. Cash prizes awarded in the categories of fiction, nonfiction, juvenile, structured and unstructured poetry. Write for this year's guidelines. (See Events, Organizations.)

Writers-In-Waiting Newsletter, 837 Archie St., Eugene, OR 97402. 503–688–5400. Contact: Bjo Ashwill. Spring & Fall Fiction/Poetry Contest (Fall deadline Nov. 15, 1988), entry fee, awards two critiques of work and copy of newsletter.

Distributors

Blackwell North America, Inc., 6024 S.W. Jean Road, Bldg. G, Lake Oswego, OR 97034. 503–684–1140.

Book Service Unlimited, Inc., 15030 Hwy. 99 S., Lynnwood, WA 98037.

Cornucopia, PO Box 85627, Seattle, WA 98145-1627. 206–323–6247. Contact: Craig Scheak. Magazine distribution, 300+ titles, resource guides focused on NW subject matter.

Himber's Books, 1380 W. Second Avenue, Eugene, OR 97402.

Homestead Book Company, 6101 22nd Ave. N.W., Seattle, WA 98107. 206–782–4532. Contact: David Tatelman. Wholesaler of books and magazines, specializing in small presses.

International Specialized Book Services, Inc., 5602 N.E. Hassalo Street, Suite F5, Portland, OR 97213.

MacRae's Indian Book Distributors, PO Box 652, 1605 Cole Street, Enumclaw, WA 98002.

New Leaf Books of Oregon Distributing Company, 1450 NE A St., Grants Pass, OR 97526. 503–474–0139. Contact: Art Bernstein. Distributes books "of special interest to Southern Oregon and the California Far North." Also self-publishing consulting.

Outlaw Books, PO Box 4466, Bozeman, MT 59772. 406–586–7248. Contact: Jeri D. Walton. Publishes and distributes cowboy poetry and Western titles.

Pacific Northwest Books, PO Box 314, Medford, OR 97501. 503–664–4442. Contact: Bert Webber.

Pacific Pipeline, Inc., 19215 66th Ave. S., Kent, WA 98032-1171. 206–872–5523. Contact: Pennie Clark. Wholesale book distributor of all categories, one specialty being NW & regional books.

Silver Bow News Distributing Company, Inc., 219 E. Park Street, Butte, MT 59701.

Western States Books Services, PO Box 855, Clackamas, OR 97015. 503–657–9838.

Yellowstone Art Center's Regional Writers Project, 401 N. 27th Street, Billings, MT 59101. 406–256–6804. Contact: Adrea Sukin/Jet Holoubek. "The Regional Writers Project is a distribution outlet for the fine literature produced by writers and small presses in Montana and a seven state region surrounding it, including the Dakotas, Idaho, Oregon, Washington and Wyoming. The Project encourages an audience for this literature by publishing an annual catalog...handles over 150 titles in the categories of poetry, fiction, nonfiction and periodicals." (See Events.)

Miscellaneous

Alaska Media Directory, 6200 Bubbling Brook Circle, Anchorage, AK 99516. Contact: Alissa Crandall. 907–346–1001. "Directory of listings of media related companies in Alaska. Includes publications; radio; television; ad, PR and marketing agencies; artists, photographers, writers; printers; typesetters, etc." Published annually. Cost: $65 for current edition; $25 for past edition.

Aperture PhotoBank, Inc., 1530 Westlake Ave. N., Seattle, WA 98109. Contact: Marty Loken. 206–282–8116. Stock photo agency.

Artist Trust, 517 Jones Bldg., 1331 3rd Ave., Seattle, WA 98101. 206–467–8734. Contact: David Mendoza. Not-for-profit arts organization, services for Washington artists, (all media): information services, advocacy and education, fellowships and grants. Quarterly newsletter.

Artists-In-Education (AIE), Oregon Arts Commission, 835 Summer St. NE, Salem OR 97301. 503–378–3625. Artists working in all disciplines may apply for short and long term residencies in schools in different regions of the state. Applications available from OAC to be submitted to desired region coordinator—addresses follow:

AIE: Benton & Linn Counties, Corvallis Art Center, 700 SW Madison, Corvallis, OR, 97333. 503–754–1551. Coordinator: Saralyn Hilde.

AIE: Columbia Gorge, Columbia Gorge Arts Council, PO Box 1063, Hood River, OR 97031. 503–386–5113. Coordinator: Dede Killeen.

AIE: Deschutes, Crook & Jefferson Counties, Central Oregon Arts Compact, Evergreen Center, 437 S. 9th St., Redmond, OR 97756. 503–923–5437 x260. Coordinator: Denissia Withers.

AIE: Douglas County, Umpqua Valley Arts Assn., PO Box 1542, Roseburg, OR 97470. 503–672–2532. Coordinator: Heidi Land.

AIE: Coos & Curry Counties, S. Coast Co. for Arts/Humanities, 170 S. Second St. Ste. 204, Coos Bay, OR 97420. 503–267–6500. Coordinator: Lionel Youst.

AIE: Eastern Oregon, Eastern Oregon Regional Arts Council, RSI House, Eastern Oregon State College, La Grande, OR, 97850. 503–963–1624. Coordinator: Anne Bell.

AIE: Jackson & Josephine Counties, Arts Council of Southern Oregon, 236 E. Main, Ashland, OR 97520. 503–482–5594. Coordinator: Brooke Friendly.

AIE: Lane County, Lane Regional Arts Council, 411 High St., Eugene, OR 97401. 503–452–2278. Coordinator: Carol Ten Eyck.

AIE: Lincoln & Tillamook Counties, Oregon Coast Council for the Arts, PO Box 1315, Newport, OR 97365. 503–265–9231. Coordinator: Babette Cabral.

AIE: Marion & Polk Counties, Salem Art Association, 600 Mission St. SE, Salem, OR 97301. 503–581–2228. Coordinator: Sara Spiegel.

AIE: Portland Metro & Clatsop County, Contemporary Crafts Assn., 3934 SW Corbett Ave., Portland, OR 97201. 503–228–2308. Coordinator: Vicki Poppen.

AIE: Statewide: Film/Video Only, NW Film & Video Center, 1219 SW Park, Portland, OR 97205. 503–221–1156. Coordinator: Ellen Thomas.

Confluence Press, Lewis Clark State College, 8th Ave. & 6th St., Lewiston, ID 83501. 208–799–2336. Contact: James R. Hepworth. Sponsors a degree program in publishing arts connected with a book publishing program. (See Classes, Contests, Events.)

Continuing Education Film Library, PO Box 1383, Portland, OR 97207. 503–464–4890. Rents films (some video available), many suitable for writing groups and classes. $5 charge for catalog.

Earth Images, PO Box 10352, Bainbridge Island, WA 98110. Contact: Terry Domico. 206–842–7793. Stock photo agency.

Elliott Press, Pacific Lutheran University, Tacoma, WA 98447. 206–535–7387. Contact: Megan Benton. Publishing and printing arts program offers English minor degree. "The Press is a working museum, where visitors may watch and try their hands at the technology that Gutenberg pioneered."

ERIC Clearinghouse on Educational Mgmt., 1787 Agate Street, University of Oregon, Eugene, OR 97403. Contact: Stuart C. Smith. 503–686–5043. "The Educational Resources Information Center (ERIC) is a decentralized nationwide network, sponsored by the National Institute of Education (NIE), and designed to collect educational documents and to make them available to teachers, administrators, researchers, students and other interested persons. ERIC publishes a monthly abstract journal, Resources in Education (RIE), which announces all documents that are acquired by ERIC and that pass its selection criteria. ERIC attempts comprehensive coverage of recently completed significant documents dealing with education."

The Foundation Center Regional Collection, Multnomah County Library, 801 SW 10th Ave., Portland, OR 97205. 503–223–7201. Contact: Meg Eisemann. Includes references such as: *Foundation Grants to Individuals*, updated every 2-3 yrs., *National Directory of Grants and Aid to Individuals in the Arts International*, updated irregularly, and *Grants & Awards Available to American Writers* updated irregularly.

KBOO, 20 S.E. 8th, Portland, OR 97214. Contact: Kathleen Stephenson or Chris Merrick. 503–231–8032. A 24 hour independent community radio station; includes poetry, story reading, interviews; "Between the Covers" is a weekly interview program with writers.

The Literary Storefront, Box 1440, Stat. A, Vancouver, BC V6C 2P7.

National Endowment for the Arts, Literature Program, 1100 Pennsylvania Ave. NW, Washington, DC 20506. 202–682–5451. Grants to individual writers and small presses.

The Northwest Information Directory, The Center for Urban Education, 1135 S.E. Salmon, Portland, OR 97214. Contact: Steve Johnson. 503–231–1285. Contains listings of over 2,000 information resources, descriptions of 600 special collections, archives, museums, government depositories, libraries, census data resources, genealogy collections, and an overview section on the information economy in the NW.

Oregon Advocates for Arts, 1313 Mill St. SE, Salem, OR 97301. 503–588–2787. Contact: Elaine Young. Statewide group of arts administrators, artists and citizens working to enhance public policy for the arts.

Oregon Center for the Book in the Oregon State Library, Oregon State Library, Salem, OR 97310. Contact: Wes Doak. 503–378–4367. A statewide program including exhibits, special collections and speakers all designed to increase awareness and appreciation of books and reading. The Center is supported with contributions by the public. It is affiliated with The Center for the Book in the Library of Congress. *Writer's Northwest Handbook* is an official resource of the Oregon Center for the Book.

Oregon Committee for the Humanities, 418 SW Washington, Rm 410, Portland, OR 97204. 503–241–0543. Contact: Robert W. Keeler. Grantmaking philanthropic organization. "Grants available for public programs involving humanities scholars; consultation grants for organizations needing humanities expertise, research grants to humanities scholars."

Oregon Historical Society, 1230 Park Ave., Portland, OR 97205. 503–222–1741. Archives and library.

Oregon Institute of Literary Arts, PO Box 42598, Portland, OR 97242. 503–223–3604. Contact: Karen Reyes. Nonprofit corporation "organized to stimulate creative writing and publishing in Oregon...." Sponsors annual Oregon Book Awards, makes grants to writers & publishers, assists schools, libraries, and the public in awareness of Oregon authors and publishers. (See Contests.)

Oregon State Archives, 1005 Broadway NE, Salem, OR 97310. 503–378–4241. Contact: John Lazuk. Publishes high school curriculum packet, historical resources, informational guides — source records on genealogy, Oregon history, law.

Photo Bank, PO Box 3069, Ketchum, ID 83340. Contact: Joe Petelle & Don Petelle. 208–726–5731. Stock-photo agency.

Poetry Exchange, c/o Horizon Books, 425 – 15th Avenue East, Seattle, WA 98112. "We are a community newsletter. The Poetry Exchange includes a calendar of literary readings, announcements about small press books, workshops, and a manuscripts wanted column. Also contains reviews & articles...Information about events can be listed for free." The newsletter serves as a regional networking tool.

Juanita B. Price, 373 Altadena, Astoria, OR 97103. 503–325–3733. A 22-page bibliography of Oregon authors and artists of children's books.

Salem Public Library, 585 Liberty SE, PO Box 14810, Salem, OR 97309. 503–588–6071. Books and magazines on authorship for writers. It is library policy to purchase books by Oregon authors. Info on Oregon authors and other topics may be obtained through the Reference/Information Dept.

The Upper Left-Hand Corner, International Self-Counsel Press Ltd., 306 W. 25th Street, North Vancouver, BC V7N 2G1. Guide to literary resources, mainly in Western Canada.

Washington State Historical Society, 315 N. Stadium Way, Tacoma, WA 98403. 206–593–2830. Contact: Gladys C. Para. "We offer researchers an archive of original papers and many thousands of photographic images in our Hewitt Research Library."

Washington State Library, Northwest Room, AJ-11, Olympia, WA 98504. 206–753–4024. Contact: Gayle Palmer. "Maintains a Washington Authors collection for books written by people born in the state or residing in Washington when the book was written.... Washington authors are encouraged to inform the State Library when they publish a book." An annual bibliography is compiled and is available on request. (See Contests).

Young & Associates, Artists in Schools, 619 Warehouse Avenue #238, Anchorage, AK 99501. Contact: Director.

Join America's most successful and soon-to-be-successful writers who read PUBLISHERS WEEKLY for profit and pleasure

Today, a serious author has to get up from the typewriter and get down to business.
The business of books.

PUBLISHERS WEEKLY has been keeping authors informed about the business of books for over 100 years. Each issue gives you a broad and colorful overview of all that's new and news-worthy in the field...

Who's writing what. What kinds of books are selling now—and what kinds will sell best a year from now. Rights and permissions—for paperbacks, movies, TV. Author tours and publicity. Industry trends and prospects—and how they affect writers, agents, publishers, and booksellers...

Book design and manufacturing. News of people in the field. Bookselling and marketing. The international scene. Media tie-ins. Calendars of upcoming events. Convention reports...

Of particular interest to you are the regular,

in-depth interviews with writers who are making news today or will be making news tomorrow. They're men and women writing in all fields—from fiction to finance, poetry to politics, and they all have valuable thoughts, experiences, ideas, and working tips to share with you.

Each issue also brings you advance reviews—by PW's own expert critics—of approximately 100 hardcover and paperback books. These reviews appear *five or ten weeks before publication dates.* So you'll always know which books will be worth looking for—long before they're on bookstore or library shelves.

Then there are the advertisements in PUBLISHERS WEEKLY—some 2800 pages a year. Surveys indicate that these book ads are particularly valuable to writers.

If you're serious about writing, the best thing to write today is your name and address on the PW subscription coupon below.

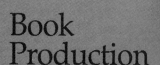

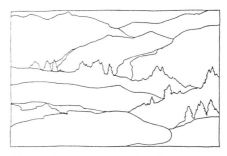